PRINCIPLES OF

Patent Claim Drafting and Patent Claim Analysis

CASES, MATERIALS,
QUESTIONS, AND
PROBLEMS

Howard A. Skaist

AMERICAN BAR ASSOCIATION
Intellectual Property
Law Section

Cover design by Amy Mandel, ABA Section of Intellectual Property Law; Jill Tedhams, ABA Design

Printed in the United States of America.

28 27 26 25 24 5 4 3 2 1

A catalog record for this book is available from the Library of Congress.

Discounts are available for books ordered in bulk. Special consideration is given to state bars, CLE programs, and other bar-related organizations. Inquire at Book Publishing, ABA Publishing, American Bar Association, 321 N. Clark Street, Chicago, Illinois 60654-7598.

www.shopABA.org

Contents

Downloadable material is available at https://ambar.org/PPCD

About the Author

Howard Skaist graduated summa cum laude, Phi Beta Kappa, and Tau Beta Pi from Princeton University in 1982 with a B.S.E.E. degree in electric engineering and computer science. He entered Duke University in 1984, simultaneously pursuing a master's degree in business administration at the Fuqua School of Business and a J.D. degree at Duke Law School. While at Duke, he served on the Editorial Board of the *Duke Law Journal*. He graduated with highest honors and Order of the Coif honors, and won the Willis Smith Award for being first in his law school class.

Immediately after graduating from Duke, he began clerking for Judge Eugene Wright on the Ninth Circuit Court of Appeals in Seattle, Washington. A year later, he entered private practice as a member of the Oregon State Bar, joining Stoel Rives, a Pacific Northwest law firm headquartered in Portland. After spending two years in the Patent Group at Stoel, Mr. Skaist became an in-house patent attorney for General Electric Company at its Corporate Research and Development Center outside Albany, New York. Eventually, he joined AT&T's Bell Laboratories as an intellectual property attorney, prior to the formation of Lucent Technologies. He returned to the Pacific Northwest in 1996 as a senior intellectual property attorney for Intel Corporation in Portland, Oregon, and in the ensuing seven years rose to become Intel's Director of Patents, where he managed a staff of more than 40, including patent attorneys, patent agents, paralegals, patent engineers, and administrative assistants. As Intel's Director of Patents, Mr. Skaist split his time between developing the substantive legal strategy for several of Intel's significant patent cases, leading several of Intel's major patent cross-licensing efforts, overseeing other patent analysis projects, and leading the strategic management of Intel's patent portfolio.

In 2003, Mr. Skaist left Intel and founded Berkeley Law & Technology Group (BLTG) before retiring in 2021. BLTG handled all aspects of patent law practice, including patent preparation and prosecution, patent strategy, portfolio building and portfolio management, patent assertion and other patent license negotiation support, patent opinion letter preparation, and strategic oversight of patent litigation. Mr. Skaist was also an adjunct professor at the Berkeley School of Law (formerly, Boalt Hall) in Berkeley, California, and at Willamette School of Law in Salem, Oregon, and has also taught patent law, copyright law, and computer law at Lewis and Clark Law School and Albany Law School. In addition, he served for several years (1998–2001) on the Editorial Board of the *AIPLA Quarterly Journal* and is a member of the Intellectual Property Law Section of the American Bar Association.

Mr. Skaist is the author of *Patent Claim Drafting Practice: Tactics, Strategy, and Analysis* published in 2023 by the Intellectual Property Law Section of the American Bar Association and will be teaching adjunct at the University of Oregon School of Law beginning in the fall of 2024. He also currently serves on the Legal Ethics Committee of the Oregon State Bar.

Chapter 1
Introduction to Basic Principles

As the esteemed Judge Giles Rich stated, in patent law, "the name of the game is the claim."[1] The interpretation of a patent claim touches virtually every aspect of patent law.[2] This first chapter introduces the subject of patent claim drafting (PCD). The notion of a patent claim is introduced as well as the rights granted by such a claim. The patent statute is also introduced.[3] The elements of a *prima facie* case in federal court are also treated. Likewise, this chapter introduces some strategic and tactical considerations when beginning to draft a set of claims for an invention.

One necessary consideration is "prior art." This has a legal meaning, which changed in 2013 when specific provisions of the America Invents Act (AIA)[4] went into effect. Thus, pre- and post-AIA definitions of "prior art" are contemplated. Related to such strategic and tactical considerations, examples

---

1. Giles S. Rich, *The Extent of the Protection and Interpretation of Claims—American Perspectives*, 21 INT'L REV. INDUS. PROP. & COPYRIGHT L. 497, 499 (1990) ("To coin a phrase, the name of the game is the claim.").

2. *See, e.g.*, Corning Glass Works v. Sumitomo Elec. U.S.A., Inc., 868 F.2d 1251, 1257 (Fed. Cir. 1989) ("A claim in a patent provides the metes and bounds of the right which the patent confers on the patentee to exclude others from making, using, or selling the protected invention.").

Donald Chisum explains the importance of claims as follows:

> Claims measure the invention for determining patentability both during examination and after issuance when validity is challenged. They also determine what constitutes infringement. A claim recites a number of elements or limitations, and will cover or "read on" only those products (or processes) that contain all such elements or limitations. Effective claims must be neither too broad (i.e., cover the prior art or matter not adequately described in the specification) nor too narrow (i.e., fail to cover all possible embodiments of the applicant's invention).

1 DONALD S. CHISUM, CHISUM ON PATENTS glossary (2024).

3. *See, e.g.*, 35 U.S.C. (2024).

4. Throughout this book, AIA refers to the Leahy-Smith America Invents Act, Pub. L. No. 112-29, 125 Stat. 284 (2011). This act was passed on September 11, 2013. The provisions that changed §§ 102 and 103 of title 35 are addressed later in this chapter. These provisions went into effect on March 16, 2013.

of how patents may be used in business are also considered via some example business situations.

As an introductory point, first understand that the scope of legal rights granted by a patent is defined by the "claims" of the patent.[5] The claims of a patent are the numbered sentences at the very end of the patent. The claims section of a patent begins with words such as "I claim," "We claim," or "What is claimed is," immediately followed by a colon. Following the colon are a succession of sequentially numbered partial sentences that complete the sentence that begins as "I claim," "We claim," or "What is claimed is."[6] Claims are, in effect, run-on sentences, since the only period in a claim occurs at the end of the claim.[7] Immediately following is a simple example of two patent claims. Claim 1 is referred to as an "independent claim" and claim 2 is referred to as a "dependent claim."[8]

EXAMPLE 1.1[9]

I claim:

1. An integrated circuit comprising: at least one metal conductor and at least one metal oxide semiconductor field effect transistor (MOSFET);

   wherein multiple contacts are coupled to the at least one metal conductor along a major axis of the at least one metal conductor to conduct current

5. *See, e.g.*, Phillips v. AWH Corp., 415 F.2d 1303, 1312 (Fed. Cir. 2005) (en banc) ("It is a 'bedrock principle' of patent law that 'the claims of a patent define the invention to which the patentee is entitled the right to exclude.'"). *See also* Constant v. Advanced Micro-Devices, Inc., 848 F.2d 1560, 1571, 7 U.S.P.Q.2d 1057, 1064 (Fed. Cir. 1988); Dollar Elec. Co. v. Syndevco, Inc., 205 U.S.P.Q. 949, 959 (E.D. Mich. 1979), *aff'd*, 669 F.2d 1370, 214 U.S.P.Q. 241 (6th Cir. 1982).

6. See *In re Fressola*, 22 U.S.P.Q.2d 1828 (Comm'r Pat. & Trademarks 1992), in which Commissioner Manbeck ruled that "[t]he single claim sentence requirement is within the [U.S. Patent and Trademark Office's (PTO's)] statutory authority and is consistent with the statutory purpose of 35 U.S.C. §112 2."

7. See Chapter 5 addressing grammar in connection with PCD.

8. See Chapter 4 addressing dependent and independent claims.

9. Illustrative example claims are presented throughout this book. The more important examples are numbered with the chapter in which the example appears and with the sequential number of the example in that chapter with these two numbers separated by a period, as shown here for Example 1.1. Thus, while most example claims have a number designation, as described, not all example claims appearing in this book are necessarily numbered. Also, for continuity and/or purposes of further explanation, and so on, some examples may be repeated in a later chapter. In those cases, for convenience, they receive another number designation in the manner described despite being identical to a claim previously treated in a prior chapter with a different number designation.

to or from the at least one metal conductor and to or from drain or source regions of the MOSFET; and

wherein the at least one metal conductor is tapered along the major axis so that during current flow the current density in the at least one metal conductor is substantially constant along the major axis.

2. The integrated circuit of claim 1, wherein the at least one metal conductor is tapered to form a shape of a trapezoid.

The main point here is that the scope of rights granted by a patent claim primarily turns on the exact words of the patent claims themselves.[10] Therefore, poor, sloppy, or not well-thought-out word selection may produce an undesirable result such that technology of value to the patentee is not *necessarily* covered by the claims of a patent. If that is the case, this will seriously reduce, if not completely eviscerate, the value of the patent at issue.

PCD is challenging because executing PCD reasonably well requires an appreciation of several complex areas: the state of patent law, the state of the technology at issue, and the state of business/economic considerations often related to the technology at issue. Furthermore, these three topics are often "moving targets." To provide a few examples, new U.S. Supreme Court and/or Federal Circuit decisions often leave uncertain the full scope of legal consequences and/or changes that may follow from those decisions. In addition, statutory changes, such as the AIA, and/or regulatory changes, promulgated by the U.S. Patent and Trademark Office (PTO), also frequently introduce change. Likewise, technological breakthroughs occurring on a weekly or daily basis may leave uncertain which technologies will remain and which will quickly be supplanted or become obsolete.

As a simple example, the movement from analog to digital modems had a significant effect on how computer networks operate. Not anticipating that change may have resulted in some patent claims that were of less value, if, for example, the claims recited analog modem technology rather than being broad enough to encompass both analog and digital modem technology.[11]

10. See Chapters 3 and 4, which address patent claim types, the parts of a patent claim, and the theory behind those parts; see also Chapter 5, which addresses principles of patent claim construction.

11. Likewise, there have been cases where the situation was reversed and because the claim was sufficiently broad to cover both analog and digital technology, the claim was held invalid because the analog technology predated the invention at issue. *Cf.* Personalized Media

Furthermore, changing economic and business conditions may also affect which technologies succeed in the marketplace and which do not. For example, difficulties in the economy may have slowed the adoption of solar technology and the adoption of more advanced cell phone networks, such as 5G and beyond. Similarly, the worldwide pandemic speeded up the adoption of technology that enables "virtual" meetings in place of "in-person" meetings. Understanding how a particular technology, especially one sought to be patented, may affect various markets may be particularly useful for PCD. As examples, changes in various markets may impact the demand for the technology at issue. Similarly, in what particular form the technology at issue will likely be sought (e.g., product demand) and/or deployed (e.g., product supply) may be particularly useful as well.

In other words, a universe of ways in which to craft a patent claim is available. To narrow this universe, there is a set of useful tools. These tools would typically include a good understanding of the technology at issue, including typical implementations. Likewise, competing technologies, as well as information about relevant markets, are also useful tools. Other tools may include how the technology is likely to be sold and/or distributed, where it likely will be manufactured, and so on. With such tools, your challenge is to craft patent claims that will hopefully sail through the PTO, although that is not all. The patent claims should also stand up to legal challenges in federal court and/or stand up to competitor scrutiny. To state this more broadly, the claims directed to a particular technical invention to be useful should successfully extract the greatest amount of value. This may occur through enforcement, such as via injunction, and/or in terms of damages, royalties, or other forms of valuable consideration.

In pursuit of this goal, we begin with an introduction to the key statutes that guide PCD. Next, we will consider the meaning of "prior art." Prior art has a specific legal meaning in this context (which changed when the relevant portion of the AIA went into force on March 16, 2013).[12] It is important that the implications of this statutory change be fully understood to be able to draft quality patent claims.

Commc'ns v. Apple, 952 F.3d 1336 (Fed. Cir. 2020) (claims avoided prior art because interpreted to mean only digital signals, rather than digital and analog signals).

12. See later parts of this chapter addressing aspects of pre- and post-AIA statutes that provide the legal meaning of "prior art." Note also that this is an area that is often tested as a major portion of the examination provided by the PTO required for admission to the patent bar.

Selected Patent Statutes

35 U.S.C. § 101. Inventions Patentable (Post-AIA)

Whoever invents or discovers any new and useful process, machine, manufacture, or composition of matter, or any new and useful improvement thereof, may obtain a patent therefor, subject to the conditions and requirements of this title.

35 U.S.C. § 102. Conditions for Patentability; Novelty (Post-AIA)

(a) NOVELTY; PRIOR ART.—A person shall be entitled to a patent unless—

(1) the claimed invention was patented, described in a printed publication, or in public use, on sale, or otherwise available to the public before the effective filing date of the claimed invention; or

(2) the claimed invention was described in a patent issued under section 151, or in an application for patent published or deemed published under section 122(b), in which the patent or application, as the case may be, names another inventor and was effectively filed before the effective filing date of the claimed invention.

(b) EXCEPTIONS.—

(1) DISCLOSURES MADE 1 YEAR OR LESS BEFORE THE EFFECTIVE FILING DATE OF THE CLAIMED INVENTION.—A disclosure made 1 year or less before the effective filing date of a claimed invention shall not be prior art to the claimed invention under subsection (a)(1) if—

(A) the disclosure was made by the inventor or joint inventor or by another who obtained the subject matter disclosed directly or indirectly from the inventor or a joint inventor; or

(B) the subject matter disclosed had, before such disclosure, been publicly disclosed by the inventor or a joint inventor or another who obtained the subject matter disclosed directly or indirectly from the inventor or a joint inventor.

(2) DISCLOSURES APPEARING IN APPLICATIONS AND PATENTS.—A disclosure shall not be prior art to a claimed invention under subsection (a)(2) if—

(A) the subject matter disclosed was obtained directly or indirectly from the inventor or a joint inventor;

(B) the subject matter disclosed had, before such subject matter was effectively filed under subsection (a)(2), been publicly disclosed by the inventor or a joint inventor or another who obtained the subject matter disclosed directly or indirectly from the inventor or a joint inventor; or

(C) the subject matter disclosed and the claimed invention, not later than the effective filing date of the claimed invention, were owned by the same person or subject to an obligation of assignment to the same person.

(c) Common Ownership Under Joint Research Agreements.—Subject matter disclosed and a claimed invention shall be deemed to have been owned by the same person or subject to an obligation of assignment to the same person in applying the provisions of subsection (b)(2)(C) if—

(1) the subject matter disclosed was developed and the claimed invention was made by, or on behalf of, 1 or more parties to a joint research agreement that was in effect on or before the effective filing date of the claimed invention;

(2) the claimed invention was made as a result of activities undertaken within the scope of the joint research agreement; and

(3) the application for patent for the claimed invention discloses or is amended to disclose the names of the parties to the joint research agreement.

(d) Patents and Published Applications Effective as Prior Art.—For purposes of determining whether a patent or application for patent is prior art to a claimed invention under subsection (a)(2), such patent or application shall be considered to have been effectively filed, with respect to any subject matter described in the patent or application—

(1) if paragraph (2) does not apply, as of the actual filing date of the patent or the application for patent; or

(2) if the patent or application for patent is entitled to claim a right of priority under section 119, 365(a), 365(b), 386(a), or 386(b), or to claim the benefit of an earlier filing date under section 120, 121, 365(c), or 386(c), based upon 1 or more prior filed applications for patent, as of the filing date of the earliest such application that describes the subject matter.

35 U.S.C. § 103. Conditions for Patentability; Non-Obvious Subject Matter (Post-AIA)

A patent for a claimed invention may not be obtained, notwithstanding that the claimed invention is not identically disclosed as set forth in section 102, if the differences between the claimed invention and the prior art are such that the claimed invention as a whole would have been obvious before the effective filing date of the claimed invention to a person having ordinary skill in the art to which the claimed invention pertains. Patentability shall not be negated by the manner in which the invention was made.

35 U.S.C. § 112. Specification (Post-AIA)

(a) In General.—The specification shall contain a written description of the invention, and of the manner and process of making and using it, in such full, clear, concise, and exact terms as to enable any person skilled in the art to which it pertains,

or with which it is most nearly connected, to make and use the same, and shall set forth the best mode contemplated by the inventor or joint inventor of carrying out the invention.

(b) CONCLUSION.*—The specification shall conclude with one or more claims particularly pointing out and distinctly claiming the subject matter which the inventor or a joint inventor regards as the invention.*

(c) FORM.*—A claim may be written in independent or, if the nature of the case admits, in dependent or multiple dependent form.*

(d) REFERENCE IN DEPENDENT FORMS.*—Subject to subsection (e), a claim in dependent form shall contain a reference to a claim previously set forth and then specify a further limitation of the subject matter claimed. A claim in dependent form shall be construed to incorporate by reference all the limitations of the claim to which it refers.*

(e) REFERENCE IN MULTIPLE DEPENDENT FORM.*—A claim in multiple dependent form shall contain a reference, in the alternative only, to more than one claim previously set forth and then specify a further limitation of the subject matter claimed. A multiple dependent claim shall not serve as a basis for any other multiple dependent claim. A multiple dependent claim shall be construed to incorporate by reference all the limitations of the particular claim in relation to which it is being considered.*

(f) ELEMENT IN CLAIM FOR A COMBINATION.*—An element in a claim for a combination may be expressed as a means or step for performing a specified function without the recital of structure, material, or acts in support thereof, and such claim shall be construed to cover the corresponding structure, material, or acts described in the specification and equivalents thereof.*

Basic Principles and Legal Formalities

What Is Considered to Be Prior Art?

Understand what constitutes prior art and how it affects claim drafting.

In general, § 101, as shown earlier, requires that an invention be "new."

Section 102 then specifies conditions that result in anticipation, meaning that the invention is not new. To complicate matters, however, § 102 was changed on March 16, 2013. Any situation likely to involve some sort of PCD should, consequently, contemplate the prior § 102 statute (pre-AIA, provided in the following section) and the current § 102 statute (post-AIA, provided earlier).

Section 103, which specifies conditions for subject matter to be nonobvious, was also changed on March 16, 2013, by the AIA. It is noted that a claim must be novel and nonobvious both pre-AIA and post-AIA, in addition to other conditions specified by statute, for someone to be entitled to a patent including that claim.[13]

Immediately following are the pre-AIA statutory §§ 102 and 103.

35 U.S.C. § 102. Conditions for Patentability; Novelty and Loss of Right to Patent (Pre-AIA)

A person shall be entitled to a patent unless—

(a) the invention was known or used by others in this country, or patented or described in a printed publication in this or a foreign country, before the invention thereof by the applicant for patent, or

(b) the invention was patented or described in a printed publication in this or a foreign country or in public use or on sale in this country, more than one year prior to the date of the application for patent in the United States, or

(c) he has abandoned the invention, or

(d) the invention was first patented or caused to be patented, or was the subject of an inventor's certificate, by the applicant or his legal representatives or assigns in a foreign country prior to the date of the application for patent in this country on an application for patent or inventor's certificate filed more than twelve months before the filing of the application in the United States, or

(e) the invention was described in—(1) an application for patent, published under section 122(b), by another filed in the United States before the invention by the applicant for patent or (2) a patent granted on an application for patent by another filed in the United States before the invention by the applicant for patent, except that an international application filed under the treaty defined in section 351(a) shall have the effects for the purposes of this subsection of an application filed in the United States only if the international application designated the United States and was published under Article 21(2) of such treaty in the English language; or

(f) he did not himself invent the subject matter sought to be patented, or

(g) (1) during the course of an interference conducted under section 135 or section 291, another inventor involved therein establishes, to the extent permitted in section 104, that before such person's invention thereof the invention was made by such other inventor and not abandoned, suppressed, or concealed, or (2) before such person's invention thereof, the invention was made in this country by another inventor who had not abandoned, suppressed, or concealed it. In determining priority of invention under this subsection, there shall be considered not only the respective dates of conception and reduction to practice of the invention, but also the reasonable diligence of one

13. Whether to apply pre-AIA sections or post-AIA sections needs to be analyzed, as discussed later in this chapter.

who was first to conceive and last to reduce to practice, from a time prior to conception by the other.

35 U.S.C. 103. Conditions for Patentability; Non-Obvious Subject Matter (Pre-AIA)

(a) A patent may not be obtained though the invention is not identically disclosed or described as set forth in section 102, if the differences between the subject matter sought to be patented and the prior art are such that the subject matter as a whole would have been obvious at the time the invention was made to a person having ordinary skill in the art to which said subject matter pertains. Patentability shall not be negatived by the manner in which the invention was made.

(b)(1) Notwithstanding subsection (a), and upon timely election by the applicant for patent to proceed under this subsection, a biotechnological process using or resulting in a composition of matter that is novel under section 102 and nonobvious under subsection (a) of this section shall be considered nonobvious if—

(A) claims to the process and the composition of matter are contained in either the same application for patent or in separate applications having the same effective filing date; and

(B) the composition of matter, and the process at the time it was invented, were owned by the same person or subject to an obligation of assignment to the same person.

(2) A patent issued on a process under paragraph (1)—

(A) shall also contain the claims to the composition of matter used in or made by that process, or

(B) shall, if such composition of matter is claimed in another patent, be set to expire on the same date as such other patent, notwithstanding section 154.

(3) For purposes of paragraph (1), the term "biotechnological process" means—

(A) a process of genetically altering or otherwise inducing a single- or multi-celled organism to—

(i) express an exogenous nucleotide sequence,

(ii) inhibit, eliminate, augment, or alter expression of an endogenous nucleotide sequence, or

(iii) express a specific physiological characteristic not naturally associated with said organism;

(B) cell fusion procedures yielding a cell line that expresses a specific protein, such as a monoclonal antibody; and

(C) a method of using a product produced by a process defined by subparagraph (A) or (B), or a combination of subparagraphs (A) and (B).

(c)(1) Subject matter developed by another person, which qualifies as prior art only under one or more of subsections (e), (f), and (g) of section 102, shall not preclude patentability under this section where the subject matter and the claimed invention were,

at the time the claimed invention was made, owned by the same person or subject to an obligation of assignment to the same person.

(2) For purposes of this subsection, subject matter developed by another person and a claimed invention shall be deemed to have been owned by the same person or subject to an obligation of assignment to the same person if—

(A) the claimed invention was made by or on behalf of parties to a joint research agreement that was in effect on or before the date the claimed invention was made;

(B) the claimed invention was made as a result of activities undertaken within the scope of the joint research agreement; and

(C) the application for patent for the claimed invention discloses or is amended to disclose the names of the parties to the joint research agreement.

(3) For purposes of paragraph (2), the term "joint research agreement" means a written contract, grant, or cooperative agreement entered into by two or more persons or entities for the performance of experimental, developmental, or research work in the field of the claimed invention.

Pre-AIA 35 U.S.C. § 102 Generally[14]

This pre-AIA statutory section (i.e., § 102) begins by operating in the negative and stating "[a] person shall be *entitled* to a patent *unless* . . . ." (emphasis added). Meeting the subsection conditions of the statute, in effect, negates novelty. Likewise, the subsections are separated by "or." Thus, meeting any one subsection would render the subject matter at issue unpatentable as being anticipated. In general, *this section is thought of as defining the scope of what constitutes prior art, an important analytic concept with respect to drafting patent claims.*[15]

Negating novelty is referred to as anticipation, which means that the invention at issue is contained in the prior art based on a strict identity test with the language of a claim.[16] In prosecution of the patent application, this would lead to a rejection of the claim at issue under § 102 as anticipated. Likewise, in federal court litigation, this would result in the patent claim being declared invalid under § 102. Strict identity under Federal Circuit law means that a single piece of prior art (such as a patent, for example, with a filing date

---

14. For a more extended treatment of pre-AIA 35 U.S.C. § 102, see Howard A. Skaist, *Patent Claim Drafting Practice: Tactics, Strategy, and Analysis*, available from the publisher of this work.

15. *See, e.g.*, 1 Chisum, *supra* note 2, § 6.02[3](c) ("Federal Circuit decisions consistently confirm that Section 102(b) bar events constitute 'prior art' for purposes of obviousness.").

16. *See, e.g.*, U.S. Water Servs. v. Novozymes A/S, 843 F.3d 1345, 1350 (Fed. Cir. 2016) ("A reference is anticipatory under 35 U.S.C. §102(b) (2006) . . . if 'the prior art reference . . . disclose[s] each and every feature of the claimed invention, either explicitly or inherently.' Eli Lilly & Co. v. Zenith Goldline Pharms., Inc., 471 F.3d 1369, 1375 (Fed. Cir. 2006).").

before the filing date of the claim at issue) includes all the elements and limitations of the patent claim at issue arranged in the same way as recited in the patent claim.[17]

Notably, a single document *might* include all the elements and limitations of the claim and *still not* anticipate.[18] For example, a patent, again, with an earlier filing date, may describe various separate pieces of hardware but an examiner might try *to combine distinctive features* of separate pieces of hardware described in the patent and reject the claim as anticipated. This would be improper. At best, such a document would be a basis for a rejection of the claim as obvious under § 103, explained in more detail later. The point of having all the elements and limitations in a single document is so that the document contains a single description, either expressly or impliedly, that includes all the elements and limitations together arranged in the manner recited in the claim. If those elements and limitations, instead, are separately shown in different pieces of hardware with different purposes and features regarding those different pieces of hardware, throughout a prior art document, for example, anticipation has not occurred.

A process of "reading" a claim on an accused device or on the prior art, illustrated later via case law, explains the axiom "that which anticipates, if later in time [literally] infringes."[19] This "reading" a claim onto prior art is the process used to determine if a claim is anticipated under § 102. It is worthy of a mention that just as claim construction is needed to determine infringement, likewise, it is needed legally to determine anticipation in a legal proceeding.[20] It almost goes without saying that as the claim drafter, you, through the words you choose and how you formulate the claims, have the ability to affect claim construction. Thus, depending on a variety of factors, a particular claim construction may either be straightforward, and benefit your client, or be somewhat tortured, which may or may not win the day in a dispute.

Along these lines, a key point to understand is that, in general, *substantively* a claim is construed consistently in a later litigation as it was construed

17. *Id.*

18. *See* Linear Tech. Corp. v. Int'l Trade Comm'n, 566 F.3d 1049 (Fed. Cir. 2009); Bos. Sci. Scimed, Inc. v. Cordis Corp., 554 F.3d 982 (Fed. Cir. 2009); Ecolochem, Inc. v. S. Cal. Edison Co., 227 F.3d 1361, 56 U.S.P.Q.2d 1065 (Fed. Cir. 2000), *cert. denied*, 532 U.S. 974 (2001).

19. See later in this chapter addressing reading a patent claim on an accused product or on the prior art.

20. *See, e.g.*, Tate Access Floors, Inc. v. Interface Architectural Res., Inc., 279 F.3d 1357 (Fed. Cir. 2002).

during examination by the PTO.[21] However, different procedural postures affect the procedural rules that may be applied. During litigation, the patent claims, being issued, are presumed valid;[22] however, during examination they are not. Likewise, during litigation, the file history is used to interpret the claims, whereas during normal examination, it is not. Finally, during examination, the claims may be modified, whereas during litigation, in general, they may not. Therefore, considering these *procedural* differences, examiners or the Patent Trial and Appeal Board (PTAB), if reviewing an examiner's rejection, are permitted to give claims their "broadest reasonable interpretation" (BRI), which is broader than the interpretation applied by a federal court in litigation. However, substantively, the claim language is to be construed consistently. Specific language of a patent claim may not be construed one way in prosecution and then have that same language construed in a different manner in litigation. This relates to a type estoppel, addressed later.[23] Notably, a key feature of the BRI standard is that the interpretation must be *reasonable* in light of the language of the claim and the specification.[24]

Two Types of Subsections: Novelty and Statutory Bars

The subsection conditions of pre-AIA § 102 may be viewed as one of two types. The first type relates to lack of novelty (i.e., anticipation) of the invention and the second type relates to "statutory bars." The primary subsections related to novelty/anticipation are subsections 102(a), 102(e), and 102(g).[25] More specifically, these subsections specify conditions that are followed by the phrase "before the invention thereof by the applicant for patent." For example, 102(a) states that "the invention was known or used by others in this country, or patented or described in a printed publication in this or a foreign country, *before the invention thereof by the applicant for patent*" (emphasis added). Thus, the invention is in the prior art if it was known or used by others in this country before it was invented by an applicant for a patent. Likewise, the invention is in the prior art if it was patented or described in a printed publication in this or a foreign country before it was invented by the applicant.

---

21. *See, e.g.*, Traxcell Techs., LLC v. Sprint Commc'n Co. LP, 15 F.4th 1121 (Fed. Cir. 2021); Traxcell Techs., LLC v. Nokia Sols. & Networks Oy, 15 F.4th 1136 (Fed. Cir. 2021).

22. *See, e.g.*, Microsoft v. i4i Ltd. P'ship, 564 U.S. 91 (2011). Furthermore, in federal court, it takes clear and convincing evidence to prove that any claims of a patent are invalid.

23. See issues regarding "claim estoppel" and "prosecution history estoppel" addressed in Chapter 5.

24. *See, e.g.*, *In re* Suitco Surface, Inc., 603 F.3d 1255, 1260 (Fed. Cir. 2011).

25. For a more extended treatment of these pre-AIA subsections, see Skaist, *supra* note 14.

Since the invention, in these examples, is in the prior art, the invention is not novel and, per the statute, the applicant "is not entitled to a patent."

Another important issue under the pre-AIA statute is how to interpret "before the invention thereof." To some extent, this is addressed by subsection 102(g). Pre-AIA, the United States was a first-to-invent country.[26] Thus, rules existed, codified in subsection 102(g), to determine priority between two inventions involving the same or quite similar subject matter, invented close in time to one another. Priority is awarded to the party that demonstrates prior invention with evidence. Subsection 102(g)(2) states (emphasis added):

> In determining priority of invention under this subsection, there shall be considered not only the respective dates of *conception* and *reduction to practice* of the invention, but also the *reasonable diligence* of one who was first to conceive and last to reduce to practice, from a time prior to conception by the other.

Per subsection 102(g)(2), dates of "conception" and "reduction to practice" are used to determine the date of invention. However, for a filed patent application, unless evidence regarding earlier dates of conception and reduction to practice are introduced (e.g., to prove the date of invention is before the date of a printed publication that is alleged to anticipate), it is presumed that *the filing date of the patent application* at issue is the date of invention.[27]

Furthermore, unless an inventor's prior work operates under one of the statutory bars of pre-AIA § 102 (such as under subsection 102(b), discussed later as a "statutory bar"), an inventor *cannot*, under pre-AIA § 102, anticipate his or her own work.[28] This follows logically from the language "before the invention thereof by the applicant for patent" in the novelty provisions of § 102. The inventor's prior work, to the extent it is related subject matter, is included as part of "the invention thereof."

The other subsections of pre-AIA 102, subsections 102(b), 102(c), and 102(d),[29] are thought of as "statutory bars."[30] This refers to the idea that these

---

26. Post-AIA, the United States is a first-to-file country with a few notable exceptions addressed in the next section.

27. Thinking in this manner will also be helpful to understand post-AIA § 102 in which the statutory language "before the invention thereof by the applicant for patent" is omitted and the relevant subsections, instead, employ statutory language regarding "before the effective filing date of the claimed invention."

28. *See, e.g.*, *In re* Costello, 717 F.2d 1346, 1349, 219 U.S.P.Q. 389, 391 (Fed. Cir. 1983).

29. For a more extended treatment of pre-AIA 35 U.S.C. § 102, see Skaist, *supra* note 14.

30. 35 U.S.C. § 102(f) is a condition that states the applicant or applicants must be inventors of the subject matter of the patent application. Notably, this provision was removed by the AIA; however, a definition of "inventor" was added that has a similar legal effect.

subsections cover actions by the applicant that can result in the applicant's forfeiture of the right to seek a patent. However, here, too, if one of these subsections of 102 is met, analytically this means the invention is included in the prior art. However, the invention is barred, not because it was invented previously. Rather, the patentee/applicant engaged in conduct that resulted in forfeiture of the right to seek patent protection and effectively made the subject matter part of the "prior art."

Pre-AIA 35 U.S.C. § 103

Section 103 and obviousness has been the subject of entire books. Legal scholars, unsuccessfully, have tried to define what makes an invention "obvious" (or not obvious such that the invention is patentable). In Europe, they refer to this requirement that an invention not be obvious as "inventive step." Obviousness is intended to be an objective standard rather than a subjective one.

The terminology "inventive step" may work better for several reasons. For one thing, it suggests more objectivity than the term "obvious" (or "not obvious"). It also helps to clarify the difference from novelty as it relates to a potential invention. The term "inventive step" clarifies that even an invention that is novel may still be unpatentable unless it demonstrates an "inventive step" over the known prior art. In other words, novel subject matter that is *less than* an inventive step from the closest known prior art is still unpatentable.

Given the complexity of obviousness, we will only cover a few basic points here.

In general, § 102 defines anticipatory prior art. However, something may qualify as prior art *without* being anticipatory. For example, a patent that predates the filing date of a patent application by more than a year may be prior art, although it may not necessarily *fully anticipate* a patent claim. This type of prior art is sometimes referred to as 102(b)/103 prior art, for example. This means it qualifies as prior art under subsection 102(b) but does not include enough elements and limitations to anticipate the patent claim at issue. Under § 103, perhaps it may be combined, if done properly, with another piece of prior art under § 103 to render the invention unpatentable. Typically, then, such prior art is combinable with another piece of prior art and the combination, if properly made, would be the basis for a rejection under subsection 103(a) during examination or, if raised in litigation, would potentially be a basis to hold a patent claim invalid.

Although § 103 has several subsections, here, we are primarily concerned with pre-AIA subsection 103(a).

Subsection 103(a) begins, "A patent may not be obtained though the invention is not identically disclosed or described as set forth in section 102 . . . ." Sections 102 and 103 are separate hurdles. If a claim is anticipated under § 102, it may not be patented; however, even if not anticipated, the patent claim may still not be patentable if the prior art meets the language of subsection 103(a) with respect to the patent claim.

The subsection then states:

> [I]f the differences between the subject matter sought to be patented and the prior art are such that the subject matter as a whole would have been obvious at the time the invention was made to a person having ordinary skill in the art to which said subject matter pertains. Patentability shall not be negatived by the manner in which the invention was made.

The statute, therefore, focuses on "the differences between the subject matter sought to be patented," which refers to the patent claim at issue, and "the prior art." These differences, "as a whole," are considered "at the time the invention was made," this latter language referring to "conception" and "reduction to practice," as suggested by the previously quoted language of subsection 102(g)(2).

The language "as a whole" is important because it means that for the purposes of subsection 103(a), *the claim must be considered as a whole*. In other words, while the claim is a collection of elements and limitations, it is not proper under this subsection (i.e., subsection 103(a)) to simply dissect the claim into separate elements and limitations and see if the prior art has each recited element and limitation. Rather, the whole may be (and typically is) greater than the sum of the parts. This typically factors into what may make an invention unobvious. For example, there may be advantages that come from combining the elements and limitations together in the manner recited in the claim that would not be present if those elements and limitations were dissected and viewed in isolation from one another.[31] Those advantages that flow from "the whole" are relevant to determining whether the invention would have been obvious. Specifically, whether, at the time the invention was made, the

31. *See, e.g.*, Panduit Corp. v. Dennison Mfg. Co., 810 F.2d 1561, 1567–68, 1 U.S.P.Q.2d 1593, 1597 (Fed. Cir. 1987), *cert. denied*, 481 U.S. 1052 (1987) ("Analysis begins with a key legal question—what is the invention claimed? Courts are required to view the claimed invention as a whole. . . ."); Ruiz v. A.B. Chance Co., 357 F.3d 1270, 1275 (Fed. Cir. 2004) ("The 'as a whole' instruction in title 35 prevents evaluation of the invention part by part. . . . This form of hindsight reasoning, using the invention as a roadmap to find its prior art components, would discount the value of combining various existing features or principles in a new way to achieve a new result—often the very definition of invention.").

invention would have been obvious to "a person having ordinary skill in the art to which said subject matter pertains."

This latter language also raises several relevant and important legal issues. What is the art to which "said subject matter pertains"? Then, for that art, what are characteristics of "a person having ordinary skill" in that art? Do they require a Ph.D.? A master's degree? Do they require a certain amount of experience in a certain industry? And so on.

Of course, when preparing the claims, there is no way to know the answers to these questions. These issues are all subject to evidence and argument in a legal proceeding. A prudent approach may be to draft narrower claims than may at first appear to be needed, sometimes referred to as a "fallback position." The general idea is to draft some patent claims narrower than the broadest claims to be presented. However, more particularly, when considering the closest known prior art to which the subject matter might pertain and even when considering someone who might have been a little *above* ordinary skill (i.e., at the time the invention was made), draft claims that you believe could still be argued to be unobvious. For the narrower claims, it may, therefore, also be prudent to have arguments for patentability using the closest known prior art in the pertinent subjects that relate to the invention. Formulate arguments around these narrow patent claims such that a "person" a little *above* ordinary skill would concede the invention would have been unobvious.

The latter may seem like a tall order; however, it is more of a way of thinking when drafting claims. As discussed, while some claims are drafted to be relatively broad, you want to make sure you have a "fallback position" if the examiner comes up with closer prior art than you expected. Therefore, try to make sure that you also have claims that are sufficiently narrow so that you are able to provide persuasive arguments for patentability, even against reasonably close art.

In this context, it is helpful to understand the nature of a rejection made under subsection 103(a) based on known prior art. As indicated, it is not sufficient for the examiner to take the elements and limitations of the claim and demonstrate that those are individually in the prior art.[32] Rather, the examiner must also demonstrate that the prior art contains the *motivation* for either combining those elements and limitations as recited in the claim or for *modifying* the elements and limitations from the prior art in a manner as recited in

32. Although examiners will, at times, do this. If so, they have not provided a legitimate (called *prima facie*) rejection under § 103. *See* PTO, Manual of Patent Examining Procedure § 2143 (9th ed. 2023) [hereinafter MPEP].

the claim.[33] Specifically, such motivations *may not* come from the patent application. The latter is referred to as using "hindsight" and is legally improper. It is not proper to reconstruct the invention based on the document that explains the invention. If the examiner is unable to demonstrate that such motivations are present in the prior art, then the examiner has not made a proper rejection under subsection 103(a).

Suppose an examiner has two pieces of prior art, A and B.[34] Typically, one, such as A, contains most of the features of the claim being rejected under subsection 103(a) as obvious. A, then, is the examiner's primary reference. However, there may be features of the claim not shown or described in A that are shown or described in B. B, then, is the examiner's secondary reference. The examiner will then formulate his or her rejection as being "based on reference A in light of reference B."[35]

The examiner must also state on the record the basis for the assertion that there is motivation to combine references A and B. In some situations, however, be aware that even a combination of A and B does not provide the elements and limitations from the patent claim in the manner recited in the patent claim, in which case the rejection is also improper.[36] The examiner has overlooked something in formulating the rejection.

Under Federal Circuit law, unfortunately, the examiner may combine *any number* of prior art references in a § 103 rejection. As an example, if the examiner also needs a reference C to meet the patent claim, the examiner will then formulate his or her rejection as "being based on reference A in light of reference B and further in light of reference C." However, as the examiner adds more pieces of prior art, some doubt may begin to increase as to whether the motivation for the proposed combination *truly* exists in the prior art. While the examiner may combine any number of references, it is likely as he or she

---

33. For a recent case on lack of motivation to combine, see Tris Pharma Inc. v. Actavis Lab'ys FL, Inc., No. 21-1495 (Fed. Cir. July 7, 2022) (non-precedential). *See also In re* Lee, 277 F.3d 1338, 1342 (Fed. Cir. 2002) ("[T]he agency tribunal must present a full and reasoned explanation of its decision. The agency tribunal must set forth its findings and the grounds thereof, as supported by the agency record, and explain its application of the law to the found facts.").

34. The examiner may also formulate a § 103 rejection on a single prior art reference; however, a recent case has cast some doubt on such rejections. *See* Raytheon v. Gen. Elec., 993 F.3d 1374 (Fed. Cir. 2021).

35. It is noted, however, that a Federal Circuit case says that designation as primary or secondary is not significant for purposes of analysis under § 103. *See, e.g., In re* Mouttet, 686 F.3d 1322, 1333 (Fed. Cir. 2012) ("where the relevant factual inquiries underlying an obviousness determination are otherwise clear," characterizing references "as 'primary' and 'secondary' is merely a matter of presentation with no legal significance") (Rich, J.).

36. *See, e.g., In re* Stepan Co., 868 F.3d 1342, 1345–46 (Fed. Cir. 2017).

adds more references to make the § 103 rejection that, in fact, the motivation needed to make such a combination is not present.

To summarize, under subsection 103(a), pre-AIA, the examiner must *do more than* show that the prior art he or she is relying upon to reject the claim meets all the elements and limitations of the claim and in the manner recited in the claim (much like in a § 102 rejection for anticipation). If the examiner cannot even accomplish the latter, his or her rejection is improper without evaluating "motivation to combine." However, even if the examiner succeeds in accomplishing the latter, he or she must *also* show that the prior art contains the motivation to combine such prior art or to modify such prior art so that those elements and limitations are combined in the manner recited in the claim. If the examiner fails to do this, the rejection is improper as well.

35 U.S.C. § 102. Conditions for Patentability; Novelty (Post-AIA)

(a) NOVELTY; PRIOR ART.—A person shall be entitled to a patent unless—

(1) the claimed invention was patented, described in a printed publication, or in public use, on sale, or otherwise available to the public before the effective filing date of the claimed invention; or

(2) the claimed invention was described in a patent issued under section 151, or in an application for patent published or deemed published under section 122(b), in which the patent or application, as the case may be, names another inventor and was effectively filed before the effective filing date of the claimed invention.

(b) EXCEPTIONS.—

(1) DISCLOSURES MADE 1 YEAR OR LESS BEFORE THE EFFECTIVE FILING DATE OF THE CLAIMED INVENTION.—A disclosure made 1 year or less before the effective filing date of a claimed invention shall not be prior art to the claimed invention under subsection (a)(1) if—

(A) the disclosure was made by the inventor or joint inventor or by another who obtained the subject matter disclosed directly or indirectly from the inventor or a joint inventor; or

(B) the subject matter disclosed had, before such disclosure, been publicly disclosed by the inventor or a joint inventor or another who obtained the subject matter disclosed directly or indirectly from the inventor or a joint inventor.

(2) DISCLOSURES APPEARING IN APPLICATIONS AND PATENTS.—A disclosure shall not be prior art to a claimed invention under subsection (a)(2) if—

(A) the subject matter disclosed was obtained directly or indirectly from the inventor or a joint inventor;

(B) the subject matter disclosed had, before such subject matter was effectively filed under subsection (a)(2), been publicly disclosed by the inventor or a joint inventor or another who obtained the subject matter disclosed directly or indirectly from the inventor or a joint inventor; or

(C) the subject matter disclosed and the claimed invention, not later than the effective filing date of the claimed invention, were owned by the same person or subject to an obligation of assignment to the same person.

(c) COMMON OWNERSHIP UNDER JOINT RESEARCH AGREEMENTS.—Subject matter disclosed and a claimed invention shall be deemed to have been owned by the same person or subject to an obligation of assignment to the same person in applying the provisions of subsection (b)(2)(C) if—

(1) the subject matter disclosed was developed and the claimed invention was made by, or on behalf of, 1 or more parties to a joint research agreement that was in effect on or before the effective filing date of the claimed invention;

(2) the claimed invention was made as a result of activities undertaken within the scope of the joint research agreement; and

(3) the application for patent for the claimed invention discloses or is amended to disclose the names of the parties to the joint research agreement.

(d) PATENTS AND PUBLISHED APPLICATIONS EFFECTIVE AS PRIOR ART.—For purposes of determining whether a patent or application for patent is prior art to a claimed invention under subsection (a)(2), such patent or application shall be considered to have been effectively filed, with respect to any subject matter described in the patent or application—

(1) if paragraph (2) does not apply, as of the actual filing date of the patent or the application for patent; or

(2) if the patent or application for patent is entitled to claim a right of priority under section 119, 365(a), 365(b), 386(a), or 386(b), or to claim the benefit of an earlier filing date under section 120, 121, 365(c), or 386(c), based upon 1 or more prior filed applications for patent, as of the filing date of the earliest such application that describes the subject matter.

35 U.S.C. § 103. Conditions for Patentability; Non-Obvious Subject Matter (Post-AIA)

A patent for a claimed invention may not be obtained, notwithstanding that the claimed invention is not identically disclosed as set forth in section 102, if the differences between the claimed invention and the prior art are such that the claimed invention as a whole would have been obvious before the effective filing date of the claimed invention to a person having ordinary skill in the art to which the claimed invention pertains. Patentability shall not be negated by the manner in which the invention was made.

35 U.S.C. § 102 (Post-AIA)

Post-AIA § 102 retains some language from pre-AIA § 102, but also has many important differences. Furthermore, the AIA adds some definitions to § 100 of title 35 that were not previously codified. These include the meaning of the terms "claimed invention," "effective filing date," "inventor," and "joint inventor" (or "coinventor"). The AIA defines the term "claimed invention" as the subject matter defined by a claim in a patent or an application for a patent. This is consistent with our previous treatment of prior law. The AIA defines the term "effective filing date" for a claimed invention in a patent or application for patent (other than a reissue application or reissued patent) as meaning the earlier of (1) the actual filing date of the patent or the application for the patent containing the claimed invention; or (2) the filing date of the earliest provisional, nonprovisional, international (e.g., Patent Cooperation Treaty (PCT) or other international treaty, such as the Paris Convention Treaty), or foreign patent application to which the patent or application is entitled to benefit or priority as to such claimed invention. We have not yet emphasized this fine point regarding priority date, but it shall be addressed shortly, and this is consistent with prior law and assumptions made throughout this book. That is, under §§ 119, 120, 121, and 365 of the statute, although a U.S. patent or patent application may have an actual filing date, it may be accorded an earlier *priority date* based on a *previous* domestic, foreign, or international patent application filing *for purposes of determining prior art* if properly handled. The AIA defines the term "inventor" as the individual or, if a joint invention, the individuals collectively, who invented or discovered the subject matter of the invention, and defines the term "joint inventor" and "coinventor" to mean any one of the individuals who invented or discovered the subject matter of a joint invention. These are also in accordance with pre-AIA law.

Current § 102 (post-AIA) operates in a comparable manner to the previous statute by stating, "A person shall be *entitled* to a patent *unless* . . . ." Thus, subsections (a)(1) and (a)(2) specify conditions that would render an invention unpatentable. Consequently, as under prior law, currently in force (post-AIA) § 102, in effect, defines "prior art."

It is evident how different in structure post-AIA § 102 is from pre-AIA § 102. For post-AIA § 102, subsection "a" defines "prior art." Subsection "b" defines "exceptions." Subsection "c" relates to common ownership and operates like subsection 103(c) of the pre-AIA statute regarding common ownership under a joint research agreement. Subsection "d" clarifies the date upon which a patent or published patent application becomes effective as prior art. This subsection, in effect, via § 365, *abolishes* the doctrine under *In re Hilmer*,[37] in which a U.S. patent that relied on a foreign-filed application for priority was only effective as prior art as of its U.S. filing date.

37. *See* 359 F.2d 859, 149 U.S.P.Q. 480 (C.C.P.A. 1966).

In many respects, currently in force (i.e., post-AIA) § 102 simplifies how the law now operates. The AIA moved the United States to a first-to-file system.[38] The distinction between subsections that operated as bars and those that operated based on "before the invention thereof by applicant" is no longer present. Instead, prior art is defined relative to the "effective filing date of the claimed invention," a statutorily defined term. Likewise, the ability to remove prior art from consideration because one is able to prove the invention "was made" before the date of the prior art is no longer available.[39] This, in essence, makes more prior art available to cite against a patent claim. Where possible, for this reason, one should seek to file a patent application in a manner so that the law as it was prior to March 16, 2013, applies to the patent claims, such as via a continuation patent application or a divisional patent application (without adding any new matter) that claims priority to a domestic patent application filed pre-AIA.[40]

Under current law, "prior art" is defined concisely in subsection 102(a) by these subsections:

> A person shall be entitled to a patent unless—
>
> (1) the claimed invention was patented, described in a printed publication, or in public use, on sale, or otherwise available to the public before the effective filing date of the claimed invention; or
>
> (2) the claimed invention was described in a patent issued under section 151, or in an application for patent published or deemed published under section 122(b), in which the patent or application, as the case may be, names another inventor and was effectively filed before the effective filing date of the claimed invention.

Subsection 102(a)(2) operates like subsection 102(e) of the previous statute in terms of defining "anticipation," although notably, all references to "in this country" are removed from current § 102. Another notable difference is the handling of commonly owned patents and patent applications, by which under subsection 102(b)(2)(C) provided earlier, "disclosures appearing in applications and patents" may be excepted from being prior art. Under prior law, this was handled by subsection 103(c), which created an exception to pre-AIA

38. With some exceptions, as described later.

39. One exception in very specific circumstances may relate to transition patent applications, addressed later in the chapter.

40. See later in this chapter addressing how the transition provisions of the AIA operate for domestic patent applications filed on or after March 16, 2013, claiming priority to domestic patent applications filed before that date.

subsection 102(e) regarding prior art for the purposes of subsection 103(a). Here, however, it is addressed by subsection 102(b)(2)(C). Post-AIA, such "disclosures appearing in applications and patents" are not prior art under either § 102 or 103 under current law; previously, the documents would remain prior art under pre-AIA subsection 102(e), but were removed from consideration for the purposes of subsection 103(a). This currently in force post-AIA exception to prior art also appears to be expanded (in comparison to the pre-AIA exception to subsection 102(e) under subsection 103(a)) based on the language of post-AIA subsection 102(b)(2)(C). The current statute specifies an exception to prior art under subsection 102(a)(2) for situations in which "the subject matter disclosed and the claimed invention, not later than the effective filing date of the claimed invention, were owned by the same person or subject to an obligation of assignment to the same person." In some cases this should ostensibly be later than was permitted under pre-AIA subsection 103(c). Despite being owned or subject to an obligation at a later time under the current statute than was permitted under the pre-AIA statute, it is still removed from being prior art.

Finally, for post-AIA subsection 102(a)(2) there appears to be an expansion of an exception to prior art relative to "by another," as specified in pre-AIA subsection 102(e). Pre-AIA this operated in accordance with inventive entity and despite the linguistic change to "names another inventor" appears to work similarly.[41] A different inventive entity for subject matter of a previously filed patent application constituted prior art as of its filing date, once published. This was true even assuming an overlap of inventors or even a superset that included an inventor, for example. This prior filed patent application was considered to be prior art "by another" per pre-AIA subsection 102(e); whereas if there is perfect identity of inventorship, it would not be prior art under subsection 102(e). However, under current law, an exception to post-AIA subsection 102(a)(2) is provided under subsection 102(b)(2)(A), again, for "disclosures appearing in applications and patents." The exception states that "the subject matter disclosed was obtained directly or indirectly from the inventor or a joint inventor." This suggests a possible broader exception because it appears to apply independent of who invented what subject matter.[42]

---

41. *See* MPEP, *supra* note 32, § 2154.01(c).

42. Although, under case law, a similar exception applied under pre-AIA subsection 102(e); however, the post-AIA exception on its face appears broader because it does not appear to distinguish which inventor or inventors specifically invented the subject matter of the prior patent or patent application being used to reject the current patent application. *See* MPEP, *supra* note 32, § 717.01(III)(B).

Subsection 102(a)(1) of post-AIA § 102 handles everything else that was handled by the other subsections of pre-AIA § 102. Specifically, subsections 102(c), 102(f), and 102(g)[43] are removed, although the new codified definition of "inventor" implicitly addresses subsection 102(f) by specifying an inventor must have invented or discovered the subject matter of the invention. Pre-AIA subsection 102(g) is not needed in a first-to-file system.

As mentioned, geographical limitations on prior art have been removed. Subsection (a)(2) of § 102, however, retains "patented," "described in a printed publication," "on sale," and "public use." The language "known or used by others" is also omitted, but there is new additional language, "otherwise available to the public."

Generally, if Congress uses the same language in a new statute replacing a previous statute, courts usually interpret this to mean that Congress desires to retain the previous construction.

In *Helsinn*,[44] this was the result reached by the Supreme Court as to the post-AIA "on sale" language of subsection 102(a)(1) despite the additional language "otherwise available to the public." It, therefore, is expected that all the common terms will be construed in the same manner as construed with respect to pre-AIA § 102. It remains to be seen how "otherwise available to the public" will be construed; however, the similarity with the language used in the European Patent Convention (EPC) to define "prior art," which states "everything available to the public," and which has been interpreted as an absolute novelty standard, has not gone unnoticed.

The exceptions in subsection (b) of post-AIA § 102 raise issues that remain unsettled, even after the *Helsinn* decision, which many had hoped would clarify the status of the "grace period" under post-AIA § 102. Under pre-AIA subsection 102(b), a one-year grace period was permitted before forfeiture of rights due to the enumerated activities, such as "public use" or placing an invention "on sale." Subsection (b)(1) of post-AIA § 102 specifies exceptions to subsection (a)(1) for "disclosures" made one year or less before the effective filing date of the claimed invention. Subsection A of that subsection states that such a "disclosure" is not prior art under subsection (a)(1) if "the disclosure was made by the inventor or joint inventor or by another who obtained the subject matter disclosed directly or indirectly from the inventor or a joint inventor."

---

43. For a more extended treatment of pre-AIA subsections of § 102, see Skaist, *supra* note 14. Also, note the special situation of subsection 102(g) and transition patent applications, addressed later in this chapter.

44. *See* Helsinn Healthcare S.A. v. Teva Pharms. USA, Inc., 139 S. Ct. 628 (2019).

An ambiguity arises because the term "disclosure" is new in the statute and undefined. Its meaning in this context continues to be debated within the patent bar. Does the term refer to the elements of subsection 102(a)(1) and thereby largely retain the grace period under prior law?[45]

A plain meaning interpretation, instead, would distinguish between activities that may or may not be accompanied by disclosure, such as the commercialization aspects under prior law regarding on sale and public use activities. Under this latter interpretation, current law has no grace period for on sale and public use activities. Rather, the grace period only applies to any accompanying disclosure. This latter interpretation, undesirable as it may be, appears more consistent with Supreme Court precedent, including *Helsinn*. For example, in that case, the Court drew a distinction between the commercial aspect of placing an invention on sale and the information made available to the public, which did not disclose details of the invention itself. On the other hand, policy considerations may suggest interpreting the statute otherwise. Interpreting "disclosure" to refer to the elements of subsection 102(a)(1), as just suggested, would encourage early disclosure by inventors, something that Congress clearly intended to encourage.

The language of subsection B of 102(b)(1) also raises questions as to its scope. It states that a disclosure one year or less before the effective filing of the claimed invention is not prior art under subsection (a)(1) if "the subject matter disclosed had, before such disclosure, been publicly disclosed by the inventor or a joint inventor or another who obtained the subject matter disclosed directly or indirectly from the inventor or a joint inventor." The scope of "publicly disclosed" is not entirely clear. The language implies but does not expressly state that "the subject matter disclosed" is identically the same as what was "publicly disclosed." For example, what if "the subject matter disclosed" was not derived in any way from that which was "publicly disclosed"? The exception, in effect, under this interpretation would give the inventor(s) a right of priority for making the public disclosure, something that the law would like to encourage from a policy perspective, but this, again, similar to the grace period issue, is not fully consistent with what may be implied by the specific statutory language.

Subsection (b)(2) specifies exceptions to (a)(2) regarding "DISCLOSURES APPEARING IN APPLICATIONS AND PATENTS."[46] Subsections A and B are similar to the exceptions to subsection (a)(1) provided under

45. This is the position of the PTO. *See* MPEP, *supra* note 32, § 2152.04.

46. Sanho v. Kaijet, case no. 2023-1336 (Fed. Cir. July 31, 2024) (concluding private sale does not meet "public disclosure" language of subsection 102(b)(2)(B)); Celanese Int'l Corp. v. ITC, Case No. 2022-1827 n.2 (Fed. Cir. Aug. 12, 2024) ("Congress also retained the one-year grace period for certain disclosures made one year or less prior to applying for patent, which was previously codified in pre-AIA Section 102(b) and is now codified in AIA Section 102(b)(1).").

subsection (b)(1) discussed previously. Subsection A of (b)(2) is like as discussed earlier with reference to subsection 102(e), although, again, it may be slightly broader, as previously discussed. Subsection B is similar to the corresponding exception under subsection (b)(1) discussed earlier with similar questions as to scope. Subsection (b)(2) also includes a subsection C excluding from prior art under subsection (a)(2) commonly owned patents and applications, similar to subsection 103(c) under the prior statute, although, again, potentially a little broader, as discussed previously.

35 U.S.C. § 103 (Post-AIA)

Post-AIA § 103 is quite similar to pre-AIA subsection 103(a). Also, pre-AIA subsections (b) and (c) were eliminated in post-AIA § 103, although subsection (c) under prior law is similar to post-AIA subsections 102(c) and 102(b)(2)(C).

Post-AIA § 103 states:

> A patent for a claimed invention may not be obtained, notwithstanding that the claimed invention is not identically disclosed as set forth in section 102, if the differences between the claimed invention and the prior art are such that the claimed invention as a whole would have been obvious before the effective filing date of the claimed invention to a person having ordinary skill in the art to which the claimed invention pertains. Patentability shall not be negated by the manner in which the invention was made.

Notably, it retains the reference to § 102 and, therefore, operates with § 102 in the manner previously described with respect to pre-AIA subsection 103(a).

The primary difference is the time at which obviousness is assessed because of the change from a first-to-invent patent system to a first-to-file patent system. Under the presently in force statute, obviousness is determined based on what would have been obvious to a person of ordinary skill in the art to which the claimed invention pertains "before the effective filing date of the claimed invention." Otherwise, current law appears to operate as the law operated under subsection 103(a). Linguistically, the statute refers to "the claimed invention" rather than "the subject matter sought to be patented" and "negated" rather than "negatived," but these are not believed to result in any substantive interpretive difference.

Questions

1. Observe that pre-AIA subsections 102(a) and 102(b) have language in common. Both state that "the invention was patented or described in a printed publication in this or a foreign country." What is the

difference in language between the two sections and what is the effect of the difference? The notable features of the common language include "patented," "described in a printed publication," and "in this or a foreign country." Compare this language with post-AIA subsection 102(a)(1).

2. How would you interpret the language "described in a printed publication"? What qualifies as "printed"?[47] What qualifies as "publication"?[48]
3. Since most countries publish issued patents, what is the difference between "patented" and "described in a printed publication" in pre- or post-AIA § 102?
4. In pre- or post-AIA § 102, must a printed publication necessarily be "enabling" as to the subject matter at issue? Same question for pre- and post-AIA § 103.
5. Post-AIA § 102 includes the language "or otherwise available to the public before the effective filing date of the claimed invention." How should this language be interpreted in light of the accompanying language "the claimed invention was patented, described in a printed publication, or in public use, on sale"? Does the exception provided under subsection 102(b)(1) provide any insight into a possible interpretation of this language?
6. Some, including the PTO,[49] have suggested that the one-year grace period provided by pre-AIA subsection 102(b) has, in effect, been retained post-AIA by subsection 102(b)(1). Compare the language of pre-AIA subsection 102(b) and the language of post-AIA subsection 102(b)(1). Is there a logical basis for this position based on the language of the statute itself?
7. It has been stated that the intent of the AIA, at least partially, was to make the United States a first-to-file country rather than a first-to-invent country. Can you identify which provision of post-AIA § 102 accomplishes that? Are the exceptions provided by post-AIA subsection 102(b) consistent or inconsistent with the notion that the United States is a first-to-file country?
8. Countries that are members of the EPC are sometimes referred to as "absolute novelty countries." In particular, Articles 54(1) and 54(2) of the EPC state:

---

47. *See In re* Enhanced Sec. Rsch., LLC, 739 F.3d 1347 (Fed. Cir. 2014).
48. *See In re* Hall, 781 F.2d 897 (Fed. Cir. 1986).
49. *See* MPEP, *supra* note 32, § 2152.04.

(1) An invention shall be considered to be new if it does not form part of the state of the art.

(2) The state of the art shall be held to comprise everything made available to the public by means of a written or oral description, by use, or in any other way, before the date of filing of the European patent application.

Is it fair to say that the United States has become an absolute novelty country as well? Why or why not?

9. What is the effect of pre-AIA subsection 102(e)(2)? What is the difference with respect to pre-AIA subsection 102(e)(1)? Note that starting in 2000, under U.S. law patent applications become published 18 months after filing unless the applicant opts out of publication. The applicant must opt out at the time of filing or the application will be published. Likewise, it is not proper to opt out if the patent application is being foreign filed. Thus, if an application that has opted out of publication in the United States is foreign filed, then the U.S. patent application is deemed abandoned by the PTO.[50]
10. For pre-AIA subsections 102(e)(1) and (e)(2), consider the interplay between the "by another" language and the "before the invention by the patent applicant" language. A general principle is that a patent applicant cannot create prior art against himself or herself except via a statutory bar (e.g., pre-AIA subsection 102(b)). What happens if a patent applicant has a previously filed patent application with subject matter relevant to a later filed patent application in which the patent applicant of the previously filed patent application has coinventors on the later filed patent application? Consider also the effect, if any, of pre-AIA subsection 103(c) in such a situation.[51]
11. Compare pre-AIA subsections 102(e)(1) and (e)(2) with post-AIA subsection 102(a)(2). Also compare pre-AIA subsection 103(c) with post-AIA subsection 102(b)(2)(C). Is there a legal difference between the effect of the former subsection relative to the latter subsection?
12. Is there a legal difference in the "by another" language in pre-AIA subsections 102(e)(1) and (e)(2) versus the "names another inventor" language of post-AIA subsection 102(a)(2)? What is the significance of post-AIA subsections 102(b)(2)(A) and 102(b)(2)(B)?

---

50. *See* 35 U.S.C. § 122; MPEP, *supra* note 32, §§ 1122–24.

51. *See* Applied Materials, Inc. v. Gemini Rsch. Corp., 835 F.2d 279, 5 U.S.P.Q.2d 1127 (Fed. Cir. 1987), *reh'g granted, opinion modified*, 15 U.S.P.Q.2d 1816 (Fed. Cir. 1988).

13. Pre-AIA subsection 102(g) is a key provision in the first-to-invent approach that existed pre-AIA. As the statutory language indicates, key concepts are "conception," "reduction to practice," and "diligence." In light of the statute, which seems more important in establishing "priority of invention," "conception," or "reduction to practice"? How would one prove "conception," "reduction to practice," and/or "diligence"? The law under this provision appears to require "corroboration" of evidence that is independent of the inventor. How might this be accomplished?[52]
14. Under Pre-AIA subsection 102(g)(2), how does one determine if something is considered "prior art"? Is there any requirement that "prior art" under subsection 102(g)(2) be public? What does it mean that "the invention was *made* by such other inventor"? What does it mean that such other inventor had "not *abandoned, suppressed, or concealed*" the invention?[53]
15. Consider pre-AIA subsection 102(a). Compare its language with post-AIA subsection 102(a)(1), which states, "or otherwise available to the public."
16. What does pre-AIA subsection 102(a) establish as "prior art" that is not already covered under the other subsections of § 102 (e.g., subsections 102(b), 102(e), and 102(g))? What does the language "known or used by others" mean? What is the difference between "known" by others versus "used" by others? Does the language "by others" imply that the knowledge or use must have been publicly available?

Claim Drafting and Prior Art

Because prior art may limit claim scope, some amount of searching the prior art is frequently associated with drafting patent claims. The prior art is the practical limit on claim scope; hence, knowing the prior art before drafting the claims and prior to taking a position before the PTO, in many instances, should provide an advantage; unfortunately, searches are notoriously poor while consuming valuable resources. In general, the higher the quality of the search, usually the more resources that are consumed.

---

52. *See In re* Costello, 717 F.2d 1346, 219 U.S.P.Q. 389 (Fed. Cir. 1983). *See also* MPEP, *supra* note 32, §§ 2138.04–.06.

53. *See In re* Bass, 474 F.2d 1276, 177 U.S.P.Q. 178 (C.C.P.A. 1973); *In re* Suska, 589 F.2d 527, 200 U.S.P.Q. 497 (C.C.P.A. 1979). *See also* MPEP, *supra* note 32, § 2138.03.

Whether to search tends to be a contextually laden decision and is considered in more detail in later sections of this book.[54] However, being able to obtain and study the best and most relevant prior art before developing or drafting the patent claims is akin to knowing your opponent's argument or position before you draft your own argument. Rarely does the law provide this opportunity to an advocate, so, *if cost is not a factor*, it may be something to consider. Unfortunately, *cost usually is a factor*. Therefore, a search may not necessarily be undertaken, or the results, again, may be quite poor in that the best and most relevant prior art may not be uncovered due to limited resources. Furthermore, despite the advantage just mentioned, in some circumstances, a search may not be needed and, if so, may unnecessarily add additional cost.[55] Still, two reasons to search for prior art are (1) if it turns out the exact subject matter has been done previously, knowing that early allows you to avoid the cost of pursuing a patent application; and (2) knowing the best prior art allows you to draft original claims that decrease the likelihood that claim elements or limitations need to be added during prosecution and, consequently, to avoid prosecution history estoppel.

As a result, as one might have inferred, some uncertainty as to the closest and most relevant prior art is likely to exist when the patent claims are submitted to the PTO. It is rarely clear at the time of filing a patent application that one has, in fact, found the best and most relevant prior art. One reason for this is because the cost of doing a completely comprehensive and thorough search would likely make pursuing a patent application prohibitively expensive. Online resources are improving so that, if needed, a useful and cost-effective search to at least uncover "low-hanging fruit" may be undertaken. More typically, however, the most careful, thorough, and, therefore, costly prior art searching is performed in conjunction with litigation or a similar type of patent assertion activity. Much more is usually at stake in a litigation (or licensing) situation than is at stake at the time an application is filed, explaining the greater allocation of resources for searching later. This may also at least partially explain why it is that new art is usually found and frequently does impact the patent claims in connection with an inter partes review (IPR) or other post-grant proceeding in the PTO, for example. These proceedings frequently result from assertion of a patent. Certainly, if serious searching is undertaken prior to filing a patent application, the art found may, in fact, be highly, if not the most, relevant art. Typically, in this situation, an expansive and aggressive posture would be appropriate when drafting the patent claims.

---

54. See later in this chapter addressing advantages and disadvantages of searching.
55. Again, considerations for the decision to search are addressed later in this chapter.

To be more precise, however, regardless of whether a search is undertaken, it is usually considered good practice that the claims submitted be as expansive as reasonably possible to secure allowance of claims that will also stand up to close legal scrutiny (e.g., in light of the *known* prior art at the time of filing). Therefore, the claims should not be so broad that they are invalid as a matter of law in light of the *known* prior art. Likewise, it is a good practice for the patent drafter[56] to have a good faith argument for patentability over the *known* prior art at the time of filing.[57] Of course, there may also be some situations in which it may be best not to "swing for the fences,"[58] addressed later.

Egbert v. Lippmann[59]
104 U.S. 333 (1881)
Supreme Court of the United States
December 12, 1881, Decided

Pfaff v. Wells Electronics, Inc
525 U.S. 55 (1998)
Supreme Court of the United States
October 6, 1998, Argued; November 10, 1998, Decided

Minerva Surgical, Inc. v. Hologic, Inc.
59 F.4th 1371
United States Court of Appeals for the Federal Circuit
February 15, 2023, Decided

Helsinn Healthcare S.A. v. Teva Pharmaceuticals USA, Inc.
139 S. Ct. 628 (2019)
Supreme Court of the United States
December 4, 2018, Argued; January 22, 2019, Decided

Questions

1. The statute at issue in *Egbert* is a predecessor statute to pre- and post-AIA § 102. Find the pre- and post-AIA subsections of § 102 statute that correspond to the statute in the case and note the differences between the three statutes.

---

56. A variety of terms are used interchangeably throughout this book without loss of generality, such as *claim drafter*, *application drafter*, *patent drafter*, *patent practitioner*, and so on.

57. Drafting principles to avoid submitting claims that "read on" known prior art will be addressed in much more detail in Chapter 6.

58. This topic is addressed in more detail later in this chapter, which addresses the advantages and disadvantages of broad claims.

59. Edited versions of the cases intended to be read are downloadable at https://ambar.org/PPCD.

2. The Court in *Egbert* cites the case *City of Elizabeth v. American Nicholson Pavement Co.*, 97 U.S. 126 (1878). What is the distinction the Court is trying to make with respect to this citation?
3. The dissent in *Egbert* says he is at a loss to distinguish between a public and a private use in light of the ruling by the majority. What are some legally arguable distinctions? Was the use commercial? Was the use experimental? Was the invention used for its intended purpose? Under the reasoning of the majority, would a nondisclosure agreement (NDA) from the inventor and signed by (i.e., agreed to) the person responsible for the public use have prevented the use from being public? Who would have to sign the NDA for it to be effective? Does that make sense? Why or why not? What is the reasoning of the majority that this was a public use despite the fact that no one other than the person wearing the corset was necessarily aware of it?
4. Do you think the facts in *Egbert* may have influenced the outcome of the case? Do you think the case would have come out the same if there was no two-year grace period after a public use? Why or why not?
5. The dissent in *Egbert* refers to another part of the statute that does not contain the word "public." What is the language of that part of the statute? Find the corresponding sections in pre- and post-AIA § 102. Is there a difference between that language and a "public use"? If so, what is the difference? Note that the majority states: "If an inventor, having made his device, gives or sells it to another, to be used by the donee or vendee, without limitation or restriction, or injunction of secrecy, and it is so used, such use is public, even though the use and knowledge of the use may be confined to *one person*."[60]
6. Does it make a difference that in *Egbert* it was not the inventor who engaged in the use that was determined to be "public"?[61]
7. *Egbert* states that it involves a "reissued-letters patent" rather than the "original letters patent." What is the Court referring to?[62]
8. What is the policy behind the "public use" and "on sale" bars? Note that in light of *Egbert* a "public use" may occur without any disclosure necessarily taking place. Is that also true with respect to placing an invention "on sale"?

60. Egbert v. Lippmann, 104 U.S. 333, 336 (1881) (emphasis added).

61. *See* Jonathan S. Masur & Lisa Larrimore Ouellette, *Real-World Prior Art*, 76 Stan. L. Rev. 703 (2024).

62. *See* 35 U.S.C. §§ 251, 252 (2024).

9. The Court in *Pfaff* points out the term "reduction to practice" is only used in subsection 102(g). Is the term used anywhere in the patent statutes today?
10. Is the term "conception" used anywhere in the patent statutes today? Was it used anywhere in the statutes pre-AIA? The Court in *Pfaff*, however, states, "The primary meaning of the word 'invention' in the Patent Act unquestionably refers to the inventor's conception rather than to a physical embodiment of that idea."[63] Is there a difference between the inventor's "conception" of the invention and the invention being ready for patenting? How clear is it when an invention is ready for patenting? Can you define an inventor's "conception"?[64]
11. Footnote 11 in *Pfaff* describes the law before this case regarding when an invention is placed on sale. Is the approach after this case better? Why or why not?
12. Justice Stevens in *Pfaff* says that the product (i.e., which contains the invention) must be the subject of a commercial offer for sale for an invention to be put "on sale." How clear is it when a commercial offer for sale has been made? What qualifies an offer as a commercial offer for sale? Must the offer be accepted? Must the offeror and/or the offeree be aware that an invention is included in the product that is being offered for sale for an invention to be placed "on sale"?
13. *Pfaff* involves pre-AIA subsection 102(b), which provided a one-year grace period. Compare the language of pre-AIA subsection 102(b) with the language of post-AIA subsection 102(a). Do you think the ruling that a reduction to practice is not required to trigger the "on sale" language of the statute would have come out differently if pre-AIA subsection 102(b) had no grace period?
14. The Court in *Pfaff* states: "It is well settled that an invention may be patented before it is reduced to practice."[65] Consider this language in light of subsection 102(g), which at the time of the decision stated: "In determining priority of invention there shall be considered not only the respective dates of conception and reduction to practice of the invention, but also the reasonable diligence of one who was first to

63. Pfaff v. Wells Elecs., Inc., 525 U.S. 55, 60 (1998).

64. *See* Hybritech Inc. v. Monoclonal Antibodies Inc., 802 F.2d 1367, 1376, 231 U.S.P.Q. 81, 87 (Fed. Cir. 1986) (Conception is the "formation in the mind of the inventor, of a definite and permanent idea of the complete and operative invention, as it is hereafter to be applied in practice.").

65. *Pfaff*, 525 U.S. at 61.

conceive and last to reduce to practice, from a time prior to conception by the other." (Note this is also included in pre-AIA subsection 102(g).) Can you reconcile the Court's statements with the language from subsection 102(g)? In general, filing a patent application that meets the requirements of the patent statute is considered to be a "constructive" reduction to practice. Also, consider that some inventions cannot feasibly be "actually" reduced to practice before they are "ready for patenting," such as a satellite or a rocket ship.

15. Note in *Pfaff* the Court's description of the litigation before this issue reached the Supreme Court. The Court states:

> The Court of Appeals reversed, finding all six claims invalid. *124 F.3d 1429 (CA Fed. 1997)*. Four of the claims (1, 6, 7, and 10) described the socket that Pfaff had sold to Texas Instruments prior to April 8, 1981. Because that device had been offered for sale on a commercial basis more than one year before the patent application was filed on April 19, 1982, the court concluded that those claims were invalid under § 102(b). That conclusion rested on the court's view that as long as the invention was "substantially complete at the time of sale," the 1-year period began to run, even though the invention had not yet been reduced to practice. *Id., at 1434*. The other two claims (11 and 19) described a feature that had not been included in Pfaff's initial design, but the Court of Appeals concluded as a matter of law that the additional feature was not itself patentable because it was an obvious addition to the prior art.[66]

Some patent attorneys haven been known to file a provisional patent application if a client discloses an upcoming and near-term bar date (e.g., pre- or post-AIA, for example, an academic paper published by the inventor coming up on its one-year anniversary) with the idea that they can make a more substantial utility patent application filing within 12 months and claim priority to the provisional patent application. Do you think such a practice has successfully dealt with the bar date?

16. *Pfaff* resolved issues regarding an invention being placed "on sale." However, the Federal Circuit in *Minerva* applied the "ready for patenting" standard from that case to a "public use" situation. Can you break down the difference in analysis for the two situations?

66. *Id.* at 59–60.

17. The court in *Minerva* states: "The 'in public use' element of the bar is met if the invention 'was accessible to the public or was commercially exploited' by the inventor. *Delano Farms Co. v. California Table Grape Comm'n, 778 F.3d 1243, 1247 (Fed. Cir. 2015)* (citation omitted); *see also Dey, L.P. v. Sunovion Pharms., Inc., 715 F.3d 1351, 1355 (Fed. Cir. 2013)* (same with minor modifications)."[67] What is the difference between being "accessible to the public" and "commercially exploited by the inventor"? Which did the court apply in *Minerva*? What is the difference between being "commercially exploited by the inventor" with respect to a "public use" and making "a commercial offer for sale" with respect to placing an invention "on sale"?
18. The court in *Minerva* also states:

    > "An invention is in public use if it is shown to or used by an individual other than the inventor under no limitation, restriction, or obligation of confidentiality" *Am. Seating, 514 F.3d at 1267.* To determine whether this occurred, the court considers, "*inter alia*, the nature of and public access to activities involving the invention [and] confidentiality obligations imposed upon observers." *Id.*; *Delano Farms, 778 F.3d at 1247.*[68]

    Why do you think the court mentions "an individual other than the inventor"?
19. The court in *Minerva* discusses a case, *Motionless Keyboard*, and states: "In *Motionless Keyboard*, the inventor disclosed his patented keyboard to various third parties. *Motionless Keyboard, 486 F.3d at 1385.* But these disclosures 'only provided a visual view of the new keyboard design without any disclosure of the' claimed technology, which involved 'enter[ing] data into a system.' *Id.*" Do you see any tension created by this authority in the distinctions between whether the invention "was accessible to the public" or "was commercially exploited"?
20. How can you reconcile *Minerva* with *Egbert* in which no one could see the corset that was the subject of the patent at issue?
21. The court in *Minerva* rejects the argument that a reduction to practice had not occurred despite the fact that further improvements were being made. How does one determine when an invention has been actually reduced to practice?[69]

---

67. Minerva Surgical, Inc. v. Hologic, Inc., 59 F.4th 1371, 1378 (Fed. Cir. 2023).
68. *Id.* at 1377.
69. *See* Brunswick Corp. v. United States, 34 Fed. Cl. 532, 584 (1995).

22. What does the Court in *Helsinn* say the phrase "otherwise available to the public" means? What, then, does this language appear to cover?
23. The Court in *Helsinn* references § 102(b)(1) of the AIA, but does not analyze it. Why does the Court not analyze this subsection in connection with its analysis of § 102(a)(1)?
24. Does § 102(b)(1) provide any insight into how to interpret § 102(a)(1)? Note that § 102(b)(1) refers to a "disclosure made 1 year or less before the effective filing date of a claimed invention." However, the statute does not define the term "disclosure." What are possible interpretations of the term "disclosure" in light of the language of the statute overall? What are possible interpretations of the term "disclosure" in light of behaviors that Congress may have wanted to encourage?[70]
25. In light of *Helsinn*, is it accurate to say that a "secret sale" that precedes the filing of a patent application with claims covering the product that was the subject of the sale will invalidate those claims if a patent issues containing those claims? Is this the factual scenario in *Helsinn*? What if the patent application includes claims that do not "read on" the product that was the subject of the sale and those claims also are contained in a patent that issues based on the patent application? Are those latter patent claims arguably valid or not?
26. Note that the Court in *Helsinn* states: "Disclosures described in § 102(a)(1) are often referred to as 'prior art.'"[71] What is the significance?
27. The case does not address what disclosures, if any, Helsinn made to the PTO with respect to its pre-filing commercial activities that were at issue in the case.[72] However, given that the situation involved a potential "on sale" bar, what needed to be disclosed?

Selected Articles of the European Patent Convention

Europe includes a set of countries in which it is common for someone filing a patent application in the United States to also file what is referred to as a "foreign counterpart." The countries of Europe quite naturally have gotten together and via treaty formed what is referred to as the "European Patent

70. *See* MPEP, *supra* note 32, § 2152.04.
71. Helsinn Healthcare S.A. v. Teva Pharms. USA, Inc., 139 S. Ct. 628, 631 (2019).
72. *See* 37 C.F.R. §§ 1.56, 1.98 (2024). *See also* Therasense v. Becton, Dickinson & Co., 649 F.3d 1276 (Fed. Cir. 2011).

Convention," which parties may use as a mechanism to file patents abroad in countries that are members of the EPC. Unfortunately, a full treatment of claim drafting issues that may arise under EPC laws and regulations is beyond the scope of this work. Nonetheless, it may be helpful or even insightful to compare basic U.S. patent doctrines or concepts with some EPC counterparts. Therefore, throughout this book, where appropriate, various articles of the EPC are provided, so that similarities and/or differences may be considered.

It is also helpful to understand how these issues may typically arise procedurally based on an initially domestically filed patent application, which is often the case. Frequently (but not always), the United States is a preferred initial jurisdiction in which to file a patent application. However, similar considerations apply if the initial filing is in a country that is a member of the Paris Convention, the EPC, and/or the PCT, as elaborated later.

Under the Paris Convention, which is an international treaty related to procedural issues around international filing of patent applications, if a patent application is initially filed in a Paris Convention member jurisdiction, then a counterpart patent application, if filed within 12 months of the initial filing in another Paris Convention member jurisdiction, will be accorded priority as if it had been filed the same day as the initial filing. Virtually all countries in the world of commercial interest are members of the Paris Convention.[73] Thus, if a patent application is filed in the United States and a counterpart patent application is filed in the European Patent Office (EPO) within 12 months, the EPO application is accorded priority based on the U.S. application. The EPO is the office designated for filing for member countries of the EPC.

Thus, the EPO does not constitute a patent office for a particular country. Instead, many countries (more than 40) in Europe (and even some technically not in Europe) are members of the EPC. By agreement, the member countries agree to follow the rules of the EPC, which are carried out by the EPO. Thus, if the EPO grants a patent application, then it can be issued in selected member countries (also referred to here as "local countries") through a process referred to as "validation" that involves paying fees and observing other local country formalities but does not require further substantive examination. After issuance by the local country, issues regarding that country's patent law, such as infringement and/or validity, are handled by the courts of that local country.

---

73. However, Taiwan is not a member of the Paris Convention. Also, be aware another treaty that arises in connection with foreign patent practice, the PCT, may not necessarily include all countries of commercial interest.

Rather than filing in the EPO, for many EPC countries, it is possible, instead, to "directly file" in selected member countries of the EPO,[74] but, if filing in multiple countries, that would require multiple prosecutions under each local country's rules and in each local country's language. Thus, filing in the EPO saves costs with one prosecution in one of three select languages (German, French, or English) under a single set of rules.[75] Thus, this is legally appealing as well as a way to reduce costs.[76]

Article 52, Patentable inventions

(1) European patents shall be granted for any inventions, in all fields of technology, provided that they are new, involve an inventive step and are susceptible of industrial application.

(2) The following in particular shall not be regarded as inventions within the meaning of paragraph 1:

(a) discoveries, scientific theories and mathematical methods;

(b) aesthetic creations;

(c) schemes, rules and methods for performing mental acts, playing games or doing business, and programs for computers;

(d) presentations of information.

(3) Paragraph 2 shall exclude the patentability of the subject-matter or activities referred to therein only to the extent to which a European patent application or European patent relates to such subject-matter or activities as such.

---

74. France, however, is one example of a country in which one may not directly file.

75. Be aware, in this context, that translation errors may potentially have a detrimental impact on legal rights.

76. Another option with respect to patent filing in Europe, which is newly available, is referred to as the "unitary patent" and is associated with the Unified Patent Court (UPC). Thus, rather than prosecute an application through the EPO and designate selected member countries for issuance, instead, a granted patent application that was prosecuted through the EPO may now be validated and issue as a "unitary patent." A unitary patent is enforceable in all the member countries of the EPC that have agreed to the terms (referred to as "enhanced cooperation") that govern unitary patents (about 25 countries so far). Furthermore, rather than be subject to the patent laws of individual countries, disputes arising with respect to a unitary patent, such as validity and/or infringement, are heard via the UPC, which was only recently created. A unitary patent has limited effect in non-member countries.

Unitary effect may be requested by the proprietor within one month of grant of a European patent, replacing validation of the European patent in the individual countries concerned. Infringement and revocation proceedings are conducted before the UPC, which decisions have a uniform effect for the unitary patent in the participating member states as a whole rather than in each country individually. The unitary patent may coexist with nationally enforceable patents ("classical" patents) in the non-participating states.

Article 53, Exceptions to patentability

European patents shall not be granted in respect of:

(a) inventions the commercial exploitation of which would be contrary to "ordre public" or morality; such exploitation shall not be deemed to be so contrary merely because it is prohibited by law or regulation in some or all of the Contracting States;

(b) plant or animal varieties or essentially biological processes for the production of plants or animals; this provision shall not apply to microbiological processes or the products thereof;

(c) methods for treatment of the human or animal body by surgery or therapy and diagnostic methods practised on the human or animal body; this provision shall not apply to products, in particular substances or compositions, for use in any of these methods.

Article 54, Novelty

(1) An invention shall be considered to be new if it does not form part of the state of the art.

(2) The state of the art shall be held to comprise everything made available to the public by means of a written or oral description, by use, or in any other way, before the date of filing of the European patent application.

(3) Additionally, the content of European patent applications as filed, the dates of filing of which are prior to the date referred to in paragraph 2 and which were published on or after that date, shall be considered as comprised in the state of the art.

(4) Paragraphs 2 and 3 shall not exclude the patentability of any substance or composition, comprised in the state of the art, for use in a method referred to in Article 53(c), provided that its use for any such method is not comprised in the state of the art.

(5) Paragraphs 2 and 3 shall also not exclude the patentability of any substance or composition referred to in paragraph 4 for any specific use in a method referred to in Article 53(c), provided that such use is not comprised in the state of the art.

Article 55, Non-prejudicial disclosures

(1) For the application of Article 54, a disclosure of the invention shall not be taken into consideration if it occurred no earlier than six months preceding the filing of the European patent application and if it was due to, or in consequence of:

(a) an evident abuse in relation to the applicant or his legal predecessor, or

(b) the fact that the applicant or his legal predecessor has displayed the invention at an official, or officially recognised, international exhibition falling within the terms of the Convention on international exhibitions signed at Paris on 22 November 1928 and last revised on 30 November 1972.

(2) In the case of paragraph 1(b), paragraph 1 shall apply only if the applicant states, when filing the European patent application, that the invention has been so displayed and files a supporting certificate within the time limit and under the conditions laid down in the Implementing Regulations.

Article 56, Inventive step

An invention shall be considered as involving an inventive step if, having regard to the state of the art, it is not obvious to a person skilled in the art. If the state of the art also includes documents within the meaning of Article 54, paragraph 3, these documents shall not be considered in deciding whether there has been an inventive step.

Article 57, Industrial application

An invention shall be considered as susceptible of industrial application if it can be made or used in any kind of industry, including agriculture.

Questions

1. Compare Article 54(1) and (2) with post-AIA subsection 102(a)(1). Does the EPC have anything like the "on sale" bar or the "public use" bar as articulated in the cases previously considered?
2. Note the exclusions under Article 52(2) and Article 53.
3. Compare Article 55 with the exceptions of post-AIA subsection 102(b).
4. Compare Article 54(3) with post-AIA subsection 102(a)(2).
5. Compare Article 56 with post-AIA § 103.

Pre- and Post-AIA Patent Application Priority

Understand the significance of priority date and its distinction from incorporation by reference; understand how these both may affect PCD.

35 U.S.C. § 120. Benefit of Earlier Filing Date in the United States

An application for patent for an invention disclosed in the manner provided by section 112(a) (other than the requirement to disclose the best mode) in an application previously filed in the United States, or as provided by section 363 or 385, which names an inventor or joint inventor in the previously filed application shall have the same effect, as to such invention, as though filed on the date of the prior application, if filed before the patenting or abandonment of or termination of proceedings on the first application or on an application similarly entitled to the benefit of the filing date of the first application and if it contains or is amended to contain a specific reference to the earlier filed application. No application shall be entitled to the benefit of an earlier filed application under this section unless an amendment containing the specific reference to the earlier filed application is submitted at such time during the pendency of the application as required by the Director. The Director may consider the failure to submit such an amendment within that time period as a waiver of any benefit under this section. The Director may establish procedures, including the requirement for payment of the fee specified in section 41(a)(7), to accept an unintentionally delayed submission of an amendment under this section.

35 U.S.C. § 121. Divisional Applications

If two or more independent and distinct inventions are claimed in one application, the Director may require the application to be restricted to one of the inventions. If the other invention is made the subject of a divisional application which complies with the requirements of section 120 it shall be entitled to the benefit of the filing date of the original application. A patent issuing on an application with respect to which a requirement for restriction under this section has been made, or on an application filed as a result of such a requirement, shall not be used as a reference either in the Patent and Trademark Office or in the courts against a divisional application or against the original application or any patent issued on either of them, if the divisional application is filed before the issuance of the patent on the other application. The validity of a patent shall not be questioned for failure of the Director to require the application to be restricted to one invention.

AIA Sections 3(n)(1) and (2)

Sections 3(n)(1) and (2) read as follows (emphasis added):

(n) Effective Date.—

(1) In General.—Except as otherwise provided in this section, the amendments made by this section shall take effect upon the expiration of the 18-month period beginning on the date of the enactment of this Act, and shall apply to any application for patent, and to any patent issuing thereon, that ***contains or contained at any time—***

(A) a claim to a claimed invention that has an effective filing date as defined in section 100(i) of title 35, United States Code, that is [after March 15, 2013]; or

(B) a specific reference under section 120, 121, or 365(c) of title 35, United States Code, to any patent or application that contains or contained at any time such a claim.

(2) INTERFERING PATENTS.—The provisions of sections 102(g), 135, and 291 of title 35, United States Code, as in effect on the day before the effective date set forth in paragraph (1) of this subsection [March 15, 2013], shall apply to each claim of an application for patent, and any patent issued thereon, for which the amendments made by this section also apply, ***if such application or patent contains or contained at any time—***

(A) a claim to an invention having an effective filing date as defined in section 100(i) of title 35, United States Code, that occurs before the effective date set forth in paragraph (1) of this subsection [March 15, 2013]; or

(B) a specific reference under section 120, 121, or 365(c) of title 35, United States Code, to any patent or application that contains or contained at any time such a claim.

35 U.S.C. § 100(i) (Post-AIA)

(i)(1)The term "effective filing date" *for a* claimed invention *in a patent or application for patent means—*

(A) if subparagraph (B) does not apply, the actual filing date of the patent or the application for the patent containing a claim to the invention; or

(B) the filing date of the earliest application for which the patent or application is entitled, as to such invention, to a right of priority under section 119, 365(a), 365(b), 386(a), or 386(b) or to the benefit of an earlier filing date under section 120, 121, 365(c), or 386(c).

AIA "Transition" Patent Applications

As mentioned, the post-AIA §§ 102 and 103 provisions took effect on March 16, 2013. However, it is important to realize that not every patent application filed on that date and after is subject to these new provisions. For example, although post-AIA §§ 102 and 103 are currently in force, technically "current law" includes pre-AIA §§ 102 and 103 *and* post-AIA §§ 102 and 103 because of legacy filings and continuations or divisionals thereof. For this reason, it is important to know which of these statutes applies to a particular patent application. Furthermore, if a patent application has the potential to be subject to pre-AIA §§ 102 and 103, and that is the desire, it is important to be aware of what sorts of actions might jeopardize that status.

The AIA transition provisions (i.e., the provisions that determine the dates on which various portions of the modified patent statute become effective) are provided in subsection 3(n) of the AIA statute. The provisions are complex, and it takes some analysis to understand how these provisions operate.[77] Likewise, in this context, one should understand the difference between a divisional, a continuation, and a continuation-in-part (CIP).[78] These are all types of patent applications having a priority date that, for our purposes, rely on an earlier filed domestic patent application.[79] These latter patent application filings are permitted under §§ 120 and 121 of title 35. These types of applications have an actual filing date later than their priority date, as we saw previously with respect to the definition of "effective filing date" in the AIA.

However, there are distinctions between these types of patent applications. In general, a continuation or divisional ***should not*** include new subject matter compared to the earlier filed application that is the basis for priority, whereas a CIP is permitted to include new subject matter compared to the earlier filed patent application that provides the basis for priority. "New subject matter" refers to content that was substantively not in the original filing. This refers to subject matter not supported by the written description. For example, if you add a new patent claim in a continuation patent application, but it is supported by the written description of the originally filed patent application, that is not new subject matter.

These distinct types of patent applications may arise in different circumstances during patent examination. For example, a common situation for the filing of a continuation patent application is when the examiner has issued a final rejection. In this situation, patent examination may often be "complete" (e.g., a final rejection may be issued) without obtaining any allowed claims. However, continuing prosecution may remain desirable because it may still

77. *See* Howard Skaist, *Patent Prosecution Across the AIA Divide: Warning to Patent Practitioners—Special Care Is Needed to Avoid Legal Malpractice*, IPWATCHDOG (Jan. 19, 2012, 7:30 AM), https://www.ipwatchdog.com/2012/01/19/patent-prosecution-across-the-aia-divide/id=21853/; Howard Skaist, *Traps for the Unwary Regarding Patent Claim Drafting and Definition of Prior Art under Leahy Smith*, IPWATCHDOG (Sept. 21, 2011, 8:00 AM), https://www.ipwatchdog.com/2011/09/21/prior-art-under-leahy-smith/id=19290/.

78. *See* MPEP, *supra* note 32, §§ 201.6, 201.7, 201.8.

79. There are some uncommon exceptions beyond the scope of the work. For example, a so-called bypass continuation or bypass CIP under 35 U.S.C. § 365 (2024) may claim priority to an internationally filed patent application, rather than a domestically filed patent application.

be possible to convince the examiner to allow at least some of the pending claims. Filing a continuation patent application requires paying another filing fee, which entitles the owner of the patent application to an additional patent examination. Here, to be clear, new subject matter is not intended to be introduced.

There are also other situations where a continuation is desirable. As another example, during patent examination, suppose the initially filed claims have been allowed. Suppose it is desirable to let those allowed claims issue, but additional unclaimed subject matter remains in the initially filed patent application. Here, too, with the filing of a continuation patent application, new subject matter is not intended to be introduced. Remember this latter example because it is potentially relevant to our discussion regarding the AIA transition provisions and will be discussed further later.

A divisional patent application is a type of continuation patent application, but if filing a divisional patent application, *one must identify it as such* to properly claim priority.[80] In general, a divisional patent application refers to a continuation patent application where the intention is to separately prosecute a subset of the initially filed patent claims. This most frequently arises when the examiner has determined that he or she will only examine a subset of the initially filed patent claims because the examiner believes multiple inventions are being claimed. He or she requires a "divisional" be filed by issuing a "restriction requirement" that requires splitting the claims into groupings reflecting the separate inventions the examiner has identified. In general, one filing fee pays for examination of one invention under patent office policy. Thus, a divisional patent application is used to retain "priority" to the subject matter of the initial patent application, while requiring another payment of a filing fee by the patent applicant to obtain examination for those claims the examiner will not examine in the initial patent application filing.[81]

An AIA "transition" patent application, in general, refers to a patent application filed on or after March 16, 2013, that claims the benefit of an earlier patent application filing made pre-AIA. Typically, these are continuation patent applications and divisional patent applications. They are referred to as AIA "transition" patent applications because the AIA transition provisions are written so that in the case of a continuation or divisional, *pre-AIA §§ 102 and 103* apply because new subject matter *should not* have been introduced in the continuation or the divisional, although these *filings take place after* March 16, 2013.

---

80. *See* MPEP, *supra* note 32, § 201.6.

81. It is noted that a similar process exists in the EPO, referred to as "unity of invention."

The transition rules are different for a CIP patent application. The typical situation for a CIP patent application is where the inventor has produced an extension or improvement to his or her initial invention, but it is not entirely clear if that extension or improvement would be patentable over the initial patent application filing. There are various legal advantages to filing a CIP patent application in this situation rather than as a separate patent application. However, a definite disadvantage, now, is that post-AIA §§ 102 and 103 will apply to all the claims of the CIP, even any claims in the CIP patent application that rely entirely on the initial patent application filing for written description support.[82]

These are the basics, but it is important to also point out a significant trap for the unwary. Recall our earlier continuation example in which the initially filed claims had been allowed. It is desirable to let those claims issue, although the initially filed patent application includes additional unclaimed subject matter.

In this situation, new claims need to be drafted for this continuation patent application. Suppose, in this example, in his or her zeal to draft valuable new patent claims, the attorney or agent involved inadvertently includes a patent claim that is *clearly* new subject matter—that is, the patent claim is clearly *not* supported by the written description of the previously filed patent application (i.e., filed before March 16, 2013). Suppose, further, that after filing the continuation patent application with the new claims, but before any action on the merits by the PTO, the attorney or agent realizes what he or she has done and cancels the unsupported claim that constitutes new subject matter.

Under this scenario, do pre-AIA §§ 102 and 103 or do post-AIA §§ 102 and 103 apply? The wording of the transition provisions indicates that *post*-AIA §§ 102 and 103 *would* apply to *all* the claims of the continuation patent application in the foregoing situation.[83] At least partially for this reason, the PTO now requires one to certify, when filing a continuation patent application claiming priority to a pre-AIA patent application, in an application data

---

82. However, one important detail is that, based on AIA § 3(n)(2), pre-AIA § 102(g) and the provisions related to interference continue to apply as well. Thus, post-AIA §§ 102 and 103 apply and make this a first-to-file patent application, meaning as to the post-AIA prior art provisions, one may not argue prior invention; however, the patent application is also subject to invalidation based on pre-AIA § 102(g) prior art. In this unique situation, per the pre-AIA § 102(g) statute, one may argue an earlier date of invention. In general, this is a "corner" case that rarely arises.

83. However, as discussed, likewise, pre-AIA § 102(g) will also apply based on AIA § 3(n)(2), again, to cover a rare situation.

sheet accompanying the continuation patent application filing, that the continuation contains no new subject matter.[84]

The upshot of the AIA transition provisions may be summarized as follows: if a patent claim is added at any time that does not have written description support in the original patent application filing, all the claims of the patent application filed on or after March 16, 2013, are subject to *post*-AIA § 102 and *post*-AIA § 103.[85] Furthermore, once such a patent claim is added, this consequence *cannot* be undone. Assuming these statutory sections apply to all the claims of a patent application, for example, as a result of adding new subject matter without written description support in the original pre-March 16, 2013, filing. Even assuming that later the new subject matter is removed (such as cancelling the claim of the previous example because, for example, it constitutes new subject matter), those statutory sections will continue to apply to all the claims of the patent application filed on or after March 16, 2013. Furthermore, recent PTAB cases support this interpretation.[86]

Now let us think for a moment about the potential consequences of the post-AIA provisions applying to a continuation application for the preceding scenario. For one thing, more prior art may now be citable against the patent claims. For example, if the date of invention under subsection 102(g)(2) (pre-AIA) is much earlier, one will still be legally foreclosed from arguing that the invention predates post-AIA § 102 prior art (*unless* the examiner or other opponent relies on pre-AIA subsection 102(g) itself for asserting that the material is prior art). To clarify, suppose the examiner cites art under post-AIA subsection 102(a)(2) on the theory that new matter has been added. Even assuming the applicant met the requirements of pre-AIA subsection 102(g)(2) as to conception, diligence, and reduction to practice, because post-AIA is "largely" a first-to-file system, assuming the filing date of this art under subsection 102(a)(2) has an earlier filing date, the applicant is unable to attempt to swear behind the document because that is not possible under post-AIA subsection 102(a)(2). (On the other hand, imagine if the examiner asserts pre-AIA subsection 102(g) having possession of non-public Massachusetts Institute of Technology documents, for example, that show conception and reduction to practice before the filing date of the patent application to which new matter had inadvertently been added. For example, a third party may have submitted

84. *See* PTO Form PTO/AIA/14.

85. However, as discussed, likewise, pre-AIA § 102(g) will also apply based on AIA § 3(n)(2).

86. *See* Microsurgical Tech., Inc. v. Regents of the Univ. of Colo., No. PGR2021-00026, Paper 12 (P.T.A.B. June 16, 2021); Rockwool Int'l A/S v. Knauf Insulation, Inc., No. PGR2022-00022, Paper 10 (P.T.A.B. July 6, 2022).

these documents to the examiner after 18-month publication of the patent application.[87] In this case, the applicant may seek to prove an earlier date of invention under pre-AIA subsection 102(g).)

However, potentially even more troubling, suppose the inventor had engaged in pre-filing commercialization activities with respect to his or her invention, but it took place within a year of the actual filing date, such as "on sale" or "public use" activities. Recall that the interpretation of post-AIA § 102 around these events is not settled, but *Helsinn* potentially implies that these events may bar an invention. Under these circumstances and this interpretation of post-AIA § 102, then, further prosecution, in theory, via the continuation patent application, potentially may be barred.

This is "in theory" because this all may happen inadvertently. For example, claims may be added that a judge in *later litigation* concludes do not have written description support in the original filing. At that time, then, the consequences of this on the validity of a patent that issued from the continuation patent application would need to be evaluated. This, of course, provides an excellent reason to make sure that drafted patent claims have written description support in any patent application to be filed.

Natural Alternatives International, Inc. v. Iancu
904 F.3d 1375
United States Court of Appeals for the Federal Circuit
October 1, 2018, Decided

Microsurgical Technology, Inc., Petitioner v. Regents of the University of Colorado, Patent Owner
United States Patent and Trademark Office
Before the Patent Trial and Appeal Board
PGR2021-00026
Patent 10,786,391 B2
Paper: 12
Date: June 16, 2021

87. *See* 35 U.S.C. § 122(b), (e) (2024).

Questions

1. What is the difference between a continuation patent application, a CIP patent application, and a divisional patent application?[88]
2. What is the difference between claiming priority to a prior filed patent application and incorporating the prior filed patent application by reference?[89]
3. What happens if a continuation patent application claims priority to a prior filed patent application, but the continuation is filed on the day the prior filed patent application issues? It has been said that a continuation patent application must maintain continuity with a prior filed patent application as to three aspects: (1) continuity of inventorship (i.e., there must be overlapping inventorship); (2) continuity of subject matter (i.e., there must be overlapping subject matter); and (3) continuity of pendency (i.e., there should be overlapping pendency). Note that § 120 states (emphasis added), "*if filed before* the patenting or abandonment of or termination of proceedings on the first application or on an application similarly entitled to the benefit of the filing date of the first application and if it contains or is amended to contain a specific reference to the earlier filed application." However, the Federal Circuit, largely employing an interpretation advanced by the PTO, has interpreted this provision so that it is sufficient to file the continuation patent application on the date of issuance of the prior filed patent application to which priority is claimed.[90] Specifically, the court relied on prior Supreme Court cases, the PTO's interpretation as set forth in the Manual of Patent Examining Procedure (MPEP), and the fact that other applicants likely relied on these prior precedents and the PTO's interpretation for the filing of continuation patent applications.
4. Note that the court in the *Natural Alternatives International* (*NAI*) case states that the MPEP does not have the force of law. Why is that the case?
5. Note that the court in the *NAI* case interprets domestic priority as forming "a single chain, growing with each additional continuation."[91] How clear is this based on the language of § 120?

---

88. *See* MPEP, *supra* note 32, §§ 201.06–.08.
89. *See* 37 C.F.R. § 1.57 (2024); MPEP, *supra* note 32, §§ 608.01(p), 2163.07(b).
90. *See* Immersion Corp. v. HTC Corp., 826 F.3d 1357 (Fed. Cir. 2016).
91. Nat. Alts. Int'l, Inc. v. Iancu, 904 F.3d 1375, 1382 (Fed. Cir. 2018).

6. Section 120 states: "The Director may establish procedures, including the requirement for payment of the fee specified in section 41(a)(7), to accept an unintentionally delayed submission of an amendment under this section." In what circumstances would this provision potentially be of assistance to an applicant?
7. What is the "tradeoff between priority and patent term"[92] mentioned by the court in the *NAI* case?
8. The court in the *NAI* case also mentioned that priority is determined on a claim-by-claim basis. What relevance does this have for drafting patent claims for a CIP patent application?
9. The decision in the *Microsurgical* case concerned a post-grant review (PGR). How is a PGR different from an IPR? Does whether an issued patent might be subject to an IPR turn on the same provision considered in the *Microsurgical* case (i.e., AIA section 3(n))?[93]
10. In *Microsurgical*, the court first engages in claim construction before addressing other issues. Why is that? What standard does the court use with respect to its claim construction?
11. The court in *Microsurgical* addresses whether the patent is eligible for PGR. What determines whether the patent is eligible for PGR? Why does the court consider the disclaimed claims in its determination? Why does the court conclude that the patent is eligible for PGR?
12. The court is initially determining on a substantive basis whether to institute the PGR, once it determines that the patent is eligible for PGR. What is the standard applied by the court to make the institution determination? What are the grounds raised by the petitioner as the basis to institute the PGR?
13. Note the grounds raised by the petitioner for institution of a PGR could have likewise been raised in a federal court litigation to invalidate the claims. In fact, the court indicates that this patent is also the subject of litigation in federal court.[94] What might be some reasons that the petitioner might prefer a PGR to federal court litigation?
14. How important is the language of the claims in resolving the grounds raised by the petitioner?
15. The court ultimately denies the request for institution of a PGR. How might this ruling potentially affect the federal court litigation?[95]

---

92. *Id.* at 1383.
93. *See* Celgene Corp. v. Peter, 931 F.3d 1342, 1349 (Fed. Cir. 2019).
94. *See* 35 U.S.C. § 325(a)(1), (a)(3) (2024).
95. *See id.* § 325(e)(2).

Reading a Claim on an Accused Product or on Prior Art; All Elements Rule

Understand the "All Elements Rule" and how it relates patent validity and patent infringement when drafting patent claims.

Lewmar Marine, Inc. v. Barient, Inc.
827 F.2d 744
United States Court of Appeals for the Federal Circuit
August 25, 1987, Decided

Godo Kaisha IP Bridge 1 v. TCL Communication Technology Holdings Ltd.
967 F.3d 1380
United States Court of Appeals for the Federal Circuit
August 4, 2020, Decided

Questions

1. The court in *Lewmar* states: "While 'the classic test of anticipation' was indeed as stated, under the current statute 'anticipation' does not carry the same meaning as before, and the 'classic test' must be modified to: That which would *literally* infringe if later in time anticipates if earlier than the date of invention."[96] What is the difference between the "classic" test and the test at the time of the case? What is the basis for the change in the test of "anticipation" to its form at the time of the case?
2. What was the prior art that Barient was relying on to anticipate the claims of the two patents at issue? Do you think it is a common occurrence that the accused infringer asserts that it has pre-existing product that invalidates the asserted patent claims? What does this suggest should be done as part of a pre-suit investigation?
3. Compare asserted claims 1 and 2 of one patent with claim 11 of the other patent. Note that only claim 11 uses "comprising." Do you have any thoughts about this regarding claim drafting and/or claim construction?
4. What was the claim construction in *Lewmar* that led to a dispute regarding whether the American Eagle included a torsion spring?

96. Lewmar Marine, Inc. v. Barient, Inc., 827 F.2d 744, 745 (Fed. Cir. 1987).

5. What is the language in *Lewmar* of claims 1 and 2 of the '580 patent that the court attempts to "read on" the American Eagle? What is the interpretation of this language by the district court that led the district court to rule that these claims were anticipated? What is the interpretation of this language that the appellate court used? What is the reason the appellate court reached a different interpretation?
6. What is Lewmar's argument that the American Eagle does not meet the district court's interpretation of claim 11? Why does the appellate court reject Lewmar's argument? Despite disagreeing with Lewmar's position, the appellate court nonetheless concludes that the American Eagle winch does not anticipate claim 11. What is the limitation the appellate court concludes is missing from the American Eagle winch? Why does the district court conclude that the limitation is met? Why does the appellate court say that the district court's interpretation was wrong?
7. Despite the conclusion that the claims are not anticipated, what would Barient need to do to argue the claims are obvious in light of the American Eagle winch?
8. Why does the appellate court in *Lewmar* remand the case back to the district court?
9. What is the usual process for a court to make a determination regarding infringement of a patent claim?
10. The court in *TCL* suggests that with respect to a technical standard, in this case long-term evolution (LTE), the approach it uses is equivalent to the usual process. Do you agree? Why or why not?
11. What is special about patent infringement with respect to a technical standard that suggests that the usual process for a court to make a determination regarding infringement should be modified in some cases?[97]
12. TCL argued that the district court erred by putting the infringement question to the jury. What was TCL's legal argument? What was IP Bridge's counterargument?
13. Ultimately, as the Federal Circuit stated in *TCL*, the case came down to "who determines the standard-essentiality of the patent claims at issue—the court, as part of claim construction, or the jury, as part of its infringement analysis" (967 F.3d at 1383)? What does the court decide regarding this question and why?

---

97. *See* Fujitsu Ltd. v. Netgear Inc., 620 F.3d 1321 (Fed. Cir. 2010).

14. The court in *TCL* makes something out of the possibility that different devices may implement a standard in different ways. How does this affect the question of whether a set of claims are standard essential and, ultimately, the question of patent infringement?
15. How might an accused infringer prove that it does not infringe the claims of a patent asserted to read on a technical standard?[98]
16. In what situation would it be the case that merely showing that an accused device complies with a technical standard would be sufficient to prove patent infringement?[99]

Verdegaal Bros. v. Union Oil Co.
814 F.2d 628
United States Court of Appeals for the Federal Circuit
March 12, 1987, Decided

Ethicon Endo-Surgery, Inc. v. United States Surgical Corp.
149 F.3d 1309
United States Court of Appeals for the Federal Circuit
June 30, 1998, Decided

Questions

1. These two cases illustrate application of the "All Elements Rule" in significantly different legal situations. Compare and contrast the differences despite application of essentially the same rule.
2. The two courts state the "All Elements Rule" differently. *Verdegaal* states: "A claim is anticipated only if each and every element as set forth in the claim is found, either expressly or inherently described, in a single prior art reference."[100]

   Ethicon states: "Infringement may be found under the doctrine of equivalents if every limitation of the asserted claim, or its 'equivalent,' is found in the accused subject matter, where an 'equivalent' differs from the claimed limitation only insubstantially."[101] Explain why the courts appear to apply different rules, but, in fact, the rules are the same.

98. *See id.*
99. *See id.*
100. Verdegaal Bros. v. Union Oil Co., 814 F.2d 628, 631 (Fed. Cir. 1987).
101. Ethicon Endo-Surgery, Inc. v. U.S. Surgical Corp., 149 F.3d 1309, 1315 (Fed. Cir. 1998).

3. The *Ethicon* court refers to the "All Elements Rule" as the "All Limitations Rule." Is there any legal significance to this difference? What is the difference between an element of a claim and a limitation of a claim?
4. Note that in *Verdegaal*, the ruling went from valid and infringed as determined in accordance with a jury verdict to invalid as a matter of law as determined by the appellate court. Does this seem like an unusual result? What does the *Verdegaal* court say is the standard of review to be applied? Why do you think with such a high standard of review that the court was nonetheless able to find the patent invalid as a matter of law? Under what subsection of pre-AIA § 102 was the patent found to be invalid? What was Verdegaal's argument that the claims at issue were not anticipated? Why did the court reject this argument?
5. Do you understand why in *Ethicon* the court was able to affirm as to claim 6, but remand as to claim 24? Observe that the court struggles a bit with what constitutes an "equivalent" with respect to a limitation. Why is that? What does the court say is the difference between an accused product not literally meeting the language of a claim and an accused product being "specifically excluded" by the language of a claim?
6. What is the difference between whether an "equivalent" differs from the claimed limitation only insubstantially and whether a component in the accused subject matter performs substantially the same function as a claimed limitation in substantially the same way to achieve substantially the same result? What does the *Ethicon* court say is the difference?

* * *

Whether the accused product or service falls within the scope of a patent claim is judged under the "All Elements Rule." To find infringement under the All Elements Rule, an accused device (or service) must contain each and every element and limitation of a single patent claim in the manner recited in the patent claim, either literally or by an equivalent.[102]

A similar rule is used to determine whether a patent claim is not novel, referred to as "anticipation." Under the All Elements Rule, for a claim to be anticipated (not novel), a single prior art reference must contain each and every element and limitation of a single patent claim in the manner recited in

102. *See, e.g.*, TIP Sys., LLC v. Phillips & Brooks/Gladwin, Inc., 529 F.3d 1364 (Fed. Cir. 2008).

the patent claim. One maxim of patent law is "that which infringes if later in time, anticipates if earlier in time." The Federal Circuit has noted the maxim should really be "that which *literally* infringes if later, anticipates if earlier."[103] This brings out the difference that a patent claim may be infringed under the doctrine of equivalents,[104] which is not literally within the scope of the patent claim (hence, referred to as "non-literal infringement"), but that doctrine is not used to determine anticipation. Nonetheless, it is helpful to think of infringement and prior art with respect to patent claims as a sort of balanced equation. With few exceptions,[105] analysis of the scope of a patent claim is the same for direct, literal infringement as it is for anticipation of that claim.

The analysis undertaken is often referred to as "reading a claim" onto the accused device or "reading a claim" onto the prior art. For purposes of literal, direct patent infringement, to determine if a patent claim is literally and directly infringed, each and every element and limitation of the claim is considered and must be found in the accused device in the manner recited in the claim. Likewise, for prior art to anticipate a patent claim, rendering it invalid, each and every element and limitation of the claim is considered and must be found in a single item of prior art in the manner recited in the claim.

Consider the following patent claim:

EXAMPLE 1.2

I claim:

1. An apparatus comprising:

   a substantially horizontally oriented, rectangularly shaped seat including four corners;

   wherein attached to a respective corner of the seat are four substantially vertically oriented legs such that the legs point in the same direction away from the seat, are oriented to be substantially mutually parallel, and are of substantially the same length.

Many will recognize that this simple claim covers a chair or a four-legged stool. The claim does not recite a chairback; nonetheless, due to the use of

103. *See* Lewmar Marine, Inc. v. Barient, Inc., 827 F.2d 744 (Fed. Cir. 1987).
104. See Chapter 5, addressing the doctrine of equivalents (DOE).
105. One exception is product-by-process claims, treated in Chapter 4.

the word *comprising*, referred to as "open" form, as long as an accused product includes all the elements and limitations in the manner recited in the claim, the claim is infringed, *even if the accused product includes other features not recited in the claim*, such as a back. However, because of the choices made for the claimed features in Example 1.2, chairs or stools that have seats of a shape other than rectangular would not be covered by the claim. The claim *cannot be read* on a circular seated stool or, similarly, a three-legged stool. Express features of the claim would be missing.

Conducting a similar analysis regarding prior art, the claim, of course, would be invalid as anticipated under current law if it were an issued claim and such a chair meeting all the elements and limitations of claim 1 were in the prior art. However, the claim is not anticipated by a circular seated stool or a three-legged stool (although the claim might be rendered obvious by such prior art). To anticipate a claim, the prior art must include each and every element and limitation in the manner recited in the claim. A four-legged stool with a rectangular-shaped seat or a four-legged chair with a rectangular-shaped seat and meeting the other limitations of the claim would anticipate the claim, if it were in the prior art. Likewise, a similar analysis regarding "comprising" applies with respect to prior art. The prior art may show additional features beyond those recited and still anticipate a patent claim.

Pleading Prima Facie Patent Infringement

Know the elements of a prima facie *case of patent infringement when drafting patent claims.*

In general, two elements must be pled and proven to make out a *prima facie* case of patent infringement:[106] (1) ownership of the patent and (2) that the accused product or service falls within the scope of at least one of the patent claims.[107]

106. In 2007, the Supreme Court decided, in *Bell Atlantic v. Twombly*, 550 U.S. 544, 562–63 (2007), that the notice pleading standard was not enough, and held for the first time that a plaintiff's factual allegations must plausibly suggest an entitlement to relief. The Court observed that the previous "no set of facts" language had "been questioned, criticized, and explained away long enough," and that the standard had "earned its retirement." The Court articulated a new standard and required that a plaintiff's complaint contain "factual allegations plausibly suggesting (not merely consistent with) an entitlement to relief."

107. *See, e.g.*, Hall v. Bed Bath & Beyond, Inc., 705 F.3d 1357, 1362 (Fed. Cir. 2013) (citing Phonometrics, Inc. v. Hosp. Franchise Sys., Inc., 203 F.3d 790, 794 (Fed. Cir. 2000)).

Whether the accused product or service falls within the scope of a patent claim is judged under the "All Elements Rule," as previously discussed. To find infringement under the All Elements Rule, an accused device (or service) must contain each and every element and limitation of a single patent claim in the manner recited in the patent claim, either literally or by an equivalent.[108]

Phonometrics, Inc. v. Hospitality Franchise Systems, Inc.
203 F.3d 790
United States Court of Appeals for the Federal Circuit
February 9, 2000, Decided

Hall v. Bed Bath & Beyond, Inc.
705 F.3d 1357
United States Court of Appeals for the Federal Circuit
January 25, 2013, Decided

Questions

1. *Phonometrics* was decided before *Twombly*, yet the Federal Circuit cites *Phonometrics* in *Hall*. Previously, the Federal Rules of Civil Procedure provided a form (i.e., Form 18) that was held to meet the applicable pleading standards for asserting patent infringement.[109] However, federal courts did away with Form 18 around 2015 and questions remained regarding how much is needed to meet *Twombly*'s "plausibility" standard. Does *Hall* meet the "plausibility" standard of *Twombly*? If so, what in *Hall* makes the claim of patent infringement plausible?
2. In *Hall*, the court distinguishes Rule 11. What is the distinction?
3. In *Phonometrics*, the Federal Circuit rejects requiring pleading all the elements of a patent claim. To be plausible, however, must the complaint provide an element-by-element analysis of at least one asserted, perhaps representative, patent claim or might that, instead, limit the scope of discovery?[110]
4. What is "pleading a case out of court"?[111]

108. *See, e.g.*, TIP Sys., LLC v. Phillips & Brooks/Gladwin, Inc., 529 F.3d 1364 (Fed. Cir. 2008).
109. *See In re* Bill of Lading, 681 F.3d 1323, 1334 (Fed. Cir. 2012).
110. *See* Bot M8 LLC v. Sony Corp. of Am., 4 F.4th 1342 (Fed. Cir. 2021).
111. *See id.*

Claim as Metes and Bounds of Invention

Understand that for purposes of claim drafting the literal scope of a patent claim defines the invention.

As previously discussed, the *scope of rights* granted by a patent claim *primarily* turns on the *exact words* of the patent claims themselves.[112] The patent claim defines the invention, whereas the rest of the patent document comprises aids to interpretation. Be aware that poor, sloppy, or not well-thought-out word selection may produce an undesirable result such that technology of value to the patentee is not *necessarily* covered by the claims of a patent. Furthermore, each separate patent claim legally constitutes a separate invention. Thus, a patent issuing with 20 separate claims covers 20 separate inventions by legal presumption. A patent claim, it is said, defines the "metes and bounds" of the invention, not unlike in real property in which the metes and bounds of a parcel of real estate are the boundaries identified by landmarks used in a "legal description" of the particular parcel of real estate. A patent claim, by analogy, identifies the legal boundaries of an invention.

Constant v. Advanced Micro-Devices, Inc.
848 F.2d 1560
United States Court of Appeals for the Federal Circuit
June 9, 1988, Decided

Johnson & Johnston Associates v. R.E. Service Co.
285 F.3d 1046
United States Court of Appeals for the Federal Circuit
March 28, 2002, Decided

Questions

1. In *Constant*, the '491 patent and the '635 patent were held invalid on summary judgment. Claims 1, 7, 8, 9, 16, 18, 21, 22, and 23 of the '491 patent were held invalid under subsection 102(b) (pre-AIA) based on a printed publication more than a year before the filing date of the patent application. How did the court interpret the term "printed publication"?

---

112. See Chapter 3, which treats the parts of a patent claim and the theory behind those parts; Chapter 4, which treats patent claim types; and Chapter 5, which treats principles of patent claim construction.

2. Regarding the '635 patent, the plaintiff/appellant argued that the random-access memory (RAM) in the claims was defined and must be understood to be a "semiconductor RAM with log2n address lines connecting the RAM through a decoder." The court stated, "The Allen and Westerfield article and Stalcup patent both use magnetic core memories instead of semiconductors."[113] Why then did the court reject appellant's argument regarding semiconductor RAM?
3. The court even agreed "the embodiments in the specification involve semiconductor RAMs."[114] Why did the court determine that this was not sufficient to avoid invalidity based on the cited documents that used magnetic core memories?
4. The court states that the appellant tried to argue that elements were missing from the documents relied upon to establish invalidity, particularly "the multiplier," which the court agrees was recited in the claims as "multiplier means." Did the documents relied upon show a "multiplier," as such? Why does the court reject the argument that this aspect of the claims was missing from the relied upon documents?
5. Why does the court reject appellant's objective indicia of obviousness?
6. *Johnson & Johnston* was decided *en banc*. Why was that necessary? Did the court necessarily need to overrule *YMB Magnex* to reach the result that it did? Note that this case went from a jury ruling of infringement to a ruling of noninfringement as a matter of law. Does the court announce an absolute rule regarding "described and not claimed subject matter" or is this simply a factor to consider in determining whether something is an equivalent?
7. How does the ruling in *Johnson & Johnston* illustrate the importance of claim language relative to the description in the specification? How does the file history and prior art factor into the court's determination of equivalency?
8. The court addresses the situation where subject matter is "disclosed and not claimed" in a patent. How should one determine if the subject matter is "not claimed" in a patent? Does that mean that the subject matter is not specifically recited in the claims? If that is not what it means, then what does it mean?
9. In addition to the court opinion, there were several concurring opinions and a dissent. There was disagreement among the judges regarding whether or not *Johnson & Johnston* made new law. Why did some

113. Constant v. Advanced Micro-Devices, Inc., 848 F.2d 1560, 1570 (Fed. Cir. 1988).
114. *Id.*

judges think that the decision did not make new law? Why did Judge Newman disagree?

10. Although the judges seem to agree that the relevant Supreme Court precedent is *Graver Tank & Manufacturing Co. v. Linde Air Products Co.*, 339 U.S. 605 (1950), there is disagreement on how it should be interpreted. Why did Judge Dyk believe that the outcome in *Johnson & Johnston* was not inconsistent with *Graver Tank*? Why did Judge Newman disagree?
11. What was Judge Rader's suggestion as alternative reasoning to explain the result in *Johnson & Johnston*? Why did Judge Lourie disagree with Judge Rader's approach? Why did Judge Newman disagree with Judge Rader's approach?
12. What was Judge Newman's view of how *Johnson & Johnston* changed the law?
13. What is the significance of footnote 2 in *Johnson & Johnston*? Does the footnote suggest that the doctrine of equivalents should or should not apply? The judges seemed to attach significance to the fact that in *Graver Tank* broader claims covering what was asserted to infringe under the doctrine of equivalents had been invalidated. Why is this different than what happened in *Johnson & Johnston*, in which claims directed to materials beyond aluminum were issued in continuation patents? It is curious that the plaintiff in *Johnson & Johnston* apparently did not sue on his other patents—what might be a possible reason?
14. Is there a way to draft claims to avoid the outcome in *Johnson & Johnston*?
15. The case describes several attempts by courts to limit the scope of the doctrine of equivalents. This also seems to be part of Judge Newman's objection. For example, Judge Rader's concurrence mentions estoppel and the prior art as limiting its scope and the element-by-element analysis as limiting scope. Another approach suggests that the claims may be interpreted to exclude the equivalent as a matter of law.[115] Likewise, as Judge Rader suggests, some cases imply that foreseeability might be a limit.[116] Here, in this case, we also see disclosure without claims (i.e., dedication) as a limit. There have also been cases that limited the doctrine of equivalents because the alleged equivalent

115. *See* Dolly v. Spalding, 16 F.3d 394, 400 (Fed. Cir. 1994).
116. *See* Sage v. Devon, 126 F.3d 1420 (Fed. Cir. 1997) (*cited by* Rader, J.).

did not possess all the advantages described in the specification.[117] Are these actual limits or merely factors to consider in the context of the technology, the claims, the specification, the file history, the prior art, and so on?[118]

16. Note that courts have suggested known interchangeability is a factor to consider in deciding whether something is an equivalent. How does this compare with the proposed approaches regarding foreseeability and described but unclaimed subject matter?[119]

Sentence Format of Claims

In claim drafting, follow the rules of grammar.

We previously explained that the claims section of a patent begins with words such as "I claim," "We claim," or "What is claimed is," immediately followed by a colon. Following the colon are a succession of sequentially numbered partial sentences that complete the sentence that begins as "I claim," "We claim," or "What is claimed is." Claims are, in effect, run-on sentences, since the only period in a claim occurs at the end of the claim. This sentence requirement is imposed by the PTO. However, other than being run-on sentences, it is probably prudent to obey the rules of grammar when preparing claims. Claims are interpreted by judges and judges are familiar with and expect wording to follow the established rules of grammar.[120]

Commissioner of Patents and Trademarks
Patent and Trademark Office (P.T.O.)

In re Application of Alfred A. Fressola
22 U.S.P.Q.2d 1828
Patent Application 07/1230,748
Attorney Docket No. 407,001
February 19, 1992
Filed: August 10, 1988

---

117. *See* Vehicular Techs. v. Titan Wheel, 212 F.3d 1377 (Fed. Cir. 2000).

118. *See* Graver Tank & Mfg. Co. v. Linde Air Prods. Co., 339 U.S. 605, 609, 85 U.S.P.Q. (BNA) 328, 330 (1950) ("What constitutes equivalency must be determined against the context of the patent, the prior art, and the particular circumstances of the case.").

119. *Cf.* Ring & Pinion Serv. Inc. v. ARB Corp., 743 F.3d 831 (Fed. Cir. 2014).

120. *See, e.g.*, Superguide v. Direct TV, 358 F.3d 870 (Fed. Cir. 2004) (applying rule of grammar to interpret claim language).

Questions

1. How did the case arise?
2. What was the standard applied by the commissioner? Do you agree that this standard was met as to the key issue raised?
3. Do you agree with historical argument advanced as a reason for keeping the practice? Why or why not?
4. Do you think the PTO has the authority to change the practice? If deciding the practice is within the PTO's statutory authority, why would changing the practice not be? Is the practice appropriately characterized as substantive or procedural? Does that matter? Note that over the years the PTO has succeeded in changing some practices but failed in other cases.
5. Why does the petitioner say the rule is *ultra vires*? Does this argument have any merit?
6. The petitioner argues that the single sentence requirement makes claims more difficult to understand. Yet, the commissioner argues that a period within a claim would make the claim indefinite. With whom do you agree and why?
7. Is it accurate to say a multiple-sentence format would make a claim more of a description than a definition?
8. Ultimately, does the commissioner seem to say that it has been that way for many years and worked, so why change?

Claim Scope Trade-Offs: Validity versus Infringement

Understand the fundamental trade-off between validity and infringement and how it drives the logic of PCD.

It has been suggested that a trade-off exists between validity (particularly under § 102, as an example) and infringement (particularly direct, literal patent infringement, again, for example). Essentially, when drafting a claim, one is attempting to craft a "goldilocks"-type claim that is narrow enough to slide by the known prior art while being broad enough to capture as many infringers as possible. As stated by Donald Chisum:

> Claims measure the invention for determining patentability both during examination and after issuance when validity is challenged. They also determine what constitutes infringement. A claim recites a number of elements

> or limitations and will cover or "read on" only those products (or processes) that contain all such elements or limitations. *Effective claims must be neither too broad (i.e., cover the prior art or matter not adequately described in the specification) nor too narrow (i.e., fail to cover all possible embodiments of the applicant's invention).*[121]

This is a tricky balance, without question. Consider the transition from analog to digital technology that took place in a number of areas of technology. Do you draft a claim that covers both because both are appearing in the market or do you draft a claim that is only digital because analog technology is well-known with respect to embodiments you intend to cover with your claim? Consider a computer or networking invention during the period when most computers included an analog modem, but it appeared that digital modems would eventually replace them.

One approach might be to include the term "modem" potentially in a dependent claim or, if needed, in the independent claim, without specifying whether it is analog or digital. In your specification, you might include an embodiment that includes an analog modem as well as an embodiment that includes a digital modem. In your claims, you then might include a further dependent claim that recites "wherein the modem comprises a digital modem." Would this approach have worked for the next case?

Personalized Media Communications, LLC v. Apple Inc.
952 F.3d 1336
United States Court of Appeals for the Federal Circuit
March 13, 2020, Decided

Questions

1. Explain the reference to the General Agreement on Tariffs and Trade (GATT) and the impact on patent term.
2. What is the issue regarding applying the BRI versus applying the *Phillips* claim construction used in federal district court? Why is that potentially important? The court in this case applied the BRI, but still considered the prosecution history. What, then, is the difference between *Phillips* claim construction and BRI?
3. The parties are arguing about whether the claim reads on an all-digital transmission signal versus a mixed analog and digital transmission

121. 1 Chisum, *supra* note 2 (emphasis added).

signal. What makes the construction of the claims with respect to this aspect so important?

4. The court draws a distinction between prosecution history statements that reflect unmistakable disavowal of subject matter and statements that inform the claim construction. What is the difference? If informing the claim construction leads to a narrower claim, why is that not, in effect, disavowal of subject matter?
5. Based only on the words of the claim, how did the Board say "receiving an encrypted digital information transmission including encrypted information" should be interpreted and why? How did Personalized Media Communications (PMC) say that language should be interpreted and why? What was the Federal Circuit's position?
6. How did the Board think that the definition of "programming" in the specification affected how the disputed language should be construed? What was the Federal Circuit's position?
7. How did the Board think the language of a related patent affected the construction of the disputed language? Why did the Federal Circuit find that this argument was not dispositive?
8. What language from the specification did PMC point out in support of its claim construction? Why did the Federal Circuit find this language supported PMC's view, but still was not dispositive?
9. What was it from the prosecution history that finally convinced the Federal Circuit to use PMC's construction?

Small Claim Errors, Large Consequences

Understand in claim drafting that small, even seemingly innocuous, errors may lead to invalidity and/or noninfringement.

There is no question that with respect to all legal documents, the exact language used is of tremendous importance. However, what may make PCD unique is the vast potential importance of every word, every comma, every colon or semicolon, and every turn of phrase. Jam-packed into what may be less than a full paragraph of words are a range of nuances and understandings. These nuances and understandings cut across a range of contextual knowledge, including legal knowledge, technical knowledge, and knowledge about the particular document being crafted in real time, among other things. In theory, one has only to look to the language of the claim itself to determine the legal rights it grants. It is a goal of claim drafting to make it so that one need only read the claim, although it is typical to resort to the specification for context, for redefinition of terminology, and so on. It is no wonder, then, that even small, seemly innocuous, mistakes in the claims have the potential to completely vitiate any potential patent claim value. Even with this understanding, you will ultimately wonder, as I have on many occasions, how it is that mistakes still manage to creep into your claims unnoticed until later. Unfortunately, depending on the mistake, once noticed, it may be too late to correct. The utmost care is always needed when it comes to claim language.

Superior Fireplace Co. v. Majestic Products Co.
270 F.3d 1358
United States Court of Appeals for the Federal Circuit
November 1, 2001, Decided

Finjan LLC v. SonicWall, Inc.
84 F.4th 963
United States Court of Appeals for the Federal Circuit
October 13, 2023, Decided

Questions

1. What was the issue raised by the court regarding the Administrative Procedure Act? Why did the court determine that a clear and convincing standard applied to the certificate of correction?
2. Why was there a question regarding whether a claim may be broadened via a certificate of correction? Why did the court reach the conclusion it did?
3. Did the court say a certificate of correction may broaden in other circumstances but not in this circumstance?
4. What do you make of this quote by the court from the *Markman* decision: "No inquiry as to the subjective intent of the applicant or PTO is appropriate or even possible in the context of a patent infringement suit. The subjective intent of the inventor when he used a particular term is of little or no probative weight in determining the scope of a claim (except as documented in the prosecution history)."[122] Does this provide any insight regarding how one might choose to draft patent claims?

122. Markman v. Westview Instruments, Inc., 52 F.3d 967, 985, 34 U.S.P.Q.2D (BNA) 1321, 1334 (Fed. Cir. 1995).

5. What should Superior Fireplace have done rather than seek a certificate of correction? Given the prosecution history, how clear is it that they would have been successful if they had pursued that angle of attack?
6. Why did the Federal Circuit remand the case to the district court? What does this tell you about how to handle situations like this case?
7. Why does Judge Dyk dissent?
8. In this case, the certificate of correction was filed within two years of patent issuance, but because the mistake was not evident in the eyes of the court, claim broadening was not permitted and the certificate of correction was invalid. Suppose, instead, the certificate of correction was filed after two years from issuance, but the mistake was evident from the file history. Do you think that certificate of correction is valid or invalid?
9. *Finjan* is another reminder of the subtlety of language and how that may ultimately be to one's disadvantage if appreciated too late. There are two claim construction issues, and both demonstrate this point in separate ways. The first is regarding the construction of "Downloadable." The parties had stipulated a meaning, but it was taken directly from two of the patents. The meaning did not fully take account of the nature of packet communications over the internet. So, this flaw was not only in the stipulation but was also arguably a feature of the patents themselves. It is a difficult issue because when inventors describe an invention, they often simplify aspects that they do not regard as relevant to the invention. The drafter must ask enough questions to get a broader understanding of the technology to make sure the claims accurately depict the technology. There is no guaranteed approach to avoid this. However, are there any ideas on how one might attempt to reduce the risk of this result when drafting claims? The dissent here makes a good point that by the construction used, almost no system operates in the way the claims are interpreted.
10. Another claim construction issue may be another potential drafting issue to try to avoid. The Federal Circuit cites several cases where this occurred. The situation arises when a claim element is introduced with an indefinite article and later is referred to with "the" or "said." In this case, it happened with respect to "computer" and in another case it happened with respect to "microprocessor." If the claimed features do not all need to be performed on the same computer or same processor, then it may be there is no infringement. Furthermore,

even if "a computer" is interpreted as "one or more computers" due to "comprising," this does not address the noninfringement argument created by the language of the claim. How might language be formulated to address this risk?

Avoiding Prior Art Admissions

Avoid making prior art admissions in drafting patent claims, in drafting patent applications, and during patent prosecution.

MPEP § 2129

2129 Admissions as Prior Art

I. ADMISSIONS BY APPLICANT CONSTITUTE PRIOR ART

A statement by an applicant in the specification or made during prosecution identifying the work of another as "prior art" is an admission which can be relied upon for both anticipation and obviousness determinations, regardless of whether the admitted prior art would otherwise qualify as prior art under the statutory categories of 35 U.S.C. 102. Riverwood Int'l Corp. v. R.A. Jones & Co., 324 F.3d 1346, 1354, 66 USPQ2d 1331, 1337 (Fed. Cir. 2003); Constant v. Advanced Micro-Devices Inc., 848 F.2d 1560, 1570, 7 USPQ2d 1057, 1063 (Fed. Cir. 1988). Where the admitted prior art anticipates the claim but does not qualify as prior art under any of the paragraphs of 35 U.S.C. 102, the claim may be rejected as being anticipated by the admitted prior art without citing to 35 U.S.C. 102.

However, even if labeled as "prior art," the work of the same inventive entity may not be considered prior art against the claims unless it falls under one of the statutory categories. Id.; see also Reading & Bates Construction Co. v. Baker Energy Resources Corp., 748 F.2d 645, 650, 223 USPQ 1168, 1172 (Fed. Cir. 1984) ("[W]here the inventor continues to improve upon his own work product, his foundational work product should not, without a statutory basis, be treated as prior art solely because he admits knowledge of his own work. It is common sense that an inventor, regardless of an admission, has knowledge of his own work.").

Consequently, the examiner must determine whether the subject matter identified as "prior art" is the inventor's own work, or the work of another. In the absence of another credible explanation, examiners should treat such subject matter as the work of another.

II. DISCUSSION OF PRIOR ART IN SPECIFICATION

Where the specification identifies work done by another as "prior art," the subject matter so identified is treated as admitted prior art. In re Nomiya, 509 F.2d 566,

571, 184 USPQ 607, 611 (CCPA 1975) (holding applicant's labeling of two figures in the application drawings as "prior art" to be an admission that what was pictured was prior art relative to the claimed improvement).

III. JEPSON CLAIMS

Drafting a claim in Jepson format (i.e., the format described in 37 CFR 1.75(e); see MPEP § 608.01(m)) is taken as an implied admission that the subject matter of the preamble is the prior art work of another. In re Fout, 675 F.2d 297, 301, 213 USPQ 532, 534 (CCPA 1982) (holding preamble of Jepson-type claim to be admitted prior art where applicant's specification credited another as the inventor of the subject matter of the preamble). However, this implication may be overcome where applicant gives another credible reason for drafting the claim in Jepson format. In re Ehrreich, 590 F.2d 902, 909–910, 200 USPQ 504, 510 (CCPA 1979) (holding preamble not to be admitted prior art where applicant explained that the Jepson format was used to avoid a double patenting rejection in a co-pending application and the examiner cited no art showing the subject matter of the preamble). Moreover, where the preamble of a Jepson claim describes the inventor's own work, such may not be used against the claims. Reading & Bates Construction Co. v. Baker Energy Resources Corp., 748 F.2d 645, 650, 223 USPQ 1168, 1172 (Fed. Cir. 1984); Ehrreich, 590 F.2d at 909–910, 200 USPQ at 510.

IV. INFORMATION DISCLOSURE STATEMENT (IDS)

Mere listing of a reference in an information disclosure statement is not taken as an admission that the reference is prior art against the claims. Riverwood Int'l Corp. v. R.A. Jones & Co., 324 F.3d 1346, 1354–55, 66 USPQ2d 1331, 1337–38 (Fed. Cir. 2003) (listing of the inventor's own prior patent in an IDS does not make it available as prior art absent a statutory basis); see also 37 CFR 1.97(h) ("The filing of an information disclosure statement shall not be construed to be an admission that the information cited in the statement is, or is considered to be, material to patentability as defined in § 1.56(b).").

MPEP § 2152.03

2152.03 Admissions

[Editor Note: This MPEP section is only applicable to applications subject to examination under the first inventor to file (FITF) provisions of the AIA as set forth in 35 U.S.C. 100 (note). See MPEP § 2159 et seq. to determine whether an application is subject to examination under the FITF provisions, and MPEP § 2131–MPEP § 2138 for examination of applications subject to pre-AIA 35 U.S.C. 102.]

The Office will continue to treat admissions by the applicant as prior art under the AIA. A statement by an applicant in the specification or made during prosecution identifying the work of another as "prior art" is an admission which can be relied upon for both anticipation and obviousness determinations, regardless of whether the admitted prior art would otherwise qualify as prior art under AIA 35 U.S.C. 102. See Riverwood Int'l Corp. v. R.A. Jones & Co., 324 F.3d 1346, 1354, 66 USPQ2d 1331, 1337 (Fed. Cir. 2003); Constant v. Advanced Micro-Devices Inc., 848 F.2d 1560, 1570, 7 USPQ2d 1057, 1063 (Fed. Cir. 1988). For a discussion of admissions as prior art, see generally MPEP § 2129.

Koninklijke Philips N.V. v. Google LLC
948 F.3d 1330
United States Court of Appeals for the Federal Circuit
January 30, 2020, Decided

Questions

1. Philips first argued that institution of the IPR was improper. Why? Did the Federal Circuit agree? If so, why did the Federal Circuit agree? What was the legal source for the law cited by the Federal Circuit to resolve this issue? If the Federal Circuit agreed, why did the Federal Circuit not rule that institution of the IPR was invalid?
2. What was Philips' second argument? Philips appears to be relying on the precise language of the IPR statute. Did the Federal Circuit agree or disagree? Why?
3. What was Philips' third argument? Why did the Federal Circuit disagree? How can one avoid this issue in the future?

Qualcomm Inc. v. Apple Inc.
24 F.4th 1367
United States Court of Appeals for the Federal Circuit
February 1, 2022, Decided

Questions

1. What do you make of footnote 1 of this case? Assume the Federal Circuit had to address the issue of whether to apply pre-AIA or post-AIA law to a continuation application that claims priority to a pre-AIA application but in which new matter is inadvertently added by a new patent claim. How would you expect the court to rule?

2. Observe that the rule on applicant's admitted prior art (AAPA) appears to be different in an IPR than it is in patent prosecution or even federal court litigation. On the other hand, it may be used for certain things in an IPR. Can you articulate the difference between what is permissible and what is not impermissible? Does this difference distinguish the *Philips* case? Why or why not?
3. What is the policy basis for the distinction drawn here regarding use of AAPA in an IPR? Does that distinction appear sound to you?
4. Can you identify the different ways that an applicant may inadvertently admit prior art in a patent application?[123]

United States Patent and Trademark Office

Under Secretary of Commerce for Intellectual Property and Director of the United States Patent and Trademark Office

Memorandum

Date: June 9, 2022

To: Members of the Patent Trial and Appeal Board

From: Katherine K. Vidal

Under Secretary of Commerce for Intellectual Property and

Director of the United States Patent and Trademark Office

Updated Guidance on the Treatment of Statements of the Applicant in the Challenged Patent in Inter Partes Reviews under § 311

Introduction

Under 35 U.S.C. § 311(b), inter partes reviews (IPRs) may be instituted only "on the basis of prior art consisting of patents or printed publications." IPR petitions sometimes rely on statements in the specification of the challenged patent, which are generally referred to as "admissions," "applicant-admitted-prior-art," or "AAPA." This Memorandum sets forth the United States Patent and Trademark Office's (USPTO) interpretation of § 311(b) and the extent to which admissions may be used in IPR proceedings. This Memorandum supersedes prior guidance, expressly the August 18, 2020, "Treatment of Statements of the

123. *See* Moshe Wilensky, *The Past and Future of Admitted Prior Art*, 21 Tex. Intell. Prop. L.J. 237 (2013).

Applicant in the Challenged Patent in Inter Partes Reviews Under § 311" (2020 Guidance). The guidance in this Memorandum shall be followed by all members of the Patent Trial and Appeal Board (PTAB or Board).[1]

[1] This Memorandum does not apply to requests for ex parte reexamination made pursuant to 35 U.S.C. § 301, et seq.

The Director issues this Memorandum under her authority to issue binding agency guidance to govern the Board's implementation of statutory provisions. *See, e.g.*, 35 U.S.C. 3(a)(2)(A); SOP2 at 1–2.

Guidance

35 U.S.C. § 311(b) provides:

> (b) Scope.—
>
> A petitioner in an inter partes review may request to cancel as unpatentable 1 or more claims of a patent only on a ground that could be raised under section 102 or 103 and only on the basis of prior art consisting of patents or printed publications.

Section 311(b) limits the prior art that may be used as "the basis" of an IPR proceeding to "patents or printed publications."

After the issuance of the 2020 Guidance, the Federal Circuit issued its decision in *Qualcomm Inc. v. Apple Inc.*, 24 F.4th 1367 (Fed. Cir. 2022), addressing the extent to which admissions can be used in IPR proceedings. The court concluded, consistent with the 2020 Guidance, that under § 311, "'patents or printed publications' that form the 'basis' of a ground for *inter partes* review must themselves be prior art to the challenged patent" and not the challenged patent itself or any admissions therein. *Qualcomm*, 24 F.4th at 1374. The court clarified that, because admissions are not prior art and therefore cannot form the basis of an IPR, it is "impermissible for a petition to challenge a patent relying on solely AAPA without also relying on a prior art patent or printed publication." *Id.* at 1377; *see, e.g.*, *Sony Corp. v. Collabo Innovations, Inc.*, IPR2016-00940, Paper 7, at 30 (PTAB Oct. 24, 2016) (denying institution of claim 1 as anticipated by AAPA); *LG Electronics, Inc. v. Core Wireless Licensing S.A.R.L.*, IPR2015-01987, Paper 7, at 18

(PTAB March 24, 2016) (denying institution on ground alleging obviousness of claims 16–28 based solely on AAPA).

Evidence of the skilled artisan's knowledge, however, remains fundamental to a proper obviousness analysis. *See KSR Int'l Co. v. Teleflex, Inc.*, 550 U.S. 398, 401 (2007); *Randall Mfg. v. Rea*, 733 F.3d 1355, 1362–63 (Fed. Cir. 2013) ("the knowledge of such an artisan is part of the store of public knowledge that must be consulted when considering whether a claimed invention would have been obvious"); *Dystar Textilfarben GmbH & Co. Deutschland KG v. C.H Patrick Co.*, 464 F.3d 1356, 1367 (Fed. Cir. 2006). The Federal Circuit has explained that because a properly conducted § 103 inquiry "necessarily depends" on the knowledge possessed by the ordinarily-skilled artisan, such knowledge must be considered in an IPR, notwithstanding the provisions of § 311(b):

> Although the prior art that can be considered in inter partes reviews is limited to patents and printed publications [under § 311], it does not follow that we ignore the skilled artisan's knowledge when determining whether it would have been obvious to modify the prior art. Indeed, under 35 U.S.C. § 103, the obviousness inquiry turns not only on the prior art, but whether "the differences between the claimed invention and the prior art are such that the claim that the claimed invention as a whole would have been obvious . . . to a person having ordinary skill in the art to which the claimed invention pertains." 35 U.S.C. § 103. Regardless of the tribunal, the inquiry into whether any "differences" between the invention and the prior art would have rendered the invention obvious to a skilled artisan necessarily depends on such artisan's knowledge.

See Koninklijke Philips v. Google, LLC, 948 F.3d 1330, 1337–39 (Fed. Cir. 2020).

Admissions are "permissible evidence in an *inter partes* review for establishing the background knowledge possessed by a person of ordinary skill in the art" and "provide a factual foundation as to what a skilled artisan would have known at the time of invention." *Qualcomm*, 24 F.4th at 1376.

Board panels should determine whether the petition relies on admissions in the specification in combination with reliance on at least one prior art patent or printed publication. *Qualcomm*, 24 F.4th at 1377.

If an IPR petition relies on admissions in combination with reliance on one or more prior art patents or printed publications, those admissions do not form "the basis" of the ground and must be considered by the Board in its patentability analysis. *Id.*

A patentee's admissions regarding the scope and content of the prior art under § 103 can be used, for example, to: (1) supply missing claim limitations that were generally known in the art prior to the invention (for pre-America Invents Act (AIA) patents) or the effective filing date of the claimed invention (for post-AIA patents); (2) support a motivation to combine particular disclosures; or (3) demonstrate the knowledge of the ordinarily-skilled artisan at the time of the invention (for pre-AIA patents) or the effective filing date of the claimed invention (for post-AIA patents) for any other purpose related to patentability. *See Qualcomm*, 24 F.4th at 1376; *see also Koninklijke Philips*, 948 F.3d at 1337–1338.

Admissions may include statements in the specification of the challenged patent such as "It is well known that . . . ," "It is well understood that . . . ," or "One of skill in the art would readily understand that . . . ," or may describe technology as "prior art," "conventional," or "well-known." *See McCoy v. Heal Sys., LLC*, 850 F. App'x 785, 789 (Fed. Cir. 2021) (non-precedential) (finding it was not an error for the Board in an IPR proceeding to accept the specification's own assertions of what was "conventional" and therefore well known in the art). Of course, parties may dispute the significance or meaning of statements in the specification or other evidence, including disputing whether specification statements constitute admissions or evidence of the background knowledge possessed by a person of ordinary skill in the art. For example, petitioners may rely on certain language in the specification identified *supra* (e.g., "It is well known that . . .") as evidence of what a skilled artisan would have known at the time of the invention, and a patent owner can choose to dispute whether the petitioner has accurately characterized the evidence it cites (e.g., offer evidence or argument that a statement in the specification does not reflect such knowledge or is not an admission). Either side may present expert testimony in support of its position. The Board shall adjudicate such disputes and determine whether the specification (or other evidence that is not "prior art consisting of patents or printed publications") properly constitutes evidence of the skilled artisan's knowledge at the time of the invention. Such situations are likely to be highly fact specific, and the Board can address them as they arise.

Because the Federal Circuit has made clear that it is appropriate in an IPR to rely on admissions in an obviousness analysis (*Qualcomm*, 274 F.4th 1376), Board panels should not exclude the use of admissions based on the number of claim limitations or claim elements the admission supplies or the order in which the petition presents the obviousness combination (e.g., prior art modified by admission or admission modified by prior art). Rather, Board panels should review whether the asserted ground as a whole as applied to each challenged claim as a whole relies on admissions in the specification in combination with reliance on at least one prior art patent or printed publication.

While 37 CFR § 42.104(b)(4) states that a petition "must specify where each element of the claim is found in the prior art patents or printed publications relied upon," this does not foreclose the limited use of admissions described in this Memorandum. Section 42.104(b) specifies what petitions must contain and requires specific information from the parties to ensure orderly proceedings, but does not narrow the scope of IPR petitions further than § 311 itself does. For example, § 42.104(b)(3) requires that petitioners include their construction of claim terms. Nevertheless, the Board does not deny petitions under § 42.104 in which petitioners assert that terms should be given their ordinary meaning. Similarly, the Board should not deny a petition in which an applicant points to general knowledge and/or a patentee's admissions regarding the scope and content of the prior art to satisfy a claim limitation. *See American Farm Lines v. Black Ball Freight Serv.*, 397 U.S. 532, 539 (1970) ("it is always within the discretion of a court or an administrative agency to relax or modify its procedural rules adopted for the orderly transaction of business before it"); *see also* 37 CFR § 42.5(b) (stating that "[t]he Board may waive or suspend a requirement of parts 1, 41, and 42").[2]

In addition to the use of admissions as described above, other AIA provisions support using evidence outside of prior art patents or printed publications when assessing §§ 102 or 103 issues in an IPR. *Qualcomm*, 24 F.4th at 1375–1376. For example, 35 U.S.C. § 312(a)(3)(B) states that an IPR petition can include "affidavits or declarations of supporting evidence and opinions." Section 314(a) indicates that the decision whether to institute the requested IPR should consider such supporting evidence. *See* 35 U.S.C. § 314(a) (the Director may institute if "the information presented in the petition" meets the applicable standard) (emphasis added). Similarly, § 316(a)(3) permits the USPTO to promulgate regulations to permit the submission of "supplemental information" by the petitioner. *See* 37 CFR § 42.123 (providing for the filing of supplemental information). Consistent with § 311, these provisions allow for an important, but limited, role for evidence other than prior art patents and printed publications in IPRs. *Qualcomm*, 24 F.4th at 1375–1376.

[2] While § 42.104 does not narrow the scope of permissible petitions under § 311, neither does it broaden it. The basis of every petition must be one or more prior art patents or printed publications.

One of the riskier things to do when preparing a patent application is to either state or in any way imply that something is prior art to the patent application filing. The reason this is risky is because such a characterization, whether express or implied, may turn out to be incorrect. If one states or implies that something is prior art to a filed patent application, this may be treated as an admission against interest that probably cannot be undone for that patent application, both during examination and even for later litigation, if it occurs.[124] Thus, any characterizations of prior art must be done with great care.

A simple rule would be to never make such a characterization, but sticking to such a rule is not so simple. For example, an examiner may require that you identify content or figures in the patent application as prior art. In addition, in explaining the benefits or advantages of an invention that would have been unobvious at the time it was made, it is often helpful to compare the subject matter with the prior art. Thus, the lesson is to be sure that something you characterize as prior art is, in fact, prior art legally, by statute, as we have discussed.

There are several ways to characterize something as prior art one should know. It may be done in the claims, as discussed next, using a Jepson-style claim or a claim format that is arguably Jepson-like. It may also be done by reciting that something is "prior art" in the specification, by labeling a figure

124. *But see* Qualcomm, Inc. v. Apple Inc., 24 F.4th 1367 (Fed. Cir. 2022) (It was error to rely on AAPA to invalidate claims in an IPR in light of the controlling statute.).

as "prior art," or it may be implied by describing something in the background section of the patent application, which should *only* describe prior art and *nothing more*.[125] As a tip, the background should be written as if the invention has not yet even been invented.

Regarding the claims, as mentioned, use of a Jepson-style claim has some risk. These claims are also discussed in more detail later.[126] 37 C.F.R. § 1.75(e) (2024) defines the structure of a Jepson claim. It states:

> Where the nature of the case admits, as in the case of an improvement, any independent claim should contain in the following order:
>
> (1) A preamble comprising a general description of all the elements or steps of the claimed combination which are conventional or known,
>
> (2) A phrase such as "wherein the improvement comprises," and
>
> (3) Those elements, steps and/or relationships which constitute that portion of the claimed combination which the applicant considers as the new or improved portion.

Jepson claims are risky because the preamble has been held to be an admission of prior art.[127] The preamble is the initial part of the claims from the beginning up to a transition word, like "comprising." If what is recited in the preamble is without question in the prior art, use of this type of claim is fine. As discussed later in connection with drafting these claims, it is best to err on the side of being cautious when drafting the preamble of a Jepson claim.[128] That is, make sure that what you recite in the preamble is prior art.

Claims that are similar in structure to Jepson claims also have some risk, although the law is less settled on this. For example, it has been argued that the claim format used in the EPC results in a prior art admission. That format uses a preamble of known or conventional elements, but then states "characterized in that" or something similar, followed by recitation of the new and improved subject matter. Similar caution should therefore be applied with this claiming style.[129]

One reason that admissions of prior art may be inadvertently made in the background section is that some practitioners accord significance to advocacy in the background section. For example, some may describe the problem at issue in the background, believing this will aid in obtaining allowance. They wish to, in essence, "tell a story" that demonstrates the innovation. In general, such

125. *See* Wilensky, *supra* note 123.
126. See Chapter 4, discussing Jepson claims.
127. *See In re* Glatt Air Techs., Inc., 630 F.3d 1026 (Fed. Cir. 2011).
128. See Chapter 4, discussing Jepson claims.
129. See Chapter 4.

motivations are not misguided. However, doing this in the background section may be deadly. For example, there is law that states recognition of the problem, where it was not previously recognized, may render an invention unobvious.[130] This rule applies even if once the problem is recognized, the solution to the problem would be obvious to one of ordinary skill. Thus, describing the problem in the background in a situation in which the problem was previously unrecognized would incorrectly imply that it had been recognized in the prior art. Again, this would be viewed as an admission against interest, removing one of the most effective legal arguments for patentability of the invention. Again, to avoid this, draft the entire background as if the invention has not yet been invented.[131]

Another form of advocacy in the background is to state: "Therefore, a need for X exists." However, if that need is not recognized in the prior art, again, you have impliedly *or even expressly* admitted that the prior art recognizes such a need.

Again, as a rule, to be cautious, do not state *anything* in the background that you are not entirely sure is well-known and in the prior art. Any advocacy of the sort just illustrated may be done in the detailed description so that you have not inadvertently implied that what you describe predates the invention.

Broadest Reasonable Interpretation

Review draft patent claims in light of the BRI.

MPEP § 2111

2111. Claim Interpretation; Broadest Reasonable Interpretation
CLAIMS MUST BE GIVEN THEIR BROADEST REASONABLE INTERPRETATION IN LIGHT OF THE SPECIFICATION

During patent examination, the pending claims must be "given their broadest reasonable interpretation consistent with the specification." The Federal Circuit's en banc decision in Phillips v. AWH Corp., 415 F.3d 1303, 1316, 75 USPQ2d 1321, 1329 (Fed. Cir. 2005) expressly recognized that the USPTO employs the "broadest reasonable interpretation" standard:

The Patent and Trademark Office ("PTO") determines the scope of claims in patent applications not solely on the basis of the claim language, but upon giving claims

---

130. See, *e.g.*, Eibel Process Co. v. Minn. & Ontario Paper Co., 261 U.S. 45 (1923).

131. *See* Wilensky, *supra* note 123. Instead, include that material in the detailed description rather than the background.

their broadest reasonable construction "in light of the specification as it would be interpreted by one of ordinary skill in the art." In re Am. Acad. of Sci. Tech. Ctr., 367 F.3d 1359, 1364[, 70 USPQ2d 1827, 1830] (Fed. Cir. 2004). Indeed, the rules of the PTO require that application claims must "conform to the invention as set forth in the remainder of the specification and the terms and phrases used in the claims must find clear support or antecedent basis in the description so that the meaning of the terms in the claims may be ascertainable by reference to the description." 37 CFR 1.75(d)(1).

See also In re Suitco Surface, Inc., 603 F.3d 1255, 1259, 94 USPQ2d 1640, 1643 (Fed. Cir. 2010); In re Hyatt, 211 F.3d 1367, 1372, 54 USPQ2d 1664, 1667 (Fed. Cir. 2000).

Patented claims are not given the broadest reasonable interpretation during court proceedings involving infringement and validity, and can be interpreted based on a fully developed prosecution record. In contrast, an examiner must construe claim terms in the broadest reasonable manner during prosecution as is reasonably allowed in an effort to establish a clear record of what applicant intends to claim. Thus, the Office does not interpret claims when examining patent applications in the same manner as the courts. In re Morris, 127 F.3d 1048, 1054, 44 USPQ2d 1023, 1028 (Fed. Cir. 1997); In re Zletz, 893 F.2d 319, 321–22, 13 USPQ2d 1320, 1321–22 (Fed. Cir. 1989).

Because applicant has the opportunity to amend the claims during prosecution, giving a claim its broadest reasonable interpretation will reduce the possibility that the claim, once issued, will be interpreted more broadly than is justified. In re Yamamoto, 740 F.2d 1569, 1571 (Fed. Cir. 1984); In re Zletz, 893 F.2d 319, 321, 13 USPQ2d 1320, 1322 (Fed. Cir. 1989) ("During patent examination the pending claims must be interpreted as broadly as their terms reasonably allow."); In re Prater, 415 F.2d 1393, 1404–05, 162 USPQ 541, 550–51 (CCPA 1969) (Claim 9 was directed to a process of analyzing data generated by mass spectrographic analysis of a gas. The process comprised selecting the data to be analyzed by subjecting the data to a mathematical manipulation. The examiner made rejections under 35 U.S.C. 101 and 35 U.S.C. 102. In the 35 U.S.C. 102 rejection, the examiner explained that the claim was anticipated by a mental process augmented by pencil and paper markings. The court agreed that the claim was not limited to using a machine to carry out the process since the claim did not explicitly set forth the machine. The court explained that "reading a claim in light of the specification, to thereby interpret limitations explicitly recited in the claim, is a quite different thing from 'reading limitations of the specification into a claim,' to thereby narrow the scope of the claim by implicitly adding disclosed limitations which have no express basis in the claim." The court found that applicant was advocating the latter, i.e., the impermissible importation of subject matter from the specification into the claim.). See also In re Morris, 127 F.3d 1048, 1054–55, 44 USPQ2d 1023, 1027–28 (Fed. Cir. 1997) (The court held that the USPTO is not required, in the course of prosecution, to interpret claims in applications in the same manner as a court would interpret claims in an infringement suit. Rather, the "PTO applies to verbiage of the proposed claims the broadest reasonable meaning of the words in their ordinary usage as they would be understood by one of ordinary skill in the art, taking into account whatever enlightenment by way of definitions or otherwise that may be afforded by the written description contained in applicant's specification.").

The broadest reasonable interpretation does not mean the broadest possible interpretation. Rather, the meaning given to a claim term must be consistent with the ordinary and customary meaning of the term (unless the term has been given a special definition in the specification), and must be consistent with the use of the claim term in the specification and drawings. Further, the broadest reasonable interpretation of the claims must be consistent with the interpretation that those skilled in the art would reach. In re Cortright, 165 F.3d 1353, 1359, 49 USPQ2d 1464, 1468 (Fed. Cir. 1999) (The Board's construction of the claim limitation "restore hair growth" as requiring the hair to be returned to its original state was held to be an incorrect interpretation of the limitation. The court held that, consistent with applicant's disclosure and the disclosure of three patents from analogous arts using the same phrase to require only some increase in hair growth, one of ordinary skill would construe "restore hair growth" to mean that the claimed method increases the amount of hair grown on the scalp, but does not necessarily produce a full head of hair.). Thus the focus of the inquiry regarding the meaning of a claim should be what would be reasonable from the perspective of one of ordinary skill in the art. In re Suitco Surface, Inc., 603 F.3d 1255, 1260, 94 USPQ2d 1640, 1644 (Fed. Cir. 2010); In re Buszard, 504 F.3d 1364, 84 USPQ2d 1749 (Fed. Cir. 2007). In Buszard, the claim was directed to a flame retardant composition comprising a flexible polyurethane foam reaction mixture. 504 F.3d at 1365, 84 USPQ2d at 1750. The Federal Circuit found that the Board's interpretation that equated a "flexible" foam with a crushed "rigid" foam was not reasonable. Id. at 1367, 84 USPQ2d at 1751. Persuasive argument was presented that persons experienced in the field of polyurethane foams know that a flexible mixture is different than a rigid foam mixture. Id. at 1366, 84 USPQ2d at 1751.

See MPEP § 2173.02 for further discussion of claim interpretation in the context of analyzing claims for compliance with 35 U.S.C. 112(b) or pre-AIA 35 U.S.C. 112, second paragraph.

In re Morris
127 F.3d 1048
United States Court of Appeals for the Federal Circuit
September 10, 1997, Decided

Questions

1. This is an appeal to the Federal Circuit of a Board decision in which an examiner's rejection was at issue. It is not typical to take an examiner's rejection all the way to the Federal Circuit, but it does happen on occasion. It is usually easier to try to negotiate with the examiner. This is a good case to keep in mind when drafting claims. Observe that the applicant did have allowed claims.
2. What was the main argument advanced by the applicant to distinguish from the art?
3. Observe that the applicant did not define the term being relied upon. The court stated:

    > We conclude that the PTO's interpretation is reasonable in light of all the evidence before the Board. As the cases cited above demonstrate, our predecessor court had on several prior occasions interpreted the term "integral" to cover more that a unitary construction. . . . Appellants' attempt to distinguish these cases misses the point. *Absent an express definition in their specification*, the fact that appellants can point to definitions or usages that conform to their interpretation does not make the PTO's definition unreasonable when the PTO can point to other sources that support its interpretation.[132]

    Thus, how did the applicants interpret the term at issue and how did the PTO interpret the term?

    This illustrates a genuine problem in drafting patent claims and patent specifications. It may be a challenge to anticipate how one will need to distinguish from the prior art. Here, without the appropriate description or definition in the specification, the applicant came up short.
4. Also take note of this language from the court:

    > The appellants urge us to consult the specification and some of the cited prior art, including Brown, and interpret the disputed language more narrowly in view thereof. When read in light of this material, according to applicants, the "true" meaning of the phrase emerges. We decline to attempt to harmonize the applicants' interpretation with the application and prior art. Such an approach puts the burden in the wrong place. *It is the applicants' burden to precisely define the invention, not the PTO's. See* 35 U.S.C. § 112 P2 ("The specification

132. *In re* Morris, 127 F.3d 1048, 1056–57 (Fed. Cir. 1997) (emphasis added).

> shall conclude with one or more claims particularly pointing out and distinctly claiming the subject matter which the applicant regards as his invention."). While it is true that the claims were not rejected on the ground of indefiniteness, this section puts the burden of precise claim drafting squarely on the applicant.[133]

Both the claims and the specification work together to make clear the precise scope intended for the claims. Also observe that it was proper for the examiner to change his mind in prosecution, which is not that uncommon. Query, if an applicant were to change his or her mind, would that be well received by a reviewing court? How would an applicant make that clear on the record?[134]

5. Why does the court say it is proper to apply the BRI in this procedural context? Note, however, that it is the broadest *reasonable* interpretation. Examiners seem to sometimes forget that part of the standard and apply the broadest possible interpretation.

In re Smith International, Inc.
871 F.3d 1375
United States Court of Appeals for the Federal Circuit
September 26, 2017, Decided

Questions

1. This is another case involving BRI, but here the Federal Circuit agrees with the applicant. In this case, this is an appeal from an *ex parte* reexamination, which is a type of prosecution. The Federal Circuit's admonition is telling here. The court states:

> We conclude that the Board's construction of "body" was unreasonably broad. Even when giving claim terms their broadest reasonable interpretation, the Board cannot construe the claims "so broadly that its constructions are *unreasonable* under general claim construction principles." *Microsoft Corp. v. Proxyconn, Inc.*, 789 F.3d 1292, 1298 (Fed. Cir. 2015) (emphasis in original). '[T]he protocol of giving claims their broadest reasonable interpretation . . . does not include giving claims a legally incorrect interpretation' 'divorced from the specification and

---

133. *Id.* at 1056 (emphasis added).
134. *See* Hakim v. Cannon Avent Grp., PLC, 479 F.3d 1313, 1318 (Fed. Cir. 2007).

> the record evidence.' *Id.* (citations and internal quotation marks omitted); *see PPC Broadband, Inc. v. Corning Optical Commc'ns RF, LLC*, 815 F.3d 747, 751–53 (Fed. Cir. 2016). . . .
>
> *The correct inquiry in giving a claim term its broadest reasonable interpretation in light of the specification is not whether the specification proscribes or precludes some broad reading of the claim term adopted by the examiner. And it is not simply an interpretation that is not inconsistent with the specification. It is an interpretation that corresponds with what and how the inventor describes his invention in the specification, i.e., an interpretation that is "consistent with the specification."* *In re Morris*, 127 F.3d 1048, 1054 (Fed. Cir. 1997) (citation and internal quotation marks omitted); *see also In re Suitco Surface*, 603 F.3d 1255, 1259–60 (Fed. Cir. 2010) [(emphasis added)].
>
> The Board emphasized that the patentee here did not act as a lexicographer, and that the specification neither defines nor precludes the examiner's reading of the term "body." Accordingly, the Board found that nothing in the specification would disallow the examiner's interpretation, rendering it "reasonable." However, following such logic, any description short of an express definition or disclaimer in the specification would result in an adoption of a broadest *possible* interpretation of a claim term, irrespective of repeated and consistent descriptions in the specification that indicate otherwise. That is not properly giving the claim term its broadest reasonable interpretation *in light of* the specification.[135]

In light of the court's clarification, how easy is it to separate a BRI analysis from an analysis of the specification and claims in accordance with the usual principles of claim construction? What was the issue regarding "body"?

2. Unfortunately, the Board tends to often side with the examiner. After all, most of the members of the Board were examiners previously. So, the approach here is not atypical. The Board concludes because a term was not defined that the examiner is free to apply his or her own definition under the guise of BRI. This case makes it clear that such an approach is wrong, but who wants to go all the way to the Federal Circuit to get that result? It demonstrates once again that, as the drafter, it is important to be quite circumspect in your drafting and to define

135. *In re* Smith Int'l, Inc., 871 F.3d 1375, 1382 (Fed. Cir. 2017).

key terms lest you be undone by an examiner, a litigation opponent, a negotiation opponent, and so on.

What is the significance of the following statement in terms of the reexamination finding some of the claims anticipated or obvious? "The PTO fails to point to any description of the body that would support its strained construction of 'body,' and its urging that the term 'body' in the '817 patent claims correspond to the 'body,' 'mandrel,' and 'cam sleeve' of Eddison is thus unsupported."[136]

3. How would you distinguish this case from *In re Morris*?

Intel Corp. v. Qualcomm Inc.
21 F.4th 784
United States Court of Appeals for the Federal Circuit
December 28, 2021, Decided

Questions

1. Other than the court saying it was applying the BRI, how clear was this from its analysis? Was there anything in the analysis that suggested it was erring on the side of a broad interpretation rather than an interpretation that was attempting to assess what the invention truly was?

136. *Id.* at 1383.

Chapter 2

Introduction to Patent Strategy and Tactics with Claim Drafting Illustrations

As the esteemed Judge Giles Rich stated, in patent law, "the name of the game is the claim."[1] The interpretation of a patent claim touches virtually every aspect of patent law.[2] The patent statute was previously introduced.[3] The elements of a *prima facie* case in federal court were also discussed previously. This chapter introduces some strategic and tactical considerations when beginning to draft a set of claims for an invention.

Related to strategic and tactical considerations, how patents may be used in some example business situations is discussed in this chapter. One necessary consideration is "prior art." As discussed, this has a legal meaning, which changed in 2013 when specific provisions of the America Invents Act (AIA)[4]

---

1. Giles S. Rich, *The Extent of the Protection and Interpretation of Claims—American Perspectives*, 21 Int'l Rev. Indus. Prop. & Copyright L. 497, 499 (1990) ("To coin a phrase, the name of the game is the claim.").

2. *See, e.g.*, Corning Glass Works v. Sumitomo Elec. U.S.A., Inc., 868 F.2d 1251, 1257 (Fed. Cir. 1989) ("A claim in a patent provides the metes and bounds of the right which the patent confers on the patentee to exclude others from making, using, or selling the protected invention.").

Donald Chisum explains the importance of claims as follows:

> Claims measure the invention for determining patentability both during examination and after issuance when validity is challenged. They also determine what constitutes infringement. A claim recites a number of elements or limitations, and will cover or "read on" only those products (or processes) that contain all such elements or limitations. Effective claims must be neither too broad (i.e., cover the prior art or matter not adequately described in the specification) nor too narrow (i.e., fail to cover all possible embodiments of the applicant's invention).

1 Donald S. Chisum, Chisum on Patents glossary (2024).

3. *See, e.g.*, 35 U.S.C. (2024).

4. Throughout this book, AIA refers to the Leahy-Smith America Invents Act, Pub. L. No. 112-29, 125 Stat. 284 (2011). This act was passed on September 11, 2013. The provisions that changed §§ 102 and 103 of title 35 were treated in detail in Chapter 1 of this book. These provisions went into effect on March 16, 2013.

went into effect. Thus, pre- and post-AIA definitions of "prior art" have been contemplated and discussed.

Many legal tasks performed today are complex and challenging and call for legal knowledge, excellent judgment, and actual experience. For example, many attorneys may have the capability to draft a simple contract. Yet, if a deal is a complex transaction, such as the sale of a business, drafting an agreement that protects the interests of the party being represented is more challenging. Likewise, attorneys are trained to understand litigation and the nuances of advocacy. However, some aspects of litigation are best learned "in the trenches."

Yet, among complex and challenging legal tasks, patent claim drafting (PCD) is recognized as one of the more difficult legal tasks to master.[5] Those less familiar with the challenge of claim drafting sometimes see drafting patent claims as more of a commodity service that anyone with both technical training and legal training can perform. However, to the extent PCD is a commodity service, then it is more like gold or silver than like pork bellies.[6]

---

5. *See, e.g.*, Topliff v. Topliff, 145 U.S. 156, 171 (1892) ("the specification and claims of a patent, particularly if the invention be at all complicated, constitute one of the most difficult legal instruments to draw with accuracy"); *see also* Festo Corp. v. Shoketsu Kinzoku Kogyo Kabushiki Co., 234 F.3d 558, 622, 56 U.S.P.Q.2d 1865, 1915–16 (Fed. Cir. 2000), *rev'd*, 535 U.S. 722 (2002), *on remand*, 344 F.3d 1359 (Fed. Cir. 2003) (en banc), *cert. denied*, 541 U.S. 988 (2004) ("In addition to the inexact fit caused by the inherent limitations of language, the language itself may not be adequately developed at the early stages when patent applications typically are filed, particularly in rapidly evolving research fields. Besides the foregoing language issues, the early patent application filings encouraged by the U.S. patent laws give rise to additional difficulties in crafting a claim that particularly points out the subject matter that the inventor regards as his invention. For inventions in rapidly evolving fields, application filings are often made while the inventions are still in their nascent stages, i.e., early in the evolutionary process, necessitating inevitable and sometimes considerable fine tuning of claim language after the initial application filings have been made. Moreover, while an inventor is often aware of relevant prior art relating to the area he is developing, he is not always fully cognizant of all of the relevant prior art until after his application has been filed, thus, again, necessitating some fine tuning of claim language after the initial application filing has been made.").

6. Patent law may be thought of as involving several branches: patent prosecution, patent litigation, and patent licensing. Patent prosecution describes the process by which an inventor, usually through the help of an attorney, files an application with the U.S. Patent and Trademark Office (PTO) for examination to obtain a patent. Patent litigation focuses on patents once issued. A patent owner whose rights have been infringed may compel an accused infringer to stop the infringing activity and/or pay for damages arising from infringement that has occurred. Patent licensing allows patent owners to generate royalty income by allowing others to practice the invention. Yet another aspect may be thought of as a cross between litigation and prosecution. The AIA created several types of legal proceedings in the PTO that may take place after a patent has issued. These proceedings are a cross between litigation and prosecution, because

Patent attorneys are often perceived as "geeks," in part because PCD requires a technical degree of some kind (or the equivalent). Patent attorneys frequently majored in electrical engineering or physics in college, whereas others also destined to enter the legal profession may have majored in history, political science, or economics.

However, billions of dollars in value quite literally can be in play, depending on the language used in the claims of a given patent. To put a finer point on the subject, over many years, there have been lots of examples of incredibly valuable technology that, if better claimed, would have resulted in an incredibly valuable patent. Understanding what went wrong and what to do to provide appropriate patent protection requires understanding PCD.

As has been discussed, first, understand that the scope of legal rights granted by a patent is defined by the "claims" of the patent.[7] The claims of a patent are the numbered sentences at the very end of the patent. Claims are, in effect, run-on sentences since the only period in a claim occurs at the end of the claim.[8]

The main point here is that the scope of rights granted by a patent claim primarily turns on the exact words of the patent claims themselves.[9] Therefore, poor, sloppy, or not well-thought-out word selection may produce an undesirable result such that technology of value to the patentee may not *necessarily* be covered by the claims of the patent at issue. If that is the case, this will seriously reduce, if not completely eviscerate, the value of the patent at issue. There are many wonderful and troubling examples where this is precisely what happened.

As one quick example of the many that are legion, simply because a word of a patent claim had an "s" on the end, meaning that the particular element or limitation of the claim was plural, the accused product was held to

---

while they take place in the PTO, they are *inter partes*, as in litigation. By contrast, patent prosecution is *ex parte*.

7. *See, e.g.*, Phillips v. AWH Corp., 415 F.2d 1303, 1312 (Fed. Cir. 2005) (en banc) ("It is a 'bedrock principle' of patent law that 'the claims of a patent define the invention to which the patentee is entitled the right to exclude.'"). *See also* Constant v. Advanced Micro-Devices, Inc., 848 F.2d 1560, 1571, 7 U.S.P.Q.2d 1057, 1064 (Fed. Cir. 1988); Dollar Elec. Co. v. Syndevco, Inc., 205 U.S.P.Q. 949, 959 (E.D. Mich. 1979), *aff'd*, 669 F.2d 1370, 214 U.S.P.Q. 241 (6th Cir. 1982).

8. *See In re Fressola*, 22 U.S.P.Q.2d 1828 (Comm'r Pat. & Trademarks 1992), in which Commissioner Manbeck ruled that "[t]he single claim sentence requirement is within the PTO's statutory authority and is consistent with the statutory purpose of 35 U.S.C. § 112 2." See Chapter 5, addressing grammar in connection with PCD.

9. See Chapter 3, which discusses the parts of a patent claim and the theory behind those parts, Chapter 4, which discusses types of patent claims, and Chapter 5, which discusses principles of patent claim construction.

not infringe the claims of the patent in suit.[10] The invention at issue and the accused product related to fireplaces. However, the claims referred to "rear walls" of a firebox that was part of the fireplace, rather than simply a "rear wall." The accused product had one rear wall. Ironically, the "s" was not in the patent claim as originally filed but was in the claim that ultimately issued. Therefore, little, almost innocuous, mistakes may, in certain circumstances, have a significant impact.[11]

The Importance of Claim Diversity and Claim Scope in Patent Strategy and Tactics

PCD may be challenging perhaps because executing PCD reasonably well requires an appreciation of several complex areas: the state of patent law, the state of the technology at issue, and the state of business/economic considerations often related to the technology at issue. Furthermore, these three topics are often "moving targets." To provide a few examples, new U.S. Supreme Court and/or Federal Circuit decisions often leave uncertain the full scope of legal consequences and/or changes that may follow from those decisions. In addition, statutory changes, such as the AIA, and/or regulatory changes, promulgated by the U.S. Patent and Trademark Office (PTO), also frequently introduce change. Likewise, technological breakthroughs occurring on a weekly or daily basis may leave uncertain which technologies will remain and which will quickly be supplanted or become obsolete.

As a simple example, the movement from analog to digital modems had a significant effect on how computer networks operate. Not anticipating that change may have resulted in some patent claims that were of less value, if, for example, the claims recited analog modem technology rather than being broad enough to encompass both analog and digital modem technology.[12]

10. *See* Superior Fireplace v. Majestic Prods., 270 F.3d 1358 (Fed. Cir. 2001).

11. There are also examples where mistakes in punctuation had dire consequences. See *Cultor Corp. v. A.E. Staley*, 224 F.3d 1328 (Fed. Cir. 2000), in which the Federal Circuit construed a claim narrowly based on a comma. See *Allen Engineering Corp. v. Bartell Industries*, 299 F.3d 1336 (Fed. Cir. 2002), where a claim did not contain any punctuation at all at the end of the limitation and the Federal Circuit found the claim indefinite under 35 U.S.C. § 112 due to a truncated limitation. Mistakes in the language of any legal document may have unfortunate consequences; however, it may be that mistakes in patent claims are more "leveraged," in the sense that a patent claim is usually shorter than the other examples of important legal documents that require custom drafting of language.

12. Likewise, there have been cases where the situation was reversed and because the claim was sufficiently broad to cover both analog and digital technology, the claim was held

Furthermore, changing economic and business conditions may also affect which technologies succeed in the marketplace and which do not. For example, difficulties in the economy may have slowed the adoption of solar technology and the adoption of more advanced cell phone networks, such as 5G and beyond. Similarly, the worldwide pandemic likely speeded up the adoption of technology that permits "virtual" meetings in place of "in-person" meetings. Understanding how a particular technology, especially one sought to be patented, may affect various markets may be particularly useful for PCD. As examples, changes in various markets may impact the demand for the technology at issue. Similarly, in what particular form the technology at issue will likely be sought (e.g., product demand) and/or deployed (e.g., product supply) may be particularly useful to understand as well.

In other words, a universe of ways in which to craft a patent claim is available. To narrow this universe, there is a set of useful tools. These tools would typically include a good understanding of the technology at issue, including typical implementations. Likewise, competing technologies, as well as information about relevant markets, are also useful tools. Other tools may include how the technology is likely to be sold and/or distributed, where it likely will be manufactured, and so on. With such tools, your challenge is to craft patent claims that will hopefully sail through the PTO, although that is not all. The patent claims should also stand up to legal challenges in federal court and/or stand up to competitor scrutiny.

In pursuit of this goal, this book introduces many important patent law doctrines in pursuit of the key principles of PCD. We begin with a discussion regarding considerations that typically limit patent claim scope. It is a generally accepted principle that broad patent claims tend to provide more value than narrow patent claims.[13] As at least an initial premise, experience suggests two primary considerations appear to typically limit the scope of patent claims that are applied for and ultimately issue from the PTO.

The first of these considerations is the so-called prior art. As already suggested, prior art has a specific legal meaning in this context (which changed when the relevant portion of the AIA went into force on March 16, 2013).[14] It is important that the implications of this change be fully understood to be

---

invalid because the analog technology predated the invention at issue. *Cf.* Personalized Media Commc'ns v. Apple, 952 F.3d 1336 (Fed. Cir. 2020) (claims avoided prior art because claim language interpreted to mean all digital signals, rather than digital and analog signals). Thus, this sword is double-edged, so to speak.

13. But see later in this chapter, treating advantages and disadvantages of broad claims.

14. See Chapter 1, treating in detail aspects of pre- and post-AIA statutes that provide the legal meaning of "prior art."

able to draft quality patent claims. The second of these considerations, however, surprising to some, tends to be *self-imposed* claim limitations primarily derived from the commercial reasons for pursuing the patent filing.

Prior Art

Because prior art may limit claim scope, some amount of searching the prior art is frequently associated with drafting patent claims. Because the prior art is the practical limit on claim scope, knowing the prior art before drafting the claims and prior to taking a position before the PTO, in many instances, should provide an advantage; unfortunately, searches are notoriously poor while consuming valuable resources. In general, the higher the quality of the search, usually the more resources that are consumed.

Whether to search tends to be a contextually laden decision and is discussed in more detail in later sections of this book.[15] However, being able to obtain and study the best and most relevant prior art before developing or drafting the patent claims is akin to knowing your opponent's best argument or position before you draft your own argument. Rarely does the law provide this opportunity to an advocate, so, *if cost is not a factor*, it may be something to consider. Unfortunately, *cost usually is a factor*. Therefore, a search may not necessarily be undertaken, or the results, again, may be quite poor in that the best and most relevant prior art may not be uncovered due to limited resources. Furthermore, despite the advantage just mentioned, in some circumstances, a search may not be needed and, if so, may unnecessarily add additional cost.[16] Still, two reasons to search for prior art are (1) if it turns out the exact subject matter has been done previously, knowing that early allows you to avoid the cost of pursuing a patent application; and (2) knowing the best prior art allows you to draft original claims that decrease the likelihood that claim elements or limitations need to be added during prosecution that would affect claim interpretation or create prosecution history estoppel (or, even perhaps, prevent lack of written description support for such needed elements and limitations).[17]

As a result, as one might have inferred, some uncertainty as to the closest and most relevant prior art is likely to exist when the patent claims are submitted to the PTO. It is rarely clear at the time of filing a patent application that one has, in fact, found the best and most relevant prior art. One

15. See later in this chapter, treating the advantages and disadvantages of searching.
16. Again, considerations for the decision to search are treated later in this chapter.
17. See Chapter 6, addressing this legal issue.

reason for this is because the cost of doing a completely comprehensive and thorough search would likely make pursuing a patent application prohibitively expensive. Online resources are improving so that, if needed, a useful and cost-effective search to at least uncover "low-hanging fruit" may be undertaken. More typically, however, the most careful, thorough, and, therefore, costly prior art searching is performed in conjunction with litigation or a similar type of patent assertion activity. Much more is usually at stake in a litigation (or licensing) situation than is at stake at the time an application is filed, explaining the greater allocation of resources for searching later. This may also at least partially explain why it is that new art is usually found and frequently does impact the patent claims in connection with an *inter partes* review (IPR) or other post-grant proceeding in the PTO, for example. These proceedings frequently result from assertion of a patent. Certainly, if serious searching is undertaken prior to filing a patent application, the art found may, in fact, be highly, if not the most, relevant art. Typically, in this situation, an expansive and aggressive posture would be appropriate when drafting the patent claims.

To be more precise, however, regardless of whether a search is undertaken, it is usually considered good practice that the claims submitted be as expansive as reasonably possible to secure allowance of claims that will also stand up to close legal scrutiny (e.g., in light of the *known* prior art at the time of filing). Therefore, the claims should not be so broad that they are invalid as a matter of law in light of the *known* prior art. Likewise, it is a good practice for the patent drafter[18] to have a good faith argument for patentability over the *known* prior art at the time of filing.[19] Of course, there may also be some situations in which it may be best not to "swing for the fences,"[20] addressed later.

Commercial Reasons for the Patent Filing

It is a well-known fact that obtaining a patent is expensive. As the comic Henny Youngman quipped, when explaining why divorces are so expensive, "it is because they are worth it!"[21] Individuals and/or entities would not seek to

18. A variety of terms are used interchangeably throughout this book without loss of generality, such as *claim drafter*, *application drafter*, *patent drafter*, *patent practitioner*, and so on.

19. Drafting principles to avoid submitting claims that "read on" known prior art will be addressed in much more detail in Chapter 6.

20. This topic is addressed in more detail later in this chapter, which addresses the advantages and disadvantages of broad claims.

21. *Henny Youngman Quotes*, BRAINYQUOTE, https://www.brainyquote.com/authors/henny-youngman-quotes (last visited May 30, 2024).

own a patent unless they believed there was something of value to be gained. Patentees expect patent assets to be commercially valuable. Companies, such as Texas Instruments (TI), AT&T, and IBM, for example, have shown this to be true with patent licensing programs that have generated significant annual revenues. Likewise, companies such as Qualcomm, Nokia, and Rambus have been able to build successful licensing businesses around a portfolio of valuable patents. Nonetheless, it is also true that the value of a given patent filing may, at best, be speculative at the time the patent application is filed.

An expectation of commercial value plays into the patent process in several ways. Often, companies or individuals have more than one technical idea capable of being pursued and, due to limited financial and/or other resources, must limit the number of applications that receive resources in the form of time and money.

Commercial value assessments are, therefore, employed to make patent application filing selections. In other words, some patent applications are not pursued so that others, believed to have more potential value, may be pursued. Typically, the patentee has a commercial goal in mind that led to the proposed patent filing. A patent application drafter may let these commercial considerations limit, or at least strongly influence, the *full* scope of the patent claims.

Although it may seem natural to allow such commercial reasons to dictate or limit claim scope, it is recommended that the commercial reasons for filing a patent application *not necessarily strictly limit* the applied for claim scope. Certainly, the drafter should understand the commercial reasons behind the proposed filing, along with the inventive subject matter, and these considerations may also prove to be a helpful starting point when drafting the claims. Furthermore, as a minimum, the filed claims should address this commercial goal or goals.

However, again, experience has shown it would be wise to not permit commercial motivations to be a *strict* limit on the *full* claim scope being pursued in the patent application. More specifically, due to some of the changes and uncertainties alluded to previously, such as changes in the technology, changes in the law, changes in the economy, and even changes in the management of the company pursuing the patent application, the motivations for filing the patent application years earlier may prove to be different from the commercial motivations for keeping and seeking to enforce the patent, once it issues.[22] Even at successful and patent-savvy technology companies, it may be long after the patent application is filed, or even issued, that management

22. It may take three to five years or even longer for a patent application to issue as a patent.

gains a *full and complete* understanding of what makes the particular technology covered by the claims valuable in the marketplace.

Thus, to summarize, a possible conclusion from the prior discussion is that uncertainty is present here, as with prior art, as discussed earlier. This existing uncertainty may be taken to suggest several things. It suggests that some amount of diversity with respect to the claims may be one way to provide a hedge in light of such uncertainties. It may also suggest taking a more expansive approach to patent claiming at the outset. It is, in essence, recommended that any and all claims that are capable of being pursued based on the technology be included in the application except where cost prohibitive; for example, typical claims to include are method claims, component claims, system claims, software claims, manufacturing claims, and so on.[23] Of course, some clients may not want to absorb the associated expense of filing with many claims, which dictates a more measured approach in which claim types are prioritized based on the situation.[24]

However, it is useful to recognize now that patents may be employed in a wide variety of circumstances, including to protect the patentee's competitive advantage against imitators, to have something to assert if a competitor with patents pursues the patentee with its patents, to obtain licensing revenue, and/or to obtain other value. A variety of different patent claims that vary in scope in diverse ways increases the likelihood that the full value of the patented technology will be extracted. Furthermore, patent claims to protect against imitation may be drafted differently from patent claims to provide defensive protection in the event a competitor asserts its patents. It follows, with this potential for significantly varying situations, that significantly varying patent claims be drafted to cover these possible eventualities. Furthermore, this is better accomplished prior to filing, rather than after the patent application has already been filed, prosecuted, and is about to issue, for example. Of course, it almost goes without saying that the patent claims must also be adequately supported by the specification of the patent application. Providing adequate patent claim support in the patent specification may avoid several legal risks, such as want of written description or the risk that undesirable limitations will be "read" into the claims from the specification.[25] These are yet additional

---

23. The *many* types of claims available to include in a patent application are introduced and treated in Chapter 4.

24. *See id.*

25. See Chapter 5, which discusses importing limitations from the specification into the claims, and Chapter 6, which discusses want of written description and other claim drafting issues that constitute non-prior art claiming issues.

reasons to consider and draft patent claims early that cover the *full* scope of the subject matter of the patent application.

Some simple examples regarding the benefits of a more expansive approach to claim drafting, as suggested, may provide perspective. A patent attorney writing an application for a component manufacturer may make a regular practice of omitting patent claims to end-product apparatuses or systems that would incorporate such components. The reasoning might be that the manufacturer, the client, or employer of the patent attorney is not likely to sue its own customers or even potential customers—that is, companies that manufacture end products that include the component. Claims may, therefore, be limited to the component sold. Furthermore, it may be reasoned, how much does claiming the component in an end product typically add in terms of patentability?

For example, a memory manufacturer, your client, may choose to omit claims to devices that employ the memory being sold, such as desktop computers, servers, cell phones, tablets, and laptops. However, as one example of changing circumstances, an original equipment manufacturer (OEM) customer of your client or perhaps a system integrator customer of your client might acquire a memory manufacturing business allowing it to produce internally the memory component supplied by your client and, potentially, reduce its costs. Now, the OEM, for example, that *was* a customer of your client *is now* a direct competitor of that client.

One might believe that, even here, patenting component claims directed to memory devices should be sufficient to handle the new situation, and this might be correct; however, keep in mind that memory is not the core business for this entity that has just become a competitor. Claims directed to the entity's core business may be more helpful if a dispute were to develop, suggesting, consequently, that claims to an end product may ultimately have value even for a component manufacturer such as your client.

In a different turn of events, perhaps a different OEM, which does not purchase the component from your client/the patentee, sues your client. Why? Doing so may reduce the supply of components to competitors of the OEM or, at least, increase the costs of competitors of the suing OEM. In such a case, having component claims in a patent owned by your client may prove less valuable against this OEM that is suing your client than having claims that cover an end product incorporating such a component. One reason is because typically the OEM suing your client will have obtained a contractual indemnity against patent infringement from its component supplier and, thus, may not be as concerned about defending a countersuit involving the component itself. However, as implied by the last example, a lawsuit that has the potential to threaten the core business of the aggressor may prove more worrisome and may even bring that company to the bargaining table before trial has concluded or even begun.

Likewise, this latter hypothetical situation may have implications related to international manufacturing and importation into the United States. For example, the company suing your client may purchase components manufactured abroad and, likewise, may have a system integrator complete assembly of the end product abroad before being imported into the United States for sale to its customers. In this scenario, again, component claims may be of little use. For example, to stop an infringing product entering the United States, U.S. Customs would need to take apart the end product as it enters the country (which almost certainly will *not* occur); however, in contrast, claims directed to the end product may be sufficient to obtain an exclusion order that would keep the infringing end product from coming into the United States for sale. In short, many factors that are difficult to know ahead of time will play into which claims might be the most useful in a lawsuit, patent license negotiation, or other business/dispute-type situation.

The real point with these examples is that the claims should be drafted so that *as many legal options as are feasible* remain available for the time when the patent may be needed. Given this starting principle, it is recommended that the commercial motivation for filing a patent application be well understood, but not necessarily be employed to *strictly* limit the *full* scope or even the type of the claims being pursued.

Business Strategy Drives Patent Strategy

Identify the business strategy and the patent strategy objective for pursuing patent protection before beginning to draft a patent claim.
Also, anticipate the possibility of changes in the law, the technology, and/or the business dynamics as you formulate and draft patent claims.

Identify the Patent Strategy Objective

A patent is a legal document; however, it has value in that it supports a business. Business strategy should and does drive patent strategy (and, more generally, intellectual property (IP) strategy).

For a company with a relatively large business involving several product lines, and perhaps even several divisions, there may be a different business strategy for each and, likewise, a different IP/patent strategy for each. For example, in the previous hypothetical, a manufacturer may manufacture a product sold to consumers, such as a mobile device, as well as manufacture components for such a device sold to system integrators of mobile (as well as other types of) devices. One example of a company like this is Samsung, which manufactures components for cell phones and other electronic devices, like memory, and also manufactures cell phones. For example, with a consumer product (e.g., a mobile device), the business strategy may be to maximize consumer appeal; whereas for components, such as chips, the business strategy may be to maximize "wafer starts" (e.g., maximize production because chips are manufactured in wafers that are then subdivided into semiconductor chips).

Similarly, these products may have various forms of IP associated with each, such as copyrights (e.g., for software and/or a graphical user interface (GUI)), trade secrets, and/or patents. Of course, a detailed discussion of other IP is beyond the scope of this work. However, this illustrates that IP strategic and tactical issues may become complex for a large business with multiple products.

Our focus here is *patent* strategy and tactics. Nonetheless, patent strategy and tactics do not exist in isolation. Rather, a larger business strategy may involve various forms of IP with different strategies associated with each. To be more specific, as an example, there may be trade secrets and know-how associated with semiconductor chip fabrication as well as patents. This is a typical occurrence. A manufacturing process that results in a product may have aspects of the process that are considered better protected as trade secrets, whereas other aspects of the process may be better protected with patents. Likewise, the result of the process may be protected with patents. The goal of trade secret protection may be to keep competitors from copying the details of a manufacturing process that provides a competitive advantage. This may also be a goal of patent protection, but patent protection may also further other goals, as discussed in more detail in the next section.

IP, particularly patents, generally supports a business by creating a *legal* barrier to entry against competition. This permits a business to protect or increase its market share and protect its profit margin. The specifics of how this may play out generally defines the patent strategy and, at a more detailed level, may define associated tactics. The line between strategy and tactics is not always a clear one; however, one way to view the difference is that patent strategy usually concerns how to approach a portfolio of patents associated with a business. In contrast, claim-level decision-making for a specific patent may be thought of as more tactical in nature.

Claim Drafting Tactical and Strategic Illustrations

The value in having a patent is that it provides a legal barrier to entry permitting a business to protect its competitive advantage. It may be thought of as protection to guard "the castle," so to speak (i.e., a core business). This relies on the exclusionary nature of a patent in that it provides exclusive rights to the subject matter protected by the patent (e.g., covered by the patent claims). It is helpful to understand that a patent does *not* give the owner a right to do something; rather, a patent gives the owner a right to *prevent others* from doing something.

Specifically, 35 U.S.C. § 154(a)(1) (2024) states (emphasis added):

> Every patent shall contain a short title of the invention and a grant to the patentee, his heirs or assigns, of *the right to exclude others* from making, using, offering for sale, or selling the invention throughout the United States or importing the invention into the United States, and, if the invention is a process, of *the right to exclude others* from using, offering for sale or selling throughout the United States, or importing into the United States, products made by that process, referring to the specification for the particulars thereof.

Thus, the owner of a patent may *prevent others* from making, using, selling, offering for sale, or importing the patented invention. The "invention" refers to subject matter that falls within the scope of the patent claims of the patent.

At a high level, *how a patent may be used reduces to a few things. One may (1) choose to rely on the exclusive nature of a patent (i.e., it may be used to prevent others from practicing the invention)*. This, however, may potentially entail enforcement, which may lead to litigation and a formal challenge to the validity of the patent. *A patent may also (2) be licensed, for royalty income or other valuable consideration (e.g., such as equity)*. Licensing a patent may advance the interests of a business by generating income, for example, while imposing a cost on a competitor who is paying the royalty income. Likewise, a license may provide information and/or partial control over your competitor in that the competitor is subject to audits and may be limited under the license to producing only a certain amount of product, for example. Consequently, this too may assist in protecting the castle. *Another use of a patent may be to (3) consummate a patent cross-license*. Some people refer to this as "design freedom." This refers to designing a product without concerns regarding patents of the other party to the cross-license. This, again, protects "the castle." A patent cross-license addresses what might otherwise be infringement of a competitor's patents. The cross-license trades patent rights instead of paying a royalty for such infringement. This protects the castle because a royalty payment would reduce the after-tax income of a business.

Patent cross-licensing is considered procompetitive by the U.S. Department of Justice and the Federal Trade Commission in that it makes technology available to market participants.[26] There are many examples, but one particularly good example is the semiconductor chip manufacturing industry.

---

26. *See* U.S. Dep't of Just. & Fed. Trade Comm'n, Antitrust Guidelines for the Licensing of Intellectual Property (2017), https://www.justice.gov/atr/IPguidelines/download.

To fabricate a semiconductor chip requires many complex technologies and no single company owns all the patents needed. Without patent cross-licensing, probably no one would be able to manufacture a semiconductor chip without infringing someone else's patents.

Finally, (4) a use of a patent, which has become more popular in recent years, is a sale or assignment of a patent.[27] For example, large companies that own large numbers of patents may find that some patents cover technology that it is no longer using or was never using. The patents, however, are business assets. One way to realize the value of these assets that are otherwise not contributing to the business is via a sale to generate income.

A way to gain an appreciation for PCD tactics and strategy is to look at some typical examples of patent claims in various situations. However, one should also be aware of the elements of a cause of action for patent infringement. At a high level, two elements must be pled and proven to make out a *prima facie* case of patent infringement: (1) ownership of the patent, and (2) that the accused product or service falls within the scope of at least one of the patent claims.[28]

Whether the accused product or service falls within the scope of a patent claim is judged under the "All Elements Rule." To find infringement under the All Elements Rule, an accused device (or service) must meet each and every element and limitation of a single patent claim in the manner recited in the patent claim, either literally or by an equivalent.[29]

A similar rule is used to determine whether a patent claim is not novel, referred to as "anticipation." Under the All Elements Rule, for a claim to be anticipated (not novel), a single prior art reference must contain each and every element and limitation of a single patent claim in the manner recited in the patent claim. One maxim of patent law is "that which infringes if later in time, anticipates if earlier in time." The Federal Circuit has noted the maxim should really be "that which *literally* infringes if later, anticipates if earlier."[30] This brings out the difference that a patent claim may be infringed under the doctrine of equivalents,[31] which is not literally within the scope of the patent claim (hence, referred to as "non-literal infringement"), but that doctrine is not used to determine anticipation. Nonetheless, it is helpful to think of

27. This might also be handled as an exclusive license, but that is less common.

28. *See, e.g.*, Hall v. Bed Bath & Beyond, Inc., 705 F.3d 1357, 1362 (Fed. Cir. 2013) (citing Phonometrics, Inc. v. Hosp. Franchise Sys., Inc., 203 F.3d 790, 794 (Fed. Cir. 2000)).

29. *See, e.g.*, TIP Sys., LLC v. Phillips & Brooks/Gladwin, Inc., 529 F.3d 1364 (Fed. Cir. 2008).

30. *See* Marine, Inc. v. Barient, Inc., 827 F.2d 744 (Fed. Cir. 1987).

31. See Chapter 5, discussing the doctrine of equivalents.

infringement and prior art with respect to patent claims as a sort of balanced equation. With few exceptions,[32] analysis of the scope of a patent claim is the same for direct, literal infringement as it is for anticipation of that claim.

The analysis undertaken, as previously discussed, is referred to as "reading a claim" onto the accused device or "reading a claim" onto the prior art. For purposes of literal, direct patent infringement, to determine if a patent claim is literally and directly infringed, each and every element and limitation of the claim must be found in the accused device in the manner recited in the claim. Likewise, for prior art to anticipate a patent claim, rendering it invalid, each and every element and limitation of the claim must be found in a single item of prior art in the manner recited in the claim.

Consider the following patent claim:

EXAMPLE 2.1

I claim:

1. An apparatus comprising:

 a substantially horizontally oriented, rectangularly shaped seat including four corners;

 wherein attached to a respective corner of the seat are four substantially vertically oriented legs such that the legs point in the same direction away from the seat, are oriented to be substantially mutually parallel, and are of substantially the same length.

Many will recognize that this simple claim covers a chair or a four-legged stool. The claim does not recite a back; nonetheless, due to the use of the word *comprising*, referred to as "open" form, as long as an accused product includes all the elements and limitations in the manner recited in the claim, the claim is infringed, even if the accused product includes other features not recited in the claim, such as a back. However, because of the choices made for the claimed features in Example 2.1, chairs or stools that have seats of a shape other than rectangular would *not* be covered by the claim. The claim *cannot be read* on a circular seated stool or, similarly, a three-legged stool. *Express features of the claim would be missing.*

---

32. One exception is product-by-process claims, further treated in Chapter 4.

Conducting a similar analysis regarding prior art, the claim, of course, would be invalid as anticipated under current law if it were an issued claim and such a chair or stool meeting all the elements and limitations of claim 1 were in the prior art. However, the claim is not anticipated by a circular seated stool or a three-legged stool (although the claim might be rendered obvious by such prior art). To anticipate a claim, the prior art must include each and every element and limitation in the manner recited in the claim. A four-legged stool with a rectangular-shaped seat or a four-legged chair with a rectangular-shaped seat and meeting the other limitations of the claim would anticipate the claim, if these items were in the prior art at the time of filing the patent application (and the patent application did not have an earlier *priority date*).[33] Likewise, a similar analysis regarding "comprising" applies with respect to prior art. The prior art may show additional features beyond those recited and still anticipate a patent claim.

With this introduction, we next consider some situations involving technology and patent claiming tactics and strategy.

Component Manufacturer

Now that we have a basic understanding of the cause of action for patent infringement and the technique of "reading" a claim on an accused device and on the prior art, we take up some claiming issues that might confront someone drafting a patent claim for a component manufacturer versus those that might confront someone drafting a patent claim for a system integrator, as examples. *The following examples provide a brief introduction to common strategic and tactical issues involving component and system-level claiming. So, do not be disheartened if you find the subject matter (e.g., wording of a good patent claim) a bit challenging. You will see similar subject matter and considerations raised throughout this book. These examples are provided as a tool to introduce some basic patent claim drafting concepts and help the reader gain some initial appreciation of a few strategic and tactical considerations in this area. This subject matter is like the first revolution on a merry-go-round. If you did not "see" it on this revolution, you will "see" it on a later revolution.*

Among other lessons, these examples illustrate the importance of understanding the technology being claimed. Examples of aspects to understand regarding the particular technical subject matter include technical value of the innovation, commercial value of a product that includes the innovation, how distribution and/or sale of such a product may take place, how use of the

33. See Chapter 1, discussing priority date. *See also, e.g.*, 35 U.S.C. §§ 119–21 (2024).

innovation might be detected, how the innovation might be used by others, how it might potentially change, and/or how it might be designed around.[34]

Claim Drafting Example

To make this more concrete, we consider a technical problem for a computer system involving transfers into or out of memory, usually to or from a peripheral device, such as a hard drive, a graphics card, a network interface card, and so on. These transfers may be thought of as transfers of *physical* signal values and/or *physical* state values.[35]

Typically, a central processing unit (CPU) (e.g., microprocessor) controls such transfers within a computer system. This approach, in which the CPU directs such transfers, has several disadvantages, however. It both ties up the resources of the CPU and it slows the transfer by adding latency due to overhead from having the CPU involved in the transfer.

A type of transfer into and out of memory was later invented, referred to as "burst mode." Although the CPU initiates such a transfer and provides a starting memory address and word count for the transfer, after initiation, the operation is controlled by a memory controller, which takes control of the system bus from the processor. After the transfer is complete, the CPU is notified and resumes control of the system bus. Besides freeing up the CPU, a memory controller has less operational "overhead" and is, therefore, able to execute transfers more quickly than a CPU.

"Burst mode," as it is called, refers to a transfer of contents into or out of sequential memory cells in a "burst," rather than transfer of contents into and out of memory a single memory cell at a time. While the initial transfer (first memory cell) in burst mode may take as long as a transfer to or from a single memory cell, the subsequent memory transfers in burst mode each take a fraction of the time. For example, it might take a 100 megahertz (MHz) 32-bit bus about five bus cycles for a transfer of the contents of one cell that involves the CPU, whereas, in burst mode, after the initial transfer, it may take a memory controller only one bus cycle per memory cell. If substantial amounts of memory cells are involved, the savings in terms of time may be significant.

"Rewind" now to when burst mode was invented and assume it was sought to be patented. Claiming burst mode operation at the component level can be tricky. Burst mode operation involves the CPU, the memory cells, the memory controller, the system bus, and, perhaps, a peripheral. However, a claim

34. See, for example, Chapter 6, which includes sections directed to many of these topics.

35. This clarifies that the invention should qualify as statutory subject matter under 35 U.S.C. § 101 (2024). *See* Arrhythmia Rsch. Tech. v. Corazonix Corp., 958 F.2d 1053 (Fed. Cir. 1992).

that includes all these elements would be infringed by a system integrator or someone selling an end product, such as a mobile device, but not necessarily by someone manufacturing only a component, such as memory with a memory controller.

To capture a memory manufacturer, therefore, burst mode should be claimed from the perspective of the memory component (which, here, includes memory and a memory controller). We start with an apparatus claim, since that covers rights to make, use, sell, offer for sale, and import the claimed invention.

The pro forma format of an apparatus claim is:

I claim:

1. An XXX comprising: A, B, and C;

   wherein the A is connected to the B and the B is connected to the C.

Hence, claim 1 completes the sentence "I claim" and ends with one period. The apparatus here is "XXX." A, B, and C are claim elements. The language after "wherein" describes or even defines the relationship of the claim elements.

To begin drafting this claim, it may be helpful to consider what might be A, B, and C, as well as XXX. For simplicity, make XXX an "apparatus," although it could be something else, such as "memory," "CPU," "mobile device," and so on. So far, we have:

I claim:

1. An apparatus comprising: . . .

Remember that a claim may be considered to define "the invention." Furthermore, the rest of the claim includes claim elements. What might be elements we could use to define this invention based on the technical description above?

Simple starting examples of an A, B, or C for this claim might be random access memory (RAM), CPU, memory controller, or system transfer bus.

Furthermore, we know that the CPU is involved at the beginning and the end. However, "in between," it is the memory controller working via the system transfer bus to move content (e.g., physical signals) into or out of memory, particularly memory cells. Previously, it was stated:

Although the CPU initiates such a transfer and provides a starting memory address and word count for the transfer, after initiation, the operation is controlled by a memory controller, which takes control of the system bus from the processor. After the transfer is complete, the CPU is notified and resumes control of the system bus.

With these elements and other description, one possible patent claim (not the only or necessarily even the best claim) might be Example 2.2.

EXAMPLE 2.2

I claim:

1. An apparatus comprising:

   random access memory (RAM) and a memory controller;

   wherein the memory controller is capable of initiating burst mode operation based, at least in part, on receipt of a request from a central processing unit (CPU);

   wherein the request is to include a memory address, a word count, and a read or a write control transfer designation; and

   wherein the memory controller is to process the request and take control of a system transfer bus.

If you think you have an inkling of the invention now, you might try to draft another apparatus claim, perhaps to a system that includes the memory, memory controller, CPU, and system bus all working together. It may not be perfect, but you have to start somewhere. Great patent practitioners are not born; rather, they are made, so to speak.

Please take note that we have previously described a technical problem that was, by construction, present *before* the invention of burst mode and the claim is intended to cover a possible technical solution to the technical problem. This approach is more typical of patent prosecution in Europe, but it is a helpful way to think about technology and patent claims.[36] This approach

36. *See* Chris Konkol, *The "Problem Solved" in* In re Wright *and* In re Dillon, IDEA J. L. & Tech. 131 (1990).

becomes especially important in connection with software-related inventions, discussed later.[37]

Observe the format of the claim used, which is quite common and makes the claim easier to comprehend. First, the claim elements or components making up the apparatus are recited (e.g., "random access memory (RAM) and a memory controller"). Then, features of those elements/components, which may include relationships between them, are recited (e.g., "wherein the memory controller is capable of . . .").

Also, as a quick point, observe the language "initiating burst mode operation *based, at least in part, on* receipt of a request from a central processing unit (CPU)." The formulation "based, at least in part, on" is a handy one to make it clear that while, here, a factor, such as a receipt of a request, may influence a feature, such as, here, initiating burst mode operation, there may be other factors as well. *Often, claim drafting amounts to making explicit what in layman's terms might be understood.* For example, if one merely stated "initiating burst mode operation based on receipt of a request from a central processing unit (CPU)," in ordinary language, it might be *understood* that this is not meant to say it is based *only* on receipt of a request from a CPU. However, on closer inspection, this precise language on its face appears to potentially leave no room for other influences. Using the exact language, "initiating burst mode operation based on receipt of a request from a central processing unit (CPU)," an opponent may persuasively argue to a court, for example, that the claim should be limited to its exact language. Case law suggests that the burden should be on the drafter as the "least cost avoider" to make sure the language is clear regarding its scope.[38]

Likewise, as another drafting point, "capable of initiating burst mode operation" might be considered a better formulation than "capable of burst mode operation." The former language might be interpreted as broader than the latter language, although this point may at first appear counterintuitive.

To appreciate this point, consider the language "capable of initiating burst mode operation and then capable of completing burst mode operation." The latter language is clearly narrower than the language "capable of initiating burst mode operation." However, due to the word "comprising," as explained previously, a memory controller that is capable of initiating burst mode operation, and

37. See Chapter 6, which addresses patent eligibility in connection with claiming software.

38. *See* Sage Prods. v. Devon, 126 F.3d 1420 (Fed. Cir. 1997). Be aware, however, that there are legal arguments to be made that one should not be limited to the exact language "initiating burst mode operation based on receipt of a request from a central processing unit (CPU)." Nonetheless, using language to make the scope of a claim more clear is a desirable goal since different judges may see the language in quotes differently.

also is capable of completing burst mode operation, is within claim language that recites "capable of initiating burst mode operation" despite not expressly reciting "capable of completing burst mode operation." Language reciting "capable of initiating burst mode operation" may also cover a memory controller that is able to initiate burst mode operation, while another system component is able to "complete" burst mode operation, hypothetically.

Now consider the language "capable of burst mode operation." Such language would probably be understood to necessarily include both being capable of "initiating" and being capable of "completing" burst mode operation. While appearing counterintuitive, "capable of initiating burst mode operation" might be considered a broader formulation than "capable of burst mode operation" because the latter language may arguably be interpreted to necessarily include a memory controller capable of initiating and capable of completing burst mode operation, whereas the former language is much less likely to be interpreted as necessarily including a memory controller capable of completing burst mode operation.

Another aspect of the claim to notice are the formulations "the request is *to include* a memory address, a word count, and a read or a write control transfer designation," "the memory controller is *to process* the request and take control of a system transfer bus," and, again, "the memory controller is *capable of* initiating burst mode operation." These particular linguistic formulations may seem a bit odd.

Rather, it might seem more natural to say "the request includes . . . ," "the memory controller processes . . . ," and "the memory controller initiates . . . ." A reason for this particular wording is that the claim is to *an apparatus rather than to a method.*

In other words, the claim is directed to a device that *is able to* perform particular operations rather than one that is *actually in operation*. It is not necessary to accomplish this through the exact linguistic approaches shown here, but it is a good idea to be sensitive to this subtlety of language when drafting patent claims. A lot more is said about this later.[39]

It is possible for a patent claim to be held invalid if it is unclear from the language whether it is directed to an apparatus or directed to a method. There are a surprising number of issued patent claims where, for example, a claim is drafted in a sloppy manner so that the claim language suggests a device or apparatus in operation. One example would be "the memory controller processes . . . ." Does this language suggest an apparatus claim or a method claim? It is quite arguable

39. See Chapters 4 and 6, discussing relevant lines of case law authority associated with so-called "functional" claim language and mixing statutory claim classes.

either way. While this alone might not be enough to render a claim invalid, if the claim language is really sloppy, it may not be clear at all which is intended. If so, the claim may be considered to be indefinite and, consequently, invalid. Later, we will walk through drafting a method claim around this same technology so that you can more clearly appreciate the differences between claiming an apparatus versus claiming a method or process.

Although the claim in Example 2.2 mentions the CPU, it is from the perspective of receipt of a burst mode request. For example, the claim could omit the source of the request by stating "based, at least in part, on receipt of a request." Similarly, the claim mentions the system bus, but, again, from the perspective of assuming control. Thus, although the CPU and system bus are mentioned in the claim, it is drafted in a manner so that at least arguably these are not needed to be present for literal direct infringement, although the accused device should still be capable to meet these limitations.[40] More specifically, these aspects of the claim are interpreted to be part of the environment of the claimed innovation. If memory is made, used, or sold with the capability claimed, that memory should infringe the claim *without* necessarily having a CPU and system bus as part of the accused product.

These features are *limitations* of the claim but are intended to not be required *elements* for infringement. One way to view this claim is that some features are limitations of the claim, but not necessarily claim elements.[41]

This might be made clearer through language added to claim 1 reciting that the CPU is external to the RAM and reciting that the request is externally derived. An additional consideration to make such an intent clear might be to add a dependent claim that expressly adds the CPU and the system bus as claim elements.[42] By presumption, claim 1 and a claim that depends from claim 1 are considered of different literal scope. *As an extension of the claim drafting problem previously raised, you might see if you can draft a claim 2, which depends from claim 1, and adds these claim elements. Because that would certainly be a tall order here, instead, we will "walk" you through the drafting process.*

So, the claims are numbered sequentially; thus, the next claim is claim 2. Typically, this claim "depends" from claim 1.[43] Therefore, it must reference

---

40. See Chapter 3, which addresses a way to view the difference between a claim element and a claim limitation. See also Chapters 4 and 6, which address functional claims and claims that mix statutory classes.

41. *See* Dawn Equip. Co. v. Ky. Farms, Inc., 140 F.3d 1009, 1014 n.1 (Fed. Cir. 1998). See Chapter 3, which addresses a way to view the difference between a claim element and a claim limitation.

42. See Chapter 6, addressing claiming higher levels of integration through dependent claims or separate independent claims.

43. See Chapter 4, addressing claim dependency.

claim 1 and will usually (as good claim drafting practice) refer to the preamble of claim 1. We, therefore, know the claim starts something like:

---

2. The apparatus of claim 1, . . .

Dependent claims always narrow the claim from which they depend. Another way to say this is that the independent claims are by construction the broadest claims of a patent. What language follows after "The apparatus of claim 1, . . ." turns on how claim 2 is intended to narrow claim 1.

In general, claim 1 recites elements, limitations, and the relationships thereof. Thus, one way to narrow claim 1 is to further clarify or describe one of these. In accordance with accepted custom, this is usually introduced by a "wherein." For example:

---

2. The apparatus of claim 1, wherein the RAM and the memory controller are mutually directly connected to one another.

Another way to narrow a claim is to introduce an entirely new claim element (or limitation, possibly). In accordance with accepted custom, this is usually introduced by a "comprising:," "further comprising:," or "and, further comprising:." For example:

---

2. The apparatus of claim 1, further comprising: the CPU.

Thus, the dependent claim suggested above might look like:

---

2. The apparatus of claim 1, comprising: the CPU and the system transfer bus, wherein the CPU is external to the RAM and memory controller, and the system transfer bus is external to the RAM and memory controller.

Such a dependency is suggested here to address infringement-type drafting considerations. This dependency is intended to increase the possibility that the claims (dependent and independent) will be interpreted in a manner that makes infringement more likely, here, by suggesting that the CPU and the system transfer bus are not elements, but are limitations, of claim 1.

A more common use of dependent claims, however, relates to adding limitations that capture potential infringers while also providing a narrower dependent claim to reduce the risk of invalidity based on prior art, yet another tactical consideration.

At the time of filing, the patent drafter does not typically know the closest prior art.[44] Rather, it may take an IPR, a litigation, or even several litigations to locate such art, for example. Therefore, dependent claims are a type of hedge that narrow the base claim so that all is not lost if prior art is found that renders the base claim (called the "independent claim"[45]) invalid. For example, perhaps subcomponents of the components of claim 1 are recited in a dependent claim. Of course, it is preferable if such subcomponents are more likely to be used in most implementations of what is claimed. In this context, consider that a request provides a starting memory cell location, the number of memory cells in the transfer, and whether the transfer is a read operation or a write operation. It seems likely that a memory controller would include registers to retain such values that would be then used as parameters to direct execution of the burst mode operation.

In that regard, perhaps one might consider this dependent claim:

---

2. The apparatus of claim 1, wherein the memory controller comprises an address register, a word count register, and a transfer mode register.

It is more likely that this claim will stand up against prior art by describing and claiming internal components of the memory controller. However, at the same time, the elements added are ones that almost any memory controller implementing burst mode would likely include, which is desirable from an infringement perspective.

Previously, claim 1 recited "an apparatus." A perhaps simpler approach, however, might be to draft a claim to an integrated circuit (IC) chip (or module) that claims the memory controller specifically, such as:

44. See later in this chapter, which addresses the advantages and disadvantages of searching.
45. See discussion of independent and dependent claims in Chapter 4.

I claim:

1. An integrated circuit (IC) comprising:

 random access memory (RAM) and a memory controller; . . .

One might then argue that the royalty base is an IC chip (or module), whereas previously an adversary might have argued that in light of the initially presented claim 1, the royalty base was potentially *only* that portion of a chip or module that includes the memory and memory controller, so that any damages are arguably less due to a smaller royalty base. One problem with the latter example, however, is that typically, a claim's "preamble" (e.g., in claim 1 as just presented, the part of the claim after the claim number and before the transition word *comprising*) is not necessarily limiting.[46] One might, therefore, to be conservative, move the IC (or module) limitation to the body of the claim (e.g., in claim 1, the part of the claim after the transition word *comprising* and the colon and before the period):

I claim:

1. An apparatus comprising:

 an integrated circuit (IC) including random access memory (RAM) and a memory controller; . . .

This might, for example, potentially affect damages by making it clearer that an entire chip (or module) rather than just a part of a chip (or module) is the royalty base.[47] These are, of course, only a few options of many potential options available to the claim drafter.

Likewise, another claim type to consider is an apparatus means-plus-function claim.[48] For most purposes, the term "means-plus-function claim" refers to a claim in which at least part of the claim recites a means for performing

46. See Chapter 3, addressing the claim preamble and the claim body.
47. See Chapter 6, which treats damages issues in connection with claim drafting.
48. See Chapter 4, addressing drafting of means-plus-function claims.

a specified function, which is permitted under 35 U.S.C. subsection 112(f).[49] These claims have many pitfalls, which are addressed in detail later.[50]

Here, tactical and strategic differences between claims construed under subsection 112(f) and claims not construed under subsection 112(f) are highlighted. 35 U.S.C. subsection 112(f) specifically states:

> (f) ELEMENT IN CLAIM FOR A COMBINATION.—An element in a claim for a combination may be expressed as a means or step for performing a specified function without the recital of structure, material, or acts in support thereof, and such claim shall be construed to cover the corresponding structure, material, or acts described in the specification and equivalents thereof.

Therefore, rather than reciting so-called structural claim elements, the claim typically[51] recites "means for . . ." and a function to be performed. The difference between structure and function in an apparatus patent claim is described as reciting what the apparatus does (i.e., function) rather than what it is (i.e., structure).[52]

Imagine how that might work for the claim of Example 2.2. Instead of "memory" or "RAM," the claim might recite "means for storing memory states." Likewise, instead of memory controller, the claim might recite "means for controlling the means for storing memory states." Likewise, the claim may recite "the means for controlling comprises means for initiating burst mode operation," and "the means for controlling comprises means for processing the request and means for taking control of a system transfer bus." Thus, such a claim might look like:

EXAMPLE 2.3

I claim:

1. An apparatus comprising:

   means for storing memory states and means for controlling the means for storing memory states;

49. Before the AIA, this was 35 U.S.C. § 112, ¶ 6; however, throughout this book it is referenced as 35 U.S.C. subsection 112(f) (2024).

50. See Chapter 4, addressing drafting of means-plus-function claims.

51. Law exists in which claims are construed under subsection 112(f) despite not reciting "means for." Generally, as treated in later sections, claims are able to be drafted to reduce the risk of such an outcome. See Chapter 4.

52. *See, e.g.*, *In re* Swinehart, 439 F.2d 210 (C.C.P.A. 1971).

wherein the means for controlling comprises means for initiating burst mode operation based, at least in part, on receipt of a request from central means for processing memory states;

wherein the request is to include a memory address, a word count, and a read or a write control transfer designation; and

wherein the means for controlling comprises means for processing the request and means for taking control of a system transfer bus.

The means-plus-function apparatus claim closely tracks the initially drafted apparatus claim. This is not required, but it is done here to make it clear that the drafter intends that the two claims are of different scope.[53] This topic is addressed more later.[54] In general, because of the language of subsection 112(f), means-plus-function claims (i.e., claims with clauses construed under subsection 112(f)) are usually narrower than similar claims without clauses construed under subsection 112(f). *Sometimes one may want a broad construction (e.g., to capture a potential infringer); sometimes one may want a narrow construction (e.g., to avoid prior art). This latter point helps explain the use of this claim type.*

Another claim to consider from a strategic and tactical perspective is a method of using claim. Many differences between apparatus and method claims exist that are relevant to patent claiming strategy and tactics. At one of the most basic levels, the set of rights granted is different. An apparatus claim provides the full set of statutory rights, which is make, use, sell, and so on.[55] On the other hand, due to an inherent nature, a method claim essentially covers "use," as in a method of using, or "make," as in a method of making or manufacturing. Apparatus claims fundamentally include more rights than method claims. At least partially for this reason, apparatus claims are usually perceived to be more valuable than method claims. However, do not read this to suggest that method claims are not valuable. In various situations, having a method claim may be important to have as an arrow in your quiver. *It is recommended to nearly always include method claims with apparatus claims for claim diversity. Many patents are written that do not follow this simple principle.*

Usually, an invention will more easily be claimed as one or the other, as a method or as an apparatus. For example, software operation is usually more

53. *But see* Mas-Hamilton Grp. v. La Gard, Inc., 156 F.3d 1206, 1214 (Fed. Cir. 1998). See Chapter 4 and drafting of means-plus-function claims.

54. See Chapter 4, addressing drafting of means-plus-function claims.

55. *See* 35 U.S.C. § 271(a) (2024).

easily described as a method. Although not a requirement, it seems logical when beginning to draft claims for an invention to begin with the claim type that is more easily drafted due to the inherent nature of the invention. In Example 2.2 for this problem, the technology seems to more easily be described as an apparatus; hence, the rationale for starting with that claim type.

Regardless, do not pass on the opportunity to claim the invention in method terms, in addition to apparatus terms. A litany of good reasons to do this exists. A method may stand up to prior art even in situations where an apparatus claim may not.[56] Depending on the limitations of the patent claim, a method claim may be infringed where an apparatus claim is not or it may be infringed in a different manner.[57] Further, a pure method claim generally is much less likely to be construed under subsection 112(f).[58] The failure to claim a method also has the potential to dedicate to the public subject matter that might have otherwise been covered.[59] Other good reasons also exist to include method claims, but these reasons should be more than sufficient.

Consider a method of use claim for the technology of this problem. While the components of the apparatus claim includes subject matter such as "memory," " memory controller," "CPU," and "system transfer bus," for a method claim, the components of the claim are operations or actions, such as "transmitting," "receiving," "transferring," and the like. Note that it can be important to draft the claim from a particular perspective, such as one of the components in operation, or perhaps the overall system in operation. Recall that, here, we are imagining a memory component manufacturer seeking patent protection; hence, as previously with the apparatus claim, it is most appropriate to draft the method claim from that perspective—here, really the perspective of the memory controller, which would typically be part of the memory product as sold.

One aspect to appreciate is the difference in drafting a method claim versus drafting an apparatus claim that flows from the preceding discussion about the set of rights for each. As indicated, a method claim recites actions or operations. A method claim is infringed by performing an action or an operation, such as when using something (for a method of using claim) or making

---

56. See Chapter 4, which introduces method claims and also addresses method claims directed to a new use of an old device.

57. *Id.*

58. *Id.*

59. *See* Johnson & Johnston Assocs. v. R.E. Serv. Co., 285 F.3d 1046 (Fed. Cir. 2002) (en banc).

something (for a method of making claim). Hence, as suggested, the claim elements are actions like "receiving," "transmitting," and so on.

For the technology previously described, therefore, a CPU may signal a memory controller to request a burst mode transfer into or out of memory. The memory controller may then signal a request to the CPU for control of the system transfer bus. The memory controller may then receive control of the system transfer bus and perform the transfer and may then signal the CPU that the transfer is complete.

From the perspective of the memory controller, therefore, a method of using claim may look like:

EXAMPLE 2.4

I claim:

1. A method comprising:[60]

   receiving a request for burst mode operation;

   transmitting a request for control of a system bus in response to the received request;

   receiving a signal granting system bus control;

   transferring signals across the system bus into or out of a group of sequential memory cells after receiving the signal granting system bus control; and

   transmitting a signal indicating completion of the signal transfer.

One way to think of a method claim is like a cooking recipe. It specifies the acts or actions to follow. In contrast, again, an apparatus may often be capable of performing an action or an operation, but it is important to *not* claim an apparatus in a manner that suggests the apparatus is actually performing such

60. *See* Seal-Flex Inc. v. Athletic Track & Ct. Constr., 172 F.3d 836 (Fed. Cir. 1999). It used to be common to state, "A method comprising the steps of:." However, it might be possible that the use of the word "step" might invoke subsection 112(f). See Chapter 4, addressing means-plus-function and step-plus-function claims. A concurrence by Judge Rader in this case suggests that "comprising the steps of" would not be a problem, but it is best to avoid such questions by good drafting practice. Therefore, "comprising the steps of" is omitted, which has now become the common practice.

actions or operations, as previously indicated.[61] Thus, an apparatus claim either recites structural elements, such as a processor or memory, or it recites that such elements are able to perform an action, to make it clear that the action itself is not being claimed, the latter being the domain of method claims.

The opportunity to claim a method of making even in situations where that is not necessarily the feature that is inventive should not be overlooked.[62] Regarding this problem, nothing about the invention appears to relate to fabrication or manufacture. Nonetheless, semiconductor chips shall be manufactured that are capable of burst mode operation. Why not include such a patent claim in one's arsenal? For example, it is becoming more common for companies, so-called fabless design houses, to outsource chip manufacturing to others. Coming up with the design does not generally by itself directly infringe a patent claim.[63] Yet, a claim directed to a company making the chip for someone else may have some value.[64]

Here is a possible method of making claim for this technology:

EXAMPLE 2.5

I claim:

1. A method of fabricating a memory controller and random access memory (RAM) comprising:

   fabricating an integrated circuit (IC) that includes a memory controller with random access memory (RAM) on the IC, wherein the memory controller and RAM are fabricated in an electrical configuration on a silicon substrate of the IC;

---

61. *See, e.g.*, IPXL Holdings v. Amazon, 430 F.3d 1377, 1384 (Fed. Cir. 2005). See Chapter 6, which addresses the problem of mixing statutory classes of patent claims in a single patent claim. *Cf.* INVT SPE LLC v. Int'l Trade Comm'n, 46 F.4th 1361 (Fed. Cir. 2022) (distinguishing between actual operation and capability of operating or performing for apparatus claims, particularly for software on a device, which tends to be functional, without discussing indefiniteness issue of mixing method and apparatus limitations).

62. A similar observation applies to method of using claims. However, this observation about method of making claims is provided here because while it is reasonably common to include method of using claims with apparatus claims, it is less common to include method of making claims unless the inventive concept is specifically related to fabrication, for example.

63. Although it might be a basis for a claim for indirect infringement; see Chapter 5, addressing indirect infringement.

64. See Chapter 4, introducing method of making claims. This is also helpful because direct patent infringement is generally easier to prove than indirect patent infringement. See Chapter 5, discussing indirect infringement.

wherein the fabricating includes forming transistors for the memory controller and RAM on the silicon substrate, wherein the transistors respectively include a source, a drain, and a gate;

wherein the fabricating further includes fabricating the memory controller to be capable of initiating burst mode operation based, at least in part, on receipt of a request from a central processing unit (CPU) in which the request is to include a memory address, a word count, and a read or a write control transfer designation; and

wherein the fabricating further includes fabricating the memory controller to be capable to process the request and take control of a system transfer bus.

Furthermore, the fabrication operations could be described more fully with dependent claims as follows, as examples:

---

2. The method of claim 1, wherein the fabricating that includes forming the transistors comprises:

   forming the gate from a conductive gate layer and an oxide layer over a silicon layer of the silicon substrate; and

   forming two doped regions in the silicon layer via ion implantation or diffusion to form the source and the drain.

3. The method of claim 2, wherein the conductive gate layer comprises a polysilicon layer; and wherein the forming the gate from the conductive gate layer comprises forming the gate from the polysilicon gate layer.

Although claims 2 and 3 describe well-known fabrication operations as long as the base claim is patentable based on the burst mode limitations, that is not a problem regarding patentability of these claims.[65]

One limiting factor to consider is how easy or difficult it would be to discover or prove infringement of a method claim, particularly a manufacturing claim. For example, if there is little or no way to discover from the end

65. See Chapter 4, addressing dependent and independent claims.

product that a particular process was used to make the end product, this technology might be better protected as a trade secret.[66]

As one example, consider that in the aircraft manufacturing industry many holes are typically created in metal structures, such as for an engine, for a fuselage, and so on. The ability to create more precise holes, more quickly, and at a cheaper cost may, therefore, provide a competitive advantage. With the advent of laser technology, it seems likely that some type of laser was developed for such processes. However, it might be difficult or nearly impossible to determine how such a hole was generated during manufacture from looking at the end product. Consequently, assuming such laser technology was developed and even assuming it was patentable at the time of its creation, a patent on such technology may be difficult to enforce. Furthermore, by filing a patent application with 18-month publication (or, if opted out, published at issuance), one would be educating one's competitors on how to perform such a process (again, a process performed behind closed doors and difficult to discover). Instead, as suggested, such technology may be better protected as a trade secret.

Another limiting factor for a fabless design house (which our client might be) seeking a manufacturing claim may be that some so-called foundries that perform manufacturing for other fabless design houses are located outside the United States.[67] Such manufacture, therefore, may at times be beyond the territorial scope of U.S. patent law for a claim of infringement under 35 U.S.C. subsection 271(a). However, there are statutes directed to extraterritorial patent infringement.[68]

That was a relatively quick survey and introduction to various approaches to claiming an invention. We will return to this example in later sections as we explore the foregoing concepts in more detail.

System Integrator

A system integrator is, in a sense, the flip side of a component manufacturer. The two frequently have a symbiotic relationship. A component manufacturer

---

66. Subject to other considerations, such as turnover in the industry and/or how easy it might be to limit knowledge of the technology to a few individuals within the company that developed it, as a few examples of considerations that may affect the desirability of trade secret protection.

67. One well-known example being Taiwan Semiconductor Manufacturing Company Limited (TSMC), which had also been planning to build one of its fabs in the United States. Note also that Intel recently announced entry into the foundry business, although most likely in and outside the United States, referred to as "Intel Foundry," to distinguish it from "Intel Business."

68. *See* 35 U.S.C. § 271(f), (g) (2024). See Chapter 4, addressing 35 U.S.C. § 271(g) (2024).

is a supplier to a system integrator. Similarly, a system integrator is a customer of a component manufacturer. It follows that many of the considerations previously highlighted are similar or even the same. For convenience, following is a description of the previous technology example from the previous section.

Claim Drafting Example

As discussed, typically, a CPU (e.g., microprocessor) controls memory transfers within a computer system. This approach has several disadvantages, however. It both ties up the resources of the CPU and it slows the transfer by adding latency due to overhead from having the CPU involved in the transfer.

A type of transfer into and out of memory was invented, referred to as "burst mode." Although the CPU initiates such a transfer and provides a starting memory address and word count for the transfer, after initiation, the operation is controlled by a memory controller, which takes control of the system bus from the processor. After the transfer is complete, the CPU is notified and resumes control of the system bus.

Burst mode refers to transfer of contents "in a burst" into or out of sequential memory cells, rather than transfer of the contents a single memory cell at a time. While the initial transfer in burst mode (i.e., first memory cell transfer) may take as long as a transfer to or from a single memory cell, the subsequent memory cell transfers each take a fraction of the time. For example, it might take a 100 MHz 32-bit bus about five bus cycles for a transfer of the contents of one memory cell that involves the CPU, whereas, in burst mode, after the initial transfer to a first memory cell, it may take one bus cycle per memory cell. If a large amount of memory cells is involved, the savings in terms of time may be significant.

Previously, our example was to claim burst mode operation at the component level. However, from the technical description, burst mode operation involves the CPU, the memory cells, the memory controller, the system bus, and, perhaps, a peripheral. A claim that includes all these elements would be infringed by a system integrator or someone selling an end product, such as a mobile device, which includes a memory controller to implement burst mode, but not necessarily by someone manufacturing or selling only the memory controller. To capture a memory manufacturer, burst mode may be claimed from the perspective of the memory component, as demonstrated in the prior section.[69]

As before, we start with an apparatus claim, since that covers rights to make, use, sell, offer for sale, and import the claimed invention. However,

69. See earlier in this chapter, addressing claims for a component manufacturer.

unlike previously, here, we claim a system of components (termed "a system claim"). It follows from the prior discussion that a primary difference here, unlike previously in Example 2.2, is that our claim should include the CPU and system bus *recited as claim elements*:

EXAMPLE 2.6

I claim:

1. An apparatus comprising:

   random access memory (RAM), a memory controller, a central processing unit (CPU), and a system transfer bus;

   wherein the memory controller is capable of initiating burst mode operation based, at least in part, on receipt of a request from the CPU;

   wherein the request is to include a memory address, a word count, and a read or a write control transfer designation; and

   wherein the memory controller is to process the request and take control of the system transfer bus.

The primary difference here, relative to Example 2.2, for example, is that the CPU and the system transfer bus are recited along with the list of other components. To infringe, these elements must specifically be present in an accused device. The claim recites an interaction of multiple components, all of which are required to be present for direct patent infringement; however, it is expected, here, that a single entity, a system integrator, such as a competitor of the patentee, will own or control all the elements of the claim so that direct infringement will be present.[70]

One may genuinely ask whether this approach of using a system-level independent claim has advantages over an approach in which there is a component-level independent claim, as in the previous section, with aspects of the overall system (e.g., CPU, system bus, etc.) being added via dependent claims, discussed and illustrated in the prior section (e.g., Example 2.2 and follow-on discussion). There are various considerations, but there is no clear answer to such a question.

70. See Chapter 6, discussing the single infringer principle and divided infringement.

One consideration may be that the claim in Example 2.6 makes it clearer that specific end products infringe, which may be beneficial in some circumstances. If dealing with U.S. Customs, as one example, and trying to enforce an exclusion order[71] against importation of these consumer end products into the United States, this claim might be more likely to be enforced than the independent claim of Example 2.2. One would not expect U.S. Customs to tear apart end products to look for infringing memory components. Yet, in theory at least, using dependent claims to cover the system should have this same legal advantage. The dependent claims may be asserted and result in an exclusion order, although the independent claim in Example 2.6 might be considered to more clearly be a system for purposes of enforcement.

One might also imagine that a system that is a combination of more elements may at least arguably be more likely to be patentable. In other words, the component interactions may provide patentability arguments. Yet, in theory at least, again, using dependent claims to cover the system, as previously discussed, should have this same legal advantage, meaning those same arguments could be made with respect to the dependent claims. Still, a tangible benefit may relate to how patent prosecution typically proceeds.

Examiners usually focus on the independent claims. Here, the independent claim of Example 2.6 might potentially be slightly more likely to be allowed than a dependent claim that amounts to the same elements and limitations. With the prior claim of Example 2.2, the examiner may reject the independent claim and then, in passing, also reject the dependent claims, without much consideration,[72] even though usually there are additional technical arguments in favor of patentability. The patent prosecutor may, in our hypothetical, then, in a response, make an argument regarding the dependent claims separately from the independent claim, if this happens. At that point, however, the examiner may be reluctant to modify his or her decision, having previously rejected all the claims.

Both approaches have some merit, an independent claim for the system and a separate independent claim for the component. In some cases, therefore, a drafter may employ both approaches.[73]

---

71. The International Trade Commission (ITC) is a quasi-judicial body in the executive branch that has the power to prevent foreign originating goods violating U.S. trade regulation laws from entering the United States by issuing exclusion orders. Thus, the ITC is one option in terms of enforcement of a U.S. patent.

72. Granted that this may not be legally appropriate, it does happen at times.

73. But *not* in a manner so that claim scope is identical in all respects between an independent claim of one claim set and a dependent claim of another set, which might otherwise produce a rejection.

Typically, a component claim is more valuable against a component manufacturer for asserting direct patent infringement and a system-level claim is more valuable against a system integrator for asserting direct patent infringement. For example, a system integrator may have a contractual indemnity against patent infringement for components that it purchases. However, typically, such indemnities are limited to the part as sold. One could certainly make a direct infringement claim against the system integrator with a memory component claim since the memory is part of the system and directly infringed. However, because of such contractual indemnities from component manufacturers, a component claim against a system integrator may be less valuable than a system-level claim.[74]

Despite these latter potential considerations, if your client is a system integrator, they may generally profess to have no interest in covering a memory manufacturer and not want to incur the extra claim fees associated with employing both approaches (i.e., system claim approach and component claim approach). This may be the case although employing both approaches would provide an ability to go after a memory manufacturer/supplier as well as a systems integrator. To clarify this point, a new application is permitted three independent claims and 20 total claims before incurring extra claim fees.[75] Thus, employing both claiming approaches may exceed these numbers of claims and result in extra claim fees.

Another consideration as to the two approaches might relate to damages, although this is also quite unclear to be sure. By claiming a system, one might try to argue for purposes of assessing damages that an entire market value effect occurs with sales of an entire system, justifying that damages be calculated using the entire system as a royalty base.[76] In essence, the notion is that the component may drive sales for the complete system due to the patented features it adds. This might be a reason to favor a system-level claim as an independent claim, for example. However, establishing application of the entire market value rule for a situation may be a legal challenge.[77] Damages based on a reasonable royalty tend to more frequently use the "smallest saleable patent-practicing unit," rather than the "entire market value," as a royalty

74. See also Chapter 6, addressing damages considerations in claim drafting. A system claim may have a larger royalty base than a component claim.

75. *See* PTO, Manual of Patent Examining Procedure § 607 (9th ed. 2023) [hereinafter MPEP].

76. *See* Finjan, Inc. v. Blue Coat Sys., Inc., 879 F.3d 1299 (Fed. Cir. 2018); Exmark Mfg. Co. v. Briggs & Stratton Power Prods. Grp., 879 F.3d 1332 (Fed. Cir. 2018). See Chapter 6, addressing damages considerations in claim drafting.

77. See Chapter 6, addressing damages considerations in claim drafting.

base.[78] The smallest saleable patent-practicing unit might be argued to be an IC or module including the memory with memory controller.

Consistent with the entire market value suggestion, however, one might attempt to draft a claim to potentially increase the royalty base by including language directed to an IC chip or module that claims the system specifically, assuming that the entire system is likely to be integrated on a single integrated chip or module, as previously illustrated in the prior section.[79]

As another example, an additional level of integration might be added with a dependent claim 2:

---

2. The apparatus of claim 1, wherein the RAM, memory controller, CPU, and system transfer bus are incorporated together in at least one of the following: a desktop computer, a laptop computer, a tablet, a smart phone, and/or a server.

Again, in some situations, a claim like this may be beneficial to assert against end products that use the system.

Typically, at the time of filing, the drafter does not know the closest prior art.[80] Rather, it may take an IPR, a litigation, or even several litigations to locate such art. Therefore, as previously illustrated in the prior section, dependent claims are a type of hedge that narrows the claim so that all is not lost if prior art is found that renders the independent claim invalid.

There are further issues to consider about the choice between an independent system claim (such as Example 2.6) and a component-level independent claim (such as Example 2.2), in which the system may, instead, be covered via dependent claims. These issues include direct versus indirect infringement, patent exhaustion, implied patent licensing, and contractual indemnities against patent infringement. We *introduce* the reader to these topics next, with more extended discussions later in this book.[81]

Direct versus indirect infringement is an important topic.[82] Basically, making, using, selling, importing, or offering to sell everything recited in a

---

78. *Id.*

79. See Example 2.2 and claim discussion following.

80. See later in this chapter, addressing the advantages and disadvantages of searching.

81. See Chapter 5, regarding indirect infringement, and Chapter 6, regarding exhaustion and implied patent licensing.

82. This topic is addressed in detail in Chapter 5.

patent claim arranged in the manner recited amounts to direct infringement;[83] making, using, selling, importing, or offering to sell a component of a patent claim that includes several components as elements or that is used in a method claim amounts to indirect infringement if done with intent to infringe.[84] In general, both types of claims may be desirable, such as for reasons just discussed. More specifically, however, a claim of direct infringement is a much easier claim to assert. Indirect infringement requires intent, as indicated, and has additional requirements.[85]

Regarding patent exhaustion and implied patent licensing, one might think, with both types of independent claims, and because *technically* the component claim and the system claim are separate inventions,[86] a sale of memory covered by one claim, such as the independent component claim, should *not* impact enforcement of the other independent (e.g., system) claim. However, sale of the memory covered by the former claim likely either "exhausts" the system claim or may result in grant of an implied license to the system claim.[87] One may still benefit from including both types of claims; however, this is an issue to keep in mind.

Patent indemnity issues as between a component supplier and a system integrator, for example, was previously introduced.[88]

For a situation like this, as for the prior situation of a component manufacturer, another claim to consider is an apparatus means-plus-function claim, discussed and illustrated in the prior section. Such claims have a long history and are statutorily permitted. For most purposes, a means-plus-function claim refers to a claim in which at least part of the claim recites a means for performing a specified function. These claims have lots of pitfalls, which are discussed in detail later.[89]

Here, tactical and strategic differences between claims construed under subsection 112(f) and claims not construed under subsection 112(f) are

83. *See* 35 U.S.C. § 271(a) (2024).

84. See Chapter 5. *See also* 35 U.S.C. § 271(b), (c) (2024).

85. See Chapter 5. Specifically, as later treated, indirect infringement generally requires some level of knowledge, unlike direct infringement, which has no scienter requirement.

86. *See, e.g.*, Dollar Elec. Co. v. Syndevco, Inc., 205 U.S.P.Q. 949, 959 (E.D. Mich. 1979), *aff'd*, 669 F.2d 1370, 214 U.S.P.Q. 241 (6th Cir. 1982) ("[E]ach claim of a patent is treated as if it was a separate patent.").

87. Perhaps even both. *See* Quanta Computer v. LG Elecs., 553 U.S. 617 (2008); Met-Coil Sys. Corp. v. Korners Unlimited, 803 F.2d 684 (Fed. Cir. 1986). See Chapter 6, addressing drafting claims with patent exhaustion and implied patent licenses in mind.

88. See the discussion earlier in this chapter.

89. See Chapter 4 for a treatment of means-plus-function *and* step-plus-function claims.

highlighted.[90] *Try drafting your own means-plus-function claim corresponding to the system covered by Example 2.6, much like Example 2.3 corresponds to Example 2.2, previously illustrated.*

The statute states that means-plus-function claims are for combinations. Therefore, a so-called *single* means claim is not permitted; however, one might mix structural elements and means-plus-function elements in a claim. For example, "memory," "memory controller," and "CPU" are likely structural features. Thus, a claim may include some structural elements and some means-plus-function elements. *Try drafting a means-plus-function apparatus claim corresponding to the system covered by Example 2.6 that mixes structural and means-plus-function elements in the claim.*

Another claim to consider from a strategic and tactical perspective is a method of using claim, as discussed in the prior section. It is recommended to nearly always include method claims (e.g., method of using and/or method of making claims) with apparatus claims for claim diversity. Many patents are written that do not follow this simple principle. *Try drafting a method of using claim for the system covered by Example 2.6, from the perspective of the CPU rather than the memory controller, which was illustrated by Example 2.4.*

Usually, an invention will more easily be claimed as one or the other, as a method or as an apparatus, as previously suggested. In Examples 2.2 and 2.6, the technology seems to more easily be described as an apparatus; hence, the rationale for starting with that claim type.

The opportunity to claim a method of making even in situations where that is not necessarily the feature that is inventive should not be overlooked, as discussed in the prior section.[91] Regarding Example 2.6, nothing about the invention appears to relate to fabrication or manufacture. However, it is becoming common for fabless design houses to generate designs and have another company manufacture the chip. Designing an infringing chip would not constitute direct infringement; however, it might constitute indirect infringement in which the company manufacturing might be the direct infringer. *Try drafting a method of making claim for the system of Example 2.6, much like Example 2.5 corresponds to Example 2.2.*

One limiting factor to consider is how easy or difficult it would be to discover or prove infringement of a method of making claim. For example, if

90. *Id.*

91. A similar observation applies to method of using claims. However, this observation about method of making claims is provided here because while it is reasonably common to include method of using claims with apparatus claims, it is less common to include method of making claims unless the inventive concept relates to manufacturing.

there is little or no way to discover from the end product that a particular process was used, this technology might be better protected as a trade secret.[92]

Another limiting factor for enforcing a claim against a fabless design house may be that typically so-called foundries that perform manufacturing for fabless design houses are located outside the United States. Such manufacture, therefore, may at times be beyond the territorial scope of U.S. patent law for infringement under 35 U.S.C. subsection 271(a). However, there are statutes directed to extraterritorial patent infringement.[93]

As indicated, we will return to this example in later sections as we explore the foregoing and other concepts in more detail.

Network Provider

The previous two sections illustrated hardware-related technology. More typically, however, today, in the predictable arts, technology involves some combination of hardware and software. In addition, quite typically innovative aspects of such technology may be embedded in software rather than hardware (or in addition to the hardware). This situation may raise challenging issues related to patent eligibility that should be kept in mind.[94]

However, at a high level, the law that has developed appears to be primarily focused on assuring that the subject matter being claimed represents a *technical* solution to a *technical* problem.[95] By staying true to this, patent eligibility issues in many cases should be able to be addressed.[96] Networking provides an illustration of the situation just mentioned, a mixture of hardware and software in which the innovation, at least today, is present primarily in the software (i.e., often the hardware comprises off-the-shelf parts).

Claim Drafting Example

Again, we consider a technical problem and then try to claim a possible technical solution. The problem, here, relates to linking or connecting otherwise physically separate private networks to operate like (e.g., mimic operation for) a single physically connected network.

92. Subject to other considerations, such as turnover in the industry and/or how easy it might be to limit knowledge of the technology to a few individuals within the company that developed it. These are a few examples of considerations that may affect the desirability of trade secret protection.

93. *See* 35 U.S.C. § 271(f), (g) (2024). See Chapter 4, addressing 35 U.S.C. § 271(g) (2024).

94. See Chapter 6, addressing patent eligibility issues and software, in particular.

95. *Id.*

96. *Id.*

For example, imagine an international business with offices in major cities, such as New York, London, Paris, Tokyo, and so on. It is desirable for the offices to be on a single network despite their physical separation. Each office represents a physically separate private network. Each network device on a local physical private network (e.g., for a particular office) is able to discover and communicate with every other network device on that local network without routing signal packets via a router. The devices on such a network are referred to as "network devices," which means that they are able to send and receive communications over the network. Typically, a network device is implemented using a computing system (e.g., a CPU and memory coupled by a bus) executing software instructions.

The problem, then, relates to linking these otherwise physically separate private networks to operate as a single private network where, again, each network device on the "created" single private so-called virtual network formed by linking the independent and physically separate private networks is able to discover and communicate with every other network device without using a router and without other sorts of technical processes that usually come into play with use of a routing table, for example.

Drawbacks of a router include use of network address translation (referred to as NAT), latency, and routing of extra but unnecessary network traffic that may "clog" the network, so to speak. In addition, a router treats as separate and independent those individual networks that are communicating via the router. Therefore, if separated by a router, a network device on one network is *not* able to discover the network devices on the other network. Specifically, signal packets communicated to a private network via a router appear as if they originate from the router.

Likewise, because of the physically separate offices, *physically* linking the separate networks so that they operate as one is not practical or even feasible. Nonetheless, so-called virtual private networks (VPNs) do exist. These, in general, link a remote network device with a physical network, but do not link multiple network devices on separate and independent private physical networks (referred to generally as "broadcast domains") in a manner to operate as a single physical network.

In an embodiment of the approach to be claimed, each physical, separate broadcast domain has a gateway device. The gateway device communicates between the physically separate broadcast domains via one or more tunnel servers. A part of one possible solution (e.g., one embodiment of the technical subject matter) includes a master controller that "provisions" the tunnel server(s) to link the physically separate broadcast domains. The tunnel server(s) may be generated and may be terminated based (at least partially) on instructions from the master controller. It is noted that the master controller is outside the "created" single "virtual" private network to be formed by the physically separate private networks (and, consequently, is outside the physically separate private networks).

For example, with two broadcast domains to be "virtually linked," the gateway device in the respective broadcast domains performs operations of discovery and emulation. A gateway device discovers the network devices on its local broadcast domain and transmits the discovered network and network devices to the master controller. The master controller then transmits the discovered network and discovered network devices of this broadcast domain to the other gateway devices of the other broadcast domains (here, in this example, one other broadcast domain) along with the network address for one or more tunnel servers to which the gateway devices (two gateway devices in this example) are instructed to direct signal packets from its local broadcast domain that are to be communicated to the other broadcast domains. The one or more tunnel servers are able to communicate signal packets between the gateway devices of the broadcast domains. Likewise, in this example, the respective gateway devices receiving the discovery of the network devices of the other broadcast domains are now able to locally emulate the other broadcast domains from receiving the discovered configuration of the network devices on the other broadcast domains.

So, imagine a physical network device 1 on a broadcast domain A in which domain A includes a gateway device B, and imagine a physical network device 2 on a broadcast domain C in which domain C includes a gateway device D. In this example, broadcast domains A and C are linked by at least one tunnel server.

If network device 1 desires to communicate with network device 2, it puts out a signal packet on its private local network for network device 2. From the normal operation of a network, that signal packet is directed to gateway device B, which, as described, is to emulate network device 2 so that it appears to device 1 as if device 2 is on its local network. Gateway device B then forwards the signal packet to the "at least one" tunnel server without modifying it, other than to encapsulate the signal packet. At the tunnel server, the encapsulation is removed to determine the intended destination of the signal packet. The tunnel server then re-encapsulates the packet in a manner so that it will be directed to gateway device D on domain C. The tunnel server is able to do so because the master controller provided the address location of gateway device D when provisioning the tunnel server. Gateway device D, after receiving the encapsulated signal packet, removes the encapsulation and puts the signal packet out on its local network, where it is directed to network device 2 through the normal operation of that local network. Thus, the signal packet is communicated as if the two domains are physically joined. No routing or NAT (which is typically performed by a router) is employed.

Observe that while the tunnel server does, in a sense, "forward" signal packets, as mentioned, it is not engaging in the technical act of *routing*, which involves use of a routing table and where the signal packet itself is modified to appear as if it originated from the router that routes it and which usually involves NAT. The two physical broadcast domains in this example are able to communicate across a larger network of intermediate and transparent network devices (e.g., the internet or World Wide Web) without signal packet routing, as is performed by a router, and without performing NAT. Another advantage is that network traffic is reduced because a router would route all the local network traffic, whereas here, only the signal packets to be communicated to the network devices of the other broadcast domain(s) are communicated via the gateway devices.

As we begin to draft a patent claim, again, notice the technique of identifying a technical problem and a possible technical solution. There are several features described here that might be patented; however, a significant one relates to permitting two (or more) physically separate broadcast domains to operate as one "virtual" broadcast domain without performing routing and without performing NAT (i.e., examples of "negative" limitations).

Here, this invention seems more naturally or inherently to be a method, so we start by drafting a method claim. The object, here, appears to be forming a "virtual broadcast domain" to virtually link at least two broadcast domains that are physically separate. Thus, a method claim might start with the following preamble:

I claim:

1. A method of forming a virtual broadcast domain by virtually linking at least a first broadcast domain with at least a second broadcast domain in which the at least a first broadcast domain and the at least a second broadcast domain are physically separate, the method comprising:

. . .

Continuing to craft, an action of the method might comprise:

"communicating signal packets between physically separate broadcast domains, wherein the communicating occurs via a gateway device."

The "communicating" may include additional actions, including:

"encapsulating signal packets in the physically separate broadcast domains" and "communicating the encapsulated signal packets between the gateway device and a tunnel server so that signal packets are able to be further communicated."

Using the foregoing as a base, recognizing the symmetry between two physically separate broadcast domains and cleaning up formalities, the following might be a method claim to cover this technology:

EXAMPLE 2.7

I claim:

1. A method of forming a virtual broadcast domain by virtually linking at least a first broadcast domain with at least a second broadcast domain in which the at least a first broadcast domain and the at least a second broadcast domain are physically separate, the method comprising:

   communicating one or more signal packets between respective physically separate broadcast domains via respective gateway devices included in the respective physically separate broadcast domains, wherein the communicating the one or more signal packets comprises:

      encapsulating the one or more signal packets in the respective physically separate broadcast domains; and

      communicating the encapsulated signal packets between the respective gateway devices and at least one tunnel server so that the one or more signal packets are communicated between the respective physically separate broadcast domains.

Several aspects are worth mentioning. As was suggested, for two broadcast domains, for example, symmetry is exploited by the claim language. It might have, instead, been drafted to describe first what happens at one broadcast domain and then at another, as later illustrated. However, with appropriate drafting, it is made shorter and broader by referring to "respective" broadcast domains and "respective" gateway devices.

Also notice use of language such as "one or more" and "at least." Such language is used to make the intended scope of the claim clearer. Coverage includes one signal packet or multiple signal packets, one tunnel server or more than one tunnel server, and two physically separate broadcast domains or more than two physically separate broadcast domains.

Finally, notice the preamble (the part of the claim before "comprising:"): "A method of forming a virtual broadcast domain by virtually linking at least a first broadcast domain with at least a second broadcast domain in which the at least a first broadcast domain and the at least a second broadcast domain are physically separate." How much of that preamble is really needed? The claim could have just as easily stated,[97] more simply:

I claim:

1. A method of forming a virtual private network comprising:

   communicating one or more signal packets between respective physically separate broadcast domains via respective gateway devices included in the respective physically separate broadcast domains, wherein the communicating the one or more signal packets comprises:

      encapsulating the one or more signal packets in the respective physically separate broadcast domains; and

      communicating the encapsulated signal packets between the respective gateway devices and at least one tunnel server so that the one or more signal packets are communicated between the respective physically separate broadcast domains.

Of course, this is a very broad claim that may not stand up to scrutiny since encapsulation was known at the time of the invention, as were tunnel servers (but *not* for this purpose).

Establishing a reasonable fallback position using dependent claims would be prudent due to the *known* art. Dependent claims could, for example, recite features, such as a master controller, the discovery and emulation performed by the gateway devices, creating the virtual broadcast domain *without* performing routing and/or NAT, and so on. Each of these features provides a reasonable basis to potentially distinguish over prior art.

97. See Chapter 3, regarding claim preambles.

Care in drafting may be appropriate for any "negative" limitations;[98] creating the virtual broadcast domain "*without* performing routing and/or NAT," and so on, are examples of negative limitations if recited in a claim. It is desirable to *expressly* have support for negative claim limitations in the written description. A prudent approach, if employing negative limitations in some independent claims, would be to include as "dependent claims" from the independent claims reciting negative limitations, affirmative or positive limitations that produce the result that is the basis for the negative limitation. Here, for example, one might try to draft the substance of the negative limitations in the independent claim via dependent claims using more affirmative language with respect to the negative limitation of a base claim. One example might be reciting "bypassing" routing and/or NAT in a claim dependent from a claim having a negative limitation, such as a dependent claim from an independent claim reciting "*without* performing routing and/or NAT."

As mentioned, here, we began with a method claim because it is usually easier to start with a claim type that more naturally relates to the technology. For example, software operation is usually more natural as a method. Here, all the hardware in this example involves standard off-the-shelf components. The innovative features all relate to software executing on the hardware devices. Here, then, a method claim is an easier initial claim to draft.

Previously, in Example 2.2, we deliberately drafted an initial claim from the perspective of only memory and a memory controller because the party that manufactures and provides the memory and memory controller may not be the same party that combines those parts with a CPU, and so on. Do we have a similar issue here, since we have separate broadcast domains and a tunnel server? It does not appear so, because one party should be operating all these elements together;[99] however, this is something to always consider or else perhaps run the risk that your claim is not infringed because it does not

98. See Chapter 6, addressing negative limitations. A recent case is *Novartis Pharmaceuticals Corp. v. Accord Healthcare, Inc.*, 38 F.4th 1013 (Fed. Cir. 2022). The case involves a negative limitation added to a drug treatment method claim during prosecution. The substantive question on appeal was whether the claim limitation lacked written description support. The initial Federal Circuit opinion by Judge O'Malley sided with the patentee; Chief Judge Moore wrote a dissent. Judge O'Malley subsequently retired and Judge Hughes was added to the panel to consider Accord's rehearing petition request. The request was granted and a new panel flipped the outcome, with Judge Hughes joining the Chief Judge's position and, therefore, the new panel ruled the claims to be invalid.

99. For example, if separate parties are operating the separate broadcast domains and separate gateway devices or if one party operates the broadcast domains and gateway devices and another party operates the tunnel server, then a "divided infringement" issue might be present. See Chapter 6, addressing the single infringer principle.

cover one single entity that owns and/or controls all the elements and limitations of the claim.[100]

Previously, we started with an apparatus claim and then drafted a method claim. Here, therefore, it would be prudent to include an apparatus claim for patent claim diversity. As before, we might begin:

---

1. An apparatus comprising: . . .

From the technical description, the gateway device performs much of the functionality. It appears that a broadcast domain includes at least one gateway device. Furthermore, a gateway device performs discovery of network devices of its broadcast domain, emulates network devices of another broadcast domain (such as for a two broadcast domain example), and encapsulates signal packets sent from a network device of its broadcast domain that are then sent to a tunnel server so that the signal packets may ultimately be sent to a network device of the other broadcast domain. This functionality may be captured as follows:

EXAMPLE 2.8

I claim:

1. An apparatus comprising:

   at least one gateway device of at least a first broadcast domain, wherein the at least one gateway device is to perform a network operation of discovery of any other network devices of the at least a first broadcast domain;

   wherein the at least one gateway device is to emulate one or more network devices of at least a second broadcast domain; and

   wherein the at least one gateway device is to encapsulate one or more signal packets of the at least a first broadcast domain to be directed to a network device of the at least a second broadcast domain and is to communicate the encapsulated one or more signal packets to at least one tunnel server.

---

100. See Chapter 6, addressing the single infringer principle.

Likewise, additional dependent claims may be written for the independent claim of Example 2.8. Observe that many of the points previously described for apparatus claim 2.2 are likewise illustrated with these apparatus claims.

---

2. The apparatus of claim 1, wherein the at least one tunnel server is to communicate the encapsulated one or more signal packets to the at least a second broadcast domain.
3. The apparatus of claim 1, wherein the at least one gateway device is to receive one or more encapsulated signal packets from the at least one tunnel server to be communicated to a network device of the at least a first broadcast domain.

Observe, here, in contrast to Example 2.7, we start from the perspective of a single broadcast domain. Starting in this manner, we are able to "construct" a local private network around the gateway device via dependent claims. Using a different approach provides claim diversity; although, we might have started from any number of perspectives. Consequently, the focus and scope of this claim is not precisely the same as the method claim (which is typically desirable for patent claim diversity), although there are overlapping features.

Notice that claim 1 of Example 2.8 recites in the first part of the claim body (the part of the claim after "comprising:"): "wherein the at least one gateway device is to perform a network operation of discovery of any other network devices of the at least a first broadcast domain." However, this is not used later in the claim. This relates to discovery information to be provided to the second broadcast domain. So, why include it here? It would broaden the claim without much downside to omit this language until dependent claims are included that are directed to using such discovery information so that a signal packet received from the "at least a second broadcast domain" is received at the gateway device of the "at least a first broadcast domain" to then be processed by the local network to be directed to a specific network device of the "at least a first broadcast domain." To take this point further, although as a matter of technology, that is how the discovery operation is used, such as for dependent claim 3, the actual claim language is not recited. Therefore, that language could be omitted entirely from claims 1 *and* 3 and/or added as a fourth dependent claim.

One aspect to appreciate is the difference in drafting a method claim versus drafting an apparatus claim that flows from the discussion about the set of rights associated with the respective claims. This was highlighted previously but is now repeated here for emphasis. A method claim recites actions or operations. As a consequence, a method claim is infringed by performing an action, such as *using* something (for a method of using) or *making* something (for a method of making). The claim elements are actions like "communicating," "encapsulating," and so on. One way to think of a method claim is like a cooking recipe with step-by-step instructions. In contrast, an apparatus is usually capable of doing actions. It is important to not claim an apparatus in a manner that suggests that it is performing such actions or operations.[101] An apparatus claim either recites structural elements, such as a processor or memory, or it recites that such elements are able or capable to perform an action to make it clear that the action itself is not being claimed, the performance of actions being the domain of method claims.[102]

The features of dependent claims 2 and 3 might have been included in the base claim; however, relegating these features to dependent claims accomplishes several things. It provides some fallback position while allowing the base claim to be broader. It also provides a way to "test" the bounds of the prior art since the examiner typically focuses on the independent claims.

Some comments on subject matter and patent eligibility are appropriate with this technology example. It is not immediately apparent from these claims that the innovation resides in software; however, it will likely be apparent from the specification. Typically, therefore, one would not expect a patent eligibility rejection here, although such rejections are becoming more common.[103]

---

101. *See, e.g.*, IPXL Holdings v. Amazon, 430 F.3d 1377, 1384 (Fed. Cir. 2005). See Chapter 6, which addresses the problem of mixing statutory classes of patent claims in a single patent claim. *Cf.* INVT SPE LLC v. Int'l Trade Comm'n, 46 F.4th 1361 (Fed. Cir. 2022) (distinguishing between actual operation and capability of operating or performing for apparatus claims, particularly for software on a device, which tends to be functional, without discussing indefiniteness issue of mixing method and apparatus limitations).

102. An exception might be typical mechanical apparatus claims that may functionally recite a limitation intended to be implemented as structure. For example, an apparatus claim might recite "a pipe operatively connected to a valve" rather than "a pipe capable of being operatively coupled to a valve." *Cf. INVT SPE LLC*, 46 F.4th 1361 (distinguishing between actual operation and capability of operating or performing for apparatus claims, particularly for software on a device, which tends to be functional, without discussing indefiniteness issue of mixing method and apparatus limitations).

103. *See* Am. Axle & Mfg., Inc. v. Neapco Holdings LLC, 939 F.3d 1355 (Fed. Cir. 2019); Yu v. Apple, 1 F.4th 1040 (Fed. Cir. 2021).

However, if such a rejection were to be made, it should be easy to overcome based on legal argument. It is well-established that the innovation may reside entirely in the software of a platform that combines hardware and software.[104]

There are several advantages to this technology beyond the scope of this discussion, including signal packet traffic engineering, creating overlay networks, and managing a complex network simply by moving icons on a screen. These aspects would or could, of course, be claimed, assuming budget is available to pursue these related inventions. However, this technology also presents an example to consider where at times what is perceived to be most valuable may not always be correct, suggesting the desirability of claiming as many features as is feasible, as previously mentioned.[105]

The aim of the technology at least in some respects was to join private and physically separate networks for separate offices, where each office includes many network devices. As mentioned, VPNs were known to be capable to connect a remote network device to a private network. However, imagine here a possible embodiment that was not an important focus of the claims in which a broadcast domain is linked with a remote device. Such an embodiment might be considered a sort of "corner" case, in that the remote device alone forms a second broadcast domain, and the remote device also operates as the gateway device for this broadcast domain of one network device. *However, notably this invention still has a technical advantage over a VPN by limiting the network traffic between broadcast domains, as one example.*

A close reading of the sample claims of Examples 2.7 and 2.8 will show that this type of embodiment *should* necessarily be covered. That this embodiment is covered, however, could be made clearer with one or more dependent claims, which could recite, for example, that the first and/or the second broadcast domain comprise a stand-alone network device.

The ability to cover such an embodiment is mentioned now, because imagine deployment just before the worldwide pandemic. After the technology is deployed, one might imagine the most popular use of the technology with customers may be use in a manner that necessarily employs a remote device. While this may not have been anticipated by the inventors, this embodiment might become so important such that additional dependent claims may be added, or even, perhaps, a separate *continuation* application claiming priority

104. *See* Enfish, LLC v. Microsoft Corp., 822 F.3d 1327 (Fed. Cir. 2016). See also Chapter 6, addressing patent eligibility in claim drafting.

105. See discussion earlier in this chapter.

to the initial patent application may be filed with new claims directed to this remote network device embodiment.

Along similar lines, as the prior discussion illustrates, in drafting the patent claims, it can be important that the language used should, as much as is feasible, not foreclose situations that, while not typical, might be attempted to avoid infringement. Again, as an example, the claims are written to make it clear that the subject matter is not limited to only two broadcast domains. The claims are drafted so that a single signal packet is covered, as well as multiple signal packets. The claims are also drafted so that a broadcast domain might comprise a gateway device or multiple gateway devices. Again, more dependent claims could also cement this latter understanding.

This is also a time to clarify good practice from what may be legally required. For example, the language used to suggest that the subject matter is not limited to only two broadcast domains may *not* be necessary, but it *is* good practice. The apparatus claim, as one example, used the language "of at least a first broadcast domain" and the language "of at least a second broadcast domain" to suggest that there may be more broadcast domains. This is also continued with the language "the at least a first broadcast domain" and the language "the at least a second broadcast domain." In other words, this may represent three or four broadcast domains or more, all of which would constitute "at least a first broadcast domain" and "at least a second broadcast domain."

On the other hand, if the claim had simply stated "a first broadcast domain," "a second broadcast domain," "the first broadcast domain," and "the second broadcast domain," it could still be argued that the claim covers additional broadcast domains. This is due to the transition word "comprising."[106] In general, "comprising" is interpreted to mean "including."[107]

Consequently, without the language in the claim, mentioned previously, one might still make a case that the claim covers more than two broadcast domains. However, with that said, there have been cases in which courts have limited claims to the exact language employed. A point to understand is that the principles or canons of claim construction, one example being as just stated regarding use of "comprising" as a transition word, represent a starting point for interpretation of the claim. Nonetheless, other factors, such as the

---

106. See treatment of transition words or phrases in patent claims in Chapter 3.

107. *See, e.g.*, Regents of Univ. of Cal. v. Eli Lilly & Co., 119 F.3d 1559 (Fed. Cir. 1997), *cert. denied*, 523 U.S. 1089 (1998) ("The word 'comprising,' . . . as is well-established, permits inclusion of other moieties."). See also the treatment of transition words in patent claims in Chapter 3.

specification, the file history, how those of ordinary skill would understand the technology, and so on, might cause a court to depart from a so-called canon of construction. With this knowledge, good practice suggests that other language (e.g., "at least," "one or more," and so on) be included so that the intent of what the claim is meant to cover is made much clearer.

As discussed in prior sections, it is also typical to include an apparatus means-plus-function claim (e.g., intended to be construed under subsection 112(f)) corresponding to the apparatus claim that is not intended to be construed under subsection 112(f), such as shown in the immediately following example.

Subsection 112(f) states that such claims (i.e., claims with a means-plus-function clause) are used for combinations. A so-called *single* means claim is not permitted; however, one might mix structural and means-plus-function clauses in a claim. In general, means-plus-function claims (i.e., claims with clauses construed under subsection 112(f)) are usually narrower than similar claims without clauses construed under subsection 112(f) primarily due to the language of the statute.

Of apparatus claim 2.8, what might be claimed as a means-plus-function clause versus employing structural elements? Certainly, the functions or operations of emulating and transmitting might be claimed using means-plus-function language. In comparison, terms such as "network device," "gateway device," and "broadcast domain" might be construed as structural.

Note that the means-plus-function claim closely tracks the previous apparatus claim. This is not required, again, but it is done to make it clear the drafter intended for the two claims to have different scope.[108] This topic is discussed more later.[109]

I claim:

1. An apparatus comprising:

   at least one gateway device of at least a first broadcast domain;

   wherein the at least one gateway device comprises means for emulating one or more network devices of at least a second broadcast domain; and

108. See Chapter 4 for a treatment of means-plus-function *and* step-plus-function claims. *But see* Mas-Hamilton Grp. v. La Gard, Inc., 156 F.3d 1206, 1214 (Fed. Cir. 1998).

109. See Chapter 4 for a treatment of means-plus-function *and* step-plus-function claims.

wherein the at least one gateway device comprises means for encapsulating one or more network communication signal packets of the at least a first broadcast domain directed to a network device of the at least a second broadcast domain and means for transmitting the encapsulated one or more network communication signal packets to at least one tunnel server.

In preceding Example 2.8, we recited a gateway device; however, in implementation, this is usually a network device in the form of a computing system with appropriate software. Therefore, we might draft the claim like this to imply broader scope, rather than as previously claimed:

EXAMPLE 2.9

I claim:

1. An apparatus comprising:

   at least one network device of at least a first broadcast domain;

   wherein the at least one network device is to emulate one or more network devices of at least a second broadcast domain; and

   wherein the at least one network device is to encapsulate one or more signal packets of the at least a first broadcast domain directed to a network device of the at least a second broadcast domain and is to communicate the encapsulated one or more signal packets to at least one tunnel server.

Of course, it would be important in the specification to clarify terms (e.g., network device, computing device, gateway device).

Also, because the technology is implemented in software, it would be typical, and prudent, to include a Beauregard claim.[110] A Beauregard claim refers to a claim that recites instructions (e.g., software instructions) stored on a "storage medium." A Beauregard claim may invite a patent eligibility rejection under § 101;[111] however, such claims can be powerful tools because they, in effect, cover the software as stored. They, in effect, may be asserted against anyone who uses, stores, sells, distributes, or generates the software. Anyone

110. See treatment of Beauregard claims in Chapter 4.
111. Because it makes it apparent that the invention is software related.

in the chain of distribution of the software may be sued, although they may not have created or used the software. In this regard, the form of the apparatus claim immediately preceding also provides guidance on drafting a Beauregard claim, such as the claim immediately following. Instead of reciting "apparatus," we are able to claim an "article," and instead of a network device, we are able to claim "executable instructions," as follows:

EXAMPLE 2.10

I claim:

1. An article comprising: a non-transitory storage medium;

   wherein the storage medium includes stored thereon executable instructions;

   wherein the instructions are executable to: emulate one or more network devices of at least a second broadcast domain, encapsulate one or more signal packets from at least a first broadcast domain to be directed to a network device of the at least a second broadcast domain, and communicate the encapsulated one or more signal packets to at least one tunnel server.

This (Beauregard) claim and the apparatus claim are quite similar in language, which reduces claim diversity in some respects (granted the apparatus claim and Beauregard claim are different claim types), but that may happen sometimes, especially if representing cost-conscious clients (because independently rewriting every independent claim can be expensive in terms of attorney time). Along similar lines, from the Beauregard claim of the immediately preceding example, it is also quite easy to now formulate a method claim that is different from the previous method claim 1 of Example 2.7, thereby adding some additional diversity.

EXAMPLE 2.11

I claim:

1. A method comprising:

   emulating one or more network devices of at least a second broadcast domain;

encapsulating one or more signal packets from at least a first broadcast domain directed to a network device of the at least a second broadcast domain; and

communicating the encapsulated one or more signal packets to the at least one tunnel server directing the encapsulated one or more signal packets to the network device of the at least a second broadcast domain.

Of course, we have now exceeded the three independent claims that are permitted with a standard filing fee and would incur extra claim fees. Five independent claims were just discussed and drafted (two method claims, an apparatus claim, a means-plus-function claim, and a Beauregard claim). One arrangement to reduce costs a bit might be to employ four independent claims (rather than the five discussed), in which we might either include two different method claims, an apparatus claim, and a Beauregard claim or, instead, perhaps, a method claim, an apparatus claim, a Beauregard claim, and a means-plus-function claim. The advantage of the former is that it employs two different approaches for a method of using. It gives up a means-plus-function claim, but those tend to be construed narrowly and tend to be included if the technical field is crowded or as a fallback position, neither of which appears needed here. Later sections address advantages and disadvantages of several types of claims, especially Beauregard and means-plus-function claims.[112]

As mentioned, this has been a quick survey and these examples may appear in later sections discussing in detail some aspects only touched upon here and/or raising new claim drafting considerations.

---

112. See Chapter 4, treating advantages and disadvantages of means-plus-function claims and Beauregard claims.

Claim Drafting Problems I

Problem 1. Kettle—Draft one independent apparatus claim and one dependent apparatus claim; also draft one independent method claim and one dependent method claim.

FIGURES:

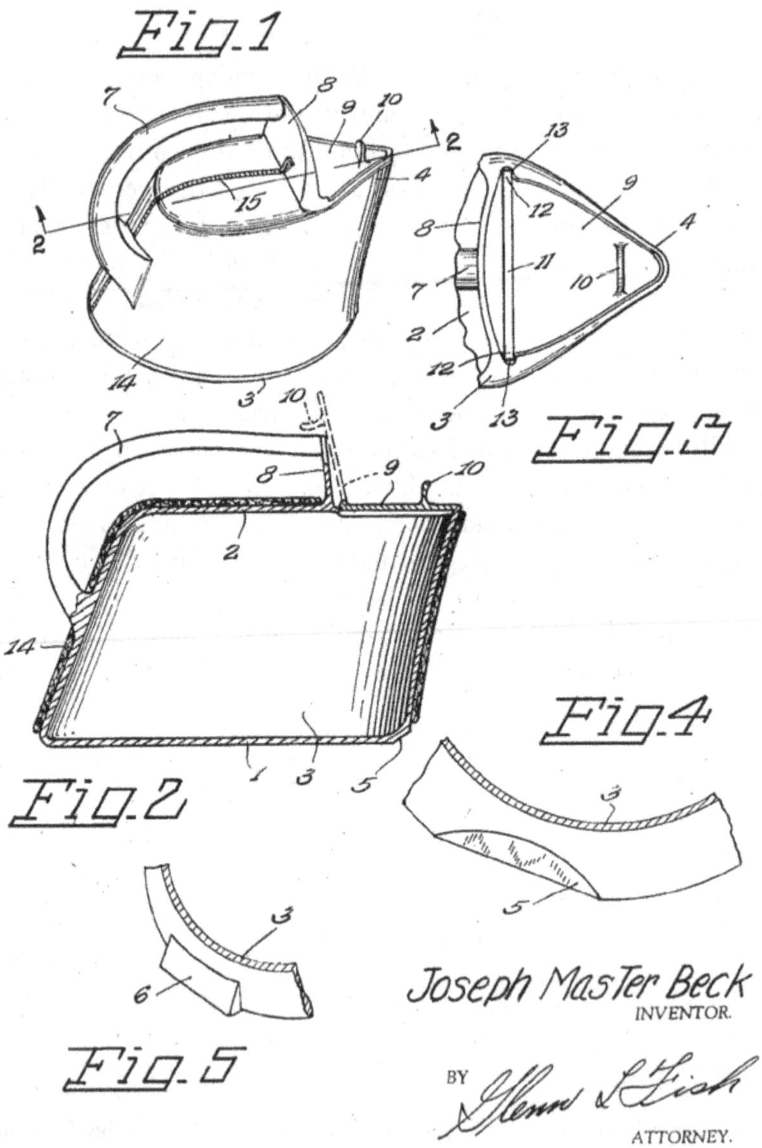

DESCRIPTION:

This invention relates to kitchenware and more particularly to a tea kettle, one object of the invention being to provide a tea kettle of such construction that water may be quickly boiled therein and easily poured from the kettle.

Another object of the invention is to so form the tea kettle that while it will remain in an upright position and not be liable to tilt over when placed upon a stove, it may be easily tilted forwardly to a pouring position when use of water in the kettle is desired.

Another object of the invention is to provide the same with an improved form of handle that may be firmly grasped when it is desired to pour water from the kettle and has a mounting for its front end that serves not only as a mounting for the handle but also as a shield to deflect steam and prevent a person's hand from being scalded while pouring hot water from the kettle.

Another object of the invention is to so form the lower portion of the front of the kettle so that when it is tilted to a pouring position while resting upon a stove or other support, the kettle will be prevented from tilting transversely.

Another object of the invention is to provide the kettle with a jacket of heat insulating material that serves to confine heat therein so that water will quickly boil, the jacket being so constructed that it can be easily applied to or removed from the kettle.

The invention is illustrated in the accompanying drawings wherein

Figure 1 is a perspective view of the improved tea kettle.

Figure 2 is a sectional view taken vertically through the kettle along the line 2-2 of Figure 1.

Figure 3 is a top plan view of the forward portion of the kettle.

Figure 4 is a fragmentary view looking at the lower portion of the front of the kettle.

Figure 5 is a view similar to Figure 4 showing a modified construction.

This improved tea kettle may be formed of any metal desired, and has a hollow body formed with a bottom 1, a top 2, and side walls 3. The side walls of the body have their upper portions tapered toward each other at the front thereof to provide a pouring spout that is open at its top, as shown in Figure 2, but the bottom of the body may be circular. It should also be noted that at the front and rear of the body the walls extend upwardly from the bottom at a forward incline. Therefore, the body has the outline of a parallelogram when viewed in vertical longitudinal section, as shown in Figure 2, and when it is desired to pour water from the kettle through the spout 4 this can be easily done by tilting the kettle forwardly without lifting it from the stove or other support upon which it is resting. The bottom of the kettle is circular and in order to prevent it from tilting transversely and causing water to be spilled while being poured from the kettle, the lower portion of the walls at the front of the kettle may be beveled, as shown in Figures 2 and 4, to provide a flat surface upon which the kettle will rest when tilted forwardly for pouring, or a block 6 that projects forwardly from the front of the kettle and serves as a fulcrum may be welded to the front of the body or formed integral therewith. By forming the kettle with the flat surface 5 or the fulcrum 6 it may be easily rocked forwardly to pour water from the spout and then returned to its normal position in which it rests upon its bottom 1 without likelihood of the kettle tilting transversely.

In order to lift the kettle, there has been provided a handle 7 which is of a goose-neck formation and extends longitudinally over the top of the body with its rear portion curved downwardly and then forwardly and united to the forwardly inclined rear portion of the walls of the body. At its front end the handle is united to a plate 8 that rises from the top 2 along the front end thereof. Referring to Figure 3, it will be seen that the plate is curved transversely of the kettle, and upon referring to Figure 2, it will be seen that it extends upwardly at a rearward incline. Therefore, when the kettle is tilted forwardly to pour hot water from the spout, the plate 8 will serve very effectively as a shield or deflector to prevent steam from striking a hand holding the handle and causing the hand to be scalded. This plate also serves as a prop or rest for the lid 9, which serves as a closure for the spout but is swung upwardly to the position indicated by dotted lines while pouring water from the kettle. The spout serves not only for pouring water from the kettle but also as a filling opening. The lid has a thumb lift 10 adjacent its front end and along its rear edge is formed with a head 11 having its ends extended to provide pintles 12, which fit into sockets or seats 13 and serve to pivotally mount the lid.

It is desired to permit water in the kettle to be quickly brought to a boiling point and in order to accomplish this, there has been provided a jacket 14 that conforms to the shape of the walls of the body and has a portion at its top adapted to cover the top 2 back of the shield or plate 9. This cover is split vertically along its back so that it may be applied to the body of the kettle, as shown in Figures 1 and 2, and in order to unite the rear edges after the jacket has been applied, there have been provided fasteners of the zipper type that securely but detachably hold the jacket in place. This jacket is formed of asbestos or any other heat insulating material desired and serves very effectively to prevent radiation of heat from the sides and the top of the kettle. Therefore, the water in the kettle may be quickly heated and also permit the kettle to be lifted without discomfort due to heat radiating therefrom.

Problem 2. Scissors—Draft one independent apparatus claim and one independent method claim.

FIGURES:

Fig 1

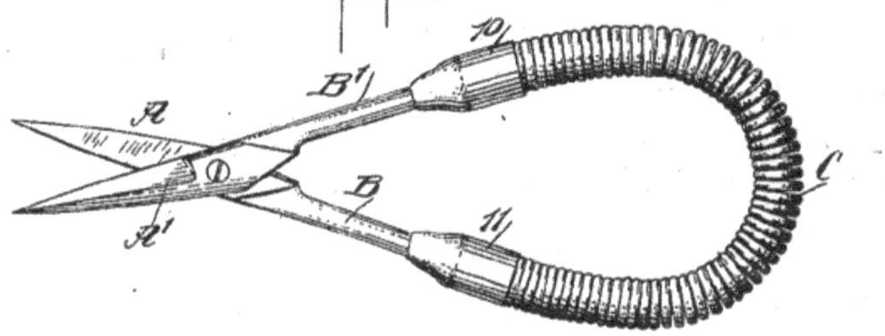

Fig 2

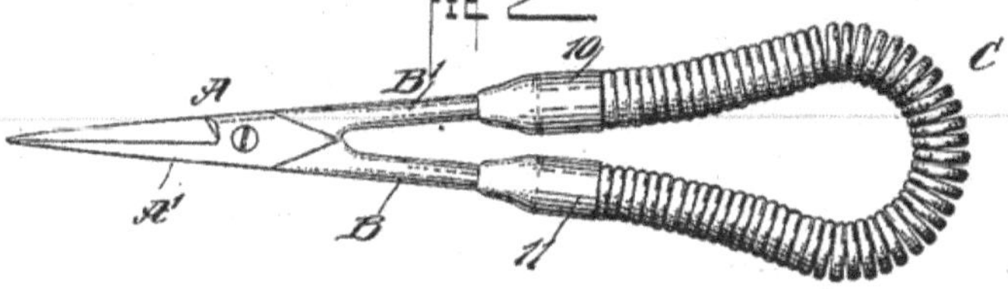

DESCRIPTION:

The purpose of the invention is to connect the shanks of scissor or shear blades by a spring that will act as a handle and normally hold the blades apart or in a position to receive an object, the blades being quickly brought into cutting action by pressing the end portions of the spring toward one another.

The invention consists in the novel construction and combination of the several parts, as will be hereinafter fully set forth, and pointed out in the claim.

Reference is to be had to the accompanying drawings, forming a part of this specification, in which similar characters of reference indicate corresponding parts in both figures.

Figure 1 is a plan view of a pair of scissors having the improvement applied, the blades being in open position; and

Figure 2 is a plan view of a pair of scissors with the improvement applied, the blades of the scissors being shown closed.

A and A' represent the blades of a pair of scissors or shears that are pivotally connected in the usual manner, and the said blades are provided with the customary shanks B and B', which heretofore have been provided with loops to receive the fingers and thumb of a hand. In the improved construction, however, the said loops or eyes are omitted, and instead of them sleeves 10 and 11, forming sockets are rigidly secured to the rear ends of the shanks B and B', and the ends of a coil-spring C are secured in these sleeves or sockets in any approved manner. This coil-spring may be of any suitable gauge of wire and may be as long as necessary and constitute the handle of the scissors or shears. When the spring-handle is secured to the shanks of the scissor-blades, said spring is bowed, and the tendency of the end portions of the spring is to move outward or away from each other. Consequently when the scissors, provided with the improved handle, are not in use, the blades will be held apart at their points. When the scissors are to be brought into action, it is simply necessary to press the end portions of the spring-handle together or in the direction of each other, whereupon the blades will close in the manner usual to scissors and shears.

Problem 3. Toilet Paper Roll Holder—Draft one independent apparatus claim and one dependent apparatus claim; also draft one independent method claim and one dependent method claim.

FIGURES:

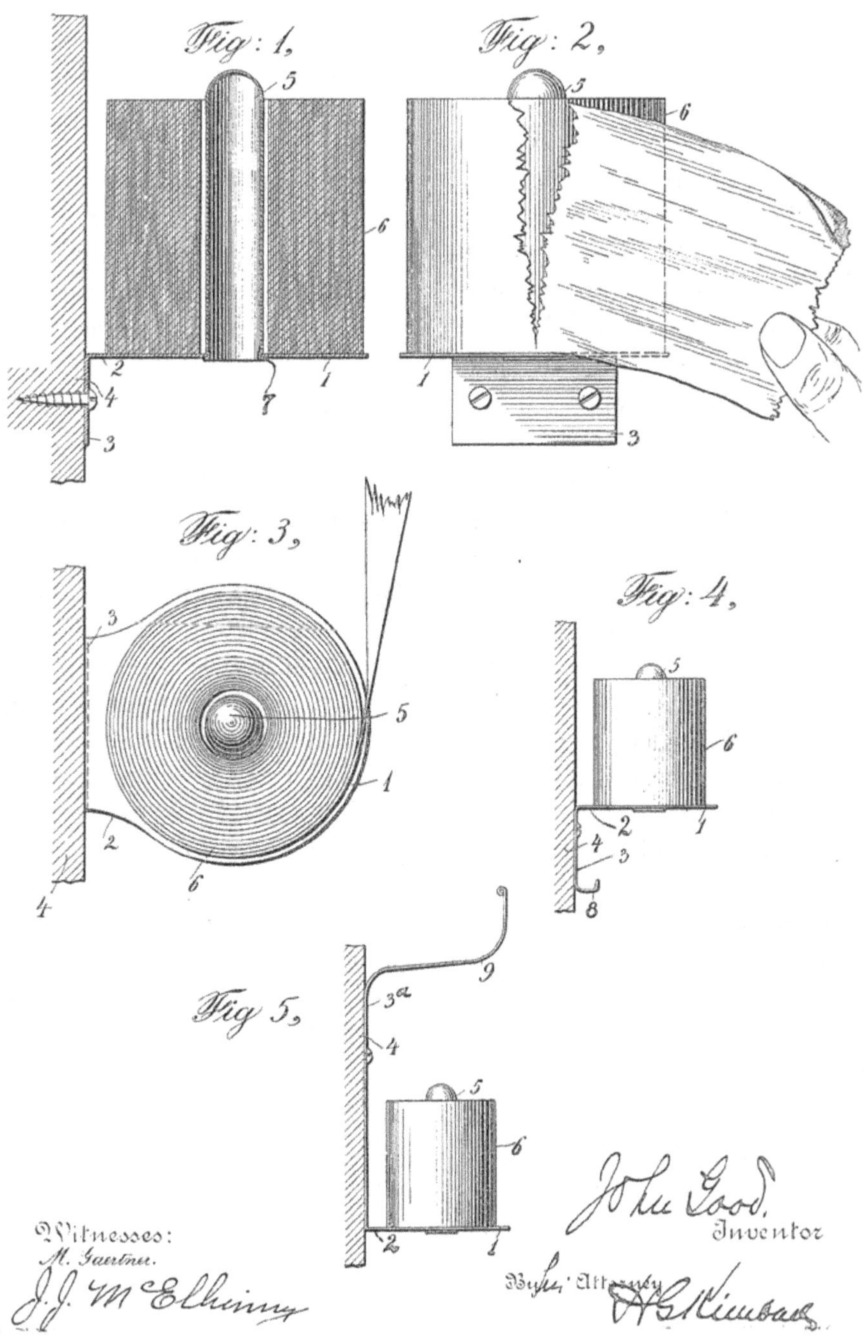

DESCRIPTION:

The invention is a dispensing holder for toilet paper rolls, and aims to simplify and reduce the cost of such devices and to provide a holder adapted for delivering the toilet paper freely and in such quantities as may be needed but without allowing the roll to spin on its support nor causing the thin tissue paper to break or tear before a sufficient length has been unwound, and also to provide a holder that will allow the paper to be withdrawn from it with equal facility from any direction or on any side, it being characteristic of the invention that the paper roll is supported in an upright and projecting relation, free from obstruction to access on any side, and is not dependent upon the presence of tearing edges or knives in contact with or surrounding the periphery of the roll, but on the contrary, and by reason of its said exposed and unobstructed disposition, provides for the side of the roll itself to be utilized as the fulcrum or edge upon which the tissue paper will tear when unwound or drawn from any direction, as hereinafter more fully described.

In the drawings forming a part hereof,

Fig. 1 is a side elevation of the new device showing the toilet paper roll in vertical section;

Fig. 2 is a front elevation of the same, showing the paper strip in the process of severance;

Fig. 3 is a top plan of Figs. 1 and 2; and

Figs. 4 and 5 are modified forms in reduced scale.

The holder comprises a horizontal base, preferably in the form of a flat smooth sheet-metal plate 1, which is rounded or circular on its front and sides and of a diameter approximately equal to the diameter of a full roll of toilet paper.

At its rearward side the plate is formed with a short neck portion 2, which terminates in a vertical flange 3, being at right angles to the plate and perforated with screw holes for attachment to a vertical wall or support, indicated at 4, whereby the device is rigidly and immovably supported in a projecting and horizontal relation therefrom. Rising from the central portion of the horizontal base there is provided a vertical post 5 that is adapted to receive and constitute a rigid pivot for the roll of toilet paper 6 placed in an upright position thereon and resting, endwise, upon the horizontal base. The latter serves as a friction table upon which the said roll revolves as the paper is drawn off and thereby provides a frictional tension for retarding or governing the unwinding of the paper, and I have discovered that the weight alone of a roll of soft tissue paper of the kind usually and preferably employed for toilet paper and of the usual and appropriate width for such paper is sufficient, when mounted upright upon a stationary base, to provide an adequate if not the most effective and satisfactory tension for the delivery and tearing of the paper strip as explained below. The friction between the end of the roll and the flat table is of course subject to some variation as the roll decreases in diameter and weight as it unwinds, but owing to the correspondingly diminishing radius of the roll, the tension on the paper strip remains substantially constant.

The upright pivot post is of somewhat less diameter than the average diameter of the internal cores of toilet paper rolls, and is preferably of a suitable length to project somewhat above the top of the roll when the latter is on the base, this dimension being desirable to prevent accidental dislodgment and also to facilitate the placing of the roll in frictional contact with the table. At its upper end the post is tapered or rounded, and is preferably free from obstruction to the removal of the roll. At its base it is connected with the friction table by a joint that provides a clean angle therewith, the table being preferably flat or flush up to the commencement of the upright cylindrical wall of the post. As shown in the drawing, the post is constructed of tubular sheet metal and secured to the table by upsetting or crimping within a central aperture provided in the latter and as indicated at 7 in Fig. 1, but other methods of attachment may be employed with equal effect.

In operation the holder is supplied with paper by placing the roll over or upon the vertical pivot post so that it rests in endwise frictional contact upon the friction table, it being immaterial which end of the roll is thus placed upon the table, inasmuch as the tension in the delivery is not dependent upon the direction of rotation. The paper may then be withdrawn or unwound for any desired length by pulling upon it in the ordinary natural manner and can be severed by then pulling downwardly or at an angle from horizontal, the tear in the paper strip taking place along the vertical line where it leaves the curvature of the roll and according to the direction from which the strip is withdrawn. The front and sides of the friction table are free and unobstructed for this purpose. As illustrated in Fig. 2, which exhibits the roll holder in front view, the paper strip is being pulled parallel with the wall 4 and then somewhat downwardly for tearing, as indicated, so that severance takes place on a transverse or vertical line exactly at the front of the roll or where the paper strip, thus withdrawn, departs from the cylindrical curvature thereof. The device may be employed for paper that has been specially perforated for the purpose of predetermining the point of severance, and such paper may be torn either along the line of the perforations or elsewhere, according as to whether such perforations coincide with the point of departure from the roll curvature or otherwise, as above explained, this being an incident of the certain degree of frictional tension produced by the free endwise support of the light tissue paper roll upon its friction table and without the aid of additional peripheral or other friction-producing devices. The invention provides for the omission of such devices inasmuch as the tension due to the weight of the roll is sufficient, as above stated, and paper of the kind referred to, being pliable and non-resilient, does not tend to unwrap or uncoil itself from the roll, so that the free or last severed end does not require to be confined or held thereto. This end will normally stand slightly off from the body of the roll on whichever side it was last torn so that it is freely accessible and can be readily grasped from any quarter. The device may, therefore, be disposed on the closet wall at any convenient point and height without regard to the direction from which the paper is to be withdrawn and without consideration of the direction in which the roll will rotate in unwinding, and its action will be uniform in all cases.

The attachment means whereby the horizontal friction table is rigidly and immovably secured to the vertical wall, comprises, in Figs. 1 to 4, a downwardly turned flange, which in Fig. 4 is outwardly bent at its free end to form a holder 8 for cigars or other articles. The invention includes, however, an upwardly bent flange 3 that is converted into a receptacle by being turned outwardly over the top of the roll, forming, with the wall or otherwise, a trough or receptacle 9, as shown for example in Fig. 5.

Claim Breadth: Is Being as Broad as Possible Always the Goal?

Drafting the Broadest Claims Possible

Understand that a range of useful and meaningful strategies may be implemented via PCD in addition to drafting the broadest possible patent claim.

When it comes to claim drafting, most people have in mind drafting to handle issues regarding prior art and creating claims that distinguish over such art. Of course, this certainly is desirable to accomplish; however, there are several other ways that a claim may fail to comply with title 35 of the U.S. Code (U.S.C.) despite *successfully* distinguishing from such prior art. Generally, in terms of prosecution of a patent application, these other ways are thought of as so-called non-art rejections during examination, in comparison with "prior art rejections." Likewise, these same non-art issues (as well as art issues, of course) may be raised in litigation after the patent has issued and various ones may also be raised in a post-issuance review of the patent, depending on the proceeding.[113]

The primary statutory sections of concern for patent claims in this regard are §§ 101, 102, 103, and 112 of title 35. These might, similarly, be thought to capture the requirements to be met for an invention to be patentable. This follows logically since the patent claims define the invention.[114]

Section 101 is the statutory basis for requiring that an invention be new and useful, that it be "statutory subject matter"[115] and "patent eligible"[116] (which overlaps with statutory subject matter, but is a separate legal consideration), and that there not be "double patenting."[117] Section 102 is the statutory basis for the principle that an invention must be novel[118] (i.e., new), providing conditions that negate novelty, and that it must be timely filed[119] (i.e., before the

113. Although the patent claims are presumed to be valid in litigation. *See, e.g.*, Nautilus, Inc. v. Biosig Instruments, Inc., 134 S. Ct. 2120 (2014).

114. *See, e.g.*, Phillips v. AWH Corp., 415 F.2d 1303, 1312 (Fed. Cir. 2005) (en banc) ("It is a 'bedrock principle' of patent law that 'the claims of a patent define the invention to which the patentee is entitled the right to exclude.'"). *See also* Constant v. Advanced Micro-Devices, Inc., 848 F.2d 1560, 1571, 7 U.S.P.Q.2d 1057, 1064 (Fed. Cir. 1988); Dollar Elec. Co. v. Syndevco, Inc., 205 U.S.P.Q. 949, 959 (E.D. Mich. 1979), *aff'd*, 669 F.2d 1370, 214 U.S.P.Q. 241 (6th Cir. 1982).

115. See Chapter 6, providing a treatment regarding statutory subject matter and patent eligibility.

116. *Id.*

117. See treatment in Chapter 4.

118. See Chapter 1, providing a treatment of pre-AIA and post-AIA novelty.

119. See Chapter 1, providing a treatment of pre- and post-AIA rights forfeiture considerations.

invention is commercialized). Section 103 is the statutory basis for the principle that the invention must be nonobvious.[120] Last, but not least, § 112 requires that the patent claims be definite[121] (i.e., not ambiguous) and is the statutory basis for means-plus-function claims.[122] These statutory sections have other specifics regarding claims (e.g., multi-dependent claims) and requirements for the specification that, if not present, may invalidate the claims (e.g., written description support, enablement).[123] Nonetheless, here, we are giving attention to claim drafting, as opposed to specification writing.

The foregoing claim drafting issues are treated in depth in other chapters of this book. Being broad, as should now be clear, while distinguishing from the prior art is *not* the *only* goal when drafting a claim. Nonetheless, here, we ask: should being as broad as possible *necessarily* be a goal at all and, if so, why?

Thus, we focus here on statutory §§ 102 and 103, which relate to prior art.[124] Being able to draft a patent claim that legally distinguishes from prior art is one of the more basic skills required of someone who crafts patent claims. Furthermore, to be able to do so requires understanding what qualifies *legally* as prior art.

This latter point is important to fully grasp. Simply because something, such as a product, an article, an idea, and so on, exists before the date of creation of an invention and, particularly, before the filing date of a patent application describing the invention at issue does not *necessarily* mean it qualifies as prior art, *at least legally*. Rather, to *legally* be prior art, it must fall under one of the subsections of 35 U.S.C. § 102.[125] Consequently, it is important to understand how those subsections operate to, in effect, define "prior art." A complication is that on March 16, 2013, the effective date of the portion of the AIA related to statutory §§ 102 and 103, these latter statutory sections changed.[126]

---

120. See Chapter 1, providing a treatment of pre-AIA and post-AIA nonobviousness.

121. See Chapter 6, providing a treatment of indefiniteness along with other issues.

122. See Chapter 4, providing a treatment of means-plus-function claims.

123. See Chapter 6, providing a treatment of many of these issues.

124. As mentioned, the other issues raised are addressed in later chapters, previously cited. Likewise, Chapter 1 provides a treatment of pre-AIA and post-AIA §§ 102 and 103.

125. *See, e.g.*, 1 Chisum, *supra* note 2, § 6.02[3](c) ("Federal Circuit decisions consistently confirm that Section 102(b) bar events constitute 'prior art' for purposes of obviousness."); Edward C. Walterscheid, *Novelty in Historical Perspective (Part I)*, 75 J. Pat. & Trademark Off. Soc'y 689 (1993); Edward C. Walterscheid, *Novelty in Historical Perspective (Part II)*, 75 J. Pat. & Trademark Off. Soc'y 777 (1993); Edward C. Walterscheid, *The Ever Evolving Meaning of Prior Art (Part 9)*, 67 J. Pat. Off. Soc'y 33 (1985); Edward C. Walterscheid, *The Ever Evolving Meaning of Prior Art (Part 5)*, 65 J. Pat. Off. Soc'y 477 (1983); Note, *Prior Art in Patent Law*, 73 Harv. L. Rev. 369, 377 (1959). See Chapter 1, addressing pre-AIA and post-AIA novelty and nonobviousness.

126. Although the AIA became law on September 16, 2011, it went into effect in stages.

Once someone understands what qualifies as prior art, that knowledge allows the individual to then dissect available and relevant prior art before drafting a patent claim. Likewise, from interviewing the inventor and reading an invention disclosure prepared by the inventor, the individual should eventually understand enough to see how the invention is different from the prior art that has been dissected. These tasks are important basic skills for being able to draft a patent claim. These skills are like basic blocking and tackling in football, as an analogy.

Now, however, comes the real challenge. The patent drafter must determine how similar or different the claim should be from the known prior art to protect the technology and still distinguish from that prior art. Furthermore, and perhaps more challenging, the patent drafter must be able to formulate that difference in words.

A claim that is overly narrow may easily distinguish from the art. However, that claim may capture few if any potential infringers that might be using the technology and, consequently, be of little commercial value. Conversely, a claim that is overly broad may capture many infringers, but might not issue as being too broad relative to the prior art. Even if the claim does issue, it may later be found invalid as being too "close" to the prior art. A trade-off between sweeping in less prior art versus capturing more infringers operates as a fundamental principle in this realm, not unlike the fundamental trade-off between bandwidth and signal-to-noise ratio in electrical engineering, as an example.[127]

The drafter is seeking to achieve a "goldilocks"-type claim that is neither too narrow nor too broad. However, that will usually depend quite a bit on the context and what may be known at the time of filing. According to one approach or theory, a broad claim should be presented such that it requires the examiner to ferret out all the close art. In this way, the prosecutor is able to craft a patent claim that leaves little or nothing "on the table" in terms of patent scope. The ideal claim, for this context, is just close enough to "ferreted out" art from which the claim patentably distinguishes and still stands up as valid under scrutiny.

It might be helpful here to recall the discussion from earlier in this chapter, discussing "what are the primary things that limit claim scope?" One is self-imposed claim limitations and the other is the prior art. Given the prior discussion, it may now be clearer why it is that these two things typically limit claim scope. First, and foremost, the claim should not read on known prior

127. See treatment in Chapter 1, "Claim Scope Trade-Offs: Validity versus Infringement."

art. Second, there should be enough difference from that art so that the claim is inventive over that art.[128] We, therefore, have come up against an area where judgment will be one's primary guide.

Also, there are a few schools of thought here, rather than a single approach. One school of thought, as alluded to earlier, is to be as broad as possible and as close to the known prior art as possible without ensnaring it by including an inventive distinction. Again, this helps to "ferret out" the close art. Another school of thought is to only be as broad as needed for the commercial setting, lest your claims be held invalid and of no use at all.[129] Yet another is to be deliberately narrow so the patent will issue quickly (and perhaps follow up with a continuation seeking broader claim scope). One may well imagine even more complex approaches.

As a practical matter, you may end up using any one of these approaches, again, depending on circumstances and client desires. The real question, then, might be: absent unusual circumstances, what should your "default" approach be? Conventional wisdom suggests that one follow the first approach: be as broad as possible and as close to the known prior art as possible without ensnaring it by including an inventive distinction. However, rather than simply accepting this, we would like to investigate whether this wisdom should apply by considering its advantages and its disadvantages. This inquiry will provide other insights about the dynamics at work in this legal situation.

A broad claim is only one of many aspects of a good claim. Rather, *a good claim is an appropriate balance between breadth, vagueness, and precision.* The claim is precise in some respects because the claim language should be specific enough to distinguish from the known prior art. This often involves some amount of detail in the language employed. For example, if the prior art shows red doorknobs, to be novel at least, the claim should recite a color other than red. For example, a recitation of "a blue doorknob" would be novel over such prior art (granted that it might be obvious, depending on other considerations). Patent claims are usually precise enough to show that the subject matter claimed is at least novel over the *known* prior art.

People sometimes confuse breadth and vagueness, the other features of a good claim. For example, "any and all electrical signals" is quite broad, but it is *not* vague. Rather, it is crystal clear. A good patent claim has breadth to cover those aspects not needed to distinguish from the known prior art. Breadth is

---

128. As suggested previously in this chapter, relying *strictly* on commercial motivations for the patent filing may result in claims that are narrower than needed.

129. This is the approach alluded to earlier in this chapter when suggesting that often commercial motivations are employed to limit claim scope.

desirable to protect the technology from those who might try to employ the technical idea in a manner that might otherwise not infringe a narrower claim. Vagueness may be appropriate, for example when it may be unclear how certain technology may be implemented among various potential choices. The future is uncertain. Being vague permits the claim to be infringed without spelling out in specific language how some aspects of the claim will be implemented.[130]

To understand vagueness better, consider, for example, a new type of razor blade for a handheld manual razor. Razor blades are a crowded art. Manufacturers are regularly coming out with designs that give a closer shave with less risk of being cut by the blade. How the blades for such razor blade cartridges are arranged is typically quite specific so the razor functions as intended. Specifics, regarding number of blades, thicknesses, juxtapositions, relative or absolute distances between blades, materials of the blades, and so on, may all be important to achieve a certain function. Likewise, these specific and *precise* details, recited in the patent claim, should assist in distinguishing the subject matter to be patented from the prior art.

However, one may imagine, in a dependent claim, it may be desirable to recite a handheld razor along with the razor blade. For one thing, the two are frequently sold together, meaning potentially larger damages and, with additional evidence, potentially having a basis for a charge of deliberate copying, which may result in up to treble damages being awarded.[131] Furthermore, this would help limit claim scope relative to prior art, such as blades in general and even relative to other types of razor blades perhaps.[132] Also, if the razor were to be sold by itself, this might still result in the ability to make out a claim

130. However, appreciate that 35 U.S.C. § 112 (2024) has a requirement that a claim not be *too* vague, hence, making it indefinite. Understanding the line that amounts to being too vague depends on context and requires judgment. Various aspects of indefiniteness are treated in later sections of this book. See Chapter 6, which treats indefiniteness along with other issues. Notably, the Federal Circuit decided a number of indefiniteness cases in 2022, suggesting that this issue may be getting more attention in litigation. These cases include Niazi Licensing Corp. v. St. Jude Med. S.C., Inc., 30 F.4th 1339 (Fed. Cir. 2022) (finding that claims to "resilient" and "pliable" catheters were indefinite); Univ. of Mass. v. L'Oreal S.A., 36 F.4th 1374 (Fed. Cir. 2022) (finding that claims to adenosine skin compositions were indefinite); ImmunoGen, Inc. v. Hirshfeld, No. 2021-1939, 2022 WL 885774, at *2 (Fed. Cir. Mar. 25, 2022) (vacating holding that "AIBW" is indefinite); ClearOne, Inc. v. Shure Acquisition Holdings, Inc., 35 F.4th 1345 (Fed. Cir. 2022) (affirming Patent Trial and Appeal Board determination that "self-similar" claim language was not indefinite); Dyfan, LLC v. Target Corp., 28 F.4th 1360, 1364 (Fed. Cir. 2022) ("code" was not in means-plus-function form and, therefore, not indefinite for lack of structural equivalents in the specification).

131. *See* 35 U.S.C. § 284 (2024).

132. Such as razor blades for electric razors, for example.

of contributory patent infringement or inducing patent infringement with respect to a "combination claim" of the blade and razor.[133]

To draft such a claim, however, may involve explaining how the cartridge and razor are joined. But there are a host of attachment mechanisms in use and many more may be possible. It might even be the case that a new attachment mechanism is created for this razor blade cartridge (and could be separately claimed). Each manufacturer likely has a favored attachment mechanism, so that the blades (or blade cartridges) are *not* interchangeable between different razors made by different manufacturers. One might, therefore, imagine claims like this:

EXAMPLE 2.12

I claim:

1. An apparatus comprising: a razor blade cartridge comprising a multiplicity of razor blades; wherein the multiplicity of razor blades . . . [description and details of new razor blade arrangement that provides the intended function].

2. The apparatus of claim 1, comprising: a handheld razor blade cartridge holder; wherein the handheld razor blade cartridge holder and the razor blade cartridge are attachable to one another for use in shaving.

How the two attach is left vague; however, this amount of vagueness should not run afoul of § 112 for being indefinite.[134] Likewise, it would be prudent to do several additional things, such as, in the specification, define for this context the term "attachable" in a reasonably broad and in a reasonably clear manner, such as "to at least temporarily join and/or temporarily connect two physically separate items so that they are able to operate as a single functional unit, such as a handheld razor blade cartridge holder and a razor blade cartridge." Furthermore, it would also be appropriate to give details of a particular attachment

133. *See* 35 U.S.C. § 271(b), (c) (2024); addressed in Chapter 5 in more detail.

134. *See* Shatterproof Glass Corp. v. Libbey-Owens Ford Co., 758 F.2d 613, 624, 225 U.S.P.Q. 634, 641 (Fed. Cir. 1985), *cert. dismissed*, 474 U.S. 976 (1985) ("The amount of detail required to be included in claims depends on the particular invention and the prior art, and is not to be viewed in the abstract but in conjunction with whether the specification is in compliance with the first paragraph of Section 112. . . .").

mechanism to be used and claim that in further dependent claims, as a fallback position to address the risk of an indefiniteness rejection being made.

The point, of course, is that good claims are broad, vague, and precise in the appropriate balance for the situation. However, people often focus on obtaining broad claims *exclusively*. Here, then, we would like to consider the advantages and the disadvantages associated with broad claims. Doing so serves several purposes. It clarifies that claims are not required to be broad. It also clarifies that while broad claims are sometimes desirable, there are associated risks. So, it may be the case that it is not always best to "swing for the fences." This, of course, is a judgment call and may involve questioning the client about their desires and goals. In general, this book advocates for drafting broad claims; *however, claim drafting is not a one-size-fits-all enterprise. Being able to adjust one's approach to the situation is the true mark of a claim drafting craftsman.*

Aside from the desire to ferret out prior art, a reason to draft broad claims is that it provides a good opening position in a negotiation. In fact, if possible, it would be prudent to draft claims broader than what may be desired or expected by the decision-maker (e.g., client, manager, overseeing attorney, etc.). Not all attorneys may agree with this latter suggestion, but most should. Technically, patent prosecution is litigation. However, as a practical matter, it is more like a negotiation. In an ideal setting, the attorney or agent presents something that is undoubtedly patent eligible and meets other "non-art" statutory requirements. In this case, the negotiation is primarily about the scope of the claims relative to the known prior art. As an advocate, the attorney desires broader claims for his or her client. As a type of protector of the public, the examiner desires narrower claims.

The situation, therefore, is like any business transaction. It is not unlike selling a house on the real estate market, for example. The two sides have their respective desires and somewhere in between is a "deal" to be made. In the house example, the market sets the backdrop for the negotiation. In the case of a patent application, the known prior art sets the backdrop. However, for the real estate example, consider this: having put your house on the market and then received your exact asking price, you may sense you have left "something on the table." Likewise, if you submit an initial set of patent claims that are allowed on the first action, similarly, you probably could have gotten broader claims allowed. Granted, you might now seek those broader claims via a continuation patent application claiming priority to your initial filing, but you might have gotten those broader claims allowed without a continuation patent application.

However, with all that said, there is a school of thought, and it does have some merit, that if you open with an overly broad set of patent claims, you may have trouble (or at least more trouble) getting *any* patent claims allowed. The thought process is that the examiner will focus on your broadest claim, which he or she may then reject. Likewise, the examiner should quickly glance through the dependent claims and may not see how any added subject matter via dependent claims makes any presented claims allowable. Thus, the examiner rejects all the claims.

On the next action, based on the prior art and reasoning to be provided, the attorney or agent may challenge the examiner's position, but the thought is that the examiner has given the case all the time he or she plans for now, and to get additional *serious* consideration from the examiner and/or further searching will require a continuation patent application, which will consume more resources, such as time and money.

Thus, advantages of broad claims include ferreting out the prior art and providing a good opening position for a negotiation. However, disadvantages include biasing the examiner against allowance, potentially raising the cost of patent prosecution.

Another potential advantage of being broad is that one may get an issued claim that is broader "at the margin" than you would otherwise have obtained.[135] The idea here is that the examiner might only be willing to fight so hard, or even, one might expect, your articulate and incisive legal arguments may convince the examiner to issue the broader claim.

Although actual data on this point is not available to the author's knowledge, most of the time the examiner rejects the initially presented claims, *regardless* of breadth or narrowness, and *regardless* of known prior art. Another way to say this is: due to his or her *bias*, regardless of what you present, the examiner will *find* a reason to reject the claims. This is not intended as a statement about a conspiracy at the PTO or a statement about competence. Rather, *this is a statement about human nature.*

This, of course, is more anecdotal than it is scientific, but may be worth this consideration at least: if you are trying to draft a claim of only sufficient breadth so that it will be allowed more easily, are you not, in a sense, *simply negotiating against yourself*? Again, examiners like to reject claims. It's their job. That is most certainly true. In general, it is reasonably likely that the examiner will at least initially reject your claims. This may be true even if you have written them to be allowable over the art you know of, and the examiner finds no

135. Further, it is entirely conceivable that you will get allowed claims that are broader than you "needed" or "expected." It generally depends on the quality of the prior art the examiner presents and the advocate's ability to distinguish that art.

better art. If you accept this latter proposition as true at least most of the time, then it seems logical, at least as an opening negotiating position, to file claims that are broader than you are truly seeking, just like no one puts their house on the market for the price they genuinely want. Rather, they always ask for more, expecting to be negotiated down to the price they want. Negotiation is a requirement in this setting—not by law, but by human nature, just as in any business transaction. *If you attempt to short circuit the negotiation process by deliberately sandbagging your initial set of claims, you will more likely end up with less than you had hoped or, even worse, less than you might have otherwise obtained.*

Another potential advantage of this potentially broader "at the margin" claim is that it is presumed valid, if issued. The burden would fall on another to show it is invalid by clear and convincing evidence in a federal court litigation. Of course, other proceedings are also available, such as *ex parte* reexamination, an IPR, or a post-grant review (PGR). A detailed discussion of these latter proceedings is beyond the scope of this book, but all have various trade-offs, including that the procedural law for IPRs and PGRs is still developing. Furthermore, it almost goes without saying that a broader claim opens one up to an attack from more prior art, a clear disadvantage; however, such is the fundamental trade-off in this discipline.

Be aware that a claim in which validity may be a close question, such as an issued broader "at the margin" claim, may still have value due to the procedural protections associated with being a claim of a patent. If a company's exposure to the claim is high (e.g., many $$$), they may prefer a more certain negotiated solution (e.g., a patent license or a covenant not to sue) to an uncertain litigation or other type of proceeding (e.g., IPR). After all, the claims after having their validity tested in one of these proceedings may emerge much stronger. A settled and reasonable negotiated solution may be better than rolling the dice.

This is typically how a rational decision-maker should operate unless the amount being requested for a license/covenant not to sue is ridiculous. Meaning, the amount is out of line with the value to the target company of avoiding a lawsuit or similar proceeding. In addition, as the patent claim drafter, you may manage the risk of invalidity of the broadest claim. For example, you may include a set of dependent claims in which one or more of these dependent claims may remain infringed, but also remains narrow enough to avoid problematic prior art. These are additional potential advantages associated with seeking broader claims.

An experienced patent attorney once told me that if you are *persistent enough*, you should be able to get a claim issued to meet your client's needs. Although this anecdotal statement is no guarantee, there still is at least an element of truth in this notion. However, this concept of persistence also implicitly points out a disadvantage of "swinging for the fences."

Your attempts at getting a broad claim issued will almost certainly result in additional cost, as mentioned. Furthermore, it will likely create more prosecution history estoppel and "claim estoppel." In general, "estoppel" refers to one being held to a position previously taken because another relied upon the position taken to their disadvantage. Under U.S. patent law, if you take a position before the PTO, you are held to that position, in theory at least, because it would disadvantage those who might rely on the written record. If, for example, you make an argument that your claim distinguishes from the prior art based on a particular interpretation of the claim language, you are not permitted to later advocate for another inconsistent interpretation. Patent law distinguishes between estoppel that affects literal claim scope (termed here "claim estoppel," but more typically viewed as "claim interpretation in light of the prosecution history"[136]) and estoppel that affects nonliteral claim scope (termed generally "prosecution history estoppel").

Of course, part of the idea of such a process is that you may argue about or even amend your claims to address previously unknown prior art found by the examiner. This is not necessarily bad; rather, it is expected. However, a claim amendment will likely create both types of estoppel and argument may also create both types of estoppel. Thus, an initial claim posture that does *not* require amendment and argument potentially might provide a better end result than one that does.

To appreciate the consequence, one should compare two hypothetical scenarios. In one, broad claims are presented that result in a protracted prosecution to secure allowance. In another, narrower claims are presented and no change to the claim language and no argument is required to secure allowance. Also, one should also compare the former hypothetical scenario with a scenario where at least some dependent claims of an initial set are allowed without amendment. The latter may result in less estoppel than may result from correspondence back and forth with the examiner that includes both various arguments and various amendments.

The point is that a greater amount of estoppel will likely result from a tortured prosecution involving several continuations, various pieces of art, and lots of attorney argument/amendment to secure allowance, than a simple "in and out" prosecution (e.g., no continuations needed). Of course, there is no way to predict which will result. This is where judgment, the specifics of the

136. What you say in prosecution will affect how the claim will be interpreted by a court in part because the public should be entitled to rely on such representations.

situation, client wishes, the technology, the art, the trade-offs just discussed, and so on, all bear on how best to draft the initial set of claims.

The bottom line is these types of considerations make PCD more than a commodity service. The issues are challenging and tend to vary by situation. In general, as a "default" approach with no special or unusual considerations, the conventional wisdom seems fairly good advice to follow while appreciating the potential consequences just discussed.

As one final comment, you might be surprised how a creative opposing counsel may come up with various arguable noninfringement arguments that you did not anticipate. Why create more opportunities for opposing counsel? Endeavor to write the broadest claim possible at the time based on the *known* prior art.

Searching the Prior Art before Drafting Patent Claims

Understand the risks and the benefits of searching the prior art before doing a search.

Another question that comes up a lot in the context of drafting patent claims is whether to conduct a prior art search and/or how much to expend in terms of resources. This was touched upon previously. Searches are, in general, notoriously poor, and high-quality searches are notoriously expensive. A mediocre-quality search should be about $2,000 to $3,000, meaning that it may uncover some relevant prior art.[137] However, if prior art to invalidate the invention exists, it may not necessarily have been uncovered. An extremely high-quality search, such as in anticipation of litigation, on the other hand, can cost $50,000 to $100,000, or more.[138]

Of course, more resources are coming online electronically, in general, to reduce searching costs so that for the same amount, a better search might be obtained. However, appreciate that searches are labor intensive, and the search quality depends significantly on the searcher. Giving a searcher a one- or two-page description of the technology with an expectation of thorough results is an expectation likely to be disappointed. For a cost-conscious client that nonetheless demands a search or for a situation where a search appears appropriate, one might suggest that the inventor use the PTO patent and published application databases. This has an advantage of increasing quality (since the inventor knows the invention technology well) while not

137. This is only a ballpark estimate based on the author's experience, not a number derived from careful studies.

138. This is only a ballpark estimate based on the author's experience, not a number derived from careful studies.

affecting out-of-pocket costs significantly. However, the client *must* also be made aware to keep careful records since forensic computer analysis has been used in the past to show that the inventor knew of prior art and did not disclose it.[139] In general, if conducting such a search, remind the client to err on the side of disclosing the art. If you submit the art in the manner specified in the PTO regulations,[140] the examiner should initial the submission, creating a presumption that it was considered and that the examiner did not find it to be material.[141]

Several advantages and disadvantages of searching have already been mentioned. Disadvantages include additional cost and marginal quality; however, advantages include that a search may at least uncover relevant art that is easy to locate, which may be used to draft the claims, and such art may be entered in the record, which supports validity if the claims issue. Some located prior art from a modestly priced search may potentially lead to including claims and description that you might have otherwise omitted. This latter point may be one of the better benefits/advantages.

The primary reason, however, most people search is to make sure the invention was not invented previously. Hence, these are typically referred to as "novelty searches." The chief benefit is to keep you from spending a lot of money to patent something that is unpatentable because it previously existed (i.e., getting a patent is expensive).

However, this reason to search may be slightly misleading. In truth, rarely does a search find the invention exactly (a plausible reason for this is discussed later). Instead, a bunch of similar technical art that may or may not bear on patentability is more typically located.

Now, keeping in mind the prior discussion, consider, for example, that an engineer who has worked in a particular technical field for 15 or 20 years comes to you with an invention. He comes to you at least believing that his invention is new because he has not seen anything like it in his 15 to 20 years of experience in the field. Plus, his visit to see you is not a mere whim. Rather, he must schedule an appointment, fit it into his busy schedule, and show up. Also, he may already know that to file a patent application will cost thousands and perhaps tens of thousands of dollars.

As a conditional probability, because he has never seen his invention during his 15 to 20 years working in the field at issue, there could be a 60 to 70 percent chance (perhaps higher) that the invention has not been done

139. *See* Eolas Techs. v. Microsoft, 399 F.3d 1325 (Fed. Cir. 2005).
140. *See* 37 C.F.R. § 1.56 (2024).
141. *See, e.g.*, MPEP, *supra* note 75, § 609.05(b).

exactly as he envisions it. Given this, is it then worth another $2,000 to $3,000 to have someone with a two-page description perform a search? The client pays a PTO filing fee of around $1,000 to $2,000 and that fee primarily pays to have the examiner search the art. So, by conducting a search in advance (especially if it is unlikely to cause the patent application to not be filed), you have, roughly, at least doubled your client's filing fees. In addition, the prior art uncovered will need to be analyzed, also raising the cost of preparing the application. So, at this point, with these considerations, such an expenditure for searching might be on the "fringe" of what might be undertaken—some might do it and some might not.

Now, let us consider additional issues related to whether to search. For one thing, there is relevant prior art that cannot be located by searching. Under the pre-AIA version of § 102, prior art under pre-AIA subsection 102(g), sometimes referred to as "secret prior art," would not be found by searching. This is material that qualifies as "prior art" by statute but is not easily accessible, such as research and development performed by others. However, this may be less of an issue due to the AIA, which removed that section and moved the United States from a first-to-invent patent system to essentially a first-to-file patent system.

However, assuming the AIA has addressed the issue just described, other potential prior art may also be problematic to locate. Under subsections 102(e) (pre-AIA) and 102(a)(2) (post-AIA), for example, various U.S. patent application filings that are published applications or published as patents, once published, constitute prior art as of their patent application filing date (*not* their publication date). If they are to be published applications, they will be unable to be located for at least 18 months of pendency following patent application filing, since that is when they are to be published. If they are designated for non-publication in the United States, they will not be published until they are issued as patents. For example, it is *not* unknown for someone to sue on a patent, only to have it invalidated by a prior filed, but later issuing patent (that was not published as a patent application at 18 months) because the patent issued after suit was filed.

For another thing, and it absolutely does happen, a search may uncover patents that could be infringed by the product that would be sold if the invention being searched were put into practice.[142] Here is the problem. Once you know about prior art that might be material to patentability of the claims to

142. This also could happen without invalidating the prior art patents or necessarily preventing patentability of the subject matter being searched. It just depends on timing, the technical description, and the scope of the issued claims.

be presented, you and your client *must* disclose it to the PTO if you file a patent application with those claims. In this hypothetical, it would be a matter of public record that you and your client knew about this patent, which your client's product may later be accused of infringing. Furthermore, under U.S. patent law, if your client knows of a patent that it may infringe and does not have a reasonable basis for a good faith belief that the allegedly infringed claims of the patent are invalid, unenforceable, or not infringed, your client could be liable for treble damages.[143] In other words, ignorance, quite literally here, is bliss. If a client, for example, does not know about a patent and infringes it, that client might be liable for lost profits and/or a reasonable royalty by statute.[144] If the client, however, knows about the patent, and infringes it anyway, the client may be liable for up to three times that amount.

Let us think about a rational decision-maker. If that decision-maker would change what it would do knowing about a patent it might infringe, it may very well want to know about that patent and the search may provide meaningful information beyond what was intended. However, if that decision-maker does not intend to alter its plans regardless of such a patent, which may sometimes be the situation, that decision-maker, if rational, would prefer *not* to know about that patent. A rational decision-maker would prefer not to know about that patent, on balance, because, at best, it may be of marginal use in deciding whether to seek patent protection on technology that may be commercialized. Realize that there is no duty to search. However, having performed a search, the inventor(s), the attorney, and the company, as the applicant, all *have* a duty to disclose information material to patentability that has been uncovered.[145] Here, it might be said that ignorance is bliss.

One way to view searching in this context is as having a "risk-adjusted" cost to the information obtained *beyond* merely the out-of-pocket cost to do the search. The real question, in context, is whether the information sought is worth that risk-adjusted cost, such as the risk that an adverse patent may be uncovered. For this reason, different companies have different policies regarding whether it is appropriate to search and/or study prior art. This is an area where reasonable minds may differ. However, what is important is to understand the reason for looking at prior art before doing so. There may, for example, be a legitimate technical reason unrelated to seeking patent protection for studying prior art. One should at least be mindful of the cost/risk associated with seeking such information before beginning.

---

143. *See* 35 U.S.C. § 284 (2024).
144. *Id.*
145. *See, e.g.*, 37 C.F.R. § 1.56 (2024).

There is yet another risk-adjusted cost to the information obtained if a search is performed. Again, these are termed "novelty searches." However, more often, such searches typically uncover what we call "103 art." This refers to prior art that by itself could *not* be used in a novelty rejection under § 102, but the uncovered prior art could potentially be used in an obviousness rejection under § 103. An examiner is permitted to combine multiple pieces of prior art for a rejection under § 103. Thus, it is entirely possible that an examiner may refuse to issue submitted claims based on a § 103 document *that you provided from a search*, despite your genuine belief that the particular § 103 document would not be a barrier to patentability. The irony is that, if you had not performed the search, the examiner might have allowed the claims. Furthermore, the search likely did not serve its main function of preventing filing of the application due to lack of novelty. Again, here, ignorance is bliss because there is nothing wrong with not conducting the search.

Appreciate that much of the previous discussion is about risk and probabilities. However, if you believe the risks just described could never happen, you would be mistaken. Granted, it is anecdotal, but all the risks described have happened to the author, and, in some instances, have occurred more than once. That does not mean that it has a high probability of occurring; however, it means it is an *actual* risk.

There are a few more additional points to consider in the context of making a fully informed decision. By doing a search, you may uncover prior art that ultimately leads you to add more dependent claims and additional technical disclosure. If you choose not to search, the burden may fall on you to be reasonably thorough in preparing a patent application with a complete description and a set of claims having wide scope. Realize you could be undone, so to speak, by a document you might have been able to amend around with appropriate written description. However, by not searching, you will not know of the document and, consequently, potentially may not create such written description support.

It is also helpful to be aware that many and perhaps even most patent-savvy technology companies and patent-savvy IP firms do *not* perform searches except in a few special circumstances. They likely believe the resources that would be used to search are better allocated to preparing a better-quality patent application. However, in contrast, also be aware that some companies in the business of getting patents and collecting significant royalties from those patents have a policy of *always* having a search performed. This may be speculative, but a plausible reason may be that this, in general, provides prior art to disclose. Like an inoculation, such prior art may help undermine a charge of inequitable conduct for deliberately withholding known prior art if litigation ensues.[146] Companies in the business of filing, issuing, and asserting patents may do things in prosecution designed to undermine commonly used patent litigation tactics. One such tactic by a defendant is usually to include a charge of inequitable conduct for withholding known, material prior art. The recommendation here, however, is to not perform a search except in special circumstances. Examples of unusual circumstances may include that the inventors are not knowledgeable about the art, or it is too hard to believe the technology at issue has not been done previously given what is known, and so on.

Also, as previously discussed, this does not necessarily mean never look at prior art. Instead, it means understand the reasons for doing so and be mindful of the risks. There are legitimate technical reasons for studying prior art but be sure you have done the cost/benefit analysis ahead of time.

Questions

1. What are the key statutory sections related to claim drafting and what legal issues relate to those statutory sections?
2. How do precision, vagueness, and breadth relate to claim drafting?
3. Summarize three schools of thought regarding how broad the claims presented to the PTO should be. What are the reasons behind each approach?
4. What is the trade-off between presenting broad versus narrow claims? What is a strategy to deal with the legal risks presented by broad versus narrow patent claims?
5. Try to articulate the difference between claim breadth and claim vagueness in words.
6. Discuss some of the advantages and some of the disadvantages of presenting broad claims to the PTO.
7. Discuss some of the advantages and disadvantages of searching the art prior to filing a patent application.

146. See Chapter 6, discussing inequitable conduct and how to avoid it.

Chapter 3
Introduction to the Patent Claim and Its Parts

Understand the constituent parts of a patent claim (preamble, transition word or phrase, and body) and how to draft a patent claim so that the separate parts are clearly identifiable.
Make where the preamble and transition phrase ends and the claim body begins clear with punctuation.

In this chapter we introduce the basics of a patent claim. This introduction involves a discussion of the constituent parts of a patent claim. In the next chapter we introduce several basic patent claim drafting concepts. These concepts include the statutorily prescribed classes or categories of claims, dependent claims versus independent claims, structure versus function, method versus apparatus, and other features of patent claims.

The Patent Claim and Its Parts

What Is a Patent Claim?

A patent claim is a set of words that are formulated to define a set of legal rights. Of course, this describes many legal documents that affect or create legal rights. In a U.S. patent, the patent claims are the numbered "run-on sentences" at the end of the patent. The claims section is at the end of the patent and begins with "I claim," "We claim," "What is claimed is that," or similar language, followed by a colon, and then a sequence of numbered partial sentences to, in effect, complete a sentence that begins with "I claim:" and so on. Therefore, each patent claim ends with a period. Omitting the period may create interpretive problems that may even result in patent claim invalidity.[1] This latter format of a patent claim is largely historical.[2]

A reason claims tend to be so cumbersome is because the words are used in a reasonably precise manner to define the "metes and bounds" of the invention being patented without reference to other material. A patent is analogous to a real estate deed that provides notice to the public regarding the property boundaries. The patent claims serve to define the boundaries of the invention so that a member of the public is on notice regarding the scope of rights granted by the patent. In this manner, members of the public being on notice are able to avoid "trespassing" on legal rights owned by another.

With a deed, however, the object of the rights associated with the deed is real estate (termed the "res") and is tangible. For intellectual property, such as a patent, the res *itself* (as opposed to the legal rights) is not tangible. Hence, the term "intellectual" property.

Patent claims cover more than simply the embodiments described in the specification. Rather, what a patent claim covers is determined by the claim language used.[3] This is one reason why patents are so valuable and the language of a patent claim so important.

By custom, there are three parts to a patent claim: a preamble, a transition word or phrase, and a claim body. Previously, we have provided several claim examples that illustrate this basic structure. In general, a patent claim includes elements and limitations that, taken together, with their relationships, constitute the literal scope of rights granted if the patent claim is issued. To be more precise, the patent claim covers the right to (exclude others from) making, using, selling, offering for sale, and importing into the United States physical structures, processes, materials, and so on that fall within the literal scope of the patent claim.

Previously, we discussed the process of "reading a claim" on an accused product (or service). It is the patent claim words that are used in patent examination to determine whether the patent claim distinguishes sufficiently from known prior art to be patentable over that known prior art. The patent claim, in general, should be construed consistently in patent litigation as it is in

1. See *Cultor Corp. v. A.E. Staley*, 224 F.3d 1328 (Fed. Cir. 2000), in which the Federal Circuit construed a claim narrowly based on a comma. See *Allen Engineering Corp. v. Bartell Industries*, 299 F.3d 1336 (Fed. Cir. 2002), where a claim did not contain any punctuation at all at the end of the limitation and the Federal Circuit found the claim indefinite under 35 U.S.C. § 112 due to a truncated limitation.

2. See *In re Fressola*, 22 U.S.P.Q.2d 1828 (Comm'r Pat. & Trademarks 1992), in which Commissioner Manpack ruled that "[t]he single claim sentence requirement is within the [U.S. Patent and Trademark Office's (PTO's)] statutory authority and is consistent with the statutory purpose of 35 U.S.C. §112 ¶ 2."

3. *See, e.g.*, Vitronics Corp. v. Conceptronic, Inc., 90 F.3d 1576 (Fed. Cir. 1996) ("We look to the words of the claims themselves . . . to define the scope of the patented invention.").

patent examination. Consequently, a similar "reading on" process is used to determine literal, direct infringement of a patent claim.

Section 101 of title 35 enumerates the statutorily permitted classes or categories of patent claims. It states (emphasis added): "Whoever invents or discovers any new and useful *process*, *machine*, *manufacture*, or *composition of matter*, or any new and useful improvement thereof, may obtain a patent therefor, subject to the conditions and requirements of this title."

The statutory classes or categories of claims are process claims (also called method claims), machine claims (also called apparatus claims), manufacture claims (also called article of manufacture claims), and composition of matter claims. The Manual of Patent Examining Procedure (MPEP) section 2106.03, provided in Chapter 4, is instructive on these categories of patentable subject matter. In Chapter 4, we give examples of claims for each category. We also discuss other types of claims that are often used.

The Patent Claim Preamble

Use claim preambles that are short and that avoid introducing claim limitations.

Previously, the basic structure of a claim was discussed as including a preamble, transition word or phrase, and claim body. This structure is primarily based on custom, but because federal courts expect this basic structure and some canons of construction revolve around this approach, it is highly recommended that it be used. Adhering to this basic approach and, furthermore, making clear your intention regarding how the language of a claim you draft clearly divides among these separate components promotes certainty regarding how the claim should be interpreted. On the other hand, major deviations from this basic structure raise the risk that the intended meaning of the claim will be more likely to be challenged with the ultimate decision as to claim scope being put in the hands of another,[4] who may interpret the claim differently from what you, the drafter, intended.

The preamble for these purposes is everything from the beginning of the claim up to but not including the transition word or phrase. How do you know which word is the transition word? Again, we recommend a structure that clearly signals your intention. Thus, we suggest you always use a colon immediately after the transition word or phrase.

Hence, here is a simple diagram of the basic structure:

[claim number]. [claim preamble] [claim transition word or words]:

[claim body].

4. Such as an examiner at the U.S. PTO.

The punctuation shown is believed important here to signal how the claim is divided into the basic components of a patent claim. Without these "signals," an opportunity exists for someone to more easily argue that part of the intended preamble is in the claim body or part of the intended claim body is in the preamble, for example. Since preambles are not necessarily limiting, this might create problems relative to a desired interpretation.

Likewise, with uncertainty where the preamble ends and the claim body begins, someone may argue that another word may be the transition word of the claim, such as "having." The issue with a transition other than "comprising" is that it may be found to be something other than open, depending on other factors.[5] If "comprising" is not employed (or one of the other well-established transition phrases), a court will endeavor to determine what might have otherwise been intended, based on the specification, file history, and so on. The claim may not be determined to be "open." The outcome, hence, may potentially turn out other than as intended.

Catalina Marketing International v. Coolsavings.com, Inc.
289 F.3d 801
United States Court of Appeals for the Federal Circuit
May 8, 2002, Decided

Questions

1. What were the number and types of claims at issue in the case?
2. Why do you think it requires review of the entire patent including the file history to determine whether a preamble is a limitation of the claim?
3. What do you think the court means by a preamble is limiting if it is "necessary to give life, meaning, and vitality"[6] to the claim?
4. The court provides a number of situations in which a preamble may be limiting and situations in which a preamble is not limiting. What are those situations? Why do you think the court says there is no "litmus test" that defines when a preamble limits a claim?
5. If a preamble is not a limitation, then what is its purpose?

---

5. *See* Crystal Semiconductor Corp. v. TriTech Microelecs. Int'l, Inc., 246 F.3d 1336, 1338 (Fed. Cir. 2001); *cf.* Moleculon Rsch. v. CBS, 793 F.2d 1261, 1271 n.8 (Fed. Cir.), *cert. denied*, 479 U.S. 1030 (1987).
6. Catalina Mktg. Int'l v. Coolsavings.com, Inc., 289 F.3d 801, 808 (Fed. Cir. 2002).

6. Do you believe the court implies that a preamble for an apparatus claim is less likely to be limiting than for a method claim? If so, why is that the case?
7. The phrase at issue is "located at predesignated sites such as consumer stores."[7] Do you see any issues with the use of the word "predesignated"? Do you see any issues with use of the language "such as"?
8. What was the basis for the court to remand claim 25 for consideration of infringement under the doctrine of equivalents but not literal infringement? Why is it relevant that Catalina did not amend or argue the language around the location of the coupon terminal? Why do you think the appellate court came to the conclusion that prosecution history estoppel (PHE) did not apply in this situation?

Arctic Cat Inc. v. GEP Power Products
919 F.3d 1320
United States Court of Appeals for the Federal Circuit
March 26, 2019, Decided

Questions

1. In *Arctic Cat*, how did the Federal Circuit in general justify the rule that preambles are not necessarily limiting?
2. How did the Federal Circuit justify that the preamble was not limiting in the particular situation of this case? Note that the title of both patent applications is "Power Distribution Module for Personal Recreational Vehicle" and each discussed personal recreational vehicles. What does this tell you about claim language versus specification language? Do you think the outcome of this issue might have been different in a lawsuit asserting the claims against a personal recreational vehicle?
3. In the case, the court states:

> We have long ruled that "a preamble is not limiting 'where a patentee defines a structurally complete invention in the claim body and uses the preamble only to state a purpose or intended use for the invention.'" *Catalina*, 289 F.3d at 808 (quoting *Rowe*, 112 F.3d at 478); *see Georgetown Rail Equip. Co. v. Holland L.P.*, 867 F.3d 1229, 1236–37 (Fed. Cir. 2017); *Deere*, 703 F.3d at 1358. That rule is grounded in the statutory distinction, in identifying the permissible subject matter of a patent

7. *Id.* at 807.

> claim, between a physical product (which may be defined in part by its claimed functional capabilities) and activities that constitute a process (which may include a new "use" of a known invention). *See* 35 U.S.C. § 101 ("process" versus "machine, manufacture, or composition of matter"); 35 U.S.C. § 100(b) (defining "process"); *MasterMine Software, Inc. v. Microsoft Corp.*, 874 F.3d 1307, 1312–16 (Fed. Cir. 2017) (explaining impermissibility of mixing products with processes in claims). In particular, the rule against giving invention-defining effect to intended-use preamble language reflects a longstanding substantive aspect of the patent statute—specifically, the "well settled" fundamental principle "that the recitation of a new intended use for an old product does not make a claim to that old product patentable."[8]

What is the distinction the court makes between products and processes? How do you interpret the explanation: "the 'well settled' fundamental principle 'that the recitation of a new intended use for an old product does not make a claim to that old product patentable'"?

4. How could the claims have been drafted to reduce the likelihood of this outcome?
5. Why do you think the drafter included language directed to a "personal recreational vehicle"?
6. Does the Federal Circuit appear to encourage or discourage the use of preambles?
7. What regulation is the only one to mention a preamble and why does it do so?
8. What do you think of the Federal Circuit's analogy with a Jepson claim?
9. What do you think of the court's diligence analysis?

Theory of the Preamble

Patents or, more precisely, patent claims, are often compared with contracts and with statutes. Patent claims have similarities with both and differences from both. A contract is a private document defining legal rights between at least two private parties. A statute is a public document and, in general, often defines rights with respect to members of the public that may be the object of the language of the statute.

8. Arctic Cat Inc. v. GEP Power Prods., 919 F.3d 1320, 1328 (Fed. Cir. 2019).

A patent claim is neither of these, but similar to each. A patent claim is like a statute in that it may restrict actions of the members of the public. Courts often refer to the "public notice function" of patent claims. However, similar to a contract and less like a statute, a patent claim creates legal rights for the owner. Yet, unlike a contract and more like a statute, those rights are with respect to members of the public, whose actions (make, use, sell, etc.), again, may be circumscribed by a patent claim or claims. Furthermore, more like a contract and less like a statute, the words of a patent claim are often the result of drafting and negotiation between two parties.[9]

For such reasons, while there is some similarity in the rules used to interpret these respective documents, there are also significant differences in the rules of interpretation that govern the three situations.

With this as background, it is worthy of mention that all three—statute, contract, and patent claim—typically include a preamble. For a contract and a statute, a preamble often states the background and/or purpose of the statute or contract, but, generally, these preambles precede the portion of these documents that are employed to define the legal rights that are being created. Consequently, for contracts and statutes, the preamble is to set the stage, so to speak, for the creation of legal rights, but does not itself, in general, affect those rights.

However, if there is ambiguity in the portion of the document that is employed to create such legal rights, courts often rely on the preamble to help resolve the ambiguity. Thus, the preamble, for contracts and statutes, may in some cases affect the legal rights created by the document, although that was not the purpose of the preamble when written.

So, it may also be said to be the case for preambles of patent claims. Generally, such language is simply a statement of intention that was not, in general, necessarily intended to affect the scope of the patent claim.[10] However, despite that general rule, there are situations identified by courts where a patent preamble may be used to limit the scope of a patent claim. In *Catalina Marketing v. Coolsavings.com*,[11] the Federal Circuit noted that no litmus test defines when a preamble limits claim scope. Thus, whether a preamble is limiting may be challenging to predict.

9. For a patent claim, it is typically an examiner and legal representative of the applicant; for a contract, it is usually the parties to the contract or their legal representatives.

10. *See Catalina Mktg.*, 289 F.3d at 808. The court also discusses that a limiting preamble "breathes life and meaning" into the claim.

11. *Id.*

Claim preambles, therefore, present a variety of risks. One risk is that the preamble will inadvertently introduce an unintended limitation into the claims. This is what most commonly occurs. However, another risk is that you may, in fact, expect the preamble to introduce a limitation to a patent claim to distinguish from the prior art (a risky approach); but a court may, instead, conclude that the preamble is not a limitation and, therefore, hold the claim invalid.[12] Likewise, if a court construes the preamble to be a limitation, then there is always the risk that the court will conclude that the limitation is not adequately supported by the specification, is not enabled by the specification, is indefinite, and so on, perhaps because at the time of drafting the claim preamble language was not given sufficiently close attention in comparison with the language of the claim body.

One possible approach to drafting preambles is to limit the preamble to recite *only* the statutory class or category of the invention such as "A method comprising:"[13] and so on. Although such a restrictive approach is not absolutely necessary, it is recommended that care be used to draft the preamble and to ensure that the preamble is short and to the point. Some simple examples are provided here.[14]

Examples:

A system	A subsystem
An apparatus	An integrated circuit
A module	A method of communicating [anything, e.g., an electronic message]
A composition of matter	
A machine	A method of operating [anything, e.g., a system]
An article	A method of processing [anything, e.g., signals]
A component	A method of manufacturing [anything, e.g., a component]
A process	

12. *See Arctic Cat Inc.*, 919 F.3d at 1320.

13. Note that "comprising" is actually not part of the preamble, but is the transition word, as explained in more detail later.

14. See Robert Kahrl & Stuart Soffer, Thesaurus of Claim Construction (2011), for additional examples of terms for use in a preamble.

A circuit	A method of using [anything, e.g., a device]
A device	A method of coding
A method	A method of decoding
A composite	A method of synthesizing
A material	A set of [anything, e.g., components]

Method claims deserve special mention in the context of preambles. It is common practice when drafting method claims to use the preamble to provide antecedent basis for words, usually tangible elements, that are then used later in the body of the claim. Consider the following example.

EXAMPLE 3.1

I claim:

1. A method of cooking pasta comprising:

   placing the pasta in boiling water; and waiting until the pasta becomes at least slightly tender.

As is clear in this example, the preamble provides antecedent basis for the word *pasta*. In this case, the preamble will likely be construed to be limiting, although perhaps, in this example, with little consequence. However, because the words of the preamble provide antecedent basis for terms used in the body of the claim, for this situation, courts usually find preambles to be limiting.[15] Of course, in this simple example, the claim could have been drafted so that the preamble did not provide antecedent basis, as follows:

I claim:

1. A method comprising:

   placing pasta in boiling water; and waiting until the pasta becomes at least slightly tender.

15. *See Catalina Mktg.*, 289 F.3d at 808.

However, for more complex method claims, drafting the claim so that the preamble does not serve this function and, consequently, is not limiting can be much trickier, depending upon the situation.

There is also a legitimate question whether one should use the preamble for antecedent basis, employ express recitations in the body for antecedent basis, or employ inferential claiming.[16] This is an area where reasonable minds may differ and different situations may suggest different approaches.

The trade-offs may be complex and require use of judgment. Generally, we recommend preambles be short and to the point to reduce uncertainty as to what may or may not be limiting. However, this suggests that antecedent basis for any hardware or tangible elements of the claim, for example, would be in the claim body. This may subject a method claim to the risk of a challenge that it is indefinite by making it unclear whether the patent claim is an apparatus claim or a method claim.[17] If the method claim is carefully drafted, however, we believe this is an acceptable risk, but it is something to consider. Following is another, more complex, example method claim in which the tangible elements are included in the preamble to provide antecedent basis rather than relying on the patent claim body, which is a legitimate alternate approach.

I claim:

1. A method of operating a module, the module including at least one integrated circuit chip comprising a plurality of series N-type metal oxide semiconductor (NMOS) field effect transistors in a series connected stack configuration that comprises at least one series NMOS field effect transistor including a body, the at least one series NMOS field effect transistor either to pass a radio frequency (RF) signal in a series enable state or to not pass the RF signal in a series disable state, the method comprising:

   electrically biasing the body of the at least one series NMOS field effect transistor of the module in the series disable state to a voltage level substantially more negative than the lowest voltage level of the following: ground, a direct current (DC) voltage level of a source of the at least one series NMOS field effect transistor of the module, and a DC voltage level of a drain of the at least one series NMOS field effect transistor of the module.

---

16. Inferential claiming is addressed in more detail later in this chapter.
17. See Chapter 6 in connection with mixing statutory classes in a single patent claim.

It is noted that this claim is a one act or action method claim.

Also, as a separate point regarding preambles, the preamble may take on added importance for an improvement claim, such as Jepson-style claims or European-style claims.[18]

SIMO Holdings, Inc. v. H.K. uCloudlink Network Technology, Ltd.
983 F.3d 1367
United States Court of Appeals for the Federal Circuit
January 5, 2021, Decided

Questions

1. The appellate court implies that there is some ambiguity regarding the preamble versus the body. How does the court resolve that issue of construction? What, instead, might be the preamble and why? Why do you think the alternate construction did not occur to the parties? Would that not have resolved the issue regarding the limiting language?
2. Note that the court says it reaches the same conclusion regardless of which interpretation of the preamble is used. However, suppose the preamble assumed by the parties had not been limiting. Might there be a problem with the claim in that instance? Where do you think the drafter would have put the colon if he had put one in?
3. Note that the district court judge simply concluded that the word "and" should mean "or." Do you think district court judges do this much? If so, why? What is the problem with such an approach?
4. Note that the court references *Superguide Corp. v. DirecTV Enterprises, Inc.*[19] and its discussion of grammar. What does this discussion tell you about drafting patent claims?
5. The court seems to state a general principle regarding parallelism and permits that to trump the specification's embodiments. When do you think a court should rely on the claim language and when do you think a court should rely on the specification in situations like this where the apparent construction would suggest a claim that probably no one infringes?

18. See Chapter 4 regarding Jepson- and European-style claims.
19. 358 F.3d 870 (Fed. Cir. 2004).

The Patent Claim Transition Word

In the predictable art, use "comprising" as the transition word or phrase.
Use other well-accepted transition phrases to vary claim scope in the unpredictable arts.
Do not introduce new or uncommon types of transition phrases in patent claims during drafting.

We often speak of the transition word; however, truly, we should refer to the transition phrase, because in many cases a transition may involve more than one word. The most common transition word is "comprising"; however, two other commonly used transition phrases are "consisting of" or "consisting essentially of." It is quite likely that the word choice for the transition may be the most important of all the words chosen for a patent claim, granted that this choice is highly circumscribed (e.g., to a limited number of possibilities).

This choice has significant importance because, more than any other words, the transition word or phrase fundamentally affects claim scope. For this reason, it is critically important that through your claim format and claim language you make it absolutely clear which word or words you intend to be the transition word or phrase.

Invitrogen Corp. v. Biocrest Manufacturing, L.P.
327 F.3d 1364
United States Court of Appeals for the Federal Circuit
May 7, 2003, Decided

Questions

1. The court addresses two claim construction issues. What are those issues?
2. Why was the district court's conclusion "the growing step (a) to mean that 'growth must be performed at a temperature within 18° C to 32° C, inclusive, and that at no time prior to freezing can the temperature of the cells exceed 32° C,'"[20] not correct according to the appellate court?
3. The court explains that during patent prosecution the originally submitted patent claim was amended. According to the court:

> When entering a rejection during prosecution of the application that led to the '797 patent, the [U.S. Patent and Trademark Office (PTO)]

20. Invitrogen Corp. v. Biocrest Mfg., L.P., 327 F.3d 1364, 1367 (Fed. Cir. 2003).

> examiner stated that 18° C to 32° C was essential to the invention. The applicants then amended the claims to replace "less than 37° C" with "18° C to 32° C" in claim 1. The applicants then stated that their amendment ensures that the claimed invention is different from prior art showing growth at 37° C. Furthermore, the applicants noted that the invention avoids undesirable effects of growth at 37° C.[21]

In light of this amendment and statements during prosecution, why does the appellate court nonetheless conclude: "The prosecution history does not show any clear and unambiguous disavowal of steps in advance of the step of growing E. coli cells in the claimed temperature range."?[22] What significance did the realization that the district court's interpretation would exclude example 3 from patent coverage have?

4. Although the patentee won ultimately, are there ways that the claim might have been drafted or remarks that might have been made during prosecution to clarify claim scope? In other words, the court concludes: "At the outset, the claim language itself does not preclude growth in advance of the first step in the claim. Step (a) of claim 1 specifies E. coli population growth at 18° C to 32° C. . . . At no point has this claim addressed or limited any activities that may have occurred before steps (a) and (b)."[23] The court reaches this result in part due to the use of the word "comprising." This is a good case to show the power of the transition "comprising" with respect to claim scope. However, since the patent prosecutor knew that the claim was intended to cover situations in which cell growth took place "before population growth at 18° C to 32° C," would it have been prudent to state on the record that the claim does not preclude cell growth at other temperatures "prior to population growth at 18° C to 32° C"? Why or why not? Are there ways that the claim might have been drafted differently to clarify scope? For example, the court interpreted the claim and prosecution history to "emphasize[] the advantages of growth at 18° C to 32° C immediately before rendering the E. coli competent."[24] What are the advantages and disadvantages of clarifying intended scope more clearly (noting that one disadvantage of the current claim is that it required an appeal to the Federal Circuit to achieve the desired claim scope)?

---

21. *Id.*
22. *Id.* at 1369.
23. *Id.*
24. *Id.*

5. Another claim construction issue related to recital of "improved competence" in the claim preamble. As we saw previously, claim preambles are not necessarily limiting. Here, however, both the district court and the appellate court found the preamble to be limiting. A reasonable question might be, was the language "improved competence" *required* in order to distinguish the claim from the prior art? If so, relying on the language added to the preamble is a bit risky since the court might have determined the preamble is not a limitation, as one party argued here. Without having the prior art ourselves, it is difficult to tell. Perhaps the limitation added to (a) was sufficient.
6. The key point, of course, is that it does not matter whether it was needed or not. Having put the argument on the record and even having amended the preamble, the patentee is held to the position taken before the PTO even if not needed to distinguish from the cited art. The patentee may not take one position before the PTO and then, having convinced the examiner to let the claims issue, take an inconsistent position in litigation. This is classic PHE. However, PHE is limited to the doctrine of equivalents. As the court stated: "While prosecution history estoppel does not apply to determining literal claim scope, statements to an examiner during prosecution before the United States Patent and Trademark Office (PTO) may also illuminate the scope of the claims."[25] This is sometimes referred to by others as "claim estoppel"; however, the Federal Circuit simply refers to it as claim interpretation (in this case, in light of the file history). However, how clear must a statement be in order to be considered a statement regarding intended claim scope?

Shire Development, LLC v. Watson Pharmaceuticals, Inc.
848 F.3d 981
United States Court of Appeals for the Federal Circuit
February 10, 2017, Decided

Questions

1. What was the factual basis for Shire filing its lawsuit against Watson?
2. What is the transition word for the claim at issue? Since it is not "consisting of" how does the issue of interpretation of "consisting of" arise?
3. What is a Markush group and why it is being used here?

---

25. *Id.* at 1367.

4. What is the presumption that applies when the language "consisting of" is used in a claim?
5. The court says there is one rare exception to the presumed interpretation of "consisting of." What is that rare exception? What do you think is the logical basis for that exception based on the discussion in the case?
6. The district court applied the exception from the *Norian v. Stryker*[26] case and found the claim to be infringed although the outer hydrophilic matrix contained magnesium stearate, a substance not included in the Markush group of 1(b) of the claim. What was the district court's rationale?
7. Here, the court treats "comprising" differently than in the prior *Biocrest* case. How do you distinguish the cases?

HZNP Medicines LLC v. Actavis Laboratories UT, Inc.
940 F.3d 680
United States Court of Appeals for the Federal Circuit
October 10, 2019, Decided

Questions

1. What was the basis for Horizon bringing a patent infringement suit against Actavis?[27]
2. Essentially, the lawsuit involved two types of patent claims. Referring to § 101, what were the types of patent claims at issue? Technically, who were the direct infringers of the two types of claims? How do these types of claims relate to 35 U.S.C. § 271(e)(2)(A)?
3. The district court construed the claims at issue and therefore ruled many claims to be indefinite on summary judgment. What were the disputed terms and what was the basis for the district court's summary judgment ruling?
4. The case also included an inducement to infringe assertion. What was the basis for this assertion? How did the district court handle the inducement to infringe assertion?
5. The case went to trial regarding the obviousness of claim 12 of the '913 patent. Why was the trial focused on that one issue alone?

---

26. 363 F.3d 1321 (Fed. Cir. 2004).
27. *See* 35 U.S.C. § 271(e)(2)(A).

6. Both the district court and the Federal Circuit found the "degrades" limitation to be indefinite. One reason was based on degradation results of the formulation impurity A results. However, another reason was "because neither the claims nor the specification disclose the means to evaluate degradation."[28] What do you think about these reasons, especially the latter one?
7. The important part of the opinion relates to the transition phrase "consisting essentially of." Again, there was bitter disagreement between the majority and the dissent. What was the issue and the positions of the majority and the dissent?
8. The majority is of the view that the language "consisting of" could have easily been used in place of "consisting essentially of." However, would that not have created an easy design around? How does 35 U.S.C. § 271(e)(2)(A) bear on this question?
9. Given the risk of indefiniteness of one linguistic formulation ("consisting essentially of") versus the risk of design around of the other formulation ("consisting of"), do you have any thoughts about the preferable formulation or at least how and/or when to use each? How easy is it to identify the basic and novel properties of claimed subject matter in a manner that does not lead to a dispute?
10. Apparently, use of "consisting essentially of" made the claims indefinite because the scope of novel properties of claimed subject matter was unclear. Which properties had unclear scope according to the district court and why? According to the Federal Circuit and why?
11. What was it about "better drying time" that made it indefinite? Do you think one of ordinary skill would be able to ascertain better drying time? Also, was there any question of an unlisted ingredient that might have affected the property of better drying time such that the scope of the claims was unclear in this case?
12. A separate question was whether the label at issue induced infringement of the method of use claims. Both the district court and the Federal Circuit ruled on summary judgment that there was no inducement. There seemed to be no question that the label might lead some users to fall within the scope of the method claim. Thus, the crucial issue seemed to be specific intent to infringe and whether that could be "inferred" from the language of the label. Given the language of the label, do you agree that this issue was resolvable as a matter of law?

---

28. HZNP Meds. LLC v. Actavis Laby's UT, Inc., 940 F.3d 680, 684 (Fed. Cir. 2019).

13. Finally, a trial was held on a single claim, claim 12 (provided in the dissent). Ultimately, the claim was held valid (as not obvious) and Actavis conceded infringement. Note that the transition word for that claim was "comprising." Given the outcome, were the formulations "consisting of" or "consisting essentially of" needed in this situation?

Theory of the Transition Word

The theory of the transition word (or phrase) follows directly from the theory of a patent claim. A patent claim is a set of elements and limitations that in combination define the metes and bounds of an invention.[29] However, one fine point about claim types relates to differences in technology. As a formal, legal matter, the patent statutes that govern U.S. patent law are neutral with respect to technology.[30]

As a patentee, one would like a claim to define, via the language used, the elements, limitations, and relationships considered to be the invention. However, likewise, from the perspective of scope of rights, if someone makes, uses, or sells a product that is exactly as recited with claim language, generally, a patentee would *not* want that individual to escape liability by simply adding something else to the product. Otherwise, it would take little effort to design around a patent claim. Such a patent system would not provide much legal protection. Hence, the use of the word "comprising."

There is also a good policy reason for this approach. In general, the idea of a patent system is for others to build on the work of the patentee. Thus, if someone, for example, builds a better mousetrap, it stands to reason that if the patent on the original mousetrap has not expired, the owner of the mousetrap patent should have rights as to the improved mousetrap (assuming the claims are properly drafted to accomplish such a result).

This point relates to the notion that, in general, most patents represent *improvements* on something that preceded the patent, often, but not necessarily, another patented technology. The system is designed with this in mind and supports the use of "comprising." A stylized example relates to the steam engine versus the combustion engine.

---

29. *See* Phillips v. AWH Corp., 415 F.2d 1303, 1312 (Fed. Cir. 2005) (en banc) ("It is a 'bedrock principle' of patent law that 'the claims of a patent define the invention to which the patentee is entitled the right to exclude.'"). *See also* Constant v. Advanced Micro-Devices, Inc., 848 F.2d 1560, 1571, 7 U.S.P.Q.2d 1057, 1064 (Fed. Cir. 1988); Dollar Elec. Co. v. Syndevco, Inc., 205 U.S.P.Q. 949, 959 (E.D. Mich. 1979), *aff'd*, 669 F.2d 1370, 214 U.S.P.Q. 241 (6th Cir. 1982).

30. *See* Dan L. Burk & Mark A. Lemley, *Policy Levers in Patent Law*, 89 VA. L. REV. 1575, 1654–55 (2003); William A. Drennan, *The Patented Loophole: How Should Congress Respond to This Judicial Invention?*, 59 FLA. L. REV. 229, 323–28 (2007).

Suppose the steam engine is invented[31] by A. The notion of an engine, being new, is broadly defined as a machine or apparatus that converts up-and-down motion (i.e., motion by pistons) to rotary motion (i.e., motion by wheels or a rotary rod, etc.). Thus, a skilled practitioner may, if extremely successful, obtain an issued claim 1 reciting:

1. A machine comprising: an engine.[32]

This claim would have been novel, nonobvious, useful, and so on, at the time the invention was made. Now, we note, that the embodiment in the technical specification is a steam engine. However, it is well established that the patent claims are not limited to the description in the specification. Furthermore, an issued claim 2 of the same patent might recite:

2. The machine of claim 1, wherein the engine comprises a steam engine.

This suggests, via claim differentiation,[33] that claim 1 has scope beyond the literal embodiment described, specifically the steam engine, a not unusual circumstance regarding patent claims and specification embodiments.[34]

In this highly stylized hypothetical, suppose after the patent has issued to A, someone, B, quite knowledgeable in combustion technology, reads it and realizes that, while it is a wonderful invention, an engine could be made to output much more "work" in terms of power or energy by using a combustion mechanism inside the engine to toggle the pistons, rather than using steam. This person, B, realizing the potential for such an invention, obtains skilled patent counsel who manages to obtain issuance of a patent with the claim (note that the steam engine patent with its claim 1 is still in force during this time):

1. A machine comprising: a combustion engine.

Again, this claim would have been novel, nonobvious, and useful at the time the invention was made. It, therefore, patentably distinguishes from the disclosure of the steam engine patent.

---

31. This is a made-up example, so please, as to technical details, permit so-called literary allowances.

32. Remember to permit literary allowances for the purpose of the overall point to be made.

33. See Chapter 4 regarding claim differentiation.

34. *But see* Lizardtech v. Earth Res. Mapping, 424 F.3d 1336 (Fed. Cir. 2005). It might be better to not add claim 2 reciting the steam engine and, instead, rely on claim 1 reciting only the engine. By providing only one embodiment and a dependent claim reciting "steam engine," claim 1 might be held invalid for lack of written description support since no more general embodiment has, presumably, been provided.

Now, in this made-up world, the question is this: who has the legal right to manufacture a combustion engine? A bit surprisingly, *no one does.* A patent claim gives you the right *to prevent others* from practicing the claim but does not grant an owner an affirmative right for the owner to practice it himself or herself.[35] This becomes particularly relevant, here, in connection with improvements and building on the patented work of others.

Thus, if B were to manufacture a combustion engine because he has the patent claim to a combustion engine, his engine would potentially infringe A's more general claim to an engine. Likewise, if A were to attempt to manufacture a combustion engine because he has a patent claim to engines generally and combustion engines are desirable to introduce to the market, A's combustion engine would potentially infringe B's combustion engine claim. In a world with rational decision-makers driven by the profit motive, A and B should consummate a cross-license so one or both might supply combustion engines to the market.

However, in the balance of value between the two patents, does A pay B because B has the hot new technology or does B pay A because A has a foundational lock on all engines generally? Of course, this is a matter of negotiation, and so on. Thus, this next point is a little speculative; however, we see today that combustion engines appear to have significantly greater demand than steam engines. It seems probable that A will pay B, assuming A wants to produce combustion engines.

Hence, the nature of technological improvements, which the patent system is designed to advance, is illustrated. It is often the latest and greatest technology that drives market demand, rather than the foundational technology, though the foundational technology, of course, is important to move the technology frontier forward.

How does this lengthy, perhaps interesting (and certainly educational) detour relate to transition words or phrases? As noted, the U.S. patent system is built upon improvements.[36] This helps explain why "comprising" is the

35. *See* 35 U.S.C. § 154(a)(1) (2024) ("Every patent shall contain a short title of the invention and a grant to the patentee, his heirs or assigns, of the right to *exclude* others from making, using, offering for sale, or selling the invention throughout the United States or importing the invention into the United States, and, if the invention is a process, of the right to *exclude* others from using, offering for sale or selling throughout the United States, or importing into the United States, products made by that process, referring to the specification for the particulars thereof.") (emphasis added).

36. Some might say incrementally small improvements; others might say incrementally sizable improvements. However, either way, improvements.

much more common and more favored transition word. It has an open format with respect to the scope of the claim.

Knowing this, then, why ever use a different transition word or phrase? This is where inherent differences in technology potentially impact the choice of a transition phrase. Let us consider some major technological and scientific areas: mechanical devices, electrical or electronic devices, software, materials science, chemistry, and biotechnology. In this order, these technologies represent a spectrum in which, moving from left to right, the technologies appear to be less predictable. By "predictable," we mean that given an invention or innovation, it becomes more difficult to extrapolate from that invention or innovation to come up with additional possible related technology that would be enabled from knowing the invention and the present state of the art.

Chemistry and biotechnology tend to be highly experimental sciences in which the properties of various combinations of known technical components are more unexpected than for mechanical devices, electronic devices, and software.[37] Hence, in patent law, the former technologies in the list in the previous paragraph are characterized more generally as being in the predictable arts and the latter technologies are characterized as being in the unpredictable arts.[38]

Imagine, for example, a chemical invention (e.g., composition of matter) such that the properties of the constituents are nothing like the properties of the result, as is usually the case in the chemical arts. Furthermore, for patentability under § 103, often the compounds or compositions of matter that result should have improved and unexpected properties relative to similar, previously known formulations.

---

37. *See* Sean Seymore, *Heightened Enablement in the Unpredictable Arts*, 56 UCLA L. Rev. 127 (2008). *See In re* Rainer, 377 F.2d 1006, 1012 (C.C.P.A. 1967) (Important considerations include "the type[s] of reactions, the state of the art, the representative nature of the examples, and the breadth of the claims."). *See also* PPG Indus., Inc. v. Guardian Indus. Corp., 75 F.3d 1558, 1564 (Fed. Cir. 1996) (explaining that "enablement is lacking . . . , because the undescribed embodiments cannot be made, based on the disclosure . . . without undue experimentation"); *In re* Prutton, 200 F.2d 706 (C.C.P.A. 1952) (holding that claims to a class of chemical compounds that were sufficiently broad to involve some speculation lack enablement notwithstanding the presence of the operative specific examples within the class); *In re* Fisher, 427 F.2d 833 (C.C.P.A. 1970).

38. *Compare In re* Vaeck, 947 F.2d 488, 496 (Fed. Cir. 1991) (noting that the requisite level of disclosure for an invention involving predictable mechanical or electrical elements is less than that required for the unpredictable arts), *with PPG Indus., Inc.*, 75 F.3d at 1564 (explaining that "enablement is lacking . . . , because the undescribed embodiments cannot be made, based on the disclosure . . . without undue experimentation"); *Prutton*, 200 F.2d 706 (holding that claims to a class of chemical compounds that were sufficiently broad to involve some speculation lack enablement notwithstanding the presence of the operative specific examples within the class).

Typically, formation of such compounds requires precise conditions. Important considerations with a composition of matter claim may include "the type[s] of reactions, the state of the art, the representative nature of the examples, and the breadth of the claims."[39] If one were to use the word "comprising" in a patent claim for a compound formulation, the patent claim could sweep in a host of other possible constituents, conditions, chemical catalysts, and so on that may not produce the desired result being described and sought to be claimed and patented. In this case, then, the claim may be invalid because its full scope would not and possibly could not be enabled or may not be sufficiently described, as is legally required.[40] The specification may describe precise conditions to produce a chemical compound, as a working example, perhaps; however, the claim language with "comprising" as the transition word may sweep in other subject matter that has not been enabled or even described because such conditions will not produce compounds literally covered by the claim or, perhaps even, compounds literally covered by the claim may not even be possible to produce.[41]

Consider Example 3.2:

EXAMPLE 3.2

I claim:

1. A composition of matter consisting of: complex compounds of the formula $M(CO)_a\ H_b\ (NH_3)_c$, in which M is a metal of the actinide series of the periodic table of the elements and each of a, b, and c is a whole number ranging from 0 to 8, such that when a is 0, b is greater than 0, and otherwise a is equal to or greater than b, and when c is greater than 0, both a and b are 0.

39. *See Rainer*, 377 F.2d at 1012.

40. *See* Juno Therapeutics, Inc. v. Kite Pharma, Inc., 10 F.4th 1330 (Fed. Cir. 2021) (written description); Trs. of Bos. v. Everlight, 896 F.3d 1357 (Fed. Cir. 2018) (enablement); Durel Corp. v. Osram Sylvania, 256 F.3d 1298, 1306–07 (Fed. Cir. 2001) (a significant number of inoperative embodiments within the scope of the claims might be sufficient to prove invalidity); *see also* Atlas Powder v. DuPont, 750 F.2d 1569, 1576–77 (Fed. Cir. 1984). *See also* Amgen v. Sanofi, 143 S. Ct. 1243 (2023).

41. For example, this would require undue experimentation. *See Everlight*, 896 F.3d 1357 (enablement); *Durel Corp.*, 256 F.3d at 1306–07 (a significant number of inoperative embodiments within the scope of the claims might be sufficient to prove invalidity); *see Atlas Powder*, 750 F.2d at 1576–77. *See also* EMI Grp. N. Am., Inc. v. Cypress Semiconductor Corp., 268 F.3d 1342 (Fed. Cir. 2001) (claims reciting scientific process found to be impossible are invalid).

2. The composition of matter in accordance with claim 1, wherein M is uranium or thorium.

3. The composition of matter in accordance with claim 2, wherein M is uranium, a is 8, b is 2, and c is 0.

4. The composition of matter in accordance with claim 2, wherein M is uranium, a is 0, b is 0, and c is 8.

For this claim, in the so-called unpredictable arts, a transition phrase is called for to limit scope and thereby avoid invalidity for lack of enablement or lack of written description that might result from use of an open-form transition word. Claim drafters may, instead, with other types of transition phrases, vary claim scope linguistically to capture more than the working examples described in the specification *without* use of an open-form transition word. As one example, for the one just preceding, precisely varying specified parameters defined by the application permits one to achieve a desired claim scope.

Again, this difference in transition phrases is a result of the inherent nature of the technology involved. In the predictable arts, a broad claim that uses the open-form "comprising" may still be enabled and potentially be sufficiently described to its full scope from only one embodiment due to the nature of the technology and the state of the art.[42]

To address this issue for the unpredictable arts, patent claims in the unpredictable arts often use "consisting of" or "consisting essentially of" as the transition, referred to as closed form and partially closed form, respectively. These transitions have a specific meaning based on canons of construction regarding patent claims; however, there are Federal Circuit cases as well that have deviated from these canons when interpreting a claim. One may view these canons as a type of "first order" analysis or, perhaps, as a weak presumption. In the appropriate circumstances, depending on claim wording, the specification, the file history, the technology, and so on, a federal court may be willing to deviate from the canon.

42. *See, e.g.*, Liebel-Flarsheim Co. v. Medrad, Inc., 358 F.3d 898, 905 (Fed. Cir. 2004); Spectra-Physics, Inc. v. Coherent, Inc., 827 F.2d 1524, 1533 (Fed. Cir. 1987) ("If an invention pertains to an art where the results are predictable, e.g., mechanical as opposed to chemical arts, a broad claim can be enabled by disclosure of a single embodiment, and is not invalid for lack of enablement simply because it reads on another embodiment of the invention which is inadequately disclosed."). However, there are cases where the Federal Circuit concluded a claim was not enabled by a single embodiment. Thus, it is best to provide multiple embodiments. *See* Chapter 6.

With this in mind, "consisting of" is used to claim the elements and limitations as recited in the claim body (i.e., closed form).[43] "Consisting essentially of" is used to claim the elements and limitations as recited in the claim body, including any additional unclaimed constituents that are of a nature or an amount to not alter the character of what is otherwise intended to be claimed as novel subject matter (i.e., partially closed form).[44]

However, one feature to know about transition words, especially in connection with compositions of matter, is that different transition words may be used within the claim to limit or enlarge scope as well. For example, imagine a silicon chip. One may, as an example, want to claim an integrated device with "comprising," but within the claim body employ "consisting of" to claim the portion of the integrated device made from the constituent materials. This sort of approach is illustrated with Example 3.3.

EXAMPLE 3.3

I claim:

1. A semiconductor device comprising:

   a substrate, the substrate consisting of a material selected from the group consisting of silicon, sapphire, gallium arsenide, magnesium oxide, zinc oxide, and silicon carbide;

   a crystalline buffer layer on the substrate consisting essentially of gallium nitride; and

   a growth layer on the buffer layer, the growth layer comprising gallium nitride and a dopant material.

---

43. *See* AFG Indus., Inc. v. Cardinal IG Co., 239 F.3d 1239 (Fed. Cir. 2001); *cf.* Norian Corp. v. Stryker Corp., 363 F.3d 1321 (Fed. Cir. 2004) (claim includes ordinary impurities of recited elements). See Chapter 4 regarding composition of matter claims.

44. *See* PPG Indus. v. Guardian Indus., 156 F.3d 1351 (Fed. Cir. 1998). See Chapter 4 regarding composition of matter claims. Note that use of "consisting essentially of" was recently held to raise an indefiniteness issue in *HZNP Medicines LLC v. Actavis Laboratories UT, Inc.*, 940 F.3d 680 (Fed. Cir. 2019). This was because a basic and novel property was indefinite. However, with this transition phrase, unclaimed constituents are to be of a nature or an amount to not alter the character of what is otherwise intended to be claimed as novel subject matter. Hence, claim scope was unclear.

For the preceding claim, "comprising" is used to join three elements, which respectively include a clause using closed form, a clause using partially closed form, and a clause using open form. The clause of the substrate element uses a format referred to as a Markush group, treated in more detail later.[45]

We have just discussed the three basic types of transition words or phrases used in patent claims and their understood meaning in accordance with basic patent law canons. We recommend these be used without deviation of language.

A long line of patent cases has construed claims so that when the word "comprising" is employed as the transition word, the claim is interpreted as open. One statement of this basic proposition is contained in the Federal Circuit case *Invitrogen v. Biocrest*.[46] This means the claim is construed to cover *more than* simply all the elements and limitations provided in the body of the claim. The claim is interpreted so that the claim is met, even if other aspects of the so-called accused product or accused process are not explicitly listed in the claim. In other words, if the listed elements and limitations are present in the relationship recited in the claim, the claim is met, for purposes of validity. An accused product or a single prior art reference may have additional aspects not recited in the claim. Nonetheless, this does not prevent the claim from being met.

In virtually all cases in the predictable arts, "comprising" should be used as the transition word. It would be unusual in the predictable arts to find all the elements and limitations of a claim present in the accused product or process, but still find that the inventive concept was not being employed, regardless of what else might also be present in the accused product or process.

It is also a good idea to follow the word "comprising" with a colon. This will make it clear that "comprising" is intended to be the transition word and that everything that follows the colon is intended to be the body of the claim. Again, it is best to have it be clear which portion of the claim is the preamble, which portion is the transition word, and which portion is the claim body. This will make it more clear which words of the claim are necessarily intended as limitations.

Sometimes in patent claims "comprised of" is used in place of "comprising." Comprising is the much more common term and, consequently, the one recommended for use. However, case law indicates that "comprised of" will be interpreted in the same manner as "comprising."[47]

---

45. *See* Chapter 4.
46. 327 F.3d 1364 (Fed. Cir. 2003).
47. *See* CIAS, Inc. v. Alliance Gaming Corp., 504 F.3d 1356, 1356–60 (Fed. Cir. 2007).

However, other less traditional terms have been employed. One example is "having." Another is "composed of."[48] It is strongly recommended that these terms *not* be employed *as a claim transition word or phrase*. Using "having" as the transition word for a patent claim, for example, is not recommended because there is some risk that the claim might otherwise not be interpreted to be "open." For example, in *Crystal v. TriTech*,[49] the Federal Circuit stated that if the transition word employed is "having," the claim may be interpreted to be open or closed, depending on the context. Here, context refers to the claim language itself, the other claims, the specification, and the file history.[50]

The Patent Claim Body

Understand the basic mechanics of how to formulate and draft a complete patent claim.

The ultimate goal of the body is to capture in words the patentable innovation. Of course, this is easier said than done. This idea may relate more, as a drafting exercise, to § 103 than to § 102.

Dawn Equipment Co. v. Kentucky Farms Inc.
140 F.3d 1009
United States Court of Appeals for the Federal Circuit
March 24, 1998, Decided

Questions

1. The Federal Circuit reverses a jury's finding of infringement under the doctrine of equivalents. However, Kentucky Farms had raised a claim construction issue. What was the issue and why did the court choose not to resolve it?
2. The claim had several means-plus-function clauses and, thus, was construed under 35 U.S.C. § 112(f) (formerly § 112, paragraph 6). According to Judge Plager's additional views and to the concurrences, this raised a complex and challenging issue under the doctrine of equivalents. What was the issue? Why did the court not need to resolve the issue? Do footnotes 3 and 5 of Judge Newman's "additional views"

48. *See AFG Indus., Inc.*, 239 F.3d 1239.
49. 246 F.3d 1336, 1338 (Fed. Cir. 2001).
50. Likewise, note that use of the word "comprising" elsewhere in the claim other than as the transition word may similarly be subject to interpretation. *See* Moleculon Rsch. v. CBS, 793 F.2d 1261, 1271 n.8 (Fed. Cir.), *cert. denied*, 479 U.S. 1030 (1987).

provide a basis to distinguish the doctrine of equivalents from a statutory equivalent under § 112?

3. Why did the court conclude that no reasonable jury could find infringement under the doctrine of equivalents in this case? Why did the court apply the function-way-result test rather than the insubstantial differences test? What did the court say about the function part of the test? The way part of the test? The result part of the test?
4. Judge Plager in footnote 1 appears to allude to a difference between a claim "element" versus a claim "limitation." However, it does not appear to make a difference in this case. Can you imagine a situation where there might be a difference between a claim element versus a claim limitation that might matter for the purposes of determining patent infringement?

INVT SPE LLC v. International Trade Commission
46 F.4th 1361
United States Court of Appeals for the Federal Circuit
August 31, 2022, Decided

Questions

1. This case is an appeal from the International Trade Commission (ITC), rather than a district court. Procedurally and substantively, it is different. For one thing, the action is brought under 19 U.S.C. § 1337 (section 337 of the Tariff Act of 1930) rather than 35 U.S.C. § 271. Section 337 of the Tariff Act of 1930, as amended, gives the ITC the authority to investigate and decide issues related to unfair competition and unfair acts in the importation and/or sale of imported goods. Under section 337, the ITC has jurisdiction to investigate claims regarding imports that infringe (1) a valid and enforceable U.S. patent; (2) a U.S. copyright registered under the Copyright Act; or (3) a U.S. trademark registered under the Lanham Act.[51] To date, the great majority of section 337 investigations involve claims of patent infringement. Thus, this is an appeal from an ITC investigation. The ITC is part of the executive branch, rather than the judicial branch; however, its rulings, once final, which involve a decision by the commission (which the president has the authority to overrule), are appealed to the Federal Circuit. Agency factual determinations are entitled to deference, as discussed in the opinion. Furthermore, its determi-

51. 19 U.S.C. § 1337(a)–(d).

nations do not result in collateral estoppel in federal court, also discussed in the opinion. Essentially, the ITC conducts investigations based on complaints and has the authority to stop the importation of goods found, for example, to infringe a U.S. patent. The ins and outs of ITC litigation is, in general, beyond the scope of this book, but see the discussion of the ITC in Chapter 5, "ITC Investigation: Another Enforcement Option." Some see an ITC exclusion order as similar to an injunction, because it keeps the accused goods from entering the United States, but without the procedural overhead of an injunction in federal court.[52] However, there are many important procedural and substantive differences between an injunction (or even preliminary injunction) and an ITC exclusion order. Regarding differences between a federal court litigation and an ITC investigation, why did the Federal Circuit rule the appeal of the '590 patent as moot?[53]

2. The Federal Circuit and the administrative law judge analyzed infringement of the one remaining patent at issue two separate ways. Why was that?
3. According to the Federal Circuit, what is a "standard essential" patent? How does this relate to the case? Why is there specific law directed to analyzing infringement of a standard essential patent? How is it different from standard patent infringement and why is it different? Why not just apply standard infringement principles to the situation?
4. The court in *INVT* says it has not imposed a specific grammatical form for "capability to perform" claims; however, note that the opinion does distinguish the language of method claims from the language of apparatus claims. An important case in this regard is *IPXL v. Amazon*,[54] addressed later in connection with invalidity due to indefiniteness.[55] The court never cites that case here, probably because invalidity due to indefiniteness does not appear to have been raised as an issue. Take a quick look now at that case. How is the situation at issue there based on the claim language different from the situation here? The court *says* it has not imposed or required a particular grammatical form regarding "capability to perform"-type claims (see, e.g., *Silicon*

52. *See* eBay Inc. v. MercExchange, 547 U.S. 388 (2006).

53. A recent Supreme Court decision has the potential to affect ITC cases since it is a type of regulatory agency. The case is *Loper Bright Enterprises v. Raimondo*, 603 U.S. ___ (2024), a landmark decision in the field of administrative law, the law governing regulatory agencies. It overruled the principle of *Chevron* deference established in *Chevron U.S.A., Inc. v. Natural Resources Defense Council, Inc.* (1984), which had directed courts to defer to an agency's reasonable interpretation of an ambiguity in a law that the agency enforces.

54. 430 F.3d 1377 (Fed. Cir. 2005).

55. *See* Chapter 6.

Graphics v. ATI Technologies, discussed in the opinion).[56] How does one distinguish method from apparatus when drafting a patent claim to avoid indefiniteness for *mixing* method limitations with apparatus limitations in one claim?[57]

5. Note that for the purpose of construing the claim, the court in *INVT* distinguishes the user device from the base station. Specifically, the court says:

   > [A]lthough the recited base station is not "a limitation on the claimed invention itself," *Nazomi Communs., Inc. v. Nokia Corp.*, 739 F.3d 1339, 1345 (Fed. Cir. 2014), in the sense that an infringer would not need to, for instance, use, make, or sell the base station, the base station's operation affects whether the claims are met, *see, e.g.*, *Advanced Software Design*, 641 F.3d at 1373–74.

   What does this mean in the context of determining patent infringement?[58]

6. In the case, the *INVT* court discusses the difference between a general-purpose computer and a special-purpose computer, stating:

   > While we have noted the principle that "apparatus claims cover what a device *is*, not what a device *does*," *Hewlett-Packard Co. v. Bausch & Lomb Inc.*, 909 F.2d 1464, 1468 (Fed. Cir. 1990), as a useful reminder that the focus of apparatus claims is the structure and not the operation or use, with computer- or software-based inventions, apparatus claims routinely depend on functional claiming to describe the apparatus. *It is the functional terms that distinguish a general purpose computer, "which can be programmed to perform very different tasks in very different ways" from a special purpose computer that is programmed to perform the particular function. Aristocrat Techs. Australia Pty Ltd. v. Int'l Game Tech.*, 521 F.3d 1328, 1333 (Fed. Cir. 2008). Therefore, what the device *does* (and

---

56. "In *Silicon Graphics*, the computer apparatus claim recited 'a rasterization circuit coupled to the processor *that rasterizes* the primitive according to a rasterization process which operates on a floating point format.' *Silicon Graphics, Inc. v. ATI Techs., Inc.*, 607 F.3d 784, 788 (Fed. Cir. 2010) (emphasis added and omitted)." INVT SPE LLC v. Int'l Trade Comm'n, 46 F.4th 1361, 1373 (Fed. Cir. 2022).

57. *See* MasterMine Software v. Microsoft, 874 F.3d 1307 (Fed. Cir. 2017).

58. See discussion later in this chapter regarding "elements/limitations and their relationship."

> how it does it) is highly relevant to understanding what the device *is*, in the computer/software context purpose.[59]

The *INVT* court cites to *Aristocrat*, but the principle articulated in *Aristocrat* originated in the case *In re Alappat*.[60] In 2015, the case *Eon Corp. v. AT&T Mobility*[61] suggested that *Alappat* may no longer be good law. Language from the *Eon Corp.* case is provided immediately following this paragraph (emphasis added). In light of the language from *Eon* and the language from *INVT*, what do you think about the continuing vitality of *In re Alappat*'s distinction between a general-purpose and a special-purpose computer or processor?[62]

Eon v. AT&T stated:

> As mentioned above, *WMS Gaming* held that the corresponding structure for a software algorithm is the algorithm. . . .
>
> Building on *Alappat*, *WMS Gaming* reasoned that "[t]he instructions of the software program that carry out the algorithm electrically change the general purpose computer by creating electrical paths within the device. These electrical paths create a special purpose machine for carrying out the particular algorithm." *WMS Gaming*, 184 F.3d at 1348. . . .
>
> *Before moving on, we note that Alappat has been superseded by Bilski, 561 U.S. at 605–06, 130 S. Ct. 3218, and Alice Corp. v. CLS Bank Int'l, — U.S. —, 134 S. Ct. 2347, 189 L. Ed. 2d 296 (2014). Nonetheless, WMS Gaming and Katz remain correctly decided. . . .* A general purpose computer is flexible—it can do anything it is programmed to do. *Id.* at 1333. Therefore, the disclosure of a general purpose computer or a microprocessor as corresponding structure for a software function does nothing to limit the scope of the claim and "avoid pure functional claiming." *Id.* As such, when a patentee invokes means-plus-function claiming to recite a software function, it accedes to the reciprocal obligation of disclosing a sufficient algorithm as corresponding structure.[63]

59. *INVT SPE LLC*, 46 F.4th at 1376–77 (some emphasis is added; some emphasis is in the original).
60. 33 F.2d 1526 (Fed. Cir. 1992).
61. 785 F.3d 616 (Fed. Cir. 2015).
62. *See* Chapter 6, "Avoid Potential Indefiniteness Issues."
63. *Eon Corp.*, 785 F.3d at 622–23.

Theory of the Claim Body

In general, if an examiner comes up with a piece of anticipatory art, per § 102, a new element or limitation may be added to the claim, to obviate the rejection.[64] Thus, "the game," so to speak, is to capture the innovation so that the claim may be said to exhibit to "an inventive step" over the closest known prior art, as discussed previously.[65]

In this regard, the language of § 103 directs a court or other decision-maker to compare differences between the prior art and the "subject matter sought to be patented" (pre-America Invents Act (AIA)) or "the claimed invention" (post-AIA) (i.e., the patent claim) "as a whole." This is important because it means that for the purposes of determining obviousness, *the claim must be considered as a whole*.

In other words, the claim is a collection of elements and limitations and associated relationships. It is not proper under § 103 to simply dissect the claim into separate elements and limitations and see if the prior art has each recited element and limitation. Rather, the whole may be (and typically is) greater than the sum of the parts. This typically factors into what would have made an invention unobvious. For example, there may be advantages that come from combining the elements and limitations together in the manner recited in the claim that would *not* be present if those elements and limitations were dissected and viewed in isolation from one another. Those advantages that flow from "the whole" are relevant to determining whether the invention would have been obvious at the time the invention was made. Specifically, such advantages may be relevant to whether, at the time the invention was made, the invention would have been obvious to "a person having ordinary skill in the art to which said subject matter pertains."

It is this aspect of the innovation that the claim body should seek to capture in language.

Furthermore, a good claim, primarily referring to the claim body, is an appropriate balance between breadth, vagueness, and precision. The claim body is precise in some respects because the claim language should be specific enough to distinguish from the *known* prior art. This often involves some amount of detail in the claim language of the claim body. For example, if the prior art shows red doorknobs, to be novel at least, the claim body should recite a color other than red. For example, a recitation in the claim body of "a blue doorknob" would be novel over such prior art (granted that it might

---

64. Assuming the specification provides written description support for that new element or limitation.

65. See Chapter 1, addressing § 103 pre- and post-America Invents Act (AIA).

have been obvious at the time the invention was made, depending on other considerations). Patent claim bodies are usually precise enough to show that the subject matter claimed is at least novel over the known prior art.

People sometimes confuse breadth and vagueness, the other features of a good claim body. For example, "any and all electrical signals" is quite broad, but it is *not* vague. Rather, it is crystal clear. A good patent claim body has breadth to cover those aspects not needed to distinguish from the *known* prior art. Breadth is desirable to protect the technology from those who might try to employ the technical idea in a manner that might otherwise not infringe a narrower claim.

Vagueness, however, may be appropriate—for example, when at the time of patenting it may be unclear how certain technology is likely to be implemented among various potential choices. The future is uncertain. Being vague permits the claim, primarily the body, to be infringed without necessarily spelling out in specific language how some aspects of the claim body will be implemented.

The point, of course, is that good claim bodies are broad, vague, and precise in the appropriate balance for the situation. Thus, the claim body should capture the innovation and employ an appropriate balance regarding precision, breadth, and ambiguity (i.e., vagueness).

Consider, again, for example, Example 2.1 from Chapter 2:

I claim:

1. An apparatus comprising:

   a substantially horizontally oriented, rectangularly shaped seat including four corners;

   wherein attached to a respective corner of the seat is a substantially vertically oriented leg such that the legs point in the same direction away from the seat, are oriented to be substantially mutually parallel, and are of substantially the same length.

This sample claim has precision and some breadth. More to the point, however, what is the innovation sought to be captured? It is not clear from the claim body. By focusing on the innovation, using claim language in the body to capture it, the aspects involving breadth and vagueness, which are to be balanced along with precision, may be better developed.

It is important, however, in performing such an evaluation, to consider the closest *known* prior art. This is a hypothetical situation. In this hypothetical world, chairs have not been invented yet. So, what did people use to sit in groups or to sit upon after becoming tired from a lot of walking, and so on? Perhaps they used very large rock formations, the ground, or trees that had fallen due to windstorms and the like. Of course, these "prior art" approaches are not convenient. To sit in groups, for example, you would need a bunch of fallen trees or boulders close together.

So, in light of this background, what might one conclude is innovative about a chair? It appears to be that it is *portable*. It provides a place to sit that is easily and conveniently portable. What would that look like in a patent claim body?

EXAMPLE 3.4

I claim:

1. An apparatus comprising: a portable seat.

Of course, this is a stylized example to illustrate a point and, hence, here, results in a possibly overly broad claim, but it *does* begin the process of formulating the claim body. A portable seat seems like it would have been novel and unobvious at the time it was made in light of *known* prior art, such as the ground or fallen trees. Also, it is useful.

Appreciate, however, if allowable, what this potentially captures compared with the previous claim: many potential follow-on improvements—wheelchairs, swivel chairs, ergonomic chairs, and so on. Many things that the previous claim would not have captured. Patents have a 20-year term. With the pace of technical change, it might be surprising how quickly products built on a fundamental concept, such as this example, may develop.

Someone, a lawyer most likely, may argue that a small boulder could be a portable seat. That may be a good point; again, Example 3.4 was a starting point. Perhaps, to distinguish from the known art, the claim should be:

EXAMPLE 3.5

I claim:

1. An apparatus comprising: a portable seat;

   wherein the portable seat includes a back oriented to be roughly perpendicular to the portable seat.

So, the claim body now includes elements (seat and back) and limitations (portable, oriented to be roughly perpendicular) that provide relationships between the elements.[66]

Claim Elements/Limitations and Their Relationship

One issue that may be confusing relates to the difference between an element and a limitation of a patent claim.[67] Likewise, if the patent claim includes elements *and* limitations, what part of the claim constitutes the relationships among claim components?

These are good questions, and the case law may not be fully consistent regarding the answers to such questions. There may be multiple ways to view the situation, although, here, we provide an internally consistent view.

The Federal Circuit has used both terms, "elements" and "limitations," to describe the words of a claim.[68] However, the Federal Circuit has expressed a preference for "limitation" over "element." In *Dawn*, as one example, the court indicates that "limitation" applies to the claim, whereas "element" applies to the accused device.[69]

It might be more helpful to consider elements, limitations, and the relationship thereof as on a spectrum. An analogy with other areas of law might also be helpful. In criminal law and in tort law, there is a notion of an "act" that is committed and also of "attendant circumstances" that must

---

66. Alternatively, perhaps, Example 3.4 is claim 1, and a claim 2 that is dependent from claim 1 adds the additional features recited in Example 3.5.

67. It is noted that 37 C.F.R. § 1.75(i) (2024) states: "Where a claim sets forth a plurality of elements or steps, each element or step of the claim should be separated by a line indentation." However, it appears that examiners rarely invoke this rule. If they were to do so, it would be as an informality objection that could easily be addressed.

68. *See, e.g.*, Festo Corp. v. Shoketsu Kinzoku Kogyo Kabushiki Co., 234 F.3d 558, 56 U.S.P.Q.2d 1865 (Fed. Cir. 2000) (en banc), *rev'd and remanded*, 535 U.S. 722 (2002), *on remand*, 344 F.3d 1359 (Fed. Cir. 2003), *cert. denied*, 541 U.S. 988 (2004) ("In our prior cases, we have used both the term 'element' and the term 'limitation' to refer to words in a claim. *See, e.g.*, *Lemelson v. United States*, 752 F.2d 1538, 1551, 224 U.S.P.Q. 526, 533 (Fed. Cir. 1985) (using the term 'element'); *Sextant Avionique, S.A. v. Analog Devices, Inc.*, 172 F.3d 817, 826–27, 49 U.S.P.Q.2d 1865, 1870–71 (Fed. Cir. 1999) (using the term 'limitation')."). In one case, the court states that it is preferable to use the term "limitation" when referring to claim language and the term "element" when referring to the accused device. *See* Dawn Equip. Co. v. Ky. Farms, Inc., 140 F.3d 1009, 1014 n.1, 46 U.S.P.Q.2d 1109, 1112 n.1 (Fed. Cir. 1998).

69. *See Dawn Equip. Co.*, 140 F.3d at 1014 n.1, 46 U.S.P.Q.2d at 1112 n.1.

be present. Perhaps one way to think of a claim is that the elements are like "the act or acts" of a tort or crime and the limitations are like "the attendant circumstances."[70]

In this construct, the elements are components recited in the claim that necessarily are present in the accused product and limitations are further clarifications about those elements that also must be met. However, to draw a subtle but potentially important difference, some limitations may not necessarily always need to be instantiated as such in the accused product, as explained later. What then of "the relationship among elements and/or limitations?" "The relationship" may refer to the relationship among the elements and may comprise all the limitations of the claim as a whole. Consider preceding Examples 2.2 and 2.6, repeated here as Examples 3.6 ("external" and "externally derived" have been added to claim 2.2) and 3.7:

EXAMPLE 3.6

I claim:

1. An apparatus comprising:

   random access memory (RAM) and a memory controller;

   wherein the memory controller is capable of initiating burst mode operation based, at least in part, on receipt of an externally derived request from an external central processing unit (CPU);

   wherein the request is to include a memory address, a word count, and a read or a write control transfer designation; and

   wherein the memory controller is to process the request and take control of an external system transfer bus.

In Example 3.6, RAM and the memory controller are claim elements in that they *must be present* in the accused product. In this claim, the CPU and transfer system bus, though recited, are part of the claim with respect to the limitations, rather than the elements, in this construct. The recited limitations must be met but, under the view presented here, the CPU and transfer system

70. *Cf.* INVT SPE LLC v. Int'l Trade Comm'n, 46 F.4th 1361 (Fed. Cir. 2022) (distinguishing in analysis of claim whether base station was part of the environment of the claims and whether to infringe one would need to make, use, or sell the base station).

bus are not required to be present for infringement of claim 1 of Example 3.6.[71] Rather, the claim itself refers to "an external CPU," "an external system transfer bus," and "an externally derived request." As an illustration, while the transfer system bus need not be present, nonetheless, the memory controller must be able to "take control of an external system transfer bus." These limitations must be capable of being met[72] for an accused product to be within the scope of claim 1 of Example 3.6.

EXAMPLE 3.7

I claim:

1. An apparatus comprising:

   random access memory (RAM), a memory controller, a central processing unit (CPU), and a system transfer bus;

   wherein the memory controller is capable of initiating burst mode operation based, at least in part, on receipt of a request from the CPU;

   wherein the request is to include a memory address, a word count, and a read or a write control transfer designation; and

   wherein the memory controller is to process the request and take control of the system transfer bus.

In Example 3.7, again, RAM and the memory controller are claim elements; however, *as now are the CPU and system transfer bus (also referred to as the system bus). These must all be present in the accused product to infringe*. In this claim, the CPU and system transfer bus are *also* part of the claim with respect to *the limitations*. The recited *limitations* must also be met, as before. However, here, as recited elements, the CPU and system bus are required to be present for infringement of claim 1 of Example 3.7, but not because of being recited in the limitations. Rather, in claim 1 of Example 3.7, these are recited to be (and are intended to be) claim elements.

71. *Cf. id.* (distinguishing in analysis of claim whether base station was part of the environment of the claims and whether to infringe one would need to make, use, or sell the base station).

72. Without modification of the accused product. *See, e.g., id.*

Cases talk of an "All Elements Rule" for patent infringement; however, sometimes this is called an "All Limitations Rule."[73]

Inferential Claiming

Generally, inferential claiming has a bad "reputation" in U.S. patent law as leading to indefiniteness. It is certainly true that unintentional inferential claiming may lead to indefiniteness; however, inferential claiming, if done intentionally and appropriately, is a powerful drafting tool and should not always be cast aside. As with all claim drafting, care and thought are required, however.

Inferential claiming, in general, means to claim something without having first provided a positive recitation thereof.[74] However, there are varying definitions, which may be termed, here, the antecedent basis view of inferential claiming and the positive recitation view of inferential claiming. This may be more easily understood by first considering a standardly used claim format, such as for an apparatus claim:

I claim:

1. An apparatus comprising:

   an element A, an element B, and an element C;[75]

   wherein [relationships among the element A, the element B, and the element C].

Employing an antecedent basis view of inferential patent claiming means to introduce an element without first employing an indefinite article, in contradiction of the format just shown.

---

73. *See* Ethicon Endo-Surgery, Inc. v. U.S. Surgical Corp., 149 F.3d 1309, 1317, 47 U.S.P.Q.2d 1272 (Fed. Cir. 1998) ("[T]he All Elements rule might better be called the All Limitations rule. It will be referred to as such throughout the remainder of this opinion."). See Chapter 1, discussing the "All Elements Rule."

74. Perhaps this approach is better described as implication claiming rather than inferential claiming since the language may be said to *imply* a feature, rather than allowing one to *infer* a feature, without first having positively recited the feature.

75. May be on separate lines per rule 37 C.F.R. § 1.75 (2024).

Consider, for example, the following claim:

EXAMPLE 3.8

I claim:

1. An apparatus comprising:

   a hip prosthesis;

   wherein the hip prosthesis includes: a ball and a socket;

   wherein the ball has an elliptical shape and the socket has a corresponding elliptical shape to receive the ball within the socket for mutual engagement;

   wherein the elliptical shape of the ball has a major axis; and

   wherein during the mutual engagement of the ball and the socket, the ball is at least able to partially rotate within the socket substantially perpendicular to the minor axis of the ball.

In this claim, we see that, in general, the claim elements are introduced first positively with an indefinite article. These include hip prosthesis, ball, socket, elliptical shape, corresponding elliptical shape, and major axis. However, we see that the term "minor axis" is *not* first introduced with an indefinite article. Nonetheless, because elliptical shape and major axis are introduced through positive recitation, we are able to *infer* that the elliptical shape also has a minor axis. Thus, indefiniteness is not a significant risk here.

With this understanding, it is easy to see how, if taken too far, this drafting approach might lead to indefiniteness. However, it is noted that the Federal Circuit has stated that recitation of a claim term without having antecedent basis does not necessarily make a claim indefinite.[76]

The positive recitation view of inferential claiming, instead, refers to not separately calling out a feature as a claim element before introducing it. This may also create potential ambiguity or at least potentially raise a question as to intended scope. As an illustration, consider the following claim similar to an example from Chapter 2, included here for convenience:

76. *See, e.g.*, Bose Corp. v. JBL, Inc., 274 F.3d 1354, 1359 (Fed. Cir. 2001); Slimfold Mfg. Co. v. Kinkead Indus., Inc., 810 F.2d 1113, 1117 (Fed. Cir. 1987).

EXAMPLE 3.9

I claim:

1. An apparatus comprising:

   random access memory (RAM) and a memory controller;

   wherein the memory controller is capable of initiating burst mode operation based, at least in part, on receipt of a request from a central processing unit (CPU);

   wherein the request is to include a memory address, a word count, and a read or a write control transfer designation; and

   wherein the memory controller is to process the request and take control of a system transfer bus.

The CPU and the system transfer bus, as examples, *are* introduced with an indefinite article, but *are not* first positively recited (in comparison with "random access memory" and "memory controller"). Under a positive recitation view of inferential claiming, the CPU and the system transfer bus (also referred to as system bus) are claimed inferentially.

As suggested in the previous section, a way to understand the latter claiming approach is that RAM and memory controller are elements and are required to be present in the accused device. The CPU and the system bus are *not* claim elements and are *not* required to be present in the accused device. The language of the claim around CPU and system bus, instead, constitutes claim limitations that clarify how the accused device is to operate when combined with a CPU and system bus. Thus, this view of inferential claiming might be thought of as related to the previous discussion[77] regarding claim elements and claim limitations. A potential ambiguity in situations such as this, however, might be which of the claim terms are specifically intended as claim elements and which of the claim terms are not intended specifically as claim elements, hence creating risk of indefiniteness or improper interpretation. This could be handled with drafting in which the request, CPU, and system bus may all be referred to as "external" or "externally derived," as previously shown with Example 3.6, and as now illustrated with Example 3.10.

---

77. See the immediately previous section of this chapter.

EXAMPLE 3.10

I claim:

1. An apparatus comprising:

   random access memory (RAM) and a memory controller;

   wherein the memory controller is capable of initiating burst mode operation based, at least in part, on receipt of an externally derived request from an external central processing unit (CPU);

   wherein the request is to include a memory address, a word count, and a read or a write control transfer designation; and

   wherein the memory controller is to process the request and take control of an external system transfer bus.

With the foregoing understanding, would the following claims in Example 3.11 be considered to use inferential claiming?

EXAMPLE 3.11

I claim:

1. A method comprising:

   receiving a request for burst mode operation;

   transmitting a request for control of a system bus in response to the received request;

   receiving a signal granting system bus control;

   transferring signals across the system bus into or out of a group of sequential memory cells after receiving the signal granting system bus control; and

   transmitting a signal indicating completion of the signal transfer.

I claim:

1. An apparatus comprising:

 a substantially horizontally oriented, rectangularly shaped seat including four corners;

 wherein attached to a respective corner of the seat is a substantially vertically oriented leg such that the legs point in the same direction away from the seat, are oriented to be substantially mutually parallel, and are of substantially the same length.

Under the antecedent basis view, probably not, but under the positive recitation view, probably so. For example, for the latter claim, it might have been more formally formulated as:

I claim:

1. An apparatus comprising:

 a seat;

 wherein the seat comprises a rectangularly shaped seat;

 wherein the rectangularly shaped seat comprises a horizontally oriented, rectangularly shaped seat;

 wherein the horizontally oriented, rectangularly shaped seat has four corners; . . .

and so on. One should recognize that the rules that discourage inferential claiming are designed to reduce claim ambiguity, which is a desirable goal because indefiniteness may invalidate a claim. On the other hand, employing a noninferential claiming approach quite strictly may also lead to a more cumbersome patent claim in terms of language, which may be a barrier to comprehension. This, of course, would be a disadvantage, as well, such as if a judge or jury is unable to comprehend the claim due to overly formalistic and exceedingly cumbersome wording. In dealing with method claims, for example, as one approach, tangible components, such as hardware, are positively recited in the preamble. Another approach, instead, may recite such tangible components "inferentially" as part of an action or action element.[78] Each approach has its benefits and disadvantages. In the first approach, the hardware elements are introduced specifically. This allows the actions or operating elements to be recited more clearly as method elements. However, one would expect and want the preamble in that situation to be limiting and should be drafted considering it as part of the body of the claim. In the second approach, it may be easier to read, although it should be carefully drafted so that antecedent basis issues do not lead to potential indefiniteness.

The risk with inferential claiming, again, arises where the possible inference (or implication, depending on your preference) creates a genuine ambiguity as to intention with respect to claim coverage. The guidance is to use approaches that lead to tighter claims if it may be done without creating ambiguity/indefiniteness.

Example 3.12 is one simple example of what not to do:

EXAMPLE 3.12

I claim:

1. An apparatus comprising:

   a portable seat.

2. The apparatus of claim 1, wherein the horizontally oriented seat has four corners.

In this example, does claim 1 have a horizontally oriented seat? One could argue that it does and one could argue that it does not. Thus, if not indefinite, at a minimum, scope is unclear. However, likewise, scope being unclear supports the position that the claim is indefinite.

78. See Chapter 4, providing examples of these approaches to method or process claims.

Chapter 4

Introduction to Various Types of Patent Claims

Understand the basic types of patent claims and what rights they are used to protect.

Patent Claim Types or Categories

35 U.S.C. § 101

Whoever invents or discovers any new and useful process, machine, manufacture, or composition of matter, or any new and useful improvement thereof, may obtain a patent therefor, subject to the conditions and requirements of this title.

MPEP § 2106.03

I. THE FOUR CATEGORIES

35 U.S.C. 101 enumerates four categories of subject matter that Congress deemed to be appropriate subject matter for a patent: processes, machines, manufactures and compositions of matter. As explained by the courts, these "four categories together describe the exclusive reach of patentable subject matter. If a claim covers material not found in any of the four statutory categories, that claim falls outside the plainly expressed scope of § 101 even if the subject matter is otherwise new and useful." In re Nuijten, 500 F.3d 1346, 1354, 84 USPQ2d 1495, 1500 (Fed. Cir. 2007).

A process defines "actions", i.e., an invention that is claimed as an act or step, or a series of acts or steps. As explained by the Supreme Court, a "process" is "a mode of treatment of certain materials to produce a given result. It is an ***act, or a series of acts****, performed upon the subject-matter to be transformed and reduced to a different state or thing." Gottschalk v. Benson, 409 U.S. 63, 70, 175 USPQ 673, 676 (1972) ([emphasis] added) (quoting Cochrane v. Deener, 94 U.S. 780, 788, 24 L. Ed. 139, 141 (1876)). See also Nuijten, 500 F.3d at 1355, 84 USPQ2d at 1501 ("The Supreme Court and this court have consistently interpreted the statutory term 'process' to require action"); NTP, Inc. v. Research in Motion, Ltd., 418 F.3d 1282, 1316, 75 USPQ2d 1763, 1791 (Fed. Cir. 2005) ("[A] process is a series of* *acts.") (quoting Minton v. Natl. Ass'n. of Securities Dealers, 336 F.3d 1373, 1378, 67 USPQ2d 1614, 1681 (Fed. Cir. 2003)). As defined in 35 U.S.C. 100(b), the term "process" is synonymous with "method."*

The other three categories (machines, manufactures and compositions of matter) define the types of physical or tangible "things" or "products" that Congress deemed appropriate to patent. Digitech Image Techs. v. Electronics for Imaging, 758 F.3d 1344, 1348, 111 USPQ2d 1717, 1719 (Fed. Cir. 2014) ("For all categories except process claims, the eligible subject matter must exist in some physical or tangible form."). Thus, when determining whether a claimed invention falls within one of these three categories, examiners should verify that the invention is to at least one of the following categories ***and*** *is claimed in a physical or tangible form.*

- *A machine is a "concrete thing, consisting of parts, or of certain devices and combination of devices." Digitech, 758 F.3d at 1348–49, 111 USPQ2d at 1719 (quoting Burr v. Duryee, 68 U.S. 531, 570, 17 L. Ed. 650, 657 (1863)). This category "includes every mechanical device or combination of mechanical powers and devices to perform some function and produce a certain effect or result." Nuijten, 500 F.3d at 1355, 84 USPQ2d at 1501 (quoting Corning v. Burden, 56 U.S. 252, 267, 14 L. Ed. 683, 690 (1854)).*
- *A manufacture is "a tangible article that is given a new form, quality, property, or combination through man-made or artificial means." Digitech, 758 F.3d at 1349, 111 USPQ2d at 1719–20 (citing Diamond v. Chakrabarty, 447 U.S. 303, 308, 206 USPQ 193, 197 (1980)). As the courts have explained, manufactures are articles that result from the process of manufacturing, i.e., they were produced "from raw or prepared materials by giving to these materials new forms, qualities, properties, or combinations, whether by hand-labor or by machinery." Samsung Electronics Co. v. Apple Inc., 137 S. Ct. 429, 120 USPQ2d 1749, 1752–3 (2016) (quoting Diamond v. Chakrabarty, 447 U.S. 303, 308, 206 USPQ 193, 196–97 (1980)); Nuijten, 500 F.3d at 1356–57, 84 USPQ2d at 1502. Manufactures also include "the parts of a machine considered separately from the machine itself." Samsung Electronics, 137 S. Ct. at 435, 120 USPQ2d at 1753 (quoting 1 W. Robinson, The Law of Patents for Useful Inventions § 183, p. 270 (1890)).*
- *A composition of matter is a "combination of two or more substances and includes all composite articles." Digitech, 758 F.3d at 1348–49, 111 USPQ2d at 1719 (citation omitted). This category includes all compositions of two or more substances and all composite articles, "'whether they be the results of chemical union or of mechanical mixture, or whether they be gases, fluids, powders or solids.'" Chakrabarty, 447 U.S. at 308, 206 USPQ at 197 (quoting Shell Dev. Co. v. Watson, 149 F. Supp. 279, 280 (D.D.C. 1957); id. at*

310 holding genetically modified microorganism to be a manufacture or composition of matter).

It is not necessary to identify a single category into which a claim falls, so long as it is clear that the claim falls into at least one category. For example, because a microprocessor is generally understood to be a manufacture, a product claim to the microprocessor or a system comprising the microprocessor satisfies Step 1 regardless of whether the claim falls within any other statutory category (such as a machine). It is also not necessary to identify a "correct" category into which the claim falls, because although in many instances it is clear within which category a claimed invention falls, a claim may satisfy the requirements of more than one category. For example, a bicycle satisfies both the machine and manufacture categories, because it is a tangible product that is concrete and consists of parts such as a frame and wheels (thus satisfying the machine category), and it is an article that was produced from raw materials such as aluminum ore and liquid rubber by giving them a new form (thus satisfying the manufacture category). Similarly, a genetically modified bacterium satisfies both the composition of matter and manufacture categories, because it is a tangible product that is a combination of two or more substances such as proteins, carbohydrates and other chemicals (thus satisfying the composition of matter category), and it is an article that was genetically modified by humans to have new properties such as the ability to digest multiple types of hydrocarbons (thus satisfying the manufacture category).

Non-limiting examples of claims that are not directed to any of the statutory categories include:

- *Products that do not have a physical or tangible form, such as information (often referred to as "data per se") or a computer program per se (often referred to as "software per se") when claimed as a product without any structural recitations;*
- *Transitory forms of signal transmission (often referred to as "signals per se"), such as a propagating electrical or electromagnetic signal or carrier wave; and*
- *Subject matter that the statute expressly prohibits from being patented, such as humans per se, which are excluded under The Leahy-Smith America Invents Act (AIA), Public Law 112-29, sec. 33, 125 Stat. 284 (September 16, 2011).*

As the courts' definitions of machines, manufactures and compositions of matter indicate, a product must have a physical or tangible form in order to fall within one of these statutory categories. Digitech, 758 F.3d at 1348, 111 USPQ2d at 1719. Thus, the Federal Circuit has held that a product claim to an intangible collection of information, even if created by human effort, does not fall within any statutory category. Digitech, 758 F.3d at 1350, 111 USPQ2d at 1720 (claimed "device profile" comprising two sets of data did not meet any of the categories because it was neither a process nor a tangible product). Similarly, software expressed as code or a set of instructions detached from any medium is an idea without physical embodiment. See Microsoft Corp. v. AT&T Corp., 550 U.S. 437, 449, 82 USPQ2d 1400, 1407 (2007); see also Benson, 409 U.S. 67, 175 USPQ2d 675 (An "idea" is not patent eligible). Thus, a product claim to a software program that does not also contain at least one structural limitation (such as a "means plus function" limitation) has no physical or tangible form, and thus does not fall within any statutory category. Another example of an intangible product that does not fall within a statutory category is a paradigm or business model for a marketing company. In re Ferguson, 558 F.3d 1359, 1364, 90 USPQ2d 1035, 1039–40 (Fed. Cir. 2009).

Even when a product has a physical or tangible form, it may not fall within a statutory category. For instance, a transitory signal, while physical and real, does not possess concrete structure that would qualify as a device or part under the definition of a machine, is not a tangible article or commodity under the definition of a manufacture (even though it is man-made and physical in that it exists in the real world and has tangible causes and effects), and is not composed of matter such that it would qualify as a composition of matter. Nuijten, 500 F.3d at 1356–1357, 84 USPQ2d at 1501–03. As such, a transitory, propagating signal does not fall within any statutory category. Mentor Graphics Corp. v. EVE-USA, Inc., 851 F.3d 1275, 1294, 112 USPQ2d 1120, 1133 (Fed. Cir. 2017); Nuijten, 500 F.3d at 1356–1357, 84 USPQ2d at 1501–03.

Independent versus Dependent Claims

Understand the different ways to narrow a claim via a dependent claim in patent claim drafting.
Use dependent claims to cover commercial embodiments, to cover different infringers, for fallback position (and claim differentiation), for higher levels of product integration, and/or to more clearly define the environment of the invention.

35 U.S.C. § 112(c), (d)

(c) Form.—

A claim may be written in independent or, if the nature of the case admits, in dependent or multiple dependent form.

(d) Reference in Dependent Forms.—

Subject to subsection (e), a claim in dependent form shall contain a reference to a claim previously set forth and then specify a further limitation of the subject matter claimed. A claim in dependent form shall be construed to incorporate by reference all the limitations of the claim to which it refers.

35 U.S.C. § 282(a)

(a) In General.—

A patent shall be presumed valid. Each claim of a patent (whether in independent, dependent, or multiple dependent form) shall be presumed valid independently of the validity of other claims; dependent or multiple dependent claims shall be presumed valid even though dependent upon an invalid claim. The burden of establishing invalidity of a patent or any claim thereof shall rest on the party asserting such invalidity.

37 C.F.R. § 1.75(b)

(b) More than one claim may be presented provided they differ substantially from each other and are not unduly multiplied.

MPEP § 608.01(m)

Form of Claims

The claim or claims must commence on a separate physical sheet or electronic page and should appear after the detailed description of the invention. Any sheet including a claim or portion of a claim may not contain any other parts of the application or other material. While there is no set statutory form for claims, the present Office practice is to insist that each claim must be the object of a sentence starting with "I (or we) claim," "The invention claimed is" (or the equivalent). If, at the time of allowance, the quoted terminology is not present, it is inserted by the Office of Data Management. Each claim begins with a capital letter and ends with a period. Periods may not be used elsewhere in the claims except for abbreviations. See Fressola v. Manbeck, 36 USPQ2d 1211 (D.D.C. 1995). Where a claim sets forth a plurality of elements or steps, each element or step of the claim should be separated by a line indentation, 37 CFR 1.75(i).

There may be plural indentations to further segregate subcombinations or related steps. In general, the printed patent copies will follow the format used but printing difficulties or expense may prevent the duplication of unduly complex claim formats.

Reference characters corresponding to elements recited in the detailed description and the drawings may be used in conjunction with the recitation of the same element or group of elements in the claims. The reference characters, however, should be enclosed within parentheses so as to avoid confusion with other numbers or characters which may appear in the claims. Generally, the presence or absence of such reference characters does not affect the scope of a claim.

Many of the difficulties encountered in the prosecution of patent applications after final rejection may be alleviated if each applicant includes, at the time of filing or no later than the first reply, claims varying from the broadest to which he or she believes he or she is entitled to the most detailed that he or she is willing to accept.

Claims should preferably be arranged in order of scope so that the first claim presented is the least restrictive. All dependent claims should be grouped together with the claim or claims to which they refer to the extent practicable. Where separate species are claimed, the claims of like species should be grouped together where possible. Similarly, product and process claims should be separately grouped. Such arrangements are for the purpose of facilitating classification and examination.

When two claims in an application comply with the requirements of 35 U.S.C. 112(d) but are duplicates, or else are so close in content that they both cover the same thing, despite a slight difference in wording, it is proper after allowing one claim to object to the other claim under 37 CFR 1.75 as being a substantial duplicate of the allowed claim. Note however, that court decisions have confirmed applicant's right to restate (i.e., by plural claiming) the invention in a reasonable number of ways. Indeed, a mere difference in scope between claims has been held to be enough. Form paragraphs 7.05.05 and 7.05.06 may be used where duplicate claims are present in an application.

See MPEP § 608.01(n), subsection II, for rejections under 35 U.S.C. 112(d) ***of dependent claims that do not specify a further limitation of the subject matter claimed. See*** *MPEP § 804* ***for double patenting rejections of claims in different applications that are not patentable over each other.***

The form of claim required in 37 CFR 1.75(e) is particularly adapted for the description of improvement-type inventions. It is to be considered a combination claim. The preamble of this form of claim is considered to positively and clearly include all the elements or steps recited therein as a part of the claimed combination.

MPEP § 608.01(n)

Dependent Claims. . . .

III. TEST FOR PROPER DEPENDENCY

In accordance with 35 U.S.C. 112(d), or pre-AIA 35 U.S.C. 112, fourth paragraph, a claim in dependent form shall contain:

(i) a reference to a claim previously set forth, and

(ii) then specify a further limitation of the subject matter claimed.

A claim in dependent form shall be construed to incorporate by reference all the limitations of the claim to which it refers.

Following the statute, the test as to whether a claim is a proper dependent claim is that it shall include every limitation of the claim from which it depends and specify a further limitation of the subject matter claimed. For example, if claim 1 recites the combination of elements A, B, C, and D, a claim reciting the structure of claim 1 in which D was omitted or replaced by E would not be a proper dependent claim, even though it placed further limitations on the remaining elements or added still other elements. A dependent claim does not lack compliance with 35 U.S.C. 112(d) simply because there is a question as to the significance of the further limitation added by the dependent claim.

The fact that a dependent claim, which is otherwise proper might relate to a separate invention that would require a separate search or be separately classified from the claim on which it depends would not render it an improper dependent claim.

The fact that the independent and dependent claims are in different statutory classes does not, in itself, render the latter improper. Thus, if claim 1 recites a specific product, a claim for the method of making the product of claim 1 in a particular manner would be a proper dependent claim since it further specifies limitations relating to the method of making the product of claim 1. Similarly, if claim 1 recites a method of making a product, a claim for a product made by the method of claim 1 could be a proper dependent claim. On the other hand, if claim 1 recites a method of making a specified product, a claim to the product set forth in claim 1 would not be a proper dependent claim if the product can be made by a method other than that recited in the base method claim, and thus, does not include the limitations of the base claim.

Examiners are reminded that a dependent claim is directed to a combination including everything recited in the base claim and what is recited in the dependent claim. It is this combination that must be compared with the prior art, exactly as if it were presented as one independent claim.

When examining a dependent claim, the examiner should determine whether the claim complies with 35 U.S.C. 112(d), which requires that dependent claims contain a reference to a previous claim in the same application, specify a further limitation of the subject matter claimed, and include all the limitations of the previous claim. If the dependent claim does not comply with the requirements of 35 U.S.C. 112(d), the examiner should reject the dependent claim under 35 U.S.C. 112(d) as unpatentable rather than objecting to the claim. See Pfizer, Inc. v. Ranbaxy Labs., Ltd., 457 F.3d 1284, 1291–92, 79 USPQ2d 1583, 1589–90 (Fed. Cir. 2006) (holding a dependent claim in a patent invalid for failure to comply with pre-AIA 35 U.S.C. 112, fourth paragraph (now 35 U.S.C. 112(d))). Although the requirements of 35 U.S.C. 112(d) are related to matters of form, non-compliance with 35 U.S.C. 112(d) renders the claim unpatentable just as non-compliance with other paragraphs of 35 U.S.C. 112 would. For example, a dependent claim must be rejected under 35 U.S.C. 112(d) if it omits an element from the claim upon which it depends or it fails to add a limitation to the claim upon which it depends.

Claims which are in improper dependent form for failing to further limit the subject matter of a previous claim, or for not including every limitation of the claim from which it depends, should be rejected under 35 U.S.C. 112(d) or pre-AIA 35 U.S.C. 112, fourth paragraph by using form paragraphs 7.36 and 7.36.01.

Innova/Pure Water, Inc. v. Safari Water Filtration Systems
381 F.3d 1111
United States Court of Appeals for the Federal Circuit
August 11, 2004, Decided

Questions

1. This case primarily turns on claim construction. Specifically, construction of the language "operatively connected." As is not unusual, the plaintiff argues for a broad construction and the defendant argues for a narrow construction. The district court had ruled for the defendant. Note that the court states that the inquiry is "an objective one." Thus, "[b]ecause the inquiry into the meaning of claim terms is an objective one, a patentee who notifies the public that claim terms are to be limited beyond their ordinary meaning to one of skill in the art will be bound by that notification, even where it may have been unintended."[1] The court then points to a fundamental challenge in claim construction: "The longstanding difficulty is the contrasting nature of the axioms that (a) a claim must be read in view of the specification and (b) a court may not read a limitation into a claim from the specification."[2] The court then quotes some famous language by Justice Jackson from *White v. Dunbar*,[3] a U.S. Supreme Court case. What is the point the court is making through this quote?
2. The court cites case law for the suggestion that claims are not limited to specification embodiments, even in situations in which only one embodiment is provided. However, be aware that the Federal Circuit has not always been consistent on this point of law. For example, although the Federal Circuit professes to not limit claims to specific embodiments, it also says that the scope of the claims may be no greater than the scope of enablement.[4] Typically, then, as a practical matter, this countervailing principle may result in the claims being limited in cases in which only a single embodiment is disclosed. With that said, however, this case is a good example in which the claims

---

1. Innova/Pure Water, Inc. v. Safari Water Filtration Sys., Inc., 381 F.3d 1111, 1117 (Fed. Cir. 2004).
2. *Id.*
3. 119 U.S. 47 (1886).
4. *See, e.g.*, Nat'l Recovery Techs., Inc. v. Magnetic Separation Sys., Inc., 116 F.3d 1190 (Fed. Cir. 1999).

were not limited to specific embodiments from the patent application. What reasoning did the court employ here to reach this result?

3. Was one factor that, in the absence of specific modifiers, words of a claim are typically to be construed in a manner that reflects the full scope of those words based on ordinary meaning?[5]
4. What effect did the interpretation of the intended or designated function of the claims have on the interpretation by the district court versus by the Federal Circuit? Did the respective courts rely on the claims or on the specification to determine this function?
5. In claim 15, the drafter used the language "operatively connected" and the language "operatively associated." Would that not normally suggest a narrower scope for "operative connected"? Why does the Federal Circuit reach a different conclusion in this instance? What standard did the Federal Circuit apply to determine whether to construe "operatively connected" in a manner consistent with the full scope of the language used?
6. How did the dependent claims and the doctrine of claim differentiation affect the appellate court's analysis?
7. Note that the appellate court also considered the prosecution history and applied the same standard applied to the specification to determine whether to interpret the language at issue consistent with the full scope of the language used. Why did the appellate court reject the argument that a statement by the examiner narrowed the scope of the language at issue?

Pfizer Inc. v. Ranbaxy Laboratories Ltd.
457 F.3d 1284
United States Court of Appeals for the Federal Circuit
August 2, 2006, Decided

Questions

1. What is the legal basis for the alleged infringement?[6]
2. Note that the litigation involves two patents, the '893 and the '995. How are the two patents related, according to the appellate court?

---

5. Johnson Worldwide Assocs., Inc. v. Zebco Corp., 175 F.3d 985 (Fed. Cir. 1999) (refusing to import a modifier for the term "coupled"); Va. Panel Corp. v. MAC Panel Co., 133 F.3d 860 (Fed. Cir. 1997) (refusing to import a modifier for the term "reciprocating").

6. See 35 U.S.C. § 271(e)(2), sometimes referred to as "artificial infringement." *See* Lilly & Co. v. Medtronic, Inc., 496 U.S. 661 (1990).

If '995 is a later, unrelated patent to the '893, why were the complaints consolidated and why does the file history of the '995 mention the '893? What does Judge Michel mean when he says the '995 is an "unrelated" patent? Why is it that the failure to disclose to the U.S. Patent and Trademark Office (PTO) the statements made about the '893 during prosecution of the '995 did not amount to inequitable conduct?

3. Why does the appellate court reject Ranbaxy's interpretation of claim 1 of the '893 patent?
4. As to claim 6 of the '995, the district court found it valid and infringed, but the Federal Circuit found claim 6 to be invalid. What is the basis for the different outcomes? How clear is it that there is no overlapping subject matter between claim 2 and claim 6 of the '995 patent? What assumptions did Judge Michel make about the claims? What do you think the claim drafter had in mind with respect to claim 6? Do you think that the specification might have shed more light on how to properly interpret these claims? Why do you think Judge Michel did not look to the specification in this situation?
5. Might the Federal Circuit outcome be different if claim 1 did not recite "pharmaceutically acceptable salts thereof"? Why or why not? What if claim 2 also recited "pharmaceutically acceptable salts thereof"? Would Ranbaxy infringe claim 6 under this latter hypothetical scenario? Why or why not?

Littelfuse, Inc. v. Mersen USA EP Corp.
29 F.4th 1376
United States Court of Appeals for the Federal Circuit
April 4, 2022, Decided

Questions

1. Compare the district court's interpretation of the dependent claims in this case (e.g., claims 8 and 9 and claims 19 and 20) with the Federal Circuit's analysis of claim 6 of the '995 patent in *Pfizer v. Ranbaxy.*
2. How did the prosecution history in this case influence the claim interpretation by the district court? By the Federal Circuit?
3. What is the significance of the "fastening stem" to the interpretation of the claims reached by the district court versus the appellate court?
4. How likely or typical would it be for the applicant here to have given up the single-piece embodiments described in the specification? Is there a principle of claim construction at work here besides simply

claim differentiation?[7] Is there at least one plausible reason why the applicant might have been willing to forego those embodiments here?

5. How important was the principle of claim differentiation to the outcome of this case? We have seen several cases that employed claim differentiation, although the court, here, states:

> We note that the presumption of differentiation in claim scope is "not a hard and fast rule." *Seachange Int'l, Inc. v. C-COR Inc.*, 413 F.3d 1361, 1369 (Fed. Cir. 2005). Indeed, "any presumption created by the doctrine of claim differentiation 'will be overcome by a contrary construction dictated by the written description or prosecution history.'" *Retractable Techs., Inc. v. Becton, Dickinson, and Co.*, 653 F.3d 1296, 1305 (Fed. Cir. 2011) (citation omitted).[8]

Why do you think the court hedged a bit in terms of relying on claim differentiation?

Theory of Dependent Claims

Understanding the legal relationship between independent and dependent claims and how that relationship may affect validity and infringement determinations is an important part of the basic principles of claim drafting. Dependent claims may also influence the interpretation of the independent claim. Hence, although the tendency in claim drafting is to focus most attention on the independent claim, the dependent claims may enhance (or unintentionally undermine) the scope of the independent claim depending on execution. Drafting a full set of claims, including one or more independent claims and many dependent claims, therefore, is usually desirable for a patent application.

In general, the relationship between an independent claim and a dependent claim is logical. 35 U.S.C. subsection 112(d)[9] discusses dependent claims.[10] It states:

---

7. *See, e.g.*, Vitronics Corp. v. Conceptronic, Inc., 90 F.3d 1576 (Fed. Cir. 1996).
8. Littelfuse, Inc. v. Mersen USA EP Corp., 29 F.4th 1376, 1380 (Fed. Cir. 2022).
9. Previously, 35 U.S.C. § 112, ¶ 4.
10. Subsection (e) of § 112 addresses multiply dependent claims, not specifically discussed here in detail. These are more commonly used in Europe. The PTO charges an extra fee for such a claim beyond fees for the dependency claim equivalent, so most applicants avoid them. *See USPTO Fee Schedule* PTO, https://www.uspto.gov/learning-and-resources/fees-and-payment/uspto-fee-schedule (last revised May 3, 2024). *See also* PTO, MANUAL OF PATENT EXAMINING PROCEDURE § 608.01(n) (9th ed. 2022) [hereinafter MPEP].

> (d) REFERENCE IN DEPENDENT FORMS.—Subject to subsection (e), a claim in dependent form shall contain a reference to a claim previously set forth and then specify a further limitation of the subject matter claimed. A claim in dependent form shall be construed to incorporate by reference all the limitations of the claim to which it refers.

Dependent claims may only narrow independent claims. That is, dependent claims add additional limitations to the independent claim and must by construction always be narrower. Therefore, the independent claim is always the broadest claim of a set of claims. This is true whether the transition word or phrase is open or closed; however, open claims may be easier to understand.[11]

Consider claims 1 and 2:

1. An apparatus comprising:

   element A, element B, and element C.

2. The apparatus of claim 1, comprising: element D.

In this example, an apparatus with A, B, and C infringes claim 1 *and* claim 2. However, an apparatus with A, B, C, and D infringes *only* claim 2.

Consider, now, this example:[12]

EXAMPLE 4.1

I claim:

1. An automobile comprising: an engine, four wheels, and a drive train;

   wherein the drive train is to transmit drive power to at least one opposing pair of the wheels.

2. The automobile of claim 1, wherein the drive train includes both forward and reverse gears and means for shifting between the gears so that the opposing pair of wheels are to be driven in either the forward or the reverse direction.

---

11. Here, in this context, a set of claims specifically refers to one independent claim followed by a series of dependent claims.

12. Adopted from the district court case *TM Patents v. IBM*, 107 F. Supp. 2d 352 (S.D.N.Y. 2000).

Claim 2 is narrower, clearly. However, one might think that an automobile with more capabilities infringes claim 2 rather than claim 1. Logically and legally, however, that would not be correct. Rather, it only *appears* that a car drivable *only* in the forward direction infringes claim 1 and a car drivable in both directions infringes claim 2. A car drivable in *both* directions would infringe *both* claim 1 and claim 2. That is, the use of "comprising" in claim 1 means that claim 1 is not restricted to a car that drives only in the forward direction.

Consequently, there may be situations where a dependent claim might "appear" to broaden the independent claim, but that would be legally improper. Usually, those situations only superficially appear to broaden, but, in terms of legal rights, narrow the independent claim (or the dependent claim, if the claim at issue depends from a dependent claim). For example, a dependent claim may seem to expand the capabilities of the subject matter of the independent claim, as shown by the preceding example. In truth, the dependent claim specifically "recites" an additional feature that may or may not be present in a literal infringement of the independent claim. For the dependent claim, the feature *must necessarily* be present for infringement, making it a narrower claim.

Dependent claims also illustrate the fundamental trade-off between infringement and validity.[13] Although a broader claim may capture more infringers, it also is open to attack based on a broader set of prior art.

One of the most common reasons for adding dependent claims, therefore, is as a sort of hedge vis-à-vis prior art. After filing, during prosecution, and even after issuance—and, perhaps, after multiple litigations—more and more prior art may be discovered. That is, one never knows exactly what the prior art contains until discovered. With dependent claims, limitations may be added so that, while discovered prior art may render broader claims invalid, other narrower, dependent claims may stand up to such art and still capture some potential infringers. In this context, it is worth noting that as a technical legal matter, a court does *not* hold a patent claim *valid*. A patent claim is presumed valid. Rather, a court holds a patent claim *not* invalid, because, at a later time, in another suit, for example, it is still possible that it may be found to be invalid in light of newly discovered prior art, for example.

---

13. *Cf.* Unique Concepts, Inc. v. Brown, 939 F.2d 1558 (Fed. Cir. 1991) (infringement and validity are separate issues so that a claim may be infringed and invalid, although there may be no liability for that infringement) (dissent by Rich, J.). See also Chapter 1, in which a case example of this trade-off is provided.

The doctrine of claim differentiation also relates to the logical structure of dependent claims. Essentially, the doctrine is a presumption that because different words are used in different claims, the claims are presumed to cover different subject matter.[14] Of course, because it is a presumption, it may be overcome based on other factors.[15] However, the doctrine may be helpful in claim drafting to suggest, via a dependent claim structure, that particular claims have a certain scope. For example, if the *dependent claims* in your claim set recite *specific features* from the specification with respect to an embodiment, the logical implication is that the claims from which those claims depend *cover broader subject matter than the embodiment*.[16]

Here, a prior example is repeated.

EXAMPLE 4.2

I claim:

1. An apparatus comprising:

   random access memory (RAM) and a memory controller;

   wherein the memory controller is capable of initiating burst mode operation based, at least in part, on receipt of an externally derived request from an external central processing unit (CPU);

   wherein the request is to include a memory address, a word count, and a read or a write control transfer designation; and

   wherein the memory controller is to process the request and take control of an external system transfer bus.

An illustrative dependent claim might be:

---

14. *See, e.g.*, Wi-LAN USA, Inc. v. Apple Inc., 830 F.3d 1347 (Fed. Cir. 2016).

15. *Id.*

16. *See, e.g.*, InterDigital Commc'ns v. Int'l Trade Comm'n, 690 F.3d 1318, 1324 (Fed. Cir. 2012) (The doctrine of claim differentiation disfavors reading a limitation from a dependent claim into an independent claim.). For a recent example of claim differentiation, see *Littelfuse, Inc. v. Mersen USA EP Corp.*, 29 F.4th 1376 (Fed. Cir. 2022), in which the Federal Circuit vacated and remanded the district court's ruling of noninfringement and emphasized that by definition, an independent claim is broader in scope than a dependent claim, and, hence, an embodiment recited in a dependent claim should also be covered by the corresponding independent claim.

2. The apparatus of claim 1, wherein the memory controller comprises an address register, a word count register, and a transfer mode register.

The implication is that if a memory controller is able to implement burst mode operation without the specific registers of claim 2, it, nonetheless, infringes claim 1. Using dependent claims and considering claim differentiation has a bootstrapping effect with respect to the base claim.

It is also noted that claim differentiation is stronger if the dependent claim adds one new feature as opposed to many new features.[17]

It is also helpful to consider the validity and infringement considerations that follow from a dependent claim structure, particularly in which the transition word is "comprising." The relationships of validity versus infringement might be thought of as being the inverse of each other. In particular, something that *literally* infringes a dependent claim should by construction *literally* infringe the independent claim.[18] This is based on the additional limitation introduced by the dependent claim that is not present in the independent claim. By contrast, a piece of prior art that invalidates an independent claim may not necessarily invalidate a dependent claim.[19] This is also based on the additional limitation introduced by the dependent claim.

Using similar reasoning, something that does not literally infringe the independent claim should not literally infringe the dependent claim, again, particularly for the transition word "comprising." The independent claim is the

17. *See* Anderson v. Fiber Composites, 474 F.3d 1361, 169–70 (Fed. Cir. 2007); Acumed v. Stryker, 483 F.3d 800, 806 (Fed. Cir. 2007).

18. The statement is qualified by "should" because there might be unusual claim formulations. For example, claim 1 may recite "consisting of A and B." Claim 2 may recite, and further "consisting of C." A product A, B, and C would appear to literally infringe claim 2 but not claim 1. However, in this latter example, claim 2 should be invalid as in *Ranbaxy*. The statement in the text is most easily understood in connection with the transition word "comprising."

The statement is also limited to literal infringement because there is a possible, but unusual, situation in which a product may infringe a dependent claim under the doctrine of equivalents (DOE) and not infringe the independent claim under the DOE. This situation was first articulated by Judge Rich in the *Wilson Sporting Goods* decision. *See* Wilson Sporting Goods v. David Geoffrey & Assocs., 904 F.2d 677 (Fed. Cir. 1990). See also Chapter 5 and its treatment of the *Wilson Sporting Goods* case.

19. *See, e.g.*, Innova/Pure Water, Inc. v. Safari Water Filtration Sys., Inc., 381 F.3d 1111, 1123 (Fed. Cir. 2004) ("[D]ependent claims are typically narrower and, by so being, are more likely to clearly distinguish the prior art. Generally speaking, this is, in part, their function.").

broadest claim of a set of claims, by construction. Consequently, a piece of prior art that invalidates a dependent claim should invalidate the independent claim.

As to issues other than prior art, the relationship of invalidity frequently may "depend" on the claims themselves. For example, an independent claim may be indefinite, but a dependent claim may potentially cure that indefiniteness. Alternatively, an independent claim may be definite, but a related dependent claim may add limitations that make the dependent claim indefinite. While the independent claim may remain definite, this might not be passed to the dependent claim due to the added limitations.

In general, dependency is a matter of substance rather than form. However, there are preferred forms for dependent claims, discussed in the next section. It is not a requirement that a dependent claim be in the same statutory class as the independent claim (although it is recommended);[20] however, it must narrow the independent claim.[21] Here is an example of the foregoing:

I claim:

1. A method comprising:

   emulating one or more network devices of at least a second broadcast domain;

   encapsulating one or more signal packets from at least a first broadcast domain to be directed to a network device of the at least a second broadcast domain; and

   communicating the encapsulated one or more signal packets to at least one tunnel server.

2. An article comprising: a nontransitory storage medium;

   wherein the storage medium has stored thereon executable instructions;

   wherein the instructions are executable to perform the method of claim 1; and

   wherein the at least one tunnel server comprises at least two tunnel servers.

---

20. See the treatment later in this chapter. See also treatment in Chapter 6 of risks associated with mixing statutory classes.

21. *See* MPEP, *supra* note 10, § 608.01(n) ("The fact that the independent and dependent claims are in different statutory classes does not, in itself, render the latter improper.").

37 C.F.R. § 1.75 (2024) addresses some aspects relevant to dependent claims. For example, subsection (b) states: "More than one claim may be presented provided they differ substantially from each other and are not unduly multiplied." The number of permissible dependent claims is generally subject to applicant discretion; however, in litigation, it may be within a court's inherent power to limit the number of dependent claims to be considered in a case due to limited judicial resources and the discretion accorded a federal district court judge.[22] That is, more is not necessarily always better.

Questions

1. Note the relationship regarding independent and dependent claims when considering claim scope with respect to direct literal patent infringement versus anticipation. For example, if an independent claim distinguishes from a piece of prior art (i.e., is not anticipated), then do the dependent claims also patentably distinguish? However, if an independent claim is anticipated, does that mean that the dependent claims are necessarily anticipated? Consider similar principles with respect to obviousness. That is, if the independent claim is not obvious in light of the prior art, does it follow that the dependent claims are also not obvious in light of the prior art? However, if an independent claim is obvious in light of the prior art, does that mean the dependent claims are necessarily obvious in light of the prior art?
2. If a product or service does not infringe an independent claim directly and literally, does it follow that the dependent claims are also not infringed directly and literally? Likewise, if a dependent claim is directly and literally infringed, does it follow that the independent claim is literally and directly infringed?
3. Is it apparent from the foregoing why independent claims typically receive more attention than dependent claims? However, it would be a mistake to think dependent claims are not important. As we have seen, courts frequently look to the dependent claims to assist in interpreting the independent claims.
4. Do these principles regarding independent and dependent claims, which primarily relate to claim scope, also apply with respect to issues such as indefiniteness, enablement, written description, or even patent eligibility?

22. *See In re* Katz Interactive Call Processing Pat. Litig., 639 F.3d 1303, 1318 (Fed. Cir. 2011).

5. For example, consider an independent claim that is indefinite; does it necessarily follow the dependent claim is indefinite? Could a dependent claim add limitations that make the claim definite despite the indefiniteness of the independent claim? Now, consider the reverse situation. If the independent claim is definite, does it necessarily follow that the dependent claim is definite? Could the added limitations in the dependent claim make the claim indefinite?
6. Now, consider written description support. If the dependent claim is supported, does it necessarily follow that the independent claim is supported? There are numerous Federal Circuit cases that address this. The independent claim may be broader than the dependent claim and may not necessarily be supported.[23] On the other hand, if the independent claim is supported, does it necessarily follow that the dependent claim is supported? Could it be that additional limitations added by the dependent claim were not mentioned or shown in the specification?[24]
7. Consider a similar analysis for enablement. Just because the independent or the dependent claim is enabled does this necessarily mean that the other is enabled? It really depends on the specification description and, furthermore, may be more or less likely depending at least partially on the predictability of the technology.
8. Consider patent eligibility of independent and dependent claims. For example, if the independent claim is patent eligible, does it necessarily follow that the dependent claim is patent eligible?[25] Does whether the technology relates to the predictable arts matter?
9. These principles are helpful to keep in mind when drafting a patent specification. That is, it is important, for example, that each claim separately be definite, have written description support, and be enabled.

---

23. *See, e.g.*, Gentry Gallery v. Berkline, 134 F.3d 1473 (Fed. Cir. 1998).

24. See treatment in Chapter 1 regarding a post-AIA patent application claiming priority to a pre-AIA patent application and whether pre-AIA or post-AIA §§ 102 and 103 apply to the post-AIA patent application.

25. See treatment of patent eligibility in Chapter 6. This may suggest a claim drafting strategy that has been overlooked. It may make sense to draft a spectrum of patent claims with respect to the issue of patent eligibility, as is recommended with respect to anticipation and obviousness.

Adding a New Element or Limitation versus Further Clarifying an Existing Element or Limitation

Understand the different ways to narrow a claim via a dependent claim in patent claim drafting.

InterDigital Communications, LLC v. International Trade Commission
690 F.3d 1318
United States Court of Appeals for the Federal Circuit
August 1, 2012, Decided

Questions

1. This is another claim construction case where the primacy between the specification and claims is at issue. Make no mistake—the words of the claims are paramount. However, likewise, the court is trying to truly figure out what the invention "is" based on the evidence before it. So, what happens when it appears that the specification provides a better or more true picture of the invention than the claim language? There certainly have been cases where that appeared to happen.[26] Is that what seems to be happening here?
2. Observe that this is an appeal from the International Trade Commission (ITC or the Commission). In this regard, the appellate court states:

> Nokia [an intervenor in the case] proposes two alternative grounds to support the Commission's decision. First, Nokia argues that that there can be no infringement in this case because the scrambling codes in the Nokia system are not transmitted. Neither the administrative law judge nor the Commission addressed that argument. The agency's decision was not predicated on that rationale, and under well-settled principles of administrative law, we are not free to accept Nokia's invitation to uphold the agency's decision on a ground not ruled on by the agency. *See SEC v. Chenery Corp.*, 318 U.S. 80, 87, 63 S. Ct. 454, 87 L. Ed. 626 (1943); *Vizio, Inc. v. Int'l Trade Comm'n*, 605 F.3d 1330, 1343 n.11 (Fed. Cir. 2010); *Mittal Steel Point Lisas Ltd. v. United States*, 542 F.3d 867, 878 n.1 (Fed. Cir. 2008). That issue, if Nokia wishes to raise it again before the Commission, may be raised on remand.[27]

---

26. *See., e.g.*, Trs. of Colum. Univ. v. Symantec Corp., 811 F.3d 1359 (Fed. Cir. 2016) (specification controlled meaning of claim terms despite rendering two claims indefinite); Lizardtech, Inc. v. Earth Res. Mapping, Inc., 424 F.3d 1336 (Fed. Cir. 2005) (claim differentiation could not trump specification where only one embodiment described).
27. InterDigital Commc'ns v. Int'l Trade Comm'n, 690 F.3d 1318, 1328–29 (Fed. Cir. 2012).

What rule does the appellate court apply in this regard for review of district court decisions?

3. This case, of course, is primarily a claim construction case, but a necessarily tricky one. The case seems to revolve around the correct interpretation of "spreading code."

   Note, however, that the majority and the dissent do not appear to be completely aligned on "the facts." The facts are in quotes because, as we shall see later in the casebook, claim construction has been ruled to be purely a matter of law. Thus, the court may see all of the following issues as legal issues rather than as factual issues. For example, the dissent states: "The Commission found, and it is not disputed, that the Nokia scrambling code does not provide a data rate differential or increase in bandwidth."[28] However, the majority states: "For example, although scrambling codes of the sort used in Nokia's accused devices do not spread data, the evidence showed that such codes, which are transmitted at the chip rate, are frequently referred to as spreading codes."[29] Likewise, whereas the majority states: "To be sure, the patents contain no express definition of 'spreading code.'"[30] Yet, the dissent states: "The common specification defines a 'spreading code' as a code having 'a much higher rate than the [subscriber unit's baseband] data' and which spreads data at a specific symbol rate called the 'spreading factor' or 'processing gain.' '966 Patent, col.2 ll.3–7."[31]

   Clearly, proper resolution of these issues would be important in reaching a construction of the *true* invention. Does spreading code generically (or loosely, as the majority put it) refer to higher data rate codes, such as those that usually accompany code division multiple access (CDMA) spreading? If so, and if it is true that Nokia's scrambling codes are transmitted at those higher rates, then the majority may have the better interpretation. Likewise, if the dissent's definition is accurate, irrespective of what Nokia does, then there seems either an internal inconsistency in the specification by calling pilot codes and access codes spreading codes or at least an issue that requires some "massaging," so to speak. Which approach based on both opinions and the recited evidence seems more plausible?

4. Notice how powerful claim differentiation turned out to be in resolution of this case. Nonetheless, one should not lose sight that it is merely a presumption. There are some cases where it did not seem

28. *Id.* at 1333.
29. *Id.* at 1327.
30. *Id.*
31. *Id.* at 1334.

to count for much of anything. Likewise, in *Lizardtech, Inc. v. Earth Resource Mapping, Inc.*,[32] all it did was lead to an invalid claim. However, when the intrinsic evidence all lines up, so to speak, if not a dispositive factor, it may still count for "making weight." Can you describe some conditions where claim differentiation is more likely to be followed when drafting claims?

* * *

Although dependency is a substantive requirement,[33] there are claim drafting conventions that have become used as a matter of custom. It is highly recommended that these be followed much like it is recommended that the format of a preamble, transition word or phrase, and claim body be employed as a matter of standard practice. These conventions are expected, and an unexplained departure might potentially suggest another meaning is intended other than the generally understood meaning.

If writing a dependent claim, logically, there are two ways to narrow the claim from which the dependent claim will depend. One way is to add a new element to the claim that is being narrowed. Consider this basic example:

---

1. An apparatus comprising:

   element A, element B, and element C.[34]

2. The apparatus of claim 1, *comprising*: element D.

Observe that in claim 2 (the dependent claim), the claim that is being depended from, here, claim 1, must be referenced. Hence, claim 2 necessarily includes elements A, B, and C. Note also that the additional element, here, D, was added using "comprising:." Some may prefer to use "and further comprising:." Likewise, a colon is used after "comprising" to highlight separation between the transition word (or phrase) and the new element. Whichever form is employed, one should do so consistently throughout the claims, again, so as not to suggest that a departure from otherwise consistent language is intended

32. 424 F.3d 1336.

33. *See* Monsanto Co. v. Syngenta Seeds, Inc., 503 F.3d 1352, 1357–58 (Fed. Cir. 2007) ("To establish whether a claim is dependent upon another, this court examines if the new claim both refers to an earlier claim and further limits that referent. *See* 35 U.S.C. §112, ¶4 (2000) ('[A] claim in dependent form shall contain a reference to a claim previously set forth and then specify a further limitation of the subject matter claimed. A claim in dependent form shall be construed to incorporate by reference all the limitations of the claim to which it refers.').").

34. *See* 37 C.F.R. § 1.75(i) (2024).

to convey a different intended meaning. The form illustrated (e.g., "comprising" rather than "and further comprising") seems the simplest to implement.

The other way to logically narrow a dependent claim is to further clarify an existing element or limitation in the claim being depended from. Here is a simple example.

---

1. An apparatus comprising: a portable seat.
2. The apparatus of claim 1, *wherein* the portable seat includes a back that is attached to the portable seat and oriented to be in a plane substantially perpendicular to a plane that includes the portable seat.

As before, the claim being "depended from" is referenced in the dependent claim. Some may ponder why this is clarifying an existing element or limitation since a (new) back element is added. That would be an astute query.

In some situations, you may employ both approaches or have a choice as to which approach is employed because, logically, the element that may be added may also result in clarifying a prior element or limitation.

For example, claim 2 might have been written as follows:

---

2. The apparatus of claim 1, *comprising*: a back; and

   wherein the back is attached to the portable seat and oriented to be in a plane substantially perpendicular to a plane that includes the portable seat.

Here, both "comprising" and "wherein" are employed because a new element is added *and* an existing element or limitation, the portable seat, is further clarified.

The latter approach is more formalistic in terms of positively reciting a new element; the former approach is a little tighter in terms of language, not unlike positive recitation inferential claiming, treated in the previous chapter.[35]

37 C.F.R. § 1.75 (2024) addresses some notable aspects relevant to dependent claims. For example, it addresses numbering and grouping in subsections (f) and (g):

35. See treatment of inferential claiming in Chapter 3.

(f) If there are several claims, they shall be numbered consecutively in Arabic numerals.

(g) The least restrictive claim should be presented as claim number 1, and all dependent claims should be grouped together with the claim or claims to which they refer to the extent practicable.

It is accepted practice that your first claim should be your broadest claim, reflected in subsection (g). If there is more than one independent claim, to the extent possible, claim 1 should be the broadest one, although there may be times where it may be unclear which independent claim is necessarily the broadest one.

Because claim numbering is consecutive, all the dependent claims for the first independent claim should be numbered consecutively after claim 1 before presenting the second independent claim. Because there are 20 claims permitted without incurring extra claim fees,[36] typically one might have a first independent claim, numbered claim 1, followed by nine dependent claims, numbered 2 to 10, and then a claim numbered 11 may be the second independent claim, also then followed by nine dependent claims, numbered 12 to 20.

Because dependent claims may skip over intervening claims, it is best to employ a form of nesting to group related claims, per subsection (g) of § 1.75. For example, the following would probably not be proper in light of subsection (g):

Claim 1: Element A—Independent claim.

An apparatus comprising: element A.

Claim 2: Element B—Depends from 1 and adds B.

The apparatus of claim 1, comprising: element B.

Claim 3: Element C—Depends from 2 and adds C.

The apparatus of claim 2, comprising: element C.

Claim 4: Element E—Depends from 2 and adds E.

The apparatus of claim 2, comprising: element E.

Claim 5: Element D—Depends from 3 and adds D.

The apparatus of claim 3, comprising: element D.

That is, claim 5 is not properly nested. For proper nesting in a complete group, the claimed content of claim 5, D, should come after claim 3. That is, claims 4 and 5 may be interchanged to achieve proper nesting. You may wonder

36. *See* MPEP, *supra* note 10, § 607.

why this is proper since new claim 5 (reciting element E) would depend from claim 2; however, claim 5, after switching claims 4 and 5 (claim 5 reciting element E), may be the start of another claim grouping that depends from claim 2. For example, a claim 6 (not shown) may now depend from claim 5 (claim 5 reciting element E), reciting F (hence, claim 5 potentially begins another nested grouping of claims). Thus, dependent claims may be thought of as groupings. With such a(n) (inter)change between claims 4 and 5 as just suggested, it should be clear that new claim 4 in substance includes the elements and limitations of claim 1, claim 2, claim 3, and claim 4—that is, A, B, C, and D. After claims 4 and 5 are interchanged for proper nesting, new claim 5 in substance includes the limitations of claim 1, claim 2, and claim 5—that is, A, B, and E.

Dependency relationships may be varied or change among the dependent claims to alter claim scope, particularly during patent prosecution. It is not uncommon, for this reason, to diagram the relationships between the independent and dependent claims for a claim set. Often this is done as a tree with the independent claim as a root node and with other nodes connected to the root node via an edge to depict a direct dependency relationship and so forth. For example, with claims 4 and 5 interchanged for proper nesting, as suggested, a claim tree diagram (Figure 4.1) would be:

Figure 4.1 Tree Showing Claim Dependency Relationships

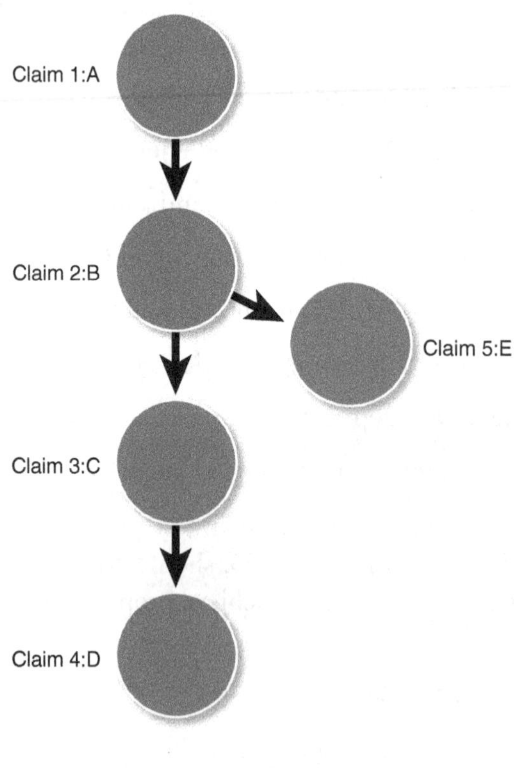

Another claim drafting fine point relates to how, in a dependent claim, to distinguish between similar, but different, elements of the independent claim. This issue of how to reference similar but different terms of an independent claim applies generally in drafting dependent claims. Consider this example claim:

---

1. An apparatus comprising:

   a hip prosthesis;

   wherein the hip prosthesis includes: a ball and a socket;

   wherein the ball has an elliptical shape and the socket has a corresponding elliptical shape to receive the ball within the socket for mutual engagement;

   wherein the elliptical shape of the ball has a major axis; and

   wherein during the mutual engagement of the ball and the socket, the ball is at least able to rotate within the socket substantially perpendicular to the minor axis of the ball.

For example, to distinguish the elliptical shape of the ball from the elliptical shape of the socket, the claim refers to "a corresponding elliptical shape." The word "corresponding" in this example serves as a "handle" so that the two elliptical shapes may be referenced in later claims without a misunderstanding that might be argued to create indefiniteness. This is a commonly used technique, and any word may suffice, but one that makes sense within the context of the claim is a good approach.[37]

Use Dependent Claims for Commercial Aspects Most Likely to Be Copied

In general, it is prudent to include in the dependent claims commercial aspects related to the invention that are more likely to be copied. This especially makes sense as a fallback position in case the independent claim, for example,

---

37. *Cf.* Pitney Bowes v. Hewlett-Packard Co., 182 F.3d 1298 (Fed. Cir. 1999) (term "spot" used in claim to mean two different things created significant claim construction issues).

is of questionable validity, while potentially bolstering a charge of willful patent infringement in the right circumstances.

Use Dependent Claims to Cover a Variety of Potential Infringers

It is also worthwhile to think about the claims from the perspective of capturing potential infringers. One way to do this is to consider the commercial value considerations with reference to why someone else may want to use the technology at issue. Does it reduce costs? Improve performance? Does it relate to compatibility? For example, is it related to a published standard, or does it address compatibility of widely used software or hardware? Does it have potential mass-market appeal? Viewing the technology from the perspective of its commercial value should make it easier to draft claims that will capture perspective infringers since this allows you to focus on the features that others will want to use and/or copy.

It is also helpful to view the claims from the perspective of how they may be used by the patentee to gain commercial advantage. For example, who are potential injunction targets? Typically, this will be the patentee's competitors. Are there companies who are potential cross-licensing targets for the patentee? Usually, this will include companies that could have patents to cover the patentee's products and who might use those patents to generate revenue. Are there potential pure licensing revenue targets for the technology? Frequently, this might include potential suppliers or customers. It is suggested that you not omit such companies from claim coverage simply due to existing business relationships with the patentee. Such relationships may change over time. Also, what about currently existing licenses and cross-licenses that may matter with respect to this technology? Sometimes such agreements may even impact the desire to file the patent application at all. Are such licenses so-called capture period licenses, meaning that patents filed or issued during a specific period remain licensed even after the term of the agreement ends, or is it a "guillotine" license, meaning that patents become unlicensed once the agreement expires? As should be clear, the answers to these questions do not only affect how the claims should be crafted but may ultimately affect whether the patent is worth pursuing since accurate answers ultimately may impact the value of the patent to the patentee.

A related consideration, although one that more frequently is an issue in foreign filing than claim drafting, is the location of these potential target companies. Where are manufacturing sites for target companies? Where are major markets for these companies? Where are corporate headquarters for these companies? It is sometimes difficult to reflect these considerations in the claims but be aware of subsections 271(f) and 271(g), which affect the ability to assert patent claims against companies in the United States that "infringe" abroad. For example, subsection 271(g) permits suit against someone who performs a process abroad that is patented in the United States, and then imports the product of that process.[38] Likewise, subsection 271(f) is meant to address various situations where acts of indirect infringement occur abroad (as if the patent were enforceable abroad), but some portion of the acts occur in the United States.[39] Without these statutes, such indirect activities may otherwise not be actionable. However, due to these statutes, indirect infringement activities pursued abroad that have a connection to the United States, as defined by these statutes, may result in actions filed against those companies in the United States for indirect patent infringement.

With the growth of the internet, a more common claim drafting problem is multiparty claims, discussed in detail later.[40] Patent claims that require several independent parties to be working in unison for direct infringement to occur are typically not infringed by anyone. This is to be distinguished from the typical or usual patent infringement situation, where there is one direct infringer and others who may aid and abet the direct infringer, making those other parties indirect infringers. For example, a claim directed to multiple servers and multiple clients where each client and each server is owned by a

38. See later in this chapter discussing § 271(g).

39. 35 U.S.C. § 271(f) (2024) states:

> (1) Whoever without authority supplies or causes to be supplied in or from the United States all or a substantial portion of the components of a patented invention, where such components are uncombined in whole or in part, in such manner as to actively induce the combination of such components outside of the United States in a manner that would infringe the patent if such combination occurred within the United States, shall be liable as an infringer.
>
> (2) Whoever without authority supplies or causes to be supplied in or from the United States any component of a patented invention that is especially made or especially adapted for use in the invention and not a staple article or commodity of commerce suitable for substantial noninfringing use, where such component is uncombined in whole or in part, knowing that such component is so made or adapted and intending that such component will be combined outside of the United States in a manner that would infringe the patent if such combination occurred within the United States, shall be liable as an infringer.

Subsection (1) is similar to inducement and subsection (2) is similar to contributory infringement. See also *Waymark Corp. v. Porta Systems Corp.*, 245 F.3d 1364 (Fed. Cir. 2001), regarding liability under subsection 271(f)(2) for exportation of a component, in which the court noted that "infringement without a completed infringing embodiment is not the norm in patent law, but it is reasonable in the context of 271(f)(2)."

40. See Chapter 6, discussing the single infringer principle.

different party will not generally result in patent infringement.[41] The claims must, in effect, be drafted from the perspective of a particular infringer. In this example, it would be wise to draft separate claims directed to individual server owners and separate claims directed to individual client owners.

Example 4.3 gives an example of covering a variety of potential infringers with an independent claim and then several dependent claims. It is a good idea to consider different potential markets and different potential infringers that claims may be drafted to cover, including manufacturers, resellers, system integrators, end users, and so on.

EXAMPLE 4.3

I claim:

1. An apparatus comprising: a flip chip.
2. The apparatus of claim 1, wherein the flip chip is incorporated in an integrated circuit (IC) chip.
3. The apparatus of claim 2, wherein the IC is part of an electronic circuit.
4. The apparatus of claim 3, wherein the electronic circuit is attached to a circuit board.
5. The apparatus of claim 4, wherein the circuit board is incorporated in a mobile device.
6. The apparatus of claim 5, wherein the mobile device is wirelessly communicatively couplable to other mobile devices via a satellite system.

Use Dependent Claims to Establish Fallback Position (and for Claim Differentiation)

As has been suggested, there are a variety of good reasons to include dependent claims from a claim drafting perspective. For example, they reduce the risk of a limitation being read into the base claim from which the dependent claim depends. They also provide written description support. They provide an additional basis to patentably distinguish from the art. They narrow scope,

41. *Id.*

which may remove problematic art but may still be broad enough to capture an infringer. Thus, *they establish a fallback position that may still be legally viable.* They also help clarify the scope of the base claim, which is another way of saying they help establish claim differentiation. They may also be used to capture the more important commercial embodiments while still implying greater claim scope.[42] They may also remove indefiniteness issues present for the base claim.[43]

Use Dependent Claims to Cover Higher Levels of Product Integration

Previously, we have given several examples of using higher levels of product integration in claims. This is also another approach to covering a variety of infringers. Example 4.3 is a good example, repeated here for convenience.

I claim:

1. An apparatus comprising: a flip chip.
2. The apparatus of claim 1, wherein the flip chip is incorporated in an integrated circuit (IC) chip.
3. The apparatus of claim 2, wherein the IC is part of an electronic circuit.
4. The apparatus of claim 3, wherein the electronic circuit is attached to a circuit board.
5. The apparatus of claim 4, wherein the circuit board is incorporated in a mobile device.
6. The apparatus of claim 5, wherein the mobile device is wirelessly communicatively couplable to other mobile devices via a satellite system.

This principle was also discussed in connection with examples of component-level claims versus system-level claims.[44] Following are several examples in which higher levels of product integration are included in dependent or in independent claims.

42. See Chapter 5, discussing legal analysis of dependent claims in the context of the DOE.
43. See Chapter 5, discussing clarifying relative claim terms to remove indefiniteness.
44. See, for example, discussion in Chapter 2 and this chapter.

Example 4.4 demonstrates in claim 1 a memory controller component base claim. Although a CPU is recited as a limitation, it is intended that it not be a claim element that must be present for infringement.[45] Claim 2 is a dependent claim that expressly recites the CPU as a claim element. Example 4.5 is similar in concept except that claim 1 includes the CPU as a claim element and claim 2 recites a higher level of integration, such as in a tablet, laptop computer, and so on.

EXAMPLE 4.4

I claim:

1. An apparatus comprising:

   random access memory (RAM) and a memory controller;

   wherein the memory controller is capable of initiating burst mode operation based, at least in part, on receipt of an externally derived request from an external central processing unit (CPU);

   wherein the request is to include a memory address, a word count, and a read or a write control transfer designation; and

   wherein the memory controller is to process the request and take control of an external system transfer bus.

2. The apparatus of claim 1, further comprising: the CPU and the system transfer bus.

EXAMPLE 4.5

I claim:

1. An apparatus comprising:

   random access memory (RAM), a memory controller, a central processing unit (CPU), and a system transfer bus;

45. See Chapter 3, discussing the body of a patent claim.

wherein the memory controller is capable of initiating burst mode operation based, at least in part, on receipt of a request from the CPU;

wherein the request is to include a memory address, a word count, and a read or a write control transfer designation; and

wherein the memory controller is to process the request and take control of the system transfer bus.

2. The apparatus of claim 1, wherein the RAM, memory controller, CPU, and system transfer bus are incorporated together in at least one of the following: a desktop computer, a laptop computer, a tablet, a smart phone, and/or a server.

Examples 4.6 and 4.8 illustrate two approaches to a method of operating a module or radio frequency (RF) module and Examples 4.7 and 4.9 show a comparable method claim except directed to operating a device integrating the technology at a higher level, here, a communication device. Of course, for Examples 4.6 and 4.8, a device integrating the technology at a higher level might have been recited in a dependent claim, rather than as an independent claim, as in Examples 4.7 and 4.9.

EXAMPLE 4.6

I claim:

1. A method of operating a module, the module including at least one integrated circuit (IC) chip comprising a plurality of N-type metal oxide semiconductor (NMOS) field effect transistors in a series connected stack configuration that comprises at least one NMOS field effect transistor including a body, the at least one NMOS field effect transistor either to pass a radio frequency (RF) signal in a series enable state or to not pass the RF signal in a series disable state, the method further comprising:

   electrically biasing the body of the at least one NMOS field effect transistor of the module in the series disable state to have a voltage level substantially more negative than the lowest voltage level of the following: ground, a DC voltage level of a source of the at least one series NMOS field effect transistor of the module, and a DC voltage level of a drain of the at least one NMOS field effect transistor of the module.

EXAMPLE 4.7

I claim:

1. A method of operating a communication device, the communication device including at least one integrated circuit (IC) chip comprising a plurality of series N-type metal oxide semiconductor (NMOS) field effect transistors in a series connected stack configuration that comprises at least one series NMOS field effect transistor including a body, the at least one series NMOS field effect transistor either to pass a radio frequency (RF) signal in a series enable state or to not pass the RF signal in a series disable state, the method further comprising:

   electrically biasing the body of the at least one series NMOS field effect transistor of the communication device in the series disable state to have a voltage level substantially more negative than the lowest voltage level of the following: ground, the DC voltage level of the source of the at least one series NMOS field effect transistor of the communication device, and the DC voltage level of the drain of the at least one series NMOS field effect transistor of the communication device.

EXAMPLE 4.8

I claim:

1. A method of operating a radio frequency (RF) module comprising at least one integrated circuit (IC) chip, the method comprising:

   inputting an input RF signal and one or more control signals to the RF module;

   outputting an output RF signal from the RF module;

   controlling, based at least in part on the one or more control signals, a silicon-on-insulator (SOI) N-type metal oxide semiconductor (NMOS) field effect transistor (FET) series connected stack configuration to either an OFF state or an ON state, the SOI NMOS FET stack configuration, comprising a plurality of NMOS FET transistors, being implemented on the at least one IC chip; and electrically biasing, based at least in part on the one or more control signals, a body of at least one NMOS FET transistor of the plurality of NMOS FET transistors of the SOI NMOS FET stack configuration with a bias voltage substantially more negative than ground during at least a portion of the OFF state of the at least one NMOS FET transistor.

EXAMPLE 4.9

I claim:

1. A method of operating a communication device including a radio frequency (RF) module that further includes at least one integrated circuit (IC) chip, the method comprising:

   controlling a silicon-on-insulator (SOI) N-type metal oxide semiconductor (NMOS) field effect transistor (FET) series connected stack configuration to either an OFF state or an ON state, the SOI NMOS FET stack configuration, comprising a plurality of NMOS FET transistors, being implemented on the at least one IC chip of the RF module of the communication device; and

   electrically biasing a body of at least one NMOS FET transistor of the plurality of NMOS FET transistors of the SOI NMOS FET stack configuration with a bias voltage substantially more negative than ground during at least a portion of the OFF state of the at least one NMOS FET transistor.

These examples show that innumerable ways to claim higher levels of integration are possible.

Claim the Environment of the Invention in Dependent Claims

While drafting broad patent claims is a laudable and valiant endeavor, it is important to remember that not all inventions are technological breakthroughs. Therefore, it is important to discuss the situation where the invention is just a relatively minor improvement on existing technology. Depending on the circumstances, for example, such claims may still provide commercial value and, in some cases, significant commercial value. Performing a search should help uncover situations where the art may be close.[46] However, regardless, it is always a good idea to make sure that you have claims directed to the "environment" of the invention.

This is meant to refer to details regarding the application of the invention that may largely be technologically independent from how the invention works.[47] Consider, for example, a simple implementation of a look-up table in a digital memory and nothing else. It is likely that a broad claim directed to such an invention is unlikely to make it through the PTO successfully. Such techniques have been known and applied for years. However, at the same time, it is reasonably likely if not highly likely that a table look-up invention, in a properly focused technical environment, and properly claimed, will make it through the PTO and also stand up in litigation. Suppose, for example, that in wireless networking technology, a table look-up implementation for directing packets from their source to their selected destination was an important aspect in a network interface card for providing the desired connection speed and that, before that, complex and time-consuming algorithms and memory accesses had to be employed. A similar point could be made in the microprocessor or graphics processor environment. As has been discussed elsewhere, it is often the recognition of the problem that makes the invention patentable.[48]

Therefore, claiming the environment of the invention provides a number of advantages. It should be done in the narrower dependent claims and, therefore, it takes advantage of claim differentiation. Further, it also addresses the issues of written description and claim construction that shall be discussed by providing additional embodiments to describe and claim. It also preserves validity, as just suggested. While the invention recited independent of the environment may or may not be patentable, claimed within the technical environment, there is a much better chance that the invention will withstand attacks on validity based upon prior art.

---

46. Although we are not necessarily recommending that a search be performed. See Chapter 2, discussing the advantages and disadvantages of searching.

47. Although, to be clear, it may be the environment of the invention that ultimately gives the invention a significant part of its value, as explained in more detail in this section.

48. *See, e.g.*, Eibel Process Co. v. Minn. & Ontario Paper Co., 261 U.S. 45 (1923); *see also* Chapter 1.

Keep the Invention Terminology Broad While Narrowing the Environment of the Invention

To draft a broad patent claim, it is often suggested that one seek to identify the smallest set of features needed for the invention/innovation as a starting point. We believe that remains correct in the appropriate circumstances (e.g., seeking patent claims that are broad). The following principles are follow-on principles for dependent claims.

We have discussed the problem-solution approach to claim drafting.[49] In some sense, the problem often helps define the invention by setting out the environment in which the invention arises.

Once the invention is realized for a particular environment, analogous environments in which the invention may be employed often become apparent. Hence, the broadest claim relates to the minimum set of features, described in the broadest terminology *and cast in the broadest environment.*[50] With this construct, the ways to narrow the subject matter relate to adding more features and narrowing (i.e., clarifying) the terminology. As discussed with respect to dependent claims, this involves the two respective formulations discussed:[51]

(1) "comprising:" or "further comprising:" (adding more features)
(2) "wherein" (narrowing/clarifying terminology)

The construct of narrowing the environment, however, as implied, may provide yet another way to look at narrowing the claims that may use either of these two formulations and, in some cases, may use both.

This notion is to narrow the environment while seeking to keep the terminology broad, as applicable (that is, in some cases, narrowing the environment may also call for narrowing terminology that describes the invention). Narrowing the environment also allows one to claim at least the commercial embodiment, but does so in dependent claims, as has previously been recommended.

Example 4.10 is primarily to cover a door jamb, which is a component of a door frame; however, the technology could be used with any frame. Hence, claim 1 is written more broadly than a door frame. The dependent claims include a window frame; however, claims 2–6 (particularly, 3–6) are used to narrow the environment, potentially providing additional ways to distinguish from prior art that may be cited or applied.

---

49. *See* Chris Konkol, *The "Problem Solved" in In re Wright and In re Dillon*, 31 IDEA J. L. & Tech. 131 (1990).

50. Again, assuming claim breath is a goal. See Chapter 2, discussing advantages and disadvantages of seeking broad claims.

51. See earlier in this chapter discussing claim drafting approaches to narrowing a claim.

EXAMPLE 4.10

I claim:

1. A frame comprising: a composite, the composite comprising:

   at least one first member comprising a composite material;

   at least one second member coupled to the first member, the second member comprising one or more materials; and

   an at least partially blended composite coating disposed over the first and the second members, the coating capable of providing structural support to the frame.

2. The frame of claim 1, wherein the frame comprises a window frame.
3. The frame of claim 1, wherein the frame comprises a door frame and the composite comprises a door jamb.
4. The frame of claim 3, wherein the door frame includes a bottom piece of the door frame and the bottom piece of the door frame comprises the door jamb.
5. The frame of claim 4, wherein the door frame includes a top piece and two side pieces.
6. The frame of claim 5, wherein one or more pieces of the door frame respectively comprise any one or any combination of the following: a metallic material, a mineral material, a ceramic material, a plastic material, or a hard fibrous material.
7. The frame of claim 1, wherein the coating is further capable of facilitating dimensional stability of the door frame.
8. The frame of claim 1, wherein the coating comprises any combination of the following: resin, substantially spherical structures, glass objects, polyvinyl acetate, a surfactant, glass micro spheres, or a wetting agent.
9. The frame of claim 1, wherein the one or more materials of the second member comprise any one or any combination of the following: a metallic material, a mineral material, a ceramic material, a plastic material, or a hard fibrous material.

Example 4.11 is the electronic switch we have previously considered that reduces analog signal corruption. It was primarily intended for wireless handsets but has a host of other applications, as recited in claim 2, including as a frequency mixer, a set-top box, a smart TV, a TiVo device, a smart console for an automobile, or an analog signal measurement device. The other dependent claims begin to narrow the environment, such as claims 6–8. For example, claim 6 recites an RF switch and includes a stack of transistors that permits higher voltage operation. Claim 7 recites the transistor as a transistor for a shunt path to ground, as used in a switch, and claim 8 recites a pass transistor path, as would be present in the electronic switch.

EXAMPLE 4.11

I claim:

1. A module comprising: at least one integrated circuit (IC) chip;

   the at least one IC chip included in the module and further including at least one field effect transistor, the at least one field effect transistor including a gate, a drain, a source, and a body;

   wherein, during at least a portion of an off state, the body of the at least one field effect transistor is to be electrically biased to have a voltage level substantially more negative than the lowest voltage level of the following: ground, the DC voltage level of the source of the at least one field effect transistor, and the DC voltage level of the drain of the at least one field effect transistor.

2. The module of claim 1, wherein the module is incorporated in at least one of the following: a frequency mixer, a wireless handset, a set-top box, a smart TV, a TiVo device, a smart console for an automobile, or an analog signal measurement device.

3. The module of claim 1, wherein the at least one field effect transistor comprises an N-type metal oxide semiconductor (NMOS) field effect transistor.

4. The module of claim 1, wherein the at least one field effect transistor is implemented in a silicon-on-insulator (SOI) technology.

5. The module of claim 1, wherein the voltage level substantially more negative than the lowest voltage level is more than one volt more negative than the lowest voltage level.

6. The module of claim 1, wherein the at least one field effect transistor is included in a stack of field effect transistors included in a radio frequency (RF) switch, the RF switch being included in the at least one IC chip.
7. The module of claim 1, wherein the at least one field effect transistor comprising a shunt transistor having a first node coupled to a first port and a second node coupled to ground, the shunt transistor to couple the first port with the ground in an on state, the shunt transistor to isolate the first port from the ground in an off state.
8. The module of claim 7, comprising:

   a second port; and another field effect transistor comprising a pass transistor having a first node coupled to the first port and a second node coupled to a second port, the pass transistor comprising a second gate, a second drain, a second source, and a second body,

   the pass transistor to couple the first port with the second port in an on state;

   the pass transistor to isolate the first port from the second port in an off state and wherein, during at least a portion of the off state of the pass transistor, the body of the pass transistor is to be electrically biased to have a voltage level substantially more negative than the lowest voltage level of the following: ground, the DC voltage level of the source of the pass transistor, and the DC voltage level of the drain of the pass transistor.
9. The module of claim 8, wherein the ports comprise RF ports.

Apparatus or Machine Claims

Understand how to draft apparatus claims and the rights covered by apparatus claims.

35 U.S.C. § 101

Whoever invents or discovers any new and useful process, machine, manufacture, or composition of matter, or any new and useful improvement thereof, may obtain a patent therefor, subject to the conditions and requirements of this title.

MPEP § 2106.03

[M]achines, manufactures and compositions of matter . . . define the types of physical or tangible "things" or "products" that Congress deemed appropriate to

patent. Digitech Image Techs. v. Electronics for Imaging, 758 F.3d 1344, 1348, 111 USPQ2d 1717, 1719 (Fed. Cir. 2014) ("For all categories except process claims, the eligible subject matter must exist in some physical or tangible form."). Thus, when determining whether a claimed invention falls within one of these three categories, examiners should verify that the invention is to at least one of the following categories ***and*** *is claimed in a physical or tangible form.*

- *A machine is a "concrete thing, consisting of parts, or of certain devices and combination of devices." Digitech, 758 F.3d at 1348–49, 111 USPQ2d at 1719 (quoting Burr v. Duryee, 68 U.S. 531, 570, 17 L. Ed. 650, 657 (1863)). This category "includes every mechanical device or combination of mechanical powers and devices to perform some function and produce a certain effect or result." Nuijten, 500 F.3d at 1355, 84 USPQ2d at 1501 (quoting Corning v. Burden, 56 U.S. 252, 267, 14 L. Ed. 683, 690 (1854)). . . .*

MPEP § 2112.01

I. PRODUCT AND APPARATUS CLAIMS—WHEN THE STRUCTURE RECITED IN THE REFERENCE IS SUBSTANTIALLY IDENTICAL TO THAT OF THE CLAIMS, CLAIMED PROPERTIES OR FUNCTIONS ARE PRESUMED TO BE INHERENT

Where the claimed and prior art products are identical or substantially identical in structure or composition, or are produced by identical or substantially identical processes, a prima facie case of either anticipation or obviousness has been established. In re Best, 562 F.2d 1252, 1255, 195 USPQ 430, 433 (CCPA 1977). "When the PTO shows a sound basis for believing that the products of the applicant and the prior art are the same, the applicant has the burden of showing that they are not." In re Spada, 911 F.2d 705, 709, 15 USPQ2d 1655, 1658 (Fed. Cir. 1990). Therefore, the prima facie case can be rebutted by evidence showing that the prior art products do not necessarily possess the characteristics of the claimed product. In re Best, 562 F.2d at 1255, 195 USPQ at 433. See also Titanium Metals Corp. v. Banner, 778 F.2d 775, 227 USPQ 773 (Fed. Cir. 1985) (Claims were directed to a titanium alloy containing 0.2–0.4% Mo and 0.6–0.9% Ni having corrosion resistance. A Russian article disclosed a titanium alloy containing 0.25% Mo and 0.75% Ni but was silent as to corrosion resistance. The Federal Circuit held that the claim was anticipated because the percentages of Mo and Ni were squarely within the claimed ranges. The court went on to say that it was immaterial what properties the alloys had or who discovered the properties because the composition is the same and thus must necessarily exhibit the properties.).

See also In re Ludtke, 441 F.2d 660, 169 USPQ 563 (CCPA 1971) (Claim 1 was directed to a parachute canopy having concentric circumferential panels radially separated from each other by radially extending tie lines. The panels were separated "such that the critical velocity of each successively larger panel will be less than the critical velocity of the previous panel, whereby said parachute will sequentially open and thus gradually decelerate." The court found that the claim was anticipated by Menget. Menget taught a parachute having three circumferential panels separated by tie lines. The court upheld the rejection finding that applicant had failed to show that Menget did not possess the functional characteristics of the claims.); Northam Warren Corp. v. D. F. Newfield Co., 7 F. Supp. 773, 22 USPQ 313 (E.D.N.Y. 1934) (A patent to a pencil for cleaning fingernails was held invalid because a pencil of the same structure for writing was found in the prior art.).

MPEP § 2114

I. INHERENCY AND FUNCTIONAL LIMITATIONS IN APPARATUS CLAIMS

Features of an apparatus may be recited either structurally or functionally. In re Schreiber, 128 F.3d 1473, 1478, 44 USPQ2d 1429, 1432 (Fed. Cir. 1997). See also MPEP § 2173.05(g). If an examiner concludes that a functional limitation is an inherent characteristic of the prior art, then to establish a prima case of anticipation or obviousness, the examiner should explain that the prior art structure inherently possesses the functionally defined limitations of the claimed apparatus. In re Schreiber, 128 F.3d at 1478, 44 USPQ2d at 1432. See also Bettcher Industries, Inc. v. Bunzl USA, Inc., 661 F.3d 629, 639–40, 100 USPQ2d 1433, 1440 (Fed. Cir. 2011). The burden then shifts to applicant to establish that the prior art does not possess the characteristic relied on. In re Schreiber, 128 F.3d at 1478, 44 USPQ2d at 1432; In re Swinehart, 439 F.2d 210, 213, 169 USPQ 226, 228 (CCPA 1971) ("where the Patent Office has reason to believe that a functional limitation asserted to be critical for establishing novelty in the claimed subject matter may, in fact, be an inherent characteristic of the prior art, it possesses the authority to require the applicant to prove that the subject matter shown to be in the prior art does not possess the characteristic relied on").

II. MANNER OF OPERATING THE DEVICE DOES NOT DIFFERENTIATE APPARATUS CLAIM FROM THE PRIOR ART

"[A]pparatus claims cover what a device ***is****, not what a device* ***does****." Hewlett-Packard Co. v. Bausch & Lomb Inc., 909 F.2d 1464, 1469, 15 USPQ2d 1525, 1528 (Fed. Cir. 1990) (emphasis in original). A claim containing a "recitation with respect to the manner in which a claimed apparatus is intended to be employed does not differentiate the claimed apparatus from a prior art apparatus" if the prior art apparatus teaches all the* *<u>structural</u>* *limitations of the claim. Ex parte Masham, 2 USPQ2d 1647 (Bd. Pat. App. & Inter. 1987) (The preamble of claim 1 recited that the apparatus was "for mixing flowing developer material" and the body of the claim recited "means for mixing . . . , said mixing means being stationary and completely submerged in*

the developer material." The claim was rejected over a reference which taught all the structural limitations of the claim for the intended use of mixing flowing developer. However, the mixer was only partially submerged in the developer material. The Board held that the amount of submersion is immaterial to the structure of the mixer and thus the claim was properly rejected.).

III. A PRIOR ART DEVICE CAN PERFORM ALL THE FUNCTIONS OF THE APPARATUS CLAIM AND STILL NOT ANTICIPATE THE CLAIM

Even if the prior art device performs all the functions recited in the claim, the prior art cannot anticipate the claim if there is any structural difference. It should be noted, however, that means-plus-function limitations are met by structures which are equivalent to the corresponding structures recited in the specification. In re Donaldson, 16 F.3d 1189, 1193, 29 USPQ2d 1845, 1848 (Fed. Cir. 1994). See also In re Robertson, 169 F.3d 743, 745, 49 USPQ2d 1949, 1951 (Fed. Cir. 1999) (The claims were drawn to a disposable diaper having three fastening elements. The reference disclosed two fastening elements that could perform the same function as the three fastening elements in the claims. The court construed the claims to require three separate elements and held that the reference did not disclose a separate third fastening element, either expressly or inherently.).

IV. DETERMINING WHETHER A COMPUTER-IMPLEMENTED FUNCTIONAL CLAIM LIMITATION IS PATENTABLE OVER THE PRIOR ART UNDER 35 U.S.C. 102 AND 103

Functional claim language that is not limited to a specific structure covers all devices that are capable of performing the recited function. Therefore, if the prior art discloses a device that can inherently perform the claimed function, a rejection under 35 U.S.C. 102 and/or 35 U.S.C. 103 may be appropriate. See In re Translogic Technology, Inc., 504 F.3d 1249, 1258, 84 USPQ2d 1929, 1935–1936 (Fed. Cir. 2007) (The claims were drawn to multiplexer circuit. The patent at issue claimed "coupled to" and "coupled to receive" between various portions of the circuitry. In reference to the claim phrase "input terminals 'coupled to receive' first and second input variables," the court held that "the claimed circuit does not require any specific input or connection . . . [a]s such, 'coupled to' and 'coupled to receive' are clearly different . . . [a]s shown in [the figures of the] patent, input terminals . . . only need to be 'capable of receiving' an input variable for the multiplexer circuit as claimed". Therefore, the specification supported the claim construction "that 'coupled to receive' means 'capable of receiving.'"); Intel Corp. v. U.S. Int'l Trade Comm'n, 946 F.2d 821, 832, 20 USPQ2d 1161, 1171 (Fed. Cir. 1991) (The court held that "programmable" claim language required only that the accused product could be programmed to perform the claimed functionality.); In re Schreiber, 128 F.3d 1473, 1478, 44 USPQ2d 1429, 1432 (Fed. Cir. 1997); In re Best, 562 F.2d 1252, 1254, 195 USPQ 430, 433 (CCPA 1977); In re Ludtke, 441 F.2d 660, 663–64, 169 USPQ 563, 566–67 (CCPA 1971); In re Swinehart, 439

F.2d 210, 212–13, 169 USPQ 226, 228–29 (CCPA 1971) ("[I]t is elementary that the mere recitation of a newly discovered function or property, inherently possessed by things in the prior art, does not cause a claim drawn to those things to distinguish over the prior art"). See MPEP § 2112 for more information.

Conversely, computer-implemented functional claim limitations may narrow the functionality of the device, by limiting the specific structure capable of performing the recited function. Nazomi Communications, Inc. v. Nokia Corp., 739 F.3d 1339, 1345, 109 USPQ2d 1258, 1262 (Fed Cir. 2014) (The claims were drawn to a CPU that can perform processing of both register-based and stack-based instructions. Appellant alleged infringement of the claims based on claim construction requiring only hardware capable of performing the claimed functionalities. Contrasted with the finding of Intel Corp. v. U.S. Int'l Trade Comm'n, 846 F.2d 821, 832, 20 USPQ2d 1161, 1171 (Fed. Cir. 1991), the court found that "[s]ince hardware cannot meet these limitations in the absence of enabling software, the claims are properly construed as claiming an apparatus comprising a combination of hardware and software capable of practicing the claim limitations.").

Computer-implemented functional claim limitations may also be broad because the term "computer" is commonly understood by one of ordinary skill in the art to describe a variety of devices with varying degrees of complexity and capabilities. In re Paulsen, 30 F.3d 1475, 1479–80, 31 USPQ2d 1671, 1674 (Fed. Cir. 1994). Therefore, a claim containing the term "computer" should not be construed as limited to a computer having a specific set of characteristics and capabilities, unless the term is modified by other claim terms or clearly defined in the specification to be different from its common meaning. Id. In Paulsen, the claims, directed to a portable computer, were rejected as anticipated under 35 U.S.C. 102 by a reference that disclosed a calculator, because the term "computer" was given the broadest reasonable interpretation consistent with the specification to include a calculator, and a calculator was considered to be a particular type of computer by those of ordinary skill in the art. Id.

When determining whether a computer-implemented functional claim would have been obvious, examiners should note that broadly claiming an automated means to replace a manual function to accomplish the same result does not distinguish over the prior art. See Leapfrog Enters., Inc. v. Fisher-Price, Inc., 485 F.3d 1157, 1161, 82 USPQ2d 1687, 1691 (Fed. Cir. 2007) ("Accommodating a prior art mechanical device that accomplishes [a desired] goal to modern electronics would have been reasonably obvious to one of ordinary skill in designing children's learning devices. Applying modern electronics to older mechanical devices has been commonplace in recent years."); In re Venner, 262 F.2d 91, 95, 120 USPQ 193, 194 (CCPA 1958); see also MPEP § 2144.04. Furthermore, implementing a known function on a computer has been deemed obvious to one of ordinary skill in the art if the automation of the known function on a general purpose computer is nothing more than the predictable use of prior art elements according to their established functions. KSR Int'l Co. v. Teleflex Inc., 550 U.S. 398, 417, 82 USPQ2d 1385, 1396 (2007); see also MPEP § 2143,

Exemplary Rationales D and F. Likewise, it has been found to be obvious to adapt an existing process to incorporate Internet and Web browser technologies for communicating and displaying information because these technologies had become commonplace for those functions. Muniauction, Inc. v. Thomson Corp., 532 F.3d 1318, 1326–27, 87 USPQ2d 1350, 1357 (Fed. Cir. 2008).

One aspect of a patent claim to keep in mind is that, in general, the whole is usually greater than the sum of the parts. In other words, it is the elements and limitations in combination, in the manner recited in the claim, that not only makes the claim unique but also unobvious. This aspect of a patent claim is expressly recognized by § 103 (post-AIA, but pre-AIA is nearly identical), which states:

> A patent for a claimed invention may not be obtained, notwithstanding that the claimed invention is not identically disclosed as set forth in section 102, if the differences between the claimed invention and the prior art are such that the claimed invention as a whole would have been obvious before the effective filing date of the claimed invention to a person having ordinary skill in the art to which the claimed invention pertains. Patentability shall not be negated by the manner in which the invention was made.

The statute, therefore, focuses on "the differences between the claimed invention," which refers to the patent claim at issue, and "the prior art." These differences, "as a whole" are considered "before the effective filing date of the claimed invention" with respect to "a person having ordinary skill in the art to which the claimed invention pertains."

The language "as a whole" means that *the claim language must be considered as a whole for purposes of determining obviousness*. In other words, while the claim is a collection of elements and limitations, it is not proper, under this section, to simply dissect the claim into separate elements and limitations and see if the prior art has each recited element and limitation. Again, the whole may be (and typically is) greater than the sum of the parts. For example, *there may be advantages that come from combining the elements and limitations together in the manner recited in the claim that would not be present if those elements and limitations were dissected and viewed in isolation from one another. Those advantages that flow from "the whole" are relevant to determining whether the invention would have been nonobvious at the time the invention was made.*[52]

---

52. *See, e.g.*, Panduit Corp. v. Dennison Mfg. Co., 810 F.2d 1561, 1567–68, 1 U.S.P.Q.2d 1593, 1597 (Fed. Cir. 1987), *cert. denied*, 481 U.S. 1052 (1987) ("Analysis begins with a key legal question—what is the invention claimed? Courts are required to view the claimed invention as a whole. . . ."); Ruiz v. A.B. Chance Co., 357 F.3d 1270, 1275 (Fed. Cir. 2004) ("The 'as a whole' instruction in title 35 prevents evaluation of the invention part by part. . . . This form of

Following are illustrative examples of apparatus or machine claims, as an introduction. Example 4.12 is an apparatus patent claim directed to an IC.

EXAMPLE 4.12

I claim:

1. An integrated circuit (IC) comprising: at least one metal conductor and at least one metal oxide semiconductor field effect transistor (MOSFET);

   wherein multiple contacts are coupled to the metal conductor along a major axis of the at least one metal conductor to conduct current to or from the at least one metal conductor and to or from drain or source regions of the MOSFET; and

   wherein the at least one metal conductor is tapered along the major axis so that during current flow the current density in the at least one metal conductor is substantially constant along the major axis.

Example 4.13 is an example of an apparatus claim directed to a stool or chair.

EXAMPLE 4.13

I claim:

1. An apparatus comprising:

   a substantially horizontally oriented, rectangularly shaped seat including four corners;

   wherein attached to a respective corner of the seat is a substantially vertically oriented leg such that the legs point in the same direction away from the seat, are oriented to be substantially mutually parallel, and are of substantially the same length.

---

hindsight reasoning, using the invention as a roadmap to find its prior art components, would discount the value of combining various existing features or principles in a new way to achieve a new result—often the very definition of invention.").

Examples 4.14 through 4.16 are examples of apparatus claims directed to memory and a memory controller.[53]

EXAMPLE 4.14

I claim:

1. An apparatus comprising:

   random access memory (RAM) and a memory controller;

   wherein the memory controller is capable of initiating burst mode operation based, at least in part, on receipt of an externally derived request from an external central processing unit (CPU);

   wherein the request is to include a memory address, a word count, and a read or a write control transfer designation; and

   wherein the memory controller is to process the request and take control of an external system transfer bus.

EXAMPLE 4.15

I claim:

1. An apparatus comprising:

   random access memory (RAM), a memory controller, a central processing unit (CPU), and a system transfer bus;

   wherein the memory controller is capable of initiating burst mode operation based, at least in part, on receipt of a request from the CPU;

   wherein the request is to include a memory address, a word count, and a read or a write control transfer designation; and

   wherein the memory controller is to process the request and take control of a system transfer bus.

53. These examples correspond to some prior examples from Chapter 2.

EXAMPLE 4.16

I claim:

1. An apparatus comprising:

   random access memory (RAM), a memory controller, a central processing unit (CPU), and a system transfer bus;

   wherein the memory controller comprises means for initiating burst mode operation based, at least in part, on receipt of a request from the CPU;

   wherein the request is to include a memory address, a word count, and a read or a write control transfer designation; and

   wherein the memory controller comprises means for processing the request and means for taking control of a system transfer bus.

Example 4.17 is an example of an apparatus claim directed to a network device for a broadcast domain of a network.

EXAMPLE 4.17

I claim:

1. An apparatus comprising:

   at least one network device of at least a first broadcast domain;

   wherein the at least one network device is to emulate one or more network devices of at least a second broadcast domain; and

   wherein the at least one network device is to encapsulate one or more signal packets of the at least a first broadcast domain directed to a network device of the at least a second broadcast domain and is to communicate the encapsulated one or more signal packets to at least one tunnel server.

One may notice several features by comparing these claim examples. Each example claim ends with a period, of course. Further, each begins with a preamble, usually stating "[a]n apparatus " or similar language. After the preamble is a transition word, in these examples "comprising," followed by a colon.

After the colon is the body of the claim, which contains the elements and limitations and associated relationships.

The structure of a patent claim that includes a preamble, transition word or phrase, and a claim body is largely by custom. However, courts use this structure to interpret the claims, so varying from it may be risky.

Instead, it is preferred to adhere to this structure and be quite clear what constitutes the preamble, the transition word or phrase, and the claim body. For example, it could be problematic if it were unclear where the preamble ends and the body begins. Likewise, it might be problematic if it were unclear which word is intended as the transition word. These issues might be problematic because, rather than receiving an interpretation as intended by the drafter, this may leave it to another decision-maker, such as an examiner, a judge, or an opponent in a license negotiation, based on an incorrect understanding, to decide how the claim should be interpreted. There may be times where a patent claim may be intended to be vague deliberately. However, the division between these basic components of a patent claim should be clear or one may risk an unintended interpretation with unknown consequences.

Another aspect to appreciate is that some claim features are described in "structural" terms and some are described in "functional" terms. It is well-recognized that both are permissible.[54] The distinction is that "structural" terms recite what the claim feature is, whereas "functional" terms recite what the claim feature does.[55] From the preceding examples, "memory," "CPU," "leg," "seat," and so on, are structural. "Means for storing," "means for processing," "to emulate," "to encapsulate," and "to communicate" are functional. Whether to use structural or functional terms is a tricky question because it may affect claim scope in ways that are not always fully predictable. The next few sections explore some of these issues. Ideally, if only for claim diversity, using both approaches is usually recommended.[56]

Another feature to appreciate is that these apparatus claims are written to make it clear that the apparatus *as claimed* is *not* operating, but rather is *capable of* operation. If there is ambiguity on this point, the claim may be indefinite and, consequently, invalid.[57]

---

54. *See, e.g., In re* Schreiber, 128 F.3d 1473 (Fed. Cir. 1997); *In re* Swinehart, 439 F.2d 210, 169 U.S.P.Q. 226 (C.C.P.A. 1971).

55. *See, e.g., Schreiber*, 128 F.3d 1473; *Swinehart*, 439 F.2d 210, 169 U.S.P.Q. 226.

56. See also treatment later in this chapter regarding means-plus-function/step-plus-func tion claims and function versus structure in claim drafting.

57. See Chapter 6, discussing the problems of having the statutory class of a patent claim be unclear. *Cf.* INVT SPE LLC v. Int'l Trade Comm'n, 46 F.4th 1361 (Fed. Cir. 2022) (distinguishing between actual operation and capability of operating or performing for apparatus

In general, the world of machine claims is separate from the world of process claims. A claim that blends these worlds risks leaving unclear which was intended, which makes claim scope unclear and may make the claim invalid.[58] It is worth the time here to study the claims to see the linguistic approaches used to make this clear from the language of the claim itself.

Yet another feature is that the claims are written with the understanding that one party owns or controls all the features claimed. This is referred to as the single infringer principle or rule. If it takes multiple independent parties acting together to meet all the limitations of a single patent claim, it may be that no one infringes the claim.[59]

This difference may be understood with reference to Examples 2.2 and 2.6 from Chapter 2 (Examples 4.14 and 4.15 in this chapter, although claim 4.14 includes the terms "external" and "externally derived" compared with claim 2.2). Example 2.2 (or Example 4.14) is specifically only intended to cover memory with a memory controller. The other limitations are directed to capabilities thereof only.[60] In contrast, Example 2.6 (or Example 4.15) is intended to cover a system that includes memory, memory controller, CPU, and system transfer bus. Thus, this latter claim is formulated to clarify which features are intended as claim elements that must be present in an accused device, here, all the features mentioned in the preceding sentence. Suppose that one *independent* party provides memory and a memory controller and another *independent* party provides a CPU and system transfer bus. Depending on other facts, it is a possibility that neither party infringes the claim of Example 2.6 (Example 4.15), although, generally, the party that integrates all these components is likely the direct infringer of this claim.

Still another aspect of these claim examples is more a matter of style than a requirement. The claims are written so that the primary claim elements are initially recited and then there is a series of "wherein" clauses that add further limitations. This is a nice style to use, but it is not required. One benefit is

---

claims, particularly for software on a device, which tends to be functional, without discussing indefiniteness issue of mixing method and apparatus limitations).

58. See Chapter 6, discussing the problems of having the statutory class of a patent claim be unclear. *Cf. INVT SPE LLC*, 46 F.4th 1361 (distinguishing between actual operation and capability of operating or performing for apparatus claims, particularly for software on a device, which tends to be functional, without discussing indefiniteness issue of mixing method and apparatus limitations).

59. See treatment in Chapter 6 of the single infringer rule. One notable exception is 35 U.S.C. § 271(g). The Federal Circuit recently held that the single infringer rule does not apply. As to a method of making claim implicated by that statutory section, there is liability without meeting the single infringer rule. *See* Syngenta Crop Prot. v. Willowood, LLC, 944 F.3d 1344 (Fed. Cir. 2019).

60. See treatment in Chapter 2; these claims are recited here as Examples 4.14 and 4.15.

that it is similar to how dependent claims are written.[61] It is easy to remove a "wherein" clause from a base claim, as with these examples, and move that limitation to a dependent claim as you draft.[62]

In contrast, some like to write claims where claim elements and/or claim limitations may instead be inferred, rather than introduced by being separately and positively recited. These claims tend to have tighter language, but so-called inferential claiming may have more interpretive risk.[63] An example from Chapter 3 partially illustrates this style. It begins:

---

1. An apparatus comprising:

   a substantially horizontally oriented, rectangularly shaped seat including four corners; . . .

The initial part of the claim body, instead, might have been written to be more like the style using "wherein" clauses, to separately and positively recite specific claim features, as follows:

---

1. An apparatus comprising: a seat;

   wherein the seat is substantially horizontally oriented;

   wherein the substantially horizontally oriented seat is rectangularly shaped . . .

Many claims are a combination of both styles in which some features are first separately and positively recited and some features are first recited in connection with a particular, more detailed limitation.[64]

Related to the formalism of first separately and positively reciting a claim element, is a formalism in which a first recitation of a feature is introduced with an indefinite article (e.g., "a" or "an")[65] and later references in the claim to that feature use either a definite article (e.g., "the") or the word "said"

61. See earlier in this chapter treating independent and dependent claims.
62. *Id.*
63. See treatment in Chapter 3 of inferential claiming.
64. *Id.*
65. There may be instances where, grammatically, an indefinite article may not be appropriate. For example, one may initially recite "four legs" but later recite either "the four legs" or "said four legs."

before the feature. This clarifies that you are discussing a previously recited feature rather than a new and separate feature.

As may be clear, these formal conventions are to make the intended scope of the patent claim reasonably clear. Often, deviations from these conventions may introduce ambiguity into the claim, which in examination may lead to a rejection or, if issued, potentially may make the claim invalid or alter its intended scope. There are some situations where such formal conventions are not observed, perhaps to make a patent claim less cumbersome and easier to comprehend. However, it is generally good practice to start by adhering to these style conventions quite rigorously and to avoid developing inadvertently sloppy drafting habits that may over time undermine the quality of the claims you draft.

An issue that can divide patent practitioners is the use of "the" versus "said" when discussing a previously recited element or limitation. Use of "said" is an age-old practice that is frequently used primarily out of custom. In general, it is good to have the facility to draft claims either way, but a default approach in the absence of client preference is recommended. Here is a simple example to show the difference:

EXAMPLE 4.18

I claim:

1. A bicycle comprising:

   a bicycle chassis and two bicycle wheels;

   wherein said wheels are able to attach to said chassis in a manner to be rotatable so that said bicycle is to be capable of being ridden with said wheels attached to said chassis.

Here is a formulation without "said":

EXAMPLE 4.19

I claim:

1. A bicycle comprising:

   a bicycle chassis and two bicycle wheels;

wherein the bicycle wheels are able to attach to the bicycle chassis in a manner to be rotatable so that the bicycle is to be capable of being ridden with the bicycle wheels attached to the bicycle chassis.

Some practitioners profess to prefer using "the" so that a patent claim is more easily understood by a lay person, such as members of a jury, for example. However, some prefer "said" due to its historical roots. Likewise, some attorneys have no real preference.

Here, however, "the" is recommended over "said" for a different reason. For a set of claims with dependencies, especially during a prosecution that may have many months between office action responses (or even longer), it becomes surprisingly easy to inadvertently intermix the use of "said" with "the," potentially raising difficult and undesired questions of interpretation.

To illustrate, for the claim of Example 4.18, consider a dependent claim as follows:

---

2. The bicycle of claim 1, wherein the wheels are respectively attached to the chassis via a bolt and nut.

This claim 2 may result in confusion. Are these the same wheels and chassis in claim 1 or different ones? Here, this ambiguity, while not ideal, may very well be resolvable. However, for complex claims with many dependencies, such ambiguities may be unresolvable, with associated legally undesirable consequences. Therefore, to ensure consistency, we recommend consistently using "the" over "said."

Structural versus Functional Elements or Limitations

Understand the difference between structural and functional claim language.

35 U.S.C. § 112(f) (Formerly 35 U.S.C. § 112, ¶ 6)

(f) Element in Claim for a Combination.—An element in a claim for a combination may be expressed as a means or step for performing a specified function

without the recital of structure, material, or acts in support thereof, and such claim shall be construed to cover the corresponding structure, material, or acts described in the specification and equivalents thereof.

In re Swinehart
439 F.2d 210
United States Court of Customs and Patent Appeals
April 1, 1971, Decided

Questions

1. The U.S. Court of Customs and Patent Appeals (CCPA) is a predecessor court to the Federal Circuit. The Federal Circuit explicitly adopted the CCPA decisions as its own binding precedent.[66] Thus, *In re Swinehart* remains good law in the Federal Circuit. The case holds that functional language is not inherently indefinite. However, how does the court reconcile its holding with *General Electric Co. v. Wabash Appliance Corp.*,[67] which is clearly binding precedent?
2. Why is there not also an issue with *Halliburton Oil Well Cementing Co. v. Walker*,[68] or is there? Note that 35 U.S.C. § 112, paragraph 6 (112, 6), today subsection 112(f), was passed by Congress to overrule *Halliburton Oil*. What is the distinction from *General Electric v. Wabash*?
3. Generally, in claim drafting a distinction is drawn between language that is "functional" and language that is "structural." The court stated it well as follows:

   > We take the characterization "functional", as used by the Patent Office and argued by the parties, to indicate nothing more than the fact that an attempt is being made to define something (in this case, a composition) by what it does rather than by what it is (as evidenced by specific structure or material, for example).[69]

   However, note the observation made by Judge Lane: "For example, a 'door' is something used to close and open a passageway; a 'nail' is an object used to hold two pieces of material together; a 'black' material is

66. *See* S. Corp. v. United States, 690 F.2d 1368 (Fed. Cir. 1982).
67. 304 U.S. 364 (1938).
68. 329 U.S. 1 (1946).
69. *In re* Swinehart, 439 F.2d 210, 212, 169 U.S.P.Q. 226 (C.C.P.A. 1971).

one incapable of reflecting visible light."[70] To drive his point home, is the term "processor" functional or structural?

4. Note that we currently have *In re Swinehart* and its progeny and we have subsection 112(f). Depending on which applies to a particular claim leads to very different legal consequences. Therefore, how does one determine which applies to a given claim? Is it possible to draft patent claims so that depending on the specifics one approach will apply instead of the other?
5. The court states: "[I]t is elementary that the mere recitation of a newly discovered function or property, inherently possessed by things in the prior art, does not cause a claim drawn to those things to distinguish over the prior art."[71] Is this correct? If so, how does one determine whether they have "invented" something new versus merely "discovered" a property or function that was "inherently" possessed?
6. What of this statement by the court:

   > Additionally, where the Patent Office has reason to believe that functional limitation asserted to be critical for establishing novelty in the claimed subject matter may, in fact, be an inherent characteristic of the prior art, it possesses the authority to require the applicant to prove that the subject matter shown to be in the prior art does not possess the characteristic relied on.[72]

   Does the PTO have this authority? If so, how would it work in practice?
7. Do you agree with this statement by the court: "It follows that when appellants' claim is read in light of that disclosure the limits it purports to define are made sufficiently clear."[73] This ultimately determined whether or not the claim is sufficiently definite, and observe that one of the judges dissented on this basis. The public notice function of patent claims is an important doctrine. The court states: "It is true that the figures reproduced in the specification indicate that the degree of transparency varies depending on such factors as the conditions employed in producing the crystal, the thickness of the crystal and the particular wavelength of the radiation transmitted. However,

70. *Id.* at 215.
71. *Id.* at 212–13.
72. *Id.* at 213.
73. *Id.* at 215.

in all cases a substantial amount of infrared radiation is transmitted."[74] Is "a substantial amount of infrared radiation is transmitted" sufficiently clear? On the other hand, the claim also says "resistant to shock." Why is that not indefinite?

Greenberg v. Ethicon Endo-Surgery, Inc.
91 F.3d 1580
United States Court of Appeals for the Federal Circuit
August 8, 1996, Decided

Questions

1. At the district court level, the court granted a motion for summary judgment of noninfringement. The ruling turned on the interpretation of "detent mechanism." While the district court determined that 112, 6 applied, the Federal Circuit disagreed. Why is it that whether 112, 6 applies has such a significant outcome on the case? What is the proper claim construction analysis if 112, 6 applies? What was the district court's claim construction analysis? What was the Federal Circuit's claim construction analysis?
2. The district court concluded that the accused products met the recited function of "detent mechanism," but was not structurally equivalent to Greenberg's approach. What does this mean in the context of applying 112, 6 to interpret the language of a patent claim?
3. The Federal Circuit concluded that 112, 6 did not apply to interpret "detent mechanism." How important was the fact that the language "means for" was not used? What is the court's analysis to determine the application of 112, 6 even in situations in which "means for" is not used?
4. The language "detent means" was used in the specification. Why did the Federal Circuit conclude that 112, 6 did not apply, despite this language?
5. How significant in the analysis is whether an attempt was being made to invoke 112, 6?
6. The court acknowledges that the language "detent mechanism" was being used in a functional manner, yet chose not to apply 112, 6. What

74. *Id.*

appears to be a significant factor on whether or not to apply 112, 6 if functional language is used in a patent claim?

Williamson v. Citrix Online, LLC
792 F.3d 1339
United States Court of Appeals for the Federal Circuit
June 16, 2015, Decided

Questions

1. Note the unusual procedural posture of this case. One part of the opinion is designated as *en banc*. What happened? Typically, for an *en banc* decision, a case is first heard by a three-judge panel. Then, either by a request by one of the parties, or *sua sponte*, there may be an *en banc* call to have the entire court hear the case (with an *en banc* call, the entire court votes on whether the case should be heard *en banc*). If there are enough votes to rehear the case before the entire court, an *en banc* hearing is docketed, the parties are notified in order to brief the judges, it becomes a matter of public record that the case is going to be heard by the entire court, and, not infrequently, for important legal issues, amicus briefs are also submitted before the hearing and, typically, a new opinion for the entire court replaces the opinion by the three-judge panel. Judge Newman suggests this approach did not occur here. She states: "An unheralded footnote, announcing en banc change of law, without notice to and participation of the interested public, is not the optimum judicial path."[75] Ultimately, then, for some reason, the entire court only decided to rule on one aspect of the case. Ostensibly, this was needed for the court to overrule its own precedent regarding 112, 6; however, it remains unclear why the entire court chose to only address the one issue and not the entire opinion, and why it was not done in the usual fashion in accordance with Federal Court protocol. Does the opinion give any suggestion for this change?
2. Judge Newman, in her dissent, discusses quite a bit of the history of 112, 6, which, apparently, starts as § 112, paragraph 3, and is now subsection 112(f). Does the legislative history affect your view of this case? One thing to know is that for many years, patent attorneys thought "means-plus-function" claims provided broad scope. It was not until

75. Williamson v. Citrix Online, LLC, 792 F.3d 1339, 1359 (Fed. Cir. 2015).

the late 1980s (recall the Federal Circuit was not established until 1982) that the Federal Circuit upon examining the provision concluded that it was a claim *narrowing* provision rather than a claim *broadening* provision.[76]

3. Given that a claim interpreted under § 112, 6 is more likely to receive a narrow interpretation, why use "means for" in a claim ever? Does the provision provide any advantages?
4. How might this case affect claim drafting in general? How does one draft a patent claim so as to not invoke § 112, 6?
5. What about the use of "step" in a patent claim? It used to be commonplace to begin a method claim with: "A method comprising the steps of:." Do you have any thoughts on this practice in light of the language of § 112, 6 and the commentary provided by P.J. Federico?[77] By analogy with "means-plus-function" claims, how do you think "step-plus-function" claims may be interpreted?[78] If we consider the policy articulated by the case, is there a basis to argue that some claims should be interpreted to invoke § 112, 6 although they do not use the word "step"? If so, how might such claims be characterized or identified?
6. Before this case, the Federal Circuit employed a strong presumption that lack of the word "means" meant § 112, 6 did not apply. After this case, there is a presumption, but it is not a strong presumption. What is the difference? Consider that originally the three-judge panel held that § 112, 6 was not invoked.
7. Observe that the claim at issue was not held invalid *under* § 112, 6. Rather, the claim was interpreted to invoke § 112, 6. That section requires that the specification describe material, acts, or structure that "correspond" to the recited function. The court in this regard specifically stated:

> The district court was correct that the specification of the '840 patent fails to disclose corresponding structure. The written description of the '840 patent makes clear that the distributed learning control module cannot be implemented in a general purpose computer, but instead must be implemented in a special purpose computer—a general purpose computer programmed to perform particular functions pursuant to instructions from program software. A special purpose

76. *See* Johnston v. IVAC Corp., 885 F.2d 1574 (Fed. Cir. 1989).
77. *See* P.J. Federico, *Commentary on the New Patent Act, in* 35 U.S.C.A. 1 (West 1954).
78. *See* O.I. Corp. v. Tekmar Co., 115 F.3d 1576 (Fed. Cir. 1997).

> computer is required because the distributed learning control module has specialized functions as outlined in the written description. *See, e.g.*, '840 patent col.5 ll.48–64. In cases such as this, involving a claim limitation that is subject to § 112, para. 6 that must be implemented in a special purpose computer, this court has consistently required that the structure disclosed in the specification be more than simply a general purpose computer or microprocessor. *E.g.*, *Aristocrat Techs. Austl. Pty Ltd. v. Int'l Game Tech.*, 521 F.3d 1328, 1333 (Fed. Cir. 2008) (citing *WMS Gaming, Inc. v. Int'l Game Tech.*, 184 F.3d 1339 (Fed. Cir. 1999)). We require that the specification disclose an algorithm for performing the claimed function. *Net MoneyIN, Inc. v. VeriSign, Inc.*, 545 F.3d 1359, 1367 (Fed. Cir. 2008). The algorithm may be expressed as a mathematical formula, in prose, or as a flow chart, or in any other manner that provides sufficient structure. *Noah*, 675 F.3d at 1312 (citing *Finisar Corp. v. DirecTV Grp., Inc.*, 523 F.3d 1323, 1340 (Fed. Cir. 2008)).[79]

Here, because the specification did not include that description, the claim was held indefinite *under* § 112, paragraph 2 (112, 2). Does this situation and outcome imply any claim drafting/specification drafting guidance? Note that the district court identified three claimed functions associated with the "distributed learning control module" term and held that one of them did not have corresponding structure.

8. What does it take to meet § 112, 2 for a claim interpreted under § 112, 6 (i.e., subsection 112(f))? The court stated, as previously shown:

> We require that the specification disclose an algorithm for performing the claimed function. *Net MoneyIN, Inc. v. VeriSign, Inc.*, 545 F.3d 1359, 1367 (Fed. Cir. 2008). The algorithm may be expressed as a mathematical formula, in prose, or as a flow chart, or in any other manner that provides *sufficient* structure. *Noah*, 675 F.3d at 1312 (citing *Finisar Corp. v. DirecTV Grp., Inc.*, 523 F.3d 1323, 1340 (Fed. Cir. 2008)).[80]

What constitutes sufficient structure, especially in the context of a formula, prose, or flowchart, as examples? The court has also stated that § 112, 6 will not be invoked for a claim that recites "*sufficient* structure." Specifically, the court said:

79. *Williamson*, 792 F.3d at 1354.
80. *Id.* at 1352 (emphasis added).

> When a claim term lacks the word "means," the presumption can be overcome and § 112, para. 6 will apply if the challenger demonstrates that the claim term fails to "recite sufficiently definite structure" or else recites "function without reciting *sufficient* structure for performing that function." *Watts*, 232 F.3d at 880.[81]

9. There is another context in which the Federal Circuit has applied a "strong" or "heavy" presumption. The court has stated that with respect to claim construction, there is a "heavy" presumption that the claim term at issue is used in a manner consistent with its ordinary and customary meaning.[82] Like here, what is the difference between a presumption and a heavy presumption?
10. The Federal Circuit also states: "To the extent the district court, in construing the claims, makes underlying findings of fact based on extrinsic evidence, we review such findings of fact for clear error."[83] Why it is that the Federal Circuit will give deference to factual findings underlying the claims construction based on extrinsic evidence, but not deference to factual findings based on intrinsic evidence?[84]
11. How should the language (emphasis added) of § 112, 6 that states "such claim *shall be construed* to cover the corresponding structure, material, or acts described in the specification *and equivalents thereof*" be interpreted? Is this intended as a reference to the doctrine of equivalents (DOE)? If not, does the DOE apply to "means-plus-function" claims? If so, how is it construed, particularly in light of the statutory language of § 112, 6?[85]
12. What do you think of Federico's statement:

> This relates primarily to the construction of such claims for the purpose of determining when the claim is infringed (note the use of the word "cover"), and would not appear to have much, if any, applicability in determining the patentability of such claims over the prior art, that is, the Patent Office is not authorized to allow a claim which "reads on" the prior art.[86]

---

81. *Id.* at 1348 (emphasis added).
82. *See* Phillips v. AWH Corp., 415 F.2d 1303 (Fed. Cir. 2005) (en banc).
83. *Williamson*, 792 F.3d at 1346.
84. *See* Teva Pharms. USA, Inc. v. Sandoz, Inc., 135 S. Ct. 831, 840–41 (2015).
85. *See* Valmont Indus., Inc. v. Reinke Mfg. Co., 983 F.2d 1039 (Fed. Cir. 1993); Kemco Sales, Inc. v. Control Papers Co., 208 F.3d 2052 (Fed. Cir. 2000).
86. Federico, *supra* note 77, at 25, 26.

Are claims under § 112, 6 interpreted differently during prosecution than during litigation?[87]

13. After the Supreme Court's *Markman* decision,[88] in general, claim construction is performed by the judge and whether an accused product or service falls within the scope of the claims, as construed by the judge, is performed by the jury. Given the unusual nature of § 112, 6, how might this work in practice? The judge, of course, determines whether § 112, 6 is invoked and, likewise, if so, determines the claimed function. But who determines the "corresponding" material, acts, or structure with respect to the claimed functions disclosed by the specification? Is this an issue of law or an issue of fact, and should this be considered part of claim construction or whether something falls within the scope of the language of the claim?[89]
14. Given the inherently functional nature of software, how does one claim software without the use of so-called nonce words? For example, in this case, the claim language at issue recited "distributed learning control module." How might this be claimed without using a "nonce word"?[90]

* * *

It is well-established that claims may be structural and that claims may be functional.[91] However, which approach may be better is a matter of judgment. Furthermore, functional language, although potentially broader on the face of the claim, has several legal pitfalls. For this and other reasons, it is recommended that both approaches to claim drafting be employed.

Again, based on the face of the claim, functional limitations appear to be broader than structural limitations; however, it is not always easy to predict whether such limitations will be interpreted as the words appear in the claim. A related issue is whether a suitable structural term exists to claim the feature sought to be covered with claim language, suggesting that resort to functional language may more or less be necessary.

Some of the complex legal issues related to functional language in patent claims emanate from how the Federal Circuit has interpreted subsection 112(f). That subsection states:

---

87. *See In re* Donaldson, 16 F.3d 1189 (Fed. Cir. 1991).
88. Markman v. Westview, 517 U.S. 370 (1996). See treatment in Chapter 5.
89. *See* Welker Bearing Co. v. PHD, Inc., 550 F.3d 1090 (Fed. Cir. 2008).
90. See example claims that cover software in Chapter 6.
91. *See, e.g., In re* Schreiber, 128 F.3d 1473 (Fed. Cir. 1997); *In re* Swinehart, 439 F.2d 210, 169 U.S.P.Q. 226 (C.C.P.A. 1971).

> (f) ELEMENT IN CLAIM FOR A COMBINATION.—An element in a claim for a combination may be expressed as a means or step for performing a specified function without the recital of structure, material, or acts in support thereof, and such claim shall be construed to cover the corresponding structure, material, or acts described in the specification and equivalents thereof.

The provision, to be invoked for an element of a patent claim, appears to require the formulation "means for [function]." However, there is Federal Circuit case law in which subsection 112(f) is invoked to interpret an element of a claim, although the word "means" does not appear in the claim.[92] This may occur, for example, where the claim term or terms at issue do not recite sufficient structure.[93] There is a presumption that the absence of use of "means" in the language of a patent claim should *not* be construed under subsection 112(f), but that presumption may be rebutted. The primary case is *Williamson v. Citrix Online*, decided *en banc*, which referred to use of "nonce words" for elements of a claim, such as the word "module," which in the context of the claim was not a recognized term of art. "Nonce words" refers to made-up words that seek to make a functional limitation appear structural. The Federal Circuit stated (note that subsection 112(f) has replaced 112, 6):

> The standard is whether the words of the claim are understood by persons of ordinary skill in the art to have a sufficiently definite meaning as the name for structure. *Greenberg*, 91 F.3d at 1583. When a claim term lacks the word "means," the presumption can be overcome and § 112, para. 6 will apply if the challenger demonstrates that the claim term fails to "recite sufficiently definite structure" or else recites "function without reciting sufficient structure for performing that function." *Watts*, 232 F.3d at 880. The converse presumption remains unaffected: "use of the word 'means' creates a presumption that § 112, ¶ 6 applies." *Personalized Media*, 161 F.3d at 703.[94]

Some terms, as a result, appear to be sufficiently structural so as to not invoke subsection 112(f). A few example claim terms in which there have been court rulings indicating particular claim terms are structural rather than functional include processor; circuit or circuitry; and digital detector. There are many other case examples that could also be cited. More specifically, as an example of the reasoning used, the Federal Circuit case *Personalized Media Communications v. International Trade Commission* states:

---

92. *See, e.g.*, Williamson v. Citrix Online, LLC, 792 F.3d 1339 (Fed. Cir. 2015) (en banc); Cole v. Kimberly-Clark Corp., 102 F.3d 524, 531 (Fed. Cir. 1996); *see also* Greenberg v. Ethicon Endo-Surgery, Inc., 91 F.3d 1580, 1584 (Fed. Cir. 1996).

93. *Williamson*, 792 F.3d 1339; *Cole*, 102 F.3d at 531.

94. *Williamson*, 792 F.3d at 1349.

> "Detector" is not a generic structural term such as "means," "element," or "device"; nor is it a coined term lacking a clear meaning, such as "widget" or "ram-a-fram." *Instead, as noted by the [administrative law judge (ALJ)] by reference to dictionary definitions, "detector" had a well-known meaning to those of skill in the electrical arts connotative of structure . . . .*[95]

Further, in some other Federal Circuit cases, functional language was permissibly used and did *not* invoke subsection 112(f).[96] That is, these cases suggest that functional language may in some situations properly and appropriately be employed in claims without using the means-plus-function format of subsection 112(f) and without necessarily being interpreted under that subsection. Presumably, despite the functional language, the claim still recited *sufficient* structure to avoid invoking subsection 112(f). We recommend using both approaches to provide diversity and to signal a different intended scope for the separate claims.[97]

However, use of functional language may still be challenging.[98] In particular, the PTO has the authority to shift the burden to the applicant with respect to functional language.[99] The CCPA decision in *In re Swinehart* stated in this regard:

---

95. 161 F.3d 696, 704–05 (Fed. Cir. 1998) (emphasis added). It is noted that *Personalized Media Communications v. International Trade Commission* was decided before the *en banc* decision *Williamson v. Citrix Online*.

96. *See, e.g.*, K-2 Corp. v. Salomon S.A., 191 F.3d 1356, 1363 (Fed. Cir. 1999) (functional language "for substantially preventing movement" did not invoke subsection 112(6)); BASF Corp. v. Johnson Matthey Inc., 875 F.3d 1360 (Fed. Cir. 2017) (functional phrase "effective to catalyze" did not involve subsection 112(6)); *see also* Enzo Biochem, Inc. v. Applera Corp., 599 F.3d 1325, 1332–33 (Fed. Cir. 2010), *reh'g and reh'g en banc denied*, 605 F.3d 1347 (Fed. Cir. 2010) ("when a claim limitation is defined in 'purely functional terms,' a determination of whether the limitation is sufficiently definite is 'highly dependent on context (e.g., the disclosure in the specification and the knowledge of a person of ordinary skill in the relevant art area)'"); Miken Composites, L.L.C. v. Wilson Sporting Goods Co., 515 F.3d 1331 (Fed. Cir. 2008) (court stated that while the term "insert" has "functional attributes," it was still a structural component); Plastic Container Corp. v. Cont'l Plastics of Okla., Inc., 607 F.2d 885, 203 U.S.P.Q. 27 (10th Cir. 1979), *cert. denied*, 444 U.S. 1018 (1980), *on remand*, 515 F. Supp. 834, 214 U.S.P.Q. 530 (W.D. Okla. 1980), *aff'd in part, rev'd in part*, 708 F.2d 1554, 219 U.S.P.Q. 26 (10th Cir. 1983) ("the idea that functional language ipso facto cannot precisely define novelty in structure was laid to rest in In re Swinehart"); *Swinehart*, 439 F.2d at 212, 169 U.S.P.Q. at 228 ("[T]here is nothing intrinsically wrong with [employing functional limitations] in drafting patent claims.").

97. *But compare* Mas-Hamilton Grp. v. LaGard, Inc., 156 F.3d 1206 (Fed. Cir. 1998) (claim without "means" interpreted under 112, 6 despite a separate, independent claim that employed "means").

98. Note that 35 U.S.C. § 112(f) (2024) also refers to "materials," suggesting applicability to composition of matter claims as well.

99. *See Swinehart*, 439 F.2d at 212, 169 U.S.P.Q. at 228.

> Additionally, where the Patent Office has reason to believe that a functional limitation asserted to be critical for establishing novelty in the claimed subject matter may, in fact, be an inherent characteristic of the prior art, *it possesses the authority to require the applicant to prove that the subject matter shown to be in the prior art does not possess the characteristic relied on.*[100]

If the PTO were to do this, it may require (1) proof that the subject matter shown to be in the prior art does not possess the characteristic sought to be claimed (proving a negative proposition is usually a challenge to establish with evidence); (2) amending the claim; or (3) arguing that for some reason the PTO has inappropriately shifted the burden.

Some features, unfortunately, may not have a feasible way to be claimed structurally. In that situation, it is suggested that a mix of structural and functional language be used so that at least the claim language at issue is not entirely devoid of structure. Consider Example 4.14 with claim language such as:

> wherein the memory controller is capable of initiating burst mode operation based, at least in part, on receipt of an externally derived request from an external central processing unit (CPU);
>
> wherein the request is to include a memory address, a word count, and a read or a write control transfer designation; and
>
> wherein the memory controller is to process the request and take control of an external system transfer bus.

The claim, here, recites "the memory controller is capable of initiating burst mode operation" and "the memory controller is to process the request and take control of an external system transfer bus." The term "memory controller" is likely structural, but the other recited limitations are more functional; however, a memory controller may be argued to support such functions.

Example 4.17 uses a similar approach reciting "network device," a potentially structural device, but adding functional limitations such as "to emulate," "to encapsulate," and "to communicate." Again, these could be argued to be operations a network device may support. With even more attention, these positions might be made even clearer through claim language and specification language. The point, here, is to pay attention to the use of structural versus functional language in the claim and to attempt to hedge your bets so

---

100. *Id.* (emphasis added).

that your claim is not construed to be limited to, essentially, your specification embodiment due to invocation of subsection 112(f).

Along these lines, it is a good idea to be mindful of the consequences should your claim, despite your best drafting efforts, be construed under subsection 112(f) during examination or in litigation. In the event subsection 112(f) is invoked, the specification *must* provide sufficient *corresponding* structure for the recited function. That is, for the function or functions recited in the claim, the specification *must* describe *corresponding* structure able to perform the recited function or functions or the claim will be invalid if issued (again, under 112, 2). Here, *corresponding* suggests that the specification is written to clearly associate the function and the structure in the description in a manner such that one of ordinary skill would comprehend the association.

If an element is construed under subsection 112(f) and the statutory requirements regarding corresponding structure are satisfied, then the claim covers, by express statutory direction, "the *corresponding* structure, material, or acts described in the specification *and equivalents*" (emphasis added). Thus, the claim, by statute, under subsection 112(f), is *literally* construed to cover embodiments in your specification that *correspond* to the functional language or to *literally* cover a *112(f) equivalent* of what is shown in the specification; however, the *literal* scope of such *112(f) equivalents* is generally exceedingly narrow.[101] In other words, equivalents falling within the statutory language of subsection 112(f) are within the literal scope of the claim.

Employing claims that *are intended* to invoke subsection 112(f)—that is, means- and step-plus-function claims—has become an issue surrounded with some controversy. Some lawyers feel strongly that such claims should be avoided due to their narrow interpretation, whereas other lawyers feel that the law may change again, or that such claims could be useful in certain situations, such as a crowded field of art. Thus, there are situations where under current law these claims may have value. We do not necessarily recommend that means- or step-plus-function claims be used or that they be avoided. *Rather, our recommendation is that if you draft claims in a way that is clearly intended to invoke subsection 112(f) (e.g., by using the word "means"), then you should also specifically include an alternate set of claims that is specifically drafted so as not to invoke subsection 112(f).* Likewise, because claims may inadvertently invoke subsection 112(f) without the use of the terms "means" or "step," it is also recommended that you take care to avoid subsection 112(f) even when not employing these terms.

---

101. *See, e.g.*, Valmont Indus., Inc. v. Reinke Mfg. Co., 983 F.2d 1039 (Fed. Cir. 1993).

One potential advantage of employing subsection 112(f) is that it provides the capability to literally cover a wide variety of associated devices where no specific word exists that might ordinarily be employed in a claim to cover them. Thus, if a means-plus-function claim is employed and the *identical* function is met by a set of described devices, so long as it is clear in the specification that the embodiments described *correspond* to the identified function, then such devices should quite arguably be covered literally by the claim.

Employing a means-plus-function claim may also provide a useful technique, for example to address the issue in *Johnson & Johnston*,[102] where subject matter disclosed in the specification was inadvertently dedicated to the public because the subject matter was not specifically covered by any of the claims of the patent. That is, because claims under subsection 112(f) are interpreted to cover embodiments in the specification, then there is a reasonable likelihood that a means-plus-function claim may cover an embodiment that you did not specifically otherwise cover with a patent claim.

A major disadvantage of means- and step-plus-function claims is that they are generally construed to be narrow. In fact, as the Federal Circuit has stated, subsection 112(f) was intended as a claim narrowing rather than a claim broadening provision. Rather than working like the DOE, the provision functions more like the reverse DOE.[103]

On the other hand, in a crowded field, a means-plus-function claim may provide some advantages. It is narrow, which may assist in distinguishing from the prior art. However, its scope may nonetheless still be quite arguable since it is a matter of interpretation what features from the specification embodiment(s) are part of the claim. This uncertainty as to scope, again, in a crowded field may have value. Furthermore, whether an accused product qualifies as a "structural equivalent" is a question of fact (after what is a structural equivalent has been construed by a court).[104] Thus, one may argue this issue should be decided by a jury; which in some situations may provide a procedural advantage.

One aspect of the narrow nature of such claims is that the recited function of the claim must be met *identically* by the accused product. This leaves little room for so-called play at the joints in terms of the claim drafting. Thus, it may, perhaps, be better to recite broad literal functions when employing such claims, but it is also important to make sure such functions are supported, as discussed immediately following. In contrast, for example, to meet the DOE,[105] the func-

102. 285 F.3d 1046 (Fed. Cir. 2002).

103. *See Valmont*, 983 F.3d at 1042.

104. *See, e.g.*, Overhead Door Corp. v. Chamberlain Grp., Inc., 194 F.3d 1261, 1273, 52 U.S.P.Q.2d 1321, 1329 (Fed. Cir. 1999) (a genuine fact issue arose whether for purposes of 112, 6 the accused software was equivalent to the patent's software).

105. See discussion in Chapter 5.

tion (under the function-way-result test) only needs to be "substantially similar," something that is looser than "identical." Thus, the Federal Circuit has even suggested that a modified function-way-result test may be employed when construing claims under subsection 112(f) where the function is met identically.[106]

Another narrow aspect of claims under subsection 112(f) is that the specification must include "corresponding structure, material or acts in support thereof," and it must be clear from the specification that such structure, material, or acts *correspond* to the recited function. For example, in *B. Braun Medical v. Abbott Laboratories*,[107] the Federal Circuit determined that a means-plus-function claim directed to a valve was not infringed where a structure included in the specification that would have arguably supported the infringement was not associated with the recited function in the specification (or prosecution history). Furthermore, in *Cardiac Pacemakers v. St. Jude Medical*,[108] the Federal Circuit invalidated a claim including a means-plus-function clause because the specification failed to disclose any structure for performing the recited function.

Means-plus-function elements are also construed to *only* cover the embodiment or embodiments described in the specification "and equivalents thereof." However, because "equivalents thereof" is construed narrowly, this is another aspect of their construction that makes these claims narrow. An equivalent for purposes of literal infringement under subsection 112(f) is an insubstantial change that adds nothing of significance.[109] Likewise, another narrowing aspect of "equivalents thereof" is the time at which whether something is an "equivalent" is evaluated. The Federal Circuit has stated that this is at the time the patent issues.[110] This is directly in contrast to the DOE, where whether something is an "equivalent" is evaluated at the time of the infringement, usually a later time.[111] Because known interchangeability is a factor in determining whether something is an equivalent,[112] evaluation of this at the time the patent issues should tend to narrow the claim.

Consistent with the preceding, the DOE has a limited role in connection with claims construed under subsection 112(f). Generally, with only limited exception, for example, if a means-plus-function element is not infringed by the accused device, then there also will *not* be infringement under the DOE. As indicated earlier, primary differences that may in only limited circumstances make the DOE applicable include the time of evaluating an equivalent, and

106. *See* Kemco Sales, Inc. v. Control Papers Co., 208 F.3d 1352 (Fed. Cir. 2000).
107. 124 F.3d 1419 (Fed. Cir. 1997).
108. 296 F.3d 1106 (Fed. Cir. 2002).
109. *See* Valmont Indus., Inc. v. Reinke Mfg. Co., 983 F.2d 1039, 1043 n.14 (Fed. Cir. 1993).
110. *See* Al-Site Corp. v. VSI Int'l, Inc., 174 F.3d 1308, 1320–21 (Fed. Cir. 1999).
111. *See* Warner-Jenkinson Co. v. Hilton Davis Chem. Co., 520 U.S. 17, 29 (1997).
112. *See id.*

that the function element for the DOE need not be met in the accused product *identically*. However, one important difference between such claims and the DOE that tends to make claims evaluated under subsection 112(f) *less* narrow is that whether the accused product is the same or "an equivalent" is evaluated "overall";[113] in contrast, the DOE is evaluated element by element.[114] An element-by-element analysis usually produces a narrower result than an "overall" analysis, as performed under subsection 112(f).

A risk exists under Federal Circuit law that a claim employing functional language that does not use the word "means" or "step" may, nonetheless, be construed under subsection 112(f). The Federal Circuit, however, has recognized that some words, while functional in nature, have acquired accepted meanings that make them less functional.[115] For example, as mentioned previously, in *Personalized Media Communications v. International Trade Commission*,[116] the Federal Circuit determined that the language "digital detector" employed in a claim should not be construed under subsection 112(f), reversing the ITC's conclusion to the contrary. Likewise, in *Apex v. Raritan Computer*,[117] the Federal Circuit determined that "circuit" should not be construed under subsection 112(f).

In the area of software, in particular, the algorithm is considered the structure at issue under subsection 112(f).[118] For this reason, not infrequently, claims interpreted under subsection 112(f) that relate to software are held invalid as not appropriately describing structure or enough structure. That is, generally it is not sufficient to merely provide a functional description.[119] Enough detail must be described to, in effect, show possession, which means sufficient detail of *how to perform the function* so that one of ordinary skill would know the scope being claimed with respect to implementing the function or operation claimed.[120]

Likewise, if a function is claimed that is not described to this level, the claim is held invalid. Therefore, in drafting claims, care is warranted to not inadvertently claim a function that is believed to be well understood, such as "transmit a signal" or "receive a signal," but for which the specification does not actually provide an implementation description.

---

113. *See* Odetics, Inc. v. Storage Tech. Corp., 185 F.3d 1259 (Fed. Cir. 1999).

114. *See* Pennwalt Corp. v. Durand-Wayland, Inc., 833 F.3d 931 (Fed. Cir. 1987) (en banc).

115. *See, e.g.*, Mas-Hamilton Grp. v. LaGard, Inc., 156 F.3d 1206 (Fed. Cir. 1998).

116. 161 F.3d 696 (Fed. Cir. 1998).

117. 325 F.3d 1364 (Fed. Cir. 2003).

118. *See, e.g.*, Eon Corp. IP Holdings, LLC v. AT&T Mobility, LLC, 785 F.3d 616, 621 (Fed. Cir. 2015).

119. *See* Blackboard, Inc. v. Desire2Learn, Inc., 574 F.3d 1371, 1383–85, 91 U.S.P.Q.2d 1481, 1491–93 (Fed. Cir. 2009); Noah Sys., Inc. v. Intuit Inc., 675 F.3d 1302 (Fed. Cir. 2012).

120. *See Blackboard, Inc.*, 574 F.3d at 1383–85, 91 U.S.P.Q.2d at 1491–93; *Noah Sys.*, 675 F.3d 1302.

Structure versus Function versus Process

Understand the difference between structural, functional, and product-by-process language.

In a previous section, structural limitations versus functional limitations were considered.[121] Similarly, we will address process limitations,[122] a topic also previously alluded to in connection with *INVT SPE LLC v. International Trade Commission*.[123] These cases and related claiming principles raise the point that some claim terms have a potential to suggest a particular type of limitation, such as a functional limitation, a structural limitation, or a process-type limitation.

It is a good idea to be mindful that claim terms have the potential to cross boundaries, such as function, structure, or process, and might be construed in more than one manner. It may, in some cases, be important to make it clear via claim language and/or specification language which is intended, especially if a lot rides on a particular interpretation.[124]

Personalized Media Communications, L.L.C. v. International Trade Commission
161 F.3d 696
United States Court of Appeals for the Federal Circuit
November 24, 1998, Decided

Questions

1. This case is provided as another example of potential uncertainty related to construing functional claim language. Whether the functional language invoked § 112, 6 was central to the ruling at the ITC and the Federal Circuit. However, in the case, the Federal Circuit did not consider all of the determinations made by the ALJ. Why not?[125]
2. Although the claims and technology were not simple, the functional language at issue was "digital detector." The ALJ ruled that this language invoked § 112, 6. What was the ALJ's reasoning? What was the

121. See the immediately preceding section, addressing structural versus functional limitations.

122. See later in this chapter, treating method or process claims.

123. 46 F.4th 1361 (Fed. Cir. 2022).

124. *See* Fromson v. Advance Offset Plate, Inc., 720 F.2d 1565, 1570, 219 U.S.P.Q. 1137, 1140 (Fed. Cir. 1983) ("That a process limitation appears in a claim does not convert it to a product by process claim."). See the treatment of product-by-process claims later in this chapter.

125. *See* Personalized Media Commc'ns, L.L.C. v. Int'l Trade Comm'n, 161 F.3d 696 n.3 (Fed. Cir. 1998) (and accompanying text).

Federal Circuit's reasoning for concluding § 112, 6 was not invoked? Do you agree with the court that the term "digital" makes the language more definite with respect to whether § 112, 6 is invoked?

3. Why did the ALJ rule that the term "digital detector" was indefinite? Why did the court conclude it was not indefinite? Can you articulate a legal explanation and a policy explanation regarding why, for the same specification, if § 112, 6 had been invoked the language would be indefinite, but because it was not invoked, the claim was definite?
4. Do you understand the distinction the court is drawing between enablement and definiteness—that is, that the claim language is definite even assuming it was not enabled? Observe that the court acknowledges that the ALJ had determined that the claim language was not enabled, but the Commission expressed no opinion. Do you think the claim language was enabled?
5. Based on the specification, the court construcd the claim language "digital detector." Note that Personalized Media Communications (PMC) proposed a much different and much narrower interpretation. Why do you think that is, given that PMC was the party asserting the patent?
6. The ALJ had ruled that claims 6 and 7 were not infringed. The court agreed on claim 6, but as to claim 7 ruled that there was not substantial evidence for the ruling that claim 7 was not infringed, and remanded the case. What was the difference between the claims that caused the court to rule that there was not substantial evidence for the noninfringement ruling? Why did the court decline to address claim 44?
7. This case was decided before *Williamson* and after *Greenberg*. Do you think the court might have ruled differently after *Williamson*? Why or why not? Given the specifics of each case, do you see these cases as relatively consistent regarding application of § 112, 6 or not?

Kamstrup A/S v. Axioma Metering UAB
43 F.4th 1374
United States Court of Appeals for the Federal Circuit
August 12, 2022, Decided

Questions

1. This case demonstrates the risk associated with language that could be interpreted as product-by-process language. Why did the court say this language was not entitled to patentable weight? This demonstrates the problem of having a limitation construed as a product-by-process

limitation. Typically, every claim element and limitation is considered material to the invention.[126]

2. What was Kamstrup required to show for the language at issue to be given patentable weight? For example, the court stated:

> Kamstrup argues that the Board erred in finding that there are no functional or structural differences between polymer structures cast in a single mold versus multiple molds. Appellant's Br. 32–34. Kamstrup states that "various structures . . . cannot be cast in a single *mold* using conventional die cast injection molding technologies." *Id.* at 34 (emphasis added); Reply 24–26.
>
> First, even if true, Kamstrup has not identified functional and structural differences between a structure "cast in one piece" and a structure manufactured using another method. Rather, the argument is merely that the claim element describes a manufacturing method with some inherent restrictions. Further, Kamstrup has not identified disclosure in the specification or prosecution history or extrinsic evidence evidencing structural and functional differences.
>
> Second, the alleged structural and functional difference that Kamstrup identifies is detached from the claims. The claims state that the structure should be "cast in *one piece*," not cast in *one mold*. '957 patent at 6:40–42 (emphasis added). The Board correctly found that the written description "focuses on reducing the number of steps required to fabricate the flow meter housing, not on casting in a single mold." *Axioma*, 2021 Pat. App. LEXIS 4956, 2021 WL 1235790, at *7 (citing '957 patent at 1:55–57, 2:6–9). While certain figures of the written description, namely Figures 5A and 5B, depict a single mold, the Board correctly found that those embodiments are narrower than the claims—which do not require use of a single mold—and correctly declined to import narrower limitations from the specification to the claims. *Id.* Substantial evidence also supports the Board's finding that the extrinsic evidence does not exclusively show that "cast in one piece" means "cast in one mold." 2021 Pat. App. LEXIS 4956, [WL] at *8.[127]

3. What was the consequence of the limitation at issue not being entitled to any patentable weight?
4. What was Kamstrup's position regarding the limitation regarding the "cavity separated from the flow tube"? Why was it rejected?

---

126. *See* Warner-Jenkinson Co. v. Hilton Davis Chem. Co., 520 U.S. 17, 29 (1997) ("Each element contained in a patent claim is deemed material to defining the scope of the patented invention.").

127. Kamstrup A/S v. Axioma Metering UAB, 43 F.4th 1374, 1382 (Fed. Cir. 2022).

* * *

For many years it remained unclear how product-by-process claims should be interpreted.[128] This was due to two Federal Circuit panels that reached different outcomes. *Scripps Clinic & Research Foundation v. Genentech, Inc.*, a 1991 Federal Circuit decision, stated that a product-by-process claim was *not* limited to products prepared by the process recited in the claims.[129] However, in *Atlantic Thermoplastics Co., Inc. v. Faytex Corp.*, a 1992 Federal Circuit decision, a different three-judge panel ruled that "process terms in product-by-process claims serve as limitations in determining infringement."[130]

These inconsistent rulings, however, did not foreclose use of such claims. Rather, the uncertainty provided a potential opportunity to argue for a desired interpretation, depending on issues related to invalidity or infringement. For a knowledgeable practitioner, product-by-process claims might be included, but with recognition of the interpretation risk. However, after nearly two decades, the Federal Circuit ultimately resolved the panel inconsistency, and the interpretation of such claims is now clear.[131] As a result of this interpretation, such claims are not generally advisable unless it is the only way to claim the subject matter at issue.[132] Part of the reason for this is that the process limitations *are not* considered for purposes of validity, but the process limitations *are* considered for purposes of infringement.[133]

Product-by-process claims represent one of the few situations where claims are *not* interpreted consistently regarding validity and infringement. As the court said in *Amgen v. F. Hoffmann-La Roche*:

> The impact of these different analyses is significant. For product-by-process claims, that which anticipates if earlier does not necessarily infringe if later. That is because a product in the prior art made by a different process can anticipate a product-by-process claim, but an accused product made by a different process cannot infringe a product-by-process claim.[134]

Thus, these claims get the worst of it, so to speak. That is, for such claims, process limitations do not help distinguish for validity purposes but may prevent a finding of infringement if not met.

---

128. *See* Atl. Thermoplastics Co., Inc. v. Faytex Corp., 970 F.2d 834, 23 U.S.P.Q.2d 1481 (Fed. Cir. 1992), *suggestion for reh'g en banc declined*, 974 F.2d 1279, 23 U.S.P.Q.2d 1801, 974 F.2d 1299, 24 U.S.P.Q.2d 1138 (Fed. Cir. 1992).

129. *See* 927 F.2d 1565, 18 U.S.P.Q.2d 1001 (Fed. Cir. 1991).

130. *See* 970 F.2d 834, 846–47, 23 U.S.P.Q.2d 1481.

131. *See* Abbott Laby's v. Sandoz, Inc., 566 F.3d 1282 (Fed. Cir. 2009) (en banc).

132. See later in this chapter addressing product-by-process claims.

133. *Id.*

134. *See* Amgen Inc. v. F. Hoffmann-La Roche Ltd., 580 F.3d 1340, 1370 (Fed. Cir. 2009).

Claim Drafting Problems II

<u>Problem 1.</u> <u>Can Opener</u>—Draft one independent apparatus claim and two dependent apparatus claims; draft an independent means-plus-function claim.

<u>FIGURES:</u>

July 12, 1955 S. W. CHAMBERS 2,712,689

ELECTRICALLY OPERATED AUTOMATIC CAN OPENER

Filed Sept. 28, 1954

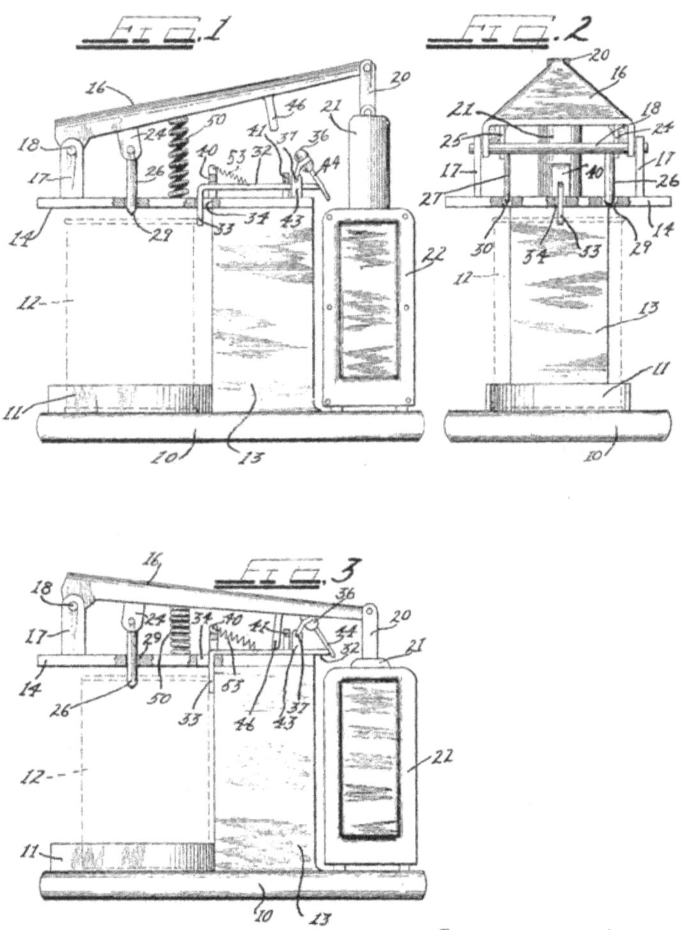

Inventor
Stanley W. Chambers

By Hill, Sherman, Meroni, Gross & Simpson Attys

DESCRIPTION:

This invention relates to an electrically operated automatic can opener for punching apertures in the top of a container to provide means for emptying the liquid contents thereof.

It is an important object of the present invention to provide a rugged and reliable electrically operated can opening apparatus that is designed to provide a powerful can opening leverage.

It is a further important object of the present invention to provide an electrically operated can opener that is automatically actuated by proper positioning of a container in relation thereto.

Still a further object of the present invention is to provide a novel and improved automatic can opening device that automatically executes an opening stroke and thereafter is automatically retracted to its initial position.

Other and further objects, features, and advantages of the present invention will be more fully apparent from the following description taken in connection with the accompanying drawings, in which:

Figure 1 is a side elevational view of a can opening apparatus according to the present invention with portions of the apparatus broken away and in section to better illustrate the construction of the device and showing the apparatus in its initial condition prior to complete insertion of a container into the apparatus;

Figure 2 is an end elevational view of the structure of Figure 1 with portions broken away and in section; and Figure 3 is a side elevational view similar to Figure 1 but illustrating the apparatus in its actuated condition.

As shown on the drawings:

Referring to Figures 1 and 2, it will be observed that the automatic can opening device of the present invention comprises a base 10 that may be secured to any suitable structure such as a table for mounting the device in a generally upright orientation. The base 10 is provided with a container guide rail 11 that at its inner portion may be contoured to conform to the diameter of a can such as indicated in dashed outline at 12 to precisely position the container in the receiving space therefor. The framework of the device further includes an upright column 13 and a generally horizontal upper deck plate 14 mounted in spaced relation above the base 10.

For providing the driving force for punching apertures in the container, a lever 16 is pivotally mounted at one end to fulcrum members 17 by means of a pivot shaft 18. At its opposite end, the lever 16 is pivotally connected to a link 20, which in turn is connected with a vertically reciprocal armature 21 of a solenoid 22 mounted on the base 10 behind the column 13. The lever 16 has depending cars 24 and 25 pivotally carrying punch members 26 and 27, which are guided for vertical movement into the container receiving space of the device by means of apertures 29 and 30 in the deck of an automatic plate 14. The punch members 26 and 27 are mounted by lever 16 in close relation to the fulcrum 17 so as to provide a substantial leverage advantage in driving the punch members into the top of the container.

For automatic actuation of the solenoid 22 upon proper positioning of a container such as 12 in the receiving space, a sensing arm 32 is provided having a downturned end 33 for engagement by the edge of the container 12 as the container is inserted into the receiving space. Movement of the container to proper position shifts the downturned end 33 in the elongated slot 34 of deck plate 14 so that the rear end or the sensing member 32 pivots a mercury switch 36 about a pivot 37 to close an energizing circuit to the solenoid 22. As seen in Figure 1, the sensing member 32 is guided by means of a pair of posts 40 and 41 having vertical slots constraining the sensing member 32 against lateral movement. The mercury switch 36 is pivotally carried by means of a further post 43 and has an extension arm 44 for engagement with the end of the sensing member 32.

As seen in Figure 3, upon completion of a downward stroke of the lever 16, a depending abutment 46 carried by the lever engages the sensing member 32 and moves it straight downwardly in the slots in posts 40 and 41.

The downward movement of the sensing member 32 results in pivoting of the mercury switch back to its original angular position shown in Figure 1 to deenergize the solenoid. Thereupon a compression spring 50 confined between the deck plate 14 and the lever 16 is effective to pivot the lever upwardly to retract the punch members 26 and 27 from the container. When the lever has reached its upper position, the container may be removed from the device. Removal of the container allows a tension spring 53 diagonally connected between post 40 and sensing member 32 to shift the sensing member horizontally and then upwardly to its initial position shown in Figure 1. The solenoid is thus automatically energized and deenergized to execute a complete opening cycle each time a container is properly positioned in the receiving space.

The operation of the can opener will now be readily apparent. As a container 12 is moved into the position shown in dotted outline in Figure 3, the edge thereof engages a downturned end 33 of a sensing member 32 and shifts the sensing member horizontally to actuate a mercury switch 36. Actuation of this switch energizes the solenoid 22 to move the lever 16 downwardly about its pivot 18 and drive the punches 26 and 27 into the top of the container. Upon completion of the downward stroke of the lever 16, the abutment 46 moves the sensing arm 32 to a lower position shown in Figure 3 to the container 12 so it may be removed. Diagonal spring 53 is so disposed that it can lift sensing member 32 to its initial position until the opened container has been removed at the end of an opening cycle.

It will be apparent that many modifications and variations may be effected without departing from the scope of the novel concepts of the present invention.

Problem 2. Brush—Draft one independent apparatus claim and two dependent apparatus claims.

FIGURES:

Feb. 15, 1938. F. J. BICKEL 2,108,742

BRUSH

Filed July 13, 1936

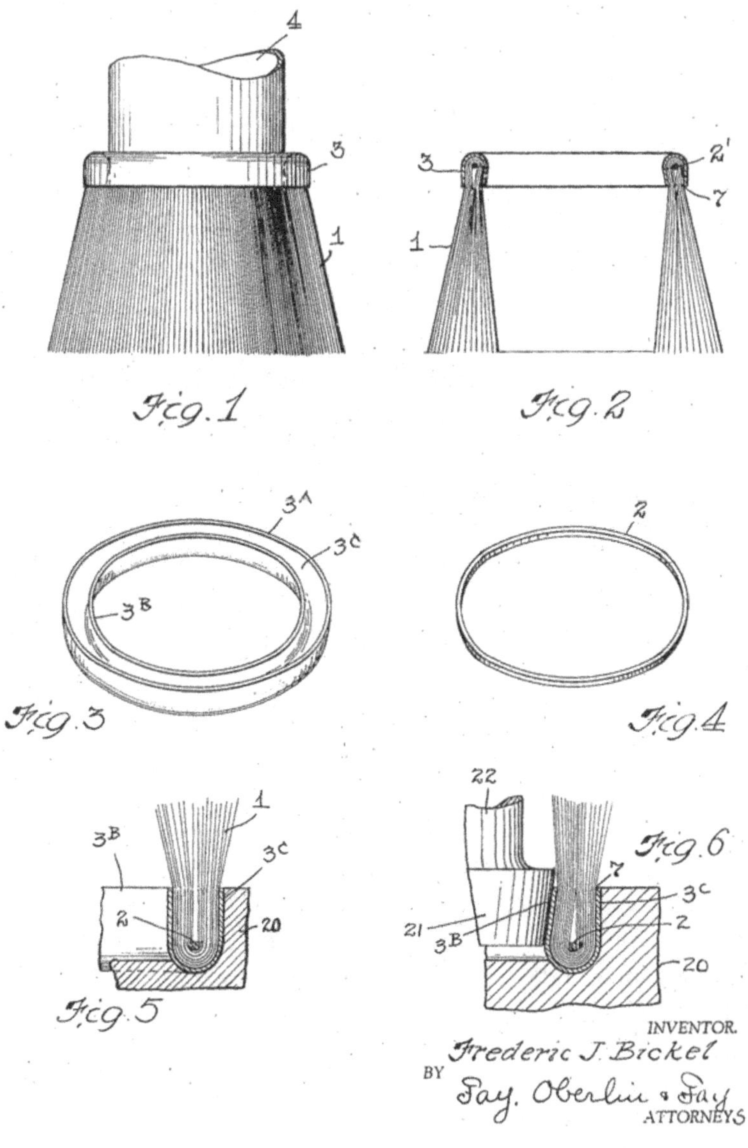

DESCRIPTION:

This invention pertains to the brush art and particularly aims to improve the manufacture and construction of hollow center end brushes.

Among the aims and purposes are the production of brushes that present certain advantages particularly for use as elements of vacuum cleaning tools; absence of rough projections or irregular junctions, edges, points, and so on, which would cause difficulty in placing the bristles during manufacture or cause injury to furniture, draperies, household ornaments, and the like, by catching, pulling, or scratching; firm gripping of the bristles without damage thereto; simplification of the manufacture of such brushes; adaptability to manufacture with economical materials and methods of construction.

To the accomplishment of the foregoing and related ends, said invention then consists of the means hereinafter fully described and particularly pointed out in the claims.

The annexed drawing and the following description set forth in detail certain means and one mode of carrying out the invention, such disclosed means and mode illustrating, however, but one of various ways in which the principle of the invention may be used.

In the accompanying drawing:

Fig. 1 is a side elevation of my brush on the end of a vacuum cleaner attachment;

Fig. 2 is a median section through the brush on an axial plane;

Fig. 3 is a perspective of the brush channel;

Fig. 4 is a perspective of a preferred form of retaining ring;

Fig. 5 is a cross section through the brush at an intermediate stage of assembly; and

Fig. 6 is a cross section through the brush, showing the final assembly step.

The brush, as completed, comprises a filling of bristles 1, looped about a ring 2, and secured in an annular channel 3, which is of slightly modified U-shape when seen in cross section in its final form, and which has its opening pointed endwise, that is, in such a direction that the bristles 1 form a cylinder instead of a disc. In use the brush is mounted on or secured to suitable holder means the principal intended purpose being to use it on a tube such as 4, which represents part of a vacuum cleaner attachment.

The inner surface of the channel 3 is placed on the tube by a sliding forced fit, or otherwise, as may be most suitable. As best shown in Figs. 2 and 6 the rim channel is somewhat narrowed at the open end to constrict the bristles at 1 and thus firmly anchor the bristles and the retaining ring against withdrawal.

In the manufacture of this brush, I have found it preferable to use an annular channel in the shape 3A, having straight inner and outer sides 3B and 3C respectively, Figs. 3 and 5. This channel is designated by the reference character 3 when the brush is in its completed form.

A preferred method of constructing the brush is to fill the channel 3A with the wall of the bristles 1 looped upon the retaining ring 2.

In the manufacture of the brush a die 20, Figs. 5 and 6, shaped to support the bottom and the outer wall 3C, is used. The filled channel 3A is placed therein, or the empty channel may be placed therein and the die also used to serve the purpose of a holder during the filling of the channel.

Fig. 5 shows, in a partly sectional fragment, the channel in the die, there filled, ready for the next step, shown in Fig. 6. A central expanding tool, such as 22, Fig. 6, conically sided with an outward upward taper, is moved down by a suitably guided and driven actuating plunger 22 to expand the inner wall of the channel 3A, thus constricting the channel top at 1. My preference is to leave the wall 3C straight both for the reason that this makes a simpler manufacturing operation, and also that it avoids excessive narrowing of the top of the channel and danger of damage to or wear upon the bristles at the portion 1. The completion of construction by the forming tool 22 is shown in Fig. 6. It will be observed that the retaining ring, as shown in Figs. 4, 5, and 6, is of rectangular cross section, the specific showing being square. I do not confine myself to this shape of retaining ring, but may use a ring of ordinary wire as at 2, Fig. 2. My preference for the ring of rectangular cross section is that it may be more cheaply made than a wire ring, by cutting off successive ends of a seamless tube of proper diameter and wall thickness. The use of square cut sections of a seamless tube has been found in practice not to be injurious to the bristles, and is more economical than making rings of round section.

From the foregoing it will be seen that I have invented a brush of simple and durable construction, free from rough or projecting parts, junctions or seams, wherein the bristles are held firmly, but without injurious pressure at the point of constriction, and have likewise invented a method of making such a brush that is simple, economical, and quick, and in some measure permits utilization of less expensive material than has heretofore been deemed necessary, but without lowering the quality of the product.

Other modes of applying the principle of my invention may be employed instead of the one explained, change being made as regards the means and steps herein disclosed, provided those stated by any of the following claims or the equivalent of such stated means be employed.

<u>Problem 3.</u> <u>Nutcracker</u>—Draft one independent apparatus claim and two dependent apparatus claims; draft an independent means-plus-function claim.

<u>FIGURES:</u>

Dec. 10, 1940. G. J. TONN **2,224,415**

NUTCRACKER

Filed April 29, 1938

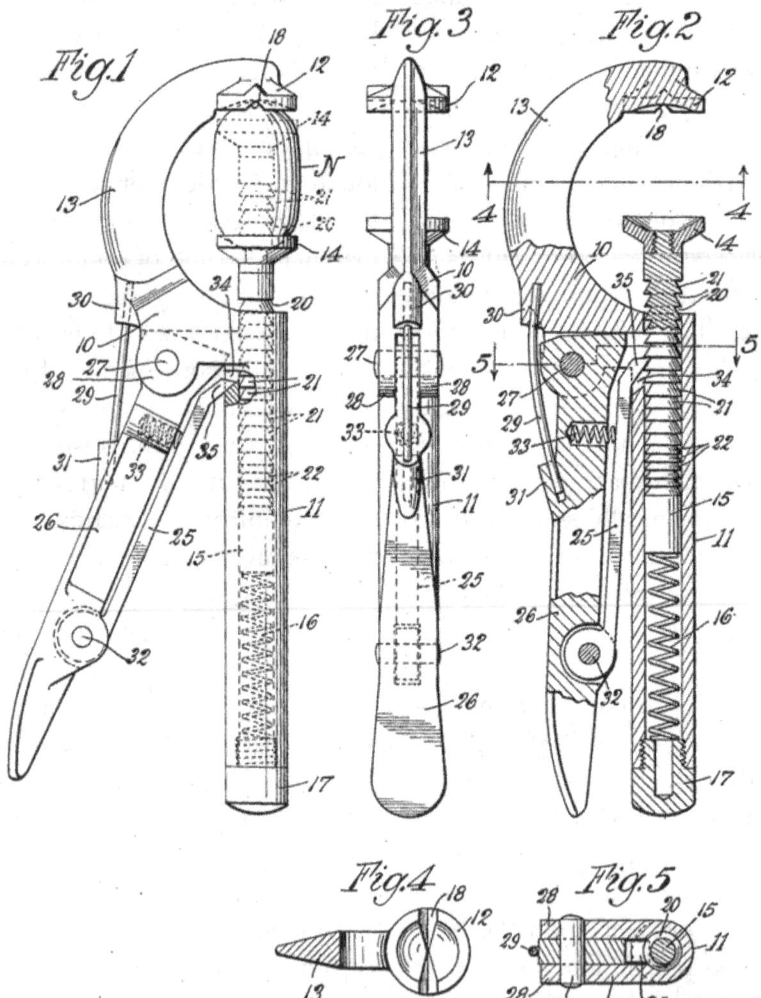

Inventor
George J. Tonn
by W. Bartlett Jones.
Attorney.

DESCRIPTION:

The present invention relates to nutcrackers and the like. It has particular reference to a device that has a limited and controllable movement.

With many varieties of nutcrackers the closing jaws are directly connected to the operating handle, and are resisted by the whole nut, that when the nut yields, the continuing applied pressure is too great for the resistance of the cracked nut. This results in crushing the meat in the nut. In some types of devices the sudden yielding of the jaws may catch the fingers or the hand to pinch or injure the same.

The object of the invention is to produce a device which has clamping jaws actuated with limited motion, which may be repeated to give a step-by-step advance.

A further object of the invention is to provide clamping jaws that are urged toward closed position so as to clamp a nut merely to position and hold it for the cracking pressure, and to provide means to actuate the cracking jaws with one or more short advances to crack the nut.

Various other and ancillary objects and advantages of the invention will appear from the following description and explanation of the invention in its presently preferred embodiment, shown in the accompanying drawing in which:

Fig. 1 represents the device holding a nut, ready to be cracked.

Fig. 2 represents the device after several step movements from the position shown in Fig. 1, the jaw being engaged to be moved.

Fig. 3 shows a view of the device of Fig. 2 looking from the left.

Fig. 4 is a cross section taken on line 4-4 of Fig. 2, showing the face of the fixed jaw.

Fig. 5 is a cross section taken on line 5-5 of Fig. 2 showing engaging parts.

The device has two relatively movable clamping or cracking jaws movable toward and away from each other. Preferably, means is provided to urge them into closed position with but slight pressure, so that they may be opened readily to insert a nut merely for holding the nut to be cracked. Independent means is operative to move into engaging position with a suitable part to give a limited movement in a direction to close the jaws with heavy pressure. This limited movement is called a step-movement, and preferably is repeated as required. The motivating device is actuated once for each step-movement, and successive actuations produce successive step-movements, giving an incremental advance.

The preferred device has a body member 10 providing a tubular handle 11 at one end and a jaw member 12 at the other. The jaw member is shown aligned with the opening of the tubular handle 11 and spaced from it. The body member has a yoke position 13 into which the article to be cracked fits when it bears against the jaw member 12. A movable jaw member 14 is carried on the end of a plunger-shaft 15, which is slidable in the tubular handle 11, preferably against a coiled compression spring 16. A threaded cap 17 is shown closing the end of the tubular handle 11 as an abutment for the spring 16. The spring 16 gives sufficient pressure to move the jaws in a closing direction simply to hold a nut. The spring is sufficiently light to permit opening the jaws by slight hand pressure to insert a nut. The face of the jaws 12 and 14 may be made as desired. Each jaw is shown with a concave face to aid in holding a nut. In addition jaw 12 has a diametrical groove 18 into which the ridges of certain nuts may be placed.

Means is provided to engage the plunger 15 to move it with heavy pressure to crack the nut. The character of said means is such as to be cooperative with certain structure associated with the plunger 15 for the desired ends. In the present form the plunger is provided with a series of obstructions or parts that may be engaged one at a time to move the shaft. Since the plunger shaft 15 as shown is round, and free to rotate in the hollow handle 11, the obstructions are circumferential. By cutting into the shaft, a series of annular grooves are formed, resembling the bottoms of partially nested cones. These provide a series of notches 21 and teeth 22 to provide a ratchet-like surface. The spacing of the teeth determines the length of the step movement or the increment of motion.

The increments may be equal or unequal. At the jaw 14 end, the increments are shown larger than at the other end. The larger increments are used where the nut is large, but when the nut or fragment of a nut is small, smaller increments 22 are used to avoid crushing after cracking.

To engage the teeth a pawl 25 moves into engaging position with a tooth 22. The pawl is then moved to push the plunger jaw onto the nut. If the nut is not cracked or insufficiently cracked, the pawl is moved back to pick up one or more teeth, and the construction may be varied to limit the number of teeth to one or more. Pivoted into the body member 10 is a complementary handle 26. Handle 26 and handle 11 shown in Fig. 2 are held in the hand for squeezing. A pivot 21 passes through spaced parallel projecting ears 28 of the body. The handle 26 is biased to open position by a suitable spring, such as spring wire 29 riding in holes in the bosses 36 and 31 located respectively on the body 10 and the handle 26. Handle 26 carries pawl 25, which is pivoted at 32 near the swinging end of handle 26. The pawl is resiliently mounted with respect to the handle. Since the pawl is of rigid structure, rather than being of resilient material, a small spring

33 is set into the handle to urge the pawl 25 away from the handle 26 and hence toward handle 11. The latter is recessed at 34 (Fig. 2) for the point 35 of the pawl 25 to enter and engage the series of teeth 22.

When the handle 26 is normally moved away from handle 11 by spring 29, pawl 25 is out of engagement with the teeth. Thus the plunger is free to slide in the handle against spring 16.

After the plunger has been given a full stroke to the limit permitted by the pawl, the handle 26 may be moved to draw the pawl back along the ratchet-like teeth 22. As illustrated, the handle may be moved part way back to pick up one tooth or all the way back, picking up two teeth. The device may readily be constructed to vary the length of the stroke and the maximum number of teeth picked up in a normal return.

In operating the device to crack a nut, for example the nut in Fig. 1, the nut is inserted by pushing the plunger from dotted-line position to full-line position; then the handle is moved from its normal position shown, to the position shown in Fig. 2. It will be observed in Fig. 1 that pawl 25 will pick up the sixth tooth, and in Fig. 2 that it still engages the sixth tooth. It can therefore be seen that if the plunger remains in the position of Fig. 2, the pawl can be partly retracted to engage the seventh tooth, or further retracted to engage the eighth tooth. Thus the user may effect a short stroke or double that short stroke in the next squeeze of the handles 26 and 11.

The pawl and ratchet device has been shown only in one relation, that is, the ratchet is moved by the pawl, but it is to be understood that this arrangement may be reversed in modifications of the structure.

The device may be modified in numerous respects without departing from the spirit and scope of the invention as set forth in the appended claim.

Method or Process Claims

Understand how to draft method claims and the rights covered by method claims. When drafting method claims, avoid "a method comprising the steps of."

MPEP § 2106.03

. . .

A process defines "actions", i.e., an invention that is claimed as an act or step, or a series of acts or steps. As explained by the Supreme Court, a "process" is "a mode of treatment of certain materials to produce a given result. It is an ***act, or a series of acts****, performed upon the subject-matter to be transformed and reduced to a different state or thing." Gottschalk v. Benson, 409 U.S. 63, 70, 175 USPQ 673, 676 (1972) ([emphasis] added) (quoting Cochrane v. Deener, 94 U.S. 780, 788, 24 L. Ed. 139, 141 (1876)). See also Nuijten, 500 F.3d at 1355, 84 USPQ2d at 1501 ("The Supreme Court and this court have consistently interpreted the statutory term 'process' to require action"); NTP, Inc. v. Research in Motion, Ltd., 418 F.3d 1282, 1316, 75 USPQ2d 1763, 1791 (Fed. Cir. 2005) ("[A] process is a series of acts.") (quoting Minton v. Natl. Ass'n. of Securities Dealers, 336 F.3d 1373, 1378, 67 USPQ2d 1614, 1681 (Fed. Cir. 2003)). As defined in 35 U.S.C. 100(b), the term "process" is synonymous with "method.". . .*

MPEP § 2112.02

I. PROCESS CLAIMS—PRIOR ART DEVICE ANTICIPATES A CLAIMED PROCESS IF THE DEVICE CARRIES OUT THE PROCESS DURING NORMAL OPERATION

Under the principles of inherency, if a prior art device, in its normal and usual operation, would necessarily perform the method claimed, then the method claimed will be considered to be anticipated by the prior art device. When the prior art device is the same as a device described in the specification for carrying out the claimed method, it can be assumed the device will inherently perform the claimed process. In re King, 801 F.2d 1324, 231 USPQ 136 (Fed. Cir. 1986) (The claims were directed to a method of enhancing color effects produced by ambient light through a process of absorption and reflection of the light off a coated substrate. A prior art reference to Donley disclosed a glass substrate coated with silver and metal oxide 200–800 angstroms thick. While Donley disclosed using the coated substrate to produce architectural colors, the absorption and reflection mechanisms of the claimed process were not disclosed. However, King's specification disclosed using a coated substrate of Donley's structure for use in his process. The Federal Circuit upheld the Board's finding that "Donley inherently performs the function disclosed in the method claims on appeal when that device is used in 'normal and usual operation'" and found that a prima facie case of anticipation was made out. Id. at 138, 801 F.2d at 1326. It was up to applicant to prove that Donley's structure would not perform the claimed method when placed in ambient light.). See also In re Best, 562 F.2d 1252, 1255, 195 USPQ 430, 433 (CCPA 1977) (Applicant claimed a process for preparing a hydrolytically-stable zeolitic aluminosilicate which included a step of "cooling the steam zeolite . . . at a rate sufficiently rapid that the cooled zeolite exhibits an X-ray diffraction pattern. . . ." All the process limitations were expressly disclosed by a U.S. patent to Hansford except the cooling step. The court stated that any sample of Hansford's zeolite would necessarily be cooled to facilitate subsequent handling. Therefore, rejections under 35 U.S.C. 102 and 103 were properly made. Applicant had failed to introduce any evidence comparing X-ray diffraction patterns showing a difference in cooling rate between the claimed process and that of Hansford or any data showing that the process of Hansford would result in a product with a different X-ray diffraction. Either type of evidence would have rebutted the rejections under 35 U.S.C. 102. A further analysis would be necessary to determine if the process was nonobvious under 35 U.S.C. 103.); Ex parte Novitski, 26 USPQ2d 1389 (Bd. Pat. App. & Inter. 1993) (The Board rejected a claim directed to a method for protecting a plant from plant pathogenic nematodes by inoculating the plant with a nematode inhibiting strain of P. cepacia. A U.S. patent to Dart disclosed inoculation using P. cepacia type Wisconsin 526 bacteria for protecting the plant from fungal disease. Dart was silent as to nematode inhibition but the Board concluded that nematode inhibition was an inherent property of the bacteria. The Board noted that applicant had stated in the specification that Wisconsin 526 possesses an 18% nematode inhibition rating.).

II. PROCESS OF USE CLAIMS—NEW AND NONOBVIOUS USES OF OLD STRUCTURES AND COMPOSITIONS MAY BE PATENTABLE

The discovery of a new use for an old structure based on unknown properties of the structure might be patentable to the discoverer as a process of using. In re Hack, 245 F.2d 246, 248, 114 USPQ 161, 163 (CCPA 1957). However, when the claim recites using an old composition or structure and the "use" is directed to a result or property of that composition or structure, then the claim is anticipated. In re May, 574 F.2d 1082, 1090, 197 USPQ 601, 607 (CCPA 1978) (Claims 1 and 6, directed to a method of effecting nonaddictive analgesia (pain reduction) in animals, were found to be anticipated by the applied prior art which disclosed the same compounds for effecting analgesia but which was silent as to addiction. The court upheld the rejection and stated that the applicants had merely found a new property of the compound and such a discovery did not constitute a new use. The court went on to reverse the obviousness rejection of claims 2–5 and 7–10 which recited a process of using a new compound. The court relied on evidence showing that the nonaddictive property of the new compound was unexpected.). See also In re Tomlinson, 363 F.2d 928, 150 USPQ 623 (CCPA 1966) (The claim was directed to a process of inhibiting light degradation of polypropylene by mixing it with one of a genus of compounds, including nickel dithiocarbamate. A reference taught mixing polypropylene with nickel dithiocarbamate to lower heat degradation. The court held that the claims read on the obvious process of mixing polypropylene with the nickel dithiocarbamate and that the preamble of the claim was merely directed to the result of mixing the two materials. "While the references do not show a specific recognition of that result, its discovery by appellants is tantamount only to finding a property in the ***old composition****." 363 F.2d at 934, 150 USPQ at 628 (emphasis in original)).*

Cochrane v. Deener
94 U.S. 780
Supreme Court of the United States
March 19, 1877, Decided

Questions

1. This is an older Supreme Court case; although it does a good job of distinguishing a process from a machine. It also shows that reissue practice has been a feature of U.S. patent law for a long time. What is the invention here generally directed to? What is the particular improvement here?
2. The suit was about six related patents, two of which were original patents and four of which were reissue patents. It is apparent from the case that the key patent is the process patent. The Court specifically states:

   > The principal patent sued on in this case was granted on the 21st of April, 1874, being a reissue of a patent granted to William F. Cochrane on the 6th of January, 1863. The original patent was numbered *37,317*, and the reissue *5,841*. The alleged invention is for a process in manufacturing flour. . . . This is the process described; but the patentee claims that it is not limited to any special arrangement of machinery.[135]

   Patent *37,321* was reissued as *6,029*. Then that reissue patent was reissued as two patents, *6,594* and *6,595*. Is it still possible today to do what happened to patent *37,321*?

135. Cochrane v. Deener, 94 U.S. 780, 784–85 (1876).

3. What is the significance of the patent to Mortimer Cogswell and John McKiernan as argued by the defendants? Why does the Court not consider this patent an issue with respect to Cochrane's patents? What is the patent to Cogswell and McKiernan directed to that is different from the patents to Cochrane? The Court makes the following interesting observation:

   > We do not perceive that the patent of Cogswell and McKiernan, if valid at all as against Cochrane (a point which will be more fully considered hereafter), affects the question in the least. That patent is not at all for the process which Cochrane claims. If valid, and if, in using his process, Cochrane is obliged to use any device secured to Cogswell and McKiernan, it does not detract in the slightest degree from his own patent. One invention may include within it many others, and each and all may be valid at the same time. This only consequence follows, that each inventor is precluded from using inventions made and patented prior to his own, except by license from the owners thereof. His invention and his patent are equally entitled to protection from infringement, as if they were independent of any connection with them.[136]

4. The rights granted by a patent are frequently misunderstood. A patent does not grant a right to do something; rather it grants a *right to prevent others* from doing something.[137] The language from the Court makes that clear. Hence, we also see that the Court discusses improvements made by the defendants to the technology but does not find that this undermines the case against them. In general, new inventions may be seen as incremental improvements over what is already known. However, what is known may have been patented by someone else. If so, it may be that you cannot practice your improvement patent without a license from the predecessor patents, despite having come up with an improvement. What should happen in a situation in which

136. *Id.* at 787.

137. *See* 35 U.S.C. § 154(a)(1) ("Every patent shall contain a short title of the invention and a grant to the patentee, his heirs or assigns, of *the right to exclude others* from making, using, offering for sale, or selling the invention throughout the United States or importing the invention into the United States, and, if the invention is a process, of *the right to exclude others from* using, offering for sale or selling throughout the United States, or importing into the United States, products made by that process, referring to the specification for the particulars thereof.") (emphasis added).

someone has a patented improvement to someone else's patented technology if the parties involved are rational?

5. The Court compares the accused process with the patented process and observes that the accused process includes improvements:

> The use of a flat screen instead of a revolving reel for bolting and cleaning the middlings is a mere matter of form. It may be an improved form, and, perhaps, patentable as an improvement; but it is at most an improvement. . . .
>
> The defendants admit that the process has produced a revolution in the manufacture of flour; but they attribute that revolution to their improvements. It may be as they say, that it is greatly due to these. But it cannot be seriously denied that Cochrane's invention lies at the bottom of these improvements, is involved in them, and was itself capable of beneficial use, and was put to such use. It had all the elements and circumstances necessary for sustaining the patent, and cannot be appropriated by the defendants, even though supplemented by and enveloped in very important and material improvements of their own.[138]

Although it is not entirely clear, it did not appear that the defendants had patents covering the specific improvements pointed out by the Court (although the Court references patents issued to Edward P. Welch being used by defendants, the Court does not discuss the specifics, which suggests it may have covered some other aspect of the defendants' machines). Suppose the defendants had patents on all the improvements discussed in the case. How might that have helped the defendants?

6. This case also provides a good example of the value of process patents. Historically, process patents are perceived quite differently than the other categories of patentable subject matter. With respect to the process patent, the Court states:

> That a process may be patentable, irrespective of the particular form of the instrumentalities used, cannot be disputed. If one of the steps of a process be that a certain substance is to be reduced to a powder, it may not be at all material what instrument or machinery is used to effect that object, whether a hammer, a pestle and mortar, or a mill. Either may be pointed out; but if the patent is not confined

138. *Cochrane*, 94 U.S. at 786–87.

> to that particular tool or machine, the use of the others would be an infringement, the general process being the same. A process is a mode of treatment of certain materials to produce a given result. It is an act, or a series of acts, performed upon the subject-matter to be transformed and reduced to a different state or thing. If new and useful, it is just as patentable as is a piece of machinery. In the language of the patent law, it is an art. The machinery pointed out as suitable to perform the process may or may not be new or patentable; whilst the process itself may be altogether new, and produce an entirely new result. The process requires that certain things should be done with certain substances, and in a certain order; but the tools to be used in doing this may be of secondary consequence.[139]

As stated in the Manual of Patent Examining Procedure (MPEP) section 2106.03, processes are "actions," whereas the other categories (machines, articles of manufacture, and compositions of matter) are "tangible." Often, apparatus claims are perceived as more valuable because they have the potential to cover the rights to make, use, and sell (in addition to offer to sell and import); however, a method claim will typically either cover the rights to make or rights to use. Thus, apparatus claims, in general, cover a wider range of potential rights. However, as the case demonstrates, a process claim has the potential, if drafted properly, to be much broader than an apparatus claim. Thus, the more valuable patent of all the patents seemed to be the process patent, at least in this case. However, also observe that Cochrane had both method and apparatus patents and there were apparatus claims that were infringed. Does this suggest a strategy for drafting patent claims?

7. What argument did the defendants make suggesting that reissue *6,594* was void? Why did the Court reject that position? Thus, if you seek a reissue patent, just as in the original patent, you are limited by the specification in terms of what you are permitted to claim. Reissues also have a limit on scope based on the "original patent" principle. What is that?

* * *

Many differences between apparatus and method claims exist that are relevant to patent claiming strategy and tactics. At one of the most basic levels, the set of rights granted by these different categories of patent claims is different. An apparatus claim provides the full set of statutory rights—that is,

139. *Id.* at 787–88.

make, use, sell, and so on.[140] On the other hand, due to an inherent nature, a method claim essentially covers "use," as in a method of using, or "make," as in a method of making or manufacturing. At least partially for this reason, apparatus claims are usually perceived to be more valuable than method claims. However, do not read this to suggest that method claims are not valuable. In various situations, having a method claim may be important as an arrow in your quiver. It is recommended to nearly always include method claims with apparatus claims for claim diversity. Many patents are written that do not follow this simple principle. Furthermore, as demonstrated by *Cochrane*, it may be that a process claim will provide significantly more coverage than an apparatus claim in terms of scope.

Usually, an invention will more easily be claimed as one or the other, that is, as a method or as an apparatus. For example, software operation is usually more easily described as a method. Although not a requirement, it seems logical when beginning to draft claims for an invention to begin with the claim type that is more easily drafted due to the inherent nature of the invention.

Regardless, do not pass on the opportunity to claim an invention in method terms (e.g., method of using and/or method of making in addition to apparatus terms). A litany of good reasons to do this exist. A method may stand up to prior art even in situations where an apparatus claim may not.[141] Depending on the limitations of the patent claim, a method claim may be infringed where an apparatus claim is not, it may be infringed in a different manner, or it may potentially result in greater damages.[142] Further, a pure method claim generally is much less likely to be construed under subsection 112(f).[143] The failure to claim a method described in the specification also has the potential to dedicate to the public subject matter that might have otherwise been covered by a method claim.[144] Other good reasons also exist to include method claims, but these reasons should be more than sufficient.

One aspect to appreciate is the difference in drafting a method claim versus drafting an apparatus claim that flows directly from the preceding discussion about the set of rights associated with each. A method claim recites actions or acts. A method claim is infringed by performing an action, an act, or an operation, such as when "using" something or "making" something. Hence,

140. *See* 35 U.S.C. § 271(a) (2024).

141. See the treatment later in this chapter regarding new use of an old device.

142. *Id. See also* Chapter 6.

143. See discussion of step-plus-function claims in this chapter.

144. *See* Johnson & Johnston Assocs. v. R.E. Serv. Co., 285 F.3d 1046, 1054 (Fed. Cir. 2002) (en banc) ("As stated in *Maxwell*, when a patent drafter discloses but declines to claim subject matter, as in this case, this action dedicates that unclaimed subject matter to the public.").

the claim elements of a method claim are actions like "receiving," "transmitting," and so on—that is, words ending in "ing."

One way to think of a method claim, for drafting purposes, is like a cooking recipe. It specifies the steps or actions to follow. Usually, therefore, method claims are easier to draft than their apparatus counterparts. As has been stated, an apparatus may be capable of performing an action, an act, or an operation, but it is important to not claim an apparatus in a manner that suggests that it is actually performing such actions or operations.[145] Thus, an apparatus claim either recites structural elements, such as a processor or memory, or it recites that such elements are able to perform an action to make it clear that the action itself is not being claimed. Claiming the action itself is the domain of method claims.

The opportunity to claim a method of making even in situations where that is *not necessarily* the feature that is inventive should also not be overlooked.[146] For example, consider an analog or digital circuit invention capable of being embedded in a silicon chip. Semiconductor or silicon chips, for example, shall be manufactured to implement such a circuit, if the inventive concept has value. If so, why not include a method of manufacturing patent claim in one's arsenal?

One may wonder how a method of making claim might be patentable if the innovation relates to something else, such as how the circuit works or how the components are arranged. With appropriate drafting, however, the claim language that recites the manufacturing operations may include language to also capture the innovation.

Consider the following example of a method of making claim corresponding to prior Example 4.14:

145. *See, e.g.*, IPXL Holdings, L.L.C. v. Amazon.com, Inc., 430 F.3d 1377, 1384 (Fed. Cir. 2005). See Chapter 6's treatment of indefiniteness from mixing statutory classes in a single claim. *Cf.* INVT SPE LLC v. Int'l Trade Comm'n, 46 F.4th 1361 (Fed. Cir. 2022) (distinguishing between actual operation and capability of operating or performing for apparatus claims, particularly for software on a device, which tends to be functional, without discussing indefiniteness issue of mixing method and apparatus limitations).

146. This point also applies to method of using claims, but those are more conventionally written along with apparatus claims. Hence, the emphasis here on method of making claims, which are not typically included with apparatus claims, except, perhaps, for semiconductor manufacturing technology.

EXAMPLE 4.20

I claim:

1. A method of fabricating a memory controller and random access memory (RAM) comprising:

 fabricating an integrated circuit (IC) that includes a memory controller with RAM on the IC, wherein the memory controller and RAM are fabricated in an electrical configuration on a silicon substrate;

 wherein the fabricating includes forming transistors for the memory controller and RAM on the silicon substrate, wherein the transistors respectively have a source, a drain, a gate, and a body;

 wherein the fabricating further includes fabricating the memory controller to be capable of initiating burst mode operation based, at least in part, on receipt of an externally derived request from an external central processing unit (CPU) in which the request is to include a memory address, a word count, and a read or a write control transfer designation; and

 wherein the fabricating further includes fabricating the memory controller to be capable to process the request and take control of an external system transfer bus.

As is shown, the claim employs language such as "wherein the fabricating further includes fabricating the memory controller to be capable of initiating burst mode operation."[147] One may ask: at the time the invention was made, would this claim have been novel, nonobvious, and useful in light of such language? The answer seems to be yes.

The usefulness of this approach may matter more as it becomes more common for companies, so-called fabless design houses, to outsource chip manufacturing to others. Specifically, coming up with the design does not

147. One might wonder whether including "fabricating" as a limitation with "memory controller to be capable of..." might raise concerns because one is more typically method language ("fabricating") and the other is more typically apparatus language ("memory controller to be capable of"). Generally, it seems that following *IPXL*, 430 F.3d at 1384, the Federal Circuit has clarified that to make a claim indefinite, it should be unclear whether the claim is intended to be an apparatus claim or a method claim. *See* Mastermine Software, Inc. v. Microsoft Corp., 874 F.3d 1307 (Fed. Cir. 2017). In this scenario, the risk of that seems acceptable.

Here, it seems from the language reasonably clear that this is intended as a method claim.

generally by itself directly infringe a patent claim.[148] Yet, a claim directed to a company making the chip for someone else would be infringed and may have some value.[149]

One limiting factor to consider is how easy or difficult it would be to discover or prove infringement of a method of manufacture claim.[150] For example, if there is little or no way to discover from the end product that a particular process was used, this technology might be better protected as a trade secret.[151]

As one example, consider that in the aircraft manufacturing industry many holes are typically created in metal structures, such as for an engine, for a fuselage, and so on. The holes may be for nuts, screws, and other types of connectors to attach various mechanical components together. The ability to create more precise holes, more quickly, and at a cheaper cost in complex metal structures may, therefore, provide a competitive advantage. With the advent of laser technology, it seems likely that some type of laser was developed for just such processes. However, it might be very difficult or nearly impossible to determine how such a hole was generated during manufacture from looking at the end product itself. Consequently, assuming such laser technology was developed and even assuming it was patentable at the time of its creation, a patent on such technology may be difficult to enforce. Furthermore, by filing a patent application that may publish 18 months after filing, one would be educating one's competitors on how to perform such a process (again, a process performed behind closed doors and difficult to discover). Instead, as suggested, such technology may be better protected as a trade secret.

Another possible limiting factor, such as for a fabless design house seeking a manufacturing claim, may be that typically so-called foundries that perform manufacturing for other fabless design houses are located outside the United States. Such manufacturing activities, therefore, may at times be beyond the territorial scope of U.S. patent law for a claim of infringement under 35 U.S.C.

148. Although it might be a basis for a claim for indirect infringement; see the treatment of indirect infringement in Chapter 5.

149. This is especially the case since direct infringement is generally easier to prove than indirect infringement. See the indirect infringement treatment in Chapter 5.

150. See the treatment of this issue more generally in Chapter 6.

151. For example, turnover in the industry and/or how easy it might be to limit trade secret knowledge of the technology within the company are a few examples of considerations that may affect the desirability of trade secret protection.

subsection 271(a). However, there are statutes directed to extraterritorial patent infringement.[152]

One thing to beware of regarding method claims is that, for years, it also used to be common practice to add to the end of a preamble of a method claim the language "the steps of," as in "A method comprising the steps of:."

It is recommended that this formulation *not* be employed. Using the word "step" anywhere in the claim, including in the preamble,[153] creates the risk that the patent claim will be interpreted to be a step-plus-function claim under 35 U.S.C. subsection 112(f) (previously, 35 U.S.C. § 112, paragraph 6).[154] Because such claims are typically given a narrow construction by courts, good practice suggests that this be avoided.

Seal-Flex, Inc. v. Athletic Track & Court Construction
172 F.3d 836
United States Court of Appeals for the Federal Circuit
April 1, 1999, Decided

Questions

1. In footnote 1, the court tells us that as to the '833 patent the noninfringement ruling was not appealed; however, the jury also determined that "Athletic Track had infringed at least one claim of [the '833 patent] under the Doctrine of Equivalents."[155] Furthermore, the jury response only identified infringement of several dependent claims of the '833 patent without a finding that any of its independent claims were also infringed. To resolve this inconsistent verdict, the district court entered judgment of noninfringement with respect to the '833 patent because "the parties agreed that 'there can be no infringement of a dependent claim unless the corresponding independent claim is

152. *See* 35 U.S.C. § 271(f), (g) (2024). See the treatment of 35 U.S.C. § 271(g) (2024) later in this chapter.

153. Technically, one might argue that "the steps of" is part of the body rather than the preamble, although it is usually followed with a colon. Since we recommend against use, we need not formally analyze whether "the steps of" is in the preamble or the body. If interpreted as part of the body, that just makes the step-plus-function issue that much riskier.

154. See discussion of step-plus-function claims in this chapter.

155. Seal-Flex Inc. v. Athletic Track & Ct. Constr., 172 F.3d 836 (Fed. Cir. 1999).

infringed.'"[156] Given that the jury indicated that at least one claim was infringed under the DOE, is this necessarily correct?[157]
2. Why do you think the parties agreed that § 112, 6 applies to the claims?
3. As Judge Rader notes, there are few step-plus-function decisions. His analysis also provides a possible basis for that. How binding is Judge Rader's concurrence? Do you find it well reasoned? What do you think about his analysis regarding "step for" versus "step of"? It used to be common to recite "A method comprising the steps of," whereas now it is generally not used. Given Judge Rader's concurrence, why do you think that is the case?
4. Note the confusion by the parties and the lower court regarding whether the claim involves a means-plus-function clause or a step-plus-function clause. Assuming Judge Rader's analysis of step-plus-function clauses in method claims is largely correct, could a method claim nonetheless involve a means-plus-function clause? Why or why not? If so, what would it look like?
5. How would you describe the difference between a function and an act? Can you provide an example?

Method of Using Claims

NTP, Inc. v. Research in Motion, Ltd.
418 F.3d 1282
United States Court of Appeals for the Federal Circuit
August 2, 2005, Decided

Questions

1. Compare apparatus claim 1 and method claim 18 of the '960 patent recited by the court. What are some formal differences? Do you see some language that could confuse method and apparatus claim distinctions?
2. What was the inventive aspect of NTP's patents at a high level?
3. Why did the court reject Research in Motion's (RIM's) pull technology construction?

156. *Id.* at 840–41.
157. *See* Wilson Sporting Goods Co. v. David Geoffrey & Assocs., 904 F.2d 677 (Fed. Cir. 1990).

4. What was the dispute regarding "processor" and regarding "information"? What was the error in the district court's jury instructions? Why did that error in a jury instruction not necessarily result in a new trial? What did the appellate court do instead?
5. What was the dispute regarding "dual pathways"? Why did the prosecution history *not* result in disclaimer or disavowal?
6. Why did the court reject the argument regarding an RF receiver and a destination processor being separate and distinct?
7. Why did the court not address the argument regarding "additional processor outside an electronic mail system"?
8. Given the issues raised by the court in footnotes 11 and 12, is the court's analysis regarding subsection 271(a) necessarily binding?
9. How did the court address the issue of having a server in Canada to relay messages and the requirements of subsection 271(a)? What is the difference between use infringement of a system and infringement of a method of using claim?
10. What do you think of footnote 13 and the court's distinctions as to the issues raised on appeal? Why does the court conclude that RIM's customers are direct infringers and that RIM is an indirect infringer of the system claims? How does the court analyze infringement of the method claims under "sale," "offer for sale," and "import" for subsection 271(a) and under subsections 271(f) and 271(g)? Note that for some unclear reason, the opinion does not directly address "make" under subsection 271(a). Perhaps it is because these method claims are clearly not directed to a method of making.

* * *

Following are several example method of using claims.

Example 4.21 is a method of using claim directed to burst mode operation of a memory controller.

EXAMPLE 4.21

I claim:

1. A method comprising:

   receiving a request for burst mode operation;

   transmitting a request for control of a system bus in response to the received request;

receiving a signal granting system bus control;

transferring signals across the system bus into or out of a group of sequential memory cells after receiving the signal granting system bus control; and

transmitting a signal indicating completion of the signal transfer.

Examples 4.22 and 4.23 are method of using claims directed to a virtual private network.

EXAMPLE 4.22

I claim:

1. A method of forming a virtual private network comprising:

communicating one or more signal packets between respective physically separate broadcast domains via a network device included in the respective physically separate broadcast domains, wherein the communicating the one or more signal packets comprises:

encapsulating the one or more signal packets in the respective physically separate broadcast domains being communicated; and

communicating the encapsulated signal packets between the respective network devices and at least one tunnel server so that the one or more signal packets are communicated between the respective physically separate broadcast domains.

EXAMPLE 4.23

I claim:

1. A method comprising:

emulating one or more network devices of at least a second broadcast domain;

encapsulating one or more signal packets from at least a first broadcast domain directed to a network device of the at least a second broadcast domain; and

communicating the encapsulated one or more signal packets to at least one tunnel server directing the encapsulated one or more signal packets to the network device of the at least a second broadcast domain.

Observe that these patent claims, although not apparatus claims, follow some of the same drafting principles. For example, these patent claims employ a preamble, a transition word or phrase, and a claim body. Each also ends with a period.

Likewise, as for apparatus claims, method claims obey the single infringer rule. One party should control the set of acts, actions, or operations recited in the claim. If some are done by one party, and some are done by another party acting independently, then it may be that no one will infringe the patent claim.[158]

However, observe there is no need for language such as "to be directed," as might typically be used in an apparatus claim directed to a "capability to perform" as opposed to actual performance.

The principles previously discussed regarding structure versus function for apparatus claims may also apply to *tangible or physical components* recited in the limitations of a method claim (to be distinguished from recited acts or actions). For example, the preceding claim examples recite "network device," "broadcast domain," and "system bus." These should be interpreted as structural, but could, instead, be claimed using functional language. A system bus might be claimed as "means for transferring signals in a system." On the other hand, the language "system bus" seems broader and it is likely structural. Of course, these points relate to tangible aspects included in the limitations of a method claim, rather than to the elements involving actions, such as "transmitting," "communicating," and so on.

One practice that used to be common was to recite in the claim "A method comprising the steps of:." This practice is less common today and, here, we also suggest avoiding it. At least one reason is to prevent someone from arguing that your method claim has a "step-plus-function" element recited that

---

158. *See, e.g.*, Limelight Networks, Inc. v. Akamai Techs., Inc., 572 U.S. 915, 921–22 (2014); Muniauction, Inc. v. Thompson Corp., 532 F.3d 1318 (Fed. Cir. 2008); BMC Res., Inc. v. Paymentech, L.P., 489 F.3d 1373, 1379–81 (Fed. Cir. 2007).

should properly be interpreted under subsection 112(f). There is not much case law on step-plus-function elements of combination claims, as was previously addressed and is also addressed further later,[159] although they may be thought of as the method "analog" of a means-plus-function element[160] of an apparatus claim. In general, claim elements interpreted under subsection 112(f) tend to be construed more narrowly than claim elements not interpreted under subsection 112(f).

However, by their very nature, specifically regarding the action elements of a method claim, such as "transmitting," "encapsulating," and so on, these are less likely to be construed under subsection 112(f). This is based on an analysis of the language of subsection 112(f) and the reasoning of Judge Rader in *Seal-Flex*.[161] Thus, invoking subsection 112(f) to interpret an act or action as a "step-plus-function" element is believed to not be particularly likely.

Subsection 112(f) states:

> (f) Element in Claim for a Combination.—An element in a claim for a combination may be expressed as a means or step for performing a specified function without the recital of structure, material, or acts in support thereof, and such claim shall be construed to cover the corresponding structure, material, or acts described in the specification and equivalents thereof.

In an apparatus claim, a means-plus-function element may recite function in place of structure via reciting "means for [function]." In a method claim, in light of the statute, a step-plus-function element may recite function in place of "acts" via the claim language "step for [function]." In the absence of the word *step*, like in the absence of "means," by analogy, an adversary trying to make this argument must *rebut a presumption against application* of subsection 112(f) by arguing that the claim recites a "function" rather than "acts." By analogy, the language would be argued to be devoid of *sufficient* "action," and assuming successful rebuttal of the presumption, would potentially be interpreted as functional and, hence, would also likely be interpreted narrowly in accordance with subsection 112(f) jurisprudence.

---

159. *See Seal-Flex Inc.*, 172 F.3d 836. A concurrence by Judge Rader suggests that "comprising the steps of" would not be a problem, but best to avoid such questions by good drafting practice.

160. See Judge Rader's concurrence in *Seal-Flex Inc.*, 172 F.3d 836. See also the treatment of means-plus-function and step-plus-function claims later in this chapter.

161. *See Seal-Flex Inc.*, 172 F.3d 836. A concurrence by Judge Rader suggests that "comprising the steps of" would not be a problem, but best to avoid such questions by good drafting practice.

What might be an example? Consider a method claim element such as "generating a Fast Fourier Transform (FFT) signal from an audio signal." Is this a function or an act? That is a reasonably tricky question and may depend quite heavily on the specification description. Typically, generating an FFT involves many separate signal processing operations that individually could be "acts." Is this claim language, then, referring to all those acts together or is the language more like a function by simply reciting a statement of a result? How would one of ordinary skill interpret this language? The point is that, in general, due at least partially to the inherent nature of language, it may be more challenging to argue that a function is recited versus an act, in comparison with arguing that a function is recited versus structure. The difference between structure and function is usually more clear linguistically than the difference between action and function. Of course, good specification drafting may also make such an argument even more challenging.

Most method claims recite some tangible components as limitations. However, care is warranted here. If a method claim recites a lot of tangible components, such as hardware, for example, and is sloppy, someone may argue it is not clear whether the claim is a method or an apparatus claim. There is not much, if any, law on this specific situation, but the argument follows from cases that have held claims invalid that were ostensibly apparatus claims but used too much language that typically appears in method claims in which the drafting was quite sloppy.[162]

There are a few approaches to help ameliorate this risk. For one thing, attempt to recite only those tangible components needed to support the claimed acts or actions, particularly in the base claim. Example 4.21 illustrates this approach since it recites the system bus, but not the CPU, the memory, or the memory controller.

It also is a good idea to stick to the form of a method claim. Consider, for example, the independent claim of Example 4.22. The network device may be a gateway device. One way to write a dependent claim adding this feature might be:

---

2. The method of claim 1, wherein the network device of the at least a second broadcast domain comprises a gateway device.

---

162. *See, e.g.*, IPXL Holdings, L.L.C. v. Amazon.com, Inc., 430 F.3d 1377, 1384 (Fed. Cir. 2005); Rembrandt Data Techs., LP v. AOL, LLC, 641 F.3d 1331 (Fed. Cir. 2011). See also the treatment of the issue of mixing statutory classes in a patent claim in Chapter 6.

This claim is easy to write and clear; however, technically, it might be argued to *not* be interpreted as a method claim by not retaining the linguistic "ing" method claim structure of claim 1. Although it may be more cumbersome and perhaps less clear, it might be desirable to retain the method claim linguistic format and write this claim so there is no question that it is a method claim, such as:

---

2. The method of claim 1, wherein the encapsulating the one or more signal packets directed to the network device comprises: encapsulating the one or more signal packets directed to a gateway device.

Another approach that is used is to recite the tangible components, such as hardware, in the preamble first, rather than inferentially in the patent claim.[163] For example, consider the method claim in Example 4.22. It could be written as follows:

I claim:

1. A method of forming a virtual private network between at least one tunnel server and at least a first and at least a second broadcast domain, the broadcast domains respectively, including one or more network devices, the method comprising:

   emulating the one or more network devices of the at least a second broadcast domain;

   encapsulating one or more signal packets from the at least a first broadcast domain directed to a network device of the at least a second broadcast domain; and

   communicating the encapsulated one or more signal packets to the at least one tunnel server directing the encapsulated one or more signal packets to the network device of the at least a second broadcast domain.

---

163. See also the treatment of inferential claiming in Chapter 3.

Since there is little meaningful law on this point, let good judgment be your guide. It is doubtful that a significant legal difference exists between the latter example claim and Example 4.22. That is, the difference appears primarily stylistic. What is most important is that it be clear from the claim language that acts or actions are being claimed.

Another useful point about method claims is that the acts, actions, or operations (e.g., elements) may be done in any order unless the language expressly states an order or through its language implies an order. The claim of Example 4.24 illustrates an implied order written from the perspective of an operational memory controller:

EXAMPLE 4.24

I claim:

1. A method comprising:

   receiving a request for burst mode operation;

   transmitting a request for control of a system bus in response to the received request;

   receiving a signal granting system bus control;

   transferring signals across the system bus into or out of a group of sequential memory cells after receiving the signal granting system bus control; and

   transmitting a signal indicating completion of the signal transfer.

For example, "transmitting a request for control of the system bus in response to the received request;" is implied to come after "receiving a request for burst mode operation."

An express order used in a claim might be to recite "first," "second," and so on, with each respective act, action, or operation. Be aware of a practice in which the claim elements are recited with letter designations like "a," "b," "c" (or something similar) added merely for convenience to refer back to specific claim elements in various dependent claims. Someone may argue such designations specify order. The problem here may be that a specific order was not intended in the base claim. Thus, avoid such a practice unless a specific order is necessarily intended. Instead, use the dependent claiming approach discussed previously, which involves using language that might be called a "handle" for the particular feature.[164]

Because of this notion regarding no specific order to the particular operations unless stated or implied, it should be relatively easy to narrow a method claim with further dependent claims that might *intellectually or logically* have been thought to come *before* the base claim's acts, actions, or operations (or in the middle of such actions or after such actions). For example, a dependent claim for Example 4.21 might be the following:

---

2. The method of claim 1, comprising: before the receiving the request for burst mode operation, at least partially directing transfer of signal values across the system bus into or out of a single, individual memory cell.

Use Infringement of a System

Understand the difference between infringing a method of use claim and use infringement of an apparatus or system claim.

Centillion Data Systems, LLC v. Qwest Communications International
631 F.3d 1279
United States Court of Appeals for the Federal Circuit
January 20, 2011, Decided

Questions

1. What new issues did the court face regarding infringement?
2. Why did the appellate court remand to the district court regarding infringement by the users?
3. How does "use" infringement by users, if present, implicate Qwest?
4. How did the appellate court analyze "use" infringement by Qwest under subsection 271(a)?
5. How did the appellate court analyze "make" infringement by Qwest under subsection 271(a)?
6. How did the appellate court rule regarding invalidity and why?

* * *

164. See discussion with respect to previous examples in this chapter, such as "corresponding elliptical shape," used in a prior example.

Another issue to consider when drafting relates to the difference between use infringement of an apparatus or system-type claim, such as a server as one example, versus infringement of a method of using claim directed to the server. Perhaps surprisingly, the Federal Circuit employs different legal analyses to the two situations.

One of the first cases to try to handle this issue was *NTP, Inc. v. Research in Motion, Ltd.*[165] The Federal Circuit distinguished claims to an apparatus or system from claims to a process, in particular, in terms of whether a system or process has been used so as to fall within subsection 271(a). It held that, for a claimed system, components of a claimed system are "used collectively." On the other hand, a claimed process is used on a step-by-step basis. In the case, it was argued that use by RIM's customers of the overall system resulted in indirect infringement by RIM for which RIM should be liable. Thus, the fundamental issue was whether RIM's customers directly infringed the claims at issue by use of RIM's email system under subsection 271(a). Interestingly, the case also partly turned on extraterritoriality because RIM had its server/relay station in Canada, not in the United States.[166]

The court stated:

> The use of a claimed system under section 271(a) is the place at which the system as a whole is put into service, *i.e.*, the place where control of the system is exercised and beneficial use of the system obtained. . . .
>
> Under section 271(a), the concept of "use" of a patented method or process is fundamentally different from the use of a patented system or device. *In re Kollar*, 286 F.3d 1326, 1332 (Fed. Cir. 2002) (recognizing "the distinction between a claim to a product, device, or apparatus, all of which are tangible items, and a claim to a process, which consists of a series of acts or steps. . . . [A process] consists of doing something, and therefore has to be carried out or performed."); *see Joy Techs., Inc. v. Flakt, Inc.*, 6 F.3d 770, 773 (Fed. Cir. 1993) ("The law is unequivocal that the sale of equipment to perform a process is not a sale of the process within the meaning of section 271(a)."). Although the Supreme Court focused on the whole operable assembly of a system claim for infringement in *Deepsouth*, there is no corresponding whole operable assembly of a process claim. A method or process consists of one or more operative steps, and, accordingly, "it is well established that a patent for a method or process is not infringed unless all steps or stages of the claimed process are utilized." *Roberts Dairy Co. v. United States*, 530 F.2d 1342, 1354, 208 Ct. Cl. 830 (Ct. Cl. 1976).

165. 418 F.3d 1282, 1319 (Fed. Cir. 2005), *cert. denied*, 546 U.S. 1157 (2006).
166. *Cf.* 35 U.S.C. § 271(f), (g) (2024), addressing extraterritorial patent infringement.

> Because a process is nothing more than the sequence of actions of which it is comprised, the use of a process necessarily involves doing or performing each of the steps recited. This is unlike use of a system as a whole, in which the components are used collectively, not individually. We therefore hold that a process cannot be used "within" the United States as required by section 271(a) unless each of the steps is performed within this country.[167]

This approach distinguishing use infringement of an apparatus claim from infringement of a method of using claim was carried forward and refined in later cases, such as *Centillion Data Systems, LLC v. QWest Communications International, Inc.*[168] and *Intellectual Ventures I LLC v. Motorola Mobility LLC.*[169] These cases require that, for patent infringement, the user put the system into service by control over the system as a whole and by obtaining benefit from it, in particular, as to *each element and limitation of the claim.* Thus, on this basis, in *Centillion*, the Federal Circuit found direct infringement by the customers and, in *Motorola Mobility*, it did not.

In *Centillion*, the court stated:

> In order to "put the system into service," the end user must be using all portions of the claimed invention. For example, in *NTP*, the end user was "using" every element of the system by transmitting a message. It did not matter that the user did not have physical control over the relays, the user made them work for their patented purpose, and thus "used" every element of the system by putting every element collectively into service.[170]

Thus, physical possession was and is not a requirement for use infringement by the customers.

By contrast, in *Motorola Mobility*, the accused infringer's customers did not obtain a benefit from the generation of delivery reports, which was an element of the claim at issue. There was no evidence the customers ever generated a delivery report. Instead, the evidence was that reports were generated by centers operated by the customers' wireless service carriers.[171]

Here, a lesson may be to take care when drafting complex apparatus/system claims that may involve use infringement by customers for services offered by a party that may own and maintain the overall system, such as where services are provided to mobile devices, for example. *That is, do not*

167. NTP, Inc. v. Research in Motion, Ltd., 418 F.3d 1282, 1317–18 (Fed. Cir. 2005).
168. 631 F.3d 1279 (Fed. Cir. 2011).
169. 870 F.3d 1320 (Fed. Cir. 2017).
170. *Centillion Data Sys.*, 631 F.3d at 1284.
171. *See Intell. Ventures I*, 870 F.3d 1320.

include elements and limitations that would not actually be initiated by the users and from which they will not actually benefit.

Likewise, in this section, we are focused on drafting method of using claims. Thus, a question might be: are we able to draft *method of using* claims that would capture a system owner/operator directly for use of an innovation by a customer?

Consider this situation. So-called visual voicemail was invented well before the introduction of the iPhone. This refers to the feature in which voicemails are transcribed so that the party to whom the voicemail is directed may read the content rather than listen to it. Visual voicemail, when invented, was one feature of an overall voicemail management system, with an inbox, somewhat similar, but distinctly separate from, an email inbox. At the time of the invention, cell phone voicemail capability was limited to serially going through and listening to voicemail messages forwarded to a wireless handset from a voicemail server.

In general, the visual voicemail innovation was initially directed at wireless handsets. The handsets might transcribe and display in a voicemail inbox received voicemails that a mobile device had at least partially transcribed. Alternately or additionally, the innovation was directed to a wireless handset that might receive transcribed voicemails from a voicemail server and display partial transcriptions in a voicemail inbox.

For example, in this latter approach, a wireless carrier might charge for a transcription service included with its voicemail service. The wireless carrier, for example, may employ a voicemail server with the capability to transcribe audio voicemails and then forward the audio voicemail and the transcription to a wireless handset. If the wireless subscriber has signed up for the transcription service, the wireless carrier would also provide software executable on the wireless handset to handle the processing and display of the voicemails and associated at least partial transcriptions in a voicemail inbox.

The question, then, might be how to draft a method claim intended to capture wireless providers that provide such a voicemail transcription service based on use of the service by one or more subscribers. Example 4.25 is an example of a possible method of using claim.

EXAMPLE 4.25

I claim:

1. A method of processing voicemail messages at a voicemail server, the method comprising:

capturing a plurality of received voicemail messages in an audio format providing a plurality of audio-formatted voicemail messages;

converting the plurality of audio-formatted voicemail messages to a plurality of corresponding text representations of the voicemail messages; and

initiating communication of the text representations of the voicemail messages and the audio-formatted voicemail messages to a mobile device, wherein a respective text representation comprises a representation of an at least partial text transcription of a corresponding converted audio-formatted voicemail message, wherein the at least partial text transcriptions of the voicemail messages are capable of being displayed via a visual voicemail inbox of a voicemail system integrated as part of the mobile device.

One reason for writing the claim to refer to a plurality of voicemail messages, which might otherwise be an "out" if someone argues they do not process a plurality of such messages, is to argue the innovation is associated with the feature of displaying *multiple* messages in a single voicemail inbox; however, one might, instead, start with a claim to individual messages and move this feature to a dependent claim. Since this claim is drafted as a method,[172] deliberately, there is not a lot of extra description regarding the server hardware, such as a processor, memory, instructions, and so on. Such hardware recitation would seem unnecessary and also should not really help much with respect to patent eligibility and § 101,[173] which is often the reason why some practitioners include hardware recitations. Also, that material should already be provided in the specification and could be added to the claim later, during prosecution if needed.

It appears that a voicemail server is able to perform the acts recited in the claim. Thus, by writing a method of using claim that reads on a voicemail server able to perform transcription that would be owned and operated by a wireless service provider, more complex questions about customer initiation of service, customer control, and/or customer benefit seem to be avoided here. It also appears here that as to this claim, the wireless provider at least will meet the control test described earlier.

172. See discussion of drafting method claims earlier in this chapter.
173. See discussion of patent eligibility in Chapter 6.

Appreciate the tricky part to drafting this claim and the hook it provides vis-à-vis wireless carriers. Ultimately, the innovation here is really associated with display of one or more at least partial transcriptions in a voicemail inbox (i.e., separate from an email inbox) on a wireless handset. It is true that wireless carriers, like AT&T, do sell handsets; however, the handsets are manufactured by others, such as Apple. Furthermore, it is likely that a wireless carrier selling a handset manufactured by someone else gets a contractual indemnity against patent infringement.

So how do we capture the wireless providers in a core business, such as wireless services, since they do not actually perform the displaying and so on? The wireless provider not only transcribes the audio voicemails, but it must also send "at least partial transcriptions" in a *format* capable of being displayed by a handset. There is really no way around doing that in the model of forwarding a transcription described. They also provide the software needed to receive the message and display it in the voicemail inbox.

The claim, therefore, has specific language directed to a "text representation" of the voicemail message as "a representation of an at least partial text transcription" in which the "at least partial text transcriptions of the voicemail messages [are] capable of being displayed via a visual voicemail inbox of a voicemail system integrated as part of the mobile device." Thus, regardless of the *format* (i.e., "representation" in the claim) actually sent, a *communication* that is *convertible* to an at least partial text transcription by a wireless handset would appear to otherwise meet the language of the claim.

A tricky question of divided infringement should be avoided by the wording of this claim. First, as noted, the software to display the message is provided by the wireless carrier. Second, per the discussion of claim elements versus claim limitations, the language regarding the "at least partial text transcriptions of the voicemail messages [are] capable of being displayed via a visual voicemail inbox of a voicemail system integrated as part of the mobile device" is a limitation rather than a method claim element.[174] Thus, there is no divided infringement.

To see this, consider first this claim:

I claim:

1. A method of processing voicemail messages at a voicemail server, the method comprising:

174. See discussion in Chapter 3; *see* INVT SPE LLC v. Int'l Trade Comm'n, 46 F.4th 1361 (Fed. Cir. 2022).

capturing a plurality of received voicemail messages in an audio format providing a plurality of audio-formatted voicemail messages;

converting the plurality of audio-formatted voicemail messages to a plurality of corresponding text representations of the voicemail messages; and

initiating communication of the text representations of the voicemail messages and the audio-formatted voicemail messages to a mobile device, wherein a respective text representation comprises a representation of an at least partial text transcription of a corresponding converted audio-formatted voicemail message, and wherein the at least partial text transcriptions of the voicemail messages are capable of being displayed.

Here, it should be pretty clear there is no divided infringement since the act is "initiating communication . . . of the voicemail messages, wherein . . . the voicemail messages are capable of being displayed." Next consider this claim:

I claim:

1. A method of processing voicemail messages at a voicemail server, the method comprising:

capturing a plurality of received voicemail messages in an audio format providing a plurality of audio-formatted voicemail messages;

converting the plurality of audio-formatted voicemail messages to a plurality of corresponding text representations of the voicemail messages; and

initiating communication of the text representations of the voicemail messages and the audio-formatted voicemail messages to a mobile device, wherein a respective text representation comprises a representation of an at least partial text transcription of a corresponding converted audio-formatted voicemail message, wherein the at least partial text transcriptions of the voicemail messages are capable of being displayed via the mobile device.

This change should not affect the divided infringement analysis (or lack thereof). It states: "initiating communication . . . of the voicemail messages . . . to a mobile device, wherein the voicemail messages are capable of being displayed via the mobile device." The claim above simply adds "wherein . . . the voicemail messages are capable of being displayed via a visual voicemail inbox of a voicemail system integrated into the mobile device." It also appears that as to this claim, the wireless provider will meet the control test described earlier.

From the method claim, it should also be easy to see how to handle an apparatus claim. It is quite similar to the approach for a Beauregard claim.[175] However, here, since this is an apparatus claim, there is not much harm in including more apparatus limitations, such as processors, memory, and so on. All servers will meet such limitations.

EXAMPLE 4.26

I claim:

1. An apparatus comprising: a server;

   wherein the server comprises one or more processors, wherein the one or more processors are coupled to one or more physical memories via one or more buses;

   wherein at least one of the one or more physical memories comprise stored instructions executable by the one or more processors; and

   wherein at least one of the one or more physical memories is capable of storing in one or more memory locations as physical memory states any results from execution by the one or more processors of the stored executable instructions;

   wherein the stored executable instructions comprise instructions, as a result of execution, at least to:

   > capture a plurality of messages in an audio format to provide a plurality of audio-formatted voicemail messages; convert the plurality of audio-formatted voicemail messages to a plurality of corresponding text representations of the voicemail messages; and initiate communication of the text representations of the voicemail messages and the audio formatted voicemail messages to a mobile device, wherein a respective text representation comprises a representation of an at least partial text transcription of a corresponding converted audio-formatted voicemail message, wherein the at least partial text transcriptions of the voicemail messages are displayable via a visual voicemail inbox of a voicemail system integrated as part of the mobile device.

175. See later in this chapter.

Observe also that this claim uses a format similar to the format for a Beauregard claim described previously and discussed in more detail later in this chapter.

New Use of an Old Device

Recognize a new use of an old device and the more challenging claim drafting issues it may present.

King Pharmaceuticals, Inc. v. Eon Labs, Inc.
616 F.3d 1267
United States Court of Appeals for the Federal Circuit
August 2, 2010, Decided

Questions

1. What was the legal basis for King's suit against Eon? Why was Elan Pharmaceuticals involved?
2. Who had the original patent on metaxalone? Why was it not in the lawsuit?
3. What did King argue was the novelty of claim 1 of the '128 patent? Why was this rejected?
4. What was King's argument regarding the patentability of the dependent claims (other than claims 21 and 22)? Why was it rejected?
5. As to claims 21 and 22 of the '128 patent, how did the district court err? Why did this, nonetheless, not keep the claims from being held invalid? What was the appellate court's reasoning? Do you think the doctrine at issue was properly applied? Why or why not? If the district court erred, how/why was the appellate court able to affirm?
6. What was the court's analysis regarding claim 1 of the '102 patent? Why did the court reject objective indicia of patentability as to claim 5?
7. Why was the district court's ruling as to Elan error?

* * *

One situation to be aware of is that a new use of an old or known device may be patentable;[176] however, it is also important to understand the

176. *See, e.g.*, Sean Seymore, *Patenting New Uses of Old Inventions*, 73 VAND. L. REV. 479 (2020); Perricone v. Medicis Pharm. Corp., 432 F.3d 1368, 1378 (Fed. Cir. 2005) ("New uses of old products or processes are indeed patentable subject matter."). One case example

parameters that affect patentability in this situation. The doctrine of inherent anticipation may limit patentability if the new use is based on an inherent characteristic of the old or known device.[177] However, if the feature is not inevitably present as "the natural result flowing from the operation [of the prior art] as taught," then it is not inherent.[178]

This inherency issue may be a technical challenge in the chemical or pharmaceutical arts, the so-called unpredictable arts.[179] The article "Patenting New Uses of Old Inventions"[180] provides a good hypothetical example of an antidepressant drug in which the patent has expired and is repatented as a treatment for irritable bowel syndrome, migraines, fibromyalgia, and functional dyspepsia. However, if the drug is able to operate as a treatment because it inhibits the uptake of serotonin in the brain, then this may not really be a new use since this may be how it *inherently* operated as an antidepressant.

Although still a real issue, it may be less of a technical issue generally for mechanical arts, electrical arts, and software, the so-called predictable arts. Typically, the science behind operation of technical innovations is usually better understood than in the unpredictable arts.

A new use is a method of using claim. The general principles of drafting method claims will therefore apply; however, also beware that the claim you draft is *sufficiently specific* lest the examiner give you a rejection by, in effect, taking the position that what you are claiming is inherent to an old structure. For example, in *In re King*, the Federal Circuit stated: "Under the principles of inherency, if a structure in the prior art necessarily functions in accordance with the limitations of a process or method claim of an application, the claim is anticipated."[181]

---

is *GlaxoSmithKline v. Teva Pharmaceuticals*, 7 F.4th 1320 (Fed. Cir. 2021), in which a drug for hypertension, carvedilol, was found to also decrease mortality for congestive heart failure.

177. *See, e.g.*, Seymore, *supra* note 176; Atlas Powder Co. v. Ireco Inc., 190 F.3d 1342, 1347 (Fed. Cir. 1999).

178. *See, e.g.*, Seymore, *supra* note 176; *In re* Oelrich, 666 F.2d 578, 581 (C.C.P.A. 1981) (quoting Hansgirg v. Kemmer, 102 F.2d 212, 214 (C.C.P.A. 1939)); *see also* Transclean Corp. v. Bridgewood Servs., 290 F.3d 1364, 1373 (Fed. Cir. 2002) ("[A]nticipation by inherent disclosure is appropriate only when the reference discloses prior art that must necessarily include the unstated limitation."). Also, be aware that a related doctrine, "inherent obviousness," might also be in play. This might arise, for example, if the inherent limitations of a reference, while not enough to anticipate the claim at issue, are combinable with another reference to render the claim obvious.

179. See Chapter 3 regarding discussion of predictable versus unpredictable arts.

180. Seymore, *supra* note 176.

181. 801 F.2d 1324, 1326 (Fed. Cir. 1986). *See* Carnegie Steel Co. v. Cambria Iron Co., 185 U.S. 403, 424–25 (1902) (explaining that a prior art device anticipates a later process if the device carries out the process in its normal operation); *In re* Ackenbach, 45 F.2d 437, 439 (C.C.P.A. 1930) ("[I]f a previously patented device, in its normal and usual operation, will

In prosecution, as an illustration, the examiner will attempt to provide a basis in fact and/or technical reasoning to support the determination that the allegedly inherent characteristic necessarily flows from the teachings of the applied prior art.[182] If a prior art device, in its normal and usual operation, would necessarily perform the method claimed, then the method claimed is anticipated by the prior art device.[183] Furthermore, when the prior art device or product is the same as the device described in the specification, the MPEP allows the examiner to presume that it will inherently perform the claimed method.[184] In this situation, a *prima facie* case of anticipation has been made by the examiner and the burden then shifts to the applicant. This is similar to the situation previously described regarding functionality where the PTO may shift the burden to the applicant.[185] If the PTO were to do this, it may require seeking to prove the characteristic is not in the prior art (e.g., proving a negative proposition, which is usually a challenge), amending the claim, or arguing that for some reason the PTO has inappropriately shifted the burden (e.g., because what is described in the specification is not the same as the prior art device).

Also recognize the disadvantages of the situation. The method claim should be specific enough to convince the examiner to allow it and yet the device is also known. In other words, it may be a challenge to obtain an allowable claim sufficiently specific and representing enough of a technical advance over a known device that it has market value because it is still sufficiently broad to capture potential infringers.[186]

Method of Making Claims

Following are several example method of manufacture (e.g., making) claims. Here is an example of a claim directed to making a cake:

---

perform the function which an appellant claims in a subsequent application for process patent, then such application for process patent will be considered to have been anticipated by the former patented device.").

182. *See Ex parte* Levy, 17 U.S.P.Q.2d (BNA) 1461, 1464 (B.P.A.I. 1990).

183. *See In re* Best, 562 F.2d 1252, 1255 (C.C.P.A. 1977).

184. *See* MPEP, *supra* note 10, § 2112.

185. See discussion earlier in this chapter.

186. In the pharmaceutical area, compare the recent cases *In re Pasteur*, No. 22-1896 (Fed. Cir. Dec. 13, 2023) (unpublished) (affirming Board's rejection in an ex parte reexamination for obviousness-type double patenting (ODP) relying at least in part on inherent anticipation), with *H. Lundbeck A/S v. Lupin Ltd.*, 87 F.4th 1361 (Fed. Cir. 2023) (where a pharmaceutical's patents had expired and a method for a new use of the pharmaceutical was patented and at issue with respect to infringement in the case; inherent anticipation was not argued).

I claim:

1. A method comprising:

   gathering constituent items in one place to make a cake, including: flour, eggs, butter, milk, and sugar;

   placing the constituent items in a mixing bowl;

   mixing the constituent items thoroughly while in the mixing bowl;

   transferring the thoroughly mixed constituent items to a cake mold;

   placing the cake mold with the thoroughly mixed items in an oven set to an appropriate temperature to bake the cake; and

   waiting an appropriate amount of time until the cake is suitably baked.

Note that terminology like "appropriate temperature" and "appropriate amount of time" should be discussed in the specification to have a fall-back position in the event of an indefiniteness rejection. Likewise, dependent claims to flesh these out would be a good idea as well. A similar approach shall be discussed later regarding negative limitations.[187]

Here is an example directed to a manufacturing process for Example 4.14:

I claim:

1. A method of fabricating a memory controller and random access memory (RAM) comprising:

   fabricating an integrated circuit (IC) that includes a memory controller with random access memory (RAM) on the IC, wherein the memory controller and RAM are fabricated in an electrical configuration on a silicon substrate;

   wherein the fabricating includes forming transistors for the memory controller and RAM on the silicon substrate, wherein the transistors respectively have a source, a drain, and a gate;

187. See the treatment of negative limitations in Chapter 6.

wherein the fabricating further includes fabricating the memory controller to be capable of initiating burst mode operation based, at least in part, on receipt of an externally derived request from an external central processing unit (CPU) in which the request is to include a memory address, a word count, and a read or a write control transfer designation; and

wherein the fabricating further includes fabricating the memory controller to be capable to process the request and take control of an external system transfer bus.

Furthermore, the fabrication operations could be described more fully with dependent claims as follows, as examples:

---

2. The method of claim 1, wherein the fabricating that includes forming the transistors having the source, the drain, and the gate comprises:

   forming the gate from a conductive gate layer and an oxide layer over a silicon layer of the silicon substrate; and

   forming two N+ regions in the silicon layer via ion implantation or diffusion to form the source and the drain.

3. The method of claim 2, wherein the forming the gate from the conductive gate layer comprises forming the gate from a polysilicon gate layer.

Although claims 2 and 3 describe well-known fabrication operations, as long as the base claim is patentable (e.g., based on the burst mode limitations), there is not a problem regarding patentability of these claims.[188] Note that the point raised earlier regarding following the method claim "linguistic structure" in dependent claims is illustrated here.

Method of making claims follow the same rules as method of using claims, although are directed to different substantive rights (i.e., the right to make). Thus, they employ a preamble, transition word or phrase, and body, and end with a period. They follow the single infringer rule, of course. They cover

188. *See In re* Fine, 837 F.2d 1071 (Fed. Cir. 1988) ("[d]ependent claims are nonobvious under section 103 if the independent claims from which they depend are nonobvious").

actual operations, acts, or actions, rather than the capability to perform an operation, act, or action. The elements consequently also use words ending in "ing." Similarly, there is no inherent order associated with the elements unless expressly stated or implied, as in the earlier example of baking a cake, illustrated here, again, for convenience.

I claim:

1. A method comprising:

    gathering constituent items in one place to make a cake, including: flour, eggs, butter, milk, and sugar;

    placing the constituent items in a mixing bowl;

    mixing the constituent items thoroughly while in the mixing bowl;

    transferring the thoroughly mixed constituent items to a cake mold;

    placing the cake mold with the thoroughly mixed items in an oven set to an appropriate temperature to bake the cake; and

    waiting an appropriate amount of time until the cake is suitably baked.

Thus, for example, "mixing the constituent items thoroughly" is followed by "transferring the thoroughly mixed constituent items."

One opportunity to be aware of in connection with method of manufacture claims is subsection 271(g). This subsection provides the ability to potentially get a type of product-by-process claim without the invalidity disadvantages.[189] The subsection states:

> Whoever without authority imports into the United States or offers to sell, sells, or uses within the United States a product which is made by a process patented in the United States shall be liable as an infringer, if the importation, offer to sell, sale, or use of the product occurs during the term of such process patent. In an action for infringement of a process patent, no remedy may be granted for infringement on account of the noncommercial use or retail sale of a product unless there is no adequate remedy under this title for infringement on account of the importation or other use, offer to sell, or

189. See later in this chapter providing a treatment of product-by-process claims.

sale of that product. A product which is made by a patented process will, for purposes of this title, not be considered to be so made after—

(1) it is materially changed by subsequent processes; or
(2) it becomes a trivial and nonessential component of another product.

Note the specific language "a product which is *made* by a process patented in the United States" (emphasis added). This provision has been interpreted to be limited to manufacturing.[190] This provision as well as subsection 271(f) are directed to "extraterritorial activities" that may ultimately result in liability for patent infringement in the United States.

For example, it is becoming more common for companies, so-called fabless design houses, to outsource chip manufacturing to others. Coming up with the design does not generally by itself directly infringe a patent claim.[191] Yet, a company making the chip for someone else could infringe a manufacturing claim absent extraterritorial considerations, potentially providing a direct infringement claim against the manufacturer and an indirect infringement claim against the customer.[192]

Let us now consider a situation in which a foundry *outside* the United States performs the aforementioned manufacturing claim (that corresponds to Example 4.14) for a U.S. company who then imports the IC with the memory controller into the United States. That U.S. company, while having not performed the process itself, may nonetheless be liable for infringement in federal court, assuming subsections (g)(1) and (g)(2) of § 271 do not apply. Furthermore, those in the chain of distribution may similarly be sued in federal court as an infringer, subject to the defenses in the statute, such as a noncommercial use, a retail sale, or the conditions of subsections (1) or (2).

Thus, subsection 271(g), in effect, gives one the equivalent of a product-by-process patent claim for this situation, but without the typical invalidity concerns that are generally present for a product-by-process claim.[193] The claim is a process claim, but subsection 271(g) creates liability for "a *product* which is made by a process patented in the United States" (emphasis added). Furthermore, the Federal Circuit has ruled that the two defenses in subsections (g)(1) and (g)(2) are not legally applicable in proceedings before the ITC, a quasi-judicial governmental body that hears and decides complaints regarding importations that may be in violation of certain U.S. trade regulation

190. *See* Bayer v. Houses Pharms., 340 F.3d 1367 (Fed. Cir. 2003).

191. Although it might be a basis for a claim for indirect infringement; see the treatment of indirect infringement in Chapter 5.

192. Note that direct infringement is generally easier to prove than indirect infringement.

193. See later in this chapter discussing product-by-process claims.

laws, including intellectual property laws.[194] Thus, one may potentially stop importation of the chips at the border of the United States without a concern regarding potential defenses under subsections (g)(1) and (g)(2).[195]

Method versus Apparatus

Understand how restriction practice and double patenting are related and draft claims with these issues in mind.

As previously suggested, in one sense the difference between a method claim versus an apparatus claim may be a matter of linguistic form. On the other hand, the difference in the rights that flow from these differences of linguistic form are substantive. This relates to an important feature of U.S. patent law to remember: *in patent claim drafting, the linguistic form of the patent claim affects the substantive scope of the claim. That is, form becomes substance.* Although there are examples of this in other areas of law, it may be more true here than in other areas. *That is, the words used critically matter.*

It is in part for this reason that we recommend including both method and apparatus claims when claiming a particular technical innovation.[196] To a technologist, the two may be largely directed to the same underlying technical subject matter. However, patent examination, analysis of infringement, the proof required to make out a case of patent infringement, the damages calculation, and, of course, the rights granted may all be quite different as between an apparatus claim and a method claim.

For these reasons, one should also be aware of PTO policy regarding the examination of multiple inventions in a patent application. In general, one patent application filing fee pays for one examination of one invention[197] or,

---

194. *See* Jennewein Biotechnologie GMBH v. Int'l Trade Comm'n, No. 2020-2220, 2021 U.S. App. LEXIS 28200 (Fed. Cir. Sept. 17, 2021); Kinik v. Int'l Trade Comm'n, 362 F.3d 1359 (Fed. Cir. 2004). See the section in Chapter 5 entitled "ITC Investigation: Another Enforcement Option."

195. Another feature of 35 U.S.C. § 271(g) is that a single entity need not perform all the claim elements. As to the method claim, there is liability without meeting the single infringer rule. *See* Syngenta Crop Prot. v. Willowood, LLC, 944 F.3d 1344 (Fed. Cir. 2019).

196. And in some cases, different types of methods, such as a method of using and a method of making.

197. *See* 37 C.F.R. § 1.142(a) (2024). This statutory section, "Requirement for restriction," states:

> If two or more independent and distinct inventions are claimed in a single application, the examiner in an office action will require the applicant in the reply to that action to elect an invention to which the claims will be restricted, this official action being called a requirement for restriction (also known as a requirement for division). Such requirement

to state a related policy, the PTO intends one invention per patent. Of course, the notion of an invention in this context requires some clarification. It is well-established that for many purposes, each patent claim defines a separate invention.[198] However, that is not what is referred to here.

For the purpose of this policy, inventions are separate and independent in that you may perform one without involving the other.[199] Hence, you might, for example, have only one set of multiple claims (e.g., one independent claim with several dependent claims) that you may for these purposes believe to be one invention. On the other hand, the examiner may believe that you are claiming three separate and independent inventions, depending on the specifics. More commonly, however, if the examiner perceives separate and independent inventions, the inventions are usually perceived to align with different claim sets, such as where you claim a method with one independent claim and multiple dependent claims and a related apparatus with another independent claim and other multiple dependent claims.

This may be illustrated most readily in semiconductor chip manufacturing. A claim may be directed to the structure of a chip to be manufactured that would have been novel and unobvious at the time the invention was made. Consider, for example, so-called flip-chip technology, also known as controlled collapse chip connection technology or its abbreviation, C4. It provides a technique for interconnecting chips to external circuitry with solder bumps that have been deposited onto the *top* surface of a chip and connect to the chip pads through the chip packaging.

The solder bumps are deposited on the chip pads on the top side of the wafer at the end of wafer processing. To mount the chip to external circuitry, it is flipped over so that its top side faces down and is aligned so that its pads align with matching pads on the external circuit, and then the solder is reflowed to make an electrical connection. This technology has advantages over wire bonding, its predecessor technology, which is much more involved to make the electrical connections, requiring fine wires be bonded to chip leads and also connected to a lead frame.

One may, therefore, imagine an apparatus claim directed, for example, to the structure of a completed chip with solder bumps on the top of the chip.

---

will normally be made before any action on the merits; however, it may be made at any time before final action.

198. *See, e.g.*, Dollar Elec. Co. v. Syndevco, Inc., 205 U.S.P.Q. 949, 959 (E.D. Mich. 1979), *aff'd*, 669 F.2d 1370, 214 U.S.P.Q. 241 (6th Cir. 1982) ("[E]ach claim of a patent is treated as if it was a separate patent.").

199. *See* MPEP, *supra* note 10, § 802.

However, a method of manufacturing claim will likely be quite different, reciting the manufacturing operations, after manufacture of silicon circuitry, for example, to create the chip packaging that includes the solder bumps that connect to the chip pads.

To explain further, in a method claim, a number of process operations may be involved to designate the location and placement of the solder bumps relative to the silicon circuitry and processing so that the solder bumps are only in the desired locations with protective external packaging covering other areas of the chip surface. An apparatus claim might not need to recite such process operations.

The PTO may take the position that these claims represent separate and independent inventions. In a nutshell, the position may be that a chip as claimed by the apparatus claim may be manufactured using a process other than the claimed manufacturing process. Similarly, the PTO may take the position that the recited manufacturing process may be used to manufacture a chip having a structure that is other than the chip structure as recited in the apparatus claim. Thus, the PTO may assert that these are separate and independent inventions, and issue a restriction requirement, which ultimately may result in the filing of a divisional patent application.[200]

Restriction and Double Patenting

35 U.S.C. § 101

Whoever invents or discovers any new and useful process, machine, manufacture, or composition of matter, or any new and useful improvement thereof, may obtain a patent therefor, subject to the conditions and requirements of this title.

35 U.S.C. § 121

If two or more independent and distinct inventions are claimed in one application, the Director may require the application to be restricted to one of the inventions. If the other invention is made the subject of a divisional application which complies with the requirements of section 120 it shall be entitled to the benefit of the filing date of the original application. A patent issuing on an application with respect to which a requirement for restriction under this section has been made, or on an application filed as a result of such a requirement, shall not be used as a reference either in the Patent and Trademark Office or in the courts against a divisional application or against the original application or any patent issued on either of them, if the divisional application is filed before the issuance of the patent on the other application. The validity of a patent shall not be questioned for failure of the Director to require the application to be restricted to one invention.

200. *See* 35 U.S.C. § 121 (2024).

35 U.S.C. § 154

(a) IN GENERAL.—

(1) CONTENTS.—

Every patent shall contain a short title of the invention and a grant to the patentee, his heirs or assigns, of the right to exclude others from making, using, offering for sale, or selling the invention throughout the United States or importing the invention into the United States, and, if the invention is a process, of the right to exclude others from using, offering for sale or selling throughout the United States, or importing into the United States, products made by that process, referring to the specification for the particulars thereof.

(2) TERM.—

Subject to the payment of fees under this title, such grant shall be for a term beginning on the date on which the patent issues and ending 20 years from the date on which the application for the patent was filed in the United States or, if the application contains a specific reference to an earlier filed application or applications under section 120, 121, 365(c), or 386(c), from the date on which the earliest such application was filed.

(3) PRIORITY.—

Priority under section 119, 365(a), 365(b), 386(a), or 386(b) shall not be taken into account in determining the term of a patent.

(4) SPECIFICATION AND DRAWING.—

A copy of the specification and drawing shall be annexed to the patent and be a part of such patent.

(b) ADJUSTMENT OF PATENT TERM.—

(1) PATENT TERM GUARANTEES.—

(A) Guarantee of prompt patent and trademark office responses.—Subject to the limitations under paragraph (2), if the issue of an original patent is delayed due to the failure of the Patent and Trademark Office to—

(i) provide at least one of the notifications under section 132 or a notice of allowance under section 151 not later than 14 months after—

(I) the date on which an application was filed under section 111(a); or

(II) the date of commencement of the national stage under section 371 in an international application;

(ii) respond to a reply under section 132, or to an appeal taken under section 134, within 4 months after the date on which the reply was filed or the appeal was taken;

(iii) act on an application within 4 months after the date of a decision by the Patent Trial and Appeal Board under section 134 or 135 or a decision by a Federal court under section 141, 145, or 146 in a case in which allowable claims remain in the application; or

(iv) issue a patent within 4 months after the date on which the issue fee was paid under section 151 and all outstanding requirements were satisfied,

the term of the patent shall be extended 1 day for each day after the end of the period specified in clause (i), (ii), (iii), or (iv), as the case may be, until the action described in such clause is taken.

(B) Guarantee of no more than 3-year application pendency.—Subject to the limitations under paragraph (2), if the issue of an original patent is delayed due to the failure of the United States Patent and Trademark Office to issue a patent within 3 years after the actual filing date of the application under section 111(a) in the United States or, in the case of an international application, the date of commencement of the national stage under section 371 in the international application, not including—

(i) any time consumed by continued examination of the application requested by the applicant under section 132(b);

(ii) any time consumed by a proceeding under section 135(a), any time consumed by the imposition of an order under section 181, or any time consumed by appellate review by the Patent Trial and Appeal Board or by a Federal court; or

(iii) any delay in the processing of the application by the United States Patent and Trademark Office requested by the applicant except as permitted by paragraph (3)(C),

the term of the patent shall be extended 1 day for each day after the end of that 3-year period until the patent is issued.

(C) Guarantee of adjustments for delays due to derivation proceedings, secrecy orders, and appeals.—Subject to the limitations under paragraph (2), if the issue of an original patent is delayed due to—

(i) a proceeding under section 135(a);

(ii) the imposition of an order under section 181; or

(iii) appellate review by the Patent Trial and Appeal Board or by a Federal court in a case in which the patent was issued under a decision in the review reversing an adverse determination of patentability,

the term of the patent shall be extended 1 day for each day of the pendency of the proceeding, order, or review, as the case may be.

(2) Limitations.—

(A) In general.—

To the extent that periods of delay attributable to grounds specified in paragraph (1) overlap, the period of any adjustment granted under this subsection shall not exceed the actual number of days the issuance of the patent was delayed.

(B) Disclaimed term.—

No patent the term of which has been disclaimed beyond a specified date may be adjusted under this section beyond the expiration date specified in the disclaimer.

(C) Reduction of period of adjustment.—

(i) The period of adjustment of the term of a patent under paragraph (1) shall be reduced by a period equal to the period of time during which the applicant failed to engage in reasonable efforts to conclude prosecution of the application.

(ii) With respect to adjustments to patent term made under the authority of paragraph (1)(B), an applicant shall be deemed to have failed to engage in reasonable efforts to conclude processing or examination of an application for the cumulative total of any periods of time in excess of 3 months that are taken to respond to a notice from the Office making any rejection, objection, argument, or other request, measuring such 3-month period from the date the notice was given or mailed to the applicant.

(iii) The Director shall prescribe regulations establishing the circumstances that constitute a failure of an applicant to engage in reasonable efforts to conclude processing or examination of an application.

(3) PROCEDURES FOR PATENT TERM ADJUSTMENT DETERMINATION.—

(A) The Director shall prescribe regulations establishing procedures for the application for and determination of patent term adjustments under this subsection.

(B) Under the procedures established under subparagraph (A), the Director shall—

(i) make a determination of the period of any patent term adjustment under this subsection, and shall transmit a notice of that determination no later than the date of issuance of the patent; and

(ii) provide the applicant one opportunity to request reconsideration of any patent term adjustment determination made by the Director.

(C) The Director shall reinstate all or part of the cumulative period of time of an adjustment under paragraph (2)(C) if the applicant, prior to the issuance of the patent, makes a showing that, in spite of all due care, the applicant was unable to respond within the 3-month period, but in no case shall more than three additional months for each such response beyond the original 3-month period be reinstated.

(D) The Director shall proceed to grant the patent after completion of the Director's determination of a patent term adjustment under the procedures established under this subsection, notwithstanding any appeal taken by the applicant of such determination.

(4) APPEAL OF PATENT TERM ADJUSTMENT DETERMINATION.—

(A) An applicant dissatisfied with the Director's decision on the applicant's request for reconsideration under paragraph (3)(B)(ii) shall have exclusive remedy by a civil action against the Director filed in the United States District Court for the Eastern District of Virginia within 180 days after the date of the Director's decision on the applicant's request for reconsideration. Chapter 7 of title 5 shall apply to such action. Any final judgment resulting in a change to the period of adjustment of the patent term shall be served on the Director, and the Director shall thereafter alter the term of the patent to reflect such change.

(B) The determination of a patent term adjustment under this subsection shall not be subject to appeal or challenge by a third party prior to the grant of the patent.

(c) CONTINUATION.—

(1) DETERMINATION.—

The term of a patent that is in force on or that results from an application filed before the date that is 6 months after the date of the enactment of the Uruguay Round Agreements Act shall be the greater of the 20-year term as provided in subsection (a), or 17 years from grant, subject to any terminal disclaimers.

(2) REMEDIES.—

The remedies of sections 283, 284, and 285 shall not apply to acts which—

(A) were commenced or for which substantial investment was made before the date that is 6 months after the date of the enactment of the Uruguay Round Agreements Act; and

(B) became infringing by reason of paragraph (1).

(3) REMUNERATION.—

The acts referred to in paragraph (2) may be continued only upon the payment of an equitable remuneration to the patentee that is determined in an action brought under chapter 28 and chapter 29 (other than those provisions excluded by paragraph (2)).

35 U.S.C. § 156[201]

(a) The term of a patent which claims a product, a method of using a product, or a method of manufacturing a product shall be extended in accordance with this section from the original expiration date of the patent, which shall include any patent term adjustment granted under section 154(b), if—

(1) the term of the patent has not expired before an application is submitted under subsection (d)(1) for its extension;

201. Citations omitted.

(2) the term of the patent has never been extended under subsection (e)(1) of this section;

(3) an application for extension is submitted by the owner of record of the patent or its agent and in accordance with the requirements of paragraphs (1) through (4) of subsection (d);

(4) the product has been subject to a regulatory review period before its commercial marketing or use;

(5)(A) except as provided in subparagraph (B) or (C), the permission for the commercial marketing or use of the product after such regulatory review period is the first permitted commercial marketing or use of the product under the provision of law under which such regulatory review period occurred;

(B) in the case of a patent which claims a method of manufacturing the product which primarily uses recombinant DNA technology in the manufacture of the product, the permission for the commercial marketing or use of the product after such regulatory review period is the first permitted commercial marketing or use of a product manufactured under the process claimed in the patent; or

(C) for purposes of subparagraph (A), in the case of a patent which—

(i) claims a new animal drug or a veterinary biological product which (I) is not covered by the claims in any other patent which has been extended, and (II) has received permission for the commercial marketing or use in non-food-producing animals and in food-producing animals, and

(ii) was not extended on the basis of the regulatory review period for use in non-food-producing animals,

the permission for the commercial marketing or use of the drug or product after the regulatory review period for use in food-producing animals is the first permitted commercial marketing or use of the drug or product for administration to a food-producing animal.

The product referred to in paragraphs (4) and (5) is hereinafter in this section referred to as the "approved product".

(b) Except as provided in subsection (d)(5)(F), the rights derived from any patent the term of which is extended under this section shall during the period during which the term of the patent is extended—

(1) in the case of a patent which claims a product, be limited to any use approved for the product—

(A) before the expiration of the term of the patent—

(i) under the provision of law under which the applicable regulatory review occurred, or

(ii) under the provision of law under which any regulatory review described in paragraph (1), (4), or (5) of subsection (g) occurred, and

(B) on or after the expiration of the regulatory review period upon which the extension of the patent was based;

(2) in the case of a patent which claims a method of using a product, be limited to any use claimed by the patent and approved for the product—

(A) before the expiration of the term of the patent—

(i) under any provision of law under which an applicable regulatory review occurred, and

(ii) under the provision of law under which any regulatory review described in paragraph (1), (4), or (5) of subsection (g) occurred, and

(B) on or after the expiration of the regulatory review period upon which the extension of the patent was based; and

(3) in the case of a patent which claims a method of manufacturing a product, be limited to the method of manufacturing as used to make—

(A) the approved product, or

(B) the product if it has been subject to a regulatory review period described in paragraph (1), (4), or (5) of subsection (g).

As used in this subsection, the term "product" includes an approved product.

(c) The term of a patent eligible for extension under subsection (a) shall be extended by the time equal to the regulatory review period for the approved product which period occurs after the date the patent is issued, except that—

(1) each period of the regulatory review period shall be reduced by any period determined under subsection (d)(2)(B) during which the applicant for the patent extension did not act with due diligence during such period of the regulatory review period;

(2) after any reduction required by paragraph (1), the period of extension shall include only one-half of the time remaining in the periods described in paragraphs (1)(B)(i), (2)(B)(i), (3)(B)(i), (4)(B)(i), and (5)(B)(i) of subsection (g);

(3) if the period remaining in the term of a patent after the date of the approval of the approved product under the provision of law under which such regulatory review occurred when added to the regulatory review period as revised under paragraphs (1) and (2) exceeds fourteen years, the period of extension shall be reduced so that the total of both such periods does not exceed fourteen years; and

(4) in no event shall more than one patent be extended under subsection (e)(1) for the same regulatory review period for any product.

(d)(1) To obtain an extension of the term of a patent under this section, the owner of record of the patent or its agent shall submit an application to the Director. Except as provided in paragraph (5), such an application may only be submitted within the sixty-day period beginning on the date the product received permission under the provision of law under which the applicable regulatory review period occurred for

commercial marketing or use, or in the case of a drug product described in subsection (i), within the sixty-day period beginning on the covered date (as defined in subsection (i)). The application shall contain—

(A) the identity of the approved product and the Federal statute under which regulatory review occurred;

(B) the identity of the patent for which an extension is being sought and the identity of each claim of such patent which claims the approved product or a method of using or manufacturing the approved product;

(C) information to enable the Director to determine under subsections (a) and (b) the eligibility of a patent for extension and the rights that will be derived from the extension and information to enable the Director and the Secretary of Health and Human Services or the Secretary of Agriculture to determine the period of the extension under subsection (g);

(D) a brief description of the activities undertaken by the applicant during the applicable regulatory review period with respect to the approved product and the significant dates applicable to such activities; and

(E) such patent or other information as the Director may require.

For purposes of determining the date on which a product receives permission under the second sentence of this paragraph, if such permission is transmitted after 4:30 P.M., Eastern Time, on a business day, or is transmitted on a day that is not a business day, the product shall be deemed to receive such permission on the next business day. For purposes of the preceding sentence, the term "business day" means any Monday, Tuesday, Wednesday, Thursday, or Friday, excluding any legal holiday under section 6103 of title 5.

(2)(A) Within 60 days of the submittal of an application for extension of the term of a patent under paragraph (1), the Director shall notify—

(i) the Secretary of Agriculture if the patent claims a drug product or a method of using or manufacturing a drug product and the drug product is subject to the Virus-Serum-Toxin Act, and

(ii) the Secretary of Health and Human Services if the patent claims any other drug product, a medical device, or a food additive or color additive or a method of using or manufacturing such a product, device, or additive and if the product, device, and additive are subject to the Federal Food, Drug, and Cosmetic Act,

of the extension application and shall submit to the Secretary who is so notified a copy of the application. Not later than 30 days after the receipt of an application from the Director, the Secretary receiving the application shall review the dates contained in the application pursuant to paragraph (1)(C) and determine the applicable regulatory review period, shall notify the

Director of the determination, and shall publish in the Federal Register a notice of such determination.

(B)(i) If a petition is submitted to the Secretary making the determination under subparagraph (A), not later than 180 days after the publication of the determination under subparagraph (A), upon which it may reasonably be determined that the applicant did not act with due diligence during the applicable regulatory review period, the Secretary making the determination shall, in accordance with regulations promulgated by such Secretary, determine if the applicant acted with due diligence during the applicable regulatory review period. The Secretary making the determination shall make such determination not later than 90 days after the receipt of such a petition. For a drug product, device, or additive subject to the Federal Food, Drug, and Cosmetic Act or the Public Health Service Act, the Secretary may not delegate the authority to make the determination prescribed by this clause to an office below the Office of the Director of Food and Drugs. For a product subject to the Virus-Serum-Toxin Act, the Secretary of Agriculture may not delegate the authority to make the determination prescribed by this clause to an office below the Office of the Assistant Secretary for Marketing and Inspection Services.

(ii) The Secretary making a determination under clause (i) shall notify the Director of the determination and shall publish in the Federal Register a notice of such determination together with the factual and legal basis for such determination. Any interested person may request, within the 60-day period beginning on the publication of a determination, the Secretary making the determination to hold an informal hearing on the determination. If such a request is made within such period, such Secretary shall hold such hearing not later than 30 days after the date of the request, or at the request of the person making the request, not later than 60 days after such date. The Secretary who is holding the hearing shall provide notice of the hearing to the owner of the patent involved and to any interested person and provide the owner and any interested person an opportunity to participate in the hearing. Within 30 days after the completion of the hearing, such Secretary shall affirm or revise the determination which was the subject of the hearing and shall notify the Director of any revision of the determination and shall publish any such revision in the Federal Register.

(3) For the purposes of paragraph (2)(B), the term "due diligence" means that degree of attention, continuous directed effort, and timeliness as may reasonably be expected from, and are ordinarily exercised by, a person during a regulatory review period.

(4) An application for the extension of the term of a patent is subject to the disclosure requirements prescribed by the Director.

(5)(A) If the owner of record of the patent or its agent reasonably expects that the applicable regulatory review period described in paragraph (1)(B)(ii), (2)(B)(ii), (3)(B)(ii), (4)(B)(ii), or (5)(B)(ii) of subsection (g) that began for a product that is the subject of such patent may extend beyond the expiration of the patent term in effect, the owner or its agent may submit an application to the Director for an interim extension during the period beginning 6 months, and ending 15 days, before such term is due to expire. The application shall contain—

(i) the identity of the product subject to regulatory review and the Federal statute under which such review is occurring;

(ii) the identity of the patent for which interim extension is being sought and the identity of each claim of such patent which claims the product under regulatory review or a method of using or manufacturing the product;

(iii) information to enable the Director to determine under subsection (a)(1), (2), and (3) the eligibility of a patent for extension;

(iv) a brief description of the activities undertaken by the applicant during the applicable regulatory review period to date with respect to the product under review and the significant dates applicable to such activities; and

(v) such patent or other information as the Director may require.

(B) If the Director determines that, except for permission to market or use the product commercially, the patent would be eligible for an extension of the patent term under this section, the Director shall publish in the Federal Register a notice of such determination, including the identity of the product under regulatory review, and shall issue to the applicant a certificate of interim extension for a period of not more than 1 year.

(C) The owner of record of a patent, or its agent, for which an interim extension has been granted under subparagraph (B), may apply for not more than 4 subsequent interim extensions under this paragraph, except that, in the case of a patent subject to subsection (g)(6)(C), the owner of record of the patent, or its agent, may apply for only 1 subsequent interim extension under this paragraph. Each such subsequent application shall be made during the period beginning 60 days before, and ending 30 days before, the expiration of the preceding interim extension.

(D) Each certificate of interim extension under this paragraph shall be recorded in the official file of the patent and shall be considered part of the original patent.

(E) Any interim extension granted under this paragraph shall terminate at the end of the 60-day period beginning on the date on which the product involved receives permission for commercial marketing or use, except that, if within that 60-day period the applicant notifies the Director of such permission and submits any additional information under paragraph (1) of this subsection not previously

contained in the application for interim extension, the patent shall be further extended, in accordance with the provisions of this section—

(i) for not to exceed 5 years from the date of expiration of the original patent term; or

(ii) if the patent is subject to subsection (g)(6)(C), from the date on which the product involved receives approval for commercial marketing or use.

(F) The rights derived from any patent the term of which is extended under this paragraph shall, during the period of interim extension—

(i) in the case of a patent which claims a product, be limited to any use then under regulatory review;

(ii) in the case of a patent which claims a method of using a product, be limited to any use claimed by the patent then under regulatory review; and

(iii) in the case of a patent which claims a method of manufacturing a product, be limited to the method of manufacturing as used to make the product then under regulatory review.

(e)(1) A determination that a patent is eligible for extension may be made by the Director solely on the basis of the representations contained in the application for the extension. If the Director determines that a patent is eligible for extension under subsection (a) and that the requirements of paragraphs (1) through (4) of subsection (d) have been complied with, the Director shall issue to the applicant for the extension of the term of the patent a certificate of extension, under seal, for the period prescribed by subsection (c). Such certificate shall be recorded in the official file of the patent and shall be considered as part of the original patent.

(2) If the term of a patent for which an application has been submitted under subsection (d)(1) would expire before a certificate of extension is issued or denied under paragraph (1) respecting the application, the Director shall extend, until such determination is made, the term of the patent for periods of up to one year if he determines that the patent is eligible for extension.

(f) For purposes of this section:

(1) The term "product" means:

(A) A drug product.

(B) Any medical device, food additive, or color additive subject to regulation under the Federal Food, Drug, and Cosmetic Act.

(2) The term "drug product" means the active ingredient of—

(A) a new drug, antibiotic drug, or human biological product (as those terms are used in the Federal Food, Drug, and Cosmetic Act and the Public Health Service Act), or

(B) a new animal drug or veterinary biological product (as those terms are used in the Federal Food, Drug, and Cosmetic Act and the Virus-Serum-Toxin

Act) which is not primarily manufactured using recombinant DNA, recombinant RNA, hybridoma technology, or other processes involving site specific genetic manipulation techniques,

including any salt or ester of the active ingredient, as a single entity or in combination with another active ingredient.

(3) The term "major health or environmental effects test" means a test which is reasonably related to the evaluation of the health or environmental effects of a product, which requires at least six months to conduct, and the data from which is submitted to receive permission for commercial marketing or use. Periods of analysis or evaluation of test results are not to be included in determining if the conduct of a test required at least six months.

(4)(A) Any reference to section 351 is a reference to section 351 of the Public Health Service Act.

(B) Any reference to section 503, 505, 512, or 515 is a reference to section 503, 505, 512, or 515 of the Federal Food, Drug, and Cosmetic Act.

(C) Any reference to the Virus-Serum-Toxin Act is a reference to the Act of March 4, 1913 (21 U.S.C. 151–158).

(5) The term "informal hearing" has the meaning prescribed for such term by section 201(y) of the Federal Food, Drug, and Cosmetic Act.

(6) The term "patent" means a patent issued by the United States Patent and Trademark Office.

(7) The term "date of enactment" as used in this section means September 24, 1984, for a human drug product, a medical device, food additive, or color additive.

(8) The term "date of enactment" as used in this section means the date of enactment of the Generic Animal Drug and Patent Term Restoration Act for an animal drug or a veterinary biological product.

(g) For purposes of this section, the term "regulatory review period" has the following meanings:

(1)(A) In the case of a product which is a new drug, antibiotic drug, or human biological product, the term means the period described in subparagraph (B) to which the limitation described in paragraph (6) applies.

(B) The regulatory review period for a new drug, antibiotic drug, or human biological product is the sum of—

(i) the period beginning on the date an exemption under subsection (i) of section 505 or subsection (d) of section 507 became effective for the approved product and ending on the date an application was initially submitted for such drug product under section 351, 505, or 507, and

(ii) the period beginning on the date the application was initially submitted for the approved product under section 351, subsection (b) of section 505,

or section 507 and ending on the date such application was approved under such section.

(2)(A) In the case of a product which is a food additive or color additive, the term means the period described in subparagraph (B) to which the limitation described in paragraph (6) applies.

(B) The regulatory review period for a food or color additive is the sum of—

(i) the period beginning on the date a major health or environmental effects test on the additive was initiated and ending on the date a petition was initially submitted with respect to the product under the Federal Food, Drug, and Cosmetic Act requesting the issuance of a regulation for use of the product, and

(ii) the period beginning on the date a petition was initially submitted with respect to the product under the Federal Food, Drug, and Cosmetic Act requesting the issuance of a regulation for use of the product, and ending on the date such regulation became effective or, if objections were filed to such regulation, ending on the date such objections were resolved and commercial marketing was permitted or, if commercial marketing was permitted and later revoked pending further proceedings as a result of such objections, ending on the date such proceedings were finally resolved and commercial marketing was permitted.

(3)(A) In the case of a product which is a medical device, the term means the period described in subparagraph (B) to which the limitation described in paragraph (6) applies.

(B) The regulatory review period for a medical device is the sum of—

(i) the period beginning on the date a clinical investigation on humans involving the device was begun and ending on the date an application was initially submitted with respect to the device under section 515, and

(ii) the period beginning on the date an application was initially submitted with respect to the device under section 515 and ending on the date such application was approved under such Act or the period beginning on the date a notice of completion of a product development protocol was initially submitted under section 515(f)(5) and ending on the date the protocol was declared completed under section 515(f)(6).

(4)(A) In the case of a product which is a new animal drug, the term means the period described in subparagraph (B) to which the limitation described in paragraph (6) applies.

(B) The regulatory review period for a new animal drug product is the sum of—

(i) the period beginning on the earlier of the date a major health or environmental effects test on the drug was initiated or the date an exemption

under subsection (j) of section 512 became effective for the approved new animal drug product and ending on the date an application was initially submitted for such animal drug product under section 512, and

(ii) the period beginning on the date the application was initially submitted for the approved animal drug product under subsection (b) of section 512 and ending on the date such application was approved under such section.

(5)(A) In the case of a product which is a veterinary biological product, the term means the period described in subparagraph (B) to which the limitation described in paragraph (6) applies.

(B) The regulatory period for a veterinary biological product is the sum of—

(i) the period beginning on the date the authority to prepare an experimental biological product under the Virus-Serum-Toxin Act became effective and ending on the date an application for a license was submitted under the Virus-Serum-Toxin Act, and

(ii) the period beginning on the date an application for a license was initially submitted for approval under the Virus-Serum-Toxin Act and ending on the date such license was issued.

(6) A period determined under any of the preceding paragraphs is subject to the following limitations:

(A) If the patent involved was issued after the date of the enactment of this section, the period of extension determined on the basis of the regulatory review period determined under any such paragraph may not exceed five years.

(B) If the patent involved was issued before the date of the enactment of this section and—

(i) no request for an exemption described in paragraph (1)(B) or (4)(B) was submitted and no request for the authority described in paragraph (5)(B) was submitted,

(ii) no major health or environmental effects test described in paragraph (2)(B) or (4)(B) was initiated and no petition for a regulation or application for registration described in such paragraph was submitted, or

(iii) no clinical investigation described in paragraph (3) was begun or product development protocol described in such paragraph was submitted,

before such date for the approved product the period of extension determined on the basis of the regulatory review period determined under any such paragraph may not exceed five years.

(C) If the patent involved was issued before the date of the enactment of this section and if an action described in subparagraph (B) was taken before the date of the enactment of this section with respect to the approved product and the commercial marketing or use of the product has not been approved before such date, the period of extension determined on the basis of the regulatory review

period determined under such paragraph may not exceed two years or in the case of an approved product which is a new animal drug or veterinary biological product (as those terms are used in the Federal Food, Drug, and Cosmetic Act or the Virus-Serum-Toxin Act), three years.

(h) The Director may establish such fees as the Director determines appropriate to cover the costs to the Office of receiving and acting upon applications under this section.

(i)(1) For purposes of this section, if the Secretary of Health and Human Services provides notice to the sponsor of an application or request for approval, conditional approval, or indexing of a drug product for which the Secretary intends to recommend controls under the Controlled Substances Act, beginning on the covered date, the drug product shall be considered to—

(A) have been approved or indexed under the relevant provision of the Public Health Service Act or Federal Food, Drug, and Cosmetic Act; and

(B) have permission for commercial marketing or use.

(2) In this subsection, the term "covered date" means the later of—

(A) the date an application is approved—

(i) under section 351(a)(2)(C) of the Public Health Service Act; or

(ii) under section 505(b) or 512(c) of the Federal Food, Drug, and Cosmetic Act;

(B) the date an application is conditionally approved under section 571(b) of the Federal Food, Drug, and Cosmetic Act;

(C) the date a request for indexing is granted under section 572(d) of the Federal Food, Drug, and Cosmetic Act; or

(D) the date of issuance of the interim final rule controlling the drug under section 201(j) of the Controlled Substances Act.

35 U.S.C. § 253

(a) In General.—Whenever a claim of a patent is invalid the remaining claims shall not thereby be rendered invalid. A patentee, whether of the whole or any sectional interest therein, may, on payment of the fee required by law, make disclaimer of any complete claim, stating therein the extent of his interest in such patent. Such disclaimer shall be in writing and recorded in the Patent and Trademark Office, and it shall thereafter be considered as part of the original patent to the extent of the interest possessed by the disclaimant and by those claiming under him.

(b) Additional Disclaimer or Dedication.—In the manner set forth in subsection (a), any patentee or applicant may disclaim or dedicate to the public the entire term, or any terminal part of the term, of the patent granted or to be granted.

37 C.F.R. § 1.142

(a) If two or more independent and distinct inventions are claimed in a single application, the examiner in an Office action will require the applicant in the reply to

that action to elect an invention to which the claims will be restricted, this official action being called a requirement for restriction (also known as a requirement for division). Such requirement will normally be made before any action on the merits; however, it may be made at any time before final action.

(b) Claims to the invention or inventions not elected, if not canceled, are nevertheless withdrawn from further consideration by the examiner by the election, subject however to reinstatement in the event the requirement for restriction is withdrawn or overruled.

37 C.F.R. § 1.321

(a) A patentee owning the whole or any sectional interest in a patent may disclaim any complete claim or claims in a patent. In like manner any patentee may disclaim or dedicate to the public the entire term, or any terminal part of the term, of the patent granted. Such disclaimer is binding upon the grantee and its successors or assigns. A notice of the disclaimer is published in the Official Gazette and attached to the printed copies of the specification. The disclaimer, to be recorded in the Patent and Trademark Office, must:

(1) Be signed by the patentee, or an attorney or agent of record;

(2) Identify the patent and complete claim or claims, or term being disclaimed. A disclaimer which is not a disclaimer of a complete claim or claims, or term will be refused recordation;

(3) State the present extent of patentee's ownership interest in the patent; and

(4) Be accompanied by the fee set forth in § 1.20(d).

(b) An applicant may disclaim or dedicate to the public the entire term, or any terminal part of the term, of a patent to be granted. Such terminal disclaimer is binding upon the grantee and its successors or assigns. The terminal disclaimer, to be recorded in the Patent and Trademark Office, must:

(1) Be signed by the applicant or an attorney or agent of record;

(2) Specify the portion of the term of the patent being disclaimed;

(3) State the present extent of applicant's ownership interest in the patent to be granted; and

(4) Be accompanied by the fee set forth in § 1.20(d).

(c) A terminal disclaimer, when filed to obviate judicially created double patenting in a patent application or in a reexamination proceeding except as provided for in paragraph (d) of this section, must:

(1) Comply with the provisions of paragraphs (b)(2) through (b)(4) of this section;

(2) Be signed in accordance with paragraph (b)(1) of this section if filed in a patent application or in accordance with paragraph (a)(1) of this section if filed in a reexamination proceeding; and

(3) Include a provision that any patent granted on that application or any patent subject to the reexamination proceeding shall be enforceable only for and during such period that said patent is commonly owned with the application or patent which formed the basis for the judicially created double patenting.

(d) A terminal disclaimer, when filed in a patent application or in a reexamination proceeding to obviate double patenting based upon a patent or application that is not commonly owned but was disqualified as prior art as set forth in either § 1.104(c)(4)(ii) or (c)(5)(ii) as the result of activities undertaken within the scope of a joint research agreement, must:

(1) Comply with the provisions of paragraphs (b)(2) through (b)(4) of this section;

(2) Be signed in accordance with paragraph (b)(1) of this section if filed in a patent application or be signed in accordance with paragraph (a)(1) of this section if filed in a reexamination proceeding; and

(3) Include a provision waiving the right to separately enforce any patent granted on that application or any patent subject to the reexamination proceeding and the patent or any patent granted on the application which formed the basis for the double patenting, and that any patent granted on that application or any patent subject to the reexamination proceeding shall be enforceable only for and during such period that said patent and the patent, or any patent granted on the application, which formed the basis for the double patenting are not separately enforced.

MPEP §§ 802.01–.02

802.01 Meaning of "Independent" and "Distinct"

35 U.S.C. 121 quoted in the preceding section states that the Director may require restriction if two or more "independent and distinct" inventions are claimed in one application. In 37 CFR 1.141, the statement is made that two or more "independent and distinct inventions" may not be claimed in one application.

This raises the question of the inventions as between which the Director may require restriction. This, in turn, depends on the construction of the expression "independent and distinct" inventions.

"Independent", of course, means not dependent, or unrelated. If "distinct" means the same thing, then its use in the statute and in the rule is redundant. If "distinct" means something different, then the question arises as to what the difference in meaning between these two words may be. The hearings before the committees of Congress considering the codification of the patent laws indicate that 35 U.S.C. 121: "enacts as law existing practice with respect to division, at the same time introducing a number of changes."

The report on the hearings does not mention as a change that is introduced, the inventions between which the Director may properly require division.

The term "independent" as already pointed out, means not dependent, or unrelated. A large number of inventions between which, prior to the 1952 Act, division had been proper, are dependent inventions, such as, for example, combination and a subcombination thereof; as process and apparatus used in the practice of the process; as composition and the process in which the composition is used; as process and the product made by such process, etc. If section 121 of the 1952 Act were intended to direct the Director never to approve division between dependent inventions, the word "independent" would clearly have been used alone. If the Director has authority or discretion to restrict independent inventions only, then restriction would be improper as between dependent inventions, e.g., the examples used for purpose of illustration above. Such was clearly not the intent of Congress. Nothing in the language of the statute and nothing in the hearings of the committees indicate any intent to change the substantive law on this subject. On the contrary, joinder of the term "distinct" with the term "independent", indicates lack of such intent. The law has long been established that dependent inventions (frequently termed related inventions) such as used for illustration above may be properly divided if they are, in fact, "distinct" inventions, even though dependent.

I. INDEPENDENT

The term "independent" (i.e., unrelated) means that there is no disclosed relationship between the two or more inventions claimed, that is, they are unconnected in design, operation, and effect. For example, a process and an apparatus incapable of being used in practicing the process are independent inventions. See also MPEP § 806.06 and § 808.01.

II. RELATED BUT DISTINCT

Two or more inventions are related (i.e., not independent) if they are disclosed as connected in at least one of design (e.g., structure or method of manufacture), operation (e.g., function or method of use), or effect. Examples of related inventions include combination and part (subcombination) thereof, process and apparatus for its practice, process and product made, etc. In this definition the term related is used as an alternative for dependent in referring to inventions other than independent inventions.

Related inventions are distinct if the inventions as claimed are not connected in at least one of design, operation, or effect (e.g., can be made by, or used in, a materially different process) and wherein at least one invention is PATENTABLE (novel and nonobvious) OVER THE OTHER (though they may each be unpatentable over the prior art). See MPEP § 806.05(c) (combination and subcombination) and § 806.05(j) (related products or related processes) for examples of when a two-way test is required for distinctness.

It is further noted that the terms "independent" and "distinct" are used in decisions with varying meanings. All decisions should be read carefully to determine the meaning intended.

802.02 Definition of Restriction

Restriction is the practice of requiring an applicant to elect a single claimed invention (e.g., a combination or subcombination invention, a product or process invention, a species within a genus) for examination when two or more independent inventions and/or two or more distinct inventions are claimed in an application.

In re Longi
759 F.2d 887
United States Court of Appeals for the Federal Circuit
April 11, 1985, Decided

Gilead Sciences, Inc. v. Natco Pharma Ltd.
753 F.3d 1208
United States Court of Appeals for the Federal Circuit
April 22, 2014, Decided

In re Cellect, LLC
81 F.4th 1216
United States Court of Appeals for the Federal Circuit
August 28, 2023, Decided

Questions

1. In *Longi*, why did the Federal Circuit previously remand this case to the Board?
2. Now, back at the Federal Circuit, what is the legal issue?
3. What is the difference between "same invention"-type double patenting and "obviousness"-type double patenting (ODP)? What is the legal rationale/policy underlying each one?
4. The applicant argues that recent changes to § 103 should affect the appellate court's analysis. What are those recent changes? How did this change affect analysis under § 103? Why was the appellate court able to conclude this change to § 103 did not affect ODP?
5. Why does the appellate court conclude ODP applies to patent assets commonly owned by an assignee rather than simply to patent assets with the same inventive entity? Could it apply where an entity owns a patent and has an exclusive license to another patent asset?[202]
6. How did patent term work for patent assets issued around the time of this case? Why might that matter? How did the patent term change on June 8, 1995, and why did it change?[203] When did the patent term adjustment (PTA) portion of § 154 go into effect?[204]

202. *See* Immunex Corp. v. Sandoz Inc., 964 F.3d 1049, 1067 (Fed. Cir. 2020).
203. *See* 35 U.S.C. § 154(c)(1).
204. *See* MPEP, *supra* note 10, § 2710.

7. For an ODP rejection in prosecution, the examiner must point to a commonly owned patent having claims that make obvious the claims of the patent application being prosecuted. In *Longi*, what is that patent? The examiner also points to some pending applications. What is the filing date and issuance date of the patent? What is the filing date of the application with rejected claims? Note the filing date of the patent is after the filing date of the patent application being rejected. Does that matter? Why or why not? If that does not matter, what does matter and why?
8. It is important to appreciate the changes that resulted from the Uruguay Round Agreements Act and then the changes due to PTA, how that affected ODP, and the interplay with terminal disclaimers. How did *Gilead* affect the determination of ODP? What about the statutory changes led to the change declared by *Gilead*? State the rule of *Gilead*.[205]
9. If after 2001 an original patent application is filed with apparatus claims and before it issues a continuation is filed by the assignee of the original patent application with method claims that largely have the limitations of the apparatus claims rewritten in the form of a method and in which neither appears to be subject to PTA, is a terminal disclaimer required? Why or why not? Suppose instead the apparatus and method claims are filed together, the examiner issues a restriction between the apparatus and method claims, and the assignee elects to prosecute the apparatus claims. Before those claims issue, the assignee files a divisional with the method claims, and again, neither appears subject to PTA. Is a terminal disclaimer needed? Why or why not? In these two hypotheticals, if a terminal disclaimer is needed, for which patent asset is the terminal disclaimer filed? After *Gilead*, how is that determined?[206]
10. In *Cellect*, the patents at issue were challenged by ex parte reexamination rather than an inter partes review (IPR). Why do you think that is the case?[207]
11. What are the implications of *Cellect* for an original patent if a continuation patent application is filed? Assume the original patent issues with PTA; do you know which will expire first? If not, how do you

205. *Cf.* Allergan v. Sun Pharma. Indus., Case No. 2024-1061 (Fed. Cir. Aug. 13, 2024) (distinguishing *Gilead* and *Cellect*, stating: "To hold otherwise—that a first-filed, first-issued parent patent having duly received PTA can be invalidated by a later-filed, later-issued child patent with less, if any, PTA—would not only run afoul of the fundamental purposes of ODP, but effectively abrogate the benefit Congress intended to bestow on patentees when codifying PTA.").
206. *Id.*
207. *Id.*

handle an ODP in the continuation? Suppose the examiner does not make an ODP rejection. Should you do a terminal disclaimer anyway? Why or why not?[208]

* * *

European Patent Office

Article 82

Unity of invention

The European patent application shall relate to one invention only or to a group of inventions so linked as to form a single general inventive concept.

As previously suggested, if you have multiple claim sets, where one set with an independent claim with multiple dependents are apparatus claims and another set of claims with one independent and multiple dependent claims are method claims, the PTO may issue a restriction requirement. The restriction requirement is asking the applicant to elect which of the two (or more) inventions the applicant desires to have examined for the particular patent application—that is, either the method claims or the apparatus claims—in the hypothetical.[209]

One may argue against restriction, but generally, for several reasons, this would not be advised. For one thing, such arguments rarely win. However, more importantly, arguments against restriction may be used by the examiner to make a § 103 rejection or even in later litigation by an adversary to assert invalidity under § 103 with respect to the nonelected patent claims.[210]

The basis for this recommendation might not be immediately intuitive; however, consider, at a higher level of granularity, the examiner's ostensible position based on his or her decision to issue a restriction requirement. The examiner's position is that the two inventions are potentially independently patentable. When you argue against that, you would be arguing, on the written record, that the inventions are *not* independently patentable. Furthermore, to advance your argument, you may make factual assertions about the technology. For example, for the flip-chip claims, you might point to similar limitations in the method and apparatus claims and argue that, due to the similar limitations, the claimed process necessarily produces the claimed chip structure or vice versa. Therefore, after the examiner finds art he or she may use to

208. *Id.*

209. Under the Patent Cooperation Treaty (PCT) and European Patent Convention (EPC), a similar concept exists, referred to as "unity of invention," under Article 82.

210. It is noted that after having searched the art, the examiner is permitted to withdraw the restriction, but this also rarely happens.

reject the "first invention"—that is, the one selected by you to be examined—the examiner, or someone else reviewing the record, may then argue that such art, when combined with your stated positions (e.g., admissions against interest) on the record against restriction, suggest that your "second invention" is also unpatentable. This is a real, rather than a theoretical, risk.

Ultimately, appreciate that a restriction requirement primarily presents a cost issue. If not for the additional cost, generally, a restriction requirement might, in some situations, be viewed as a positive development. It means that there may be two patents for roughly the amount of attorney drafting work of one patent application. However, the cost issues usually are not irrelevant. To preserve the claims that are not elected for immediate examination, a divisional patent application is filed.[211] In addition to paying another filing fee, this also means another, separate prosecution with associated costs, perhaps before a different examiner, another issue fee payment if successful in prosecution, and additional maintenance fees after issuance.

On the one hand, if cost is not a significant issue, having two patents often appears better to outsiders than having one, especially for smaller- to medium-sized companies interested in finding investors. For large companies, it may not matter as much that two rather than one patent might be obtained for a company with a sizable patent portfolio, but likewise cost may be less of an issue for such companies.

On the other hand, a significant legal benefit in this context, from a restriction requirement, is that, by statute,[212] if the appropriate rules and procedures are followed, then a restriction requirement provides a safe harbor against an attack on one of the patents based on ODP, which might otherwise be used to invalidate a patent. Appreciating this legal benefit requires some explanation.

ODP is a judicially created doctrine.[213] It has become a legally complex topic at least partly due to various statutory changes over the years to the patent term that had to be reconciled by courts with the underlying policy behind the ODP doctrine.

ODP came into existence to address potential patent system abuses. One potential abuse relates to a patentee attempting to extend patent coverage of an invention beyond its statutory term by later filing another patent application for an otherwise obvious variation of a patented innovation. For example, pharmaceutical companies have been accused of this with respect to

211. See Chapter 1, addressing divisional patent applications in connection with a discussion of domestic priority.

212. *See* 35 U.S.C. § 121 (2024).

213. *See, e.g., In re* Longi, 759 F.2d 887, 893 (Fed. Cir. 1985).

blockbuster drugs in which, as an example, the follow-on patent application filing is directed to a straightforward extended-release version of the initial blockbuster drug.

This potential abuse was "solved" by requiring that a "terminal disclaimer" be filed, meaning that the term of the second patent that extends past the term of the first patent is terminally disclaimed so that the two patents expire at the same time.[214] Patent term, however, was changed so that patent applications claiming domestic priority to an earlier patent application have their term limited by the filing date (i.e., plus 20 years) of the originally filed patent application (it had been 17 years from issuance of the particular patent). Furthermore, the statutory term was further changed in part to account for delay in patent issuance and delays due to obtaining the approval from another federal agency, such as the U.S. Food and Drug Administration, before being able to bring a product to market.

Although initially principles around ODP, which were similar to obviousness under § 103 (although for ODP, rather than § 103, the reference used for a rejection was not prior art but, in general, a prior issued patent to the assignee), seemed simple, they became more complex with statutory changes and system imperfections, such as PTO delay in issuing a patent, including situations in which the first filed patent issues later than the second filed patent and/or other similar complications related to patent term extension (PTE) or patent term adjustment (PTA).[215]

Another potential abuse was addressed by ODP. As a matter of policy, members of the public should not be subject to the risk of liability to two separate parties owning separate patents over what may essentially be viewed as one invention. Here, again, one invention is understood to include its obvious variations.

For example, suppose a drug company has a blockbuster drug to reduce or remove stammering by an individual and the drug is covered by a patent.

---

214. *See* MPEP, *supra* note 10, § 1490 ("35 U.S.C. 253(b) and 37 CFR 1.321(a) and (b) also provide for the filing by a patentee or applicant of a terminal disclaimer which disclaims or dedicates to the public the entire term or any terminal part of the term of a patent or patent to be granted."). The PTO has recently proposed a change to terminal disclaimers. The proposed rule would require the patent owner to agree that the patent would be unenforceable if it is tied to another patent by a terminal disclaimer that has an invalidated claim based on prior art; however, there have been lawsuits to block this rule going into effect on the grounds that the PTO does not have the authority to issue such a rule.

215. *See* Novartis AG v. Ezra Ventures LLC, 909 F.3d 1367 (Fed. Cir. 2018); 35 U.S.C. §§ 154, 156 (2024).

Suppose the company then seeks and has issued a patent for an obvious extended-release version of the drug.

The term extension issue may be addressed through the mechanism of using the filing date of the initial patent application filing to limit the term of the second patent (e.g., via a terminal disclaimer); however, what if both patents are in force at the same time and the drug company decides to sell the patent covering the extended-release drug? In that scenario, a competitor might decide to obtain a license of the first patent from the drug company that developed the drug, but do so after the extended-release patent has been sold. That license, if granted, most likely would not protect the competitor from potential liability to the company that purchased the patent that covers the extended-release drug if the competitor also manufactures such a drug.

This latter situation is also handled with a "terminal disclaimer." For the terminal disclaimer to be effective to prevent invalidity of the patent covering the extended-release drug, by the terms of the terminal disclaimer, the two patents must be commonly assigned.[216] To be clear, without the terminal disclaimer, the patent covering the extended-release drug, if an obvious variation, would be invalid, even assuming the patents expire on the same day.[217] Likewise, however, with the terminal disclaimer on file with the PTO, the patent covering the extended-release drug is not invalid for ODP; however, by express language in the terminal disclaimer, the two patents must be commonly assigned, and a violation of this restriction would render the patent subject to the terminal disclaimer unenforceable (in this hypothetical, the extended-release drug patent).

One way to view the situation is that the description and claims to obvious variations should have been included in the originally filed patent application. A terminal disclaimer, with its term restrictions and common assignment requirements, in effect creates a functional equivalent. That is, an equivalent from a rights perspective to a single patent that includes the initial subject matter and the obvious variations.

---

216. *See* 37 C.F.R. § 1.321(c)(3) (2022) ("A terminal disclaimer, when filed to obviate judicially created double patenting in a patent application . . . must: (3) Include a provision that any patent granted on that application or any patent subject to the reexamination proceeding shall be enforceable only for and during such period that said patent is commonly owned with the application or patent which formed the basis for the judicially created double patenting."); *see also* MPEP, *supra* note 10, § 1490 ("35 U.S.C. 253(b) and 37 CFR § 1.321(a) and (b) also provide for the filing by a patentee or applicant of a terminal disclaimer which disclaims or dedicates to the public the entire term or any terminal part of the term of a patent or patent to be granted.").

217. Assuming obviousness-type patenting is present.

Now, consider a reverse situation. The original application, as in our flip-chip situation, *does* include these *potentially* obvious variations, but suppose the PTO responds with a restriction requirement. Given this, it only seems appropriate (and is the case) that the applicant, now required by the PTO to separate into two patent applications subject matter that out of an abundance of caution the applicant filed as one patent application, should be given a safe harbor against invalidity based on ODP. It is notable, however, that this safe harbor may be easily lost if care is not taken. For one thing, after the restriction requirement and election of claims to prosecute, the nonelected claims must be filed as a divisional[218] patent application. Likewise, it must be done without having filed an intervening continuation patent application.[219] In addition, because claims may change during prosecution, the issued claims of the divisional must be consonant with the original restriction requirement to fall within the safe harbor.[220]

218. *See* 35 U.S.C. § 121 (2022).

219. *See* G.D. Searle LLC v. Lupin Pharms. Inc., 790 F.3d 1349, 1354 (Fed. Cir. 2015) (citing Geneva Pharms., Inc. v. GlaxoSmithKline PLC, 349 F.3d 1373, 1382 (Fed. Cir. 2003); Amgen Inc. v. F. Hoffmann-La Roche Ltd., 580 F.3d 1340, 1353 (Fed. Cir. 2009)).

220. *See id.* (citing *Geneva Pharms.*, 349 F.3d at 1382; *Amgen*, 580 F.3d at 1353).

Claim Drafting Problems III

<u>**Problem 1.**</u> <u>Brush</u>—Draft one independent method claim and two dependent method claims.

<u>**FIGURES:**</u>

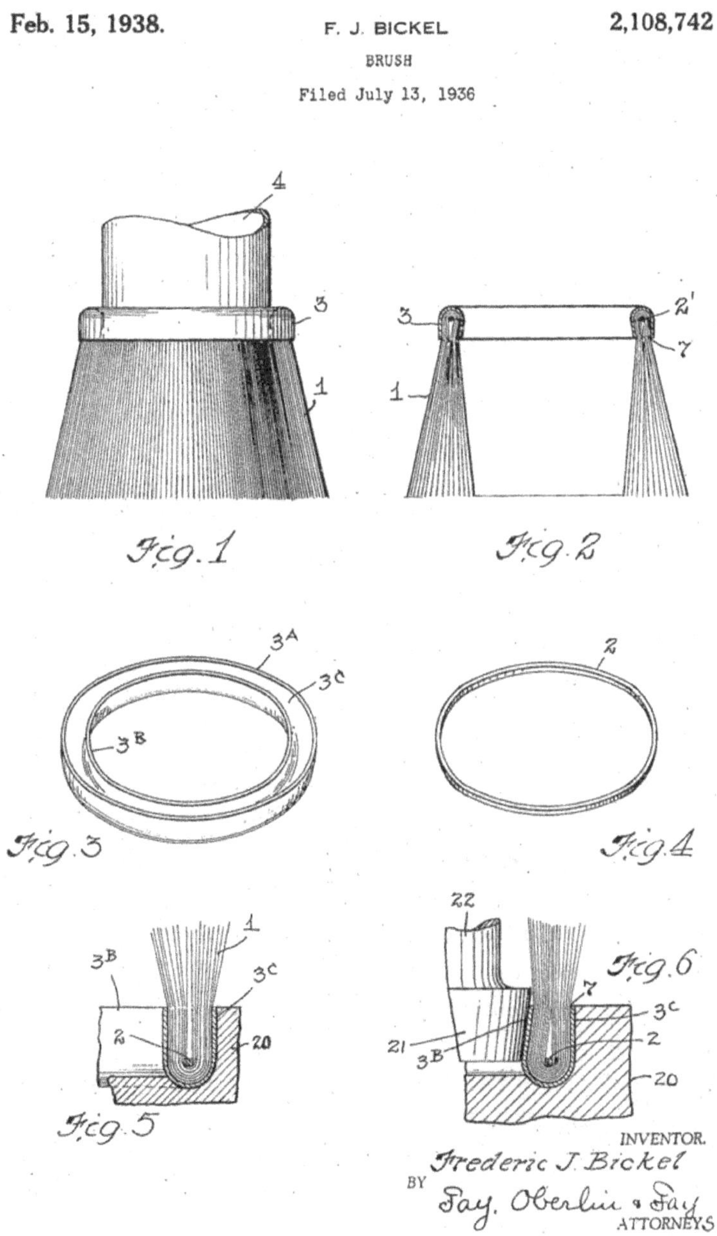

DESCRIPTION:

This invention pertains to the brush art and particularly aims to improve the manufacture and construction of hollow center end brushes.

Among the aims and purposes are the production of brushes that present certain advantages particularly for use as elements of vacuum cleaning tools; absence of rough projections or irregular junctions, edges, points, and so on, which would cause difficulty in placing the bristles during manufacture or cause injury to furniture, draperies, household ornaments, and the like, by catching, pulling, or scratching; firm gripping of the bristles without damage thereto; simplification of the manufacture of such brushes; adaptability to manufacture with economical materials and methods of construction.

To the accomplishment of the foregoing and related ends, said invention then consists of the means hereinafter fully described and particularly pointed out in the claims.

The annexed drawing and the following description set forth in detail certain means and one mode of carrying out the invention, such disclosed means and mode illustrating, however, but one of various ways in which the principle of the invention may be used.

In the accompanying drawing:

Fig. 1 is a side elevation of my brush on the end of a vacuum cleaner attachment;

Fig. 2 is a median section through the brush on an axial plane;

Fig. 3 is a perspective of the brush channel;

Fig. 4 is a perspective of a preferred form of retaining ring;

Fig. 5 is a cross section through the brush at an intermediate stage of assembly; and

Fig. 6 is a cross section through the brush, showing the final assembly step.

The brush, as completed, comprises a filling of bristles 1, looped about a ring 2, and secured in an annular channel 3, which is of slightly modified U-shape when seen in cross section in its final form, and which has its opening pointed endwise, that is, in such a direction that the bristles 1 form a cylinder instead of a disc. In use the brush is mounted on or secured to suitable holder means the principal intended purpose being to use it on a tube such as 4, which represents part of a vacuum cleaner attachment The inner surface of the channel 3 is placed on the tube by a sliding forced fit, or otherwise, as may be most suitable. As best shown in Figs. 2 and 6 the rim channel is somewhat narrowed at the open end to constrict the bristles at 1 and thus firmly anchor the bristles and the retaining ring against withdrawal.

In the manufacture of this brush, I have found it preferable to use an annular channel in the shape 3A, having straight inner and outer sides 3B and 3C respectively, Figs. 3 and 5. This channel is designated by the reference character 3 when the brush is in its completed form.

A preferred method of constructing the brush is to fill the channel 3A with the wall of the bristles 1 looped upon the retaining ring 2.

In the manufacture of the brush a die 20, Figs. 5 and 6, shaped to support the bottom and the outer wall 3C, is used. The filled channel 3A is placed therein, or the empty channel may be placed therein and the die also used to serve the purpose of a holder during the filling of the channel.

Fig. 5 shows, in a partly sectional fragment, the channel in the die, there filled, ready for the next step, shown in Fig. 6. A central expanding tool, such as 22, Fig. 6, conically sided with an outward upward taper, is moved down by a suitably guided and driven actuating plunger 22 to expand the inner wall of the channel 3A, thus constricting the channel top at 1. My preference is to leave the wall 3C straight both for the reason that this makes a simpler manufacturing operation, and also that it avoids excessive narrowing of the top of the channel and danger of damage to or wear upon the bristles at the portion 1. The completion of construction by the forming tool 22 is shown in Fig. 6. It will be observed that the retaining ring, as shown in Figs. 4, 5, and 6, is of rectangular cross section, the specific showing being square. I do not confine myself to this shape of retaining ring, but may use a ring of ordinary wire as at 2, Fig. 2. My preference for the ring of rectangular cross section is that it may be more cheaply made than a wire ring, by cutting off successive ends of a seamless tube of proper diameter and wall thickness. The use of square cut sections of a seamless tube has been found in practice not to be injurious to the bristles, and is more economical than making rings of round section.

From the foregoing it will be seen that I have invented a brush of simple and durable construction, free from rough or projecting parts, junctions, or seams, wherein the bristles are held firmly, but without injurious pressure at the point of constriction, and have likewise invented a method of making such a brush that is simple, economical, and quick, and in some measure permits utilization of less expensive material than has heretofore been deemed necessary, but without lowering the quality of the product.

Other modes of applying the principle of my invention may be employed instead of the one explained, change being made as regards the means and steps herein disclosed, provided those stated by any of the following claims or the equivalent of such stated means be employed.

Problem 2. Ultraviolet Light Filter—Draft a method of using claim and two dependent claims and a method of making claim and two dependent claims.

FIGURES:

U.S. Patent Apr. 20, 1993 Sheet 1 of 6 5,204,773

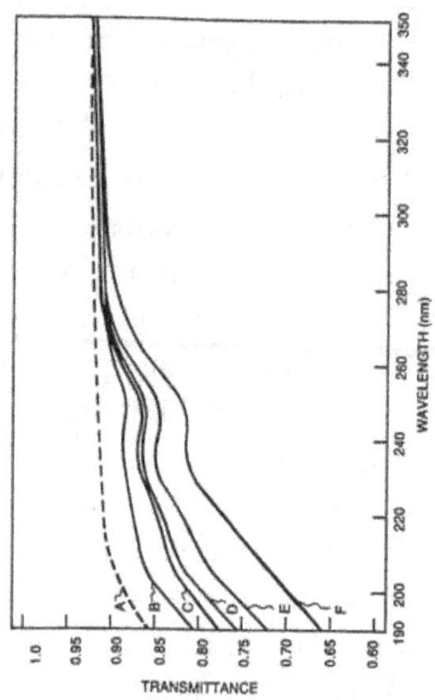

FIG. 1

U.S. Patent Apr. 20, 1993 Sheet 2 of 6 5,204,773

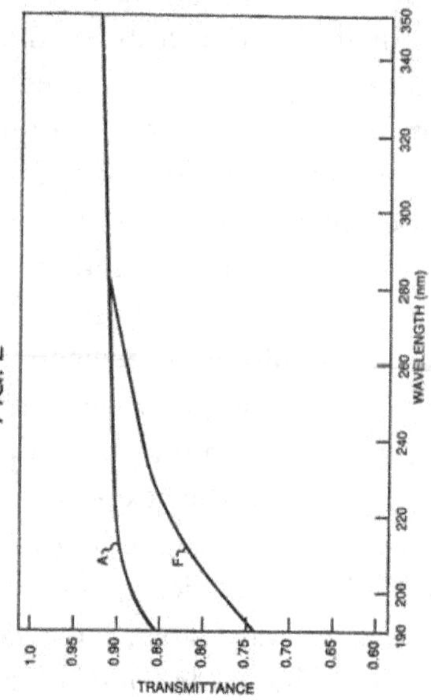

FIG. 2

U.S. Patent Apr. 20, 1993 Sheet 3 of 6 5,204,77

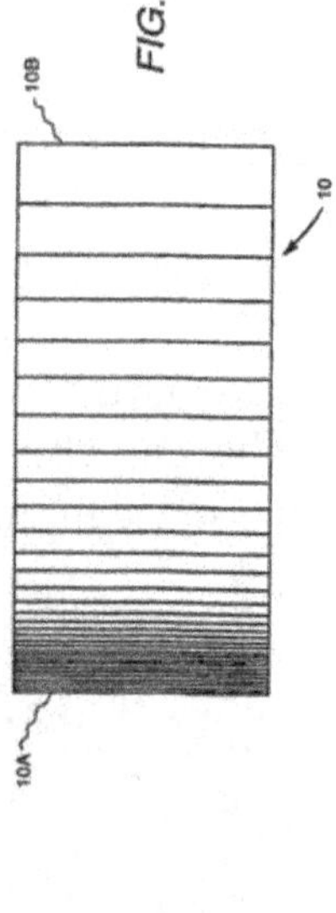

FIG. 3

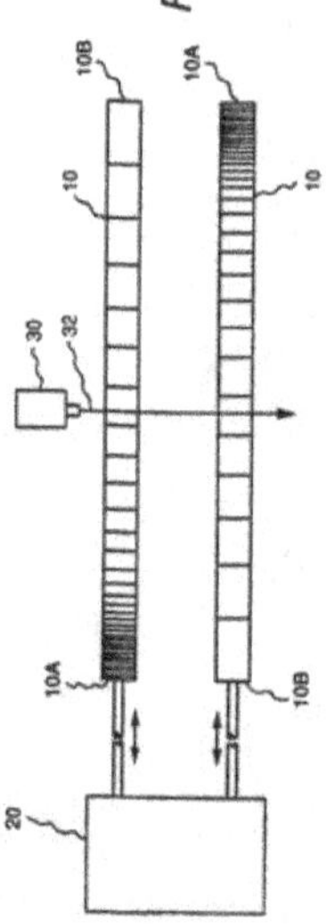

FIG. 4

U.S. Patent Apr. 20, 1993 Sheet 4 of 6 5,204,773

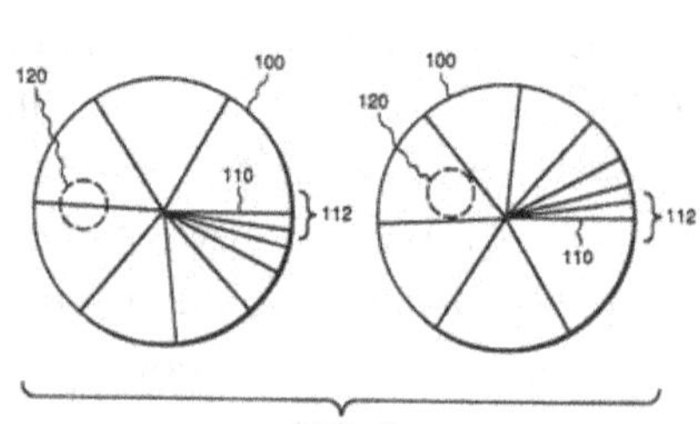

FIG. 5

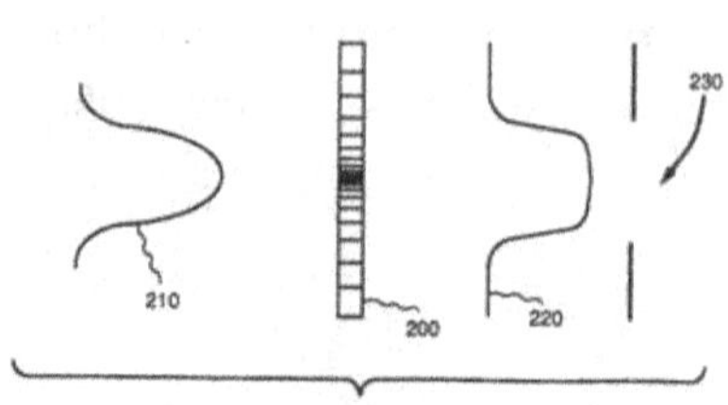

FIG. 6

U.S. Patent Apr. 20, 1993 Sheet 5 of 6 5,204,773

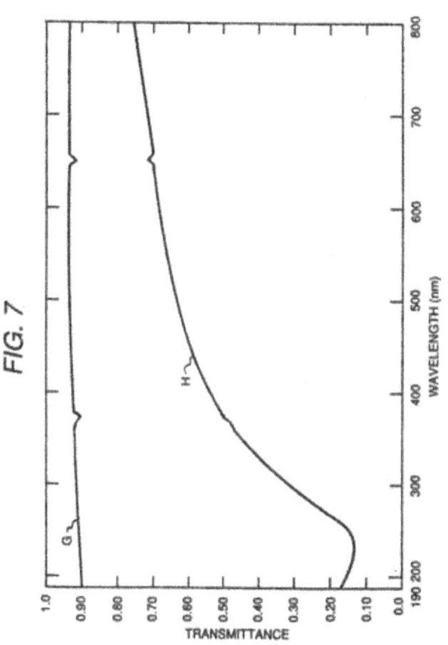

U.S. Patent Apr. 20, 1993 Sheet 6 of 6 5,204,773

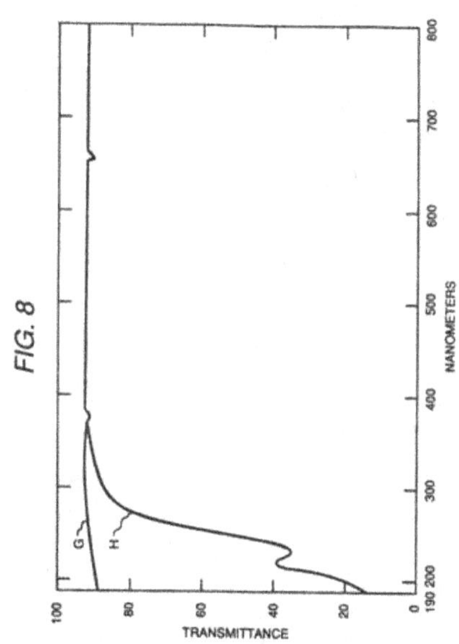

DESCRIPTION:

BACKGROUND OF THE INVENTION

1. Field of the Invention

The present invention relates to the field of filters and, more particularly, to the field of filters for ultraviolet light.

2. Background Information

The use of ultraviolet laser light to ablate material from a workpiece in order to modify the shape of the workpiece is used in a number of fields. In most such systems, a fixed laser pulsed energy results in the ablation of a fixed quantity of material from the workpiece. Typically, a pulsed excimer laser is employed for such ablation processes. These lasers typically emit their laser beam at 193 nm or 248 nm. Since the excimer laser is a pulsed laser, each pulse to which a workpiece is exposed ablates the same quantity of material for a uniform workpiece. Where it is desired to remove a quantity of material that is not an integral multiple of the quantity removed by one pulse, additional control is required. One way of adjusting the amount of material ablated per pulse is to change the beam fluence by changing the laser power. This technique suffers from a variety of disadvantages, including reduction of the power to the point where the beam becomes unstable or nonreproducible. Further, adjustment of the power of the laser is a relatively slow process. Alternatively, a variable beam expander may be employed. However, such expanders are expensive and reduce the collimation of the laser beam. Available commercial ultraviolet light filters cannot be used to reduce the intensity of the ultraviolet light because the ultraviolet light damages their filter properties.

Consequently, there is a need for an improved technique for adjusting the intensity of ultraviolet light.

OBJECTS OF THE INVENTION

Accordingly, a primary object of the present invention is to provide an ultraviolet light filter that may be used to control the intensity of an excimer laser without damage to the filter.

Another object of the present invention is to provide a system for rapidly adjusting the intensity of an excimer laser beam.

Another object of the present invention is to provide an improved technique for modifying the beam energy profile of an ultraviolet light beam.

SUMMARY OF THE INVENTION

The above and other objects, which will become apparent from the specification as a whole, including the drawings, are achieved in accordance with the present invention by distributing an ultraviolet light absorbing chemical species within an ultraviolet light transmissive substrate.

In accordance with one embodiment, a quartz or other ultraviolet light transmissive substrate is ion implanted with an ultraviolet light absorbing chemical species and then annealed to stabilize the distribution of that ultraviolet light absorbing chemical species. The result is a stable ultraviolet light filter.

In accordance with another embodiment, a pair of such filters having graded distributions of the ultraviolet light absorbing chemical species are positioned in series in the optical path of an ultraviolet beam and the degree of attenuation is adjusted by relative movement of the two substrates to change the quantity of ultraviolet light absorbing chemical species in the path of the ultraviolet light beam.

In accordance with another embodiment, the implanted pattern of ultraviolet absorbing chemical species is tailored to modify the energy profile across a beam passing therethrough. In particular, with a beam having a Gaussian energy distribution, an absorption pattern that leaves the emerging beam with a flat energy distribution enables uniform removal of material across the area treated by the resulting beam.

BRIEF DESCRIPTION OF THE DRAWINGS

The subject matter that is regarded as the invention is particularly pointed out and distinctly claimed in the concluding portion of the specification. The invention, however, both as to organization and method of practice, together with further objects and advantages thereof, may best be understood by reference to the following description taken in connection with the accompanying drawings in which:

FIG. 1 is a graph showing the as-implanted transmission characteristics of a plurality of filters having different densities of phosphorus;

FIG. 2 is a graph showing the characteristics of one of the FIG. 1 samples after annealing;

FIG. 3 is a plan view illustration of a variable density filter in accordance with the present invention;

FIG. 4 is a stylized illustration of an ultraviolet light intensity control system employing two filters like that in FIG. 3;

FIG. 5 is a plan view illustration of an alternative configuration for the filters of the FIG. 4 system;

FIG. 6 illustrates modification of the energy profile of an ultraviolet laser beam;

FIG. 7 is a graph showing the as-implanted transmission characteristics of a filter having a density of lead ion implanted; and

FIG. 8 is a graph showing the characteristics of the FIG. 7 sample after annealing.

DETAILED DESCRIPTION

In accordance with the present invention, an ultraviolet light filter is fabricated from a quartz substrate that is substantially transparent to ultraviolet light or fabricated from another ultraviolet light transmissive substrate by ion implanting into the substrate a chemical species that absorbs ultraviolet light at the frequency of interest.

Six quartz Suprasil II substrates, each 1x1x1/16 inch, were obtained from Heraeus. One of these was kept as a control sample (A) and the other five (B–F) were ion implanted with various dosages of phosphorus, as shown in the accompanying table. It will be understood that other materials substantially transparent to ultraviolet light would provide effective substrates for ion implantation, such as magnesium fluoride or calcium fluoride. Quartz was employed in this particular embodiment primarily due to its ready availability.

TABLE

Sample Implant	A	B	C	D	E	F
1×10^{15} ions/cm^2	—	X	—	X	—	X
5×10^{15}	—	—	X	X	—	X
1×10^{16}	—	—	—	—	X	X
Total dose	0	1×10^{15}	5×10^{15}	6×10^{15}	1×10^{16}	1.6×10^{16}

The transmittance spectrum for each of these samples was then measured and is shown in the graph in FIG. 1. The curve for sample A in FIG. 1 shows that the quartz substrate is substantially transparent to ultraviolet light for wavelengths in the range of approximately 190 nanometers to 350 nanometers. It will be noted from FIG. 1 that the ultraviolet light transmittance decreased with increasing implantation dose. Samples A and F were then annealed with 5,000 pulses of excimer laser light at a pulse fluence of 0.5 W/cm^2 and their transmittance spectrum remeasured as illustrated in FIG. 2. As can be seen, the transmittance curve is unchanged for the control sample A, but has changed for sample F as a result of this annealing. Samples A and F were then exposed to an additional 10,000 pulses of the excimer laser and their transmittance curves remeasured. The curves for samples A and F were identical to that in FIG. 2.

A quartz substrate like those described above was also obtained for ion implantation with lead. A portion G of the substrate was not ion implanted and a portion H was implanted with a total dose of 1×10^{16} $ions/cm^2$. The transmittance spectrum of both portions was measured and is shown in the graph in FIG. 7. The curve for portion G in FIG. 7 shows that the quartz substrate is substantially transparent to ultraviolet light for wavelengths in the range of approximately 190 nanometers to 800 nanometers. These portions were then annealed with 20,000 pulses of excimer laser light at a pulse fluence of 0.5 W/cm^2 and their transmittance spectrum was remeasured as illustrated in FIG. 8. Only the ion implanted portion of the substrate has a transmittance curve that changed as a result of the annealing. Exposure to 10,000 additional pulses of excimer laser light produced identical curves.

Thus, the initial exposure of the implanted substrates to ultraviolet light annealed the filters' characteristics to a stable state. While this annealing was done by use of a laser beam, the annealing may also be done by thermal treatment in a manner well-known in the semiconductor industry, if desired.

The stability of the transmittance spectrums over the large number of pulses establishes the stability of this type of filter for use in controlling attenuation of excimer laser and other ultraviolet light beams. FIGS. 2 and 8 respectively provide the information to calculate the dosage of phosphorus or lead to achieve a particular transmittance. For example, twice the dosage of these respective samples will double the difference between the transmittance resulting from a single dose and the transmittance of the control sample. While these specific samples were implanted with either phosphorus or lead, it will be understood that other elements and species may be employed as the ultraviolet light absorbing chemical species. Phosphorus and lead were used in these experiments because of their ready availability in an available implantation apparatus. In general, a filter may be fabricated from any element or species capable of being implanted; however, appropriate chemical species may be determined by reference to handbooks of the light absorbance spectra of chemical species. Furthermore, once a dosage of chemical species has been ion implanted, one skilled in the art may produce a graph as illustrated in FIGS. 2 and 8 to calculate the dosage to achieve a particular transmittance. It will be appreciated by those skilled in the art that materials having a relatively high atomic weight compared to phosphorus, such as arsenic, boron, gold, xenon, radon, or uranium, should result in transmission of less ultraviolet light for approximately the same dose of the particular material. Nonetheless, it will be understood that other factors may also affect the capability of an ion implanted material to absorb ultraviolet light. Furthermore, depending on the filter application, the shape of the resulting transmittance curve for a particular range of wavelengths may make a particular material more or less desirable for use as the ultraviolet light absorbing chemical species.

The intensity of an excimer laser beam may be adjusted by substituting different filters having different densities in its light path. However, that is a relatively slow process and exhibits a granularity determined by the difference in densities of the various filters.

In FIG. 3, a rectangular filter 10 having a graded distribution of ultraviolet light absorbing chemical species is illustrated in schematic plan view. The denser placement of the lines at the left-hand side 10A of the filter indicates a greater concentration of the absorbing species than the wider placement of the lines at the right-hand side 10B of the filter. Such a graded distribution may be provided by ion implantation through an aperture while translating the filter substrate behind the aperture at an increasing velocity to reduce the quantity of ions implanted in the later exposed portions of the substrate. As will be appreciated by those skilled in the art, for situations where a filter having a graded distribution is unnecessary, an ultraviolet light filter in accordance with the present invention may also be fabricated by thermal doping, as is well-known in the art, instead of by ion implantation.

A pair of variable density filters 10 of the type shown in FIG. 3 are shown in FIG. 4 positioned in series along the path of an ultraviolet light beam 32 from a laser 30. A system 20 for translating the two filters relative to each other controls the quantity of the ultraviolet light absorbing chemical species disposed in the path of the ultraviolet light beam 32 whose intensity is to be controlled. The system 20 can be a linear motor, a stepper motor, or any other appropriate mechanism. For a maximum control range, both filters should be movable. However, only one needs to be movable in order to provide adjustable attenuation.

In FIG. 4, filters 10 are positioned with their distribution gradients in opposed relation whereby sliding their heavy distribution ends 10A toward each other increases attenuation while sliding those ends away from each other decreases attenuation with the attenuation being constant across the filter pair in any given position of the filter pair. In this manner, the ultraviolet light beam is affected uniformly by the filter, whereas either filter alone would result in a gradient in the attenuation across the beam. In FIG. 5, an alternative configuration 100 for filters for use in an intensity control system is illustrated in plan view. These two filters 100 are circular and are implanted with an ultraviolet light absorbing chemical species gradient, which is an arc of a circle. When positioned in series, the degree of attenuation for a beam located in the region 120 is controlled by rotating the two filters relative to each other. To maintain uniform attenuation, the portions 112 of these disks should not be brought into alignment with the beam because of the abrupt change in absorbing species concentration at the line 110. Where circular filters are employed in a system similar to that shown in FIG. 4, intensity control is provided by rotating the filters relative to each other rather than sliding them as in the FIG. 4 embodiment.

If it is desired to change the relative energy fluence across the spot of a laser or other ultraviolet light beam, then a filter may be implanted with an ultraviolet light absorbing chemical species distribution that is circularly symmetric (for a circularly symmetric beam energy profile) and varies radially. With a higher density at the center of such a circular distribution, more attenuation is provided in the center of a beam centered on that spot, and with a minimum distribution at the center, more attenuation is provided along the periphery of such a beam. A structure of this type in which the center of the beam is attenuated more than the outside of the beam has great utility in laser ablation systems in which it is desired to remove a uniform amount of material across the entire area being treated. In particular, a filter 200 is fabricated whose absorption characteristics are the inverse of the laser beam energy profile, as shown in FIG. 6. Passing a laser beam having the energy profile 210 through this filter attenuates the central portion of the beam to provide an emerging beam having an energy profile 220, which is substantially flat across that portion of the beam. The beam may then be limited to that flat energy portion by passing it through an appropriate aperture 230. This distribution may be elliptically symmetric or circularly symmetric in accordance with the symmetry of the beam's energy profile.

In the absence of this technique, the initial beam is normally limited to the very center of the beam and then expanded to provide a wider beam having substantially uniform energy across the beam. That is much less energy efficient than the inventive technique because so little of the beam is actually used and it has the further disadvantage of requiring expensive beam expanders and substantially more volume.

The implantation of the ultraviolet light absorbing chemical species into the quartz or other ultraviolet light transmissive substrate and its distribution within the interior of the quartz or other substrate, rather than along its surface, provides several advantages including prevention of removal of the absorbing species either by abrasion or evaporation with the result that the absorption is constant over time. While it is presently preferred to implant the ultraviolet light absorbing species into the quartz or other ultraviolet light transmissive substrate, it should be recognized that such species may also be introduced into the quartz or other substrate during the formation of the substrate.

It will be recognized that the attenuation effects of two such filters positioned in series is cumulative. Consequently, the order of the filters is unimportant to such use.

While the invention has been described in detail herein in accord with certain preferred embodiments thereof, many modifications and changes therein may be effected by those skilled in the art. Accordingly, it is intended by the appended claims to cover all such modifications and changes as fall within the true spirit and scope of the invention.

<u>Problem 3.</u> <u>Pencil Sharpener</u>—Draft an independent apparatus claim and two dependent claims.

<u>FIGURES:</u>

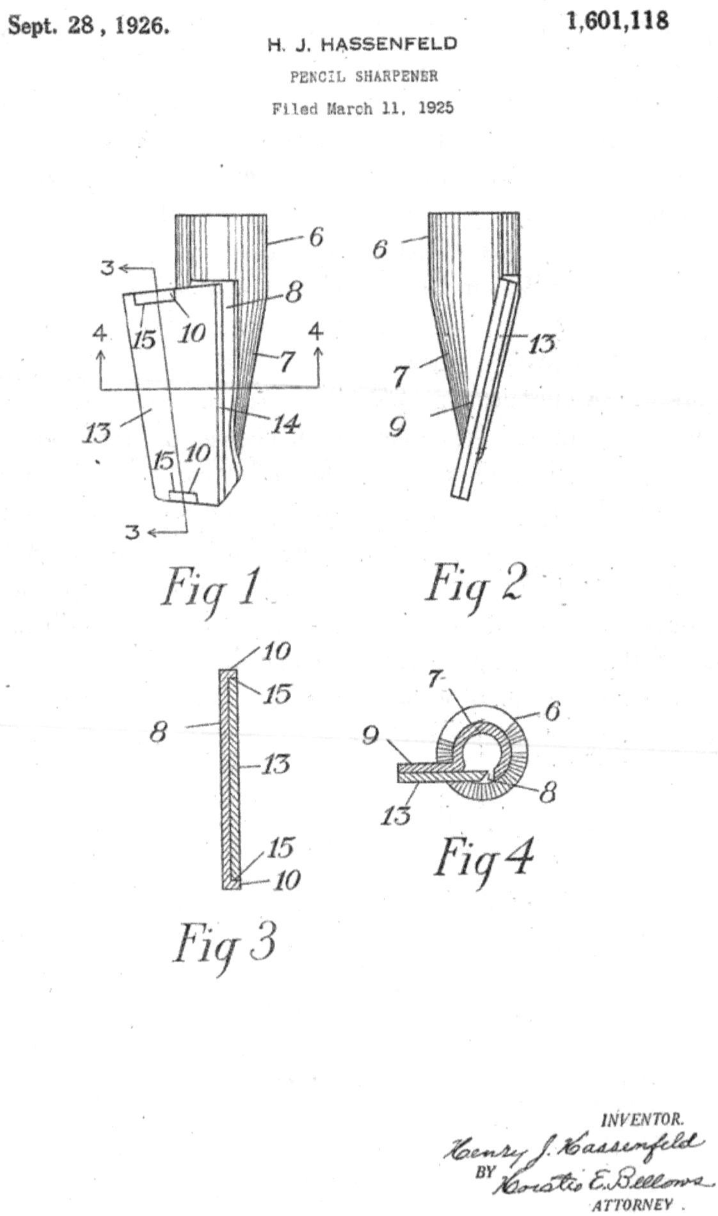

DESCRIPTION:

My invention relates to pencil sharpeners of that type that comprises a conical sharpening socket and is rotatable by engaging the thumb and finger of the operator.

The essential object of my invention is to avoid in the construction of my device the necessity of employing solder, electric welding, or screws, and thus secure a maximum of strength at a minimum cost.

To the above enumerated ends essentially, but not exclusively, my invention consists in such parts and in such combinations of parts as fall within the scope of the appended claim.

In the accompanying drawings that form a part of this specification:

Figure 1 is a side elevation of a sharpener embodying my invention.

Figure 2 is a similar elevation of the same taken at an angle of 95 degrees from the showing in Figure 1, and

Figures 3 and 4 are sections on line 3-3 and 4-4 respectively of Figure 1.

Like reference characters indicate like parts throughout the views.

My device comprises a tubular member or body 6, integral with which is a conical socket or head 7 provided with a longitudinal slot 8 upon one of whose edges is formed a lateral tongue 9 provided upon its top and bottom with lugs 10. A knife blade 13 rests upon the tongue and its beveled lateral edge 14 extends into the slot 8. The blade is provided with rectangular cavities 15 in its top and bottom edges. The lugs 10 are bent and forced by swaging or otherwise into the cavities 15 where they are tightly held by friction.

It will be observed that the described construction permits the formation of the parts from initially flat metallic blanks. Further that the attachment of the blade by interlocking integral lugs not only insures a permanent and firm engagement of the blade, but avoids the expensive use of screws and the costly process of welding.

Composition of Matter Claims

Understand how to draft composition of matter claims and the rights covered by composition of matter claims.

MPEP § 2106.03

[M]achines, manufactures and compositions of matter . . . define the types of physical or tangible "things" or "products" that Congress deemed appropriate to patent. Digitech Image Techs. v. Electronics for Imaging, 758 F.3d 1344, 1348, 111 USPQ2d 1717, 1719 (Fed. Cir. 2014) ("For all categories except process claims, the eligible subject matter must exist in some physical or tangible form."). Thus, when determining whether a claimed invention falls within one of these three categories, examiners should verify that the invention is to at least one of the following categories ***and*** *is claimed in a physical or tangible form. . . . [emphasis added]*

- *A composition of matter is a "combination of two or more substances and includes all composite articles." Digitech, 758 F.3d at 1348–49, 111 USPQ2d at 1719 (citation omitted). This category includes all compositions of two or more substances and all composite articles, "'whether they be the results of chemical union or of mechanical mixture, or whether they be gases, fluids, powders or solids.'" Chakrabarty, 447 U.S. at 308, 206 USPQ at 197 (quoting Shell Dev. Co. v. Watson, 149 F. Supp. 279, 280 (D.D.C. 1957); id. at 310 holding genetically modified microorganism to be a manufacture or composition of matter).*

In re Prutton
28 C.C.P.A. 1343
United States Court of Customs and Patent Appeals
July 2, 1941, Decided

Questions

1. This case involves an appeal from a ruling by the Board of Appeals of the PTO. Currently, this is referred to as the Patent Trial and Appeal Board (PTAB). Likewise, the CCPA was an Article I court hearing matters under Article I of the U.S. Constitution (rather than Article III) within the jurisdiction of the executive branch. In 1982, the jurisdiction of the CCPA was transferred to the newly created Federal Circuit, an Article III court in the judicial branch under the Constitution.[221] The claims at issue appear reasonably broad and there are several related

221. The Federal Circuit has adopted the decisions from the CCPA as its own precedent. *See* S. Corp. v. United States, 690 F.2d 1368 (Fed. Cir. 1982).

applications/patents to the one before the appellate court. What are the potentially related applications and how are they related to the application at issue? Why does the appellant say they are relevant?

2. The appellate court says it does not need to analyze the cited art against the patent application at issue. Why is that? What, then, does the appellate court need to analyze?
3. The Board of Appeals ruled that claims 28 and 29 were not patentable over the cited references. What are the appellant's arguments that the decision is wrong?
4. The appellant tried to rely on application no. 760,038 to antedate Ralston and Lincoln. Why was that position rejected?
5. The Board of Appeals also ruled that the appellant could not rely on application no. 737,070 to antedate Ralston and Lincoln. Why was that?
6. There were several issues about what was disclosed by 737,070. The appellant had argued that it disclosed *one specific example of halogenated cyclic ketones*. Why did the Board of Appeals rule that to be insufficient?
7. There was also a question whether the appellant's application disclosed any specific example of a halogenated *alkylated* cyclic ketone. How was that issue resolved by the appellate court?
8. Note that the application on appeal was a continuation in part (CIP) of 737,070 rather than a continuation. In the case of a CIP, there are some crucial requirements that must be satisfied in order to antedate references between the filing of the first application and the CIP. What are those requirements?
9. It appears that the appellate court relied on the fact that the 737,070 application disclosed not one, but six specific examples of halogenated cyclic ketones. However, this was not argued to the Board of Appeals or even mentioned in the request for reconsideration. However, these six examples are now argued before the appellate court. Why is this argument not waived?
10. Assuming the argument just mentioned is not waived and that the 737,070 application discloses use of an alkyl radicle, still that application does not antedate Clark, also cited by the examiner and used to reject the claims. Why did the examiner reject the claims on Clark? Why did the appellate court reject the examiner's position?

AFG Industries, Inc. v. Cardinal IG Co.
239 F.3d 1239
United States Court of Appeals for the Federal Circuit
February 6, 2001, Decided

Questions

1. What type of claim is claim 1 of the '532 patent? Is it process, apparatus, or composition of matter? Note that the *Digitech* court (quoting the Supreme Court) states that a composition of matter is a "combination of two or more substances and includes all composite articles."[222] Is it product by process? If so, why was that not raised? What might have been a better way to draft the claim and why?
2. The claim uses the transition language "composed of." Why was that problematic? What principle does the court use to resolve the issue of interpretation of this particular language? Ultimately, the court treats the language to mean "consisting essentially of." Will it therefore always be interpreted in that manner? Why or why not? Recall prior discussion of this language and recent case law that could suggest such language may result in claim indefiniteness. Do you think here there was some risk of indefiniteness from the reasoning of the previously discussed case law? Why or why not?
3. The claim does not use the term "interlayer," yet the court thinks it is important to construe this term. Why?
4. Observe the knotty questions that come up: What is a "layer"? What is an "interlayer"? If the same material is deposited twice, is that one layer or two layers? What is a "top coat"? How is that different than a "layer"? Does the language "formed on" imply that material may not be interposed between layers? How could the claim drafter have made it easier to understand the intended meaning behind such language? Do you think the term "layer" comes up in patent claims frequently?
5. There was also a dispute regarding the meaning of the term "comprising." Do you think this is a serious argument or a frivolous one? Why do you think the court ruled that the term was meant to be open?
6. Both parties focus on whether the claim, particularly "layer" or "interlayer," should be interpreted with respect to a chemically uniform material. What does the appellate court think of that approach? The appellate court seems to come up with an interpretation of "layer" not argued by either party. What is that interpretation? Why did the appellate court come up with that interpretation? Do you find the appellate court's interpretation more meaningful than those advanced

222. Digitech Image Techs., LLC v. Elecs. for Imaging, Inc., 758 F.3d 1344, 1348–49, 111 U.S.P.Q.2d 1717, 1719 (Fed. Cir. 2014). *See* MPEP, *supra* note 10, § 2106.03.

by the parties? As an advocate for either side, however, do you see an issue in cases where that happens? Could this happen in a case where the appellate court resolves the legal (and, perhaps, even factual) issues *without* even a remand? If that were to happen, what then is the recourse of either or both parties, if any? Note, in this case, the appellate court remanded to the district court. Why did the appellate court remand here? But for that, do you think the appellate court would have decided the case without remand?

7. The appellate court says this case is the inverse of what happened in *Vitronics Corp. v. Conceptronic, Inc.* What is the point being made by the appellate court? Who wrote the *Vitronics* opinion?

* * *

Examples 4.27 through 4.30 are examples of composition of matter patent claims.

The following is a patent claim directed to a complex compound.

EXAMPLE 4.27

I claim:

1. A composition of matter consisting of: complex compounds of the formula $M(CO)_a\ H_b\ (NH_3)_c$, in which M is a metal of the actinide series of the periodic table of the elements and each of a, b, and c is a whole number ranging from 0 to 8, such that when a is 0, b is greater than 0, and otherwise a is equal to or greater than b, and when c is greater than 0, both a and b are 0.

2. The composition of matter in accordance with claim 1, wherein M is uranium or thorium.

3. The composition of matter in accordance with claim 2, wherein M is uranium, a is 8, b is 2, and c is 0.

4. The composition of matter in accordance with claim 2, wherein M is uranium, a is 0, b is 0, and c is 8.

The following is a claim directed to a roofing underlaying garment material (and a dependent claim).

EXAMPLE 4.28

I claim:

1. A composition of matter comprising: a material comprising:

   a first composite layer consisting of:

   a first non-woven fabric layer;

   a second non-woven fabric layer; and

   a film layer between the first and second non-woven fabric layers;

   a second composite layer comprising:

   a third non-woven fabric layer;

   a glass-fiber net reinforcement layer to form a grid on the third non-woven fabric layer, wherein the glass-fiber net reinforcement layer comprises a glass-fiber fabric web;

   a second film layer on the glass-fiber net reinforcement layer; and

   a fourth non-woven fabric layer on the second film layer; and

   an asphalt layer between the first composite layer and the second composite layer.

2. The composition of matter of claim 1, wherein the material comprises a roofing underlaying garment material.

Example 4.29 is an independent claim, including dependent claims, directed to a door jamb that includes a composition of matter.

EXAMPLE 4.29

I claim:

1. A door jamb for a door frame comprising: a composite, the composite comprising:

   at least one first member comprising a composite material;

   at least one second member coupled to the first member, the second member comprising one or more materials; and an at least partially blended composite coating disposed over the first and the second members, the coating capable of providing structural support to the door frame.

2. The door jamb of claim 1, wherein the coating is further capable of facilitating bonding between the first and second members.
3. The door jamb of claim 1, wherein the coating is further capable of facilitating dimensional stability of the door frame.
4. The door jamb of claim 1, wherein the coating comprises any number or combination of the following: resin, substantially spherical structures, glass objects, polyvinyl acetate, a surfactant, glass micro spheres, or a wetting agent.
5. The door jamb of claim 1, wherein the composite material further comprises any number or combination of the following: a metallic material, a mineral material, a ceramic material, a plastic material, or a hard fibrous material.

Example 4.30 is a patent claim directed to synthesized zinc oxide crystals.

EXAMPLE 4.30

I claim:

1. A composition of matter comprising: synthesized zinc oxide crystals, wherein the synthesized zinc oxide crystals include one or more synthesized zinc oxide crystals having fabricated intra-crystalline porosity, wherein the fabricated intra-crystalline porosity consists essentially of intra-crystalline porosity beyond incidental intra-crystalline porosity.
2. The composition of matter of claim 1, wherein pores in the fabricated intra-crystalline porosity comprise pores of substantially uniform size, shape, and/or density.
3. The composition of matter of claim 1, wherein pores in the fabricated intra-crystalline porosity comprise pores of an average pore diameter in the range from approximately 1 nm to approximately 100 nm.

Compositions of matter more frequently arise in the unpredictable arts, such as in chemistry or in biotechnology, although not necessarily. A composition of matter is not limited to chemistry or biotechnology. Also, some chemistry has become reasonably predictable from being well studied, such as silicon-related processing for the manufacture of silicon chips. In general, any type of composition of matter, so long as it would have been novel, nonobvious, and useful at the time it was made, would be appropriate to claim. These claims can be quite important.

We have discussed that apparatus claims cover make, use, sell, and so on, whereas method claims cover make or use. One might think of this as a type of claim domination. That is, anything that infringes the dominated claim infringes the dominant claim, but there are other things that also infringe the dominant claim. Apparatus claims, for example, may dominate related method claims, such as method of using claims, because apparatus claims cover make, use, sell, and so on. In a similar manner, composition of matter claims may dominate related apparatus claims and method claims.

As an example, consider the continual search for new types of memory materials. In general, this amounts to seeking a substance able to be put in one of two states (e.g., writing to memory) and then being able to determine the state of the substance (e.g., reading from memory). Of course, silicon is an important substance used today for memory devices.

Suppose a substance is invented that is cheap to make and easy to create in which, if it is heated and then cooled in one way, it has a particular resistance; whereas, if it is heated and then cooled in another way, it has a different and distinct resistance. Further, suppose this heating and cooling can be done quickly (on the order of a picosecond) and it may be done to the substance hundreds of millions of times without degrading this property.[223] Also, the volume of material needed for a memory cell is small, such as a cubic nanometer. Likewise, suppose the substance is patented with a composition of matter claim in which the composition of matter is claimed as a type of "improved memory material."[224] Now, any apparatus or method that is made from or uses this "improved memory material" would constitute patent infringement of this composition of matter claim. Thus, the composition of matter claim, in a sense, dominates these other types of claims, such as apparatus and method, that may later be filed as the technology continues to develop.

The Supreme Court has stated "composition of matter" means "all compositions of two or more substances and all composite articles, whether they

223. This hypothetical is similar to how phase-change memory (PCM) and other new types of memory materials operate.

224. This would not generally be sufficient, of course. This is just provided as a "handle" for discussion purposes.

be the results of chemical union, or of mechanical mixture, or whether they be gases, fluids, powders or solids."[225] Composite articles may also be claimed as articles of manufacture—such as roofing, a bathtub or countertop, a door jamb, and so on.

Typically, the claim recites the constituent components and how they are to be combined, such as amounts and conditions (e.g., temperature, pressure, flow rates, catalysts, etc.). The purpose or use of the composition may or may not be stated. Likewise, a composition of matter claim may cover short-lived or intermediate compositions of an overall chemical process.

Composition of matter claims may at times use a transition word or phrase other than "comprising." The word *comprising* is understood to be open form. For some composition of matter claims, this may produce a rejection or result in invalidity either for undue breadth in the unpredictable arts and/or for failing to enable or provide written description support for the full scope of the claim.[226] For example, it may require quite specific conditions to produce a particular composition of matter. Using "comprising," however, would imply the composition of matter could be produced with other conditions or substances, for example. Thus, the claim would on its face appear to cover many more inoperative embodiments than operative embodiments[227] or the claim could be said to fail to be enabled or described sufficiently as to its full scope,[228] rendering it invalid.

---

225. *See* Diamond v. Chakrabarty, 447 U.S. 303, 308 (1980).

226. *See* Juno Therapeutics, Inc. v. Kite Pharma, Inc., 10 F.4th 1330 (Fed. Cir. 2021) (written description); Trs. of Bos. v. Everlight, 896 F.3d 1357 (Fed. Cir. 2018) (enablement); Durel Corp. v. Osram Sylvania, 256 F.3d 1298, 1306–07 (Fed. Cir. 2001) (a significant number of inoperative embodiments within the scope of the claims might be sufficient to prove invalidity); *see* Atlas Powder v. DuPont, 750 F.2d 1569, 1576–77 (Fed. Cir. 1984). *See also* EMI Grp. N. Am., Inc. v. Cypress Semiconductor Corp., 268 F.3d 1342 (Fed. Cir. 2001) (claims reciting scientific process found to be impossible are invalid). *See* Sean Seymore, *Heightened Enablement in the Unpredictable Arts*, 56 UCLA L. Rev. 127 (2008). *See also* Amgen Inc. v. Sanofi, 143 S. Ct. 1423 (2023) (patents claiming all antibodies that bound to specific amino acids on a specific naturally occurring protein and blocked that protein from impairing the body's mechanism for removing LDL cholesterol from the bloodstream failed to meet the enablement requirement of 35 U.S.C. § 112(a) where the described roadmap or proposal for conservative substitution for finding functional antibodies forced scientists to engage in random trial-and-error discovery).

227. *See Durel Corp.*, 256 F.3d at 1306–07 (a significant number of inoperative embodiments within the scope of the claims might be sufficient to prove invalidity); *see Atlas Powder*, 750 F.2d at 1576–77. *See also EMI Grp.*, 268 F.3d 1342 (claims reciting scientific process found to be impossible are invalid).

228. *See Juno Therapeutics*, 10 F.4th 1330 (written description); *Trs. of Bos.*, 896 F.3d 1357 (enablement); *Durel Corp.*, 256 F.3d at 1306–07 (a significant number of inoperative embodiments within the scope of the claims might be sufficient to prove invalidity); *see Atlas Powder*, 750 F.2d at 1576–77. *See also EMI Grp.*, 268 F.3d 1342 (claims reciting scientific process

To address this, such claims often use "consisting of" or "consisting essentially of" as the transition,[229] referred to as closed form and partially closed form, respectively. These transitions have a specifically understood meaning that relates to canons of construction regarding patent claims, as previously explained, and discussed in more detail later; however, there are Federal Circuit cases as well that have deviated from these canons when interpreting a claim. One may view these canons as a type of "first order" analysis or, perhaps, as a weak presumption. In the appropriate circumstances, depending on claim wording, the specification, the file history, the technology, and so on, a federal court may be willing to deviate from the applicable canon or canons.

With this in mind, "consisting of" is used to claim the elements and limitations as recited in the claim body (e.g., closed form).[230] "Consisting essentially of" is used to claim the elements and limitations as recited in the claim body including any additional unclaimed constituents that are of a nature or an amount to not alter the character of what is otherwise intended to be claimed as novel subject matter (e.g., partially closed form).[231] Treatment regarding the important topic of transition words or phrases was provided earlier in Chapter 3.[232]

However, one important aspect to know about transition words, especially in connection with compositions of matter, is that different transition words may be used *within the claim body* to limit or enlarge scope as well. For example, suppose our "improved memory material" easily integrates into a silicon chip. One may want to claim an integrated device using "comprising," but, within the claim body, employ "consisting of" to claim the portion of the integrated device made from the constituents for our "improved memory material." This approach was illustrated earlier with Example 4.28, and Example 4.31 is another example to illustrate the concept, although technically the following is an apparatus claim with composition of matter clauses.

---

found to be impossible are invalid). *See* Seymore, *supra* note 226. *See also Amgen*, 143 S. Ct. 1423 (patents claiming all antibodies that bound to specific amino acids on a specific naturally occurring protein and blocked that protein from impairing the body's mechanism for removing LDL cholesterol from the bloodstream failed to meet the enablement requirement of 35 U.S.C. § 112(a) where the described roadmap or proposal for conservative substitution for finding functional antibodies forced scientists to engage in random trial-and-error discovery).

229. See Chapter 3's treatment of transition words or phrases.

230. *See* AFG Indus. v. Cardinal IG Co., 239 F.3d 1236 (Fed. Cir. 2001); *cf.* Norian Corp. v. Stryker Corp., 363 F.3d 1321 (Fed. Cir. 2004) (claim includes ordinary impurities of recited elements).

231. *See* PPG Indus. v. Guardian Indus., 156 F.3d 1351 (Fed. Cir. 1998); see Chapter 3's treatment of transition words or phrases.

232. See Chapter 3's treatment of transition words or phrases.

EXAMPLE 4.31

I claim:

1. A semiconductor device comprising:

a substrate, the substrate consisting of a material selected from the group consisting of silicon, sapphire, gallium arsenide, magnesium oxide, zinc oxide, and silicon carbide;

a crystalline buffer layer on the substrate consisting essentially of gallium nitride; and

a growth layer on the buffer layer, the growth layer comprising gallium nitride and a dopant material.

For this claim, "comprising" is used to join three elements, which respectively include a clause using closed form, partially closed form, and open form. Also, the clause of the substrate element uses a format referred to as a Markush group, discussed in more detail later.[233] Query, in light of recent case law, what is the scope of the clause using the transition phrase "consisting essentially of"?

Composition of matter claims are frequently used for alloy or other types of mixtures having specific properties. Likewise, as examples, aspects about the crystal structure or about the microstructure might be claimed. Usually, however, for patentability, an improved, unexpected property should be shown, such as with respect to mechanical, thermal, electrical, optical, or other properties.

One issue to be aware of in this context is inadvertent use of "product-by-process" limitations.[234] Words that may be the past tense of a verb that suggests a process, as illustrated in Example 4.29, may have some risk. There, "coating," "blended," or "disposed over" are illustrative examples. A common word used that may be another example is "formed." The nature of materials technology may often lend itself to this sort of description. This sort of language is highlighted here because, if interpreted to be a product-by-process limitation, the language would be subject to the rules governing product-by-process claims,

233. See later in this chapter regarding the treatment of Markush groups.

234. See earlier in this chapter regarding a treatment of this claiming trap in conjunction with the Federal Circuit case *Kamstrup A/S v. Axioma Metering UAB*, 43 F.4th 1374 (Fed. Cir. 2022).

which increases risk of invalidity and/or may result in limitations not being given patentable weight.[235]

However, the Federal Circuit has ruled that such language might not be "product-by-process," but "structural" if used in a nonprocess sense. An example might be as for an apparatus claim.[236] Still, some may challenge that. Care is needed to draft the claims and the specification to support the argument that the language is structural, rather than "product-by-process."

For a composition of matter claim, use of functional language may also be challenging.[237] The PTO has the authority to shift the burden to the applicant with respect to functional language.[238] The CCPA decision in *In re Swinehart* stated in this regard:

> Additionally, where the Patent Office has reason to believe that a functional limitation asserted to be critical for establishing novelty in the claimed subject matter may, in fact, be an inherent characteristic of the prior art, *it possesses the authority to require the applicant to prove that the subject matter shown to be in the prior art does not possess the characteristic relied on.*[239]

If the PTO were to do this it may require seeking to prove the characteristic is not in the prior art being applied (e.g., proving a negative proposition with evidence is usually a challenge), amending the claim, or arguing that for some reason the PTO has inappropriately shifted the burden.

Markush Group Claims

Understand how to draft Markush group claims and how to draft similar claims without using a Markush group.

---

235. See later in this chapter discussing validity issues regarding product-by-process claims. For a recent case, see *Kamstrup A/S*, 43 F.4th 1374 (finding that the PTAB properly construed a product-by-process claim element as not entitled to patentable weight).

236. *See* Fromson v. Advance Offset Plate, Inc., 720 F.2d 1565, 1570, 219 U.S.P.Q. 1137, 1140 (Fed. Cir. 1983) ("That a process limitation appears in a claim does not convert it to a product by process claim."); *cf.* AFG Indus. v. Cardinal IG Co., 239 F.3d 1236 (Fed. Cir. 2001) (product-by-process issue not raised (probably overlooked), although claim was susceptible to such an interpretation).

237. Note that 35 U.S.C. § 112(f) (2023) also refers to "materials," suggesting applicability to compositions of matter.

238. *See In re* Swinehart, 439 F.2d 210, 169 U.S.P.Q. 226 (C.C.P.A. 1971).

239. *Id.* at 213 (emphasis added).

MPEP § 2117

2117 Markush Group

I. MARKUSH CLAIM

A "Markush" claim recites a list of alternatively useable members. In re Harnisch, 631 F.2d 716, 719–20, 206 USPQ 300, 302–304 (CCPA 1980); Ex parte Markush, 1925 Dec. Comm'r Pat. 126, 127 (1924). The listing of specified alternatives within a Markush claim is referred to as a Markush group or Markush grouping. Abbott Labs v. Baxter Pharmaceutical Products, Inc., 334 F.3d 1274, 1280–81, 67 USPQ2d 1191, 1196–97 (Fed. Cir. 2003) (citing to several sources that describe Markush groups). Claim language defined by a Markush grouping requires selection from a closed group "consisting of" the alternative members. Id. at 1280, 67 USPQ2d at 1196. See MPEP § 2111.03, subsection II, for a discussion of the term "consisting of" in the context of Markush groupings.

Treatment of claims reciting alternatives is not governed by the particular format used (e.g., alternatives may be set forth as "a material selected from the group consisting of A, B, and C" or "wherein the material is A, B, or C"). See, e.g., the Supplementary Examination Guidelines for Determining Compliance with 35 U.S.C. 112 and for Treatment of Related Issues in Patent Applications ("Supplementary Guidelines"), 76 Fed. Reg. 7162 (February 9, 2011). Claims that set forth a list of alternatives from which a selection is to be made are typically referred to as Markush claims, after the appellant in Ex parte Markush, 1925 Dec. Comm'r Pat. 126, 127 (1924). Although the term "Markush claim" is used throughout the MPEP, any claim that recites alternatively usable members, regardless of format, should be treated as a Markush claim. Inventions in metallurgy, refractories, ceramics, chemistry, pharmacology and biology are most frequently claimed under the Markush formula, but purely mechanical features or process steps may also be claimed by using the Markush style of claiming. See, e.g., Fresenius USA, Inc. v. Baxter Int'l, Inc., 582 F.3d 1288, 1297–98, 92 USPQ2d 1163, 1170–1172 (Fed. Cir. 2009)(claim to a hemodialysis apparatus required "at least one unit selected from the group consisting of (i) a dialysate-preparation unit, (ii) a dialysate-circulation unit, (iii) an ultrafiltrate-removal unit, and (iv) a dialysate-monitoring unit" and a user/machine interface operably connected thereto); In re Harnisch, 631 F.2d 716, 206 USPQ 300 (CCPA 1980) (defining alternative moieties of a chemical compound with Markush groupings).

A Markush grouping is proper if the members of a group share a single structural similarity and a common use. See subsections II–IV, below, for guidelines regarding the determination of whether a Markush grouping is improper.

See MPEP § 2111.03 and MPEP § 2173.05(h) for discussions of when a Markush grouping may be indefinite under 35 U.S.C. 112(b) (e.g., if the list of alternatives is not a closed grouping, or if a Markush group is so expansive that persons skilled in the art cannot determine the metes and bounds of the claimed invention).

See MPEP § 803.02 for information pertaining to the election, search, and examination of claims that include at least one Markush grouping.

II. IMPROPER MARKUSH GROUPING

A Markush claim may be rejected under judicially approved "improper Markush grouping" principles when the claim contains an improper grouping of alternatively useable members. A Markush claim contains an "improper Markush grouping" if either: (1) the members of the Markush group do not share a "single structural similarity" or (2) the members do not share a common use. Supplementary Guidelines at 7166 (citing In re Harnisch, 631 F.2d 716, 721–22, 206 USPQ 300, 305 (CCPA 1980)).

Where a Markush grouping describes part of a combination or process, the members following "selected from the group consisting of" (or a similar introductory phrase) must be substitutable, one for the other, with the expectation that the same intended result would be achieved. Multilayer Stretch Cling Film Holdings, Inc. v. Berry Plastics Corp., 831 F.3d 1350, 1357, 119 USPQ2d 1773, 1779 (Fed. Cir. 2016) ("It is generally understood that . . . the members of the Markush group . . . are alternatively usable for the purposes of the invention . . . .") (citations omitted). Where a Markush grouping describes part of a chemical compound, regardless of whether the claim is limited to a compound per se or the compound is recited as part of a combination or process, the members following "selected from the group consisting of" (or similar introductory phrase) need not share a community of properties themselves; the propriety of the grouping is determined by a consideration of the compound as a whole. See Harnisch, 631 F.2d at 722, 206 USPQ at 305 ("in determining the propriety of a Markush grouping the compounds must be considered as wholes and not broken down into elements or other components"). See also In re Jones, 162 F.2d 479, 481, 74 USPQ 149, 151 (CCPA 1947) ("In determining the propriety of a Markush grouping, moreover, the compounds which are grouped must each be considered as a whole and should not be broken down into elements or other components").

The alternatives defined by the Markush group are either alternative chemical compounds as a whole (e.g., if a claim includes a compound R-OH wherein R is selected from the group consisting of methyl, propyl, and butyl, then the alternatives are methanol, propanol, or butanol) or in the context of a combination or process, the alternatives from which a selection is to be made (e.g., the alternatives in a list following the phrase "selected from the group consisting of"). The alternatives (1) share a "single structural similarity" when they belong to the same recognized physical or chemical class or to the same art-recognized class, and (2) share a common function or use when they are disclosed in the specification or known in the art to be functionally equivalent in the context of the claimed invention. See Supplementary Guidelines at 7166 and subsection II.A, below.

Where a Markush grouping describes alternative chemical compounds, whether by words or chemical formulas, and the compounds do not appear to be members of a recognized physical or chemical class or members of an art-recognized class, the members are considered to share a "single structural similarity" and common use when the alternatively usable compounds share a substantial structural feature that is essential to a common use. Ex parte Hozumi, 3 USPQ2d 1059, 1060 (Bd. Pat. App. & Int. 1984). See also subsection II.B, below.

A. "Single Structural Similarity"—Members of a Physical, Chemical, or Art-Recognized Class

Members of a Markush group share a "single structural similarity" when they belong to the same recognized physical or chemical class or to the same art-recognized class. A recognized physical class, a recognized chemical class, or an art-recognized class is a class wherein there is an expectation from the knowledge in the art that members of the class will behave in the same way in the context of the claimed invention. In other words, each member could be substituted one for the other, with the expectation that the same intended result would be achieved. For example, in the context of a claim covering a disposable diaper, a limitation "the fastener selected from the group consisting of a pressure sensitive adhesive and complementary release material, a complementary hook and loop structure, a snap, and a buckle" would likely be considered an art recognized class because a review of the prior art would establish that it was well known that each member could be substituted for each other with the expectation that the intended result (repositionable and refastenable) would occur.

Note that where a Markush group includes only materials from a recognized scientific class of equivalent materials or from an art-recognized class, "the mere existence of such a group in an application tend[s] to prove the equivalence of its members and when one of them [is] anticipated the group [is] therefore rendered unpatentable, in the absence of some convincing evidence of some degree of non-equivalency of one or more of the remaining members." In re Ruff, 256 F.2d 590, 598–99, 118 USPQ 340, 348 (CCPA 1958) ("[A]ctual equivalence is not enough to justify refusal of a patent on one member of a group when another member is in the prior art. The equivalence must be disclosed in the prior art or be obvious within the terms of Section 103." Id. at 599, 118 USPQ at 348).

Thus, a Markush grouping is ordinarily proper if all the members of the group belong to a recognized class (whether physical, chemical, or art recognized) and are disclosed in the specification to possess at least one property in common which is mainly responsible for their function in the claimed invention, and it is clear from their very nature or from the prior art that all members possess this property. See also MPEP § 803.02.

B. Common Use Flows From Substantial Structural Feature

Where a Markush grouping describes alternative chemical compounds, whether by words or chemical formulas, and the alternatives do not belong to a recognized class as explained in subsection II.A, above, the members of the Markush grouping may still be considered to be proper where the alternatives share a substantial structural feature that is essential to a common use.

For example, in Harnisch, the claims were directed to a Markush group of coumarin derivatives disclosed to be useful as dyes. The claimed coumarin derivatives were not members of a recognized chemical class, encompassing "polyfused N-heterocyclics, cyclic, acyclic and aromatic amines, aryloxyalkylamines, amides, sulfonamides, [and] phthalimides" among others. Harnisch, 631 F.2d at 718, 206 USPQ at 302. Furthermore, they were not members of an art-recognized class ("[n]owhere in the record has it been established or even alleged that the variety of compounds included within the explicit scope of the claims are recognized by the art as being functionally equivalent" (Id.)). However, the court found that the Markush grouping was proper because the claimed compounds, viewed as a whole, all share a coumarin group and the property of being a dye. See also In re Jones, 162 F.2d 479, 481, 74 USPQ 149, 151 (1947).

See also Ex parte Hozumi, 3 USPQ2d 1059, 1060 (Bd. Pat. App. & Int. 1984). See subsection IV, below, for a discussion of the Harnisch and Hozumi decisions.

III. REJECTION BASED ON IMPROPER MARKUSH GROUPING

When an examiner determines that the species of a Markush group do not share a single structural similarity or do not share a common use, then a rejection on the basis that the claim contains an "improper Markush grouping" is appropriate (see subsection II). Note that this is a rejection on the merits and may be appealed to the Patent Trial and Appeal Board in accordance with 35 U.S.C. 134 and 37 CFR 41.31(a)(1). Use Form Paragraph 8.40 to reject a claim on the basis that it includes an improper Markush grouping.

In accordance with the principles of compact prosecution, a rejection based on an improper Markush grouping should be made in the first action on the merits after presentation of the claim with the improper Markush grouping (e.g., first Office action on the merits or next Office action following presentation of the claim). In addition, if the examiner determines that one or more claims include an improper Markush grouping, the examiner should also require the applicant to elect an alternative or group of indistinct alternatives for search and examination (i.e., an election of species), if such an election requirement was not previously made. See MPEP § 803.02 for more information on election of species requirements in Markush claims. Note that if a written provisional election of species requirement must be made separate from the first Office action on the merits, it should not include a rejection on the basis of an improper Markush grouping. Any appropriate improper Markush grouping rejection should be made in an Office action on the merits.

The examiner should include suggestions for the applicant as to how to overcome the rejection, e.g., by suggesting a proper Markush grouping based on the specification as filed and/or by suggesting that applicant set forth each alternative (or grouping of patentably indistinct alternatives) within an improper Markush grouping in a series of independent or dependent claims. There may be more than one way to formulate a proper Markush grouping. The examiner should not suggest any grouping that clearly would not meet the requirements of 35 U.S.C. 112(a). For example, the examiner should not suggest a grouping that meets the requirements for a proper Markush grouping, but would clearly lack adequate written description if presented in a separate claim.

In addition to a rejection based on an improper Markush grouping, the claim should also be rejected under 35 U.S.C. 112(b) if one skilled in the art cannot determine the metes and bounds of the Markush claim due to an inability to envision all of the members of the Markush grouping. In other words, if a boundary cannot be drawn separating embodiments encompassed by the claim from those that are not, the claim is indefinite and should be rejected under 35 U.S.C. 112(b). See also MPEP § 2173.05(h).

The claim should be examined for patentability with respect to all other conditions of patentability (e.g., 35 U.S.C. 101, 102, 103, 112, and nonstatutory double patenting). As explained with regard to election of species practice as set forth in detail in MPEP § 803.02, the search need not be extended to species that fall outside a proper Markush grouping.

The improper Markush grouping rejection of the claim should be maintained until (1) the claim is amended such that the Markush grouping includes only members that share a single structural similarity and a common use; or (2) the applicant presents convincing arguments why the members of the Markush grouping share a single structural similarity and common use (i.e., are members of a physical, chemical, or art-recognized class that share a common use, or are chemical compounds that share a substantial structural feature that is essential to the common use). In addition, even if the applicant does not take action sufficient to overcome the improper Markush grouping rejection, when all of the claims are otherwise in condition for allowance the examiner should reconsider the propriety of the improper Markush grouping rejection. If the examiner determines that in light of the prior art and the record as a whole the alternatives of the Markush grouping share a single structural similarity and a common use, then the rejection should be withdrawn. Note that no Markush claim can be allowed until any improper Markush grouping rejection has been overcome or withdrawn, and all other conditions of patentability have been satisfied.

MPEP § 2173.05(h)

2173.05(h) Alternative Limitations

I. MARKUSH GROUPS

A claim which recites a list of alternatives to define a limitation is an acceptable claim construction which should not necessarily be rejected as confusing under 35

U.S.C. 112(b) or as improper. See MPEP § 2117 for guidelines regarding the determination of whether a Markush grouping is improper.

Treatment of claims reciting alternatives is not governed by the particular format used (e.g., alternatives may be set forth as "a material selected from the group consisting of A, B, and C" or "wherein the material is A, B, or C"). See, e.g., the Supplementary Examination Guidelines for Determining Compliance with 35 U.S.C. 112 and for Treatment of Related Issues in Patent Applications ("Supplementary Guidelines"), 76 Fed. Reg. 7162, 7166 (February 9, 2011). Claims that set forth a list of alternatives from which a selection is to be made are typically referred to as Markush claims, after the appellant in Ex parte Markush, 1925 Dec. Comm'r Pat. 126, 127 (1924). The listing of specified alternatives within a Markush claim is referred to as a Markush group or Markush grouping. Abbott Labs v. Baxter Pharmaceutical Products, Inc., 334 F.3d 1274, 1280–81, 67 USPQ2d 1191, 1196–97 (Fed. Cir. 2003) (citing to several sources that describe Markush groups).

See MPEP § 2117 for a general discussion of Markush claims and guidelines regarding the determination of whether a Markush grouping is improper, and MPEP § 803.02 for a discussion of election requirements in Markush claims.

A Markush grouping is a closed group of alternatives, i.e., the selection is made from a group "consisting of" (rather than "comprising" or "including") the alternative members. Abbott Labs., 334 F.3d at 1280, 67 USPQ2d at 1196. If a Markush grouping requires a material selected from an open list of alternatives (e.g., selected from the group "comprising" or "consisting essentially of" the recited alternatives), the claim should generally be rejected under 35 U.S.C. 112(b) as indefinite because it is unclear what other alternatives are intended to be encompassed by the claim. If a claim is intended to encompass combinations or mixtures of the alternatives set forth in the Markush grouping, the claim may include qualifying language preceding the recited alternatives (such as "at least one member" selected from the group), or within the list of alternatives (such as "or mixtures thereof"). Id. at 1281. See also MPEP § 2111.03.

A Markush grouping may include a large number of alternatives, and as a result a Markush claim may encompass a large number of alternative members or embodiments, but a claim is not necessarily indefinite under 35 U.S.C. 112(b) for such breadth. In re Gardner, 427 F.2d 786, 788, 166 USPQ 138, 140 (CCPA 1970) ("Breadth is not indefiniteness."). In certain circumstances, however, a Markush group may be so expansive that persons skilled in the art cannot determine the metes and bounds of the claimed invention. For example, if a claim defines a chemical compound using one or more Markush groups, and that claim encompasses a massive number of distinct alternative members, the claim may be indefinite under 35 U.S.C. 112(b) if one skilled in the art cannot determine its metes and bounds due to an inability to envision all of the compounds defined by the Markush group(s). In such a circumstance, a rejection of the claim for indefiniteness under 35 U.S.C. 112(b) is appropriate.

The use of Markush claims of diminishing scope should not, in itself, be considered a sufficient basis for objection to or rejection of claims. However, if such a practice renders the claims indefinite or if it results in undue multiplicity, an appropriate rejection should be made.

Similarly, the double inclusion of an element by members of a Markush group is not, in itself, sufficient basis for objection to or rejection of claims. Rather, the facts in each case must be evaluated to determine whether or not the multiple inclusion of one or more elements in a claim renders that claim indefinite. The mere fact that a compound may be embraced by more than one member of a Markush group recited in the claim does not necessarily render the scope of the claim unclear. For example, the Markush group, "selected from the group consisting of amino, halogen, nitro, chloro and alkyl" should be acceptable even though "halogen" is generic to "chloro." See, e.g., Eli Lilly & Co. v. Teva Parenteral Meds., 845 F.3d 1357, 1371, 121 USPQ2d 1277, 1287 (Fed. Cir. 2017) (redundancy of including both "vitamin B12" and "cyanocobalamin" (which were recognized on the record as referencing the same compound) within a Markush group of methylmalonic acid lowering agents did not render the claims indefinite).

II. "OPTIONALLY"

Another alternative format which requires some analysis before concluding whether or not the language is indefinite involves the use of the term "optionally." In Ex parte Cordova, 10 USPQ2d 1949 (Bd. Pat. App. & Inter. 1989) the language "containing A, B, and optionally C" was considered acceptable alternative language because there was no ambiguity as to which alternatives are covered by the claim. A similar holding was reached with regard to the term "optionally" in Ex parte Wu, 10 USPQ2d 2031 (Bd. Pat. App. & Inter. 1989). In the instance where the list of potential alternatives can vary and ambiguity arises, then it is proper to make a rejection under 35 U.S.C. 112(b) and explain why there is confusion.

Amgen Inc. v. Amneal Pharmaceuticals LLC
945 F.3d 1368
United States Court of Appeals for the Federal Circuit
January 7, 2020, Decided

Amgen Inc. v. Sanofi
598 U.S. 594
Supreme Court of the United States
March 27, 2023, Argued; May 18, 2023, Decided

Questions

1. What was the claim construction issue in *Amneal* and how does it relate to Markush group claims?
2. Do you think the court's distinction of *Multilayer Stretch Cling Film Holdings, Inc. v. Berry Plastics Corp.*[240] was correct? Why or why not?
3. Do you believe both "comprising" and "at least one" were needed to get the construction of the claim reached by the Federal Circuit? Why or why not?
4. Writing dependent claims for claims that use "consisting of" can be tricky. Note that in *Multilayer* the court held claim 10 invalid. If the court had considered the use of "comprising" do you think the same outcome would have been reached? Does the *Amneal* case suggest a claim drafting principle?
5. What do you think about this language from claim 1 that was not in dispute:

   > wherein the composition is for the treatment of at least one of hyperparathyroidism, hyperphosphonia, hypercalcemia, and elevated calcium phosphorus product[241]?

6. The following illustrates one of the claims (claim 19) at issue in *Sanofi*:

   > 1. An isolated monoclonal antibody, wherein, when bound to PCSK9, the monoclonal antibody binds to at least one of the following residues: S153, I154, P155, R194, D238, A239, I369, S372, D374, C375, T377, C378, F379, V380, or S381 of SEQ ID NO:3, and wherein the monoclonal antibody blocks binding of PCSK9 to LDLR.
   > 19. The isolated monoclonal antibody of claim 1 wherein the isolated monoclonal antibody binds to at least two of the following residues S153, I154, P155, R194, D238, A239, I369, S372, D374, C375, T377, C378, F379, V380, or S381 of PCSK9 listed in SEQ ID NO:3.[242]

   Is claim 19 a Markush group clam? Why or why not? Could these have been written using traditional Markush group format? Whether in traditional format or not, what is the problem with claim 19? What does this tell you about Markush group claims? Does this suggest you should use such claims or suggest that you should not use such claims (i.e., either traditional Markush group claims or claims like claim 19)?

---

240. 831 F.3d 1350 (Fed. Cir. 2016).
241. Amgen Inc. v. Amneal Pharms. LLC, 945 F.3d 1368 (Fed. Cir. 2020).
242. Amgen Inc. v. Sanofi, 987 F.3d 1080, 1083 (Fed. Cir. 2021).

What differences do you perceive between traditional Markush group claim format versus a claim written like claim 19?

7. Note that the Supreme Court does not present the claims at issue. What aspect of these claims is the Court focused on? What claim drafting guidance does this suggest?

* * *

Another claim type frequently in use, in particular in the chemical area, is referred to as a Markush group or Markush expression. This claim is named after the case on which it is based, *Ex parte Markush*.[243] Markush groups are seen most frequently in the unpredictable arts but may also be employed in the predictable arts.

Markush groupings are, in general, fine to employ; however, it is important to employ a good form for such a claim. The concept of the claim is to name a genus of certain specified claim elements, such as, for example, materials, when there is no commonly accepted generic expression to cover the subject matter to be claimed.[244] A common claim form is, for example:

I claim:

A process for etching silicon, comprising:

treating the surface of the silicon with an acid selected from the group consisting of sulfuric acid, nitric acid, and phosphoric acid.

However, this may not be the preferred form. One reason is that the use of "consisting of" introduces some risk that the claim may be construed narrowly to cover using only acid and nothing else, and likewise these particular acids only (i.e., referred to as "closed" form). Instead, a better form introduces a "comprising" before the Markush group so that it is clear the claim element is not necessarily limited to the Markush group, such as the following:[245]

243. 1925 Dec. Comm'r Pat. 126, 340 O.G. 839.
244. *See* MPEP, *supra* note 10, § 2173.05(h).
245. *See Amgen Inc.*, 945 F.3d 1368.

I claim:

A process for etching silicon, comprising:

treating the surface of the silicon with a substance comprising an acid selected from the group consisting of sulfuric acid, nitric acid, and phosphoric acid.

This claim may yet be further refined. What if someone used a combination of acids? Would there be infringement? Probably, because the combination would literally include one of the recited acids and we have introduced a "comprising." Still, it would be better if it were clearer that combinations of acids out of the group infringe. Here is one way to do this:

A process for etching silicon, comprising:

treating the surface of the silicon with a substance comprising at least one acid selected from the group consisting of sulfuric acid, nitric acid, and phosphoric acid.

Now, it is clearer that a combination of acids from the group infringe. Perhaps yet another way that is arguably even clearer might be:

A process for etching silicon, comprising:

treating the surface of the silicon with a substance comprising at least one acid selected from the group consisting of sulfuric acid, nitric acid, phosphoric acid and any combinations thereof.

Likewise, it may be appropriate to, instead, employ the form "consisting essentially of" in some situations, but beware of the potential risks of indefiniteness.[246]

246. See the discussion of "consisting essentially of" in Chapter 3.

Appreciate that a Markush group has certain legal requirements that, if not met, may invalidate the claim. Also, appreciate that where a Markush group lists several elements of the group, if any one member of the group is found in the prior art, along with the other limitations of the claim in addition to the Markush group, then the claim would be anticipated. MPEP section 2117 (2023) discusses features of a Markush group:

> A "Markush" claim recites a list of alternatively useable members. *In re Harnisch*, 631 F.2d 716, 719–20 (CCPA 1980); *Ex parte Markush*, 1925 Dec. Comm'r Pat. 126, 127 (1924). The listing of specified alternatives within a Markush claim is referred to as a Markush group or Markush grouping. *Abbott Labs v. Baxter Pharmaceutical Products, Inc.*, 334 F.3d 1274, 1280–81, 67 USPQ2d 1191, 1196–97 (Fed. Cir. 2003) (citing to several sources that describe Markush groups). Claim language defined by a Markush grouping requires selection from a closed group "consisting of" the alternative members. *Id.* at 1280, 67 USPQ2d at 1196. *See* MPEP § 2111.03 (2023), subsection II, for a discussion of the term "consisting of" in the context of Markush groupings. . . .
>
> Inventions in metallurgy, refractories, ceramics, chemistry, pharmacology and biology are most frequently claimed under the Markush formula, but purely mechanical features or process steps may also be claimed by using the Markush style of claiming. *See, e.g., Fresenius USA, Inc. v. Baxter Int'l, Inc.*, 582 F.3d 1288, 1297–98 (Fed. Cir. 2009) (claim to a hemodialysis apparatus required "at least one unit selected from the group consisting of (i) a dialysate-preparation unit, (ii) a dialysate-circulation unit, (iii) an ultrafiltrate-removal unit, and (iv) a dialysate-monitoring unit" and a user/machine interface operably connected thereto); *In re Harnisch*, 631 F.2d 716, 206 USPQ 300 (CCPA 1980) (defining alternative moieties of a chemical compound with Markush groupings).
>
> A Markush grouping is proper if the members of a group share a single structural similarity and a common use.
>
> *See* MPEP § 2111.03 (2023) and MPEP § 2173.05(h) (2023) for discussions of when a Markush grouping may be indefinite under 35 U.S.C. 112(b) (e.g., if the list of alternatives is not a closed grouping, or if a Markush group is so expansive that persons skilled in the art cannot determine the metes and bounds of the claimed invention). . . .
>
> A Markush claim may be rejected under judicially approved "improper Markush grouping" principles when the claim contains an improper grouping of alternatively useable members. A Markush claim contains an "improper Markush grouping" if either: (1) the members of the Markush group do not share a "single structural similarity" or (2) the members do not share a common use. See, e.g., the *Supplementary Examination Guidelines for Determining Compliance with 35 U.S.C. 112 and for Treatment of Related Issues in Patent Applications ("Supplementary Guidelines")*, 76 Fed. Reg. 7162, 7166 (February 9, 2011).

As noted in the MPEP, Markush groups work for both the predictable and unpredictable arts. For example, a large group of dependent claims might be combined into a single Markush group claim. With that said, it is suggested that Markush groups be limited to the areas in which they are more commonly used, such as metallurgy, refractories, ceramics, chemistry, pharmacology, and biology. Rather, use of a Markush group may make a straightforward claim more confusing, particularly with respect to the proper use of "and" versus "or." One example of such confusion is the case *SuperGuide v. DirecTV*,[247] addressed later.

An advantage of a Markush group is that it is a way to claim subject matter broadly. That is, a Markush group permits a claim to read on many embodiments, particularly with respect to many substances. However, we shall also see that this may be accomplished without a Markush group.[248]

Of course, extremely broad claims also have risks, particularly in the unpredictable arts.[249] For example, such claims may be held invalid for lack of enablement or lack of written description.[250]

There are other risks as well. For one thing, the language may fail to meet the legal requirements of a Markush group.[251] In addition, the wording might be improper. That is, the language may use "or" rather than "and."

One issue to appreciate with Markush groups is that they came into existence at a time when the PTO took the position that the use of "or" was considered indefinite since it permitted the claim to cover alternatives. Today, courts and even the PTO both recognize that "or" does not necessarily make a claim indefinite.[252]

The Markush group claim format was an approach to get the equivalent of "or" without using the word expressly.[253] That is, the formulation "at least one . . . selected from the group consisting of A, B, *and* C" is equivalent to "at least one of the following: A, B, *or* C." This may create some confusion regarding proper use of "and" versus "or." A good example is the case *Super-*

---

247. 358 F.3d 870 (Fed. Cir. 2004). The use of "and" in what was not a traditional Markush group formulation resulted in a claim interpretation that prevented the claim from being infringed.

248. See the discussion later in this chapter; see *Amgen Inc. v. Sanofi*, 987 F.3d 1080 (Fed. Cir. 2021), *aff'd*, 598 U.S. 594 (2023), in which at least millions of potential substances fell within the scope of the claims at issue. The claims used a technique described later in this chapter.

249. See discussion of the unpredictable arts in Chapter 3.

250. *Id.*

251. *See, e.g.*, MPEP, *supra* note 10, § 2173.05(h).

252. Although, once in a while, an examiner will issue an indefiniteness rejection for the use of "or."

253. Of course, since such a claim was definite, one would think that would have been a clear basis to conclude use of "or" is not necessarily indefinite.

Guide v. DirecTV.[254] The claim construction issue concerned the language "at least one of A, B, and C." The Federal Circuit stated:

> The next phrase for construction is "at least one of" which appears in Claim 1: *at least one of a desired program start time, a desired program end time, a desired program service **and** a desired program type*. SuperGuide and Gemstar argue that only one of the four criteria is necessary; Defendants assert that one of each is necessary. . . . SuperGuide's position that "at least one of" refers only to one category of the criteria instead of to one of each category "would contradict the clear purpose of the invention as described in the written description, depicted in [Figure 4a], and recited in claim 1. Such an assertion would also impermissibly read the preferred embodiment out of claim 1." *Crystal Semiconductor*, 246 F.3d at 1349; *accord, Sandisk Corp. v. Lexar Media, Inc.*, 91 F. Supp. 2d 1327, 1330–32 (N.D. Cal. 2000) (Claim language "partitioning the memory cells within the individual sectors into at least a user data portion and an overhead portion" meant the memory cells within the individual sectors were partitioned "into at least a user data portion and an overhead portion."). Here, the claim language is "at least one of" followed by the term "a desired," a term which is repeated for each category. *Moreover, the final category is introduced by "and* a desired" *which is conjunctive not disjunctive. Thus, the phrase "at least one of" means at least one of each desired criterion; that is, at least one of a desired program start time, a desired program end time, a desired program service and a desired program type.*[255]

Consequently, of course, there was no infringement. Although it is only a theory, the formulation construed in *SuperGuide* shows up frequently enough in claims that it suggests some practitioners are confused about the usage of "and" in a Markush group and the use of "or" in a claim that does not employ a Markush group.

SuperGuide is not the only Federal Circuit case to implicate use of "and" versus use of "or."[256] This issue—that is, use of "and" versus "or" in a claim—is sufficiently unclear but is important enough with respect to infringement[257] that it is recommended, in general, to use "and/or" in claims except where it makes no sense and to address this in the specification. For example, language such as the following may be employed:

---

254. 358 F.3d 870 (Fed. Cir. 2004).

255. *Id.* at 888 (emphasis added).

256. *See* Kustom Signals, Inc. v. Applied Concepts, 264 F.3d 1326 (Fed. Cir. 2001); Brown v. 3M, 265 F.3d 1349 (Fed. Cir. 2001); *cf.* Kaufman v. Microsoft, No. 21-1634 (Fed. Cir. May 20, 2022) (affirming interpretation of "and" in claim as meaning "or" based on usage in specification).

257. Consider the *SuperGuide* case in which the use of "and" resulted in no infringement.

> Unless otherwise indicated, in the context of the present patent application, the term "or" if used to associate a list, such as A, B, or C, is intended to mean A, B, and C, here used in the inclusive sense, as well as A, B, or C, here used in the exclusive sense. With this understanding, "and" is used in the inclusive sense and intended to mean A, B, and C; whereas "and/or" can be used in an abundance of caution to make clear that all of the foregoing meanings are intended, although such usage is not required.[258]

Following are two examples of claims employing a Markush group in the formulation we described earlier so that, for example, "substance" is not limited to the particular Markush group in Example 4.32.

EXAMPLE 4.32

I claim:

1. A process for etching silicon, comprising:

   treating the surface of the silicon with a substance comprising at least one acid selected from the group consisting of sulfuric acid, nitric acid, phosphoric acid, and any combinations thereof.

EXAMPLE 4.33

I claim:

1. A semiconductor device comprising:

   a substrate, the substrate comprising at least one material selected from the group consisting of silicon, sapphire, gallium arsenide, magnesium oxide, zinc oxide, silicon carbide, and any combinations thereof;

   a crystalline buffer layer on the substrate consisting essentially of gallium nitride; and

   a growth layer on the buffer layer, the growth layer comprising gallium nitride and a dopant material.

As noted, however, an equivalent claim for Example 4.32 might be:

258. *See Ex parte* Gross, No. 2011-005628 (P.T.A.B. May 22, 2014) (approving use of "and/or" in patent claims); *cf. Kaufman*, No. 21-1634 (affirming interpretation of "and" in claim as meaning "or" based on usage in specification).

I claim:

1. A process for etching silicon, comprising:

   treating the surface of the silicon with a substance comprising at least one of the following: sulfuric acid, nitric acid, or phosphoric acid.

A similar formulation might be:

I claim:

1. A process for etching silicon, comprising:

   treating the surface of the silicon with a substance comprising at least one of the following: sulfuric acid, nitric acid, phosphoric acid, or any combination thereof.

Another similar formulation might be (in conjunction with the boilerplate specification language proposed earlier):

I claim:

1. A process for etching silicon, comprising:

   treating the surface of the silicon with a substance comprising at least one of the following: sulfuric acid, nitric acid, and/or phosphoric acid.

Note that the MPEP suggests these formulations will be viewed as Markush groups. In general, any formulation involving alternatives appears to be considered a Markush group based on the MPEP. Of course, the examiner must recognize and appreciate the issue. It does not appear that case law has adopted this view.[259] It is in part for these reasons that it is recommended that Markush groups be used with claims in the unpredictable arts

259. It is noted, however, that the EPC appears to have a view similar to the MPEP.

but that the preceding alternative formulations be used in the predictable arts. That is, this recommendation is an attempt to balance prosecution risk with enforcement risk.

Article of Manufacture Claims

Understand the differences between article claims and apparatus claims when drafting patent claims and the respective situations that call for each.

35 U.S.C. §§ 171–173

Some aspects of these provisions were amended by the AIA.

35 U.S.C. § 171 Patents for Designs

(a) IN GENERAL.—Whoever invents any new, original, and ornamental design for an article of manufacture may obtain a patent therefor, subject to the conditions and requirements of this title.

(b) APPLICABILITY OF THIS TITLE.—The provisions of this title relating to patents for inventions shall apply to patents for designs, except as otherwise provided.

(c) FILING DATE.—The filing date of an application for patent for design shall be the date on which the specification as prescribed by section 112 and any required drawings are filed.

35 U.S.C. § 172 Right of Priority

The right of priority provided for by subsections (a) through (d) of section 119 shall be six months in the case of designs. The right of priority provided for by section 119(e) shall not apply to designs.

35 U.S.C. § 173 Term of Design Patent

Patents for designs shall be granted for the term of 15 years from the date of grant.

MPEP § 2106.03

The other three categories (machines, manufactures and compositions of matter) define the types of physical or tangible "things" or "products" that Congress deemed appropriate to patent. Digitech Image Techs. v. Electronics for Imaging, 758 F.3d 1344, 1348, 111 USPQ2d 1717, 1719 (Fed. Cir. 2014) ("For all categories except process claims, the eligible subject matter must exist in some physical or tangible form."). Thus, when determining whether a claimed invention falls within one of these three categories, examiners should verify that the invention is to at least one of the following categories and is claimed in a physical or tangible form. . . .

- *A manufacture is "a tangible article that is given a new form, quality, property, or combination through man-made or artificial means." Digitech, 758 F.3d at 1349, 111 USPQ2d at 1719–20 (citing Diamond v. Chakrabarty, 447 U.S. 303, 308, 206 USPQ 193, 197 (1980)). As the courts have explained, manufactures are articles that result from the process of manufacturing, i.e., they were produced "from raw or prepared materials by giving to these materials new forms, qualities, properties, or combinations, whether by hand-labor or by machinery." Samsung Electronics Co. v. Apple Inc., 580 U.S. __, 120 USPQ2d 1749, 1752–3 (2016) (quoting Diamond v. Chakrabarty, 447 U.S. 303, 308, 206 USPQ 193, 196–97 (1980)); Nuijten, 500 F.3d at 1356–57, 84 USPQ2d at 1502. Manufactures also include "the parts of a machine considered separately from the machine itself." Samsung Electronics, 137 S. Ct. at 435, 120 USPQ2d at 1753 (quoting 1 W. Robinson, The Law of Patents for Useful Inventions § 183, p. 270 (1890)). . . .*

It is not necessary to identify a single category into which a claim falls, so long as it is clear that the claim falls into at least one category. For example, because a microprocessor is generally understood to be a manufacture, a product claim to the microprocessor or a system comprising the microprocessor satisfies Step 1 regardless of whether the claim falls within any other statutory category (such as a machine). It is also not necessary to identify a "correct" category into which the claim falls, because although in many instances it is clear within which category a claimed invention falls, a claim may satisfy the requirements of more than one category. For example, a bicycle satisfies both the machine and manufacture categories, because it is a tangible product that is concrete and consists of parts such as a frame and wheels (thus satisfying the machine category), and it is an article that was produced from raw materials such as aluminum ore and liquid rubber by giving them a new form (thus satisfying the manufacture category). Similarly, a genetically modified bacterium satisfies both the composition of matter and manufacture categories, because it is a tangible product that is a combination of two or more substances such as proteins, carbohydrates and other chemicals (thus satisfying the composition of matter category), and it is an article that was genetically modified by humans to have new properties such as the ability to digest multiple types of hydrocarbons (thus satisfying the manufacture category).

MPEP § 2114

Apparatus and Article Claims—Functional Language

For a discussion of case law which provides guidance in interpreting the functional portion of means-plus-function limitations see MPEP § 2181–§ 2186.

I. INHERENCY AND FUNCTIONAL LIMITATIONS IN APPARATUS CLAIMS

Features of an apparatus may be recited either structurally or functionally. In re Schreiber, 128 F.3d 1473, 1478, 44 USPQ2d 1429, 1432 (Fed. Cir. 1997). See also MPEP § 2173.05(g). If an examiner concludes that a functional limitation is an inherent characteristic of the prior art, then to establish a prima case of anticipation or obviousness, the examiner should explain that the prior art structure inherently possesses the functionally defined limitations of the claimed apparatus. In re Schreiber, 128 F.3d at 1478, 44 USPQ2d at 1432. See also Bettcher Industries, Inc. v. Bunzl USA, Inc., 661 F.3d 629, 639–40, 100 USPQ2d 1433, 1440 (Fed. Cir. 2011). The burden then shifts to applicant to establish that the prior art does not possess the characteristic relied on. In re Schreiber, 128 F.3d at 1478, 44 USPQ2d at 1432; In re Swinehart, 439 F.2d 210, 213, 169 USPQ 226, 228 (CCPA 1971) ("where the Patent Office has reason to believe that a functional limitation asserted to be critical for establishing novelty in the claimed subject matter may, in fact, be an inherent characteristic of the prior art, it possesses the authority to require the applicant to prove that the subject matter shown to be in the prior art does not possess the characteristic relied on").

II. MANNER OF OPERATING THE DEVICE DOES NOT DIFFERENTIATE APPARATUS CLAIM FROM THE PRIOR ART

"[A]pparatus claims cover what a device ***is****, not what a device* ***does****." Hewlett-Packard Co. v. Bausch & Lomb Inc., 909 F.2d 1464, 1469, 15 USPQ2d 1525, 1528 (Fed. Cir. 1990) (emphasis in original). A claim containing a "recitation with respect to the manner in which a claimed apparatus is intended to be employed does not differentiate the claimed apparatus from a prior art apparatus" if the prior art apparatus teaches all the <u>structural</u> limitations of the claim. Ex parte Masham, 2 USPQ2d 1647 (Bd. Pat. App. & Inter. 1987) (The preamble of claim 1 recited that the apparatus was "for mixing flowing developer material" and the body of the claim recited "means for mixing . . . , said mixing means being stationary and completely submerged in the developer material." The claim was rejected over a reference which taught all the structural limitations of the claim for the intended use of mixing flowing developer. However, the mixer was only partially submerged in the developer material. The Board held that the amount of submersion is immaterial to the structure of the mixer and thus the claim was properly rejected.).*

III. A PRIOR ART DEVICE CAN PERFORM ALL THE FUNCTIONS OF THE APPARATUS CLAIM AND STILL NOT ANTICIPATE THE CLAIM

Even if the prior art device performs all the functions recited in the claim, the prior art cannot anticipate the claim if there is any structural difference. It should be noted, however, that means-plus-function limitations are met by structures which are equivalent to the corresponding structures recited in the specification. In re Donaldson, 16 F.3d 1189, 1193, 29 USPQ2d 1845, 1848 (Fed. Cir. 1994). See also In re Robertson,

169 F.3d 743, 745, 49 USPQ2d 1949, 1951 (Fed. Cir. 1999) (The claims were drawn to a disposable diaper having three fastening elements. The reference disclosed two fastening elements that could perform the same function as the three fastening elements in the claims. The court construed the claims to require three separate elements and held that the reference did not disclose a separate third fastening element, either expressly or inherently.).

IV. DETERMINING WHETHER A COMPUTER-IMPLEMENTED FUNCTIONAL CLAIM LIMITATION IS PATENTABLE OVER THE PRIOR ART UNDER 35 U.S.C. 102 AND 103

Functional claim language that is not limited to a specific structure covers all devices that are capable of performing the recited function. Therefore, if the prior art discloses a device that can inherently perform the claimed function, a rejection under 35 U.S.C. 102 and/or 35 U.S.C. 103 may be appropriate. See In re Translogic Technology, Inc., 504 F.3d 1249, 1258, 84 USPQ2d 1929, 1935–1936 (Fed. Cir. 2007) (The claims were drawn to multiplexer circuit. The patent at issue claimed "coupled to" and "coupled to receive" between various portions of the circuitry. In reference to the claim phrase "input terminals 'coupled to receive' first and second input variables," the court held that "the claimed circuit does not require any specific input or connection . . . [a]s such, 'coupled to' and 'coupled to receive' are clearly different . . . [a]s shown in [the figures of the] patent, input terminals . . . only need to be 'capable of receiving' an input variable for the multiplexer circuit as claimed". Therefore, the specification supported the claim construction "that 'coupled to receive' means 'capable of receiving.'"); Intel Corp. v. U.S. Int'l Trade Comm'n, 946 F.2d 821, 832, 20 USPQ2d 1161, 1171 (Fed. Cir. 1991) (The court held that "programmable" claim language required only that the accused product could be programmed to perform the claimed functionality.); In re Schreiber, 128 F.3d 1473, 1478, 44 USPQ2d 1429, 1432 (Fed. Cir. 1997); In re Best, 562 F.2d 1252, 1254, 195 USPQ 430, 433 (CCPA 1977); In re Ludtke, 441 F.2d 660, 663–64, 169 USPQ 563, 566–67 (CCPA 1971); In re Swinehart, 439 F.2d 210, 212–13, 169 USPQ 226, 228–29 (CCPA 1971) ("[I]t is elementary that the mere recitation of a newly discovered function or property, inherently possessed by things in the prior art, does not cause a claim drawn to those things to distinguish over the prior art"). See MPEP § 2112 for more information.

Conversely, computer-implemented functional claim limitations may narrow the functionality of the device, by limiting the specific structure capable of performing the recited function. Nazomi Communications, Inc. v. Nokia Corp., 739 F.3d 1339, 1345, 109 USPQ2d 1258, 1262 (Fed Cir. 2014) (The claims were drawn to a CPU that can perform processing of both register-based and stack-based instructions. Appellant alleged infringement of the claims based on claim construction requiring only hardware capable of performing the claimed functionalities. Contrasted with the finding of Intel Corp. v. U.S. Int'l Trade Comm'n, 846 F.2d 821, 832, 20 USPQ2d 1161, 1171

(Fed. Cir. 1991), the court found that "[s]ince hardware cannot meet these limitations in the absence of enabling software, the claims are properly construed as claiming an apparatus comprising a combination of hardware and software capable of practicing the claim limitations.").

Computer-implemented functional claim limitations may also be broad because the term "computer" is commonly understood by one of ordinary skill in the art to describe a variety of devices with varying degrees of complexity and capabilities. In re Paulsen, 30 F.3d 1475, 1479–80, 31 USPQ2d 1671, 1674 (Fed. Cir. 1994). Therefore, a claim containing the term "computer" should not be construed as limited to a computer having a specific set of characteristics and capabilities, unless the term is modified by other claim terms or clearly defined in the specification to be different from its common meaning. Id. In Paulsen, the claims, directed to a portable computer, were rejected as anticipated under 35 U.S.C. 102 by a reference that disclosed a calculator, because the term "computer" was given the broadest reasonable interpretation consistent with the specification to include a calculator, and a calculator was considered to be a particular type of computer by those of ordinary skill in the art. Id.

When determining whether a computer-implemented functional claim would have been obvious, examiners should note that broadly claiming an automated means to replace a manual function to accomplish the same result does not distinguish over the prior art. See Leapfrog Enters., Inc. v. Fisher-Price, Inc., 485 F.3d 1157, 1161, 82 USPQ2d 1687, 1691 (Fed. Cir. 2007) ("Accommodating a prior art mechanical device that accomplishes [a desired] goal to modern electronics would have been reasonably obvious to one of ordinary skill in designing children's learning devices. Applying modern electronics to older mechanical devices has been commonplace in recent years."); In re Venner, 262 F.2d 91, 95, 120 USPQ 193, 194 (CCPA 1958); see also MPEP § 2144.04. Furthermore, implementing a known function on a computer has been deemed obvious to one of ordinary skill in the art if the automation of the known function on a general purpose computer is nothing more than the predictable use of prior art elements according to their established functions. KSR Int'l Co. v. Teleflex Inc., 550 U.S. 398, 417, 82 USPQ2d 1385, 1396 (2007); see also MPEP § 2143, Exemplary Rationales D and F. Likewise, it has been found to be obvious to adapt an existing process to incorporate Internet and Web browser technologies for communicating and displaying information because these technologies had become commonplace for those functions. Muniauction, Inc. v. Thomson Corp., 532 F.3d 1318, 1326–27, 87 USPQ2d 1350, 1357 (Fed. Cir. 2008).

For more information on the obviousness determination, see MPEP § 2141.

Samsung Electronics Co. v. Apple Inc.
580 U.S. 53
Supreme Court of the United States
October 11, 2016, Argued; December 6, 2016, Decided

Questions

1. This case involves a long-running dispute between Apple and Samsung. Generally, intellectual property attorneys often overlook the opportunity to file a design patent. It is a very different animal than a utility patent, but as this case demonstrates, in the right circumstances may be quite valuable. In recent years, the law related to design patents appears to be in the process of being rewritten by the Federal Circuit.[260] Also, be aware that the AIA modified sections 171–173 that relate to term and priority. Furthermore, rights under a design patent may overlap with other types of intellectual property rights, such as copyright and/or trade dress (e.g., section 43(a) of the Lanham Act). This overlap is beyond the scope of this work; however, recognize that copyrights may apply to works of applied art (e.g., an ornamental lamp[261]) and trade dress may apply to objects (e.g., shape of a Coca-Cola bottle as an identification of source of the product; also as a form of unfair competition such as "passing off," etc.). Is this decision limited to design patents or does it apply to utility patents as well?
2. While it is true that an article of manufacture may be an end product or a component thereof, why does the statute necessarily imply that, for the purposes of determining damages under § 289, the Federal Circuit approach may not be correct?

   The statute explicitly states:

   > *Whoever during the term of a patent for a design, without license of the owner, (1) applies the patented design, or any colorable imitation thereof, to any article of manufacture for the purpose of sale, or (2) sells or exposes for sale any article of manufacture to which such design or colorable imitation has been applied shall be liable to the owner to the extent of his total profit, but not less than $250, recoverable in any United States district court having jurisdiction of the parties.*

   Thus, the key language appears to be:

   > *Whoever . . . applies the patented design . . . to any article of manufacture . . . shall be liable to the owner to the extent of his total profit. . . .*

   In this case, the so-called component was not available for sale as such from the owner of the patented design. Why does it not make sense

260. *See* Egyptian Goddess v. Swisa, 543 F.3d 665 (Fed. Cir. 2008); LKQ Corp. v. GM Glob. Tech. Operations LLC, 71 F.4th 1383 (Fed. Cir. 2024) (en banc).

261. *See* Mazer v. Stein, 347 U.S. 201 (1954).

to apply the statute, calling for a "total profits" remedy, to the entire article as a whole? In fact, one could argue that was the ostensible intent since Congress knew that such articles might be components of a larger product, as perhaps implied by the language "total profit." What reasoning does the Court apply, and do you agree?

3. Is the damages statute for a design patent the same statute regarding damages for a utility patent or is it a different statute? Note the language of subsection 171(b) that states: "*The provisions of this title relating to patents for inventions shall apply to patents for designs, except as otherwise provided.*" How do you interpret this statutory language?
4. The court applies a broad interpretation to "articles of manufacture." Other than processes, what might be excluded from "article of manufacture"—that is, appears covered under a different statutory category of § 101? Does an article of manufacture include machines or apparatuses? What might be some differences, if any? Does the Court suggest or imply differences or not? Is an iPhone a machine or an apparatus or an article of manufacture? Does an article of manufacture include a composition of matter? Again, what might be some differences, if any? Does the Court suggest or imply differences or not? Is a COVID vaccine an article of manufacture? Is it a composition of matter? Is there subject matter that might legally fall into several categories of § 101?
5. Given that the Court ruled that "the term 'article of manufacture' is broad enough to embrace both a product sold to a consumer and a component of that product, whether sold separately or not,"[262] how is one to apply § 289? Any ideas or thoughts on how it should be applied depending on the situation? Also, is it relevant whether a component potentially the subject matter of a design patent is ever seen by a consumer of the end product, for example? Why or why not?
6. The Court states:

> Patent protection is available for a "new, original and ornamental design for an article of manufacture." 35 U. S. C. § 171(a). A patentable design "gives a peculiar or distinctive appearance to the manufacture, or article to which it may be applied, or to which it gives form." *Gorham Co.* v. *White*, 81 U.S. 511, 14 Wall. 511, 525, 20 L. Ed. 731 (1872). This Court has explained that a design patent is infringed "if, in the eye of an ordinary observer, giving such attention as a purchaser

262. Samsung Elecs. Co. v. Apple Inc., 580 U.S. 53, 60 (2016).

> usually gives, two designs are substantially the same." *Id.*, at 528, 14 Wall. 511, 525, 20 L. Ed. 731.[263]

Apple's design patent D604,305 is provided with the *Samsung v. Apple* case. What part of the patent is the claim? Observe that the patent went through reexamination, which is available for both design patents and utility patents. Why do you think Apple had this patent reexamined?

* * *

Article of manufacture claims are like apparatus claims. In fact, one may wonder what the difference might be to recite, for the same claim body:

"An apparatus comprising:" versus
"An article comprising:"

The answer may be more an issue of style.[264] However, although the preamble is not usually limiting,[265] it is good practice to ensure that the words you use in the preamble are broad enough to encompass all potential infringements. Hence, out of caution, "apparatus" may often be favored, as arguably broader.

With that said, there are times when "article" is more descriptive and consequently more appropriate than "apparatus." An article is thought of more as a physical object without moving parts, in comparison with an apparatus.[266]

The rules discussed for an "apparatus" or "machine" claim are the same for an article of manufacture. Obey the single infringer rule; include a preamble, transition word, and body; include a period at the end; and be mindful of the difference between function, structure, and process.

Beauregard Claims

Understand how to draft and use Beauregard claims.

MPEP § 2111.05

2111.05 Functional and Nonfunctional Descriptive Material [R-07.2022]

USPTO personnel must consider all claim limitations when determining patentability of an invention over the prior art. In re Gulack, 703 F.2d 1381, 1385, 217 USPQ 401, 403–04 (Fed. Cir. 1983). Since a claim must be read as a whole, USPTO

263. *Id.* at 55–56.
264. *See* MPEP, *supra* note 10, § 2106.03.
265. *See, e.g.*, Catalina Mktg. Int'l v. Coolsavings.com, Inc., 289 F.3d 801 (Fed. Cir. 2002).
266. *See* MPEP, *supra* note 10, § 2106.03.

personnel may not disregard claim limitations that include printed matter. See Id. at 1384, 217 USPQ at 403; see also Diamond v. Diehr, 450 U.S. 175, 191, 209 USPQ 1, 10 (1981). The first step of the printed matter analysis is the determination that the limitation in question is in fact directed toward printed matter. "Our past cases establish a necessary condition for falling into the category of printed matter: a limitation is printed matter only if it claims the content of information." See In re DiStefano, 808 F.3d 845, 848, 117 USPQ2d 1265, 1267 (Fed. Cir. 2015). "[O]nce it is determined that the limitation is directed to printed matter, [the examiner] must then determine if the matter is functionally or structurally related to the associated physical substrate, and only if the answer is 'no' is the printed matter owed no patentable weight." Id. at 850, 117 USPQ2d at 1268. If a new and nonobvious functional relationship between the printed matter and the substrate does exist, the examiner should give patentable weight to printed matter. See In re Lowry, 32 F.3d 1579, 1583–84, 32 USPQ2d 1031, 1035 (Fed. Cir. 1994); In re Ngai, 367 F.3d 1336, 70 USPQ2d 1862 (Fed. Cir. 2004); In re Gulack, 703 F.2d 1381, 1385, 217 USPQ 401, 403–04 (Fed. Cir. 1983). The rationale behind the printed matter cases, in which, for example, written instructions are added to a known product, has been extended to method claims in which an instructional limitation is added to a method known in the art. Similar to the inquiry for products with printed matter thereon, in such method cases the relevant inquiry is whether a new and nonobvious functional relationship with the known method exists. See In re DiStefano, 808 F.3d 845, 117 USPQ2d 1265 (Fed. Cir. 2015); In re Kao, 639 F.3d 1057, 1072–73, 98 USPQ2d 1799, 1811–12 (Fed. Cir. 2011); King Pharmaceuticals Inc. v. Eon Labs Inc., 616 F.3d 1267, 1279, 95 USPQ2d 1833, 1842 (Fed. Cir. 2010).

I. DETERMINING WHETHER A FUNCTIONAL RELATIONSHIP EXISTS BETWEEN PRINTED MATTER AND ASSOCIATED SUBSTRATE

A. EVIDENCE SUPPORTING A FUNCTIONAL RELATIONSHIP

To be given patentable weight, the printed matter and associated product must be in a functional relationship. A functional relationship can be found where the printed matter performs some function with respect to the product to which it is associated. See Lowry, 32 F.3d at 1584, 32 USPQ2d at 1035 (citing Gulack, 703 F.2d at 1386, 217 USPQ at 404). For instance, indicia on a measuring cup perform the function of indicating volume within that measuring cup. See In re Miller, 418 F.2d 1392, 1396, 164 USPQ 46, 49 (CCPA 1969). A functional relationship can also be found where the product performs some function with respect to the printed matter to which it is associated. For instance, where a hatband places a string of numbers in a certain physical relationship to each other such that a claimed algorithm is satisfied due to the physical structure of the hatband, the hatband performs a function with respect to the string of numbers. See Gulack, 703 F.2d at 1386–87, 217 USPQ at 405.

B. EVIDENCE AGAINST A FUNCTIONAL RELATIONSHIP

Where a product merely serves as a support for printed matter, no functional relationship exists. These situations may arise where the claim as a whole is directed towards conveying a message or meaning to a human reader independent of the supporting product. For example, a hatband with images displayed on the hatband but not arranged in any particular sequence was found to only serve as support and display for the printed matter. See Gulack, 703 F.2d at 1386, 217 USPQ at 404. Another example in which a product merely serves as a support would occur for a deck of playing cards having images on each card. See In re Bryan, 323 Fed. App'x 898 (Fed. Cir. 2009) (unpublished). In Bryan the applicant asserted that the printed matter allowed the cards to be "collected, traded, and drawn"; "identify and distinguish one deck of cards from another"; and "enable[] the card to be traded and blind drawn". However, the court found that these functions do not pertain to the structure of the apparatus and were instead drawn to the method or process of playing a game. See also Ex parte Gwinn, 112 USPQ 439, 446–47 (Bd. Pat. App. & Int. 1955), in which the invention was directed to a set of dice by means of which a game may be played. The claims differed from the prior art solely by the printed matter in the dice. The claims were properly rejected on prior art because there was no new feature of physical structure and no new relation of printed matter to physical structure. For example, a claimed measuring tape having electrical wiring information thereon, or a generically claimed substrate having a picture of a golf ball thereupon, would lack a functional relationship as the claims as a whole are directed towards conveying wiring information (unrelated to the measuring tape) or an aesthetically pleasing image (unrelated to the substrate) to the reader. Additionally, where the printed matter and product do not depend upon each other, no functional relationship exists. For example, in a kit containing a set of chemicals and a printed set of instructions for using the chemicals, the instructions are not related to that particular set of chemicals. In re Ngai, 367 F.3d at 1339, 70 USPQ2d at 1864.

II. FUNCTIONAL RELATIONSHIP BETWEEN PRINTED MATTER AND ASSOCIATED SUBSTRATE MUST BE NEW AND NONOBVIOUS

Once a functional relationship between the product and associated printed matter is found, the investigation shifts to the determination of whether the relationship is new and nonobvious. For example, a claim to a color-coded indicia on a container in which the color indicates the expiration date of the container may give rise to a functional relationship. The claim may, however, be anticipated by prior art that reads on the claimed invention, or by a combination of prior art that teaches the claimed invention.

III. MACHINE-READABLE MEDIA

When determining the scope of a claim directed to a computer-readable medium containing certain programming, the examiner should first look to the relationship between the programming and the intended computer system. Where the programming performs some function with respect to the computer with which it is associated, a functional relationship will be found. For instance, a claim to computer-readable medium programmed with attribute data objects that perform the function of facilitating retrieval, addition, and removal of information in the intended computer system, establishes a functional relationship such that the claimed attribute data objects are given patentable weight. See Lowry, 32 F.3d at 1583–84, 32 USPQ2d at 1035.

However, where the claim as a whole is directed to conveying a message or meaning to a human reader independent of the intended computer system, and/or the computer-readable medium merely serves as a support for information or data, no functional relationship exists. For example, a claim to a memory stick containing tables of batting averages, or tracks of recorded music, utilizes the intended computer system merely as a support for the information. Such claims are directed toward conveying meaning to the human reader rather than towards establishing a functional relationship between recorded data and the computer.

A claim directed to a computer readable medium storing instructions or executable code that recites an abstract idea must be evaluated for eligibility under 35 U.S.C. 101. See MPEP § 2106.

MPEP § 2112.01 (III)

III. PRODUCT CLAIMS—NONFUNCTIONAL PRINTED MATTER DOES NOT DISTINGUISH CLAIMED PRODUCT FROM OTHERWISE IDENTICAL PRIOR ART PRODUCT

Where the only difference between a prior art product and a claimed product is printed matter that is not functionally related to the product, the content of the printed matter will not distinguish the claimed product from the prior art. In re Ngai, 367 F.3d 1336, 1339, 70 USPQ2d 1862, 1864 (Fed. Cir. 2004) (Claim at issue was a kit requiring instructions and a buffer agent. The Federal Circuit held that the claim was anticipated by a prior art reference that taught a kit that included instructions and a buffer agent, even though the content of the instructions differed, explaining "[i]f we were to adopt [applicant's] position, anyone could continue patenting a product indefinitely provided that they add a new instruction sheet to the product."). See also In re Gulack, 703 F.2d 1381, 1385–86, 217 USPQ 401, 404 (Fed. Cir. 1983) ("Where the printed matter is not functionally related to the substrate, the printed matter will not distinguish the invention from the prior art in terms of patentability. . . . [T]he critical question is whether there exists any new and unobvious functional relationship between the printed matter and the substrate."); In re Miller, 418 F.2d 1392, 1396 (CCPA 1969) (finding a new and nonobvious relationship between a measuring cup and writing showing how to "half" a recipe); In re Seid, 161 F.2d 229, 73 USPQ

431 (CCPA 1947) (matters relating to ornamentation only which have no mechanical function cannot be relied upon to patentably distinguish the claimed invention from the prior art); In re Xiao, 462 Fed. App'x 947, 950–51 (Fed. Cir. 2011) (non-precedential) (affirming an obviousness rejection of claims directed to a tumbler lock that used letters instead of numbers and had a wild-card label instead of one of the letters); In re Bryan, 323 Fed. App'x 898, 901 (Fed. Cir. 2009) (non-precedential) (printed matter on game cards bears no new and nonobvious functional relationship to game board).

The court has extended the rationale in the printed matter cases, in which, for example, written instructions are added to a known product, to method claims in which "an instruction limitation" (i.e., a limitation "informing" someone about the existence of an inherent property of that method) is added to a method known in the art. King Pharmaceuticals, Inc. v. Eon Labs, Inc., 616 F.3d 1267, 1279, 95 USPQ2d 1833, 1842 (2010). Similar to the inquiry for products with printed matter thereon, for such method cases the relevant inquiry is whether a new and nonobvious functional relationship with the known method exists. In King Pharma, the court found that the relevant determination is whether the "instruction limitation" has a "new and unobvious functional relationship" with the known method of administering the drug with food. Id. The court held that the relationship was non-functional because "[i]nforming a patient about the benefits of a drug in no way transforms the process of taking the drug with food." Id. That is, the actual method of taking a drug with food is the same regardless of whether the patient is informed of the benefits. Id. "In other words, the 'informing' limitation 'in no way depends on the method, and the method does not depend on the 'informing' limitation.'" Id. (citing In re Ngai, 367 F.3d 1336, 1339 (Fed. Cir. 2004)); see also In re Kao, 639 F.3d 1057, 1072–73, 98 USPQ2d 1799, 1811–12 (Fed. Cir. 2011).

In re Lowry
32 F.3d 1579
United States Court of Appeals for the Federal Circuit
August 26, 1994, Decided

In re Beauregard
53 F.3d 1583
United States Court of Appeals for the Federal Circuit
May 12, 1995, Decided

Questions

1. These cases have the printed matter doctrine underlying them. How is the printed matter doctrine relevant? Why does the printed matter doctrine not apply to the printed matter in *Lowry*?

2. What is the difference between functional and nonfunctional printed matter?
3. *In re Beauregard* does not provide the claims at issue. However, computer readable media (CRM) claims have been described by patent practitioners as an example of a Beauregard type of patent claim. What is the difference between a Beauregard claim and the claims at issue in *In re Lowry*?
4. Technically, *In re Beauregard* is not a decided case.[267] Why do you think Beauregard-type claims have not been challenged in litigation? Why do you think Beauregard claims on their face (e.g., as a claiming style) have not been challenged as being directed to an abstract idea?
5. Into which class or category of claim type from § 101 does a Beauregard claim fall? Could it be considered an apparatus? Why or why not?
6. With respect to protecting computer software, what advantages do Beauregard claims have over method claims or apparatus claims?
7. When it comes to CRM claims, why do you think it is commonplace to recite "non-transitory"?[268]

* * *

35 U.S.C. § 101 is the statutory source for court pronouncements regarding what is statutory subject matter—that is, subject matter that is capable of being claimed by a patent claim. A line of Supreme Court cases[269] has indicated that mathematical algorithms are not patentable subject matter. However, this line of authority, for a while, left unclear whether software, for example computer programs, was patentable subject matter.

Today, although the Supreme Court has not specifically opined on the latter issue, it is generally accepted, based both on court decisions and on PTO policy, that computer programs are an acceptable subject for patent claiming. To many, the case *In re Beauregard*,[270] which has led to a particular claiming style referred to as "Beauregard" claims, was an important turning point.

In some ways, it is ironic, because there is no Federal Circuit decision in the *Beauregard* case itself; however, many people believe they know how the case would have come out if the Federal Circuit had decided it—in favor of the patentee. The case itself was between IBM and the PTO over a claiming

267. *See, e.g.*, *Ex parte* Bo Li, No. 2008-2131 (B.P.A.I. Nov. 6, 2008).
268. *See In re* Nuijten, 515 F.3d 1361 (Fed. Cir. 2008); *see Ex parte* Mewherter, No. 2012-007692 (P.T.A.B. May 8, 2013).
269. *See* Diamond v. Diehr, 450 U.S. 175 (1981).
270. 53 F.3d 1583 (Fed. Cir. 1995).

style that claimed software embodied on a storage medium of some sort, such as a floppy, disk, or CD. Here is one example of such a claim:

I claim:

1. An article comprising: a storage medium having stored thereon, instructions, that when executed, result in performance of the following method:

   Action A;

   Action B;

   Action C.

The PTO, at the time, would likely have taken the position that a claim like this one constitutes unpatentable subject matter, like the position it initially took in the *Beauregard* case itself.

However, while the case was on appeal before the Federal Circuit and waiting to be heard, the patent commissioner asked that the case be dismissed, settling the dispute. Soon after that occurred, in 1996, the PTO then published guidelines regarding this claim type.[271] Since then, probably tens of thousands, if not hundreds of thousands or even millions, of patents have issued from the PTO containing such so-called Beauregard claims.[272]

One advantage of employing Beauregard claims, of course, is that it provides the capability to pursue an infringer where the infringement occurs because infringing software is merely stored, such as on a server, a hard drive, a CD, or even a floppy. Therefore, it is recommended that Beauregard claims nearly always be employed in patent applications where a potential embodiment of the invention includes software. It is also noted that several different forms of Beauregard claims are possible. The form of such a claim from the prior section is improved in the explanation that follows.

It is also noted that another similar claim type had at one time cropped up as well, although it was quite experimental at the time it was introduced. Some refer to these as "propagating signal" claims. The idea here was to claim the signals themselves as subject matter—that is, "signals per se."

271. *See* MPEP, *supra* note 10, § 2106.
272. This is an educated guess, not based on any careful study.

Although, as with Beauregard claims, such claims have many potential forms, one example of such a claim might be:

I claim:

1. A signal comprising: propagating energy that, when received, results in performance of the following method:

   Action A;

   Action B;

   Action C.

However, as to the latter claim type, it was ultimately ruled to be nonstatutory.[273] Use of this claim type, therefore, of course, is not recommended.

The general idea of a Beauregard or CRM claim is to claim software stored on a "storage medium," such as on a flash drive, a hard disk drive, and so on. However, the claim recites features of the software in a manner so that it is clear the software is *not* operating, analogous to the manner of claiming previously mentioned for apparatus claims. These claims have become quite commonly used. This is most likely because anyone in the chain of distribution of the software can be sued. Software is always stored on some type of storage medium.

Although most of these claims refer to a "machine readable storage medium" or "computer readable storage medium," a question may be whether this is narrower than needed. Why not just recite "storage medium"?

Similarly, a lot of examples do not clearly distinguish the claim preamble from the claim body. Some claims, for example, recite "A computer readable storage medium having stored thereon executable computer instructions comprising . . . ."

In this latter claim, is the transition word "having" or is it "comprising"? If it is "having," then the claim is subject to the argument that it is not an "open format claim." Furthermore, is this format nonstatutory because "computer readable storage medium" is the preamble and, consequently, not necessarily limiting? Recall that the Federal Circuit never resolved the issue regarding whether the claim in the *Beauregard* case was necessarily statutory.

---

273. *See In re* Nuijten, 500 F.3d 1346 (Fed. Cir. 2007).

Consider this hypothetical claim example:

I claim:

1. A storage medium having stored thereon computer readable software instructions that, when executed by a computer, cause to be performed a method of transmitting signals over a network comprising:

   Action A;

   Action B;

   Action C.

From the face of this claim, it is not entirely clear whether the entire preamble is "a storage medium" or whether it is everything that precedes the word "comprising." One problem with this ambiguity is that it permits an opponent to take the position that best suits his or her case and it permits a court to go along with that position. As previously indicated, preambles are not always limiting, whereas the words in the body of the claim are.[274] Thus, in this example, it is not entirely clear whether the words between "having" and "comprising" necessarily limit the scope of the claim or not.

A clearer approach would be to recite:

I claim:

An article comprising:

a storage medium including stored thereon . . .

Here, it is clear that "comprising" is the transition word and that "storage medium" is within the claim body.

Another issue that may arise with this claim type is whether it might be interpreted to cover "signals per se,"[275] an issue discussed as nonstatutory previously. This concern is based in part on the notion that the PTO is permitted

274. See Chapter 3, addressing the patent claim preamble and patent claim body for a patent claim.

275. *See Nuijten*, 500 F.3d 1346.

to apply the broadest reasonable interpretation to a claim. In theory, perhaps a wire transmitting an electrical signal along it, as a type of transitory storage medium for the signal, would qualify as a "storage medium." Whether this is a real concern or not, some examiners will not issue a Beauregard claim unless it recites "nontransitory," so that it clearly does not cover signals per se. For this reason, it is a good idea to describe a "nontransitory storage medium" in your specification so that there is clear written description support, if needed, for the following:

I claim:

An article comprising:

a nontransitory storage medium including stored thereon executable instructions to . . .

Appreciate that "nontransitory" does not exclude memory states stored on a *temporary* basis (versus a *transitory* basis), as is done with RAM, for example. However, clarifying this in the specification would be prudent.

Another issue to appreciate is that the language of the claim reciting features of the software may be functional, raising the issues described regarding structural and functional language.[276]

Fortunately, there is another formulation for a Beauregard claim that may address this concern. It uses a concept explained previously with respect to method claims. Method claims are more difficult to attack as being functional because they recite "acts" or "actions."[277] Hence, a Beauregard claim might, instead, have the following form:

I claim:

1. An article comprising: a nontransitory storage medium;

   wherein the storage medium includes stored thereon executable instructions; and

---

276. See discussion of structural versus functional claiming earlier in this chapter.

277. See earlier in this chapter discussing functionality in the context of method of using claims.

wherein the instructions are executable to perform a method comprising the following:

Action A;

Action B; and

Action C.

This may, to a large extent, address the functionality issue. One may wonder if this claim could be attacked as having unclear scope for mixing method claim terminology with apparatus claim terminology, a potential indefiniteness issue previously raised.[278] However, at least two Federal Circuit cases addressed a similar issue. These cases provide a strong reasoned basis for concluding that such a claim as the preceding would not be indefinite for mixing statutory classes if carefully drafted.[279]

To demonstrate this, recall Example 2.11 similar to this method claim as an illustration:

I claim:

A method comprising:

emulating one or more network devices of at least a second broadcast domain;

encapsulating one or more signal packets from at least a first broadcast domain to be directed to a network device of the at least a second broadcast domain; and

communicating the encapsulated one or more signal packets to at least one tunnel server.

---

278. *See, e.g.*, IPXL Holdings, L.L.C. v. Amazon.com, Inc., 430 F.3d 1377, 1384 (Fed. Cir. 2005). See also Chapter 6, addressing mixing statutory classes.

279. *See* Microprocessor Enhancement Corp. v. Tex. Instruments Inc., 520 F.3d 1367 (Fed. Cir. 2008); HTC Corp. v. IPCom GmbH & Co., 667 F.3d 1270, 101 U.S.P.Q.2d 1518 (Fed. Cir. 2012).

Using the alternate Beauregard claim format immediately preceding, a Beauregard claim might be:

I claim:

1. An article comprising: a nontransitory storage medium;

   wherein the storage medium includes stored thereon executable instructions; and wherein the instructions are executable to perform a method comprising the following:

   emulating one or more network devices of at least a second broadcast domain;

   encapsulating one or more signal packets from at least a first broadcast domain to be directed to a network device of the at least a second broadcast domain; and

   communicating the encapsulated one or more signal packets to at least one tunnel server.

In some cases, it might be desirable to include more hardware such as:

I claim:

1. An article comprising: a nontransitory storage medium;

   wherein the storage medium includes stored thereon executable instructions; and wherein the instructions are executable by a processor to perform a method comprising the following:

   emulating one or more network devices of at least a second broadcast domain;

   encapsulating one or more signal packets from at least a first broadcast domain to be directed to a network device of the at least a second broadcast domain; and

   communicating the encapsulated one or more signal packets to at least one tunnel server.

Some forms may include additional hardware. Here is an example:

I claim:

1. An article comprising: a nontransitory storage medium;

   wherein the nontransitory medium has stored thereon executable instructions for execution by at least one computing device in which the at least one computing device includes at least one processor and at least one memory comprising at least the nontransitory storage medium; the at least one processor to fetch the instructions from the at least one memory of the at least one computing device for execution on the at least one processor of the at least one computing device; the at least one computing device to execute the fetched instructions on the at least one processor of the at least one computing device; and the at least one computing device to store in the at least one memory of the at least one computing device results, if any, of having executed the fetched instructions on the at least one processor of the at least one computing device; wherein the instructions are executable to perform a method comprising the following:

   emulating one or more network devices of at least a second broadcast domain;

   encapsulating one or more signal packets from at least a first broadcast domain to be directed to a network device of the at least a second broadcast domain; and

   communicating the encapsulated one or more signal packets to at least one tunnel server.

Notice that despite the additional hardware limitations, ultimately the claim is written to cover:

---

1. An article comprising: a nontransitory storage medium; wherein the nontransitory medium has stored thereon executable instructions . . . .;

   wherein the instructions are executable to perform a method comprising the following:

emulating one or more network devices of at least a second broadcast domain;

encapsulating one or more signal packets from at least a first broadcast domain to be directed to a network device of the at least a second broadcast domain; and

communicating the encapsulated one or more signal packets to at least one tunnel server.

Improvement Claims

Understand the risks of claims that expressly call out the improvement when drafting patent claims.

Improvement claims are included as a separate type of claim; however, most, if not all, patent claims represent an improvement. The language of § 101 specifically states (emphasis added): "Whoever invents or discovers any new and useful process, machine, manufacture, or composition of matter, *or any new and useful improvement thereof*, may obtain a patent therefor, subject to the conditions and requirements of this title."

Here, therefore, by improvement claim, we mean a very specific type of claim in which the improvement is *specifically identified*. In the United States, these are referred to as Jepson claims. Europe also employs a similar claim format in which the improvement is introduced with the phase "characterized in that."[280]

The key feature of these claim types is that the preamble recites known prior art. Normally, under U.S. law, a question exists whether the preamble is limiting. However, because, for a Jepson claim, there is a reasonable, if not likely, risk that the preamble would constitute an admission of prior art,[281] a prudent approach would *assume* the preamble *is* limiting.

---

280. Throughout this book, where relevant, comparable provisions from the EPC are provided, particularly those that may have the potential to affect claim drafting.

281. *See* Kegel Co. v. AMF Bowling, Inc., 127 F.3d 1420, 1426 (Fed. Cir. 1997) ("Jepson form allows a patentee to use the preamble to recite 'elements or steps of the claimed invention which are conventional or known.' 37 C.F.R. § 1.75(e) (1996).").

Jepson Claims

37 C.F.R. § 1.75(e)

Where the nature of the case admits, as in the case of an improvement, any independent claim should contain in the following order:

(1) A preamble comprising a general description of all the elements or steps of the claimed combination which are conventional or known,

(2) A phrase such as "wherein the improvement comprises," and

(3) Those elements, steps and/or relationships which constitute that portion of the claimed combination which the applicant considers as the new or improved portion.

MPEP § 2129

III. JEPSON CLAIMS

Drafting a claim in Jepson format (i.e., the format described in 37 CFR 1.75(e); see MPEP § 608.01(m)) is taken as an implied admission that the subject matter of the preamble is the prior art work of another. In re Fout, 675 F.2d 297, 301, 213 USPQ 532, 534 (CCPA 1982) (holding preamble of Jepson-type claim to be admitted prior art where applicant's specification credited another as the inventor of the subject matter of the preamble). However, this implication may be overcome where applicant gives another credible reason for drafting the claim in Jepson format. In re Ehrreich, 590 F.2d 902, 909–910, 200 USPQ 504, 510 (CCPA 1979) (holding preamble not to be admitted prior art where applicant explained that the Jepson format was used to avoid a double patenting rejection in a co-pending application and the examiner cited no art showing the subject matter of the preamble). Moreover, where the preamble of a Jepson claim describes the inventor's own work, such may not be used against the claims. Reading & Bates Construction Co. v. Baker Energy Resources Corp., 748 F.2d 645, 650, 223 USPQ 1168, 1172 (Fed. Cir. 1984); Ehrreich, 590 F.2d at 909–910, 200 USPQ at 510.

Kegel Co. v. AMF Bowling, Inc.
127 F.3d 1420
United States Court of Appeals for the Federal Circuit
September 17, 1997, Decided

Questions

1. Is claim 7 in Jepson claim format? Did the court conclude that the preamble limited the scope of the claim? Did the court conclude that the preamble was known (e.g., constituted prior art)?

2. If the court concluded that the preamble was limiting and that it was an admission of what was known, how did this impact the claim construction, if at all?
3. If the court concluded that the preamble was limiting and that it was an admission of what was known, how did this affect the infringement analysis? How did this affect the invalidity analysis?
4. Was the fact that claim 7 was in Jepson format damaging at all to the invalidity analysis or the infringement analysis?
5. Would your preference be to use claims in Jepson format or to not use claims in Jepson format? Why or why not?
6. Observe that the European Patent Office (EPO) uses a claim format similar to a Jepson format. If this format were used in a foreign counterpart to a U.S. patent, but not in the U.S. patent itself, do you think it could affect a court's claim construction of the claims of the U.S. patent? If so, how? Do you think the foreign counterpart would be considered intrinsic evidence or extrinsic evidence?

* * *

We discuss Jepson claims here. However, we mention improvement-style claims as used in Europe (i.e., the European Patent Convention (EPC)) at the end of this section for completeness.

37 C.F.R. § 1.75(e) defines the structure of a Jepson claim. It states:

> Where the nature of the case admits, as in the case of an improvement, any independent claim should contain in the following order:
>
> > (1) A preamble comprising a general description of all the elements or steps of the claimed combination which are conventional or known,
> > (2) A phrase such as "wherein the improvement comprises," and
> > (3) Those elements, steps and/or relationships which constitute that portion of the claimed combination which the applicant considers as the new or improved portion.

The PTO for years has encouraged the use of Jepson claims, although practitioners are less enamored with this type of claim. The PTO likes this claim format because it identifies in language what is considered to be prior art, as stated in part (1) of § 1.75(e). Practitioners, on the other hand, are wary because cases have held the preamble constitutes an admission of prior art (even if that admission is not correct).[282]

282. *Id.*

Two considerations, therefore, apply here. First, it is essential to confirm that what you believe to be prior art is, in fact, prior art. Second, it is equally essential to draft the preamble with care to ensure it *correctly* characterizes what you have confirmed to be prior art.

Consider Example 4.15. Per § 1.75, a Jepson claim for that example claim might look like:

I claim:

1. An apparatus including a central processing unit (CPU) coupled to random access memory (RAM) via a system transfer bus, wherein the improvement comprises: a memory controller coupled to the RAM;

   wherein the memory controller is capable of initiating burst mode operation based, at least in part, on receipt of a request from the CPU;

   wherein the request is to include a memory address, a word count, and a read or a write control transfer designation; and

   wherein the memory controller is to process the request and take control of the system transfer bus.

A comparison of Example 4.15 with the previously drafted claim illustrates that the primary change was to move elements from the body to the preamble. Also, appreciate the conservative nature of this claim. It, in effect, admits that a computing system including a CPU coupled to RAM via a system transfer bus is known prior art. While this preamble is reasonably broad, it also appears to be factually correct. Furthermore, although memory controllers were known, the claim does not recite "memory controller" in the preamble; however, this stance is defensible because of the additional limitations also included in the claim body.

Recall that while Example 4.15 dealt with a system, Example 4.14 dealt with a component of a system. A tricky aspect of Example 4.14 was to draft the claim so that it was clearly directed to a component, rather than a system, although the claim in Example 4.14, like Example 4.15, recited the CPU and system bus to properly claim the invention. Here, interestingly, a Jepson claim might make distinguishing Examples 4.14 and 4.15 easier to accomplish, such as follows, for Example 4.14:

I claim:

1. An apparatus including random access memory (RAM), wherein the improvement comprises: a memory controller coupled to the RAM;

   wherein the memory controller is capable of initiating burst mode operation based, at least in part, on receipt of an externally derived request from an external central processing unit (CPU);

   wherein the request is to include a memory address, a word count, and a read or a write control transfer designation; and

   wherein the memory controller is to process the request and take control of an external system transfer bus.

With this claim structure or format, it seems clearer that the claim is specifically directed to RAM and a memory controller, especially in light of Federal Circuit law that "when this form is employed, the claim preamble defines not only the context of the claimed invention, but also its scope."[283] However, again, it is also easy to see by inspection that the primary difference is moving RAM into the claim preamble. Likewise, the risk of an inadvertently incorrect admission here is not great since the preamble seems to at most admit that RAM is known.

For completeness, here, these claims could be made to conform to EPC practice by replacing "wherein the improvement comprises" with "characterized in that" as follows, for the claim immediately preceding:

I claim:

1. An apparatus including random access memory (RAM), wherein the RAM is characterized in that it includes: a memory controller;

   wherein the memory controller is capable of initiating burst mode operation based, at least in part, on receipt of an externally derived request from an external central processing unit (CPU);

283. *See* Rowe v. Dror, 112 F.3d 473 (Fed. Cir. 1997).

wherein the request is to include a memory address, a word count, and a read or a write control transfer designation; and

wherein the memory controller is to process the request and take control of an external system transfer bus.

EPO—Two-Part Claim—Rule 43(1)

(1) The claims shall define the matter for which protection is sought in terms of the technical features of the invention. Wherever appropriate, claims shall contain:

(a) a statement indicating the designation of the subject-matter of the invention and those technical features which are necessary for the definition of the claimed subject-matter but which, in combination, form part of the prior art;

(b) a characterising portion, beginning with the expression "characterised in that" or "characterised by" and specifying the technical features for which, in combination with the features stated under sub-paragraph (a), protection is sought.

Component-Level Claims

Understand the difference between component-level . . .

In prior chapters, differences between component-level claims and system-level claims, including examples of each,[284] have been suggested. These concepts arise frequently enough and are important enough that we are providing additional illustrative examples of these concepts.

Here, we introduce an example of some semiconductor technology to highlight this difference in claim types. First, we describe the technology at issue.

A metal oxide semiconductor (MOS) transistor ***body*** *made from silicon may be electrically biased, in this example, by a negative voltage.* The reason, as explained in more detail later, is to reduce noise corrupting analog signals being transmitted via an electrical or electronic switch that includes the transistor. A typical electronic switch, for example, may include an MOS transistor operating as a pass gate and another MOS transistor operating as a shunt gate in close proximity. It was not fully understood originally that these transistors in close proximity in an electrical switch may affect linear performance of the switch due to mutual electrical inductance between the transistors.

284. See Chapter 2, providing various illustrative examples.

In a switch, such as an RF switch, commonly used in cell phones, for example, one transistor, called a pass gate, may be ON to pass an oscillating analog signal (such as in RF transmission or RF reception). However, while that pass gate is ON to pass the analog signal, there is another transistor, referred to as a shunt gate, which is OFF while the pass gate is ON. Conversely, the shunt gate is ON while the pass gate is OFF. Essentially, the shunt gate grounds the switch during the time the switch is off (e.g., while the pass gate is OFF). For example, multiple switches may be in parallel so that some are OFF while others are ON. The technical problem, not previously understood, is that while the pass gate was ON and has a time varying analog signal passing through it, mutual inductance from the shunt gate could corrupt the analog signal propagating through the pass gate. MOS transistors may be P-channel (also called P-type) MOS (PMOS) transistors or N-channel (also called N-type) MOS (NMOS) transistors. In this example, for simplicity, we consider an NMOS transistor embodiment of an electrical switch.

The electrical switch (or modulator, which also employs a similar transistor structure) may be implemented in an IC and the IC may be part of a module. Typically, an electronic switch has multiple signal paths. Typically, for example, a path to pass an analog signal may be implemented as a pass gate. A path to not pass the analog signal, which may be implemented as a shunt gate, again, is an example.

To be more specific, during ordinary operation without the benefit of the invention, holes in the shunt gate transistor typically accumulate near the transistor gate (while the shunt transistor is in the OFF state). Typically, an NMOS transistor is turned ON by applying a positive voltage to the gate. Hence, for the shunt gate, the gate may have zero volts or a negative voltage applied to turn it OFF. However, relative to the drain voltage and source voltage of the shunt gate, that zero or negative voltage attracts holes that accumulate underneath the gate while the shunt transistor is OFF.

While the shunt transistor is OFF, the pass transistor is ON and a time varying analog signal passes through the pass gate. This swing in voltage experienced by the pass gate transistor, as it permits the analog signal to propagate, induces movement in the holes that have accumulated under the gate of the shunt transistor, despite the shunt transistor being OFF, due to the close proximity of the shunt gate transistor and the pass gate transistor. Likewise, as the holes under the shunt gate are induced to move via the varying analog signal passing through the pass gage, that positive voltage movement, in this example, then mutually affects the analog signal, introducing nonlinear electrical effects. These nonlinear induced harmonics reduce the quality of the analog signal. For example, signal corruption due to the mutual induction may cause a signal being received by a cell phone to drop or may cause a signal being transmitted to be dropped at the receiving cell phone. As suggested, however, this signal corruption may be handled *by using an electrical (negative) body biasing of the NMOS transistor of the shunt gate*. The negative body voltage pulls the holes away from the gate. This, therefore, reduces the noise that might otherwise corrupt the analog signal passing through the pass gate (e.g., NMOS transistor). By applying a negative voltage to the body of the shunt transistor, while, for example, the gate is at zero volts, holes that might otherwise accumulate under the gate are then pulled or attracted away from the gate by the negative bias on the transistor body. With a sufficient negative voltage, the holes are sufficiently attracted away from the gate so that the mutual inductance effects described are negligible enough to not interfere with signal transmission and reception.

Example 4.34 is an example component-level claim. The claim covers an NMOS transistor capable of being appropriately electrically body biased. Again, without the strong negative bias claimed, mutual electrical induction effects between the NMOS transistors of an RF switch may result in corruption of the analog signal passing through the switch. Without the negative body bias on the transistor of the shunt gate, charge may accumulate in the body of the transistor, in particular immediately below the gate. Furthermore, the analog signal may induce movement of that charge within the transistor body due to the time varying nature of the analog signal. That charge movement (of holes in this example), occurring in the transistor that is OFF, may then, through mutual electrical effects, corrupt the analog signal passing through the transistor that is ON.

Claim Examples

EXAMPLE 4.34

I claim:

1. A device comprising: at least one N-type metal oxide semiconductor field effect transistor (NMOSFET), the at least one NMOSFET including a source, a gate, a drain, and a body;

   wherein the at least one NMOSFET is further included in an electrical configuration at least to control the at least one NMOSFET transistor to either an OFF state or an ON state;

   wherein the electrical configuration is at least further to electrically bias the body of the at least one NMOSFET at least in a portion of the OFF state of the at least one NMOSFET to a DC voltage level substantially more negative than at least one of the following: ground, the DC voltage level of the source, and the DC voltage level of the drain.

Appreciate that in some respects this claim is rather *specific*, but in other ways it is quite *open ended*. As mentioned previously, good claims achieve a "balance between precision, breadth and vagueness."[285] The claim specifically covers "at least one N-type metal oxide semiconductor field effect transistor." Any device that has an NMOSFET body biased as claimed would infringe. There would not be a reason to bias an NMOSFET body as claimed, other than to avoid the signal corruption explained earlier.

However, while the claim is *clear* as to the type of transistor and to the type and amount of bias on the body, it is quite *vague* about how that bias is implemented. It states: "the at least one NMOSFET is further included in an electrical configuration" and "the electrical configuration is at least further to electrically bias the body of the at least one NMOSFET."

Furthermore, observe the use of the language "at least in a portion of the OFF state of the at least one NMOSFET." This language is to address an issue like the issue of "when" in the *Renishaw* case.[286] It may be a challenge to legally establish that a bias is applied precisely at a particular time, such as the exact time a transistor is in the OFF state. This language makes it clear that such precise timing is not required.

As a claim to a component, this claim is extremely powerful. The transistor may be included in an electrical switch. The electrical switch may be one of many switches on an IC. Although not required for infringement, all the transistors for all the switches on the IC may operate in this manner. Likewise, the IC could be included in a module and the module may be part of a consumer device, such as a cell phone, as simply one example of a consumer device that uses such switches. Note that due to the "comprising," all these things—switch, IC, module, and cell phone, would, at least theoretically, be included within the scope of the claim without being expressly "called out" as such in claim 1.

Claim 1, therefore, carries a threat of an injunction against anyone who manufactures or deals in these parts. Also, since many of these parts are manufactured abroad and imported into the United States, there may also be a threat

285. See Chapter 2, introducing this principle.

286. Renishaw PLC v. Marposs Societá per Azioni, 158 F.3d 1243 (1998). See Chapter 5, discussing the *Renishaw* case.

of an exclusion order from the ITC.[287] Exclusion orders from the ITC are much easier to get than injunctions from a federal court. One problem, however, for such an exclusion order may be how to distinguish infringing product from noninfringing product by inspection. An exclusion order is enforced by U.S. Customs, which must inspect imported goods to find infringing product. Regardless, this is not a bad component claim. One would expect it to worry anyone using this technology without a patent license.

Another issue, however, may relate to monetary damages. One issue is royalty base. Unfortunately, the law of damages for patent infringement may be more of an art than a science. However, typically, damages may be based on a reasonable royalty rather than lost profits.[288]

Relying on the reasonable royalty remedy in the statute requires considering a hypothetical transaction.[289] In that transaction, usually there is a royalty rate and a royalty base. The royalty base represents the value of what the claim covers. So, for a chip that sells potentially for a few dollars, what is the value of a transistor on a chip that may contain tens of thousands of transistors? Considering even that the transistors in the switches of the IC may all be biased in this manner, perhaps, a few cents? Now we consider the royalty rate. Again, this is mostly speculation, but a 10 percent royalty rate might be considered on the high side. Thus, while the claim may pose quite a threat in terms of the ability to potentially stop the manufacturer or distributer, it may be less of a monetary threat, although with high product volume it might be a reasonable monetary threat.

Of course, it is easy to add dependent claims that include higher levels of integration and that would certainly be something to be done. However, quite frequently, in an assertion posture as part of a negotiation, focus is placed on the base claim, unless it is believed invalid due to art, for example. It seems like it might be a challenge to convince someone to ignore the base claim and only consider the dependent claims to determine a royalty base. In a litigation, however, this may arise as a "hypothetical" negotiation, in which many, many factors are considered.[290] The scope of the claim is not irrelevant in this

---

287. See Chapter 5, addressing patent enforcement in the ITC.

288. Lost profits may arise, but usually does so in very specific situations. *See* 35 U.S.C. § 284 (2023). It states, in part: "Upon finding for the claimant the court shall award the claimant damages adequate to compensate for the infringement, but in no event less than a reasonable royalty for the use made of the invention by the infringer, together with interest and costs as fixed by the court."

289. *See* Finjan, Inc. v. Blue-Coat Sys., Inc., 879 F.3d 1299 (Fed. Cir. 2018); Exmark Mfg. Co. v. Briggs & Stratton Power Prods. Grp., 879 F.3d 1332 (Fed. Cir. 2018).

290. See Chapter 6, addressing drafting patent claims with monetary damages in mind.

analysis;[291] thus, as was suggested in connection with Example 2.2 in Chapter 2 and as is treated in Chapter 6, having the base claim directed to an IC or a module may increase the royalty base from a transistor of an IC or module.

System-Level Claims

. . . and system-level claims and the reasons for each.

One may genuinely ask whether an approach of using a system-level independent claim has advantages over an approach in which there is a component-level independent claim. Aspects of the overall system may be added via dependent claims. There are various considerations, but there is no clear answer to such a question. In the previous section, we discuss the possible issue of monetary damages and royalty base; however, given the numerous factors considered,[292] that is far from clear.

One consideration may be that a system-level claim may make it clearer that specific end products infringe, which may be beneficial in some circumstances. If dealing with U.S. Customs, a system-level claim, such as to a consumer electronic device, may be much more likely to be enforced. One would not expect Customs to tear apart end products to look for infringing components so that a system-level claim, rather than a component-level claim, may be desirable. Yet, in theory at least, using dependent claims to cover the system should have this same legal advantage. That is, the dependent claims may be asserted and may also result in an exclusion order from the ITC to be enforced by U.S. Customs. However, an independent system claim might be considered to more clearly be a system.

One might also imagine that a system that is a combination of more elements may at least arguably be more likely to be patentable. In other words, the component interactions may provide potential patentability arguments.[293] Yet, in theory at least, again, using dependent claims to cover the system should have this same legal advantage. That is, those same arguments could be made with respect to dependent claims.

---

291. *See id.*

292. *See, e.g.*, Georgia-Pacific Corp. v. U.S. Plywood Corp., 318 F. Supp. 1116 (S.D.N.Y. 1970), *modified and aff'd*, 446 F.2d 295 (2d Cir. 1971), *cert. denied*, 404 U.S. 870 (1971).

293. Although that potential benefit may not necessarily be immediately apparent in this example, one might, for example, make arguments about the path from and to the antenna of a cell phone for the analog signal that is no longer corrupted and, hence, sufficiently linear for purposes of wireless communications.

Still, a tangible benefit may relate to how patent prosecution typically proceeds for a pending patent application. Examiners usually focus on the independent claims. An independent claim of multiple components might potentially be slightly more likely to be allowed than a dependent claim that amounts to the same elements and limitations. That is, for a simple component claim, the examiner may reject the independent claim and then, in passing, also reject the dependent claims, without much consideration,[294] even though there may be additional technical arguments in favor of patentability for the dependent claims. The patent prosecutor may, in our hypothetical, then, in response to a rejection, make an argument regarding the dependent claims separately from the independent claim, if this happens (i.e., the examiner rejects the dependent claims without much consideration). At that point, however, the examiner may be reluctant to modify his or her decision, having previously rejected all the claims.

Both approaches, consequently, have some merit—that is, an independent claim for the system and a separate component-level independent claim using dependent claims to then cover the system. In some cases, therefore, a drafter may employ both approaches.[295]

Typically, a component claim is more valuable against a component manufacturer for asserting direct patent infringement and a system-level claim is more valuable against a system integrator for asserting direct patent infringement. For example, a system integrator may have a contractual indemnity against patent infringement for components that it purchases. However, typically, such indemnities are limited to the part as sold. One could certainly make a direct infringement claim against the system integrator with a component claim if the component is a part of the system. The component claim would be directly infringed. However, because of contractual indemnities from component manufacturers, a component claim against a system integrator may be less valuable than a system-level claim.[296] The system claim may threaten the core business with no indemnity; whereas the component claim is not directed to a core business of the integrator and the integrator may have a contractual indemnity against patent infringement from the component manufacturer.

---

294. Granted that this may not be legally appropriate, it does happen at times.

295. But not in a manner so that claim scope is identical in all respects between an independent claim of one claim set and a dependent claim of another set, which might otherwise produce a rejection.

296. But see Chapter 6 regarding using higher levels of integration in claim drafting.

Despite these latter potential considerations, if your client is a system integrator, it may generally profess to have no interest in covering a component manufacturer and not want to incur extra claim fees that would be likely (e.g., system claim approach and component claim approach would result in more claims). Specifically, a new application is permitted three independent claims and 20 total claims before incurring extra claim fees.[297] However, as suggested, employing both approaches would provide an ability to go after a component manufacturer/supplier as well as a systems integrator.

Another consideration as to the two approaches might relate to monetary damages. This may matter in several ways, potentially; however, damages law is quite unclear in this regard. By claiming a system, one might, in an appropriate situation, try to argue for purposes of assessing damages that an entire market value effect occurs with sales of an entire system, potentially justifying damages be calculated using the entire system as a royalty base.[298]

In essence, the notion is that the whole is greater than the sum of the parts. This might be a reason to favor a system-level claim as an independent claim, for example, in appropriate situations.[299] However, the entire market value principle is a challenge to establish legally. Damages based on a reasonable royalty tend to more frequently use the "smallest saleable patent practicing unit" (SSPPU), rather than the entire market value, as a royalty base. The SSPPU, here, might be argued to be an IC, for example, which would at least be better than a transistor as a royalty base.

Consistent with the entire market value suggestion, however, one might attempt to draft a claim to potentially increase the royalty base by including language directed to a communications device, such as a wireless phone, for example, that claims a module specifically, assuming that a module is likely to be integrated. A system claim at a higher integration level, such as a consumer product, may be beneficial to assert against end products that use the system.

The strategy here is to increase the royalty base through claim drafting. Several factors affect how a court may determine royalty base for damages;

---

297. *See* MPEP, *supra* note 10, § 607. This lack of interest by a system integrator may *change*, such as with the example of Chapter 2, in which the system integrator's memory supplier expands its business to system integration or is acquired by a system integrator and becomes a direct competitor. *See* Chapter 2.

298. *See* Finjan, Inc. v. Blue-Coat Sys., Inc., 879 F.3d 1299 (Fed. Cir. 2018); Exmark Mfg. Co. v. Briggs & Stratton Power Prods. Grp., 879 F.3d 1332 (Fed. Cir. 2018). *See* Chapter 6.

299. For example, with the sample claims that follow, one might argue that the claimed mechanism to reduce noise in an analog signal drives the sale of a wireless phone. This position is not without merit.

however, one factor is definitely how the invention is claimed.[300] Here, there are a variety of levels of integration one might seek to employ—switch, IC, module, and communications device. The preferred level, of course, depends on likely targets.

It might be appropriate to have several system claims at different levels of integration. The two that appear promising here are the module and the communications device. Modules are common enough these days that a chip manufacturer may still be likely to integrate the chip into a module. Whereas a chip may be worth a few dollars, such as $3, a module may be worth tens of dollars, such as $30 to $50. However, a communications device would be worth hundreds of dollars at least, if not a thousand dollars or more. Thus, in this example, higher levels of integration might increase a potential royalty base by a factor of ten per level, roughly.

Claim Examples

EXAMPLE 4.35

I claim:

1. A radio frequency (RF) module comprising: at least one integrated circuit (IC) chip;

   the at least one IC chip included in the RF module and further including at least one field effect transistor, the at least one field effect transistor including a gate, a drain, a source, and a body;

   wherein, during at least a portion of an off state, the body of the at least one field effect transistor is to be electrically biased to have a voltage level substantially more negative than the lowest voltage level of the following: ground, the DC voltage level of the source of the at least one field effect transistor, and the DC voltage level of the drain of the at least one field effect transistor.

300. *See Exmark Mfg. Co.*, 879 F.3d at 1348 ("Using the accused lawn mower sales as the royalty base is particularly appropriate in this case because the asserted claim is, in fact, directed to the lawn mower as a whole.").

The preceding claim integrates the transistor at the module level, although the IC is also recited. The term "module" is used in the preamble and in the claim body to address the argument that the preamble is not limiting. Note that the claim recites an "RF module," which is probably the most likely implementation. Nonetheless, "RF" is a limitation that may be omitted here and added through a dependent claim. Other limitations might be added, such as via dependencies, that would not make infringement less likely but might add more substance regarding a module such as reciting other ICs, input and output ports, connections, chip or module packaging, and so on. The broadened base claim, without reciting RF, is shown in Example 4.36.

EXAMPLE 4.36

I claim:

1. A module comprising: at least one integrated circuit (IC) chip;

   the at least one IC chip included in the module and further including at least one field effect transistor, the at least one field effect transistor including a gate, a drain, a source, and a body;

   wherein, during at least a portion of an off state, the body of the at least one field effect transistor is to be electrically biased to have a voltage level substantially more negative than the lowest voltage level of the following: ground, the DC voltage level of the source of the at least one field effect transistor, and the DC voltage level of the drain of the at least one field effect transistor.

A similar approach might be employed to claim a communications device. Likewise, features of the communications device might be claimed, such as for a wireless smart phone, a tablet, or a laptop. Likewise, dependencies may include that the IC or module is included in the communications channel of a communications device and may be coupled to an antenna of the device, and so on.

Additional dependencies may also drill down on features of the technology since not all the prior art is necessarily known (i.e., as a hedge against presently unknown prior art). For example, the passing transistor and shunting transistor *switch* structure may be claimed for an electrical switch. Also, implementation technologies likely to be used, such as SOI transistor structure and/or thin-film silicon structures, may be recited, to narrow the claim. Features of the biasing structure might also be recited. Note that similar features could be dependencies for the preceding Example 4.35 or 4.36, illustrating a component-level claim.[301]

Among other lessons, these examples illustrate the importance of understanding the technology being claimed, including aspects such as its technical value, its commercial value, how it might be distributed or sold, how use might be detected, how it might be used, how it might potentially change, and how it might be designed around.[302]

In our examples, we typically have described a technical problem (e.g., here, corruption of an analog signal) that was present before the invention. The claim is then intended to cover a possible technical solution to the technical problem. This approach is more typical of patent prosecution in Europe, but it is a helpful way to think about technology and patent claims.[303] This approach becomes especially important in connection with software-related inventions, discussed later.[304]

Often, claim drafting amounts to making explicit what in layman's terms might be understood without being expressly stated. For example, as one illustration, the language "during at least a portion of an off state" makes explicit what might be understood by a layperson. However, if not clarified expressly with claim language, you are likely stuck with the exact language used, as happened in *Renishaw* with the use of "when." According to the Federal Circuit, the burden is typically on the drafter as the "least cost avoider" to make sure the language is clear regarding its scope.[305]

Means-Plus-Function/Step-Plus-Function Claims[306]

Understand the complex legal issues related to claim language interpreted under 35 U.S.C. subsection 112(f).

In prior sections, means-plus-function and even step-plus-function clauses have come up mostly to address the topic of functional language. Do

301. See later in this chapter, illustrating intermediate and narrow scope claims.
302. See, for example, Chapters 5 and 6, discussing many of these principles/issues.
303. *See* Konkol, *supra* note 49.
304. *See* Chapter 6.
305. *See* Sage Prods. v. Devon Indus., 126 F.3d 1420 (Fed. Cir. 1997).
306. The PTO in March 2024 released a memo to the examining corps regarding means- and step-plus-function claims. *See* Memorandum from Vaishali Udupa, Commissioner for Patents, PTO, to All Patent Examiners, re: Resources for Examining Means-Plus-Function and Step-Plus-Function Claim Limitations (35 U.S.C. 112(f)) (Mar. 18, 2024), https://www.uspto.gov/sites/default/files/documents/112f-memo.pdf.

not forget what you learned from reading previous cases. Now we address additional fine points of such clauses.

O.I. Corp. v. Tekmar Co.
115 F.3d 1576
United States Court of Appeals for the Federal Circuit
May 22, 1997, Decided

Chiuminatta Concrete Concepts, Inc. v. Cardinal Industries
145 F.3d 1303
United States Court of Appeals for the Federal Circuit
May 14, 1998, Decided

WMS Gaming Inc. v. International Game Technology
184 F.3d 1339
United States Court of Appeals for the Federal Circuit
July 20, 1999, Decided

WSOU Investments LLC v. Google LLC
Nos. 2022-1063, 2022-1065, 2023 U.S. App. LEXIS 27763
United States Court of Appeals for the Federal Circuit
October 19, 2023, Decided

Questions

1. The *Tekmar* case preceded the *Seal-Flex* case, and was cited therein. *Tekmar*, like *Seal-Flex*, represents one of the few decided Federal Circuit cases on step-plus-function claims; however, the approach of these cases appears consistent. The appellate court determined that the district court erred in its construction of apparatus claim 17. What was the error? Why was the appellate court able to affirm the ruling as to this claim despite the error by the district court?
2. The appellate court says it could not find structure to go with the means-plus-function clause of claim 17. Why was this not alone fatal to O.I.'s case?
3. Why does the court say it will not apply claim differentiation to claim 17? Do you find this compelling?
4. Note this language by the appellate court regarding applying § 112, 6 to method claim 9:

> If we were to construe every process claim containing steps described by an "ing" verb, such as passing, heating, reacting, transferring, etc. into a

> step-plus-function limitation, we would be limiting process claims in a manner never intended by Congress. Accordingly, we conclude that the "passing" limitations of claim 9 are not step-plus-function limitations subject to the requirements of section 112, Para(s) 6.[307]

Why was the district court's error in this regard here also harmless?

5. Why did the appellate court reject the parallelism argument between the method and apparatus claims?
6. Why did the appellate court reject infringement under the DOE?
7. In *Chiuminatta*, what was the claim construction error made by the district court in ruling that claim 11 of '499 was literally infringed? Why did the appellate court say a ruling under the DOE is also precluded by analysis with respect to literal infringement? What is a situation where the court says there could be infringement under the DOE of a claim with a means-plus-function clause despite there being no literal infringement?
8. What does the appellate court mean by this statement: "An element of a device cannot be 'not equivalent' and equivalent to the same structure. *See, e.g., Dawn Equip. Co. v. Kentucky Farms Inc.*, 140 F.3d 1009, 46 U.S.P.Q.2d (BNA) 1109, 1115–18 (Fed. Cir. 1998) (Plager, J., additional views)."[308]?
9. Although there is no infringement regarding apparatus claim 11 of '499, there is infringement of the method claims of '675. However, that infringement was induced infringement rather than direct infringement. What was the evidence of induced infringement? What was different about the method claims that permitted finding infringement on summary judgment, whereas the apparatus claim was held not to be infringed on summary judgment?
10. What was the issue raised by Cardinal regarding prior art and obviousness and representations made during reexamination of the '675 to the examiner that resulted in allowance? Why did the district court reject the argument? Why did the Federal Circuit agree?
11. In *WMS Gaming*, the court reasoned that in claim 1, the language "randomly selecting one of said plurality of assigned numbers" was necessarily limited to one number. What was the court's basis for that construction? Be aware that the Federal Circuit has applied this

307. O.I. Corp. v. Tekmar Co., 115 F.3d 1576, 1583 (Fed. Cir. 1997).

308. Chiuminatta Concrete Concepts, Inc. v. Cardinal Indus., 145 F.3d 1303, 1311 (Fed. Cir. 1998).

sort of reference back reasoning several times in construing patent claims.[309]

12. In *WMS Gaming*, why did the Federal Circuit say claim 1 was not literally infringed? What test did the Federal Circuit use to determine whether there was infringement of a means-plus-function clause? What was the structure of a means-plus-function clause in this situation?
13. On what basis did the Federal Circuit find infringement by equivalents of claim 1?
14. Why did the appellate court remand the finding of willfulness?
15. As to obviousness of the IGT patent, what did the appellate court say was not shown in the prior art?
16. How did the appellate court view the objective indicia?
17. As to damages, what was the significance of the stipulation by WMS that IGT manufactures slot machines?
18. Why did the Federal Circuit affirm the ruling to not grant a new trial?
19. In *WSOU Investments v. Google*, as to the '045 patent, why did the appellate court conclude that "processor" did not connote sufficient structure to avoid 112, 6? Why did the appellate court rule that the specification did not provide sufficient corresponding structure? Why does that make the claim invalid under 112, 2 (now, 112(b)) rather than 112, 6 (now, 112(f))?
20. In contrast to '045, why did the Federal Circuit rule that the claim in the '875 patent was not to be construed under 112, 6 (now, 112(f))? What was different from the '045 patent claim?

EPO—Guidelines, Part F, Chapter IV, Section 6.5 (2023)

A claim may broadly define a feature in terms of its function, i.e. as a functional feature, even where only one example of the feature has been given in the description, if the skilled person would appreciate that other means could be used for the same function (see also FIV, 2.1 and 4.10). For example, "terminal position detecting means" in a claim might be supported by a single example comprising a limit switch, it being evident to the skilled person that e.g. a photoelectric cell or a strain gauge could be used instead. In general, however, if the entire contents of the application are such as to convey the impression that a function is to be carried out in a particular way, with no

309. For a recent case, see *Salazar v. AT&T Mobility LLC*, 64 F.4th 1311, 1313 (Fed. Cir. 2023).

intimation that alternative means are envisaged, and a claim is formulated in such a way as to embrace other means, or all means, of performing the function, then objection arises. Furthermore, it may not be sufficient if the description merely states in vague terms that other means may be adopted, if it is not reasonably clear what they might be or how they might be used.

As is well-known, 35 U.S.C. subsection 112(f) (previously, 35 U.S.C. § 112, paragraph 6) specifically authorizes by statute a special claim type, but also specifies how that claim type must be construed. The statute states (emphasis added):

> *An element in a claim* for a combination *may be expressed as a means* or a step *for performing a specified function without the recital of structure*, material, or acts in support thereof, and such claim shall be construed to cover the corresponding structure, materials, or acts described in the specification and equivalents thereof.

The statute has been interpreted, in essence, to mean that a claim element (note that a "means-plus-function" claim must be a claim for a combination) may be expressed in the form "means for [function]," such as "means for transmitting," and this functional form is permissible, providing the element is construed appropriately. The element is construed to cover the embodiment or embodiments, more specifically, the "corresponding structure, material, or acts," in the specification, and "equivalents thereof." Thus, if the specification describes a wire coupled to a signal generator, for example, then the "means for transmitting" is likely to be construed to be the wire (and equivalents thereof).

In one sense, the concept of the statute is that you may claim an element in terms of what it does (function), rather than what it is (structural embodiments). For years, patent attorneys were of the view that such claims would obtain a broad construction since such claims were broad on their face and, perhaps, due to the presence of the language "and equivalents thereof" in the statute. However, in the late 1980s and early 1990s, in a sequence of cases, the Federal Circuit made clear that 112, 6 (now, subsection 112(f)) was a claim *narrowing* statute rather than a claim broadening statute.[310]

The rationale was largely based on the history of the statute, which was passed to overrule a Supreme Court case, *Halliburton Oil Well Cementing Co. v. Walker*.[311] The case held functional claims at the point of novelty to be invalid as being overly broad. Thus, in the Federal Circuit's view, while Congress

310. *See* Johnson v. IVAC Corp., 885 F.2d 1574, 1580 (Fed. Cir. 1989).
311. 329 U.S. 1 (1946).

intended to overrule that case, it also intended such claims to be narrow. Thus, the additional range provided by "equivalents thereof" was interpreted to be quite narrow.[312] Furthermore, the Federal Circuit made clear that the term "equivalents" in subsection 112(f) and the DOE are separate and distinct (though related) concepts.[313] To put a finer point on it, the equivalents in subsection 112(f) are technically considered to be *a part of the literal scope* of the means-plus-function claim, whereas the DOE is a type of nonliteral patent infringement.[314]

The state of the law regarding the construction of means-plus-function claims[315] may be stated as follows. To infringe a claim including such a means-plus-function element, the accused product must perform the function recited in the element *identically*. Furthermore, the accused product must be the same as the embodiment or embodiments shown in the specification to be corresponding to that function, or the accused product must be an equivalent to the embodiment or embodiments shown in the specification. Here, "an equivalent" is construed narrowly to mean an insubstantial change that adds nothing of significance to the structure, material, or acts disclosed in the patent specification.[316]

The line of precedent on step-plus-function claims[317] is much shorter than means-plus-function claims, despite the same statutory origin. Thus, subsection 112(f) has also been interpreted to mean that "[a]n element in a claim for a combination may be expressed as a . . . step for performing a specified function without the recital of . . . acts in support thereof, . . ."

According to the Federal Circuit, "step" in a method claim is the corresponding word for "means" in an apparatus claim.[318] Likewise, whereas a means-plus-function element avoids the need to recite "structure" in the claim, a step-plus-function claim avoids the need to recite "acts." While it appears that the Federal Circuit has yet to interpret a method claim to be a step-plus-function claim, the interpretation would be like that indicated earlier for means-plus-function claims.

312. *See, e.g.*, Valmont Indus., Inc. v. Reinke Mfg. Co., 983 F.2d 1039, 1043 (Fed. Cir. 1993).

313. *See id.* at 1043 n.14; *see Chiuminatta Concrete Concepts*, 145 F.3d 1303.

314. See Chapter 5, addressing the DOE.

315. For our purposes, a means-plus-function claim is a claim with at least one means-plus-function clause or element.

316. *See Valmont*, 983 F.2d at 1043 n.14.

317. A step-plus-function claim has a similar definition for our purposes as a means-plus-function claim: a claim with at least one step-plus-function clause or element.

318. *See* O.I. Corp. v. Tekmar Co., 115 F.3d 1576, 1583 (Fed. Cir. 1997).

In an apparatus claim, a means-plus-function element may recite function in place of structure via reciting "means for [function]." In a method claim, due to the statute, a step-plus-function element may recite function in place of "acts" via the claim language "step for [function]." In the absence of the word "step," it is expected, like in the absence of "means," by analogy, an adversary trying to make this argument must rebut a presumption against application of subsection 112(f) by arguing that the claim recites a "function" rather than "acts." That is, by analogy, the language would be argued to be devoid of sufficient "action," and assuming successful rebuttal of the presumption would, therefore, be interpreted as functional.

What might be an example? Consider a method claim element such as: "generating a Fast Fourier Transform (FFT) signal from an audio signal." Is this a function or an act? That is a reasonably tricky question and may depend quite heavily on the specification description. Typically, generating an FFT involves many separate signal processing operations that individually could be "acts." Is the FFT example language (i.e., "generating . . .") referring to all such acts together or is this language more like a function by simply reciting a statement of a result (i.e., "generating an FFT signal . . .")? How would one of ordinary skill interpret this language? The point is that, in general, due at least partially to the inherent nature of language, it may be more challenging to argue that a function is recited versus an act. For structure, on the other hand, it is easier to argue a function is recited even without the word "means." Of course, good specification drafting may also make it challenging to argue that the acts of a method claim be interpreted under subsection 112(f). Again, there is not much case law on step-plus-function elements of combination claims.[319] In general, claim elements interpreted under subsection 112(f) tend to be construed more narrowly than claim elements not interpreted under subsection 112(f). It is, therefore, expected that if subsection 112(f) were applied to the actions of a method claim, resulting in a functional interpretation, it would result in a narrower interpretation of the claim.

However, by their very nature, regarding specifically the action elements of a method claim, such as "transmitting," "encapsulating," and so on, these are less likely to be construed under subsection 112(f). This is based on analysis of the language of subsection 112(f) and the reasoning in Judge Rader's

319. *See* Seal-Flex Inc. v. Athletic Track & Ct. Constr., 172 F.3d 836 (Fed. Cir. 1999). A concurrence by Judge Rader suggests that "comprising the steps of" would not be a problem, but best to avoid such questions by good drafting practice, especially since the concurrence does not bind the court. In fact, one member of the panel felt that the question under 112, 6 was not properly before the court.

concurrence from *Seal-Flex*.[320] Thus, invoking subsection 112(f) to interpret an act or action as a "step-plus-function" element is believed to not be particularly likely. Nonetheless, we recommend avoiding use of the word "step" in claims unless the intention is to deliberately invoke subsection 112(f).

Employing claims that *are intended* to invoke subsection 112(f)—that is, means- and step-plus-function claims—has become an issue surrounded with some controversy. Some lawyers feel strongly that such claims should be avoided due to their narrow interpretation. Other lawyers feel that the law may change again and/or such claims could be useful. There are situations where under current law these claims may have value. We do not necessarily recommend that means- or step-plus-function claims be used or that they be avoided. *Rather, our recommendation is that if you draft claims in a way that is clearly intended to invoke subsection 112(f) (e.g., by using the word "means"), then you should also specifically include an alternate set of claims that is specifically drafted so as not to invoke subsection 112(f).* Likewise, because claims may inadvertently invoke subsection 112(f) without the use of the terms "means" or "step," it is also recommended that you take care to draft claims so as to avoid subsection 112(f) even when not employing the terms "step" and/or "means."

With that said, one potential advantage of employing subsection 112(f) is that it provides the capability to literally cover a wide variety of associated devices where no specific word exists that might ordinarily be employed in a claim to cover them. Thus, if a means-plus-function claim is employed and the *identical* function is met by a set of described devices, so long as it is clear in the specification that the embodiments described *correspond* to the identified function, then such devices should quite arguably be covered literally by the claim.

Employing a means-plus-function claim may also provide a useful technique, for example, to address the issue in *Johnson & Johnston*, where subject matter disclosed in the specification was inadvertently dedicated to the public because the subject matter was not specifically covered by any of the claims of the patent. Claims under subsection 112(f) are interpreted to cover embodiments in the specification. This suggests a reasonable likelihood that a means-plus-function claim may cover an embodiment that you did not specifically otherwise cover with a patent claim.

A major disadvantage of means- and step-plus-function claims is that they are generally construed to be narrow. In fact, as the Federal Circuit has stated, subsection 112(f) was intended as a claim narrowing rather than a claim

320. *Id.*

broadening provision. Rather than working like the DOE, the provision functions more like the reverse DOE.[321]

On the other hand, in a crowded field, a means-plus-function claim may provide some advantages. It is narrow, which may assist in distinguishing from the prior art. However, its scope may nonetheless still be quite arguable since it is a matter of interpretation what features from the specification embodiment(s) are part of the claim. This uncertainty as to scope, again, in a crowded field, may have value. Furthermore, whether something qualifies as an "equivalent" is a question of fact.[322] Thus, one may argue this issue should be decided by a jury, which in some situations may provide a procedural advantage.

One aspect of the narrow nature of such claims is that the recited function of the claim must be met *identically* by the accused product. This leaves little room for so-called play at the joints in terms of the claim drafting. Thus, it may, perhaps, be better to recite broad literal functions when employing such claims, but it is also important to make sure such functions are supported, as discussed immediately following. In contrast, for example for a means-plus-function clause to meet the DOE,[323] the function (under the function-way-result test) only needs to be "substantially similar," something that is looser than "identical." Thus, the Federal Circuit has even suggested that a modified function-way-result test may be employed when construing claims under subsection 112(f) where the function is met identically.[324]

Another narrow aspect of claims under subsection 112(f) is that the specification must include "corresponding structure, material or acts in support thereof," and it must be clear from the specification that such structure, material, or acts *correspond* to the recited function. For example, in *B. Braun Medical v. Abbott Laboratories*,[325] the Federal Circuit determined that a means-plus-function claim directed to a valve was not infringed where a structure included in the specification that would have arguably supported the infringement was not associated with the recited function in the specification (or prosecution

321. *See Valmont*, 983 F.3d at 1042.

322. *See, e.g.*, Overhead Door Corp. v. Chamberlain Grp., Inc., 194 F.3d 1261, 1273, 52 U.S.P.Q.2d 1321, 1329 (Fed. Cir. 1999) (a genuine fact issue arose whether for purposes of 112, 6 the accused software was equivalent to the patent's software; note, however, that whether something is corresponding structure to the function of a means-plus-function clause is a claim construction issue).

323. See discussion in Chapter 3.

324. *See* Kemco Sales, Inc. v. Control Papers Co., 208 F.3d 1352 (Fed. Cir. 2000).

325. 124 F.3d 1419 (Fed. Cir. 1997).

history). Furthermore, in *Cardiac Pacemakers v. St. Jude Medical*,[326] the Federal Circuit invalidated a claim including a means-plus-function clause because the specification failed to disclose any structure for performing the recited function.

Means-plus-function elements are also construed to *only* cover the embodiment or embodiments described in the specification "and equivalents thereof." However, because "equivalents thereof" is construed narrowly, this is another aspect of their construction that makes these claims narrow. An equivalent for purposes of literal infringement under subsection 112(f) is an insubstantial change that adds nothing of significance.[327] Likewise, another narrowing aspect of "equivalents thereof" is the time at which whether something is an "equivalent" is evaluated. The Federal Circuit has stated that this is at the time the patent issues.[328] This is directly in contrast to the DOE, where whether something is an "equivalent" is evaluated at the time of the infringement, usually a later time.[329] Because known interchangeability is a factor in determining whether something is an equivalent,[330] evaluation of this at the time the patent issues with respect to subsection 112(f) should tend to narrow the claim relative to the DOE. On the other hand, with respect to interpreting the literal language of a claim that does not relate to subsection 112(f), the language is interpreted post-AIA as of the time of filing the patent application.[331]

Consistent with the preceding, the DOE has a limited role in connection with claims construed under subsection 112(f). Generally, with only limited exception, for example if a means-plus-function element is not infringed by the accused device, then there also will *not* be infringement under the DOE. As indicated earlier, primary differences that may in only limited circumstances make the DOE applicable include the time of evaluating an equivalent, and that the function element for the DOE need not be met in the accused product identically. However, one important difference between such claims and the DOE that tends to make claims evaluated under subsection 112(f) *less* narrow is that whether the accused product is the same or "an equivalent" is evaluated "overall";[332] in contrast, the DOE is evaluated element by element.[333]

---

326. 296 F.3d 1106 (Fed. Cir. 2002).
327. *See* Valmont Indus., Inc. v. Reinke Mfg. Co., 983 F.2d 1039, 1043 n.14 (Fed. Cir. 1993).
328. *See* Al-Site Corp. v. VSI Int'l, Inc., 174 F.3d 1308, 1320–21 (Fed. Cir. 1999).
329. *See* Warner-Jenkinson Co. v. Hilton Davis Chem. Co., 520 U.S. 17, 29 (1997).
330. *See id.*
331. *See, e.g.*, SmithKline Beecham v. Aptox, 365 F.3d, 1306, 1313 (Fed. Cir. 2004).
332. *See* Odetics, Inc. v. Storage Tech. Corp., 185 F.3d 1259 (Fed. Cir. 1999).
333. *See* Pennwalt Corp. v. Durand-Wayland, Inc., 833 F.3d 931 (Fed. Cir. 1987) (en banc).

An element-by-element analysis usually produces a narrower result than an "overall" analysis, as performed under subsection 112(f).

A risk exists under Federal Circuit law that a claim employing functional language that does not use the word "means" or "step" may, nonetheless, be construed under subsection 112(f). The Federal Circuit, however, has recognized that some words, while functional in nature, have acquired accepted meanings that make them less functional.[334] For example, in *Personalized Media Communications v. International Trade Commission*,[335] the Federal Circuit determined that the language "digital detector" employed in a claim should not be construed under subsection 112(f), reversing the ITC's conclusion to the contrary. Likewise, in *Apex v. Raritan Computer*,[336] the Federal Circuit determined that "circuit" should not be construed under subsection 112(f).

Some of the complex legal issues related to functional language in patent claims emanate from how the Federal Circuit has interpreted subsection 112(f). The provision, to be invoked for an element of a patent claim, appears to require the formulation "means for [function]." However, there is Federal Circuit case law in which subsection 112(f) is invoked to interpret an element of a claim although the word "means" does not appear in the claim.[337]

This may occur, for example, where the claim term or terms at issue do *not* recite sufficient structure.[338] There is a presumption that in the absence of use of "means" in the language of a patent claim, such language should *not* be construed under subsection 112(f), but that presumption may be rebutted. The primary case is *Williamson v. Citrix Online*, decided *en banc*, which referred to use of "nonce words" for elements of a claim, such as the word "module," which in the context of the claim was not a recognized term of art. "Nonce words" refers to made-up words that seek to make a functional limitation appear structural. The Federal Circuit stated (note that subsection 112(f) has replaced 112, 6):

> Our consideration of this case has led us to conclude that such a heightened burden is unjustified and that we should abandon characterizing as "strong" the presumption that a limitation lacking the word "means" is not subject to § 112, para. 6. That characterization is unwarranted, is uncertain in meaning

334. *See, e.g.*, Mas-Hamilton Grp. v. LaGard, Inc., 156 F.3d 1206 (Fed. Cir. 1998).

335. 161 F.3d 696 (Fed. Cir. 1998).

336. 325 F.3d 1364 (Fed. Cir. 2003).

337. *See, e.g.*, Williamson v. Citrix Online, LLC, 792 F.3d 1339 (Fed. Cir. 2015) (en banc); Cole v. Kimberly-Clark Corp., 102 F.3d 524, 531 (Fed. Cir. 1996); *see also* Greenberg v. Ethicon Endo-Surgery, Inc., 91 F.3d 1580, 1584 (Fed. Cir. 1996).

338. *See, e.g.*, *Williamson*, 792 F.3d 1339 (en banc); *Cole*, 102 F.3d at 531; *see also Greenberg*, 91 F.3d at 1584.

> and application, and has the inappropriate practical effect of placing a thumb on what should otherwise be a balanced analytical scale. It has shifted the balance struck by Congress in passing § 112, para. 6 and has resulted in a proliferation of functional claiming untethered to § 112, para. 6 and free of the strictures set forth in the statute. Henceforth, we will apply the presumption as we have done prior to *Lighting World*, without requiring any heightened evidentiary showing and expressly overrule the characterization of that presumption as "strong." We also overrule the strict requirement of "a showing that the limitation essentially is devoid of anything that can be construed as structure."
>
> The standard is whether the words of the claim are understood by persons of ordinary skill in the art to have a sufficiently definite meaning as the name for structure. *Greenberg*, 91 F.3d at 1583. When a claim term lacks the word "means," the presumption can be overcome and § 112, para. 6 will apply if the challenger demonstrates that the claim term fails to "recite sufficiently definite structure" or else recites "function without reciting sufficient structure for performing that function." *Watts*, 232 F.3d at 880. The converse presumption remains unaffected: "use of the word 'means' creates a presumption that § 112, ¶ 6 applies." *Personalized Media*, 161 F.3d at 703.[339]

Some terms, as a result, appear to be sufficiently structural to not invoke subsection 112(f).[340] A few example claim terms in which there have been court rulings indicating some claim terms are structural rather than functional include processor (although a recent case also determined that, for the particular situation, the term "processor" was not used as a structural term of art[341]); circuit or circuitry; and digital detector. There are many other case examples that could also be cited. More specifically, as an example of the reasoning used, the Federal Circuit case *Personalized Media Communications v. Thomson* states:

> "Detector" is not a generic structural term such as "means," "element," or "device"; nor is it a coined term lacking a clear meaning, such as "widget" or "ram-a-fram." *Instead, as noted by the ALJ by reference to dictionary definitions,*

339. *Williamson*, 792 F.3d at 1349.

340. *See* Dyfan, LLC v. Target Corp., 28 F.4th 1360 (Fed. Cir. 2022); Zeroclick, LLC v. Apple Inc., 891 F.3d 1003, 1008 (Fed. Cir. 2018) ("the mere fact that the disputed limitations incorporate functional language does not automatically convert the words into means for performing such functions"). *See Greenberg*, 91 F.3d at 1583 ("Many devices take their names from the functions they perform. The examples are innumerable, such as 'filter,' 'brake,' 'clamp,' 'screwdriver,' or 'lock.'"); VDPP LLC v. Vizio, Inc., No. 21-2040 (Fed. Cir. Mar. 25, 2022) ("processor" and "storage" do not invoke subsection 112(f)) (nonprecedential).

341. *See* WSOU Invs. LLC v. Google LLC, Nos. 2022-1063, 2022-1065, 2023 U.S. App. LEXIS 27763 (Fed. Cir. Oct. 19, 2023).

"detector" had a well-known meaning to those of skill in the electrical arts connotative of structure . . . .[342]

Further, in some other Federal Circuit cases, functional language was permissibly used and did *not* invoke subsection 112(f).[343] These cases suggest that functional language may in some situations be properly and appropriately employed in claims *without* using the means-plus-function format of subsection 112(f) and *without* necessarily being interpreted under that subsection. Presumably, despite the functional language, the claim still recited sufficient structure to avoid invoking subsection 112(f). We recommend using a number of potential approaches if you intend to use functional language (e.g., functional language with and/or without "means"; functional language without "means" and with sufficient structure; functional language without "means" using words that have an established meaning in the art, and nonfunctional language with "sufficient structure" and without a means-plus-function clause) to provide diversity and to signal a different intended scope for the separate claims.[344]

Some features, unfortunately, may not have a feasible way to be claimed structurally. In that situation, it is suggested a mix of structural and functional language be used so that at least the claim language at issue is not entirely devoid of structure. Consider Example 4.14, previously discussed, with claim language such as:

---

342. Personalized Media Commc'ns v. Int'l Trade Comm'n, 161 F.3d 696, 704–05 (Fed. Cir. 1998) (emphasis added). It is noted that *Personalized Media Communications v. International Trade Commission* was decided before the *en banc* decision *Williamson v. Citrix Online*.

343. *See, e.g.*, K-2 Corp. v. Salomon S.A., 191 F.3d 1356, 1363 (Fed. Cir. 1999) (functional language "for substantially preventing movement" did not invoke subsection 112(6)); BASF Corp. v. Johnson Matthey Inc., 875 F.3d 1360 (Fed. Cir. 2017) (functional phrase, "effective to catalyze," did not involve subsection 112(6)); *see also* Enzo Biochem, Inc. v. Applera Corp., 599 F.3d 1325, 1332–33 (Fed. Cir. 2010), *reh'g and reh'g en banc denied*, 605 F.3d 1347 (Fed. Cir. 2010) ("when a claim limitation is defined in 'purely functional terms,' a determination of whether the limitation is sufficiently definite is 'highly dependent on context (e.g., the disclosure in the specification and the knowledge of a person of ordinary skill in the relevant art area)'"); Miken Composites, L.L.C. v. Wilson Sporting Goods Co., 515 F.3d 1331 (Fed. Cir. 2008) (court stated that while the term "insert" has "functional attributes," it was still a structural component); Plastic Container Corp. v. Cont'l Plastics of Okla., Inc., 607 F.2d 885, 203 U.S.P.Q. 27 (10th Cir. 1979), *cert. denied*, 444 U.S. 1018 (1980), *on remand*, 515 F. Supp. 834, 214 U.S.P.Q. 530 (W.D. Okla. 1980), *aff'd in part, rev'd in part*, 708 F.2d 1554, 219 U.S.P.Q. 26 (10th Cir. 1983) ("the idea that functional language ipso facto cannot precisely define novelty in structure was laid to rest in In re Swinehart"); *In re* Swinehart, 439 F.2d 210, 212, 169 U.S.P.Q. 226, 228 (C.C.P.A. 1971) ("[T]here is nothing intrinsically wrong with [employing functional limitations] in drafting patent claims.").

344. *But see* Mas-Hamilton Grp. v. LaGard, Inc., 156 F.3d 1206 (Fed. Cir. 1998) (claim without "means" interpreted under 112, 6 despite a separate independent claim that employed "means").

wherein the memory controller is capable of initiating burst mode operation based, at least in part, on receipt of an externally derived request from an external central processing unit (CPU);

wherein the request is to include a memory address, a word count, and a read or a write control transfer designation; and

wherein the memory controller is to process the request and take control of an external system transfer bus.

The claim language, here, recites "the memory controller is capable of initiating burst mode operation" and "the memory controller is to process the request and take control of an external system transfer bus." The term "memory controller" is likely structural, but the other recited limitations are more functional; however, a memory controller may be argued to support such functions.

Example 4.17, discussed earlier, uses a similar approach reciting "network device," a potentially structural device, but adding functional limitations such as "to emulate," "to encapsulate," and "to communicate." Again, these could be argued to be operations a network device may support. With even more attention, these positions might be made even clearer through claim language and specification language. The point, here, is to pay attention to the use of structural versus functional language in the claim and attempt to hedge your bets so that your claim is not construed to be limited to, essentially, your specification embodiment due to invocation of subsection 112(f).

Previously, in Example 4.34, a component claim was illustrated. Following is Example 4.37, a claim using means-plus-function language.

EXAMPLE 4.37

I claim:

1. A device comprising: at least one N-type metal oxide semiconductor field effect transistor (NMOSFET), the at least one NMOSFET including a source, a gate, a drain, and a body;

   wherein the at least one NMOSFET is further included in a configuration means at least to control the at least one NMOSFET transistor to either an OFF state or an ON state;

wherein the configuration means comprises an electrical bias means to at least electrically bias the body of the at least one NMOSFET at least in a portion of the OFF state of the at least one NMOSFET to a DC voltage level substantially more negative than at least one of the following: ground, the DC voltage level of the source, and the DC voltage level of the drain.

This claim should provide some diversity because Example 4.34 should not be construed under subsection 112(f), while this claim should be construed under subsection 112(f). The analysis of claim scope, therefore, should be significantly different.

It is also a good idea to be mindful of the consequences should your claim, despite your best drafting efforts, be construed under subsection 112(f) during examination or in litigation. In the event subsection 112(f) is invoked, the specification *must* provide sufficient *corresponding* structure for the recited function. That is, for the function or functions recited in the claim, the specification *must* describe *corresponding* structure able to perform the recited function or functions or the claim will be invalid if issued. Here, *corresponding* suggests that the specification is written to clearly associate the function and the structure in the written description in a manner such that one of ordinary skill would comprehend the association.

If an element is construed under subsection 112(f) and the statutory requirements regarding corresponding structure are satisfied, then the claim covers, by express statutory direction, "the *corresponding* structure, material, or acts described in the specification *and equivalents*" (emphasis added).

Thus, the claim, by statute, construed *literally* under subsection 112(f) may be infringed by embodiments in your specification that *correspond* to the functional language or by a *112(f) equivalent* of what is shown in the specification; however, the scope of such *112(f) equivalents* is generally exceedingly narrow.[345]

In the area of software, in particular, the algorithm is considered the structure at issue under subsection 112(f).[346] For this reason, not infrequently, claims interpreted under subsection 112(f) that relate to software are held invalid as not appropriately describing structure or enough structure. That is, generally it is not sufficient to merely provide a functional description, even

345. *See, e.g.*, Valmont Indus., Inc. v. Reinke Mfg. Co., 983 F.2d 1039 (Fed. Cir. 1993).

346. *See, e.g.*, Eon Corp. IP Holdings, LLC v. AT&T Mobility, LLC, 785 F.3d 616, 621 (Fed. Cir. 2015).

assuming that is sufficient to enable one of ordinary skill in the art.[347] Enough detail must be described to, in effect, show possession, which means sufficient detail of *how to perform the function* so that one of ordinary skill *would know the scope being claimed* with respect to implementing the function or operation claimed.[348]

Likewise, if a function is claimed via a means-plus-function clause that is not described to this level, the claim is held invalid. Therefore, in drafting claims, care is warranted to not inadvertently claim a function that is believed to be well understood, such as "transmit a signal" or "receive a signal," but for which the specification does not actually provide an implementation description.

Structure versus Function Revisited

Understand the subtle claim drafting issues related to claiming a device capable of infringing.

Intel Corp. v. International Trade Commission
946 F.2d 821
United States Court of Appeals for the Federal Circuit
September 17, 1991, Decided

Fantasy Sports Properties v. Sportsline.com, Inc.
287 F.3d 1108
United States Court of Appeals for the Federal Circuit
April 24, 2002, Decided

ParkerVision, Inc. v. Qualcomm Inc.
903 F.3d 1354
United States Court of Appeals for the Federal Circuit
September 13, 2018, Decided

Questions

1. *Intel v. International Trade Commission* is a complex case involving many patents and legal issues. We will touch on the most interesting ones.

347. *See* Blackboard, Inc. v. Desire2Learn, Inc., 574 F.3d 1371, 1383–85, 91 U.S.P.Q.2d 1481, 1491–93 (Fed. Cir. 2009); Noah Sys., Inc. v. Intuit Inc., 675 F.3d 1302 (Fed. Cir. 2012).

348. *See Blackboard, Inc.*, 574 F.3d at 1383–85, 91 U.S.P.Q.2d at 1491–93; *Noah Sys.*, 675 F.3d 1302.

There is a dispute regarding the scope of the license between Intel and Sanyo. Here, the issue revolves around so-called foundry rights and the "Sanyo" limitation. How did the ALJ and the Federal Circuit reach the conclusion that the "Sanyo" limitation does not include foundry rights? Note that several later decisions attempt to address this issue of foundry rights in other Intel license agreements, but not as favorably as this case.[349]

2. The '084 patent raises special issues of infringement and validity. What was the validity issue raised? How does the resolution in this case compare with current law for a pre-AIA patent application? What type of claim is claim 1 of the '084 patent? Why did the ALJ rely on the DOE to say that claim 1 was infringed? Why does GI/M try to argue indirect infringement and why does the court reject that position? Regarding infringement, the Federal Circuit stated:

> GI/M also contends that the Commission's finding of infringement under the doctrine of equivalents is incorrect because, although GI/M's "old" design 51 Series EPROMs are *capable* of performing page mode addressing, the EPROMs were never sold to operate in page mode. No customer was ever told how to convert the chip to page mode operation—or even that such conversion was possible. GI/M argues that an alleged infringer must intend its parts to be used in an infringing fashion and cites *Fromberg, Inc. v. Thornhill*, 315 F.2d 407, 415, 137 U.S.P.Q. (BNA) 84, 89 (5th Cir. 1963), in support of its argument. As noted by Intel, there is no intent element to *direct* infringement. *See* 35 U.S.C. § 271(b) and (c). *Fromberg* deals with induced and contributory infringement and is therefore inapposite. Because the language of claim 1 refers to "programmable selection means" and states "whereby *when* said alternate addressing mode is selected" (emphases added), the accused device, to be infringing, need only be capable of operating in the page mode. Contrary to GI/M's argument, actual page mode operation in the accused device is not required.[350]

3. What does this suggest regarding the particular claim formulation used by Intel?

349. *See, e.g.*, Intel Corp. v. ULSI Sys. Tech., Inc., 995 F.2d 1566 (Fed. Cir. 1993); Cyrix Corp. v. SGS-Thomson Microelectronics, 77 F.3d 1381 (Fed. Cir. 1996).
350. Intel Corp. v. Int'l Trade Comm'n, 946 F.2d 821, 842 (Fed. Cir. 1991).

4. How does *Fantasy* distinguish *Intel*?[351]
5. In *ParkerVision v. Qualcomm*, what is the distinction drawn by the appellate court in apparatus claims that recite "capable of" versus those that recite "configured to"?[352] What category do the *Intel* claims fall into? What category do the *Fantasy* claims fall into?
6. In *ParkerVision v. Qualcomm*, why and how does the appellate court distinguish the method claims from the apparatus claims?
7. What do these cases suggest regarding different formulations for functional limitations in apparatus claims? What are the trade-offs regarding validity versus infringement? What does this suggest regarding method claims with respect to these different functional formulations?
8. Why does the appellate court reject ParkerVision's lack of motivation to combine the references for the IPR?

* * *

Use of functional language may be challenging due primarily to 35 U.S.C. subsection 112(f).[353] Some functional terms, however, appear to be sufficiently structural to not invoke subsection 112(f). Further, in some Federal Circuit cases, functional language was permissibly used and did *not* invoke subsection 112(f).[354]

---

351. Compare the analysis in *INVT SPE LLC v. International Trade Commission*, 46 F.4th 1361 (Fed. Cir. 2022), from Chapter 3.

352. Compare the analysis in *INVT SPE LLC*, 46 F.4th 1361, from Chapter 3. *See also* Aspex Eyewear, Inc. v. Marchon Eyewear, Inc., 672 F.3d 1335 (Fed. Cir. 2012); *In re* Giannelli, 739 F.3d 1375 (Fed. Cir. 2014).

353. Note that subsection 112(f) also refers to "materials," suggesting applicability to composition of matter claims as well.

354. *See, e.g.*, K-2 Corp. v. Salomon S.A., 191 F.3d 1356, 1363 (Fed. Cir. 1999) (functional language "for substantially preventing movement" did not invoke subsection 112(6)); BASF Corp. v. Johnson Matthey Inc., 875 F.3d 1360 (Fed. Cir. 2017) (functional phrase, "effective to catalyze," did not involve subsection 112(6)); *see also* Enzo Biochem, Inc. v. Applera Corp., 599 F.3d 1325, 1332–33 (Fed. Cir. 2010), *reh'g and reh'g en banc denied*, 605 F.3d 1347 (Fed. Cir. 2010) ("when a claim limitation is defined in 'purely functional terms,' a determination of whether the limitation is sufficiently definite is 'highly dependent on context (e.g., the disclosure in the specification and the knowledge of a person of ordinary skill in the relevant art area)'"); Miken Composites, L.L.C. v. Wilson Sporting Goods Co., 515 F.3d 1331 (Fed. Cir. 2008) (court stated that while the term "insert" has "functional attributes," it was still a structural component); Plastic Container Corp. v. Cont'l Plastics of Okla., Inc., 607 F.2d 885, 203 U.S.P.Q. 27 (10th Cir. 1979), *cert. denied*, 444 U.S. 1018 (1980), *on remand*, 515 F. Supp. 834, 214 U.S.P.Q. 530 (W.D. Okla. 1980), *aff'd in part, rev'd in part*, 708 F.2d 1554, 219 U.S.P.Q. 26 (10th Cir. 1983) ("the idea that functional language ipso facto cannot precisely define novelty in structure was laid to rest in In re Swinehart"); *In re* Swinehart, 439 F.2d 210, 212, 169 U.S.P.Q. 226, 228 (C.C.P.A. 1971) ("[T]here is nothing intrinsically wrong with [employing functional limitations] in drafting patent claims.").

A line of Federal Circuit authority is directed to claiming a device with a so-called *capability* of infringing. One way to view such cases is as another spin on functional language. It is not uncommon to see language in claims such as "adapted to" and "configured to," in connection with functional language. Other formulations include "capable of," "the capability to," as well as ". . . for . . ." (which is similar to "means for" and may be more likely to invoke subsection 112(f)), and ". . . to. . . ."

There could be issues with some of these formulations, particularly "adapted to" and "configured to." For one thing, examiners do not like them, so they are reasonably likely to be rejected. Second, there is some Federal Circuit law that has construed some of these linguistic formulations narrowly (although, interestingly, without invoking subsection 112(f)).[355] Third, one could make the noninfringement argument that the accused product is not "configured" or "adapted." This might be an especially strong argument in connection with software, which is often configured. Usually the word "adapted," "configured," and so on is not needed. Thus, including it suggests some intent that it have this meaning, which might not be the case.

However, as suggested by cases like *ParkerVision*, these claims with a narrower interpretation may also be more difficult to invalidate. That is, such claims will likely be interpreted that the apparatus is actually performing the function or is ready to perform the function, whereas functional language, like "to x," "for x," or "capable of x," is likely to be interpreted more broadly as presently containing the capability, but in a manner that may involve some type of activation.

One case addressing these functional phrases is *Aspex Eyewear v. Marchon Eyewear*.[356] In that case, the district court had construed "adapted to" narrowly and the construction was challenged on appeal. The Federal Circuit agreed with the narrow construction, stating:

> Aspex's first objection to the court's ruling on that limitation is that it construes the phrase "adapted to" too narrowly; that phrase, according to Aspex, should be interpreted to mean "suitable for" rather than "made to." As the parties have noted, the phrase "adapted to" is sometimes used in claim drafting to carry the broader meaning proposed by Aspex, and sometimes to carry a narrower meaning closer to that proposed by the defendants. *In this case, we conclude that the narrower meaning is correct.*
>
> In common parlance, the phrase "adapted to" is frequently used to mean "made to," "designed to," or "configured to," but it can also be used in a

355. *See Aspex Eyewear*, 672 F.3d 1335; *Giannelli*, 739 F.3d 1375.
356. 672 F.3d 1335.

> broader sense to mean "capable of" or "suitable for." *See* Webster's Third New International Dictionary 24 (1968) ("suited by nature, character, or design to a particular use, purpose, or situation"); 1 Oxford English Dictionary 139 (2d ed. 1989) ("fitted; fit, suitable . . . modified to fit new situations"). The way the phrase is used in amended claim 23 of the '545 patent supports the district court's conclusion that a narrower definition, such as "configured to," applies here. *See Sta-Rite Indus., LLC v. ITT Corp.*, 682 F. Supp. 2d 738, 753 (E.D. Tex. 2010) (construing "adapted to," in context, to mean "designed or configured to," not "having the capacity to"); *Boston Scientific Corp. v. Cordis Corp.*, 2006 U.S. Dist. LEXIS 94329, 2006 WL 3782840 (N.D. Cal. Dec. 20, 2006) (construing "adapted to," in light of patent as a whole, to mean "configured to," not "capable of").[357]

Two years later, the Federal Circuit used similar analysis to reverse and remand the Board's affirmance of an examiner's obviousness rejection. In the case *In re Giannelli*, the court stated:

> The claims of the '261 application specifically require a "first handle portion adapted to be moved from a first position to a second position by a pulling force . . . in a rowing motion." Response to Office Action, No. 10/378,261, at 2 (Apr. 12, 2006). We have noted that, "the phrase 'adapted to' is frequently used to mean 'made to,' 'designed to,' or 'configured to,' . . ." *Aspex Eyewear, Inc. v. Marchon Eyewear, Inc.*, 672 F.3d 1335, 1349 (Fed. Cir. 2012). *Although the phrase can also mean "'capable of' or 'suitable for,'" id., here the written description makes clear that "adapted to," as used in the '261 application, has a narrower meaning, viz., that the claimed machine is designed or constructed to be used as a rowing machine whereby a pulling force is exerted on the handles.*
>
> The written description of the '261 application describes how the position of the handles relative to the primary and secondary lever arms and the resistance mechanism renders them "adapted" to be moved by the user's pulling force. For example, the application states that the exercise machine "enables a user to maintain biomechanical alignment of the user's wrist and forearm during performance of the exercise, while maintaining a consistent resistance applied to the muscles, in the stability of an exercise machine." '261 application, at 3. The location of those handles relative to the other components is one of their structural attributes that enables performance of the rowing motion against the selected resistance. '261 application, at 4 ("The declining, substantially linear path [of the pulled handles] enables the user to maintain proper biomechanical alignment of the force angle being applied to the grip. This allows for a fairly consistent torque application at the shoulder throughout the range of motion of the exercise."). Consequently, the relevant

357. *Id.* at 1349 (emphasis added).

> question before the Board was whether the apparatus described in the '447 patent was "'made to,' 'designed to,' or 'configured to,'" allow the user to perform a rowing exercise by pulling on the handles as claimed in the '261 application. . . .
>
> Because the Board's analysis began with the premise that "adapted to" meant "capable of," its affirmance of the examiner's rejection also contained no explanation why or how a person having ordinary skill in the art would modify the prior art chest press machine to arrive at the apparatus of the '261 application. And because the initial burden was not met, Giannelli was not obligated to submit additional evidence to rebut the examiner's findings of pulling capability. *See In re Rijckaert*, 9 F.3d 1531, 1532 (Fed. Cir. 1993) ("Only if that burden [of establishing a prima facie case] is met, does the burden of coming forward with evidence or argument shift to the applicant."). The Board thus erred in affirming the conclusion of the examiner that the '447 patent apparatus rendered obvious the claimed invention of the '261 application.[358]

Good practice, therefore, suggests avoiding formulations like "adapted to" or "configured to" and the like. Instead, just say "to . . . ," assuming, of course, a broader meaning is desired.

Language such as "capable of" or "the capability to" seems to more often receive a broader scope from courts, as suggested in the previous two cases. This approach to claiming may be quite powerful in some situations. For example, software or semiconductor chips may have many different features. A customer may not necessarily use or even be aware of all such features. Yet, it may be powerful to draft a claim such that so long as the software or chip, for example, has the capability to perform the feature, direct patent infringement is present.

Two cases that relate to this issue are *Intel v. International Trade Commission*[359] and *Fantasy Sports v. SportsLine*.[360] A crucial issue seems to be the presence of a limitation that may be met by an accused product even if not activated or used by a customer, as an example.

In general, the topic of claiming a device capable to infringe may be tricky in some situations. In the *Intel* case, an early and influential case on this topic, the feature was so-called page mode addressing. Generally, to use page mode addressing required setting a bit in a chip. However, the language of the claim was such that as long as the capability to use page mode addressing was

---

358. *Giannelli*, 739 F.3d at 1380–81 (emphasis added).
359. 946 F.2d 821, 832 (Fed. Cir. 1991).
360. 287 F.3d 1108 (Fed. Cir. 2002).

present in a device, such as enabled by setting a bit, then infringement was present *even if the bit was not actually set.*

The claim at issue recited:

---

1. In an integrated circuit (IC), read-only memory having n address lines used for accessing p words in one addressing mode, an improvement for providing an alternate addressing mode, comprising:

   programmable selection means for selecting said alternate addressing mode; storage means for storing at least one signal; an address buffer coupled to one of said n address lines, said buffer also being coupled to said storage means and said programmable selection means, the output of said buffer being controlled by said signal stored in said storage means when said alternate addressing mode is selected, whereby when said alternate addressing mode is selected said p words in said memory may be selected with less than n address signals.

Cleverly, the claim recited: "programmable selection means . . . when said alternate addressing mode is selected said p words in said memory may be selected with less than n address signals." The issue, therefore, was whether the alleged infringing product necessarily infringed if it had this alternative addressing mode capability, but the mode was not being used.

In affirming the ITC ruling finding infringement, the Federal Circuit stated:

> Both the multiplexer and the address buffer use an addressing signal to select a particular memory cell from an incoming address pin or latch. Thus, the accused circuits infringe claim 1 under the doctrine of equivalents because they perform substantially the same function in substantially the same way to obtain the same result as the invention claimed in the '084 patent. . . .
>
> GI/M also contends that the Commission's finding of infringement under the doctrine of equivalents is incorrect because, although GI/M's "old" design 51 Series EPROMs are capable of performing page mode addressing, the EPROMs were never sold to operate in page mode. No customer was ever told how to convert the chip to page mode operation—or even that such conversion was possible. GI/M argues that an alleged infringer must intend its parts to be used in an infringing fashion and cites *Fromberg, Inc. v. Thornhill*, 315 F.2d 407, 415, 137 USPQ 84, 89 (5th Cir. 1963), in support of its argument. As noted by Intel, there is no intent element to direct infringement.

> See 35 U.S.C. § 271(b) and (c). *Fromberg* deals with induced and contributory infringement and is therefore inapposite. Because the language of claim 1 refers to "programm*able* selection means" and states "whereby *when* said alternate addressing mode is selected" (emphases added), the accused device, to be infringing, need only be capable of operating in the page mode. Contrary to GI/M's argument, actual page mode operation in the accused device is not required.[361]

More recent cases employ a similar analysis. For example, in *Fantasy Sports v. SportsLine*,[362] the Federal Circuit reversed and remanded a district court ruling of summary judgment of no infringement due to the presence of genuine and material issues of fact requiring resolution.

The issue was whether the accused software met a limitation or, instead, was modifiable to meet the limitation. The former would be infringing, whereas the latter would not. The court referenced the *Intel* case in its discussion. The Federal Circuit stated:

> *Intel* involved a claim to a memory chip in an integrated circuit having, *inter alia*, "*programmable* selection means for selecting [an] alternate addressing mode." *Id.* at 831, 20 USPQ2d at 1170 (emphasis added). The defendant in *Intel* argued that even though its products could be modified to infringe that claim, the fact that those products were capable of infringing alone could not support a finding of infringement. *Id.* at 832, 20 USPQ2d at 1171. Although we concluded that the defendant's products did infringe, we explained our basis for doing so as follows: "Because *the language of claim 1* refers to '*programmable* selection means' . . . the accused device, to be infringing, need only be capable of operating in the page mode." *Id.* (emphases added). *Intel* therefore does not stand for the proposition, as argued by Fantasy, that infringement may be based upon a finding that an accused product is merely capable of being modified in a manner that infringes the claims of a patent. *See High Tech Med. Instrumentation, Inc. v. New Image Indus., Inc.*, 49 F.3d 1551, 1555–56, 33 USPQ2d 2005, 2008–09 (Fed. Cir. 1995) (distinguishing *Intel* and holding that the fact that the accused device could be altered in way that satisfies the claim term "rotatably coupled" did not *per se* justify a finding of infringement); *see also Telemac Cellular Corp. v. Topp Telecom, Inc.*, 247 F.3d 1316, 1330, 58 USPQ2d 1545, 1554 (Fed. Cir. 2001) ("[T]hat a device is capable of being modified to operate in an infringing manner is not sufficient, by itself, to support a finding of infringement."). *Rather, as in every infringement analysis, the language of the claims, as well as the nature of the accused product, dictates whether an infringement has occurred.*

361. *Intel Corp.*, 946 F.2d at 833.
362. 287 F.3d 1108.

> In the present case, claim 1 is directed to "[a] computer for playing football," and thus the claims of the '603 patent read on a computer executing fantasy football game software. Claim 1 also sets forth a number of functionally defined means that that software must contain, including a "means for scoring . . . bonus points" for unusual scoring plays. Software is a set of instructions, known as code, that directs a computer to perform specified functions or operations. Thus, the software underlying a computer program that presents a user with the ability to select among a number of different options must be written in such a way as to enable the computer to carry out the functions defined by those options when they are selected by the user. Therefore, although a user must activate the functions programmed into a piece of software by selecting those options, the user is only activating means that are *already present in the underlying software*. Otherwise, the user would be required to alter the code to enable the computer to carry out those functions. Accordingly, in order to infringe the '603 patent, the code underlying an accused fantasy football game must be written in such a way as to enable a user of that software to utilize the function of awarding bonus points for unusual plays such as out-of-position scoring, without having to modify that code. In other words, an infringing software must include the "means for scoring . . . bonus points" regardless whether that means is activated or utilized in any way.[363]

A recent Federal Circuit case may muddy slightly how to interpret such limitations; however, the basic conclusion regarding claims that include limitations with the capability to infringe remains intact, or so it appears. In *INVT SPE LLC v. International Trade Commission*,[364] the Federal Circuit affirmed the ITC's determination that the respondents did not violate 19 U.S.C. § 1337. INVT had alleged that the importation and sale of long-term evolution (LTE)-compliant personal electronic devices infringed U.S. Patent Nos. 6,760,590 (the '590 patent) and 7,848,439 (the '439 patent). The ITC determined that the asserted claims were not essential to the LTE standard and that the accused products did not infringe the asserted claims.

However, before reaching this conclusion, it was necessary to construe the claims at issue, in particular, the claims of the '439 patent, which related to wireless communication systems, specifically an improvement to adaptive modulation and coding (AMC), which is a technique used to transmit signals in an orthogonal frequency division multiplexing (OFDM) system. Claim 1 of the '439 patent recited:

363. *Id.* at 1117–19 (some emphasis in original, some added).
364. *See* 46 F.4th 1361 (Fed. Cir. 2022).

1. A communication apparatus comprising:

[a] a channel estimating section that carries out a channel estimation per subband;

[b] a parameter deciding section that decides modulation parameters and coding parameters per subband group comprised of a plurality of the subbands, based on a result of the channel estimation per subband;

[c] a parameter information transmission section that transmits, to a communicating party, parameter information indicating the modulation parameters and the coding parameters decided at the parameter deciding section;

[d] a receiving section that receives a signal containing data modulated and encoded on a per subband group basis at the communicating party using the modulation parameters and the coding parameters of the parameter information transmitted at the parameter information transmission section;

[e] a data obtaining section that demodulates and decodes the received signal received at the receiving section on a per subband group basis using the modulation parameters and the coding parameters decided at the parameter deciding section, and obtains the data contained in the received signal; and

[f] a pattern storage section that stores in advance patterns for selecting subbands constituting the subband groups wherein the parameter deciding section decides the modulation parameters and the coding parameters per subband group comprised of the subbands selected based on the patterns stored in the pattern storage section.

INVT asserted that compliance with the LTE communications standard required infringing this claim. The key limitations in dispute were elements [d] and [e], which stated:

[d] a receiving section that receives a signal containing data modulated and encoded on a per subband group basis at the communicating party using the modulation parameters and the coding parameters of the

parameter information transmitted at the parameter information transmission section;

[e] a data obtaining section that demodulates and decodes the received signal received at the receiving section on a per subband group basis using the modulation parameters and the coding parameters decided at the parameter deciding section, and obtains the data contained in the received signal[.]

At the ITC, a dispute regarding interpretation of these elements related to whether this language required "actual operation" or merely "the capability for performing." The ITC determined that the language required actual operation; however, the ITC also determined that the language was not shown to be LTE compliant and also determined separately that the accused devices had not been shown to meet the claim language at issue regardless of whether it was LTE compliant.

On appeal, INVT challenged the interpretation of the claims as requiring actual operation. In this regard, the Federal Circuit agreed with INVT that the language required the capability for performing rather than actual operation, but, nonetheless, concluded that the language still had not been shown to be LTE compliant and also that the accused devices had not been shown to meet the limitations at issue.

Here, the Federal Circuit stated:

> Our cases have held that sometimes a device only needs to be "capable of operating" according to a claimed limitation, for a finding of infringement. *See Finjan*, 626 F.3d at 1204. Other times, a device does not infringe unless it actually operates as claimed. *See ParkerVision, Inc. v. Qualcomm Inc.*, 903 F.3d 1354, 1361 (Fed. Cir. 2018) (*discussing Ball Aerosol & Specialty Container, Inc. v. Ltd. Brands, Inc.*, 555 F.3d 984 (Fed. Cir. 2009)). *Whether infringement requires actual performance of the recited functions by the accused device depends on the claim language. See Finjan*, 626 F.3d 1204 (*citing Fantasy Sports Props. v. Sportsline.com, Inc.*, 287 F.3d 1108, 1118 (Fed. Cir. 2002)); *see also ParkerVision, Inc.*, 903 F.3d at 1361 (articulating a distinction between configuration-type and capability type claims).
>
> *Possibly the most straightforward example of this is the common distinction between method claims and apparatus claims. See, e.g., Finjan*, 626 F.3d at 1203–05. In *Finjan*, this court held that Finjan's "non-method claims describe capabilities without requiring that any software components be 'active' or 'enabled.'" *Id.* at 1204–05. The court, therefore, upheld a finding of infringement for products in which the accused proactive-scanning software module was locked when sold by the defendants. *Id.* at 1205; *see also id.* at 1203–04

(*distinguishing Southwest Software, Inc. v. Harlequin Inc.*, 226 F.3d 1280, 1291 (Fed. Cir. 2000), in which the accused software product required a manual step to activate the patented feature, but the claim at issue was a method claim). In contrast, Finjan's method claims were not infringed by the accused products because those claims required actual performance of each claimed step; there was no evidence that proactive scanning was performed in the United States. *Id.* at 1206 ("To infringe a method claim, a person must have practiced all steps of the claimed method." (*quoting Lucent Techs. v. Gateway, Inc.*, 580 F.3d 1301, 1317 (Fed. Cir. 2009))). *Cf. ParkerVision, Inc.*, 903 F.3d at 1363 (similarly differentiating apparatus claims and method claims in the patent invalidity context). However, differences exist between apparatus claims as well, depending on the claim language. *We have construed some apparatus claims to require an infringing device to actually perform and operate according to the functional terms recited in the claim.* The intervenors cite two such cases, *Cross Medical* and *Ball Aerosol*. *See Intervenors' Br.* 64, 67–68. We have construed other apparatus claims to require only capability, such as in *Finjan* and *Silicon Graphics*. . . .

In *Cross Medical*, we rejected the argument that the limitation "anchor seat means which has a lower bone interface operatively joined to said bone segment" could be met merely by an interface that was capable of contacting bone. *Cross Med. Prods., Inc. v. Medtronic Sofamor Danek, Inc.*, 424 F.3d 1293, 1305–06 (Fed. Cir. 2005). *Instead, the claim language "operatively joined" required that the interface and the bone segment be connected and in contact such that the device effectively performed posterior stabilization. Id.* at 1306. Direct infringement did not occur until the device was connected to the bone, which a surgeon performed, not the allegedly infringing device maker. *Id.* at 1310–14. . . .

Intervenors emphasize that the *Cross Medical* claims included the present-tense verb "has," similar to the present-tense verbs "demodulates" and "decodes" in the '439 claims. But this court's construction in *Cross Medical* was based on "operatively joined," not "has." Intervenors do not provide any analysis of *Ball Aerosol*. While the *Ball Aerosol* claim is atypical for its recitation, within a mechanical device claim, of how a component is to be used or operated—somewhat akin to computer device claims, which commonly include functional language—it ultimately has little relevance for construing INVT's claims.

Because of the nature of the technology, computer and software claims typically use functional language to define the invention. Functional language is used to define and delimit otherwise generic or interchangeable general purpose computer hardware, which can be programmed to perform an unlimited array of functions. In other words, the recited operative steps a computer- or software-based device undertakes is what defines what a computer-implemented invention is. We have frequently construed such functional language as not requiring actual performance of those operative steps for infringement purposes. Moreover, we have not required claims to adhere to a specific grammatical form to find that the claim is drawn to capability, contrary to the Commission's and the intervenors' contentions. . . .

The [final initial determination (FID)] relied primarily on *Finjan* and the absence of "for performing"-type claim language, providing little else for why the '439 claims require actual operation. The intervenors argue that simple-present-tense words are enough to require actual operation, *see Intervenors' Br.* 65, 67, but *Silicon Graphics* shows that is not true. *In fact, based on just claim language, we see very little significance in the difference between a limitation that might recite "a data obtaining section for demodulating and decoding" (Finjan-style) and one that recites "a data obtaining section that demodulates and decodes" (the actual '439 claim language), for determining on which side of the capability/actual-operation line the claims fall.*

Like with the claims in *Finjan* and *Silicon Graphics*, we find that the asserted '439 claims are directed to capability—as in a device that includes "software components with specific purposes," programmed to have the ability to perform the operative steps: namely, a "receiving section" that can receive a signal containing data modulated and encoded using the parameters decided at user device, and a "data obtaining section" that can demodulate and decode the signal using the parameters decided at the user device. *Finjan*, 626 F.3d at 1204–05. *In other words, the claims recite a device with the capability of performing the recited functions when in operation without any modification or further programming.*[365]

Thus, the court interpreted the language of the claim, such as "a data obtaining section that demodulates and decodes," to recite a device with the capability of performing the recited functions apparently in part because the language at issue involves a device that includes "software components with specific purposes," programmed to have the ability to perform the operative steps. Despite this, however, the court affirmed as to noninfringement.

For our purposes, in light of this precedent, the analysis seems clear. If the claim requires that a device have the capacity to perform a function, one who makes, uses, or sells, and so on, a device with that capacity without the patent owner's authority is a direct infringer even if the capacity is not actually used.[366]

---

365. *Id.* at 1371–74 (emphasis added).

366. It is noted that there appears to be some tension between this case and the case *IPXL Holdings v. Amazon.com*, 430 F.3d 1377, 1384 (Fed. Cir. 2005). See also Chapter 6, addressing the issue of mixing statutory classes. However, it may be that the *IPXL v. Amazon* line of authority had not been argued and, furthermore, the court seems here to have interpreted the claim language in a manner that may not make the claim language indefinite because it involves a device that includes "software components with specific purposes," programmed to have the ability to perform the operative steps. We, nonetheless, continue to recommend drafting apparatus

To illustrate such a claim for such a situation, consider, for example, this technical problem. On modern computers, the address space of programs is typically provided a special region of memory described as the stack. The stack is primarily intended for fast allocation and deallocation of regions of memory, called frames, for use by a particular function operation (a "function operation" refers to code to perform an operation; the term is intended to distinguish it from a mathematical function). Data objects allocated in a frame of a particular function operation are considered to be "private" to that frame by default; however, there are ways for unscrupulous individuals to violate this protocol and improperly access the frame of a particular function operation. This may occur via malware with the intention to interfere with normal computer operation. Furthermore, there are no standard methods to prevent this from occurring at program runtime in state-of-the-art computers today.

One way to prevent such malware interference is to limit access to the stack memory locations of the particular function operation by another function operation *unless* the other function operation has had a *pointer granting access passed to it* by the particular function operation during the execution of the processor instructions.

This may, for example, be a feature included in a microprocessor in which the feature may be turned on and off. Example 4.38 is a possible claim.

EXAMPLE 4.38

I claim:

1. An apparatus comprising: an integrated circuit (IC); wherein the IC comprises a processor;

   wherein the processor comprises memory management capability with memory to be connected to the processor and to be accessed during execution of one or more programs, wherein the execution of the one or more programs comprises execution of processor instructions by the processor;

   wherein the memory management capability includes the capability to maintain flow control between the execution of function operations to be implemented via the processor instructions;

claims in a manner to avoid the risk of mixing statutory classes. Even in this case, the court acknowledged "*[p]ossibly the most straightforward example of this [difference] is the common distinction between method claims and apparatus claims.*" *INVT SPE LLC*, 46 F.4th at 1371.

> wherein the capability to maintain flow control between the execution of function operations to be implemented via the processor instructions comprises the processor, during execution of the processor instructions, to limit access of another function operation to read from or write to stack memory address locations to be reserved for a particular function operation unless the another function operation has had a pointer to grant access passed to it by the particular function operation during the execution of the processor instructions.

Thus, the claim recites

> the memory management capability includes the capability to maintain flow control between the execution of function operations . . . ;
>
> wherein the capability to maintain flow control between the execution of function operations . . . comprises the processor, during execution of the processor instructions, to limit access of another function operation to read from or write to stack memory address locations to be reserved for a particular function operation unless the another function operation has had a pointer to grant access passed to it by the particular function operation during the execution of the processor instructions.

A processor with this capability whether activated or used would therefore infringe this claim.

Product-by-Process Claims

Understand how to draft product-by-process claims, the risks of such claims, and how to get equivalent protection in some situations without using them.

35 U.S.C. § 271(g)

Whoever without authority imports into the United States or offers to sell, sells, or uses within the United States a product which is made by a process patented in the United States shall be liable as an infringer, if the importation, offer to sell, sale, or use of the product occurs during the term of such process patent. In an action for infringement of a process patent, no remedy may be granted for infringement on account of the noncommercial use or retail sale of a product unless there is no adequate remedy under this title for infringement on account of the importation or other use, offer to sell, or sale of that product. A product which is made by a patented process will, for purposes of this title, not be considered to be so made after—

(1) it is materially changed by subsequent processes; or

(2) it becomes a trivial and nonessential component of another product.

MPEP §§ 2113, 2173(p)

2113 Product-by-Process Claims

I. PRODUCT-BY-PROCESS CLAIMS ARE NOT LIMITED TO THE MANIPULATIONS OF THE RECITED STEPS, ONLY THE STRUCTURE IMPLIED BY THE STEPS

"[E]ven though product-by-process claims are limited by and defined by the process, determination of patentability is based on the product itself. The patentability of a product does not depend on its method of production. If the product in the product-by-process claim is the same as or obvious from a product of the prior art, the claim is unpatentable even though the prior product was made by a different process." In re Thorpe, 777 F.2d 695, 698, 227 USPQ 964, 966 (Fed. Cir. 1985) (citations omitted) (Claim was directed to a novolac color developer. The process of making the developer was allowed. The difference between the inventive process and the prior art was the addition of metal oxide and carboxylic acid as separate ingredients instead of adding the more expensive pre-reacted metal carboxylate. The product-by-process claim was rejected because the end product, in both the prior art and the allowed process, ends up containing metal carboxylate. The fact that the metal carboxylate is not directly added, but is instead produced in-situ does not change the end product.). Furthermore, "[b]ecause validity is determined based on the requirements of patentability, a patent is invalid if a product made by the process recited in a product-by-process claim is anticipated by or obvious from prior art products, even if those prior art products are made by different processes." Amgen Inc. v. F. Hoffmann-La Roche Ltd., 580 F.3d 1340, 1370 n 14, 92 USPQ2d 1289, 1312, n 14 (Fed. Cir. 2009). See also Purdue Pharma v. Epic Pharma, 811 F.3d 1345, 117 USPQ2d 1733 (Fed. Cir. 2016). However, in the context of an infringement analysis, a product-by-process claim is only infringed by a product made by the process recited in the claim. Id. at 1370 ("a product in the prior art made by a different process can anticipate a product-by-process claim, but an accused product made by a different process cannot infringe a product-by-process claim").

The structure implied by the process steps should be considered when assessing the patentability of product-by-process claims over the prior art, especially where the product can only be defined by the process steps by which the product is made, or where the manufacturing process steps would be expected to impart distinctive structural characteristics to the final product. See, e.g., In re Garnero, 412 F.2d 276, 279, 162 USPQ 221, 223 (CCPA 1979) (holding "interbonded by interfusion" to limit structure of the claimed composite and noting that terms such as "welded," "intermixed," "ground in place," "press fitted," and "etched" are capable of construction as structural limitations). See also In re Nordt Dev. Co., 881 F.3d 1371, 1375–76, 125 USPQ2d 1817, 1820 (Fed. Cir. 2018) (holding "the specification demonstrates that 'injected molded' connotes an integral structure," and discussing several cases since Garnero that held "limitations to convey structure even when they also describe a process of manufacture").

II. ONCE A PRODUCT APPEARING TO BE SUBSTANTIALLY IDENTICAL IS FOUND AND A PRIOR ART REJECTION IS MADE, THE BURDEN SHIFTS TO THE APPLICANT TO SHOW AN NONOBVIOUS DIFFERENCE

"The Patent Office bears a lesser burden of proof in making out a case of prima facie obviousness for product-by-process claims because of their peculiar nature" than when a product is claimed in the conventional fashion. In re Fessmann, 489 F.2d 742, 744, 180 USPQ 324, 326 (CCPA 1974). Once the examiner provides a rationale tending to show that the claimed product appears to be the same or similar to that of the prior art, although produced by a different process, the burden shifts to applicant to come forward with evidence establishing an nonobvious difference between the claimed product and the prior art product. In re Marosi, 710 F.2d 799, 803, 218 USPQ 289, 292–33 (Fed. Cir. 1983) (The claims were directed to a zeolite manufactured by mixing together various inorganic materials in solution and heating the resultant gel to form a crystalline metal silicate essentially free of alkali metal. The prior art described a process of making a zeolite which, after ion exchange to remove alkali metal, appeared to be "essentially free of alkali metal." The court upheld the rejection because the applicant had not come forward with any evidence that the prior art was not "essentially free of alkali metal" and therefore a different and nonobvious product.).

See also Ex parte Gray, 10 USPQ2d 1922 (Bd. Pat. App. & Inter. 1989) (The prior art disclosed human nerve growth factor (b-NGF) isolated from human placental tissue. The claim was directed to b-NGF produced through genetic engineering techniques. The factor produced seemed to be substantially the same whether isolated from tissue or produced through genetic engineering. While the applicant questioned the purity of the prior art factor, no concrete evidence of an nonobvious difference was presented. The Board stated that the dispositive issue is whether the claimed factor exhibits any unexpected properties compared with the factor disclosed by the prior art. The Board further stated that the applicant should have made some comparison between the two factors to establish unexpected properties since the materials appeared to be identical or only slightly different.).

III. A REJECTION BASED ALTERNATIVELY ON 35 U.S.C. 102 OR 103 FOR PRODUCT-BY-PROCESS CLAIMS HAS BEEN APPROVED BY THE COURTS

"[T]he lack of physical description in a product-by-process claim makes determination of the patentability of the claim more difficult, since in spite of the fact that the claim may recite only process limitations, it is the patentability of the product claimed and not of the recited process steps which must be established. We are therefore of the opinion that when the prior art discloses a product which reasonably appears to be either identical with or only slightly different than a product claimed in a product-by-process claim, a rejection based alternatively on either section 102 or section 103 of the statute is eminently fair and acceptable. As a practical matter, the Patent Office is not equipped to manufacture products by the myriad of processes put before it and then obtain prior art products and make physical comparisons therewith." In re Brown, 459 F.2d 531, 535, 173 USPQ 685, 688 (CCPA 1972). Office personnel should note that reliance on the alternative grounds of 35 U.S.C. 102 or 35 U.S.C. 103 does not eliminate the need to explain both the anticipation and obviousness aspects of the rejections.

2173.05(p) Claim Directed to Product-By-Process or Product and Process

There are many situations where claims are permissively drafted to include a reference to more than one statutory class of invention.

I. PRODUCT-BY-PROCESS

A product-by-process claim, which is a product claim that defines the claimed product in terms of the process by which it is made, is proper. Purdue Pharma v. Epic Pharma, 811 F.3d 1345, 1354, 117 USPQ2d 1733, 1739 (Fed. Cir. 2016); In re Luck, 476 F.2d 650, 177 USPQ 523 (CCPA 1973); In re Pilkington, 411 F.2d 1345, 162 USPQ 145 (CCPA 1969); and In re Steppan, 394 F.2d 1013, 156 USPQ 143 (CCPA 1967). A claim to a device, apparatus, manufacture, or composition of matter may contain a reference to the process in which it is intended to be used without being objectionable under 35 U.S.C. 112(b) or pre-AIA 35 U.S.C. 112, second paragraph, so long as it is clear that the claim is directed to the product and not the process.

An applicant may present claims of varying scope even if it is necessary to describe the claimed product in product-by-process terms. Ex parte Pantzer, 176 USPQ 141 (Bd. App. 1972).

II. PRODUCT AND PROCESS IN THE SAME CLAIM

A single claim which claims both an apparatus and the method steps of using the apparatus is indefinite under 35 U.S.C. 112(b) or pre-AIA 35 U.S.C. 112, second paragraph. See In re Katz Interactive Call Processing Patent Litigation, 639 F.3d 1303, 1318, 97 USPQ2d 1737, 1748–49 (Fed. Cir. 2011). In Katz, a claim directed to "[a] system with an interface means for providing automated voice messages . . . to certain of said individual callers, wherein said certain of said individual callers digitally enter data" was determined to be indefinite because the italicized claim limitation is not directed to the system, but rather to actions of the individual callers, which creates confusion as to when direct infringement occurs. Katz, 639 F.3d at 1318, 97 USPQ2d at 1749 (citing IPXL Holdings v. Amazon.com, Inc., 430 F.3d 1377, 1384, 77 USPQ2d 1140, 1145 (Fed. Cir. 2005), in which a system claim that recited "an input means" and required a user to use the input means was found to be indefinite because it was unclear "whether infringement . . . occurs when one creates a system that allows the user [to use the input means], or whether infringement occurs when the user actually uses the input means."); Ex parte Lyell, 17 USPQ2d 1548 (Bd. Pat. App. & Inter. 1990) (claim directed to an automatic transmission workstand and the method of using it held ambiguous and properly rejected under 35 U.S.C. 112, second paragraph).

In contrast, when a claim recites a product and additional limitations which focus on the capabilities of the system, not the specific actions or functions performed by the user, the claim may be definite under 35 U.S.C. 112(b) or pre-AIA 35 U.S.C. 112, second paragraph. See Mastermine Software, Inc. v. Microsoft Corp., 874 F.3d 1307, 124 USPQ2d 1618 (Fed. Cir. 2017).

Abbott Laboratories v. Sandoz, Inc.
566 F.3d 1282
United States Court of Appeals for the Federal Circuit
May 18, 2009, Decided

Questions

1. The majority decision in *Abbott* is confusing without the context provided by the dissenting opinions. Another way to obtain context would be to read *Atlantic Thermoplastics v. Faytex*,[367] an opinion also authored by Judge Rader. That case created a conflict between panel decisions until *Abbott* ostensibly resolved the conflict *en banc* in 2009. Thus, the conflict existed for 17 years. What was the law before *Scripps* and *Atlantic Thermoplastics*?
2. What do you think of the justification offered in *Atlantic Thermoplastics v. Faytex*[368] for not following *Scripps*?
3. What was the law in accordance with *Scripps*?
4. What was the law in accordance with *Atlantic Thermoplastics*?
5. What was the law in accordance with *Abbott*?

367. 970 F.2d 834, 23 U.S.P.Q.2d 1481 (Fed. Cir. 1992).
368. *Id.* n.2, 23 U.S.P.Q.2d 1481.

6. Judge Newman and Judge Rader have two different views of how product-by-process claims evolved. Can you summarize the respective views?[369] Which one seems more credible?
7. Judge Newman dissents on both procedural and substantive grounds. What do you think about her dissent on procedural grounds? This is another *en banc* decision in which the usual *en banc* process in accordance with Federal Court protocol had not been followed.[370] Judge Newman in her dissent explains in detail how the process should work, but, here, was not followed. Yet, it is asserted that the section of the opinion regarding product-by-process claims was decided *en banc*, again, to deal with inconsistent court precedent created by opinions by two different three-judge panels. Why do you think that in these situations the court chose this unusual route to overrule its own precedent while ignoring its own procedural rules?
8. As demonstrated by the lengthy opinions, product-by-process claims have a long and complex history and raise challenging issues. In terms of claim drafting basics, it has been previously noted how courts perceive apparatus (or product-type) claims quite differently from process claims. Process claims were dealt with in more detail in the preceding sections of this book. However, starting with the premise that these two types of claims are fundamentally different,[371] it should not be a tremendous surprise that interpretive challenges may arise for claims that may not clearly fall into one class (e.g., apparatus or product-type) or the other class (e.g., method or process), as might be said of product-by-process claims due to their hybrid nature. How should such claims be interpreted in prosecution and in litigation?
9. Although *Abbott Laboratories* settled the split in Federal Circuit precedent, it did not really do a good job of making clear the approach now in place for product-by-process claims. A better case, previously cited, is *Amgen Inc. v. F. Hoffmann-La Roche Ltd.*, which states:

> For product-by-process claims, that which anticipates if earlier does not necessarily infringe if later. That is because a product in the prior art made by a different process can anticipate a product-by-process

369. *See Atl. Thermoplastics*, 970 F.2d 834, 23 U.S.P.Q.2d 1481.
370. The other decision is *Williamson v. Citrix Online, LLC*, 792 F.3d 1339 (Fed. Cir. 2015) (en banc).
371. For example, the wording, the scope of rights, the interpretation, and so on, are different.

claim, but an accused product made by a different process cannot infringe a product-by-process claim.[372]

One perhaps unintended consequence to be aware of in this context is inadvertent use of "product-by-process" limitations—words in an apparatus claim that could be viewed as a process limitation. Typical examples are words that may be the past tense of a verb that suggests a process, such as "coating," "blended," or "disposed over," which are illustrative examples. A common word used that may be another example is "formed." The nature of materials technology, as an example, may often lend itself to this sort of description. This sort of language is highlighted here because, if interpreted to be a product-by-process limitation, the language would be subject to the rules governing product-by-process claims, which increases risk of invalidity. Short of avoiding the use of such words in an apparatus or product claim, how might one reduce the risk that these terms are interpreted to be product-by-process limitations?

10. At times the distinction between functional language and process-type language may be blurred in Federal Circuit cases. The prior question dealt with structure versus process limitations. This question highlights functional versus process limitations. How can one be sensitive to these issues and draft appropriately to reduce risk in both situations?
11. Why did the appellate court permit the Japanese patent prosecution to affect the claim construction? Was this intrinsic or extrinsic evidence and why?
12. Can you explain Abbott's plain language argument, that "*obtainable* by" introduces an optional process, whereas "*obtained* by" would introduce limiting process steps?
13. Can you explain this position of the appellate court:

> If this court were to strip the process elements from the claims, as Abbott would urge, for infringement purposes, there would then be nothing to differentiate independent claim 2 from independent claim 5. After all, if those claims are not bound by the process terms but only "define" the basic cefdinir compound, then each of the claims recite the same thing, over and over again.[373]

---

372. Amgen Inc. v. F. Hoffmann-La Roche Ltd., 580 F.3d 1340, 1369–70 (Fed. Cir. 2009).
373. Abbott Laby's v. Sandoz, Inc., 566 F.3d 1282, 1295 (Fed. Cir. 2009).

Why might that be an issue? Why does Judge Rader profess to reject it?

* * *

Product-by-process claims are a complex subject. Not even the judges appear to agree on why they exist and how they should be interpreted. Thus, for many years it was unclear how product-by-process claims should be interpreted.[374] This was due primarily to two Federal Circuit panels that reached different outcomes. *Scripps Clinic & Research Foundation v. Genentech, Inc.*, a 1991 Federal Circuit decision, stated that a product-by-process claim was *not* limited to products prepared by the process recited in the claims.[375] However, in *Atlantic Thermoplastics Co., Inc. v. Faytex Corp.*, a 1992 Federal Circuit decision, a different three-judge panel ruled that "process terms in product-by-process claims serve as limitations in determining infringement."[376]

These potentially inconsistent rulings did not necessarily foreclose use of such claims. One case discussed applying a process limitation for purposes of infringement, whereas the other case, while less clear, seemed to suggest otherwise. Rather, the uncertainty provided a potential opportunity to argue for a desired interpretation, depending on issues related to invalidity or infringement.

For a knowledgeable practitioner, product-by-process claims might be included, but with recognition of the interpretation risk. However, after nearly two decades, the Federal Circuit ultimately resolved the panel inconsistency, and the interpretation of such claims is now clear.[377] As a result of this interpretation, such claims are not generally advisable unless it is the *only* way to claim the subject matter at issue. Part of the reason for this is that the process limitations *are not* considered for purposes of validity, but the process limitations *are* considered for purposes of infringement.[378]

Product-by-process claims represent one of the few situations where claims are interpreted differently for validity than they are for infringement. As the court said in *Amgen v. F. Hoffmann-La Roche*:

> The impact of these different analyses is significant. For product-by-process claims, that which anticipates if earlier does not necessarily infringe if later. That is because a product in the prior art made by a different process can

374. *See id.*

375. *See* 927 F.2d 1565, 18 U.S.P.Q.2d 1001 (Fed. Cir. 1991).

376. *See* 970 F.2d 834, 23 U.S.P.Q.2d 1481.

377. *See Abbott Laby's*, 566 F.3d 1282 (en banc).

378. For a recent case, see *United Therapeutics Corp. v. Liquidia Technologies*, 74 F.4th 1360 (Fed. Cir. 2023), in which claims of a patent were determined to be product-by-process and were held to be anticipated by a prior art product.

anticipate a product-by-process claim, but an accused product made by a different process cannot infringe a product-by-process claim.[379]

The format of a product-by-process claim might look like:

---

1. An apparatus comprising: product X;

 wherein product X is to be produced by:

  action 1;

  action 2; and

  action 3.

One issue to be aware of in this context is inadvertent use of "product-by-process" limitations.[380] Words that may be the past tense of a verb that suggests a process, as discussed earlier in this chapter, for example, may have some risk. Thus, "coating," "blended," or "disposed over" are illustrative examples. A common word used that may be another example is "formed." The nature of materials technology may often lend itself to this sort of description. This sort of language is highlighted here because, if interpreted to be a product-by-process limitation, the language would be subject to the rules governing product-by-process claims, which increases risk of invalidity.[381]

Although previously it was thought there was some potential advantage to the use of product-by-process claims even with the uncertainty in the law regarding their scope for validity and infringement, in 2009 the Federal Circuit resolved the issue in an *en banc* decision.[382] As a result, as indicated, the process limitations of a product-by-process claim *are not* considered for purposes of validity, but the process limitations of the claim *are* considered for purposes of infringement.

This, of course, means that to be patentable, the claim must distinguish from the prior art *without* considering the process limitations. However, if that

379. *See* Amgen Inc. v. F. Hoffmann-La Roche Ltd., 580 F.3d 1340, 1369–70 (Fed. Cir. 2009).

380. See earlier in this chapter.

381. *See* Kamstrup A/S v. Axioma Metering UAB, 43 F.4th 1374 (Fed. Cir. 2022) (affirming that the PTAB properly construed a product-by-process claim element as not entitled to patentable weight).

382. *See* Abbott Laby's v. Sandoz, Inc., 566 F.3d 1282 (Fed. Cir. 2009).

is the case, why include the process limitations, in the independent claim at least? One might include process limitations in a dependent claim. However, in that case, the dependent claim would seem to not help distinguish from the prior art. Thus, these claims offer some disadvantages with few advantages.

One situation where a product-by-process claim might arguably be of use is where there is no other way to describe the product being made other than by referring to the particular process; however, if, again, one could write a patentable claim despite ignoring the process limitations, then the situation would appear to be the one just described. One could write a patentable independent claim without process limitations, which would capture more infringers.

Despite these concerns, it seems that product-by-process claims do show up a lot in pharmaceutical patents. This may be somewhat like the original reason for using such claims under "the rule of necessity." It may be a challenge to characterize the pharmaceutical product in some way other than by its manufacturing process.

There might be a possible advantage to a product-by-process claim, assuming a patentable claim may be crafted. Previously, under the rule of necessity, the power of a product-by-process claim was typically seen with a manufacturing process. A method claim to the process is only infringed by the manufacturer. Once something is made by the process and sold, it is beyond the scope of the process claim. However, with a product-by-process claim, in theory at least, a distributer or purchaser of the manufactured product would be suable based on a product within the scope of the claim. This would be especially powerful assuming the process limitations are ignored for patentability *and* for infringement, as in *Scripps*. Unfortunately, that is not the current Federal Circuit law. It may be, however, that even with the process limitations affecting claim scope, such a claim has some of the power just described in connection with product distribution by a competitor.

In what follows, however, we discuss a very specific situation under 35 U.S.C. subsection 271(g) that might be used in a similar fashion to sue distributors or purchasers of a manufactured product prepared by a patented process. With that provision, one may get the power of a product-by-process claim without the disadvantages of Federal Circuit jurisprudence. Rather, using this provision, the validity and infringement considerations are in balance.

For starters, there may be a bit of subtlety in appreciating how a product-by-process claim might differ from other claims, like an apparatus claim or a method claim, as such. Consider first the following relatively simple process claim directed to manufacturing a thin-film SOI-IC. At one time, the following claim would have been new and nonobvious.

EXAMPLE 4.39

I claim:

1. A method of fabrication comprising:

fabricating an integrated circuit (IC);

wherein the fabricating includes forming at least a plurality of N-type metal oxide semiconductor field effect transistors (NMOSFETs) by forming a source, a drain, a gate, and a body for respective NMOSFETs of the plurality in a thin-film silicon layer of a silicon-on-insulator (SOI) substrate;

wherein the forming the source, the drain, the gate, and the body for the respective NMOSFETs of the plurality comprises:

forming the gate from a conductive layer and an oxide layer over the thin film silicon layer of the SOI substrate; and

forming two N+ regions in the thin film silicon layer of the SOI substrate via ion implantation or diffusion to form the source, the drain, and the body;

wherein the fabricating further includes fabricating one or more layers of metallization over the thin film silicon layer; and

coupling the one or more layers of metallization to the plurality of NMOSFETs into an electrical configuration.

Next, consider a claim for fabricating an RF switch in a thin-film SOI-IC. Perhaps one might try to argue this is a product-by-process claim, but by its terms it is a method claim.

EXAMPLE 4.40

I claim:

1. A method of fabricating a radio frequency (RF) switch comprising:

fabricating an integrated circuit (IC) that includes the RF switch;

wherein the fabricating includes forming at least a plurality of N-type metal oxide semiconductor field effect transistors (NMOSFETs) by forming a source, a drain, a gate, and a body for respective NMOSFETs of the plurality in a thin-film silicon layer of a silicon-on-insulator (SOI) substrate;

wherein the forming the source, the drain, the gate, and the body for the respective NMOSFETs of the plurality comprises:

forming the gate from a conductive layer and an oxide layer over the thin film silicon layer of the SOI substrate; and

forming two N+ regions in the thin film silicon layer of the SOI substrate via ion implantation or diffusion to form the source, the drain, and the body;

wherein the fabricating further includes fabricating one or more layers of metallization over the thin film silicon layer;

wherein the one or more layers of metallization to couple the plurality of NMOSFETs into a stack to pass an RF signal through the stack of NMOSFETs in an ON state of the stack of NMOSFETs;

wherein the one or more layers of metallization to couple the plurality of NMOSFETs of the stack to not pass an RF signal through the stack of NMOSFETs in an OFF state of the stack of NMOSFETs; and

wherein the one or more layers of metallization to couple an electrical bias to the body of the respective NMOSFETs at least in a portion of the OFF state of the stack to have a DC voltage level substantially more negative than a lowest voltage level of the following: ground, a DC voltage level of the source of the respective NMOSFETs, and a DC voltage level of the drain of the respective NMOSFETs.

One might perhaps argue that the last three "wherein" clauses are not in method format. Thus, to keep the claim "clean," so to speak, the method claim might, instead, be crafted as follows:

EXAMPLE 4.41

I claim:

1. A method of fabricating a radio frequency (RF) switch comprising:

fabricating an integrated circuit (IC) that includes the RF switch;

wherein the fabricating includes forming at least a plurality of N-type metal oxide semiconductor field effect transistors (NMOSFETs) by forming a source, a drain, a gate, and a body for respective NMOSFETs of the plurality in a thin film silicon layer of a silicon-on-insulator (SOI) substrate;

wherein the fabricating further includes fabricating one or more layers of metallization over the thin film silicon layer;

coupling the plurality of NMOSFETs into a stack via the one or more layers of metallization to pass an RF signal through the stack of NMOSFETs in an ON state of the stack of NMOSFETs;

coupling the plurality of NMOSFETs of the stack via the one or more layers of metallization to not pass an RF signal through the stack of NMOSFETs in an OFF state of the stack of NMOSFETs; and

coupling an electrical bias to the body of the respective NMOSFETs via the one or more layers of metallization at least in a portion of the OFF state of the stack to have a DC voltage level substantially more negative than a lowest voltage level of the following: ground, a DC voltage level of the source of the respective NMOSFETs, and a DC voltage level of the drain of the respective NMOSFETs.

Now, it appears a challenge to argue this is not a method claim. Next, consider Example 4.42, which might be considered a product-by-process claim.

EXAMPLE 4.42

I claim:

1. A device comprising: a plurality of N-type metal oxide semiconductor field effect transistors (NMOSFETs), respective NMOSFETs of the plurality including a source, a gate, a drain, and a body;

   wherein the plurality of NMOSFETs are fabricated on an integrated circuit (IC);

   the respective NMOSFETs are fabricated from the source, the drain, the gate, and the body are formed in a thin-film silicon layer of a silicon-on-insulator (SOI) substrate;

   wherein the source, the drain, the gate, and the body for the respective NMOSFETs of the plurality are formed in a manner that comprises the following:

the gate is formed from a conductive layer and an oxide layer over the silicon layer of the SOI substrate; and

two N+ regions are formed in the silicon layer of the SOI substrate via ion implantation or diffusion to form the source, the drain, and the body;

wherein one or more layers of metallization are fabricated over the silicon layer;

wherein the one or more layers of metallization couple the plurality of NMOSFETs into a stack to pass a radio frequency (RF) signal through the stack of NMOSFETs in an ON state of the stack of NMOSFETs;

wherein the one or more layers of metallization couple the plurality of NMOSFETs of the stack to not pass an RF signal through the stack of NMOSFETs in an OFF state of the stack of NMOSFETs; and

wherein the one or more layers of metallization couple an electrical bias to the body of the respective NMOSFETs at least in a portion of the OFF state of the stack so that DC voltage level is substantially more negative than a lowest voltage level of the following: ground, a DC voltage level of the source of the respective NMOSFETs, and a DC voltage level of the drain of the respective NMOSFETs.

However, appreciate that there is not a tremendous amount of process in this claim. Nonetheless, as discussed, for the claim to be patentable, the key features are in the structure. Perhaps one could argue that "fabricated" and "formed" are structural limitations, although this seems like a long shot in this context. Nonetheless, appreciate that many of these linguistic issues are subtle and subject to interpretation and argument. Description in the specification may shift the balance as well regarding interpretation issues.

Example 4.43 is another example of a product-by-process claim for a different technology:

EXAMPLE 4.43

I claim:

1. An apparatus comprising: a mesh;

the mesh including plastic;

the plastic heated to a temperature sufficient to make the plastic malleable;

the malleable plastic then rolled, extruded, and cut to form a mesh-shaped plastic;

the mesh-shaped plastic then being cooled to a temperature sufficient to harden the plastic of the mesh-shaped plastic after having been rolled, extruded, and cut.

As suggested, one important legal opportunity to be aware of in connection with method of manufacture claims is 35 U.S.C. subsection 271(g). This section provides the ability to potentially get a type of product-by-process claim without the invalidity disadvantages discussed earlier. The section states:

> Whoever without authority imports into the United States or offers to sell, sells, or uses within the United States a product which is made by a process patented in the United States shall be liable as an infringer, if the importation, offer to sell, sale, or use of the product occurs during the term of such process patent. In an action for infringement of a process patent, no remedy may be granted for infringement on account of the noncommercial use or retail sale of a product unless there is no adequate remedy under this title for infringement on account of the importation or other use, offer to sell, or sale of that product. A product which is made by a patented process will, for purposes of this title, not be considered to be so made after—
>
> (1) it is materially changed by subsequent processes; or
> (2) it becomes a trivial and nonessential component of another product.

Note the specific language "a product which is *made* by a process patented in the United States" (emphasis added). This provision has been interpreted to be limited to manufacturing.[383] This provision as well as subsection 271(f) are directed to "extraterritorial activities" that may ultimately result in liability for patent infringement in the United States.

For example, it is becoming more common for companies, so-called fabless design houses, to outsource chip manufacturing to others. Coming up with the design does not generally by itself directly infringe a patent claim.[384] Yet, a company making the chip for someone else could infringe a manufacturing claim absent extraterritorial considerations.[385]

---

383. *See* Bayer v. Houses Pharms., 340 F.3d 1367 (Fed. Cir. 2003).

384. Although it might be a basis for a claim for indirect infringement; see Chapter 5, addressing indirect infringement.

385. See earlier in this chapter discussing method of making claims. Direct infringement is generally easier to prove than indirect infringement, as discussed in Chapter 5.

Let us consider a situation in which a foundry *outside* the United States performs the claim of Example 4.39 for a U.S. company that then imports the manufactured IC into the United States. That U.S. company, while having not performed the process itself, is nonetheless liable for infringement in federal court assuming subsections (g)(1) and (g)(2) do not apply. Furthermore, those in the chain of distribution may similarly be sued in federal court as an infringer, subject to the defenses in the statute, such as a noncommercial use, a retail sale, or the conditions of subsections (g)(1) or (g)(2).

This section, in effect, gives one the equivalent of a product-by-process patent claim for this situation, but without the invalidity concerns previously raised for a product-by-process claim.[386] Furthermore, the Federal Circuit has ruled that the two defenses in subsections (g)(1) and (g)(2) are not legally applicable in proceedings before the ITC, a quasi-judicial governmental body that hears and decides complaints regarding importations that may be in violation of certain U.S. trade regulation laws, including intellectual property laws.[387] Thus, one may potentially stop importation of the chips at the border of the United States without a concern regarding potential defenses under subsections (g)(1) and (g)(2).[388]

Employ a "Hedge" Strategy to Claiming: Use Patent Claim Diversity

As explained, at the time a patent application is filed, the patentee has one view of the prior art. However, that is a view that evolves throughout the life of a patent. During prosecution, prior art is uncovered that was not known at the time of filing. Likewise, the patent issuing is not the end of the matter. The claims of a patent are presumed valid. If the patent is challenged or asserted, then more art comes to the fore. Even after a litigation, more prior art may be uncovered in later litigations. A patent is not held valid by a court. Rather, a patent is presumed valid. A court at best may declare a patent *not invalid*. Consequently, it is still possible for validity of the patent claims to be tested.

---

386. *See* Jennewein Biotechnologie GMBH v. Int'l Trade Comm'n, No. 2020-2220, 2021 U.S. App. LEXIS 28200 (Fed. Cir. Sept. 17, 2021); Kinik v. Int'l Trade Comm'n, 362 F.3d 1359 (Fed. Cir. 2004).

387. *See Jennewein Biotechnologie GMBH*, 2021 U.S. App. LEXIS 28200; *Kinik*, 362 F.3d 1359.

388. Another feature of subsection 271(g) is that a single entity need not perform all the claim elements. As to the method claim, there is liability without meeting the single infringer rule. *See* Syngenta Crop Prot. v. Willowood, LLC, 944 F.3d 1344 (Fed. Cir. 2019).

In such a situation, a prudent drafter would be wise to employ a wide spectrum of patent claims from quite broad to quite narrow *in scope* with claims also falling in the range of intermediate scope. Likewise, *various claim types* should be employed, and in the dependent claims, features should be mixed and matched based on judgment about which features are likely to provide strong patentability arguments and which features are likely to be copied by others who may sell similar products or provide similar services.

In General, Draft Claims of Varying Scope and of Varying Type

The patent claims should expressly recite the broadest and the narrowest embodiments of the invention, including multiple claims for multiple embodiments between the broadest and the narrowest; include a picture claim.
To add to claim diversity, draft claims to make "design around" more difficult and increase the relative ease of detecting (and proving) infringement.

For good practice, therefore, the patent claims should include claims of varying scope and of varying type. It is specifically recommended that multiple embodiments be disclosed and claimed, including the broadest and the narrowest embodiments of the invention, and embodiments between the broadest and the narrowest. There are several reasons for this recommendation.

For one thing, as previously suggested, it is a good principle of claim drafting to make the drafter's intent as clear as possible from the face of the claims themselves. Drafting the claims to expressly cover multiple embodiments assists this effort. It makes clearer to others looking at the claims what is intended to be a broad claim, an intermediate claim, and a narrow claim, and how the words of the claims and the order of the claims are structured to communicate such claim breadth and claim narrowness. Of course, it is likewise important that the specification also recite these embodiments, and they be clearly understood to present examples of broad, intermediate, and narrow scope, although preferably *without* using such labels per se.[389]

Another advantage of this approach is that it reduces the risk of limitations being read into the claims from the specification. It is difficult to predict

389. It is important to remember that while we recommend drafting claims as broad as the prior art will allow (depending, of course, on context), there remains uncertainty as to whether you have the closest and most relevant prior art. Thus, those intermediate and narrow claims may become quite important.

when a court will read a limitation from the specification into the claims and when it will not.[390]

This was done, for example, in *Toro Co. v. White Consolidated Industries*.[391] The Federal Circuit limited the term "including" to mean "permanently affixed to and included as part of." Thus, the court read a limitation from the specification into the claims. In *Toro*, the patent at issue disclosed and claimed a convertible vacuum-blower for use in vacuuming or blowing leaves and small debris, depending on the selected mode. The design employed a removable cover that was *physically attached* to a restriction ring. The restriction ring was used to increase the velocity of air in the blower mode by reducing the diameter of the air intake opening. The accused product, on the other hand, had a restriction ring *physically separate from* the cover. Therefore, because the Federal Circuit reached a different construction of the word "including," the Federal Circuit reversed the district court's summary judgment of patent infringement.

Likewise, *Watts v. XL Systems*[392] and *Wang Laboratories v. America Online*[393] were two more cases where limitations were read from the specification into the claims. Of course, these are not the only examples. For example, in *SciMed Life Systems v. Advanced Cardiovascular Systems*,[394] a claim for a catheter, having guide wire and inflation lumens that were "separate" from one another, was interpreted to read only on coaxial lumens and not side-by-side lumens. Likewise, in *Bell Atlantic v. Covad Communications*,[395] the Federal Circuit interpreted a claim to an asymmetric digital subscriber line (ADSL) data transmission system with adjustable variable rate functionality that employed the term "mode." The Federal Circuit interpreted the language to cover only three specific "modes" of operation recited in the specification. Furthermore, in *Renishaw v. Marposs*,[396] the Federal Circuit interpreted the term "when," used in a claim to a touch probe for automated manufacturing, to mean the probe was triggered as soon as possible after contact with the work piece rather than simply "at or after the time that" contact with the work piece occurred.

The point, of course, is not to list every case where a limitation was ever read from the specification into the claims, but, rather, to demonstrate that

390. See Chapter 5, addressing claim construction and importing claim limitations from the specification into the claims.
391. 199 F.3d 1295, 1301 (Fed. Cir. 1999).
392. 232 F.3d 877 (Fed. Cir. 2000).
393. 197 F.3d 1377 (Fed. Cir. 1999).
394. 242 F.3d 1337 (Fed. Cir. 2001).
395. 262 F.3d 1258 (Fed. Cir. 2001).
396. 158 F.3d 1243 (Fed. Cir. 1998).

the risk this may happen is substantial. However, drafting the claims so that multiple embodiments are covered, including the broadest and the narrowest, should reduce this risk.

Because these embodiments are specifically covered in the claims, it makes it less likely that a court will read a limitation into a claim where the limitation is not specifically intended.[397] In many of the cases just cited, one of the difficulties was that the specification recited only one or only a few embodiments. This situation made it easier for the court to read limitations from the specification into the claim or claims at issue. In contrast, the more embodiments in the specification *with corresponding claims*, the more likely it is that a court will not read a limitation into a claim where that limitation is not intended.

Another advantage of this approach is that it reduces the risk that claims will be held invalid for lack of written description. Several well-known Federal Circuit cases, including *Gentry Gallery v. Berkline Corp.*,[398] *Tronzo v. Biomet*,[399] and *Toro v. Ariens*,[400] have found patent claims to be invalid under 35 U.S.C. § 112 for failing to satisfy the written description requirement. In these cases, the court determined that the specification failed to provide support for recited limitations in the claims. This is a risk associated with disclosing a single or only a few embodiments. By, instead, describing and claiming multiple embodiments from broadest to narrowest, the risk of lack of written description is reduced because explicit textual support is provided at the time of filing, at a minimum, by the claims themselves.

One risk avoided, then, is that a court will conclude in later litigation that added claims are broader than the specification intended to support those claims. For example, in *Gentry*, the patent related to a section sofa having two parallel reclining seats. In the embodiment disclosed in the specification, two push-button recliner controls were mounted on a console positioned between the two recliners. The broadest claim at filing specified the location of the controls as upon the center console; however, claims were later added that did not specify the location of the recliner controls specifically. The Federal Circuit, therefore, held the later-added claims to be invalid because the patent did not support location of the recliner controls other than on the center console.

---

397. *See, e.g.*, InterDigital Commc'ns v. Int'l Trade Comm'n, 690 F.3d 1318, 1324 (Fed. Cir. 2012) (The doctrine of claim differentiation disfavors reading a limitation from a dependent claim into an independent claim.).

398. 134 F.3d 1473 (Fed. Cir. 1998).

399. 156 F.3d 1154 (Fed. Cir. 1998).

400. 232 F.3d 915 (Fed. Cir. 2000) (nonprecedential).

The recommended approach also avoids the risk that a court will conclude that a narrow claim is not supported by the specification. For example, in *Purdue Pharma v. Faulding Inc.*,[401] the claims related to a method for treating pain by administering an analgesic. A claim added after filing related to concentration in a patient's blood (defined by a ratio) 24 hours after administration. The claim specified the ratio as greater than two. According to the court, the examples in the specification did not emphasize this limitation as "an important defining quality of the formulation." Thus, the court held the claim invalid for failing to satisfy the written description requirement under 35 U.S.C. § 112.

An independent advantage, of course (i.e., of having a set of claims of varying scope that includes narrow claims, intermediate claims, and broad claims), is that this increases the chances of capturing infringers while decreasing the chances of reading on the prior art. The more different ways an invention is claimed, the more opportunities exist to capture infringers that might otherwise escape liability. Likewise, even if a thorough prior art search may have taken place, there is still some uncertainty regarding whether the best and closest prior art has been found. Also, it may be that a search has not been conducted. In both instances, claiming the invention a variety of ways from broad to narrow helps mitigate that risk by providing more opportunities to avoid potentially difficult prior art that may later crop up.

Broad Scope Claims

As an illustration of drafting claims from broad to narrow scope, the previous technology examples related to transistor body biasing and visual voicemail are employed. Note that these are two quite different technologies to provide diverse examples.

Observe that we provide a single set of claims for each as an example; however, a patent application would include other claim sets with different independent claims and likely different claim types. For example, we illustrate transistor body biasing with apparatus claims, but we would also expect, perhaps, a set with another different independent apparatus claim and a set with an independent method of using claim in a complete application. One might also employ means-plus-function claims and/or method of making claims, provided the client is willing to absorb extra claim fees. We begin with a broad independent claim in these examples.

401. 230 F.3d 1320 (Fed. Cir. 2000).

EXAMPLE 4.44

I claim:

1. A radio frequency (RF) module comprising: at least one integrated circuit (IC) chip;

   the at least one IC chip is included in the RF module and further includes at least one field effect transistor, the at least one field effect transistor includes a gate, a drain, a source, and a body;

   wherein, during at least a portion of an off state, the body of the at least one field effect transistor is to be electrically biased to have a voltage level substantially more negative than the lowest voltage level of the following: ground, the DC voltage level of the source of the at least one field effect transistor, and the DC voltage level of the drain of the at least one field effect transistor.

Example features recited include:

1. Claim recites an RF module.
2. Claim recites the RF module includes an IC chip.
3. Claim recites that the IC chip includes at least one field effect transistor including a gate, a drain, a source, and a body.
4. Claim recites the at least one field effect transistor is in the off state.
5. Claim recites the body of the at least one field effect transistor is electrically biased to a voltage level.
6. Claim recites the voltage level of the electrical bias is substantially more negative than the lowest voltage level of ground, the DC voltage level of the source, and the DC voltage level of the drain.

Observe that while claim 1 is reasonably broad, it clearly has specific limitations that permit the ability to distinguish even this broad claim from the prior art. The reasons for these features should be clear from the prior technology discussion.[402] Most are for patentability arguments, but the recitation of a module and an IC may aid enforcement.

402. See earlier in this chapter introducing this technology example.

EXAMPLE 4.45

I claim:

1. A method of processing voicemail messages at a voicemail server, the method comprising:

   capturing a plurality of received voicemail messages in an audio format to provide a plurality of audio-formatted voicemail messages;

   converting the plurality of audio-formatted voicemail messages to a plurality of corresponding text representations of the voicemail messages; and

   initiating communication of the text representations of the voicemail messages and the audio-formatted voicemail messages to a mobile device, wherein a respective text representation comprises a representation of an at least partial text transcription of a corresponding converted audio-formatted voicemail message, the at least partial text transcriptions of the voicemail messages to be displayed via a visual voicemail inbox of a voicemail system integrated as part of the mobile device.

Example features recited include:

1. Claim recites processing of voicemail messages (plural) at a voicemail server.
2. Claim recites capturing audio-formatted voicemail messages and converting to text representations.
3. Claim clarifies and recites that a text representation comprises a representation of an at least partial text transcription of a corresponding audio-formatted voicemail message.
4. Claim recites that communication of the text representations of the voicemail messages and the audio-formatted voicemail messages is to a mobile device and is initiated.
5. Claim recites that the at least partial text transcriptions of the voicemail messages are to be displayed via a visual voicemail inbox of a voicemail system integrated as part of the mobile device.

Observe that while claim 1 is reasonably broad, it clearly has specific limitations that permit the ability to distinguish even this broad claim from the prior art. The reasons for these features should be clear from the prior discussion.[403]

403. *See id.*

Intermediate and Narrow Scope Claims

Continuing with the two previous technical examples, here, for the transistor body biasing technology example, are claims 2–10, which might be half of the claims of a complete patent application. Usually, patent applications are filed with 20 claims and three independent claims. The other ten claims might be another independent claim with nine dependent claims, or two more independent claims each with four dependent claims, and so on.

EXAMPLE 4.46

2. The radio frequency (RF) module of claim 1, wherein the at least one field effect transistor comprises an N-type metal oxide semiconductor (NMOS) field effect transistor.
3. The RF module of claim 1, wherein the at least one field effect transistor is implemented in a silicon-on-insulator (SOI) technology.
4. The RF module of claim 1, wherein the voltage level substantially more negative than the lowest voltage level is more than one volt more negative than the lowest voltage level.
5. The RF module of claim 1, wherein the body of the at least one field effect transistor is electrically coupled to an accumulated charge sink.
6. The RF module of claim 1, wherein the at least one field effect transistor during the at least a portion of the off state is to be electrically biased so as to improve the linearity of the at least one field effect transistor relative to the at least one field effect transistor not electrically biased to have a voltage level substantially more negative than the lowest voltage level of the following: ground, the DC voltage level of the source of the at least one field effect transistor, and the DC voltage level of the drain of the at least one field effect transistor.
7. The RF module of claim 1, wherein the at least one field effect transistor during the at least a portion of the off state is to be electrically biased so as to reduce nonlinear harmonic and/or intermodulation distortion of RF signals to be propagated by the module, reduction via the at least one field effect transistor being relative to the at least one field effect transistor not electrically biased to have a voltage level substantially more negative than the lowest voltage level of the following: ground, the DC voltage level of the source of the at least one field effect transistor, and the DC voltage level of the drain of the at least one field effect transistor.

8. The RF module of claim 7, wherein the power of a third harmonic of the RF signals to be propagated via the RF module is to be lower than –30 dBm at an operating power of +35 dBm power.

9. The RF module of claim 1, wherein the at least one field effect transistor is included in a stack of field effect transistors included in an RF switch, the RF switch being included in the at least one integrated circuit (IC) chip.

10. The RF module of claim 1, wherein the body of the at least one field effect transistor is electrically coupled to at least two accumulated charge sinks.

Example features recited include:

1. Claims recite NMOSFETs.
2. Claims recite SOI technology.
3. Claims recite "substantially more negative" is more than one volt "more negative."
4. Claims recite an accumulated charge sink.
5. Claims recite linearity improvement relative to a transistor without a body biased electrically negative so as to be in the off state.
6. Claims recite reduction of nonlinear harmonic and/or intermodulation distortion relative to a transistor without a body biased electrically negative so as to be in the off state.
7. Claims recite the power of a third harmonic of the RF signals to be propagated via the RF module is to be lower than –30 dBm at an operating power of +35 dBm power.
8. Claims recite that the at least one transistor is included in a transistor stack.

All these claims via dependency are necessarily narrower than claim 1. Some are not significantly narrower than claim 1, whereas some claims do seem narrow, such as feature 7, for example.

Continuing with the voicemail processing technology example are claims 2–7.

EXAMPLE 4.47

---

2. The method of claim 1, and further comprising:

receiving and processing the plurality of text representations for display of the at least partial text transcriptions via the visual voicemail inbox of the voicemail system integrated as part of the mobile device.

3. The method of claim 1, wherein the initiating communication of the text representations of the voicemail messages and the audio-formatted voicemail messages to the mobile device further includes initiating communication of one or more voicemail identifiers for respective voicemail messages of the plurality of voicemail messages, the one or more voicemail identifiers also displayable with the at least partial text transcriptions via the visual voicemail inbox as one or more visual voicemail indicators.
4. The method of claim 3, wherein, for a particular voicemail message, the one or more visual voicemail indicators include at least one of the following: a time of a telephone call associated with the particular voicemail message; a date of the telephone call associated with the particular voicemail message; and/or a telephone number for the telephone call associated with the particular voicemail message.
5. The method of claim 3, wherein the initiating communication further includes initiating communication of a plurality of telephone numbers associated with the plurality of voicemail messages, the telephone numbers displayable via the visual voicemail inbox as one of the one or more visual voicemail indicators in a manner so that the telephone numbers are selectable to call at least one of the telephone numbers.
6. The method of claim 1, wherein the initiating communication comprises initiating communication of one or more voicemail identifiers for respective voicemail messages to the mobile device displayable via the visual voicemail inbox as one or more visual voicemail indicators for respective voicemail messages along with the at least partial text transcription of the respective voicemail messages via the visual voicemail inbox of the voicemail system integrated as part of the mobile device.
7. The method of claim 1, wherein the initiating communication further includes initiating communication of the text representations of the voicemail messages and the audio-formatted voicemail messages, wherein the text transcriptions respectively comprise an at least partial text transcription displayable in a manner so that a displayed telephone number in at least one of the at least partial text transcriptions is selectable to call the telephone number that is displayed.

Example features recited include:

1. Claims recite receiving and processing the plurality of text representations for display.

2. Claims recite initiating communication of one or more voicemail identifiers for respective voicemail messages.
3. Claims recite particulars regarding voicemail indicators, for example a time of a telephone call associated with the particular voicemail message; a date of the telephone call associated with the particular voicemail message; and/or a telephone number for the telephone call associated with the particular voicemail message.
4. Claims recite that displayable telephone numbers are selectable to call at least one of the telephone numbers.
5. Claims recite a displayed telephone number in at least one of the at least partial text transcriptions is selectable to call the telephone number that is displayed.

All these claims via dependency are necessarily narrower than claim 1. In general, all seem of intermediate scope or narrower. Note how all are written in method claim format. Observe that claim 2 may have a divided infringement issue compared with the other claims because it recites receiving and processing performed by the mobile device, which is potentially separately operated from the server; however, to the extent that the software that does the receiving and processing is provided and perhaps even controlled by those controlling the voicemail server, then this may arguably not be divided infringement.

Picture Claims

A picture claim refers to a claim that includes all or nearly all the limitations of the narrowest embodiment of an invention. Such a claim, in essence, is sufficiently detailed as to form or create a "picture." Although we have recommended that you use claim differentiation as one technique for claiming the narrow embodiments, we also recommend the use of picture claims separately as well. Picture claims, of course, provide some of the advantages previously discussed. For example, they reduce the risk of lack of written description; however, there are additional advantages as well.

Employing picture claims may avoid the need to add rewritten claims in response to a PTO rejection. This, of course, has the potential to reduce prosecution history estoppel, although it will depend on the circumstances.[404] In addition, it is likely to save prosecution time by avoiding the need for an amendment, as just indicated, and, therefore, avoid the need to wait for the

404. *See* Honeywell Int'l v. Hamilton Sundstrand Corp., 370 F.3d 1131 (Fed. Cir. 2004) (en banc).

examiner's response to that amendment. Therefore, it may save money for your client, as well as a portion of the patent term.[405]

Another benefit of a picture claim is that it may lead to having at least one claim allowed in the first office action.[406] If not, this also gives you a good sense of where the examiner stands regarding your added limitations, suggesting you have work ahead to further distinguish from the art or to convince the examiner he or she has overlooked something.

Typically, a picture claim is an independent claim. This means it should get serious consideration from the examiner, which is desirable. One technique that is not as good might be to have, through a series of related dependencies, a claim that is a picture claim *in theory* because it includes all the important limitations. There are several reasons this is not as good. First, not being an independent claim, it may not get as much examiner attention. Furthermore, from the face of the claim, all its limitations are not immediately apparent. Rather, one needs to trace through a series of dependencies to appreciate its limitations. For this reason, it may not appear as narrow to the examiner.

Finally, employing picture claims may reduce the risk of dedicating disclosed subject matter to the public by forcing the patent drafter to be careful and claim everything that is disclosed. In *Johnson & Johnston Associates v. R.E. Service Co.*,[407] the Federal Circuit held, *en banc*, that subject matter disclosed in a specification that is not claimed is dedicated to the public. Of course, a picture claim would not necessarily have solved the problem in that case. The claims at issue related to fabrication of a printed circuit board. The claims recited aluminum and the patentee was attempting to use the DOE to also encompass steel, although steel had been disclosed as a possible material in the specification. Therefore, in some sense, the claim at issue in *Johnson & Johnston* was too narrow. However, writing picture claims is a good claim drafting practice to ensure that nothing mentioned in the specification that should be claimed is overlooked. As mentioned in connection with the discussion of means-plus-function claims,[408] including such claims is another way to avoid the problem in *Johnson & Johnston*.

There was a time when picture claims were commonly employed. Today, with the costs of filing having gone up considerably and with an increased

---

405. Delays in prosecution may affect the term of the patent. *See* 35 U.S.C. § 154 (2024).

406. On the other hand, some have expressed the concern that due to presence of the picture claim, perhaps that is all the examiner is willing to allow. If so, this could be seen as a disadvantage of a picture claim.

407. 285 F.3d 1046 (Fed. Cir. 2002) (en banc).

408. See the treatment of means-plus-function claims in this chapter.

focus on cost cutting, such claims are no longer typical. However, due to its potential benefits, a picture claim might be a third independent claim in a set of 20 claims or it might be a fourth independent claim in a set of 20 claims, at an additional cost of around $600 or $700 for a large entity.

Draft Claims to Make "Design Around" More Difficult

Another aspect of having a diverse set of claims is to draft claims to prevent or make "design around" more difficult. It is best if the claims may be drafted so that the only design around alternative is the prior art. It is impossible to cover the prior art with a claim, of course; however, presumably, the prior art approaches are inferior and less desirable than employing the technology associated with the invention. Preventing design around is such an important consideration that it may be a factor in the application of the DOE.

For example, in *Sage Products v. Devon Industries*,[409] the Federal Circuit held that no equivalents to the literal claims existed because the claims were drafted in a manner that made it "foreseeable" at the time of drafting that they could be easily designed around. This is sometimes referred to as the "foreseeability" limit to the DOE. Of course, this case may be unusual due to the simplicity of the invention and how easily the claims were to design around. The invention related to a receptacle for used medical debris, such as hypodermic needles. The concept, therefore, was that once the debris was placed in the receptacle it should not be easily removable. The claims, however, specifically recited elements, such as a precise location for the opening of the receptacle relative to the "top," and so on, making design around relatively easy. However, the court said that as between the public and the patentee, the burden should be on the patentee to prepare clear and broad claims, if desired. In other words, the DOE should not be used to, in essence, forgive claim drafting errors like overly narrow claims.

Nonetheless, the Supreme Court case *Festo Corp. v. Shoketsu Kinzoku Kogyo Kabushiki Co.*[410] also lends credence to the notion, suggested above, that a limited design around potential of the claims may result in a limited opportunity under the DOE. In that case, the Supreme Court created a presumption with respect to prosecution history estoppel in connection with an amendment of

---

409. 126 F.3d 1420 (Fed. Cir. 1997); *cf.* Ring & Pinion Serv. Inc. v. ARB Corp., 743 F.3d 831 (Fed. Cir. 2014).

410. 535 U.S. 722 (2002).

pending patent claims. The Court stated: "A patentee's decision to narrow his claims through amendment may be *presumed* to be a general disclaimer of the territory between the original claim and the amended claim."[411] However, according to the Court, the patentee is entitled to rebut this presumption: "The patentee must show that at the time of the amendment one skilled in the art could not reasonably be expected to have drafted a claim that would have literally encompassed the alleged equivalent."[412] Thus, it is fair to say that after *Festo*, design around considerations took on additional importance in connection with claim drafting.

It is important to consult with the inventors and technical personnel to make sure that all possible alternatives are thoroughly considered, evaluated, and, if appropriate, disclosed and claimed. Note that in addition to addressing the design around issues, as just discussed, including such claims as alternatives should also reduce the risk of a limitation being imported from the specification into the claims and reduce the risk that a court will conclude that the claims are not adequately supported in the specification.

A valuable technique is to review the claims with the inventors word by word. This will uncover both design around opportunities and potentially the closest prior art known to the inventor, which, in most if not all cases, must then be disclosed to the PTO. Another helpful exercise is to ask the inventors how they might attempt to design around their own invention once you have shown them the claims.

Following are examples of claims easily designed around. Potential ways to design around Example 4.48 include the shape of the seat, its orientation, the number and orientation of the legs, and so on. Inherently, a claiming approach that relies on claiming embodiments rather than the inventive concept invites design around opportunities.

EXAMPLE 4.48

I claim:

1. An apparatus comprising:

   a substantially horizontally oriented, rectangularly shaped seat including four corners;

411. *Id.* at 740 (emphasis added).
412. *Id.* at 741.

wherein attached to a respective corner of the seat is a substantially vertically oriented leg such that the legs point in the same direction away from the seat, are oriented to be substantially mutually parallel, and are of substantially the same length.

Instead, this might be claimed as a portable seat, which captures more effectively the inventive concept or innovation.[413]

Example 4.49 is a more subtle potential design around example.

EXAMPLE 4.49

I claim:

1. A method of forming a virtual private network comprising:

   communicating one or more signal packets between respective physically separate broadcast domains via a gateway device included in the respective physically separate broadcast domains, wherein the communicating the one or more signal packets comprises:

      encapsulating the one or more signal packets in the respective physically separate broadcast domains to be communicated; and

      communicating the encapsulated signal packets between the respective gateway devices and at least one tunnel server so that the one or more signal packets are communicated between the respective physically separate broadcast domains.

If this were the initial claim, one might argue *implicitly* that a broadcast domain includes more than one network device. This is further suggested by the reference to a gateway device, suggesting a gateway for other network devices on the domain. However, it is possible for a domain to consist of one device. Whether or not this claim covers that situation may come down to an analysis of the specification and the file history.

There are several ways to attempt to handle this potential design around opportunity with claim drafting. For one thing, "gateway device" may be

413. See Chapter 3, discussing this example in more detail.

changed to "network device," since a gateway device is really a network device, particularly in an embodiment employing a single device domain, as illustrated here.

I claim:

1. A method of forming a virtual private network comprising:

   communicating one or more signal packets between respective physically separate broadcast domains via a network device included in the respective physically separate broadcast domains, wherein the communicating the one or more signal packets comprises:

      encapsulating the one or more signal packets in the respective physically separate broadcast domains to be communicated; and

      communicating the encapsulated signal packets between respective network devices and at least one tunnel server so that the one or more signal packets are communicated between the respective physically separate broadcast domains.

Furthermore, adding a dependent claim reciting a single network device domain would leave little doubt regarding an embodiment with a single network device and that the base claim is intended to cover domains of one network device or more than one network device.

---

2. The method of claim 1, wherein at least one of the respective physically separate broadcast domains comprises a stand-alone network device.

However, one weakness with this claim is that it is not provided in method claim format, as shown here, which may be preferrable for a set of method claims.

---

2. The method of claim 1, wherein the communicating one or more signal packets between the respective physically separate broadcast domains comprises communicating the one or more signal packets between the

respective broadcast domains in which at least one physically separate broadcast domain comprises a stand-alone network device.

Draft Claims to Increase Relative Ease of Detecting (and Proving) Infringement

This is another area where it is recommended that you consult closely with the inventors and technical personnel who are familiar with the technology to ensure that this issue is addressed as completely as possible. There are a variety of ways that patent infringement is typically detectable. Therefore, ask technical personnel about whether those ways might apply and then draft the claims to enhance the possibility of detection.

For example, often certain features are likely to be mentioned in advertising literature, on a website, in a data sheet, and the like. One instance of this is a feature related to a published standard. If so, this is a feature where detecting its presence is relatively easy and claiming that feature will likely improve the value of the claims to the patentee. Of course, claiming features that are apparent rather than latent, or features that are relatively easy to test, such as those related to the input or output terminals of a chip, for example, is recommended. Also, claiming the ultimate end product in addition to the process of producing it, assuming that is possible, will make detecting infringement easier. This assumes the end product is easier to obtain and test than the process for making it. For example, if the invention is a process of applying a moisture-resistant coating to ICs, claim the moisture-resistant chip as well. Frequently, detecting infringement of the manufacturing process is difficult because it requires access to the potential infringer's factory; however, the chip may usually be purchased and closely examined.

It is also helpful to think in terms of features that will quickly eliminate products that do not infringe from consideration, even if it may not definitely produce an infringing product without significantly more investigation. Such features have the beneficial effect of limiting the scope of products to investigate to a reasonable number. For example, if the invention will reduce power consumption over the prior art, this may be a feature worth claiming even assuming there may be other reasons unrelated to the invention that may also reduce power consumption. At least those products that do not reduce power consumption measurably are easy to eliminate early. This is often an overlooked technique to improve ease of detecting infringement. Features that improve the ability to detect infringement add value, even where presence of the feature is not dispositive of infringement.

In addition to detecting infringement, the ability to easily prove infringement if a lawsuit were to result can be quite important (or where there is a significant threat of a lawsuit, such as a private negotiation). As claim drafters, we try to precisely identify what makes the invention innovative. However, this precise aspect may at times be quite a challenge to prove. It might be helpful in such circumstances to look for a sort of "proxy" measurement or feature that also relates to the innovation, but is much easier to demonstrate with evidence. Again, consulting the inventors, as the technical experts, may be useful here.

Example 4.50 is a claim to the switch technology we have used to illustrate some claim drafting principles.[414]

EXAMPLE 4.50

I claim:

1. A device comprising: at least one integrated circuit (IC); the at least one IC comprising:

   a shunt transistor having a first node coupled to a port and a second node coupled to ground, the shunt transistor comprising an accumulated charge control N-type MOSFET (NMOSFET) and wherein:

      the accumulated charge control NMOSFET comprises a gate, a drain, a source, a gate oxide layer, and a body, and an accumulated charge sink region connected to the body;

      the shunt transistor to couple the first port with the second port in a shunt transistor first state;

      the shunt transistor to isolate the first port from the second port in a shunt transistor second state, and wherein the shunt transistor is to have a bias voltage applied to the accumulated charge sink region to remove or otherwise control, via the accumulated charge sink region, charge that, without the bias voltage applied, would accumulate in the body in the shunt transistor second state; and

      the bias voltage to be substantially negative with respect to ground.

414. See earlier in this chapter, discussing this example.

Here, the invention is claimed in terms of the innovation. That is, to remove or otherwise control (e.g., limit) charge that might otherwise accumulate in the body of a transistor. It is this charge accumulation in a transistor (termed here "a shunt transistor") proximate to a transistor passing an analog signal that would otherwise corrupt the analog signal being passed.

While a technically accurate patent claim, an issue might be proving that charge would accumulate in the transistor body but for the claimed technology. The problem is that it would require building computer models of transistor operation to prove this. This could be done but it would be expensive and, of course, one can expect a battle of experts regarding the transistor models. Unfortunately, the judge and jury are unlikely to understand the transistor models of the technology enough to assess who should be believed.

However, if the shunt transistor body is properly biased in the off state, then signal corruption or nonlinear harmonics are reduced. Therefore, instead, simply claim the bias voltage as applied in the off state of the shunt transistor for the broadest claim. This is easier to prove. It also is broader than Example 4.50. The charge accumulation aspects may also be claimed in dependencies as fallback positions if needed to distinguish from prior art.

In addition, other more detectable and provable features may be included in dependent claims, as illustrated in Example 4.51.

EXAMPLE 4.51

I claim:

1. A device comprising: at least one integrated circuit (IC) chip; the at least one IC chip including at least one N-type metal oxide semiconductor field effect transistor (NMOSFET);

   wherein at least one NMOSFET transistor of the plurality includes a source, a gate, a drain, and a body;

   wherein the at least one NMOSFET transistor is further included in an electrical configuration within the at least one IC chip, the electrical configuration to at least control the at least one NMOSFET transistor to either an ON state or an OFF state based at least on one or more control signals; and wherein the electrical configuration is at least further to electrically bias the body of the at least one NMOSFET transistor to a DC voltage level substantially more negative than ground at least in a portion of the OFF state of the at least one NMOSFET transistor.

2. The device of claim 1, wherein the at least one field effect transistor is implemented in a silicon-on-insulator (SOI) technology.
3. The device of claim 1, wherein the voltage level substantially more negative than ground is more than one volt more negative than ground.
4. The device of claim 1, wherein the at least one field effect transistor during the at least a portion of the off state is to be electrically biased so as to improve the linearity of the at least one field effect transistor relative to the at least one field effect transistor not electrically biased to have a voltage level substantially more negative than ground.
5. The device of claim 1, wherein the at least one field effect transistor during the at least a portion of the off state is to be electrically biased so as to reduce nonlinear harmonic and/or intermodulation distortion of signals to be propagated by the IC, reduction via the at least one field effect transistor being relative to the at least onc field effect transistor not electrically biased to have a voltage level substantially more negative than ground.

Claim 2 refers to SOI technology, which is relatively easy to detect and prove. Claim 3 refers to a specific voltage amount below ground. Claims 4 and 5 refer to measures easy to detect and prove—improved signal linearity and reduced nonlinear harmonic and/or intermodulation distortion, respectively. These features, such as the latter two, are not only easy to detect and prove but also provide further distinctions from the prior art beyond the base claim.

Chapter 5

Introduction to Claim Construction and Principles of Patent Infringement

Understand the differences between direct patent infringement and indirect patent infringement as well as the differences between literal patent infringement and non-literal patent infringement when drafting patent claims.

In this chapter, we discuss the *Markman v. Westview Instruments, Inc.*[1] case, a U.S. Supreme Court decision, and the *Phillips v. AWH Corp.*[2] case, an *en banc* Federal Circuit decision. These decisions continue to have a major impact on the interpretation of patent claims. One may, in fact, think in terms of a post-*Markman* era of claim construction in patent law due to the significance of how claim language interpretation changed after the *Markman* decision.

Understanding how federal courts interpret patent claims assists in drafting patent claims and leads to some basic claim drafting principles, as introduced later. Key categories of patent infringement include direct patent infringement, literal patent infringement, indirect patent infringement, and patent infringement under the doctrine of equivalents (DOE).[3]

Legal Framework for Claim Construction

Understand why Markman hearings exist, their importance in claim construction, and how that may affect patent claim drafting.

Following the Supreme Court's decision in *Markman*, a host of substantive and procedural questions emerged that were not resolved by that decision and required lower courts to fill in the blanks, so to speak. In the time since then, many issues, procedural and substantive, have become reasonably well settled. This body of law represents the existing legal framework for claim

1. 517 U.S. 370 (1996).
2. 415 F.3d 1303 (Fed. Cir. 2005) (en banc).
3. Another type is referred to as imputed patent infringement but is far less common.

construction. Our primary focus relates to understanding the substantive legal issues that could be of use in claim drafting.

Markman v. Westview Instruments, Inc.
517 U.S. 370
Supreme Court of the United States
January 8, 1996, Argued; April 23, 1996, Decided

Questions

1. The *Markman* case provides some history of the use of patent claims. According to the Court, it was not until about 1870 that claims came into use. It was commonplace to use what is termed an "omnibus claim," which is sometimes used in some foreign jurisdictions. It might state something like: "An apparatus substantially as shown and described." Today, the Manual of Patent Examining Procedure (MPEP) specifically instructs examiners to reject such claims.[4] Any theories on why practice evolved from relying on the specification to a practice that requires a claim to "define" the claimed invention? What is the statutory section of title 35 that such a claim would seem to violate? One may legitimately wonder about the effectiveness of the present system. For example, issues under § 101 and patent eligibility may well be a reflection of the fact that claims may do a poor job of truly identifying an innovation.[5] Furthermore, as addressed later, despite the *Markman* decision, which put claim construction in the hands of the federal judge, the reversal rate for claim construction is about where it was before that decision.[6]
2. Before the *Markman* decision how do you think questions of claim construction were handled? Under such an approach how likely do you think it was that the claims were being appropriately construed? Do you believe that juries are able to understand the scope of patent claims without some guidance by a federal judge? How helpful, then,

4. *See* U.S. Patent and Trademark Office, Manual of Patent Examining Procedure § 2173.05(r) (9th ed. 2023).

5. See Chapter 6, addressing patent eligibility issues.

6. There have been various studies and there is some variance in terms of how decisions are counted, but typically the reversal rate for claim construction ruling ranges from a low of about one-third to a high of about two-thirds. In general, then, an estimate of a 50 percent reversal rate is probably a good guess. For a shorthand, although not precisely accurate, for purposes of discussion, we will refer to this as "the 50 percent reversal rate."

is the guidance provided by the federal judge? Do you believe a federal judge is able to understand the scope of patent claims? What are some barriers to either the jury or a judge being able to understand the scope of particular patent claims? Are there any procedural benefits to having the federal judge construe the patent claims? Do you think the complexity of patent claims, including whether a proper interpretation is reached, undermines due process?

3. Note that we have seen rulings go from a jury decision in favor of one party to, on appeal, the Federal Circuit ruling summary judgment for the other party (i.e., without a remand). Note that sometimes the case is remanded and sometimes it is not. Be aware that there have been Federal Circuit cases where the Federal Circuit came up with a claim construction that was not advanced by either party and then proceeded to decide the case without remand (e.g., on grounds of summary judgment, etc.). What concerns do these possible outcomes raise?
4. Does the *Markman* decision say anything about the distinction between issues of law and issues of fact and how these issues might be allocated between a judge and jury, and/or the appropriate standard of review on appeal for legal versus factual issues? Is claim construction an issue of law or an issue of fact? Does your answer tell you the appropriate standard of review on appeal?
5. As suggested by footnote 6 to question 1 and discussed in at least one of the additional opinions in *Cybor* (next case addressed), studies suggest that there is little impact on the reversal rate by having the judge construe the claims rather than the jury. With a 50 percent reversal rate of a district court's claim construction, as a litigant who loses regarding claim construction, what are you likely to do? What is the problem, then, with such a reversal rate as a matter of policy? What does it tell you regarding certainty of the law surrounding claim construction? (Recall one of the justifications for relegating claim construction was to promote uniformity in the law.) As a claim drafter, what strategy does it suggest?
6. Do you think these issues regarding claim construction (e.g., an unusually high reversal rate) are a failing by the Federal Circuit or do you think there is something inherent in the issues that come up during claim construction that leads to this lack of certainty?
7. Claim construction is often compared with contract or statutory interpretation; however, some aspects of the rules of construction are different. Do you think if some of the same principles from those

analogies were adopted that it might lead to greater certainty and predictability regarding claim interpretation? Can you provide examples? Any theories on why the rules are different for claim construction in some fundamental ways?

8. The Federal Circuit professes to try to figure out what the patent claims *truly* mean. Do you think figuring that out is possible? Why do you think Markman was pushing so hard to get the Court to let claim construction go to the jury?
9. After the *Markman* decision, it appears that in any case there are decisions that are properly for the court and decisions that are properly for the jury. Can you articulate what those respective domains amount to? How might a court inadvertently invade the area related to the jury? If that were to happen, what would be the remedy by an appellate court to correct it in a given case?
10. It is important to appreciate that claim construction may touch every important issue in a patent case. It is, perhaps, the single most important legal issue in a patent case. Can you provide examples of some issues in a patent case that might be impacted by the claim construction, other than simply validity and infringement? Certain practices have emerged in connection with claim construction in light of the *Markman* decision, treated later.

Cybor Corp. v. FAS Technologies, Inc.
138 F.3d 1448
United States Court of Appeals for the Federal Circuit
March 25, 1998, Decided

Questions

1. What is *Markman I* referred to by the court versus *Markman II* also referred to by the appellate court? Does *Markman I* have any continuing vitality as a legal decision binding on lower courts? Why or why not?
2. According to the appellate court, it took this case *en banc* to resolve a conflict in lower court decisions. What was that conflict? How did the appellate court choose to resolve that conflict? Does this create an issue in connection with claim construction? How do federal appellate courts usually resolve a mixed question of fact and law (i.e., what is the usual standard of review)? Is claim construction a purely legal question or a mixed question? How does the *en banc* decision in this case review factual issues that may arise in connection with claim construction (i.e., what standard of review is an appellate court to apply to such issues)?

3. The court, in footnote 5, suggests some controversy around the *Fromson v. Anitec Printing Plates, Inc.* decision.[7] Can you articulate the legal issue alluded to by the appellate court in its footnote and how the court appears to resolve the issue?
4. What is the question raised by the appellate court in footnote 7 that it chose not to answer in this case? How would you argue that it is an issue for the jury? How would you argue that it is an issue for the court?
5. The appellate court observes that this decision took place before the *Markman* decision by the Supreme Court was available. Despite this the *en banc* court does not feel a new trial is necessary. Why is that?
6. What is the crux of Cybor's argument that it does not infringe? How does the Federal Circuit reconcile the argument by Cybor with statements made during prosecution of the patent claims at issue? How clear is it from the file history what subject matter the patentee relinquished for this patent?
7. FAS argues that because Cybor is willful, the district court was required to enhance the award of damages. Why does the Federal Circuit say that is not a correct description of the law?
8. There seems discord among the judges of the Federal Circuit regarding the meaning of the *Markman* decision as it relates to how properly to characterize the determinations that must be made during claim construction with respect to issues of law versus issues of fact. This, then, affects the appropriate standard of review to apply to such determinations made by a lower court. Can you summarize the key differences in the views articulated through the different opinions in this case?
9. What is the point being made by the concurrence in judgment by Judges Newman and Mayer about the consequences of the affirmance of infringement? The concurrence stated:

> However, if the court is correct that claim construction is purely and solely a question of law to be reviewed *de novo* on appeal, it could not affirm the judgment of infringement. Infringement was determined in this case by a jury at the same time that it was asked to construe these claims by resolving factual disputes about their meaning and to determine whether the scope of these claims should be limited by arguments made during prosecution of the patent. Ordinarily, a jury's verdict of infringement permits us to presume the existence of factual findings necessary to that verdict. But we are in no way entitled to

7. 132 F.3d 1437 (Fed. Cir. 1997).

presume factual findings or even to rely on the verdict of infringement where neither the jury, nor the judge on a motion for judgment as a matter of law, articulated a construction of the claims upon which the findings are premised. As explained above, there are five possible combinations of claim term interpretations and findings of paragraph 112(6) equivalents that could have led the jury to its infringement verdict. In light of the possibilities, it is difficult to imagine how the court can affirm the jury's finding of infringement based upon its own *de novo* claim construction, which merely presumes a claim construction by the district court and that admits of no deference to the findings of fact.

The effect of allowing such a combination of presumptions in this case has been to deny Cybor meaningful review of anything more than the district judge's decision not to apply prosecution history estoppel, since it was the only legal determination that can be located outside of those presumptions. Not surprisingly, this is the decision Cybor contests most strenuously on appeal. The effect has also been to allow this court to presume that it made the same claim construction as the jury, without so much as articulating its own construction of these two claim terms, and then to presume that the jury's infringement finding is still valid. Penultimately, Cybor is left with little more than the ability to make presumptions as to our own claim interpretations in any motion it may file for reconsideration. Worse still is the message the court is sending to district courts: we will affirm a finding of infringement as long as the district court avoids articulating its construction of the claims—which coincidentally leaves us free to arrive at our own constructions—and as long as we can presume that the jury used our constructions to arrive at that finding of infringement.[8]

10. What do you think about Judge Rader's suggestion to provide more deference to the district court judge? Rader provides some advantages. What are some disadvantages? How much deference do you think he has in mind? Clear error deference? Substantial evidence deference?
11. A fixture in patent claim construction appears to be a decided preference for intrinsic evidence over extrinsic evidence. The additional views expressed by Judges Newman and Mayer appear to question the wisdom of this approach. As we shall see, how to appropriately

8. Cybor Corp. v. FAS Techs., Inc., 138 F.3d 1448, 1471–73 (Fed. Cir. 1998).

weigh intrinsic versus extrinsic evidence appears to divide the court until the *en banc* decision, *Phillips*. What are some of the pros and cons for letting or for not letting extrinsic evidence be accorded significant weight in comparison to intrinsic evidence during the claim construction calculus?

Markman Decision and *Markman* Hearings

The Supreme Court's *Markman v. Westview Instruments* decision fundamentally changed how patent claims are interpreted under U.S. patent law. Before that decision, interpretation of patent claims was usually relegated to the jury along with the determination whether patent infringement had occurred. However, in the *Markman* decision, the Supreme Court determined that how claims are construed should be performed by the judge rather than the jury for federal court patent litigation. This was a policy-based decision emanating from the view that construing claims is more legal (province of the judge) than it is factual (province of the jury). The Court believed having the judge construe the claims would lead to greater consistency in how claims are construed.[9]

Nonetheless, the Seventh Amendment provides a right to jury trial in patent cases. Thus, the jury makes the factual determination of whether the accused product or accused service falls within the scope of the patent claims, once properly construed. Hence, determination of patent infringement is a two-step process: (1) construing the claims and (2) determining whether the accused product or accused service falls within the construed claim scope.

Interestingly, despite the rationale provided for the decision, studies of Federal Circuit decisions before and after *Markman* suggest that having a judge construe the claims has had little impact on appellate court reversal rates, which is typically around 50 percent, depending on the study.[10]

---

9. The *Markman* decision did not resolve the standard of review an appellate court should apply to lower court determinations regarding claim construction. That issue was resolved by the *en banc* decision *Cybor Corp. v. FAS Technologies, Inc.*, 138 F.3d 1448 (Fed. Cir. 1998), to be de novo review. However, a later Supreme Court decision clarified that for subsidiary factual issues related to extrinsic evidence (as opposed to intrinsic evidence) a clear error standard should be applied on appeal. *See* Teva Pharms. USA, Inc. v. Sandoz, Inc., 574 U.S. 318 (2015).

10. *See* Christian A. Chu, *Empirical Analysis of the Federal Circuit's Claim Construction Trends*, 16 Berkeley Tech. L.J. 1075, 1143 (2001); Kimberly A. Moore, *Markman Eight Years Later: Is Claim Construction More Predictable?*, 9 Lewis & Clark L. Rev. 231, 232–34 (2005); Michael Saunders, *A Survey of Post-*Phillips *Claim Construction Cases*, 22 Berkeley Tech. L.J. 215, 233 (2007); Andrew T. Zidel, *Patent Claim Construction in the Trial Courts: A Study Showing the Need for Clear Guidance from the Federal Circuit*, 33 Seton Hall L. Rev. 711, 743 (2003).

Thus, as a result of *Markman*, the judge interprets the patent claims and instructs the jury as to the meaning thereof. The jury then determines whether patent infringement has occurred in light of the evidence presented and the court's claim construction. This division should generally be kept in mind, because it is important to *not* have a federal court in a given case, under the guise of claim construction, inadvertently invade the domain left for jury decision.[11]

Soon after the decision, a procedural mechanism, referred to as a "*Markman* hearing," came into existence, in which parties present respective positions to a federal judge regarding how the patent claims should be interpreted. The Supreme Court case did not address the procedural issue of holding a hearing. Thus, it was left to lower courts to figure out how and when to conduct such hearings.

It bears mention that how the patent claims are construed touches every important issue in a patent infringement case. Consequently, the rules surrounding such hearings were and are quite important. Some federal jurisdictions that frequently hear patent cases, such as the Northern District of California,[12] have fashioned local rules to govern such proceedings.

Typically, *Markman* hearings are held reasonably early in a patent case, after a certain amount of discovery has taken place. Of course, this is not required, but it is a common practice. The claim construction found early in the case may be revisited later; however, it is more desirable to time the hearing in a manner so that revisiting claim construction is not needed. Likewise, it is not unusual for a *Markman* hearing to be combined with a hearing regarding a motion for summary judgment. This often aids court efficiency because claim interpretation may resolve the case, allowing an immediate appeal to the Federal Circuit regarding the claim construction found by the district court.

Table 5.1 provides a typical example of how filings leading up to a *Markman* hearing may be docketed in federal court. This is simply provided as an illustration. Other courts may docket these and other items differently.

---

11. *Cf.* Acumed LLC v. Stryker Corp., 483 F.3d 800, 806 (Fed. Cir. 2007) ("[A] sound claim construction need not always purge every shred of ambiguity. The resolution of some line-drawing problems—especially easy ones like this one—is properly left to the trier of fact.").

12. *See Patent Local Rules*, N.D. Cal., https://www.cand.uscourts.gov/rules/patent-local-rules/ (last revised Oct. 19, 2023) (providing patent local rules for the Northern District of California).

Table 5.1 Filings Leading Up to a *Markman* Hearing[13]

1. Case management conference
2. Disclosure of asserted claims and infringement contentions
3. Invalidity contentions
4. Identification of claim terms to be construed
5. Preliminary claim constructions
6. Joint claim construction statement
7. Close of claim construction discovery
8. Opening claim construction brief
9. Responsive claim construction brief
10. Reply claim construction brief
11. *Markman* hearing
12. Claim construction order

As shown, there is usually an initial conference to set time lines, and so on. Then asserted claims are identified and infringement and invalidity contentions are exchanged. Following that, claims to be construed are identified by respective sides, initial claim constructions are exchanged, and a joint claim construction statement is produced. After close of claim construction discovery, an initial or opening claim construction brief is filed, followed by a responsive brief and a reply brief. This all leads up to the *Markman* hearing itself, which typically results in a claim construction order.

ITC Investigation: Another Enforcement Option

The most common form of enforcement of intellectual property (IP) rights, particularly patent rights, occurs by bringing a lawsuit in federal district court. Unfortunately, federal court litigation may not fully address the needs of a patent holder whose products are copied and sold in the United States by a foreign entity *without the authority to do so*. Seeking redress against a foreign entity importing so-called knockoffs into the United States may be especially challenging. Federal court remedies and procedures may, at times, permit a foreign entity to infringe on patent rights without full redress of those rights. Examples include that federal courts have jurisdiction and venue requirements that may be limited to specific locales,[14] and that federal court legal remedies may be limited. As an example, the requirements for an injunction against an infringer are quite stringent.[15] In essence, to obtain a federal court injunction,

13. *Id.*

14. *See* Tom Schaumberg, *Advantages of International Trade Commission Practice: Gaining an Edge over Infringing Imports*, 25 Comput. & Internet Law. 19 (2008).

15. *Id.*

one must show that the patent holder cannot be made whole with monetary damages.[16] Consequently, the International Trade Commission (ITC or the Commission), a federal agency with quasi-judicial power, is becoming a more popular choice for patent enforcement.[17] While having some advantages relative to federal court, the ITC may also have some disadvantages relative to federal court. Consequently, one of the more effective strategies for redress against foreign entities importing goods into the United States that infringe on an entity's patents is a parallel strategy of enforcement in federal court *and* in the ITC.[18]

Some important differences between federal court litigation and an ITC investigation suggest several advantages for ITC enforcement. For example, while a lawsuit is typically limited to a particular locale based on principles of jurisdiction and venue, an ITC investigation is not limited in this respect.[19] The investigation and resulting exclusion order from the ITC are directed to the goods at issue, rather than to the parties involved or to a particular location.[20] Thus, the ITC with its broad powers may be more effective against goods sold throughout the United States.[21] One potential disadvantage, on the other hand, is that a broad ITC exclusion order may affect sales by the foreign entity to an existing customer of the patent holder. This may detrimentally affect the patent holder's relationship with that customer. As to remedies, exclusion orders capable of issuing from the ITC may provide the functional equivalent of a federal court-issued injunction because such an order prevents foreign goods from entering the country. Obtaining an injunction in a federal lawsuit, however, may often be more challenging due to stringent requirements applied by federal courts to issue an injunction.[22] The ITC also offers an advantage from a discovery perspective.[23] Discovery orders issued by a U.S. court are typically limited to the United States; however, a discovery order to a foreign entity issued by the ITC, even if seeking evidence from outside the United States, usually receives compliance because noncompliance may lead to exclusion of the entity's goods from the United States.[24] The differ-

---

16. *Id.*
17. *Id.*; Mark J. Abate & Calvin E. Wingfield Jr., *Pleading Requirements in the ITC and Tips to Starting an Investigation on the Right Foot*, IP LITIGATOR, Mar./Apr. 2009, at 8.
18. *See* Schaumberg, *supra* note 14.
19. *Id.*; Abate & Wingfield, *supra* note 17.
20. *See* Schaumberg, *supra* note 14; Abate & Wingfield, *supra* note 17.
21. Schaumberg, *supra* note 14; Abate & Wingfield, *supra* note 17.
22. *See* Schaumberg, *supra* note 14.
23. *Id.*
24. *Id.*

ent decision-makers for the two proceedings also suggests an advantage in the ITC. The administrative law judges (ALJs) and Commission members of the ITC are well-versed in patent law and technology, while district court judges and juries often are not.[25] Some have even suggested that the ITC is like a trial-level patent court due to its expertise. This difference from federal practice and procedure may also explain the significantly higher affirmance rate for ITC decisions taken on appeal relative to district court decisions.[26] Furthermore, there are no juries in the ITC, which is typically an advantage for the patent holder, primarily because, again, ITC judges are well-versed in patent law.[27] Because an action in the ITC is an investigation and not a lawsuit, counterclaims by the importer are not permitted, another advantage for the patent holder. From an enforcement perspective, the ITC also provides an advantage in terms of time frame to completion. ITC investigations are usually completed in 12–15 months, which puts pressure on the entity whose goods are being imported.[28] In contrast, a federal district court case may last two to five years or longer before a final decision is issued, at times due to procedural opportunities by the defendant to drag it out. Another advantage associated with an ITC investigation is that a district court will stay (i.e., hold in abeyance) a lawsuit pending outcome of a Commission investigation.[29] A further advantage is that the ITC will rarely stay its investigation for a parallel U.S. Patent and Trademark Office (PTO) proceeding involving the patents at issue, such as a patent reexamination, for example.[30] This is in direct contrast to a district court that often might stay the lawsuit in favor of the parallel PTO proceeding.[31] This strategic situation gives the patent holder an opportunity to secure a win in the ITC before battling things out in federal court.

There are a few areas, however, where a federal district court lawsuit may be more advantageous. For one thing, damages are available in federal district court, but not in the ITC. The complaint process for an ITC investigation is much more complex and document intensive.[32] One must establish with evidence the presence of "importation" and an affected "domestic industry" for an investigation in the ITC to proceed, *in addition to* proving the typical elements

25. *Id.*
26. *Id.*
27. *Id.*
28. *Id.*
29. *Id.*
30. *See* Abate & Wingfield, *supra* note 17.
31. *Id.*
32. *See* Schaumberg, *supra* note 14; Abate & Wingfield, *supra* note 17.

of a patent infringement case.[33] Federal district courts, by contrast, employ a pleading standard where the basis for the lawsuit needs to be explained in the complaint with sufficient facts pled to show that it is plausible that the asserted claim can be established.[34] Detailed and more specific allegations come later in the suit. Furthermore, once a complaint is filed in federal court, it is relatively easy to amend if the amendment is timely and with good cause. A complaint in an ITC investigation, after having been filed, is relatively difficult to amend.[35] Federal courts also typically use *Markman* hearings early in the lawsuit to interpret the patent claims, which tends to focus the issues for the case and may even resolve the dispute without trial.[36] As previously noted, a *Markman* hearing is a special proceeding in federal court patent litigation in which each side presents its position on the correct interpretation of the patent claims to a federal district judge.[37] Ultimately, this important question is then decided *exclusively* by the district court judge in a *Markman* order.[38] Also, federal district court rulings, such as a *Markman* order, may have a *res judicata* effect (e.g., be binding on future litigation between the parties).[39] ITC investigations rarely conduct *Markman* hearings and the orders from the ITC are not binding on federal courts and, consequently, have no *res judicata* effect.[40] Federal courts, in general, have an inherent contempt power with respect to the parties to obtain compliance with orders and rulings. The ITC does not have a contempt power, but the threat of exclusion of an entity's goods for noncompliance is a powerful incentive.[41] Furthermore, decisions by the Commission may become political (e.g., requiring the approval of the president),[42] while the constitutional separation of powers between the judicial branch and the executive branch generally tends to keep courts isolated from political pressures. Also, there is some enforcement risk of an ITC exclusion order, not present for a district court ruling due to a federal court's inherent contempt power, depending on the nature of the product at issue. U.S. Customs may

---

33. Schaumberg, *supra* note 14; Abate & Wingfield, *supra* note 17.
34. *See* Abate & Wingfield, *supra* note 17.
35. *Id.*
36. *See* Peter S. Menell et al., *Patent Claim Construction: A Modern Synthesis and Structured Framework*, 25 Berkeley Tech. L.J. 713 (2010).
37. *Id.*
38. *Id.*
39. *See* Schaumberg, *supra* note 14.
40. *Id.*
41. *Id.*
42. For example, during the Obama administration, President Obama, largely on political grounds, did not approve an ITC exclusion order that resulted from a complaint by a foreign entity against a U.S. company.

not be able to identify infringing product by simple product inspection (e.g., infringing software or an infringing chip may be buried deep in a system-level product being imported). If U.S. Customs is not able to verify infringement by inspection, the goods are permitted to enter the United States.

Given the trade-offs between a federal court lawsuit and an ITC investigation, one strategy to get the benefits of both may be to engage in parallel proceedings.[43] One benefit might be timing because both may be filed concurrently, but the federal suit is likely to be stayed until the conclusion of the ITC investigation.[44] Filing the suit in federal court with a stay is a type of preemptive strike preventing the potential defendant from "shopping" for a more sympathetic court by attempting to file in federal court first.[45] Meanwhile, the ITC investigation may proceed at its accelerated pace. If there is a decision to ultimately go forward with a federal court litigation after the ITC investigation, this may draw the process out considerably, but an ongoing ITC investigation with the threat that a pending federal suit that has been stayed may proceed later might be a sufficient legal threat to get early resolution with an adverse party. A key benefit of a parallel strategy is the potential to stop future importation (e.g., via the ITC) *and* recover damages for past infringement (via federal court).[46] Likewise, proceeding with the ITC investigation first should benefit a stayed lawsuit for the patent holder. For example, the ITC discovery may be transferred to the lawsuit.[47] In addition, the analysis at the ITC, in which the ALJs are well-versed in patent law, may influence a federal court judge in a district court case. Likewise, by proceeding with a federal district court case, the binding *res judicata* effect of a federal court decision will ultimately be obtained.

Nonetheless, there are also challenges with a parallel enforcement strategy. For one thing, both parties experience a "war on two fronts," so to speak. This suggests greater costs related to the dispute and a greater distraction for management, whose main occupation should be running the business of the particular entity. Likewise, potentially, there may be a longer time to full resolution for a parallel enforcement strategy. In general, these issues may affect both the importer and the patent holder. The advantage here may, thus, be to the larger entity of the two having greater resources to handle such burdens.

---

43. *See* Schaumberg, *supra* note 14.
44. *Id.*
45. *Id.*
46. *Id.*
47. *Id.*

Of course, a loss in the ITC for either entity would have a potentially negative impact overall and certainly may affect the district court litigation.

Unfortunately, in today's international economy, the fact that IP rights, particularly patents rights, are country-based may be a barrier to extracting full value from owning such rights. A foreign entity importing so-called knockoffs into the United States may fall outside the powers of a federal court in some situations. Federal court remedies and procedures, based on principles of fairness and governmental authority, are not entirely equipped to handle situations that typically may arise in a worldwide economy. The ITC, a federal agency with quasi-judicial power, is becoming a more popular venue for patent enforcement, but while having some advantages over federal court, it may also have some disadvantages relative to federal court in part due to its federal agency status. However, notably, it is not hampered by some of the procedural limits imposed on federal courts. Thus, it appears that the most effective strategy for redress against foreign entities importing goods into the United States that infringe on an entity's patents is a parallel strategy that pursues enforcement in federal court and in the ITC; however, this assumes adequate resources by the patent holder to pursue such a strategy.

Intrinsic Evidence versus Extrinsic Evidence

Understand the difference between intrinsic and extrinsic evidence and the significance of each in claim interpretation and in claim drafting.

From the *Markman* decision until around 2005, the state of claim construction was not entirely clear as different panels of judges emphasized what was termed "intrinsic evidence" while others emphasized what was termed "extrinsic evidence." Rather than work our way forward, we will start where the law ultimately settled and visit the decisions that shaped the path to the end result. The seminal case on claim construction is the *en banc* decision *Phillips*. However, appreciate that even after *Phillips*, differences remain at the margins as some panels apply the principles of *Phillips* quite rigorously, while others, although in general adhering to the fundamental principles, use reasoning that may not be pristine in an effort to discover what they come to believe is the *true* meaning of the claims.

Phillips v. AWH Corp.
415 F.3d 1303
United States Court of Appeals for the Federal Circuit
July 12, 2005, Decided

Questions

1. In many ways, although quite well-reasoned, the *Phillips* decision is a complex one, touching on many of the issues we have seen in some prior cases. It is helpful to trace the history to the *en banc* decision if only to see the different ways the same claims at issue had been quite differently construed. For example, how did the district court initially construe the claims and why? After that, how did the three-judge panel hearing the case on appeal construe the claims and why? Likewise, one judge on the panel dissented. Why did that judge dissent and how did he want the claims construed? Then we have the *en banc* decision. How did the full court construe the claims and why? Thus, we have a number of different views on what the claims could mean, plus several of the concurring opinions and dissenting opinions also expressing different views about the methodology and/or the ultimate outcome. Is it no wonder that the reversal rate on district court claim construction hovers around 50 percent?
2. One way to view *Phillips*, as the appellate court itself states several times, is as a return to the construct of the appellate court's *Markman I* decision, and its *Vitronics* decision,[48] which we will consider later in this chapter. However, in *Phillips*, the appellate court clarifies some issues that were not entirely clear following *Markman I* and *Vitronics*. Thus, *Phillips*, truly, is the authoritative and most influential guide to patent claim construction. With the majority opinion, the concurrences, and the dissents, readily apparent are some key aspects that had divided the appellate court. What are some of those issues?
3. However, it might be more accurate to say that *Phillips* provided a methodology for uniting fundamentally differing approaches to claim construction—an approach that primarily employs ordinary and customary meaning (derived from extrinsic evidence) with an approach that primarily employs intrinsic evidence. The benefit of the approach adopted is that it is essentially a weighted totality of the circumstances approach, which is highly flexible. Given the potential variability of claim terms, especially due to its highly technological nature, flexibility seems appropriate. However, that same flexibility may be its undoing as well. District courts have no clear guidance on how to weigh the different examples of evidence. Even experienced

48. Vitronics Corp. v. Conceptronic, Inc., 90 F.3d 1576 (Fed. Cir. 1996).

judges may well each reach different results under such an approach, illustrated by the different constructions reached by different judges in this very case. Exacerbating this issue is the debate regarding the appropriate standard of review. Is it fair to say that no one knows the meaning of the claims until the Federal Circuit rules on what they mean (raised by Judge Rader in his dissent in *Cybor*)?

4. One key (but not the only) aspect, as implied earlier, revolves around the division between intrinsic and extrinsic evidence and how to respectively weigh each during the claim construction phase. What is intrinsic evidence? What is extrinsic evidence? What are the appellate court's rationales for favoring intrinsic evidence over extrinsic evidence? Given those rationales, why is it that some panels overweighted extrinsic evidence and underweighted intrinsic evidence? Why is it that the *en banc* majority rejects that approach? What do they say would be the systematic claim construction error that would likely result from using such an approach consistently? However, does the *en banc* court give appropriate guidance regarding how to weigh these different sources of evidence? For example, is it clear in what situations the prosecution history should be given more weight? Is it clear in what situations extrinsic evidence should be given more weight?
5. What role, if any, do dictionaries and similar sources play in the claim construction process? Are the materials intrinsic or extrinsic? What is ordinary and customary meaning and how does a court determine it? Once the court determines the ordinary customary meaning, does that necessarily guide how the claims are to be interpreted? Why or why not? If not, what then is the role of the ordinary and customary meaning?
6. After *Phillips*, how clear is the difference between interpreting the claims in light of the specification and reading a limitation from the specification into the claims? Can you articulate the difference?
7. Why did the district court determine that the claims should be construed under § 112, paragraph 6 (112, 6)? Why did the appellate panel disagree but determine that the term "baffle" should have a restricted meaning? Why did the *en banc* majority ultimately disagree with the three-judge panel regarding how to construe "baffle"? In light of the facts, do these different interpretations affect the infringement case against the defendant? How should a court use extrinsic evidence? When is it improper to resort to extrinsic evidence?
8. In addition to the pecking order between intrinsic and extrinsic evidence, there is also a pecking order, so to speak, regarding the different

types of intrinsic evidence. What are those different types and what is the pecking order? Despite the existence of a pecking order, so to speak, is it clear how to weigh the claims with respect to the specification and how to weigh each of those with respect to the file history? Is applied prior art extrinsic evidence or intrinsic evidence? What about cited prior art that is not applied?

9. Judge Mayer argues that claim construction should be treated like obviousness where the conclusion is legal but is based on factual underpinnings. What are examples of factual underpinnings in claim construction? Is it true that a trial judge is in a better position than an appellate court to assess these things? What might be examples of disadvantages of relying on factual findings by the trial judge?
10. What do you make of the following paragraphs from the majority opinion?

> In our order granting rehearing *en banc*, we asked the parties to brief various questions, including the following: "Consistent with the Supreme Court's decision in *Markman v. Westview Instruments*, 517 U.S. 370, 134 L. Ed. 2d 577, 116 S. Ct. 1384 (1996), and our *en banc* decision in *Cybor Corp. v. FAS Techs., Inc.*, 138 F.3d 1448 (Fed. Cir. 1998), is it appropriate for this court to accord any deference to any aspect of trial court claim construction rulings? If so, on what aspects, in what circumstances, and to what extent?" After consideration of the matter, we have decided not to address that issue at this time. We therefore leave undisturbed our prior *en banc* decision in *Cybor*.

Teva Pharmaceuticals USA, Inc. v. Sandoz, Inc.
574 U.S. 318
Supreme Court of the United States
October 15, 2014, Argued; January 20, 2015, Decided

Questions

1. Which approach do you find more persuasive, that a patent is more like a statute or more like a contract?
2. Do you find the Court's ultimate division here between intrinsic and extrinsic evidence odd? Conclusions about intrinsic evidence are reviewed de novo, but conclusions about extrinsic evidence are reviewed for clear error. Would it not make more sense to apply de novo review or apply clear error review to all findings or conclusions regarding the evidence?

3. How much of a difference do you think treating extrinsic evidence this way will make? Consider this case, for example. The question of indefiniteness is still a legal question. Thus, despite the change in standard of review to the factual findings, do you think the ultimate determination changed?[49]
4. Note that there has been mention that some deference is given to the trial judge even with de novo review. Would this be a better approach? Why or why not?
5. The dissenters suggest dire consequences from the majority's opinion. Have those consequences come to pass? Why or why not?
6. It seems that either approach, de novo review or clear error review, has its problems in this context. Given that, which approach do you think does the least harm and why?

* * *

The *Markman* decision was handed down by the Supreme Court in 1996. Not long after, that same year, the Federal Circuit decided the *Vitronics Corp. v. Conceptronic, Inc.*[50] case. That case reads like a "how-to" guide on claim construction. One of the more fundamental aspects of the decision was the distinction between intrinsic and extrinsic evidence for purposes of claim construction. Furthermore, within each of these respective categories, there was a pecking order to the evidence regarding greater preference/reliance and lesser preference/reliance.

In general, intrinsic evidence was and is preferred over extrinsic evidence. Part of the rationale in *Vitronics* was the public notice aspect associated with patent claims. Typically, someone reviewing a patent record would be unaware of what extrinsic evidence might be used to interpret the patent claims for a given patent.

Intrinsic evidence was and is the patent claims, the patent specification, and the prosecution history, generally in that order of preference.[51] Extrinsic evidence technically is any evidence that is not intrinsic. A typical order of preference is technical dictionaries and treatises, technical publications,

49. *See* Teva Pharms. USA, Inc. v. Sandoz, Inc., 789 F.3d 1335 (Fed. Cir. 2015).

50. 90 F.3d 1576.

51. Intrinsic evidence also includes cited prior art and might include foreign counterpart patent applications if included in the file history. *See, e.g.*, *Vitronics*, 90 F.3d 1576. *See also* Apple v. Motorola, 757 F.3d 1286 (Fed. Cir. 2014); Glaxo Grp. Ltd. v. Ranbaxy Pharms., Inc., 262 F.3d 1333, 1337 (Fed. Cir. 2001); Tanabe Seiyaku Co., Ltd. v. Int'l Trade Comm'n, 109 F.3d 726, 733 (Fed. Cir. 1997).

general dictionaries, and expert witness (typically other than attorney or inventor) testimony.[52]

Essentially, the job of the court is to figure out what the claims *truly* mean as best as possible using the intrinsic and extrinsic evidence. One tricky aspect relates to the ordinary and customary meaning of a claim term, which has a role in patent claim interpretation. There is a heavy presumption that claim terms are used in a manner that is consistent with their ordinary and customary meaning at the time of filing the patent application.[53] This presumption may be overcome expressly or by implication based on the intrinsic evidence. Yet, to make such determinations often involves looking to extrinsic evidence as well. Thus, in the period up to 2005, there were lines of cases and divisions on the Federal Circuit regarding the appropriate weight to accord the intrinsic evidence, often in the form of the specification, relative to extrinsic evidence, often in the form of technical dictionaries. One of the primary concerns that led to this division was the concern to *not* read limitations from the specification into the claims.[54]

To resolve the lines of cases and unify these divisions, the Federal Circuit decided the *Phillips* case *en banc* in 2005. Today, that decision represents the most comprehensive statement regarding the use of intrinsic and extrinsic evidence to interpret patent claims. *Phillips* reaffirms the principles of *Vitronics*. However, it clarifies that *Vitronics*, in the search for the ordinary and customary meaning of claim terms, did not create rigid rules regarding (1) use of dictionaries, technical treatises, and so on; (2) preventing consultation of extrinsic evidence to supplement the court's understanding of such terms and technology; and (3) a particular *temporal order* in which evidence is to be consulted by a federal judge (this is not the same as preference order, which remains a feature of claim construction). Thus, while there is a pecking order as to the intrinsic and extrinsic evidence as a guide, the real goal is to determine what the claims *truly* mean. This determination is not subject to rigid rules and, per *Phillips*, it may be appropriate in some circumstances to depart from the general guidelines *so long as a court does not use extrinsic evidence to modify or contradict the intrinsic evidence*.

The court's job, consequently, is to determine whether claim terms are used in a manner consistent with the ordinary and customary meaning of those terms at the time of filing. If so, the court is to determine the ordinary

52. *See, e.g.*, Solomon v. Kimberly-Clark Corp., 216 F.3d 1372 (Fed. Cir. 2000) (testimony of inventor and his attorney concerning claim construction entitled to little or no consideration).

53. *See, e.g.*, Johnson Worldwide Assocs. v. Zebo Corp., 175 F.3d 985, 989 (Fed. Cir. 1999).

54. See treatment of the *Texas Digital* case later in this chapter.

and customary meaning of such claim terms. If not, the court is to determine the special meaning accorded such terms, generally, in light of the intrinsic evidence.

As suggested, *Vitronics* established a pecking order of intrinsic evidence as follows: patent claims, patent specification, patent file history. Again, *Phillips* reaffirmed the importance of intrinsic evidence and this pecking order, but with some clarifications.

It is now well-established patent law that the starting point for claim construction is always the words of the claims themselves. Although this principle, by itself, should not be particularly surprising to patent attorneys, one of the clearer statements of the principle is found in *Vitronics Corp. v. Conceptronic, Inc. Markman v. Westview Instruments, Inc.* (Supreme Court) made it clear that, for policy reasons, patent claim construction is a function that should always be performed by judges, rather than juries. Therefore, relatively soon after that watershed Supreme Court decision, the Federal Circuit handed down the *Vitronics* decision, which, even today, provides an excellent "how-to" guide for claim construction. Likewise, the principles of *Vitronics* were reaffirmed in an *en banc* decision by the Federal Circuit in *Phillips v. AWH*,[55] as has been suggested.

The invention in *Vitronics* related to a technique for using solder to surface-mount components or circuit devices to circuit boards. The components passed through various ovens providing a variety of heat zones. The zones, including the last zone, in particular, were set at temperatures to heat the solder to a higher temperature than the component itself, thereby making the solder adhere more solidly. This heating process apparently caused the solder to reflow in a way that formed a more solid connection. The claims specifically indicated that the solder needed to be heated to its "solder reflow temperature," which was intended to be higher than the temperature of the components. However, as one might expect, a dispute ensued over the meaning of "solder reflow temperature," the language used in the patent claims.

It appears from the case that if the term were to be construed in a manner consistent with the relevant art, rather than the manner in which it was used in the specification, then the defendant would *not* be infringing. Vitronics, of course, asserted that it had clearly imparted a special meaning to this particular claim terminology in the patent application, acting as its own lexicographer. The lower court, however, sided with the defendant, relying principally on extrinsic evidence regarding the meaning in the art.

55. 415 F.3d 1303 (Fed. Cir. 2005) (en banc).

On appeal, the Federal Circuit reversed and remanded and, in a well-formulated opinion written by Judge Michel, provided a relatively clear set of guidelines for district court judges to follow when construing patent claims. The Federal Circuit went out of its way to specify a particular pecking order with respect to the intrinsic evidence that a court should follow when attempting to construe a claim—namely, the claims, specification, and prosecution history. The Federal Circuit stated:

> *First, we look to the words of the claims themselves* . . . .
>
> Although words in a claim are generally given their ordinary and customary meaning, *a patentee may choose to be his own lexicographer and use terms in a manner other than their ordinary meaning, as long as the special definition of the term is clearly stated in the patent specification or file history*. . . .
>
> [S]econd, it is always necessary to review the specification to determine whether the inventor used any terms in a manner inconsistent with their ordinary meaning. . . . *Usually, it [the spec] is dispositive; it is the single best guide to the meaning of a disputed term.*
>
> Third, the court may also consider the prosecution history of the patent, if in evidence. . . . [T]he record before the Patent and Trademark Office is often of critical significance in determining the meaning of claims.[56]

For our purposes, then, one important pronouncement from *Vitronics*, as indicated by the preceding quote, is that claim construction *always* begins with the claim language itself.

This recognition is critical to providing good representation before the PTO and to obtaining patents of value that will likely be enforceable in federal court. *Vitronics* suggests, and other cases have also suggested, if the intrinsic evidence is clear, then claim construction should, for all practical purposes, be complete.[57] *Phillips* loosened this a bit by clarifying that a court is always free to consult extrinsic evidence, so long as the intrinsic evidence is not modified or contradicted. However, Federal Circuit cases that came after *Vitronics* also included a similar point regarding reliance on intrinsic evidence.[58] There is no doubt regarding the preference for intrinsic evidence and no doubt that among the intrinsic evidence the importance of the claims is paramount.

To be clear, the claim language defines the grant of rights. The other intrinsic evidence aids interpretation. The patent drafter, then, may provide

56. *Vitronics*, 90 F.3d at 1582–83 (emphasis added).

57. Although Vitronics was not fully consistent on this point, which aided the confusion. *See infra* note 62.

58. *See, e.g.*, Mantech Env't Corp. v. Hudson Env't Servs., 152 F.3d 1368 (Fed. Cir. 1998); Comark Commc'ns, Inc. v. Harris Corp., 156 F.3d 1182, 1186–87 (Fed. Cir. 1998).

the best representation by preparing simple, straightforward claims that are as clear as possible as to their intended meaning from the very face of the claim.[59]

Vitronics also clearly states that the specification *must* be consulted as part of the claim construction process, as confirmed by the preceding quote. However, *Vitronics* further clearly states that the specification is consulted primarily to determine whether the claim terms are used in the specification in a manner consistent with their ordinary meaning. Therefore, if the claim terms are used consistently in the specification, then, at least in principle, there may be little need for further consultation of the specification to interpret the claims.[60] To restate this, for claim construction, the words of the claims are of paramount importance, and the claim language in some cases may virtually alone determine the scope of claim coverage (after consulting the specification to verify that the terms are used consistently). This is an ideal, of course. More frequently, resorting to the specification in greater detail to establish context, and so on, may be needed; however, there is little harm in shooting for the ideal when drafting claims since achieving it has occurred in previous examples of patent litigation.[61]

After *Vitronics*, there were still questions about substantive claim construction. Again, the period up to 2005 resulted in some splintering in approach among judges on the Federal Circuit. This appeared to become more pronounced, particularly in the period 2002–2005.

More specifically, how to appropriately treat dictionaries appeared to vary at times, from being important as an unbiased source for ordinary and customary meaning to not being quite so important relative to intrinsic evidence since dictionaries are extrinsic evidence. Thus, the proper process for claim construction was unclear at times.

Furthermore, how to treat extrinsic evidence in general was in question. *Vitronics* appeared to suggest that it required claim language ambiguity *before* resort to such evidence was appropriate.[62] However, other Federal Circuit

59. This preference for being clear on the face of the claim has also risen to be of importance in another area, the jurisprudence surrounding § 101. See Chapter 6, discussing patent eligibility.

60. See *Straight Path IP Group, Inc. v. Sipnet EU S.R.O.*, 806 F.3d 1356 (Fed. Cir. 2015), which states the specification plays a "more limited role" when the claim term has an especially "plain" meaning.

61. *See, e.g.*, *Mantech*, 152 F.3d 1368; *Comark Commc'ns*, 156 F.3d at 1186–87; *cf.* McGill Inc. v. John Zink Co., 736 F.2d 666 (Fed. Cir. 1984) (consulting specification and prosecution history to determine the proper interpretation of "recovered liquid hydrocarbon absorbent").

62. *See* Vitronics Corp. v. Conceptronic, Inc., 90 F.3d 1576, 1583 (Fed. Cir. 1996) ("In most situations, an analysis of the intrinsic evidence alone will resolve any ambiguity in a disputed

decisions suggested otherwise, in that claim language should not be divorced from the context of usage.[63]

This division in approach became pronounced in the *Texas Digital*[64] case, which suggested that, so as not to import limitations from the specification into the claims, an unbiased dictionary definition took on greater importance than was suggested under *Vitronics*. Likewise, the case suggested a particular temporal order in which a court was to consider (not simply a precedence order, but a temporal order of consideration) evidentiary sources, such as the specification (intrinsic) versus dictionaries or technical treatises (extrinsic). The approach suggested greater importance for extrinsic sources than articulated in *Vitronics*.

To resolve these separate lines of cases, the Federal Circuit took a panel decision, *Phillips v. AWH*, *en banc*. The principles articulated in *Phillips* remain true today, although disagreement at the margins on some fine points appears to affect decisions by the appellate court.

The invention in the case concerned modular, steel-shell panels that can be welded together to form vandalism-resistant walls. The panels were especially useful in building prisons because they were load bearing and impact resistant, while also insulating against fire and noise. There had been an arrangement with a company, AWH, made under a patent (the '798 patent) to Phillips to market and sell the panels; however, after the arrangement ended, Phillips found evidence that AWH continued to sell the panels and instituted a lawsuit in federal district court.

In the district court case, regarding patent infringement, the district court focused on the language of claim 1, which recited "further means disposed inside the shell for increasing its load bearing capacity comprising internal steel baffles extending inwardly from the steel shell walls."[65] The district court

---

claim term. In such circumstances, it is improper to rely on extrinsic evidence."). *But see id.* at 1584 n.6 ("Although technical treatises and dictionaries fall within the category of extrinsic evidence, as they do not form a part of an integrated patent document, they are worthy of special note. Judges are free to consult such resources at any time in order to better understand the underlying technology and may also rely on dictionary definitions when construing claim terms, so long as the dictionary definition does not contradict any definition found in or ascertained by a reading of the patent documents.").

63. *See, e.g.*, Home Diagnostics, Inc. v. Lifescan, Inc., 381 F.3d 1352, 1355 (Fed. Cir. 2004) ("This court construes the meaning of claim language according to its usage and context."); Metabolite Laby's, Inc. v. Lab'y Corp. of Am. Holdings, 370 F.3d 1354, 1360, 71 U.S.P.Q.2d 1081 (Fed. Cir. 2004), *cert. dismissed*, 126 S. Ct. 2921 (2006) ("[t]his court sets the meaning of claim terms by ascertaining their technological and temporal context").

64. *See* Tex. Digital Sys., Inc. v. Telegenix, 308 F.3d 1193 (Fed. Cir. 2002).

65. Phillips v. AWH Corp., 415 F.3d 1303, 1309 (Fed. Cir. 2005) (en banc).

interpreted this language as "a means . . . for performing a specified function," subject to 35 U.S.C. § 112, paragraph 6,[66] which provides that such a claim "shall be construed to cover the corresponding structure, material, or acts described in the specification and equivalents thereof." Looking to the specification of the '798 patent, the court noted that "every textual reference in the specification and its diagrams show baffle deployment at an angle other than 90 to the wall faces" and that "placement of the baffles at such angles creates an intermediate interlocking, but not solid, internal barrier." The district court therefore ruled that, for purposes of the '798 patent, a baffle must "extend inward from the steel shell walls at an oblique or acute angle to the wall face" and must form part of an interlocking barrier in the interior of the wall module.[67] Because Phillips could not prove infringement under that claim construction, the district court granted summary judgment of noninfringement, and an appeal by Phillips followed.

In the appeal to a panel of appellate judges, the majority sustained the district court's summary judgment of noninfringement, although on different grounds. A dissenting judge,[68] however, would have reversed the summary judgment of noninfringement.

The appellate panel first determined that because the asserted claims of the '798 patent contained a sufficient recitation of structure, the district court erred by construing the term "baffles" to invoke the "means-plus-function" claim format authorized by 112, 6. Nonetheless, the panel concluded that the patent used the term "baffles" in a restrictive manner. Based on the patent's written description, the panel held that the claim term "baffles" excluded structures that extend at a 90-degree angle from the walls. The panel noted that the specification repeatedly referred to the ability of the claimed baffles to deflect projectiles and that it described the baffles as being "disposed at such angles that bullets which might penetrate the outer steel panels are deflected."[69]

In addition, the panel observed that nowhere in the patent was there any disclosure of a baffle projecting from the wall at a right angle and that baffles oriented at 90 degrees to the wall were found in the prior art. Based on "the specification's explicit descriptions," the panel concluded "that the patentee regarded his invention as panels providing impact or projectile resistance and that the baffles must be oriented at angles other than 90." The panel

66. Currently, 35 U.S.C. § 112(f) (2024).
67. *Phillips*, 415 F.3d at 1309.
68. Judge Dyk.
69. *Phillips*, 415 F.3d at 1310.

added that the patent specification "is intended to support and inform the claims, and here it makes it unmistakably clear that the invention involves baffles angled at other than 90."[70] The panel therefore upheld the district court's summary judgment of noninfringement.

The Federal Circuit court agreed to rehear the *Phillips* appeal *en banc*, largely based on the points made by the dissent regarding how the approach of the decision deviated from Federal Circuit precedent. Ultimately, the portion of the panel's decision addressed to the issue of infringement was reversed.

The *en banc* court decision begins:

> *The principal question that this case presents to us is the extent to which we should resort to and rely on a patent's specification in seeking to ascertain the proper scope of its claims.*
>
> This is hardly a new question. The role of the specification in claim construction has been an issue in patent law decisions in this country for nearly two centuries. We addressed the relationship between the specification and the claims at some length in our en banc opinion in *Markman v. Westview Instruments, Inc.*, 52 F.3d 967, 979–81 (Fed. Cir. 1995) *(en banc)*, *aff'd*, 517 U.S. 370, 116 S. Ct. 1384, 134 L. Ed. 2d 577 (1996). We again summarized the applicable principles in *Vitronics Corp. v. Conceptronic, Inc.*, 90 F.3d 1576 (Fed. Cir. 1996), and more recently in *Innova/Pure Water, Inc. v. Safari Water Filtration Systems, Inc.*, 381 F.3d 1111 (Fed. Cir. 2004). *What we said in those cases bears restating, for the basic principles of claim construction outlined there are still applicable, and we reaffirm them today. We have also previously considered the use of dictionaries in claim construction. What we have said in that regard requires clarification.*[71]

The appellate court continues:

> It is a "bedrock principle" of patent law that "the claims of a patent define the invention to which the patentee is entitled the right to exclude." *Innova*, 381 F.3d at 1115; *see also Vitronics*, 90 F.3d at 1582 ("we look to the words of the claims themselves . . . to define the scope of the patented invention"); *Markman*, 52 F.3d at 980 ("The written description part of the specification itself does not delimit the right to exclude. That is the function and purpose of claims."). . . .
>
> *We have frequently stated that the words of a claim "are generally given their ordinary and customary meaning."* *Vitronics*, 90 F.3d at 1582; *see also Toro Co. v. White Consol. Indus., Inc.*, 199 F.3d 1295, 1299 (Fed. Cir. 1999); *Renishaw PLC v. Marposs Societa' per Azioni*, 158 F.3d 1243, 1249 (Fed. Cir. 1998). *We have*

70. *Id.*
71. *Id.* at 1312 (emphasis added).

> *made clear, moreover, that the ordinary and customary meaning of a claim term is the meaning that the term would have to a person of ordinary skill in the art in question at the time of the invention, i.e., as of the effective filing date of the patent application. See Innova*, 381 F.3d at 1116 ("A court construing a patent claim seeks to accord a claim the meaning it would have to a person of ordinary skill in the art at the time of the invention."); *Home Diagnostics, Inc. v. LifeScan, Inc.*, 381 F.3d 1352, 1358 (Fed. Cir. 2004) ("customary meaning" refers to the "customary meaning in [the] art field"); *Ferguson Beauregard/Logic Controls v. Mega Sys., LLC*, 350 F.3d 1327, 1338 (Fed. Cir. 2003) (claim terms "are examined through the viewing glass of a person skilled in the art"); *see also PC Connector Solutions LLC v. SmartDisk Corp.*, 406 F.3d 1359, 1363 (Fed. Cir. 2005) (meaning of claim "must be interpreted as of [the] effective filing date" of the patent application); *Schering Corp. v. Amgen Inc.*, 222 F.3d 1347, 1353 (Fed. Cir. 2000) (same).
>
> *The inquiry into how a person of ordinary skill in the art understands a claim term provides an objective baseline from which to begin claim interpretation. See Innova*, 381 F.3d at 1116. That starting point is based on the well-settled understanding that inventors are typically persons skilled in the field of the invention. . . .[72]

The appellate court provides five strong rationales as to why extrinsic evidence is less reliable than intrinsic evidence:

> *We have viewed extrinsic evidence in general as less reliable than the patent and its prosecution history in determining how to read claim terms, for several reasons.* First, extrinsic evidence by definition is not part of the patent and does not have the specification's virtue of being created at the time of patent prosecution for the purpose of explaining the patent's scope and meaning. Second, while claims are construed as they would be understood by a hypothetical person of skill in the art, extrinsic publications may not be written by or for skilled artisans and therefore may not reflect the understanding of a skilled artisan in the field of the patent. Third, extrinsic evidence consisting of expert reports and testimony is generated at the time of and for the purpose of litigation and thus can suffer from bias that is not present in intrinsic evidence. The effect of that bias can be exacerbated if the expert is not one of skill in the relevant art or if the expert's opinion is offered in a form that is not subject to cross-examination. *See Senmed, Inc. v. Richard-Allan Med. Indus., Inc.*, 888 F.2d 815, 819 n.8 (Fed. Cir. 1989). Fourth, there is a virtually unbounded universe of potential extrinsic evidence of some marginal relevance that could be brought to bear on any claim construction question. In the course of litigation, each party will naturally choose the pieces of extrinsic evidence most favorable to

72. *Id.* at 1312–13 (emphasis added).

> its cause, leaving the court with the considerable task of filtering the useful extrinsic evidence from the fluff. *See Daubert v. Merrell Dow Pharms., Inc.*, 509 U.S. 579, 595, 113 S. Ct. 2786, 125 L. Ed. 2d 469 (1993) ("Expert evidence can be both powerful and quite misleading because of the difficulty in evaluating it."). Finally, undue reliance on extrinsic evidence poses the risk that it will be used to change the meaning of claims in derogation of the "indisputable public records consisting of the claims, the specification and the prosecution history," thereby undermining the public notice function of patents. *Southwall Techs.*, 54 F.3d at 1578.[73]

The appellate court summarizes as follows:

> *In sum, extrinsic evidence may be useful to the court, but it is unlikely to result in a reliable interpretation of patent claim scope unless considered in the context of the intrinsic evidence.* Nonetheless, because extrinsic evidence can help educate the court regarding the field of the invention and can help the court determine what a person of ordinary skill in the art would understand claim terms to mean, it is permissible for the district court in its sound discretion to admit and use such evidence. *In exercising that discretion, and in weighing all the evidence bearing on claim construction, the court should keep in mind the flaws inherent in each type of evidence and assess that evidence accordingly.*[74]

Finally, the appellate court, for a second time in the opinion, reaffirmed *Vitronics* and other similar cases, stating:

> In *Vitronics*, this court grappled with the same problem and set forth guidelines for reaching the correct claim construction and not imposing improper limitations on claims. 90 F.3d at 1582. *The underlying goal of our decision in* ***Vitronics*** *was to increase the likelihood that a court will comprehend how a person of ordinary skill in the art would understand the claim terms. See id.* at 1584. *In that process, we recognized that there is no magic formula or catechism for conducting claim construction. Nor is the court barred from considering any particular sources or required to analyze sources in any specific sequence, as long as those sources are not used to contradict claim meaning that is unambiguous in light of the intrinsic evidence. See id.* at 1583–84; *Intel Corp. v. VIA Techs., Inc.*, 319 F.3d 1357, 1367 (Fed. Cir. 2003). For example, a judge who encounters a claim term while reading a patent might consult a general purpose or specialized dictionary to begin to understand the meaning of the term, before reviewing the remainder of the patent to determine how the patentee has used the term. *The sequence of steps used by the judge in consulting various sources is not important; what matters is for the court to attach the appropriate weight to be assigned to those*

73. *Id.* at 1318–19 (emphasis added).
74. *Id.* at 1319 (emphasis added).

sources in light of the statutes and policies that inform patent law. Vitronics, 90 F.3d at 1582. *In* ***Vitronics****, we did not attempt to provide a rigid algorithm for claim construction, but simply attempted to explain why, in general, certain types of evidence are more valuable than others.* ***Today, we adhere to that approach and reaffirm the approach to claim construction outlined in that case***, in *Markman*, and in *Innova*. . . .[75]

Ordinary and Customary Meaning

Understand what "ordinary and customary meaning" is and its role in claim interpretation (and consequently claim drafting).

Comark Communications, Inc. v. Harris Corp.
156 F.3d 1182
United States Court of Appeals for the Federal Circuit
September 9, 1998, Decided

Questions

1. Why did Harris argue the district court's claim construction of "video delay circuit" was flawed? What did the appellate court say was the role of claim language vis-à-vis the specification description? Why did the appellate court say that in this case resort to the specification was not needed? Is this inconsistent with the principle that the specification must always be considered? Why or why not?
2. Did the appellate court say it was applying the ordinary and customary meaning? If so, what language used by the appellate court suggests it was applying the ordinary and customary meaning?
3. What was the appellate court's (and the district court's) observation regarding claim differentiation?
4. Did the jury conclude that claims 1 and 14 were infringed literally or under the DOE? On what basis was Harris challenging the sufficiency of the evidence? Why did the appellate court say that in this context the challenge was insufficient? What did Harris need to show to prevail on this point?
5. Why did Harris's opinion letter of noninfringement fail to keep it from being found liable for willful infringement? What does this tell you about the pitfalls of reliance on an opinion letter of noninfringement to avoid being found willful?

75. *Id.* at 1324 (emphasis added).

Johnson Worldwide Associates v. Zebco Corp.
175 F.3d 985
United States Court of Appeals for the Federal Circuit
April 27, 1999, Decided

Questions

1. It is always helpful to be aware of the procedural posture of a case. What is the procedural posture of this case? What were the terms in the claim in which claim interpretation was disputed? What narrow interpretation did the defendant propose? Can you come up with any other arguments for an interpretation of either of the words disputed based solely on the language of the claim itself? Is it clear that the claim is necessarily limited to a heading lock? Why or why not?
2. What do you think of the principle stated in the case: "Varied use of a disputed term in the written description demonstrates the breadth of the term rather than providing a limited definition."[76] If the same term is used in different senses, why does that necessarily imply breadth? Could it imply that the term is indefinite? What might be argued to be different in this situation to suggest the term is not indefinite?
3. What do you think of this statement by the appellate court: "Rather, this exchange is an example of how carefully-crafted arguments in support of patentability can avoid creating ambiguous or adverse prosecution history."[77] Do you necessarily agree with the appellate court that this accurately describes the exchange in question? Why or why not? The defendant uses the specification to argue that "coupled" should be limited to a mechanical or physical coupling. Although the appellate court did not accept the argument, are there other reasons why that argument should not fly with respect to claim 1? Is "electrically coupled" being "physically coupled"? Is "electrically coupled" being "mechanically coupled"? When the term "coupled" is used in the claim body, does it refer to the same "coupled" used in the preamble?
4. Note that the appellate court says there is a "heavy" presumption in favor of the ordinary and customary meaning. How is that different from a regular or ordinary presumption?
5. This case provides a number of claim drafting lessons. Do you think defining the words that turned out to be disputed would have helped

76. Johnson Worldwide Assocs. v. Zebo Corp., 175 F.3d 985, 991 (Fed. Cir. 1999).
77. *Id.* at 993.

or would have hurt the plaintiff? What do you think about the appellate court's statement regarding the situations in which a claim term is given a meaning other than its ordinary and customary meaning? Can you think of other potential situations? Observe this comment by the appellate court: "General descriptive terms will ordinarily be given their full meaning; modifiers will not be added to broad terms standing alone."[78] Is it always clear when "the patentee has chosen to be his or her own lexicographer"?

Thorner v. Sony Computer Entertainment America LLC
669 F.3d 1362
United States Court of Appeals for the Federal Circuit
February 1, 2012, Decided

Questions

1. Does *Thorner* represent a change in emphasis by the Federal Circuit or just a different panel?
2. What is the difference between redefinition and disavowal? Is the appellate court making this more exacting than it has been previously or are these merely differences at the margin?
3. Compare the question regarding construction of "flexible" with issues of degree and indefiniteness. The appellate court states: "The task of determining the degree of flexibility, the degree of rigidity that amounts to 'semi-rigid,' is part of the infringement analysis, not part of the claim construction."[79] Is there not an argument here that the use of "flexible" in this context without more clarity makes the claim indefinite?[80]

Evolusion Concepts, Inc. v. HOC Events, Inc.
22 F.4th 1361
United States Court of Appeals for the Federal Circuit
January 14, 2022, Decided

78. *Id.* at 989.
79. Thorner v. Sony Comput. Ent. Am. LLC, 669 F.3d 1362, 1369 (Fed. Cir. 2012).
80. However, compare *Acumed LLC v. Stryker Corp.*, 483 F.3d 800, 806 (Fed. Cir. 2007) ("[A] sound claim construction need not always purge every shred of ambiguity. The resolution of some line-drawing problems—especially easy ones like this one—is properly left to the trier of fact.").

Questions

1. The appellate court states:

> The specification supports the ordinary-meaning interpretation of "magazine catch bar." *Phillips*, 415 F.3d at 1315 ("[C]laims must be read in view of the specification, of which they are part." (internal quotation marks and citation omitted)). The specification nowhere limits the scope of a "magazine catch bar" to exclude factory-installed ones from the assembly that achieves the fixed-magazine goal. Nor, contrary to a suggestion made by Juggernaut, does it explain that only a customized or modified magazine catch bar, one necessarily different from what was factory installed, may be used on the firearm. It simply explains that the described embodiments of the invention all include a "magazine catch bar" that can be securely attached to the lower receiver of the firearm, and consistently describes the component in generic terms. *Id.*, col. 2, line 65, through col. 3, line 2; *see also id.*, col. 5, lines 5–7.
>
> Juggernaut argues, and Evolusion concedes, that the disclosed embodiments do not illustrate [original equipment manufacturer (OEM)] magazine catch bars. *See id.*, figs. 3 & 4. But that cannot make a difference in this case. *We have repeatedly held that "it is not enough that the only embodiments, or all of the embodiments, contain a particular limitation to limit claims beyond their plain meaning." Unwired Planet, LLC v. Apple, Inc.*, 829 F.3d 1353, 1359 (Fed. Cir. 2016) (internal quotation marks and citation omitted).[81]

   What was the district court's mistake? The appellate court says: "The district court relied primarily on one sentence of the specification to conclude that the specification excludes a factory-installed magazine catch bar: 'The invention is a permanent fixture added to a semi-automatic firearm by removing the standard OEM magazine catch assembly and installing the invention.'"[82] However, it appears that the primary mistake was how the district court construed claim 15. Can you articulate the error?

2. How should the district court have first proceeded? The appellate court states: "We begin with the claim-construction issue presented respecting claims 1 and 8. . . . The question is whether the term

---

81. Evolusion Concepts, Inc. v. HOC Events, Inc., 22 F.4th 1361, 1366–67 (Fed. Cir. 2022) (emphasis added).

82. *Id.* at 1367.

'magazine catch bar' in the asserted claims includes a factory-installed magazine catch bar."[83] So, the district court should have started with the broadest claims and determined if they were used in the specification consistently with the ordinary and customary meaning. What does this tell you about how to draft patent claims?

3. Why did it not matter that the specification did not include an embodiment that showed using the factory-installed magazine bar?
4. In analyzing claim 15, how important is the use of the indefinite article to the appellate court's analysis? What if the claim had used a definite article? What does this tell you about how to draft claims?

Sisvel International S.A. v. Sierra Wireless, Inc.
81 F.4th 1231
United States Court of Appeals for the Federal Circuit
September 1, 2023, Decided

Questions

1. In the apparatus claim of the '196 patent, is the claim open or closed? What is the transition word or phrase?
2. Observe that in this case, the rules of claim construction applied rigidly lead to a broad interpretation that renders the claims unpatentable despite narrower embodiments in the specification. What does this suggest regarding claim drafting?
3. What claim term is in dispute? How did the Patent Trial and Appeal Board (the Board) construe it? Is this the ordinary and customary meaning and why? How did Sisvel argue it should be construed? Why is this not the ordinary and customary meaning? Why is Sisvel trying to limit its claims to the embodiments of its patent?
4. What are the two ways the appellate court says the ordinary and customary meaning would not apply? What language did the appellate court quote from the specification and why did that support its claim interpretation?
5. Why did the Board refuse to enter Sisvel's substitute claim for claim 10? Do you agree with the court's analysis of the substitute claim?

* * *

83. *Id.* at 1365.

An important job for the court is to determine whether terms are used in the claims in accordance with the ordinary and customary meaning of those terms as of the filing date of the patent application.[84] There is a "heavy" presumption in favor of ordinary and customary meaning rather than a specialized meaning,[85] although this presumption may be overcome. As made clear by *Vitronics* and *Phillips*, a court reviews multiple sources, intrinsic and extrinsic, to arrive at the ordinary and customary meaning.

Although there is a presumption of ordinary meaning, the actual goal of the court is to determine what the patent claims *truly* mean, not simply the ordinary meaning of such terms. Ordinary meaning is simply a baseline used to assist in reaching the goal of what the claims mean.[86] Thus, determining ordinary meaning may exhibit some amount of fluidity as a court reviews and compares the various sources available to it.

The language of the patent claims takes a paramount role; however, patent claims in the abstract may not always provide clear guidance.[87] In accordance with Federal Circuit jurisprudence, the next most important source is the specification. According to the court, it is "the single best guide."[88] Furthermore, with true meaning as the goal, various doctrines of claim interpretation may push or pull on ordinary meaning so that a court may find the true meaning.[89]

A number of principles have been discussed in this book so far. Many of them are used to guide a court to determine ordinary meaning and/or to guide a court to determine what the claim terms mean. Some basic principles, as discussed, include construing the claims and specification and the file history as a single package from the perspective of one of ordinary skill in the art and reviewing this package in its entirety with respect to the time period of the invention at issue—that is, the *effective* filing date. Again, while extrinsic evidence may be considered, it may not modify or contradict the intrinsic evidence. Furthermore, as stated, there is a "heavy" presumption that the claim terms are used consistent with ordinary and customary meaning.

Doctrines that push or pull on ordinary meaning relate to various aspects of the claims, specification, and file history, including the following: how what is believed to be inventive is specifically described; whether the specification

---

84. *See, e.g.*, Phillips v. AWH Corp., 415 F.3d 1303 (Fed. Cir. 2005) (en banc).
85. *Id.*
86. *Id.*
87. *Id.*
88. *Id.*; Vitronics Corp. v. Conceptronic, Inc., 90 F.3d 1576 (Fed. Cir. 1996).
89. *See* Menell et al., *supra* note 36, app.

contains multiple embodiments; whether some embodiments are described as preferred over others; whether terms are used in a slavishly consistent manner or are used in a manner that is varied and demonstrates breadth; how the prior art is characterized relative to subject matter sought to be patented; what advantages are described regarding the subject matter sought to be patented; whether any scope regarding the subject matter is disavowed in the specification or during prosecution, including claim amendments in response to art; whether terms are defined in the specification or file history; and whether terms are used in a manner that creates ambiguity as to meaning or scope.[90]

Thus, the court's job is a complex one in terms of balancing many considerations as it reviews intrinsic and extrinsic evidence. As claim drafters that appreciate the process of claim construction and the doctrines that govern, our job is to adopt approaches that are more likely to lead to a broader interpretation of the claims, other things being equal (unless there is specific knowledge that suggests this is not the best approach), while also making it reasonably clear from the words used the precise claim scope actually intended. While the conventional wisdom is to create a record suggesting broad claims, it is also important to appreciate that there is uncertainty regarding the scope of the prior art. Thus, it may also be important that the specification include support for claims that have a narrower interpretation (and include those claims in the claims you present in prosecution).

Use of Dictionaries

Understand the distinction between dictionaries and other types of extrinsic evidence; understand the history of dictionary use in claim interpretation and how dictionaries might aid patent claim drafting.

CCS Fitness, Inc. v. Brunswick Corp.
288 F.3d 1359
United States Court of Appeals for the Federal Circuit
May 3, 2002, Decided

Questions

1. What was the procedural posture of this case? Who authored the opinion?
2. What was the claim term in dispute?
3. Observe that this case precedes *Phillips* and again refers to the "heavy presumption" of ordinary and customary meaning. Do you think the "heavy presumption" survives *Phillips*? Why or why not?

---

90. *See id.*

4. What do you think of the defendant's claim construction arguments? Why do you think the appellate court ruled for the plaintiff?
5. This case precedes *Williamson v. Centrix*.[91] Do you think if it had been decided after *Williamson* the result might have been different?
6. Do you think "member" is a term of art?
7. The appellate court cites *Johnson Worldwide*,[92] which discussed two ways to modify the ordinary and customary meaning of a claim term. This case, however, says there are four rather than two ways. What are the two additional ways?
8. What do you think of the following statements by the appellate court?

> "If an apparatus claim recites a general structure without limiting that structure to a specific subset of structures, we will generally construe the term to cover all known types of that structure" that the patent disclosure supports. *Renishaw*, 158 F.3d at 1250, 48 USPQ2d at 1122. Sensibly enough, our precedents show that dictionary definitions may establish a claim term's ordinary meaning. *Rexnord Corp. v. Laitram Corp.*, 274 F.3d 1336, 1344, 60 USPQ2d 1851, 1855 (Fed. Cir. 2001).[93]

and

> [C]ontrary to the district court's analysis here, our case law makes clear that a patentee need not "describe in the specification every conceivable and possible future embodiment of his invention." *Rexnord*, 274 F.3d at 1344, 60 USPQ2d at 1856 (citations omitted).[94]

9. Is it at all surprising that the appellate court credited the inventor's affidavit over Life Fitness's (a division of Brunswick Corp.) expert? Why or why not?
10. Why did the appellate court not limit the reciprocating member to how it was shown in the figures of the patent?
11. Why did the appellate court not apply 112, 6? What does this situation and this case suggest with respect to claim drafting?
12. How did the appellate court distinguish these cases: *Scimed Life Systems, Inc. v. Advanced Cardiovascular Systems, Inc.*, 242 F.3d 1337 (Fed. Cir. 2001), *Watts v. XL Systems, Inc.*, 232 F.3d 877 (Fed. Cir. 2000), *Toro Co. v. White Consolidated Industries, Inc.*, 199 F.3d 1295 (Fed. Cir. 1999), and *Ethicon Endo-Surgery, Inc. v. U.S. Surgical Corp.*, 93 F.3d

---

91. 792 F.3d 1339 (Fed. Cir. 2015) (en banc).
92. Johnson Worldwide Assocs. v. Zebco, 175 F.3d 985 (Fed. Cir. 1999).
93. CCS Fitness v. Brunswick Corp., 288 F.3d 1359, 1366 (Fed. Cir. 2002).
94. *Id.*

1572 (Fed. Cir. 1996)? What is it that you think is different in these cases based on the appellate court's description of when to depart from the ordinary and customary meaning?

13. Do you think that a well-known term to describe the plaintiff's structure did not seem to exist may have influenced the appellate court's decision? Why or why not?

Texas Digital Systems v. Telegenix, Inc.
308 F.3d 1193
United States Court of Appeals for the Federal Circuit
October 16, 2002, Decided

Questions

1. Certainly, the *Telegenix* case is most known for its logic indicating that extrinsic evidence sources, including dictionaries and the like, may have some preference over intrinsic evidence due to a lack of bias and due to a desire to avoid reading limitations from the specification into the claims. For example, the appellate court states, referring to dictionaries, encyclopedias, and treatises publicly available at the time a patent issues: "Indeed, these materials may be the most meaningful sources of information to aid judges in better understanding both the technology and the terminology used by those skilled in the art to describe the technology." The *Telegenix* court also states: "categorizing them as 'extrinsic evidence' or even a 'special form of extrinsic evidence' is misplaced and does not inform the analysis." And further states: "By examining relevant dictionaries, encyclopedias and treatises to ascertain possible meanings that would have been attributed to the words of the claims by those skilled in the art, and by further utilizing the intrinsic record to select from those possible meanings the one or ones most consistent with the use of the words by the inventor, the full breadth of the limitations intended by the inventor will be more accurately determined and the improper importation of unintended limitations from the written description into the claims will be more easily avoided."[95] Why does *Phillips* say this approach is not entirely correct?
2. However, *Telegenix* is a quite complex case dealing with many complex issues. From reading the case, it is easy to see how difficult it may be

95. Tex. Digital Sys., Inc. v. Telegenix, 308 F.3d 1193, 1205 (Fed. Cir. 2002).

for a court to adhere to the black letter claim construction principles, such as interpreting the claims in light of the specification without reading limitations from the specification into the claims. Again, it may no longer be too surprising that the rate of reversal of a claim construction by a district court may hover around 50 percent. What is the procedural posture of the case and why does it matter here, in particular how the district court chose to interpret the claims? What is Telegenix seeking on appeal?

3. Having laid out the intended approach, the appellate court addresses many examples of disputed claim language considered by the district court. Before addressing how the appellate court handled the interpretation of the claims by the district court, note that several of the claims include the terminology "display unit." It does not appear that anyone argued that this might qualify as a means-plus-function clause. Do you think that might be a colorable argument?
4. First, the appellate court addresses the claim language "repeatedly substantially simultaneously activating." How does the district court construe this language? How does Telegenix argue that the district court erred? How does Texas Digital Systems (TDS) argue that the district court is correct? Why do you think Telegenix is making the argument it does? How does the appellate court ultimately resolve the dispute?
5. How did the district court construe "selectively controlling the durations of the time intervals of activation"? What does Telegenix argue? What does TDS argue? Why do you think TDS argues for the construction that it does? How does the appellate court resolve the dispute? Why is the appellate court's approach not considered reading limitations from the specification into the claims in this instance?
6. How did the district court construe "color control means"? How did Telegenix argue that the district court erred? Why did the appellate court agree?
7. The construction of "display areas" and "background area" appears a bit complex. How helpful was the appellate court's reference to external dictionaries ultimately relative to intrinsic evidence? Why is the appellate court's approach not considered reading limitations from the specification into the claims in this instance?
8. How did the district court construe "pattern"? What did Telegenix argue? What did TDS argue? Why do you think they took these respective positions? Why did the appellate court say the '514 patent

is unrelated? Why did the appellate court rule that the examiner's reasons for allowance did not limit the scope of this language?

9. How did the district court construe "means for selectively activating said display light sources"? Why did the appellate court rule the district court was in error? Does the appellate court interpret the function of this language more narrowly than the claim recites? Why or why not?
10. How did the district court construe "converter means"? Why did the appellate court rule the district court was in error? The appellate court states: "There is no dispute that 'converter means' is a means-plus-function limitation within the meaning of section 112, paragraph 6."[96] However, could not one argue that recitation of a "converter" provides sufficient structure to rebut the presumption?
11. How did the district court construe "first means" and "second means"? Why did the appellate court rule the district court was in error?
12. How did the district court construe "control means for selectively coupling said light sources"? How did the appellate court say it should have been construed?
13. What does this case tell you about the interpretation of means-plus-function claims or means-plus-function clauses thereof?
14. What is considered prejudicial error with respect to jury instructions regarding claim interpretation and how is it demonstrated to a reviewing court?
15. What standard of review did the appellate court apply with respect to rulings about the admissibility of evidence? What was Telegenix trying to show with engineer Brent Brown's testimony? Why was corroboration of Brown's testimony required by the district and appellate courts?
16. What is the issue being raised with respect to the *Wine Railway Appliance Co. v. Enterprise Railway Equipment Co.*[97] case and § 287?

* * *

After *Vitronics*, although dictionaries and technical treatises were deemed extrinsic evidence, the Federal Circuit appeared to treat those sources differently from other types of extrinsic evidence, seeing such sources as unbiased, relative to expert testimony. In general, it seemed federal courts were

96. *Id.* at 1213.
97. 297 U.S. 387 (1936).

permitted to consult such sources at any time during claim construction.[98] However, *Vitronics* appeared to suggest that extrinsic evidence should not generally be consulted unless there was a genuine claim ambiguity.[99]

It is fair to say that a perception was created that dictionaries and the like had a special status in claim construction relative to other types of extrinsic evidence. However, Federal Circuit cases were not entirely consistent and different panels of judges seemed to take different stances. The special status treatment of dictionaries reached a pinnacle in the *Texas Digital* case.[100]

This issue at least in part led to the *en banc* decision in *Phillips*. The *Phillips* case, therefore, addressed the line of cases, epitomized by *Texas Digital*, and clarified the appropriate status of dictionaries and the like, stating:

> [S]ome of this court's cases have suggested a somewhat different approach to claim construction, in which the court has given greater emphasis to dictionary definitions of claim terms and has assigned a less prominent role to the specification and the prosecution history. . . .
>
> Although the concern expressed by the court in *Texas Digital* was valid [to avoid reading limitations from the specification into the claims], the methodology it adopted placed too much reliance on extrinsic sources such as dictionaries, treatises, and encyclopedias and too little on intrinsic sources, in particular the specification and prosecution history. . . .
>
> The main problem with elevating the dictionary to such prominence is that it focuses the inquiry on the abstract meaning of words rather than on the meaning of claim terms within the context of the patent. *Properly viewed, the "ordinary meaning" of a claim term is its meaning to the ordinary artisan after reading the entire patent.* Yet heavy reliance on the dictionary divorced from the intrinsic evidence risks transforming the meaning of the claim term to the artisan into the meaning of the term in the abstract, out of its particular

---

98. *See* Vitronics Corp. v. Conceptronic, Inc., 90 F.3d 1576 n.6 (Fed. Cir. 1996) ("Although technical treatises and dictionaries fall within the category of extrinsic evidence, as they do not form a part of an integrated patent document, they are worthy of special note. Judges are free to consult such resources at any time in order to better understand the underlying technology and may also rely on dictionary definitions when construing claim terms, so long as the dictionary definition does not contradict any definition found in or ascertained by a reading of the patent documents."); *cf.* Home Diagnostics, Inc. v. Lifescan, Inc., 381 F.3d 1352, 1355 (Fed. Cir. 2004) ("This court construes the meaning of claim language according to its usage and context."); Metabolite Laby's, Inc. v. Lab'y Corp. of Am. Holdings, 370 F.3d 1354, 1360, 71 U.S.P.Q.2d 1081 (Fed. Cir. 2004), *cert. dismissed*, 126 S. Ct. 2921 (2006) ("[t]his court sets the meaning of claim terms by ascertaining their technological and temporal context").

99. *See Vitronics*, 90 F.3d at 1583 ("In most situations, an analysis of the intrinsic evidence alone will resolve any ambiguity in a disputed claim term. In such circumstances, it is improper to rely on extrinsic evidence.").

100. See discussion in immediately preceding sections.

context, which is the specification. *The patent system is based on the proposition that claims cover only the invented subject matter. . . .*

The problem is that if the district court starts with the broad dictionary definition in every case and fails to fully appreciate how the specification implicitly limits that definition, the error will systematically cause the construction of the claim to be unduly expansive. The risk of systematic overbreadth is greatly reduced if the court instead focuses at the outset on how the patentee used the claim term in the claims, specification, and prosecution history, rather than starting with a broad definition and whittling it down.

Dictionaries, by their nature, provide an expansive array of definitions. General dictionaries, in particular, strive to collect all uses of particular words, from the common to the obscure. By design, general dictionaries collect the definitions of a term as used not only in a particular art field, but in many different settings. In such circumstances, it is inevitable that the multiple dictionary definitions for a term will extend beyond the "construction of the patent [that] is confirmed by the avowed understanding of the patentee, expressed by him, or on his behalf, when his application for the original patent was pending." *Goodyear Dental Vulcanite Co. v. Davis*, 102 U.S. 222, 227, 26 L. Ed. 149 (1880). Thus, the use of the dictionary may extend patent protection beyond what should properly be afforded by the inventor's patent. *See Smith v. Snow*, 294 U.S. 1, 14, 55 S. Ct. 279, 79 L. Ed. 721 (1935) ("if the claim were fairly susceptible of two constructions, that should be adopted which will secure to the patentee *his actual invention*") (emphasis added). For that reason, we have stated that "a general-usage dictionary cannot overcome art-specific evidence of the meaning" of a claim term. *Vanderlande Indus. Nederland*, 366 F.3d at 1321; *see also Renishaw*, 158 F.3d at 1250, *quoting Liebscher v. Boothroyd*, 46 C.C.P.A. 701, 258 F.2d 948, 951 (CCPA 1958) ("Indiscriminate reliance on definitions found in dictionaries can often produce absurd results. . . . One need not arbitrarily pick and choose from the various accepted definitions of a word to decide which meaning was intended as the word is used in a given claim. The subject matter, the context, etc., will more often than not lead to the correct conclusion.").

Even technical dictionaries or treatises, under certain circumstances, may suffer from some of these deficiencies. There is no guarantee that a term is used in the same way in a treatise as it would be by the patentee. In fact, discrepancies between the patent and treatises are apt to be common because the patent by its nature describes something novel. *See Autogiro*, 384 F.2d at 397 ("Often the invention is novel and words do not exist to describe it. The dictionary does not always keep abreast of the inventor. It cannot.").

Moreover, different dictionaries may contain somewhat different sets of definitions for the same words. A claim should not rise or fall based upon the preferences of a particular dictionary editor, or the court's independent decision, uninformed by the specification, to rely on one dictionary rather than

> another. Finally, the authors of dictionaries or treatises may simplify ideas to communicate them most effectively to the public and may thus choose a meaning that is not pertinent to the understanding of particular claim language. *See generally* Ellen P. Aprill, *The Law of the Word: Dictionary Shopping in the Supreme Court*, 30 Ariz. St. L.J. 275, 293–314 (1998). The resulting definitions therefore do not necessarily reflect the inventor's goal of distinctly setting forth his invention as a person of ordinary skill in that particular art would understand it.
>
> *As we have noted above, however, we do not intend to preclude the appropriate use of dictionaries. Dictionaries or comparable sources are often useful to assist in understanding the commonly understood meaning of words and have been used both by our court and the Supreme Court in claim interpretation. See Exhibit Supply Co. v. Ace Patents Corp.*, 315 U.S. 126, 134, 62 S. Ct. 513, 86 L. Ed. 736 (1942) (relying on dictionaries to construe the claim term "embedded"); *Weber Elec. Co. v. E.H. Freeman Elec. Co.*, 256 U.S. 668, 678, 41 S. Ct. 600, 65 L. Ed. 1162 (1921) (approving circuit court's use of dictionary definitions to define claim terms); *Renishaw*, 158 F.3d at 1247–53 (approving the use of dictionaries with proper respect for the role of intrinsic evidence). *A dictionary definition has the value of being an unbiased source "accessible to the public in advance of litigation." Vitronics, 90 F.3d at 1585. As we said in Vitronics, judges are free to consult dictionaries and technical treatises at any time in order to better understand the underlying technology and may also rely on dictionary definitions when construing claim terms, so long as the dictionary definition does not contradict any definition found in or ascertained by a reading of the patent documents.*[101]

The Federal Circuit in *Phillips* then addressed the issue of reading limitations from the specification into the claims:[102]

> *[W]e recognize that the distinction between using the specification to interpret the meaning of a claim and importing limitations from the specification into the claim can be a difficult one to apply in practice. See Comark Communications, Inc. v. Harris Corp.*, 156 F.3d 1182, 1186–87 (Fed. Cir. 1998) ("there is sometimes a fine line between reading a claim in light of the specification, and reading a limitation into the claim from the specification"). *However, the line between construing terms and importing limitations can be discerned with reasonable certainty and predictability if the court's focus remains on understanding how a person of ordinary skill in the art would understand the claim terms.* For instance, although the specification often describes very specific embodiments of the invention, we have repeatedly warned against confining the claims to those

101. Phillips v. AWH Corp., 415 F.3d 1303, 1319–23 (Fed. Cir. 2005) (en banc) (emphasis added).

102. See discussion in immediately preceding sections.

> embodiments. *See, e.g., Nazomi Communications, Inc. v. ARM Holdings, PLC*, 403 F.3d 1364, 1369 (Fed. Cir. 2005) (claims may embrace "different subject matter than is illustrated in the specific embodiments in the specification"); *Liebel-Flarsheim*, 358 F.3d at 906–08; *Teleflex*, 299 F.3d at 1327; *SRI Int'l v. Matsushita Elec. Corp. of Am.*, 775 F.2d 1107, 1121 (Fed. Cir. 1985). *In particular, we have expressly rejected the contention that if a patent describes only a single embodiment, the claims of the patent must be construed as being limited to that embodiment. Gemstar-TV Guide*, 383 F.3d at 1366. That is not just because section 112 of the Patent Act requires that the claims themselves set forth the limits of the patent grant, but also because persons of ordinary skill in the art rarely would confine their definitions of terms to the exact representations depicted in the embodiments.
>
> To avoid importing limitations from the specification into the claims, it is important to keep in mind that the purposes of the specification are to teach and enable those of skill in the art to make and use the invention and to provide a best mode for doing so. *See Spectra-Physics, Inc. v. Coherent, Inc.*, 827 F.2d 1524, 1533 (Fed. Cir. 1987). One of the best ways to teach a person of ordinary skill in the art how to make and use the invention is to provide an example of how to practice the invention in a particular case. *Much of the time, upon reading the specification in that context, it will become clear whether the patentee is setting out specific examples of the invention to accomplish those goals, or whether the patentee instead intends for the claims and the embodiments in the specification to be strictly coextensive. See SciMed Life Sys.*, 242 F.3d at 1341. *See Snow v. Lake Shore M.S. Ry. Co.*, 121 U.S. 617, 630, 7 S. Ct. 1343, 30 L. Ed. 1004 (1887) (it was clear from the specification that there was "nothing in the context to indicate that the patentee contemplated any alternative" embodiment to the one presented).
>
> In the end, there will still remain some cases in which it will be hard to determine whether a person of skill in the art would understand the embodiments to define the outer limits of the claim term or merely to be exemplary in nature. *While that task may present difficulties in some cases, we nonetheless believe that attempting to resolve that problem in the context of the particular patent is likely to capture the scope of the actual invention more accurately than either strictly limiting the scope of the claims to the embodiments disclosed in the specification or divorcing the claim language from the specification.*[103]

Thus, a federal court may consult dictionaries and the like at any time so long it does not modify or contradict the intrinsic evidence. However, it is noted that the tension between the intrinsic (e.g., importance of specification) and extrinsic evidence (e.g., importance of ordinary meaning) that led to the

103. *Phillips*, 415 F.3d at 1323–24 (emphasis added).

Federal Circuit's *en banc* decision in *Phillips* remains. For example, in *MySpace, Inc. v. Graphon Corp.*,[104] a Federal Circuit panel, per Judge Plager, stated:

> One approach is to focus on the invention disclosed in the patent: "[t]ry to understand what the inventor has invented (what he says is his contribution in the art) and then choose the claim meaning that best fits the invention." . . . The other is to focus on the words that the prosecuting lawyer used to craft the claims and "then apply legal rules of construction to divine the meaning of the claim." . . . While this is insightful regarding the approaches highlighted in one or another of our cases, it is an oversimplification to suggest that these are competing theories; rather, they are complementary. An inventor is entitled to claim in a patent what he has invented, but no more. . . . He can, however, claim less, to avoid prior art or for any other reason. Therefore, in construing a claim there are two limiting factors—what was invented, and what exactly was claimed. To determine the former—what was invented—we look at the entire patent, with particular attention to the specification (the written description of the invention and the several claims made). To determine the latter—what exactly was claimed—the focus is on the precise words of the particular claim or claims at issue; the written description and preferred embodiments are aids in understanding those words. In the case before us, proper claim construction requires that we understand what the invention encompasses as well as how the claims are stated.[105]

Hence, the appellate court clarified that consulting dictionaries or technical treatises is clearly permissible at any time; however, such extrinsic evidence may never be used to contradict or modify the intrinsic evidence. The court pointed out the benefits and disadvantages of such sources, which a district court should consider when reviewing such sources. The court also recognized the tension previously expressed[106] between interpreting claims in light of the specification and importing limitations from the specification into the claims. Some cases from the Federal Circuit are strict regarding the presumption of ordinary and customary meaning, such as *Thorner v. Sony Computer Entertainment America*, whereas other cases use the specification "to point the way," such as *Renishaw*, employing what appears to be a lesser standard than a clear and unambiguous redefinition or disavowal. We recommend a spectrum of patent claims from quite broad to quite narrow to address these uncertainties.[107]

---

104. *See* 672 F.3d 1250 (Fed. Cir. 2012).

105. *Id.* at 1256.

106. See treatment later in this chapter.

107. *Id.* See also Chapter 4, regarding employing a spectrum with respect to claim scope and claim type.

Patentee as Lexicographer

Understand why and when to use express definitions of claim terms in patent claim drafting.

Autogiro Co. of America v. United States
384 F.2d 391
United States Court of Claims
October 13, 1967, Decided

Questions

1. What is the statutory basis for a suit in the Court of Claims? How is that different from a federal court suit for patent infringement, for example under 28 U.S.C. subsection 1338(a)? Why is there no mention of a jury in this case?
2. *Autogiro* is famous for this language:

   > An invention exists most importantly as a tangible structure or a series of drawings. A verbal portrayal is usually an afterthought written to satisfy the requirements of patent law. This conversion of machine to words allows for unintended idea gaps which cannot be satisfactorily filled. Often the invention is novel and words do not exist to describe it. The dictionary does not always keep abreast of the inventor. It cannot. Things are not made for the sake of words, but words for things. To overcome this lag, patent law allows the inventor to be his own lexicographer. Chicago Steel Foundry Co. v. Burnside Steel Foundry Co., 132 F.2d 812 (7th Cir. 1943); Stuart Oxygen Co. Ltd. v. Josephian, 162 F.2d 857 (9th Cir. 1947); Universal Oil Products Co. v. Globe Oil & Refining Co., 137 F.2d 3 (7th Cir. 1943), aff'd 322 U.S. 471 (1944).[108]

   Do you think this accurately reflects the policy behind an inventor being his or her own lexicographer?
3. The court appears to rely heavily upon objects of the invention to construe the patent claims. What are your thoughts about this in connection with drafting patent claims?
4. If the patentee is truly the lexicographer, does that suggest that claim terms should be defined? Are there times when it may be better to define claim terms and times when it may be better not to do so? What are reasons to define claim terms and what are reasons not to define

---

108. Autogiro Co. of Am. v. United States, 384 F.2d 391, 396–97 (Ct. Cl. 1976).

claim terms? Is there a risk that the ordinary meaning of claim terms may change over time? Should courts use the ordinary meaning at the time the application is filed or at the time the application is issued? What does *Telegenix* say? What does *Phillips* say? What about at the time of the infringement?[109]

5. Would there be any point to explicitly defining claim terms in a patent to be consistent with its ordinary and customary meaning? Is there an approach to defining a claim term in a manner so that the claim term is at least arguably open-ended?
6. The court raises an issue it refers to as "late claiming." What is the court referring to? Is that a problem here? Is that usually a problem while a patent application is pending? The court seems to believe little will be gained by determining the "invalidity" of patent claims not found to be infringed. However, this case was decided in 1967. Is this still true today?[110] What about validity? Does a court hold a patent valid? Why or why not? Is there a difference between a patent claim being "valid" in comparison to being "presumed valid"? If so, what is the difference?

Vitronics Corp. v. Conceptronic, Inc.
90 F.3d 1576
United States Court of Appeals for the Federal Circuit
July 25, 1996, Decided

Questions

1. Procedurally, why did Vitronics concede at trial that the district court was required to grant judgment as a matter of law in favor of Conceptronic?
2. What were the competing definitions of "solder reflow temperature"? What was the evidence supporting each proposed definition?
3. What evidence did the district court indicate that it relied upon to support its construction of solder reflow temperature?

---

109. *See* SuperGuide Corp. v. DirecTV Enters., Inc., 358 F.3d 870 (Fed. Cir. 2004); Mark A. Lemley, *The Changing Meaning of Claim Terms*, 104 Mich. L. Rev. 101 (2005). *See also* Kevin Emerson Collins, The Reach of Literal Claim Scope into After-Arising Technology: On Thing Construction and the Meaning of Meaning (2008), https://www.repository.law.indiana.edu/facpub/1754; Joshua D. Sarnoff, *Correcting Misunderstandings of Literal Infringement Scope Regarding After-Arising Technologies Protected by the Doctrine of Equivalents*, 53 Akron L. Rev. 767 (2019), https://ideaexchange.uakron.edu/akronlawreview/vol53/iss4/1.

110. *See* Blonder Tongue v. Univ. of Ill. Found., 402 U.S. 313 (1971); *compare* Parklane Hosiery Co., Inc. v. Shore, 439 U.S. 322 (1979).

4. The court states: "In most situations, an analysis of the intrinsic evidence alone will resolve any ambiguity in a disputed claim term. In such circumstances, it is improper to rely on extrinsic evidence." However, in footnote 6, the court also states:

> Although technical treatises and dictionaries fall within the category of extrinsic evidence, as they do not form a part of an integrated patent document, they are worthy of special note. Judges are free to consult such resources at any time in order to better understand the underlying technology and may also rely on dictionary definitions when construing claim terms, so long as the dictionary definition does not contradict any definition found in or ascertained by a reading of the patent documents.[111]

   How easy is it to reconcile these two statements? Does *Phillips* clarify this?

5. The court also states:

> No doubt there will be instances in which intrinsic evidence is insufficient to enable the court to determine the meaning of the asserted claims, and in those instances, extrinsic evidence, such as that relied on by the district court, may also properly be relied on to understand the technology and to construe the claims. See Markman, 52 F.3d at 979, 34 USPQ2d at 1329. Extrinsic evidence is that evidence which is external to the patent and file history, such as expert testimony, inventor testimony, dictionaries, and technical treatises and articles. Id. at 980, 34 USPQ2d at 1330. However, as we have recently re-emphasized, extrinsic evidence in general, and expert testimony in particular, may be used only to help the court come to the proper understanding of the claims; it may not be used to vary or contradict the claim language. Id. at 981, 34 USPQ2d at 1331. Nor may it contradict the import of other parts of the specification. Indeed, where the patent documents are unambiguous, expert testimony regarding the meaning of a claim is entitled to no weight.[112]

   Later the court further states:

> Once again, however, reliance on such evidence is unnecessary, and indeed improper, when the disputed terms can be understood from a

---

111. Vitronics Corp. v. Conceptronic, Inc., 90 F.3d 1576, 1583–85 (Fed. Cir. 1996).
112. *Id.* at 1584.

> careful reading of the public record. See Kearns v. Chrysler Corp., 32 F.3d 1541, 1547, 31 USPQ2d 1746, 1750 (Fed. Cir. 1994). Nor may it be used to vary claim terms from how they are defined, even implicitly, in the specification or file history.[113]

What rationale does the court use to justify that extrinsic evidence may not be used to vary or contradict the claim language, the specification, or the file history?

6. Given the accepted meanings of liquidus temperature and reflow temperature, is there a way Vitronics might have either defined the claim terms or worded the claim to avoid confusion with similar terms of art? If possible, what would have been the benefit of using such terminology?

* * *

That a patentee may act as his or her own lexicographer has a long pedigree in patent law, both at the Supreme Court[114] and the Federal Circuit.[115] However, it is not necessarily easy to establish that a special meaning is being used, rather than the ordinary and customary meaning. Several cases state that redefinition by the patentee may be done expressly or by implication. However, whether express or implied, it must be clear.[116]

In this regard, the *Phillips* decision states:

> The importance of the specification in claim construction derives from its statutory role. The close kinship between the written description and the claims is enforced by the statutory requirement that the specification describe the claimed invention in "full, clear, concise, and exact terms." 35 U.S.C. § 112, para. 1; *see Netword, LLC v. Centraal Corp.*, 242 F.3d 1347, 1352 (Fed. Cir. 2001) ("The claims are directed to the invention that is described in the specification; they do not have meaning removed from the context from which they arose."); *see also Markman v. Westview Instruments, Inc.*, 517 U.S. 370, 389, 116 S. Ct. 1384, 134 L. Ed. 2d 577 (1996) ("[A claim] term can be defined only in a way that comports with the instrument as a whole."). In light of the statutory directive that the inventor provide a "full" and "exact" description of the claimed invention, the specification necessarily informs the proper construction of the claims. *See Merck Co. v. Teva Pharms. USA, Inc.*, 347 F.3d 1367, 1371 (Fed. Cir. 2003) ("A fundamental rule of claim construction is that terms in a patent document are construed with the meaning with which they are presented in the patent document. Thus claims must be

---

113. *Id.*
114. *See, e.g.*, United States v. Adams, 383 U.S. 39 (1966).
115. *See, e.g.*, CCS Fitness v. Brunswick Corp., 288 F.3d 1359 (Fed. Cir. 2002).
116. *See, e.g.*, Thorner v. Sony Comput. Ent. Am. LLC, 669 F.3d 1362 (Fed. Cir. 2012).

construed so as to be consistent with the specification, of which they are a part.") (citations omitted).

In *Renishaw*, this court summarized that point succinctly:

> Ultimately, the interpretation to be given a term can only be determined and confirmed with a full understanding of what the inventors actually invented and intended to envelop with the claim. The construction that stays true to the claim language and most naturally aligns with the patent's description of the invention will be, in the end, the correct construction.

Consistent with that general principle, our cases recognize that the specification may reveal a special definition given to a claim term by the patentee that differs from the meaning it would otherwise possess. In such cases, the inventor's lexicography governs. See CCS Fitness, Inc. v. Brunswick Corp., 288 F.3d 1359, 1366 (Fed. Cir. 2002). In other cases, the specification may reveal an intentional disclaimer, or disavowal, of claim scope by the inventor. In that instance as well, the inventor has dictated the correct claim scope, and the inventor's intention, as expressed in the specification, is regarded as dispositive. See SciMed Life Sys., Inc. v. Advanced Cardiovascular Sys., Inc., 242 F.3d 1337, 1343–44 (Fed. Cir. 2001).[117]

In general, in light of this law, we recommend that claim terms be broadly and expressly defined in the specification, but in a manner consistent with ordinary and customary meaning. In this manner, one need not necessarily take a position during prosecution whether the ordinary meaning applies or whether the term has a special meaning. Rather, one may argue that under either approach, the same conclusion is reached with respect to claim scope relative to cited art, and so on.

Interpreting Claims in Light of the Specification Compared with Reading a Limitation from the Specification into the Claims

In claim drafting, understand the tension between reading a limitation from the specification into the claims and interpreting the claims in light of the specification; draft the claims to deal with the associated risks.

Mantech Environmental Corp. v. Hudson Environmental Services
152 F.3d 1368
United States Court of Appeals for the Federal Circuit
August 13, 1998, Decided

117. Phillips v. AWH Corp., 415 F.3d 1303, 1316 (Fed. Cir. 2005) (en banc) (emphasis added).

Questions

1. This is an instructive case on claim construction. Notice how the appellate court initially derives meaning from the language of the claims alone and then verifies whether that meaning is consistent with the specification. Did the appellate court consider the ordinary and customary meaning? Did the appellate court apply the ordinary and customary meaning? Why or why not? Is this an example of an appellate court interpreting the claims in light of the specification or reading a limitation from the specification into the claims?
2. What does the appellate court say regarding the district court's use of extrinsic evidence?
3. Does this case provide any insight regarding how to draft the patent claims vis-à-vis the specification?

Renishaw PLC v. Marposs Societa' per Azioni
158 F.3d 1243
United States Court of Appeals for the Federal Circuit
September 16, 1998, Decided

Questions

1. This is an appeal from a bench trial in which the district court found noninfringement due to one missing limitation. Given the nature and complexity of the claim in the case, is it surprising that the noninfringement ruling hinged on a common everyday term such as "when"?
2. The court spent some time trying to explain the tension between the twin axioms or canons: (1) one may not read a limitation into a claim from the written description, but (2) a claim must be read in view of the specification of which it is a part. In this case, the court asserted that the term "when" operated as a "hook" that linked the preferred embodiment to the claim: "To the extent that these passages refer to the preferred embodiment, they cannot be read into the claims without some hook. The claim term 'when' is that hook."[118] Hence, according to the court, this is an example of reading the claim in light of the specification rather than reading a limitation from the specification into the claim. However, does a "hook" not exist in most cases? Take for example *Johnson Worldwide*.[119] In that case, the term was "heading

118. Renishaw PLC v. Marposs Societa' per Azioni, 158 F.3d 1243, 1253 (Fed. Cir. 1998).
119. Johnson Worldwide Assocs. v. Zebco, 175 F.3d 985 (Fed. Cir. 1999).

signal." However, despite the fact that the embodiment used the "motor heading" and the "heading signal," the court did not read the claim that narrowly. Thus, is this a case where the court read the preferred embodiment into the claim when it did not need to do so? Why or why not?

3. The court laid out a number of claim construction principles. The question may be whether the court followed them. For example, the court said "Absent a special and particular definition created by the patent applicant, terms in a claim are to be given their ordinary and accustomed meaning." The court also said: "The patentee's lexicography must, of course, appear 'with reasonable clarity, deliberateness, and precision' before it can affect the claim."[120] The court also said:

> Thus, when a claim term is expressed in general descriptive words, we will not ordinarily limit the term to a numerical range that may appear in the written description or in other claims. *See Modine Mfg.*, 75 F.3d at 1551, 37 U.S.P.Q.2D (BNA) at 1612. Nor may we, in the broader situation, add a narrowing modifier before an otherwise general term that stands unmodified in a claim. *See, e.g., Bell Communications*, 55 F.3d at 621–22, 34 U.S.P.Q.2D (BNA) at 1821 (faulting the district court for interpreting claim term "associating" to cover only explicit, and not implicit, association); *Specialty Composites*, 845 F.2d at 986–87, 6 U.S.P.Q.2D (BNA) at 1604 (refusing to limit the recited claim term "plasticizer" to external plasticizers where skilled artisans used the term broadly). For example, if an apparatus claim recites a general structure (*e.g.*, a noun) without limiting that structure to a specific subset of structures (*e.g.*, with an adjective), we will generally construe the claim to cover all known types of that structure that are supported by the patent disclosure. *See, e.g., Virginia Panel Corp. v. MAC Panel Co.*, 133 F.3d 860, 865–66, 45 U.S.P.Q.2D (BNA) 1225, 1229 (Fed. Cir. 1997) (claim term "reciprocating" is given its ordinary meaning and not limited to mere linear reciprocation); *Sjolund v. Musland*, 847 F.2d 1573, 1581–82, 6 U.S.P.Q.2D (BNA) 2020, 2027 (Fed. Cir. 1988) (refusing to limit claim term "baffle" to only rigid baffles and term "panel" to only panels of lattice construction).[121]

How well did the court follow these principles in the case?

120. *Id.* at 1249.
121. *Id.* at 1250.

4. Should the term "when" have received its ordinary and customary meaning or did the patentee provide a "special and particular definition" made clear "with reasonable clarity, deliberateness, and precision"? Was the term "when" used with a narrowing modifier or was it unmodified? Note, however, that the court also said:

 > Ultimately, the interpretation to be given a term can only be determined and confirmed with a full understanding of what the inventors actually invented and intended to envelop with the claim. *See Markman v. Westview Instruments, Inc.*, 517 U.S. 370, 389, 38 U.S.P.Q.2D (BNA) 1461, 1470, 134 L. Ed. 2d 577, 116 S. Ct. 1384 (1996). The construction that stays true to the claim language and most naturally aligns with the patent's description of the invention will be, in the end, the correct construction.[122]

 Can this latter set of principles (e.g., the construction that most naturally aligns with the patent's description) be reconciled with the former set of principles (e.g., presumption of ordinary and customary meaning unless a special meaning is made clear either explicitly or at least with "reasonable clarity, deliberateness, and precision")? Which set of principles did the court ultimately apply? Why do you think the court chose to interpret "when" narrowly in this case?
5. Is it fair to say that as much as the court would like to have a set of claim construction principles to follow in nearly every case (note that the court specifically says no canon of construction is absolute), in reality, in some cases (perhaps depending on the panel) the court is very rigid and applies those canons formalistically whereas in other cases the court is less rigid and a bit more flexible in trying to discern what it perceives the claims *truly* mean? What different claim drafting strategies do these approaches suggest?
6. Of course, the claim construction turned on the specification, as is often the case in situations involving the twin axioms. However, is there something the claim drafter might have done here in advance if trying to anticipate how one might avoid infringement?

122. *Id.* at 1251.

Toro Co. v. White Consolidated Industries, Inc.
199 F.3d 1295
United States Court of Appeals for the Federal Circuit
December 10, 1999, Decided

Questions

1. This case has several claim construction issues. The appellate court states early: "White argues that the district court incorrectly construed the terms 'air inlet cover' and 'attachment means for removably securing' in claim clause [5], and 'cover including means for increasing the pressure' in clause [6]."[123] The more challenging issues relate to the interpretation of "cover including means for increasing the pressure." However, the other issues should also be addressed. Is "attachment means for removably securing" interpreted under 112, 6 by the district court and the appellate court? How is the function "removably securing" interpreted? Is there some irony here between this issue in clause [5] and the issue in clause [6] because, here, apparently, it does not matter whether the air inlet cover may be completely separated from the housing (but later, it does matter whether the restriction ring is physically attached for patent infringement)? The appellate court states: "The district court correctly held that it is irrelevant whether the cover in the accused device is attached to the housing, for clause [5] relates only to the attachment means for removably securing the cover to the air inlet opening."[124] On what basis did the appellate court determine that the accused "hinge and latch" approach infringed the claim language despite the fact that the patent described a "tab and detent" approach?
2. As to the claim language "cover including means for increasing the pressure," this is another claim construction case where the question is whether the court is interpreting the claims in light of the specification or reading limitations into the claims from the specification. Here, the dissenting opinion and the majority opinion seem to have different views of the facts of the case. The dissent states:

   > The court mistakenly takes the described embodiment to be unique, inferring that the specification teaches that embodiment alone. The court notes that "the specification shows only a structure whereby

123. Toro Co. v. White Consol. Indus., Inc., 199 F.3d 1295, 1298 (Fed. Cir. 1999).
124. *Id.* at 1300.

> cover and ring are permanently attached to each other. This was not simply the preferred embodiment; it was the only embodiment." On the contrary, the specification does not claim such uniqueness and describes another embodiment, specifically one in which the flow restriction ring is not permanently attached to the cover. Everywhere the word "embodiment" is used to denote what is described in the specification of the '528 patent, it is used in the phrase "*a preferred* embodiment." More important, the inventor contrasts the preferred embodiment not, as the court thinks, with disadvantageous prior art, but rather with a less-preferred embodiment of the invention at hand: a blower with a replaceable, i.e., non-attached, ring. As the inventor states, the method of construction of the preferred embodiment, in which the flow restriction ring is indeed built into, and thus "part of," the air inlet cover, is advantageous in that "it automatically restricts the size of air inlet . . . without having the operator manually insert or remove a replaceable ring." '528 patent, col. 7, ll. 6–12. But as noted above, there is no prior art for the flow restriction ring, so that such a ring in any form was part of the invention. In particular, an owner-replaceable ring, i.e., one not attached, was clearly part of the invention, and is described by element [6] of claim 16 of the '528 patent. In short, an "included" but definitely not "attached" flow restriction ring is a feature of an embodiment of the invention, but not the preferred embodiment.[125]

Does this difference regarding the facts help explain the different conclusions regarding construction of the word "including"?

3. Is the outcome in this case troubling, even under the majority's view of the facts? Questions might be asked, such as: Should the term "including" have received its ordinary and customary meaning or did the patentee provide a "special and particular definition" made clear "with reasonable clarity, deliberateness, and precision"? Was the term "including" used with a narrowing modifier or was it unmodified? Is this a case where the court limited the claims to the preferred embodiment, despite the majority opinion saying otherwise?
4. What do you think explains the majority's construction of the word "including" (assuming that the dissent is wrong and an embodiment without the ring attached was not disclosed, per the majority opinion)? Is it that the majority believes that the patentee only *meant* to cover

125. *Id.* at 1303.

an attached restriction ring in light of the entire document? However, assuming that is true, how relevant is the patentee's *actual* intent here? Are not the claims construed under an objective, rather than a subjective, standard?[126] Objectively, is it not reasonable to assume that if the patentee had meant physically attached, the patentee would have said so in the patent claim?[127]

5. Again, what claim drafting approaches make sense in light of the claim construction uncertainty?

Free Stream Media Corp. v. Alphonso Inc.
996 F.3d 1355
United States Court of Appeals for the Federal Circuit
May 11, 2021, Decided

Questions

1. This case involves two related patents. The procedural posture is an appeal by Free Stream of summary judgment of noninfringement as to one patent ('668) and a cross-appeal by Alphonso of a denial to grant a motion to dismiss of the other patent ('356) as being patent ineligible. Thus, the lower court ruled that the subject matter of one of the patents was patent eligible, but ruled by summary judgment that the other patent was not infringed. The Federal Circuit reversed the refusal to grant the motion to dismiss, finding the subject matter of the applicable patent ('356) ineligible for patenting under § 101. The noninfringement ruling ('668) was based on a construction of the claims; the court affirmed the claim construction and therefore did not reach the summary judgment of noninfringement. Patent ineligibility is a serious issue getting a lot of attention in patent federal court litigation. Why did the district court find the subject matter patent

126. *See* Innova/Pure Water, Inc. v. Safari Water Filtration Sys., Inc., 381 F.3d 1111, 1116 (Fed. Cir. 2004) ("The inquiry into the meaning that claim terms would have to a person of skill in the art at the time of the invention is an objective one.").

127. *Cf.* Tun-Jen Chiang & Lawrence B. Solum, *The Interpretation-Construction Distinction in Patent Law*, 123 Yale L.J. 530 (2013) ("What *Phillips* really represents is a conflict about the underlying goal of claim construction: is it to give effect to the linguistic meaning of text, or is it to tailor patent scope to the real invention? As we will explain, these two goals are fundamentally different, and the inquiry becomes incoherent—and uncertain—when judges oscillate between them.").

eligible? What does Alphonso argue to the Federal Circuit regarding why the district court was wrong?

2. As to the '356 patent, Free Stream and Alphonso have completely different perspectives regarding the claims. Whereas the district court had been convinced regarding the view advanced by Free Stream, Alphonso convinced the Federal Circuit that the district court was wrong. What are these separate views?
3. Thus, Free Stream tries to characterize the claims as an improvement to computer functionality, which if correct should arguably make the claims patent eligible. The Federal Circuit took a much closer look at the '356 claims and specification. The analysis by the Federal Circuit is somewhat important because this is the same analysis the Federal Circuit would apply to any patent claims under § 101. Thus, the appellate court states:

> Further, this court has explained that a relevant inquiry at *Alice* Step 1 is "whether the claims in the[] patent[] focus on a specific means or method that improves the relevant technology or are instead directed to a result or effect that itself is the abstract idea and merely invoke generic processes and machinery." *McRO, Inc. v. Bandai Namco Games Am. Inc.*, 837 F.3d 1299, 1314 (Fed. Cir. 2016). Indeed, in response to Samba's arguments, Alphonso asserts that Samba "failed to identify any language in the '356 patent claims relating to overcoming the supposed communication barriers between a television and a mobile device." Appellee's Reply Br. at 4; *see also id.* at 5 ("[t]he claims do not explain in any way *how* the supposed communication barriers are overcome"); *see also id.* at 5 ("the claims do not describe *how* the purported 'barriers to communication imposed by the sandbox' are overcome"). As "reflected repeatedly in our cases," a claim must "ha[ve] the specificity required to transform [the] claim from one claiming only a result to one claiming a way of achieving it" to avoid ineligibility. *SAP Am., Inc. v. InvestPic, LLC*, 898 F.3d 1161, 1167–68 (Fed. Cir. 2018) (collecting cases). As a result, a claim is ineligible if it "fail[s] to recite a practical way of applying an underlying idea . . . [and] instead [is] drafted in such a result-oriented way that [it] amount[s] to encompassing 'the principle in the abstract' no matter how implemented." *Interval Licensing LLC v. AOL, Inc.*, 896 F.3d 1335, 1343 (Fed. Cir. 2018). *All that is required at the eligibility phase is that the claim itself "must identify 'how' that functional result is achieved by limiting the claim scope to structures specified at some level of concreteness, in the case of a product claim,*

> *or to concrete action, in the case of a method claim." Am. Axle & Mfg., Inc. v. Neapco Holdings LLC*, 967 F.3d 1285, 1302 (Fed. Cir. 2020). Here, Samba asserts that its invention allows devices on the same network to communicate where such devices were previously unable to do so. The asserted claims provide for how that is achieved only by stating that the mechanism used to achieve this communication is by piercing or otherwise overcoming a mobile device's security sandbox. But the asserted claims do not at all describe how that result is achieved.[128]

Is there another way to state the principle being applied that the claims must do more than simply claim a result in an abstract manner?

4. Thus, Free Stream loses on patent eligibility for the '356. The appellate court then reviews claim construction of the '668 (which was actually performed by a Texas federal court before consolidation in California of both lawsuits on the two related patents). What was the claim term at issue? How was it construed by the district court? How did Free Stream want it construed? Why do you think Free Stream wanted it construed this way?
5. Did the district and appellate courts apply a special meaning or the ordinary and customary meaning? Free Stream argues that both under plain meaning and based on the intrinsic evidence, "communication session" should include "one-way" communication rather than simply "bi-directional" communication. How clear do you think it is that the ordinary and customary meaning includes one-way communication? How would you argue that it is included? How would you argue that it is not included? How does the appellate court distinguish one-way communication from bi-directional communication? What do you think of the distinction?

Intel Corp. v. Qualcomm, Inc.
21 F.4th 801
United States Court of Appeals for the Federal Circuit
December 28, 2021, Decided

Questions

1. Again, what is the procedural posture of this case and how does that, if it does, affect the claim construction?

---

128. Free Stream Media Corp. v. Alphonso Inc., 996 F.3d 1355, 1363 (Fed. Cir. 2021) (emphasis added).

2. Why did the court conclude Intel had Article III standing? Any thoughts on why the settlement between Qualcomm and Apple and the sale to Apple of Intel's modem business did not affect Intel's Article III standing?
3. Why is the standard of review of factual findings substantial evidence rather than clear error? What is the difference? Why did the appellate court apply the broadest reasonable interpretation (BRI) standard rather than the *Phillips* standard? Does this appear to make any difference?
4. What is the disputed term? Why did the court not accept the reasonable and customary meaning as proposed by Intel? Why are none of the proposed definitions adequate? Why is it so difficult to come up with an appropriate construction here? Is this an example where a claim term definition might have been a better approach? Who would be helped here by a clear definition—Intel or Qualcomm?
5. What is the issue regarding means-plus-function claim interpretation and why does the procedural posture make this problematic? If claims 16 and 17 are held indefinite, who is most likely to benefit—Intel or Qualcomm? Why does the appellate court say, even if the claims are indefinite, that the Board may still be able to determine whether or not they are unpatentable? Do you think this analysis makes sense?
6. What do you think the appellate court means regarding its statement in footnote 2?

* * *

As suggested, some tension is present between some canons of claim construction. This makes it difficult to predict with confidence how a court may apply the appropriate canon in a given situation. Consequently, it is believed to be better to include a spectrum of patent claims that cover the subject matter at a broad level of specificity, at an intermediate level of specificity of detail, and at a narrow level of specificity.[129] Also, in this manner, one may be reasonably assured that such claims are supported by the written description, because the written patent claims are part of the written description.

One canon is that claims are to be interpreted in light of the specification of which they are a part.[130] Another canon is that it is improper under the guise of claim interpretation to import a limitation from the specification into the claims.[131] The latter principle even applies where a specification provides a

129. See Chapter 4, suggesting claiming multiple embodiments, from broadest to narrowest.

130. *See, e.g.*, SimpleAir, Inc. v. Sony Ericsson Mobile Comm'cns AB, 820 F.3d 419, 429–38 (Fed. Cir. 2016); Phillips v. AWH Corp., 415 F.3d 1303, 1315 (Fed. Cir. 2005) (en banc).

131. *See, e.g.*, *Phillips*, 415 F.3d at 1313 (en banc); Leibel-Flarsheim Co. v. Medrad, Inc., 358 F.3d 898, 913 (Fed. Cir. 2004). For a recent example, see *Lowe v. ShieldMark, Inc.*, No. 2021-2164,

single embodiment unless the specification evidences a clear intention to limit the claims to that single embodiment. The claims are not to be limited to that single embodiment.[132]

However, navigating between these two canons is not quite so easy as stating them. The Federal Circuit itself has recognized the difficulty.[133] An early case that clearly illustrates this challenge is *Renishaw v. Marposs*.[134]

The invention concerned a touch probe used to measure very fine distances (e.g., dimensions) of machined parts. It appears that the accused product met every limitation of the claim at issue but one, whose interpretation was in dispute. The patent claim at issue recited that "the probe generat[es] a trigger signal *when* said sensing tip contacts an object and said stylus holder is thereby deflected relative to said housing."[135]

The ultimate question was the meaning of "when." The specification described the invention in a manner that suggested there was virtually no appreciable delay between contacting an object and generating a trigger signal. However, the accused product had an appreciable delay due to its method of operation. Despite this contrast, the term "when" more generally may be understood to not mean simply "at the time of." Rather, it may be understood to also include within a short time thereafter. Claim terms are heavily presumed to be interpreted in accordance with their ordinary and customary meaning,[136] unless clearly redefined in the specification to have a different meaning.

The Federal Circuit discussed the tension between the two canons in the opinion:

> Renishaw, of course, alludes to a familiar pair of claim construction canons: (a) one may not read a limitation into a claim from the written description, but (b) one may look to the written description to define a term already in a claim limitation, for a claim must be read in view of the specification of which it is a part. These two rules lay out the general relationship between the claims and the written description. *See Vitronics Corp. v. Conceptronic, Inc.*, 90 F.3d 1576, 1582, 39 USPQ2d 1573, 1576 (Fed. Cir. 1996); *Markman*

2022 WL 636100 (Fed. Cir. Mar. 4, 2022), in which the Federal Circuit held that the lower court erred by importing terms from the specification into the claims.

132. *See, e.g.*, *Leibel-Flarsheim*, 358 F.3d at 905.

133. *See, e.g.*, *Phillips*, 415 F.3d at 1323 (en banc); Comark Commc'ns, Inc. v. Harris Corp., 156 F.3d 1182, 1186–87 (Fed. Cir. 1998).

134. 158 F.3d 1243 (Fed. Cir. 1998).

135. *Id.* at 1245 (emphasis added).

136. *See, e.g.*, Azure Networks, LLC v. CSR PLC, 771 F.3d 1336, 1347–48 (Fed. Cir. 2014); Aventis Pharms. Inc. v. Amino Chems. Ltd., 715 F.3d 1363, 1373 (Fed. Cir. 2013).

> *v. Westview Instruments, Inc.*, 52 F.3d 967, 979–80, 34 USPQ2d 1321, 1329–30 (Fed. Cir. 1995) (in banc), *aff'd*, 517 U.S. 370, 116 S. Ct. 1384, 134 L. Ed. 2d 577, 38 USPQ2d 1461 (1996). As rules at the core of claim construction methodology, they provide guideposts for a spectrum of claim construction problems.
>
> Thus, where there are several common meanings for a claim term, the patent disclosure serves to point away from the improper meanings and toward the proper meaning. Ultimately, the interpretation to be given a term can only be determined and confirmed with a full understanding of what the inventors actually invented and intended to envelop with the claim. *See Markman v. Westview Instruments, Inc.*, 517 U.S. 370, 389, 116 S. Ct. 1384, 134 L. Ed. 2d 577, 38 USPQ2d 1461, 1470 (1996). The construction that stays true to the claim language and most naturally aligns with the patent's description of the invention will be, in the end, the correct construction.[137]

The appellate court, hence, resolves the question by looking at how the term "when" is used in the description. The appellate court, for instance, states:

> For example, in describing the invention's place within the prior art, the '904 patent notes: "When the stylus contacts a workpiece surface, a trigger signal is generated by the probe, which is used to trigger the taking of a reading of the instantaneous position of the movable spindle, quill or arm." Col. 1, ll. 36–42. Likewise, the Summary of the Invention states that the preferred embodiment of the probe "includes means for providing a signal when said stylus contacts a workpiece," col. 3, ll. 28–29, and that the movable elements are displaced "out of said rest position when said stylus contacts a workpiece," col. 3, ll. 21–22.
>
> Statements in the "Description of Preferred Embodiments" also use the term "when" to describe a time very close to the precise instant that the stylus contacts the object to be measured and not some appreciable time thereafter. . . .[138]

Thus, concluding that "when" means "at the time of," the Federal Circuit stated:

> These passages make abundantly clear that "when" in the patent means at the time of, and not some appreciable time thereafter. *See Autogiro Co.*, 384 F.2d at 397, 155 USPQ at 702–03 ("[W]ords must be used in the same way in both the claims and the specification.").
>
> To the extent that these passages refer to the preferred embodiment, they cannot be read into the claims without some hook. The claim term "when"

---

137. *See Renishaw*, 158 F.3d at 1248.
138. *See id.* at 1252–53.

> is that hook. Each of the preceding passages above show that the patentee wanted "when" to mean as soon as possible after contact. In contrast, Renishaw's preferred construction of "when," which would sweep in any time whatsoever after contact, is so broad that it would require us to ignore the abounding statements in the written description that point decidedly the other way.[139]

The court is trying to be helpful with its "hook" analogy. However, this approach logically pushes the question back to how specifically or generally a claim term is to be understood from the usage of that term in the specification. It seems a court will not have difficulty locating such "a hook" for those cases in which it wants to import a limitation from the specification.

How clear and unmistakable is it that the drafter intended to "redefine" the term "when" from its ordinary and customary meaning? If the patent draftsman had perceived the precise issue that might later be raised, there is little doubt the specification would have clarified the point and even the claim language itself. Thus, concluding noninfringement from such a general term in the claim, while demonstrating good lawyering by those representing the defendant, does not give sufficiently clear guidance regarding the difference between construing claims in light of the specification and importing limitations. Yet, *Renishaw* is heavily cited and held out as an example of a case that clarifies the difference.

A drafting lesson, here, might be to be circumspect in the use of everyday language and endeavor to uncover potential interpretations that might lead to noninfringement, and revise claim and specification language accordingly. In this regard, it is generally considered good practice to review claims with an eye toward possible design around opportunities so that claims may be redrafted before filing so as to cover such noninfringement opportunities.[140]

Express/Implied Meaning of Claim Terms

In claim drafting, consider the risks associated with expressly defining claim terms versus impliedly defining claim terms; draft claims appropriately.

A similar tension exists between impliedly defining a claim term versus importing limitations from the written description. For example, a specification may employ terms in an idiosyncratic manner, terms may be highly technical, or terms may be coined by an inventor.[141] Likewise, claim terms may also

---

139. *See id.*

140. See Chapter 4, treating how to make designing around patent claims more difficult.

141. *See, e.g.*, Phillips v. AWH Corp., 415 F.3d 1303, 1313 (Fed. Cir. 2005) (en banc).

be expressly defined. Generally, it has been recognized that the specification is reviewed to resolve such ambiguities.[142]

SciMed Life Systems, Inc. v. Advanced Cardiovascular Systems, Inc.
242 F.3d 1337
United States Court of Appeals for the Federal Circuit
March 14, 2001, Decided

Bell Atlantic Network Services, Inc. v. Covad Communications Group, Inc.
262 F.3d 1258
United States Court of Appeals for the Federal Circuit
August 17, 2001, Decided

SuperGuide Corp. v. DirecTV Enterprises, Inc.
358 F.3d 870
United States Court of Appeals for the Federal Circuit
February 12, 2004, Decided

Irdeto Access, Inc. v. Echostar Satellite Corp.
383 F.3d 1295
United States Court of Appeals for the Federal Circuit
September 14, 2004, Decided

Silicon Graphics, Inc. v. ATI Technologies, Inc.
607 F.3d 784
United States Court of Appeals for the Federal Circuit
June 4, 2010, Decided

Grace Instrument Industries, LLC v. Chandler Instruments Co., LLC
57 F.4th 1001
United States Court of Appeals for the Federal Circuit
January 12, 2023, Decided

Questions

1. In *SciMed*, according to the appellate court, is the claim term at issue expressly or implicitly redefined? What do you think about the analysis under the DOE? At what point is a structure necessarily "excluded from being an equivalent" by the language of the claims in comparison

142. *See, e.g.*, Straight Path IP Grp., Inc. v. Sipnet EU S.R.O., 806 F.3d 1356, 1361 (Fed. Cir. 2015).

to simply not meeting the literal language of the claims? What do you think of the concurrence by Judge Dyk?

2. In *Bell Atlantic*, despite the broad nature of the term "mode," the appellate court makes a persuasive case for redefinition by implication. Would it have helped Bell Atlantic if, instead, it had provided an express definition of "mode" consistent with its ordinary and customary meaning and then stated that it was merely providing an illustrative embodiment that was not intended to limit the scope of the patent claims? How does one know when a claim term has been redefined by implication? Note this statement by the appellate court: "[W]hen a patentee uses a claim term throughout the entire patent specification, in a manner consistent with only a single meaning, he has defined that term 'by implication.'"[143] However, will this not occur even when a redefinition is not intended? Is it not considered good practice to use terms consistently throughout a specification? If terms are used inconsistently, does that not invite ambiguity or indefiniteness? What is a way to vary use of terms without being inconsistent? Also, note that in the analysis under the DOE the appellate court stated that "if a court determines that a finding of infringement under the doctrine of equivalents 'would entirely vitiate a particular claim element,' then the court should rule that there is no infringement under the doctrine of equivalents."[144] Is this a different principle or just another way of stating the principle from *SciMed*, that where "the scope of the claim was limited in a way that plainly and necessarily excluded a structural feature that was the opposite of the one recited in the claim, that different structure could not be brought within the scope of patent protection through the doctrine of equivalents"?[145]
3. In *SuperGuide*, did the court apply the ordinary and customary meaning of "regularly received television signal" as it would have been understood by one of ordinary skill in the art at the time of filing? Did it apply a special meaning based on the patentee acting as his own lexicographer? Did the court apply the ordinary and customary meaning of "regularly received television signal" as it would have been understood by one of ordinary skill in the art at the time of infringement?[146]

143. Bell Atl. Network Servs., Inc. v. Covad Comm'cns Grp., Inc., 262 F.3d 1258, 1298 (Fed. Cir. 2001).

144. *Id.* at 1279–80.

145. SciMed Life Sys., Inc. v. Advanced Cardiovascular Sys., Inc., 242 F.3d 1337, 1346 (Fed. Cir. 2001).

146. *See* Ring & Pinion Serv. Inc. v. ARB Corp., 743 F.3d 831 (Fed. Cir. 2014).

How persuasive is this point: "Had the patentees intended to limit the disputed claim terms to 'analog' technology, they could have easily done so by explicitly modifying the disputed claim language with the term 'analog.'"[147] How should technology developed after the patent application was filed affect the construction of the claims? Is it that the claim drafter needs to draft claims that take later-developed technology into account or does the law surrounding claim construction take this into account?[148]

Note this statement by the court:

> We begin our review of the district court's construction of the asserted claim by agreeing with Gemstar that the court improperly relied on cases involving means-plus-function claims to conclude that later or "after-arising technologies" cannot fall within the literal scope of the claim at issue. Method and apparatus claims not written in means-plus-function format are not necessarily limited to that disclosed in the specification but rather are defined by the language of the claims themselves. *See SRI*, 775 F.2d at 1121 ("It is the claims that measure the invention.").[149]

Observe that Judge Rader disagrees with the literal construction that would include digital signals but states: "Because I agree with the court that there is at least a triable issue as to infringement of the '578 patent under the doctrine of equivalents, I concur in the result as to the '578 patent."[150]

Of course, perhaps it was a lucky accident that the claims did not refer to analog signals. If the claims had, despite after-arising technology, certainly the claims would have been limited to analog signals. What does this point suggest about drafting claims in which the implementation of various technical aspects may be subject to change or technical advancements?

4. In *SuperGuide*, do you see any indefiniteness issues with the language "desired format"?
5. *SuperGuide* is also well-known for its construction of "at least one of the following: A, B *and* C." Unfortunately, it appears that, before this case, patent attorneys quite commonly used this formulation, which

---

147. SuperGuide Corp. v. DirecTV Enters., Inc., 358 F.3d 870, 880 (Fed. Cir. 2004).
148. Lemley, *supra* note 109. *See also* Collins, *supra* note 109; Sarnoff, *supra* note 109.
149. *SuperGuide Corp.*, 358 F.3d at 877.
150. *Id.* at 898.

it is recommended be avoided. Compare this claim language with a Markush group formulation.[151] Note that the court relied on the ordinary and customary meaning of "and." Do you think that if it had been made expressly or implicitly clear that the formulation "A, B, and C" could also be understood to mean "A, B, or C" that this would have changed the result?

6. In *Irdeto*, it appears that the patentee's flaw was directing the examiner to the specification regarding the meaning of claim terms because the ordinary and customary meaning was broader. Of course, in the face of close prior art, one might well imagine that a narrower meaning, if the specification provides one, might be preferred. The point, of course, is to appreciate that with respect to claim language, these possibilities—ordinary and customary meaning, express meaning, and/or implied meaning—hedging may be best because the prior art and the accused device may not be fully known or may potentially be "moving targets." Hence, different situations may call for different positions as to what the claim terms mean. During prosecution, how might one hedge their position in this regard?
7. In *Silicon Graphics*, how did the court construe "rasterization process," "scan conversion," and "sl0e5"? What approach did the court use to construe them—ordinary and customary meaning, express definition, or implied definition?
8. Why did the appellate court conclude that the immunity provision in the Microsoft license did not necessarily protect ATI from liability as to the '327 patent?
9. In *Grace*, the appellate court said the district court's reliance on dictionaries to understand "enlarged chamber" was wrong. Why was that an error?
10. The district court had held some claims to be invalid because the district court found the term "enlarged chamber" to be indefinite. What was the district court's view in this regard? What did the appellate court say was the correct view?
11. The appellate court also analyzed the claim language "*means for driving said rotor to rotate located in at least one bottom section.*" There were quite a few issues argued by Grace regarding this language; however, the appellate court determined that the district court was correct.

151. See Chapter 4, treating Markush group claim formulations. See also later in this chapter regarding following the rules of grammar.

How did the appellate court analyze the language to conclude that the district court was correct?

12. Do you think the claim construction might have gone more in favor of Grace if they had not used means-plus-function language for this aspect of the claim? For example, how might this element have been claimed to favor Grace based on the arguments Grace presented regarding construction of this element?

While a specification may *expressly* redefine a claim term, the Federal Circuit has also recognized that this may occur *by implication* without express definition *if it is clear*.[152] Previously, we discussed the tension between reading the claims in light of the specification and importing limitations into the claims from the specification. Likewise, it may be said a tension exists between reading the claims in light of the specification and concluding the occurrence of claim term redefinition by implication. The difference may be a fine one.

One example case is *Thorner v. Sony*,[153] which, like *Renishaw*, involved an issue of claim construction. The district court had construed "attached to said pad" in a manner so that the defendant, Sony, did not infringe. The district court held that "the specification redefines 'attached' by implication." The district court reasoned that the word "attached" was limited to attached to the outside of an object because the embodiments in the specification consistently use the term "attached" to indicate affixing an actuator to the outer surface of an object and used the word "embedded" when referring to an actuator inside an object. For additional support for the notion that "attached" and "embedded" have different meanings, the district court pointed to claim 1, which used the word "attached," and dependent claim 10, which used the word "embedded."

Following claim construction by the district court, the parties stipulated to noninfringement by the accused products so that the claim construction by the district court could be appealed to the Federal Circuit.

In *Thorner*, the appellate court stated, regarding claim construction:

> Our case law is clear, claim terms must be given their plain and ordinary meaning to one of skill in the art. *Phillips*, 415 F.3d at 1316. The plain meaning of the term "attached" encompasses either an external or internal attachment. We must decide whether the patentee has redefined this term to mean only

152. *See* Irdeto Access, Inc. v. Echostar Satellite Corp., 383 F.3d 1295, 1300 (Fed. Cir. 2004); Bell Atl. Network Servs., Inc. v. Covad Comm'cns Grp., Inc., 262 F.3d 1258, 1268 (Fed. Cir. 2001).

153. 669 F.3d 1362 (Fed. Cir. 2012).

attachment to an external surface. As Sony argues, the specification repeatedly uses the term "attached" in reference to embodiments where the actuators are "attached to [an] outer side." '941 patent col.33 ll.40–41. In fact, the specification never uses the word "attached" when referring to an actuator located on the interior of a controller. We hold that this does not rise to the level of either lexicography or disavowal. Both exceptions require a clear and explicit statement by the patentee. *CCS Fitness*, 288 F.3d at 1366; *Teleflex*, 299 F.3d at 1325. It is not enough that the patentee used the term when referencing an attachment to an outer surface in each embodiment. *See Kara Tech.*, 582 F.3d at 1347–48. In fact, the specification explains that an actuator was "attached to [an] outer surface." *See* '941 patent col.33 ll.40–41. If the applicant had redefined the term "attached" to mean only "attached to an outer surface," then it would have been unnecessary to specify that the attachment was "to [an] outer surface" in the specification. We conclude that the term attached should be given its plain and ordinary meaning. The specification does not redefine attached nor is there any disavowal.[154]

The appellate court further stated:

The fact that the specification uses the two terms "attached" and "embedded" as alternatives does not require a different result. *See, e.g.*, *id.* col.32 l.66. There is nothing inconsistent about the applicant's use of the narrower term, "embedded," to describe embodiments affixed to an internal surface. The plain and ordinary meaning of embedded, "attached within," is narrower than "attached." Hence it makes sense that the applicant would want to use embedded when it meant to explicitly claim attached to the inside only. That does not mean the word attached automatically means attached to the external surface, as opposed to the broader plain meaning—attached to either the interior or exterior.

It is true that in certain pre-*Phillips* cases, we held that use of two terms as alternatives could amount to an implicit redefinition of the terms. *See Bell Atl. Network Servs., Inc. v. Covad Commc'ns Grp., Inc.*, 262 F.3d 1258, 1271 (Fed. Cir. 2001). But the "implied" redefinition must be so clear that it equates to an explicit one. In other words, a person of ordinary skill in the art would have to read the specification and conclude that the applicant has clearly disavowed claim scope or has acted as its own lexicographer. Simply referring to two terms as alternatives or disclosing embodiments that all use the term the same way is not sufficient to redefine a claim term.

Other parts of the claim and specification also support this construction. The claim at issue requires a "flexible pad." The only embodiment in the specification that includes flexible material is the seat cushion 510 shown in

154. *See id.* at 1367–68.

Figure 2. The specification states that "the tactile feedback seating unit 510 is a semi-rigid flexible foam structure . . . with a plurality of actuators embedded within the foam structure." '941 patent col.37 ll.6–10. Thus, the only flexible embodiment in the specification has embedded actuators. If we agreed with Sony that "attached" must mean attached to an outer surface, then the claim would exclude the only flexible embodiment disclosed in the specification. This is further evidence that the term "attached" should have its plain and ordinary meaning which includes either internal or external attachments.

We hold that the term "attached to said pad" should be given its plain and ordinary meaning which encompasses either internal or external attachment. Because the parties based the stipulation of noninfringement on the district court's erroneous construction of this claim term, we vacate and remand.[155]

It is helpful to compare the approach of the panel in *Renishaw* with the approach of the panel in *Thorner v. Sony*. It is true that *Renishaw* is an earlier case compared with *Thorner*; however, *Renishaw* is repeatedly cited throughout Federal Circuit claim construction jurisprudence. Furthermore, many other examples along the lines of *Renishaw* continued to be decided in the years following that decision. The point, then, is to show, by contrast, that various legal outcomes are possible, depending on the context. It may even be the situation that the particular three-judge panel suggests a particular outcome or approach. The best way to hedge one's bets is to make sure the desired interpretation follows both from the clear language of the claims as well as the clear description in the specification.

Throughout the post-*Markman* era in which claim construction was determined to be a court function, a tension is evident on the Federal Circuit illustrated by the comparison between *Renishaw* and *Thorner*. On the one hand, the court would like a consistent set of rules that gives predictability. These principles include the presumption of ordinary meaning and that any deviation requires a clear and unmistakable redefinition in the specification. On the other hand, principles also exist that the specification should be used to point the way to a proper claim construction. Thus, a construction may be sought that aligns with specification usage. However, this latter principle appears to be applied in a manner that is not as exacting or is without the same high evidentiary showing as suggested by principles that apply the presumption of ordinary meaning and that require a clear and unmistakable redefinition in the specification. Hence, close cases are harder to resolve.

For the drafter, the "game," so to speak, is to ensure either approach leads to the same construction. This is discussed more later, but it would be best

155. *Id.*

that a definition of a key claim term provided in the specification align as much as possible with the known and understood ordinary meaning. This permits being true to the presumption of ordinary meaning while also abiding by the principle that definitions of claim terms in the specification are clear and unmistakable.

Categories of Claim Terminology

In claim drafting, consider and identify different categories of claim terminology to appreciate where disputes over claim term meaning may arise.

Terminology finding its way into claims may be viewed in different categories. A reason for viewing claim terms in this manner is that the particular category may affect the likelihood that the claim term meaning will be disputed and, therefore, potentially construed by a court if a litigation were to ensue. The category may also suggest how a court is likely to treat the term. For example, claim terms may be divided into four categories. These are lay terms, technical terms, patent law terms of art, and terms of degree.[156] A close variation of this approach was suggested by individuals who have studied and engaged in patent litigation.[157]

Of course, it may not always be clear which category a claim term may fall into; however, perceiving claim terms in this manner may aid claim drafting (as well as specification drafting) by focusing attention on the terms used and the likelihood of a dispute as to meaning, especially for particular words, so that one may take extra care regarding use in drafting.

For example, as to patent law terms of art, these typically have an adjudicated meaning and should, therefore, be used in a manner consistent with that meaning. Clear examples include "comprising" and other transition phrases, previously discussed.[158] These are the primary examples for this category. Another example might be "plurality." However, there are other terms commonly used in claims that might be considered a patent law term of art but may also be viewed as in another category.[159] A good example is "substantially," discussed here as a term of degree.

For all these examples, appreciate that particular adjudicated meaning may be affected by the facts in a particular situation, so that the meaning of

156. Terms of degree may be thought of as a subcategory of patent law terms of art but require special attention due to the risk of indefiniteness associated with this category of terms.

157. *See* Menell et al., *supra* note 36.

158. See, for example, Chapter 3, discussing patent claim transition words or phrases.

159. *See* Menell et al., *supra* note 36, tbl. B (listing terms commonly construed by the Federal Circuit).

these terms may change in a given situation.[160] A good example is the indefinite article "a" or "an." Although in patent law, this should mean one or more as a term of art, cases exist that have held otherwise based on unusual facts.[161] Thus, it is suggested that such terms be used in the specification in a manner so that intended meaning is clear and, if appropriate, expressly defined. Patent applications often employ boilerplate language near the beginning or end of the specification for such purposes.

For terms of degree, use and meaning may be able to be significantly affected via drafting. Terms of degree often include words that might be viewed as a patent law term of art (e.g., substantially) or as lay terminology (e.g., about). However, terms of degree are identified as a separate term category because without some clarity as to meaning, there is a risk of a claim using the term being held indefinite.[162]

The legal standard for indefiniteness is different for examination than it is for litigation.[163] The rationale for the difference is that a patent claim has a presumption of validity. A court will not find a patented claim indefinite unless the claim interpreted in light of the specification and the prosecution

160. *See* Medrad, Inc. v. MRI Devices Corp., 401 F.3d 1313, 1318 (Fed. Cir. 2005) (Interpretations of the same word or phrase in separate patents may diverge because (1) "[a] patentee may define a particular term in a particular way, and in that event the term will be defined in that fashion for purposes of that particular patent, no matter what its meaning in other contexts"; (2) "claim terms are typically given their ordinary and accustomed meaning as understood by one of ordinary skill in the pertinent art, and the generally understood meaning of particular terms may vary from art to art"; and (3) "[e]ven absent an express definition of a term in the specification or prosecution history, or a clearly established understanding of the meaning of the term in the art, the manner in which the term is used in the patent may dictate a definition that differs from the definition that would be given to the same term in a different patent with a different specification or prosecution history.").

161. *See* TiVo, Inc. v. EchoStar Commc'ns Corp., 516 F.3d 1290, 1303 (Fed. Cir. 2008) (term "a" or "an" interpreted to be singular); Aug. Tech. Corp. v. Camtek, Ltd., 655 F.3d 1278, 1282 (Fed. Cir. 2011) (term "a wafer" interpreted to mean one and only one wafer). *See Medrad*, 401 F.3d at 1318 (Interpretations of the same word or phrase in separate patents may diverge because (1) "[a] patentee may define a particular term in a particular way, and in that event the term will be defined in that fashion for purposes of that particular patent, no matter what its meaning in other contexts"; (2) "claim terms are typically given their ordinary and accustomed meaning as understood by one of ordinary skill in the pertinent art, and the generally understood meaning of particular terms may vary from art to art"; and (3) "[e]ven absent an express definition of a term in the specification or prosecution history, or a clearly established understanding of the meaning of the term in the art, the manner in which the term is used in the patent may dictate a definition that differs from the definition that would be given to the same term in a different patent with a different specification or prosecution history.").

162. *Cf.* Grace Instrument Indus., LLC v. Chandler Instruments Co., LLC, 57 F.4th 1001 (Fed. Cir. 2023).

163. *See In re* Packard, 751 F.3d 1307 (Fed. Cir. 2014).

history fails to "inform those skilled in the art about the scope of the invention with reasonable certainty."[164] In contrast, during examination, examiners apply the BRI. In this regard, MPEP section 2173.02(I) (2023) states:

> Patented claims are not given the broadest reasonable interpretation during court proceedings involving infringement and validity, and can be interpreted based on a fully developed prosecution record. While "absolute precision is unattainable" in patented claims, the definiteness requirement "mandates clarity." *Nautilus, Inc. v. Biosig Instruments, Inc.*, 527 U.S. 898, 910, 110 USPQ2d 1688, 1693 (2014). A court will not find a patented claim indefinite unless the claim interpreted in light of the specification and the prosecution history fails to "inform those skilled in the art about the scope of the invention with reasonable certainty." *Id.* at 899, 110 USPQ2d at 1689.
>
> The Office does not interpret claims when examining patent applications in the same manner as the courts. *In re Packard*, 751 F.3d 1307, 1312, 110 USPQ2d 1785, 1788 (Fed. Cir. 2014); *In re Morris*, 127 F.3d 1048, 1054, 44 USPQ2d 1023, 1028 (Fed. Cir. 1997); *In re Zletz*, 893 F.2d 319, 321–22, 13 USPQ2d 1320, 1321–22 (Fed. Cir. 1989). During prosecution the Office construes claims by giving them their broadest reasonable interpretation consistent with the specification in an effort to establish a clear record of what the applicant intends to claim. Such claim construction during prosecution may effectively result in a lower threshold for ambiguity than a court's determination. *Packard*, 751 F.3d at 1323–24, 110 USPQ2d at 1796–97 (Plager, J., concurring). However, applicant has the ability to amend the claims during prosecution to ensure that the meaning of the language is clear and definite prior to issuance or provide a persuasive explanation (with evidence as necessary) that a person of ordinary skill in the art would not consider the claim language unclear. *In re Buszard*, 504 F.3d 1364, 1366, 84 USPQ2d 1749, 1750 (Fed. Cir. 2007) (claims are given their broadest reasonable interpretation during prosecution "to facilitate sharpening and clarifying the claims at the application stage"); *see also In re Yamamoto*, 740 F.2d 1569, 1571, 222 USPQ 934, 936 (Fed. Cir. 1984); *In re Zletz*, 893 F.2d 319, 322, 13 USPQ2d 1320, 1322 (Fed. Cir. 1989); *Ex parte McAward*, Appeal 2015-006416 (PTAB Aug. 25, 2017) (precedential).

As suggested, one example of a term of degree may be "substantially." Although often seen as a patent law term of art, its meaning could be clarified in the specification, and/or perhaps the term may be given a technical meaning in the particular context so that it may then be construed as a technical term by a court in an appropriate situation. For example, if "substantially" were defined using a reasonably objective technical standard, that term would

164. *See* Nautilus, Inc. v. Biosig Instruments, Inc., 572 U.S. 898 (2014).

then likely be understood by one of ordinary skill and, similarly, be interpreted in a manner that one of ordinary skill would likely employ.

Consider this claim as an example:

EXAMPLE 5.1

I claim:

1. A method of operating a module, the module including at least one integrated circuit (IC) chip comprising a plurality of series N-type metal oxide semiconductor (NMOS) field effect transistors configured in a series connected stack configuration that comprises at least one series NMOS field effect transistor including a body, the at least one series NMOS field effect transistor either to pass a radio frequency (RF) signal in a series enable state or to not pass the RF signal in a series disable state, the method comprising:

   electrically biasing the body of the at least one series NMOS field effect transistor of the module in the series disable state to have a voltage level substantially more negative than the lowest voltage level of the following: ground, a DC voltage level of a source of the at least one series NMOS field effect transistor of the module, and a DC voltage level of a drain of the at least one series NMOS field effect transistor of the module.

The claim refers to "a voltage level *substantially* more negative than the lowest voltage level of the following." The specification may assign a value, such as more than one volt, or perhaps clarify in the context the intended meaning of "substantially." Here, for example, since the transistor is biased to be in a "disable state," "substantially more negative" could mean a voltage level more negative so that the "at least one series NMOS field effect transistor" is clearly electrically off.

Even without some language in the specification, if issued, a claim using the term "substantially" might not necessarily be held indefinite. A court may be able to clarify meaning from the particular context, for example;[165] however, depending on importance, this may become a term whose meaning is disputed, increasing uncertainty as to what the claims cover. Thus, aside from the risk of being indefinite, another good reason to clarify meaning is

165. *Cf. Grace Instrument Indus.*, 57 F.4th 1001.

to reduce uncertainty as to claim scope. Other examples of terms of degree include "approximately" and "about."[166]

Another category of terms are technical terms. To illustrate, for the claims discussed in the examples of Chapter 2, the technical terms include "burst mode," "memory controller," "central processing unit (CPU)," "system bus," and so on. Claim scope will necessarily turn on how these terms are interpreted. *It is, therefore, important that these terms have express definitions, but as has been suggested, using definitions that are also consistent with ordinary meaning*. The law is well established that if these types of terms are disputed then the court must construe these terms for the jury.[167]

A final category of terms are lay terms, which basically includes terms not in one of the preceding categories. Recognizing these terms may be useful when drafting because these terms are less likely to be construed by a court. The court construes terms for the jury, but, for some terms, it may not aid the jury in its deliberations to have the court provide a construction. The jury will understand these words without an interpretation.[168] These are common, everyday words. However, care is justified to make sure words that may seem like lay terms are not technical terms, terms of degree, or even patent law terms of art. A good example of the latter is "a" or "an," discussed earlier. This seems like a lay term, but it would probably be better viewed as a patent law term of art.

Onc source for possible patent terms of art is the article "Patent Claim Construction: A Modern Synthesis and Structured Framework" by Peter S. Menell, Matthew D. Powers, and Steven C. Carlson. The article contains a table of terms that courts have commonly construed.[169] Another source is the *Thesaurus of Claim Construction*.[170]

One should appreciate that viewing terms in this manner is not a science, so to speak, and involves significant use of judgment. This approach is introduced, however, as one way to spot which claim terms are more likely to raise legal issues in litigation and should perhaps receive special drafting attention.

---

166. *See* Menell et al., *supra* note 36, tbl. B (listing terms commonly construed by the Federal Circuit).

167. *See* O2 Micro Int'l Ltd. v. Beyond Innovation Tech. Co., 521 F.3d 1351, 1362 (Fed. Cir. 2008) (holding that failure to construe the term "only if" was error where parties engaged in technical dispute over its scope).

168. *See* Acumed LLC v. Stryker Corp., 483 F.3d 800, 806 (Fed. Cir. 2007) ("[A] sound claim construction need not always purge every shred of ambiguity. The resolution of some line-drawing problems—especially easy ones like this one—is properly left to the trier of fact.").

169. *See* Menell et al., *supra* note 36, tbl. B (listing terms commonly construed by the Federal Circuit).

170. *See* Robert Kahrl & Stuart Soffer, Thesaurus of Claim Construction (2011).

Claim Drafting in Light of Claim Construction and Principles of Patent Infringement

Having discussed *Markman* and claim construction principles in some detail, we may now discuss a set of basic claim drafting principles that follow logically from these principles of claim construction. One or two we have stated or implied previously, but, here, we discuss these as principles derived from an understanding of claim construction and, if appropriate, provide examples for purposes of illustration.

Direct, Literal Infringement

One thing to appreciate, which will be developed throughout this chapter, is that there are several types of patent infringement, and each has associated legal rules. Much is based on § 271 of the statute (which, however, was a codification of case law). Thus, court development is also a basis for these types of patent infringement and the differences.

The most straightforward patent infringement is direct, literal infringement, which derives from subsection 271(a). That section states: "Except as otherwise provided in this title, whoever without authority makes, uses, offers to sell, or sells any patented invention, within the United States or imports into the United States any patented invention during the term of the patent therefor, infringes the patent."

Thus, the acts that result in patent infringement are making, using, offering for sale, selling, or importing into the United States the patented invention. As has been noted, the patented invention is quite literally defined by the claims.[171] Thus, an accused product must meet the "All Elements Rule" that applies for a claim. The accused product must meet each and every element and limitation of the particular claim literally for literal patent infringement.

If each and every element and limitation is met literally (including how they are arranged), then this constitutes direct, literal infringement of the patent claim at issue. Another way to infringe a patent claim directly is to infringe it nonliterally. This relates to the DOE, which is a type of infringement created by federal courts in light of the policies behind patent law. We treat the principles related to the DOE later in this chapter.[172] As just stated, it is often said that to infringe a patent claim requires that each element and limitation of the patent claim be met by the accused device (or accused ser-

171. *See, e.g.*, Phillips v. AWH Corp., 415 F.3d 1303 (Fed. Cir. 2005) (en banc).
172. See a treatment later in this chapter of patent infringement under the DOE.

vice) either *literally* or *equivalently*. This statement is referring to direct patent infringement but includes both literal and nonliteral infringement.

Another type of patent infringement is indirect patent infringement. This topic was introduced in Chapter 2 through examples. The legal basis for indirect patent infringement is statutory subsections 271(b) and (c), which state:

> (b) Whoever actively induces infringement of a patent shall be liable as an infringer;
>
> (c) Whoever offers to sell or sells within the United States or imports into the United States a component of a patented machine, manufacture, combination or composition, or a material or apparatus for use in practicing a patented process, constituting a material part of the invention, knowing the same to be especially made or especially adapted for use in an infringement of such patent, and not a staple article or commodity of commerce suitable for substantial noninfringing use, shall be liable as a contributory infringer.

These sections are treated in much more detail later in this chapter.[173] In general, these sections are directed to someone who in some manner aids and abets a direct infringer but does not otherwise directly infringe the patent claim at issue. Hence, the name "indirect infringement." As with direct infringement, this infringement may occur literally or nonliterally.

At the Start of Drafting, Consider the Types of Direct Infringement and the Business and Economic Considerations Surrounding the Invention

When beginning to draft patent claims, it is helpful to have in mind a type of patent infringement. Typically, one begins with direct, literal patent infringement since it is the easiest to make out (to show with evidence) legally. As discussed later, for indirect infringement or nonliteral infringement, more things must generally be proven to establish in federal court that these types of patent infringement have occurred.

Not unlike our discussion in Chapter 4 regarding claim types, such as apparatus claims, method of making claims, and method of using claims, it is helpful when beginning to draft claims to think about the types of acts that might constitute direct, literal infringement for a patent claim you are beginning to draft. The goal of patent claim drafting is to create an asset that has commercial value and aids the business and patent strategy of a client/patentee. The more the claims cover potential acts of direct infringement, the more valuable the patent will be and the more the asset will support such strategies.

173. See later treatment of indirect infringement.

As discussed previously, the acts of patent infringement protected by a patent claim are making, using, selling, offering for sale, and importing the claimed invention. There are a number of possible and related questions to ponder that will aid in drafting a patent claim. For example, how is the invention likely to be infringed by another? Will it be copied? Will it be infringed via a technical specification that companies voluntarily meet, such as USB, PCI, or Bluetooth? Will others develop technology along the lines of the invention because it provides performance or cost advantages? Will an infringer *sell* a competitive product or *offer* a competitive service? Will an infringer *manufacture* abroad and *import* into this country? Will they have someone else *manufacture* for them? Will there be multiple *manufacturers* for different components and then will integration be performed by a system integrator? How easy is it to avoid infringing by using a different approach? How easy is it to know whether someone else is infringing? Chapter 2 discusses various scenarios to see how the possibilities may be varied and may impact desired claim scope. Some of these issues are also treated in more detail in other chapters.[174]

You may not have all the answers to all the possible questions, but it is still important to think about them to begin the process of drafting a patent claim of appropriate scope. As demonstrated in Chapter 2, the economics and the business details matter if the claims are to be valuable. Likewise, the business and IP strategies of the client/patentee matter. This section is to highlight that initially understanding these issues or initially thinking about them may be a good way to start, in particular as it relates to literal, direct claim scope.

Make Claim Coverage Clear from the Face of the Claims

It is now well-established patent law that the starting point for claim construction is always the words of the claims themselves. Although this principle, by itself, should not be particularly surprising to patent attorneys, a clear statement of the principle is found in *Vitronics Corp. v. Conceptronic, Inc.*,[175] treated previously. In *Markman v. Westview Instruments, Inc.*,[176] the U.S. Supreme Court made it clear that, for policy reasons, patent claim construction is a function that should always be performed by judges, rather than juries. Therefore, relatively soon after that watershed Supreme Court decision, the

174. See Chapter 4, discussing reducing opportunities for designing around patent claims and increasing the likelihood of detecting patent infringement.

175. 90 F.3d 1576, 1582 (Fed. Cir. 1996).

176. 517 U.S. 370, 372 (1996).

Federal Circuit handed down the *Vitronics* decision, which, even today, provides an excellent "how-to" guide for claim construction. As shown earlier, the principles of *Vitronics* were reaffirmed in the *en banc* decision by the Federal Circuit in *Phillips v. AWH.*[177]

In *Vitronics*, the Federal Circuit went out of its way to specify a particular pecking order with respect to the intrinsic evidence that a court should follow—namely, the claims, specification, and prosecution history—when attempting to construe a claim:

> *First, we look to the words of the claims themselves* . . . .
>
> Although words in a claim are generally given their ordinary and customary meaning, a patentee may choose to be his own lexicographer and use terms in a manner other than their ordinary meaning, as long as the special definition of the term is clearly stated in the patent specification or file history. . . .
>
> Second, it is always necessary to review the specification to determine whether the inventor used any terms in a manner inconsistent with their ordinary meaning. . . . Usually, it [the spec] is dispositive; it is the single best guide to the meaning of a disputed term.
>
> Third, the court may also consider the prosecution history of the patent, if in evidence. . . . The record before the Patent and Trademark Office is often of critical significance in determining the meaning of claims.[178]

For our purposes, then, one important pronouncement from *Vitronics*, as indicated by the preceding quote, is that claim construction begins with the claim language itself.

To a patent claim drafter, this recognition is critical to providing good representation before the PTO and to obtaining enforceable patents of value. What it means, in essence, is that if the claims are clear on their face, then claim construction may in some cases be complete.[179] The patent drafter, then, may provide the best representation by preparing simple, straightforward claims that are clear as to their intended meaning.

Vitronics does state that the specification *must* be consulted as part of the claim construction process, as confirmed by the preceding quote. However, the specification is often consulted primarily to determine whether the claim terms are used in the specification in a manner consistent with their ordinary

177. 415 F.3d 1303 (Fed. Cir. 2005) (en banc).

178. *Vitronics*, 90 F.3d at 1582–83 (emphasis added).

179. See, for example, *Straight Path IP Group, Inc. v. Sipnet EU S.R.O.*, 806 F.3d 1356 (Fed. Cir. 2015), which stated the specification played a "more limited role" when the claim term had an especially "plain" meaning.

meaning. Therefore, if the claim terms are used consistently in the specification in this manner, then, at least in principle, there is no need for further consultation of the specification to further interpret the claims. To restate this, for claim construction, it is the words of the claims that are paramount.

Various Federal Circuit cases have clearly established that if the claims are clear on their face and the specification is entirely consistent, then the specification need not be used to further limit the claims.[180] In such circumstances, claim construction should be based on the claim language itself. For example, in *Mantech Environmental Corp. v. Hudson Environmental Services*,[181] at issue was the meaning of the disputed claim term "well" in a groundwater monitoring system for reducing the levels of hydrocarbon contaminants.

Mantech argued that the term "well" referred to a structure able to perform either the function of monitoring or the function of injecting test fluid into the groundwater, or both. Hudson's experts, not surprisingly, testified that the term "well" was limited to a structure that performed both monitoring and injecting. In the accused systems, not all the wells performed both functions. It is worth noting, in this context, that the preferred embodiment in the application showed *only a well capable of performing both*.

The court determined that the specification was entirely consistent with the claims. The court's claim construction was based strictly on the claim language, which recited a series of wells, at least one of which had to be used for injecting test fluid, and at least one of which had to be used for monitoring. In other words, the claims were written so that it was not required, either expressly or impliedly, that a well perform both functions. This ultimately controlled how the court construed the claims at issue.

The Federal Circuit specifically stated: "If the written description supports the definition of the term that is apparent from the claim limitation, then reading in a further limiting definition [based upon the specification] would be improper."[182] Therefore, while a well could perform both functions, *and* the preferred embodiment showed a well capable of performing both functions, the claims and specification did not require this narrow construction. According to the court, the term "well" *as used in the claims* was not and should not have been limited in such a manner. The appellate court further stated: "The district court erred because it, in essence, incorporated from the preferred embodiment into the claims a narrow definition for the term 'well.'"[183]

180. *See id.*
181. 152 F.3d 1368 (Fed. Cir. 1998).
182. *Id.* at 1374.
183. *Id.* at 1375.

A similar result occurred in *Comark Communications v. Harris Corp.*[184] The key language of the claim in dispute related to a "video delay circuit." The invention related to ultrahigh frequency (UHF) television transmission equipment. Comark had developed a common amplification system that allowed audio and video signals to be amplified together, thereby saving hardware. However, this also created cross-modulation, so Comark also devised an invention to reduce the cross-modulation distortions. It is the latter invention that was the subject of the suit.

The defendant attempted to limit the claims to the specific embodiment shown in the specification; however, the court reasoned that because the specification was entirely consistent with the claims, there was no need to consult the specification for claim construction or to limit the claims in the manner proposed. The Federal Circuit stated:

> Despite our repeated statements that limitations from the specification are not to be read into the claims, Harris nonetheless argues that the term "video delay circuit" should be read "in light of the specification" to include a limitation that the video delay circuit must also function to compensate for delay introduced to the video signal by the IF vision modulator. We have previously stated that "while . . . claims are to be interpreted in light of the specification and with a view to ascertaining the invention, it does not follow that limitations from the specification may be read into the claims." We recognize that there is sometimes a fine line between reading a claim in light of the specification and reading a limitation into the claim from the specification. However, we believe that Harris advocates the latter rather than the former.
>
> *In this case, the term "video delay circuit" has a clear and well-defined meaning. This term is not so amorphous that one of skill in the art can only reconcile the claim language with the inventor's disclosure by recourse to the specification.* . . . Harris is indeed correct that the specification clearly discloses that the video delay circuit functions to compensate for delay introduced to the video signal being processed by the IF vision modulator by introducing a similar delay to the same video signal in the correct path. However, *the language of the specification does not at all aid in our interpretation of the phrase "video delay circuit." It simply details how the video delay circuit is to be used in a single embodiment of the invention. It in no way sheds light on either the meaning of the term to the inventor, or the common meaning of the term to one of skill in the art.*[185]

The court, thus, appears to recognize it will be true that the specification, out of necessity, provides an embodiment that is likely narrower than

184. 156 F.3d 1182 (Fed. Cir. 1998).

185. *Id.* at 1186–87 (emphasis added) (citations omitted).

the language of the claims. This is necessitated in some measure from the requirements of enablement and best mode, which require a relatively detailed description of operation directed to one of ordinary skill in the art. The claims, however, have no such requirements of enablement or best mode, independent of the specification itself. Therefore, if the specification uses the terms of the claim consistently, then the fact that the specification may contain an embodiment narrower than the claims should not, by itself, be a valid justification for limiting those claim terms to that narrow embodiment. It is further noted that in addition to *Vitronics*, both *Mantech* and *Comark* are regularly cited by the Federal Circuit as good law.

A more recent case is *Evolusion Concepts v. HOC Events*.[186] Based on the specification, the district court had ruled that the term "magazine catch bar" *excluded* a factory-installed magazine catch bar. The Federal Circuit reversed and stated:

> The specification supports the ordinary-meaning interpretation of "magazine catch bar." *Phillips*, 415 F.3d at 1315 ("[C]laims must be read in view of the specification, of which they are part." (internal quotation marks and citation omitted)). The specification nowhere limits the scope of a "magazine catch bar" to exclude factory-installed ones from the assembly that achieves the fixed-magazine goal. Nor, contrary to a suggestion made by Juggernaut, does it explain that only a customized or modified magazine catch bar, one necessarily different from what was factory installed, may be used on the firearm. It simply explains that the described embodiments of the invention all include a "magazine catch bar" that can be securely attached to the lower receiver of the firearm, and consistently describes the component in generic terms. *Id.*, col. 2, line 65, through col. 3, line 2; *see also id.*, col. 5, lines 5–7. Juggernaut argues, and Evolusion concedes, that the disclosed embodiments do not illustrate OEM magazine catch bars. *See id.*, figs. 3 & 4.
>
> But that cannot make a difference in this case. We have repeatedly held that "it is not enough that the only embodiments, or all of the embodiments, contain a particular limitation to limit claims beyond their plain meaning." *Unwired Planet, LLC v. Apple, Inc.*, 829 F.3d 1353, 1359 (Fed. Cir. 2016) (internal quotation marks and citation omitted). Here, nothing in the specification suggests that factory (or OEM) provenance of a bar disqualifies it from being part of the invention if, as a structural matter, it is a magazine catch bar under the ordinary meaning. And nothing in the specification suggests that factory (or OEM) installation precludes the possession of the structural features required by the invention. The specification reiterates the background principle that the claims are not limited to the illustrated embodiments. '845

186. 22 F.4th 1361 (Fed. Cir. 2022).

> patent, col. 4, lines 46–53. And it describes and illustrates at least one embodiment in which the magazine catch bar is a separate element from the upper tension bar, *id.*, col. 5, lines 5–10, 17–20; *id.*, fig. 3, reinforcing the idea that there is no requirement to replace each individual component in the assembly in order to replace the assembly as a whole.[187]

Of course, there are Federal Circuit cases that have introduced limitations from the specification into the claims. As the previous quote from *Comark* makes clear, the line between interpreting the claims in light of the specification, which is permissible, and reading limitations from the specification into the claims, which is impermissible, is a fine one indeed.[188] For example, in *Medegen MMS, Inc. v. ICU Medical, Inc.*,[189] Judge Walker, a district court judge sitting by designation, dissented from the decision and asserted that the issues before the Federal Circuit present "a conundrum often faced by district courts when construing" claim terms. He cited the "twin axioms" of claim construction that produced the conundrum that "[o]n the one hand, claims 'must be read in view of the specification,'" while "[o]n the other hand, it is improper to read a limitation from the specification into the claims." The problem with these axioms, according to Judge Walker, is that "the axioms themselves seldom provide an answer, but instead merely frame the question to be resolved."[190]

Thus, it may be difficult to predict in advance which way a court may lean, for example toward a broader construction employing ordinary and customary meaning or toward a narrower construction relying on the specification to impart a narrow meaning.[191] Of course, it may be that the ordinary and customary meaning may also suggest a narrower interpretation and it might be in some cases that the intrinsic evidence may impose a broader meaning than that—which may be a more desirable situation and may depend on the accused product or service and the prior art. In *Medegen*, the Federal Circuit determined that the district court had read limitations from the specification into the claims.

---

187. *Id.* at 1367.

188. See *CCS Fitness v. Brunswick Corp.*, 288 F.3d 1359 (Fed. Cir. 2002), also written by Judge Michel, as simply one example, which provides a logical framework for analyzing when it is appropriate to depart from the ordinary and customary meaning of a claim term and when such a departure is not appropriate. The typical reason is because the drafter has demonstrated an intent to depart from the ordinary and customary meaning in either the specification or the file history of the patent.

189. 317 F. App'x 982 (Fed. Cir. 2009).

190. *Id.* at 988–89.

191. See earlier in this chapter.

By contrast, however, in *Bell Atlantic Network Services v. Covad Communications Group*,[192] despite the claims including a relatively broad term "mode," the Federal Circuit, in a case involving digital subscriber loop (DSL) communications technology, interpreted the terminology "different modes" narrowly. The patent claims required transceiver modems to selectively operate in one of a plurality of "different modes" over a network. Thus, the claim recited "different modes," which was interpreted by the Federal Circuit to refer to only one of the *three* specific modes described in the specification. According to the Federal Circuit, the patentee had redefined the term "mode" *by implication*. To help reduce the risk of this eventuality, it is strongly recommended to both describe and claim multiple embodiments of varying scope.[193]

To recap, when drafting patent claims, the best claims are those where the drafter's intent is clear on the face of the claims themselves. This should be a guiding principle in claim drafting. It is, of course, possible that you may come in contact with a judge who prefers the line of authority in which limitations are read into the claims from the specification over the line of authority suggesting otherwise. Likewise, a judge may lean toward applying the ordinary and customary meaning of claims, which may be broad, but could, instead, be narrow. In fact, in high-quality patent claim drafting practice (PCDP), it is largely assumed that such scenarios may happen, and you are encouraged to draft the patent application—that is, both the claims *and the specification*—in a manner so that some terms are construed broadly, some terms are construed narrowly, and some are construed to have intermediate scope. This approach is intended to reduce the risk that broad terms will be construed narrowly or vice versa. As has been alluded, ways to do this include employing claims of varying scope and type,[194] defining the key terms used in the claims,[195] and covering multiple embodiments (fully described in the specification) with an array of verbal formulations that are logically consistent and employ a hierarchy of terms.[196] For those situations, therefore, the next sections and later chapters develop a set of principles to follow to draft the patent claims (and provide appropriate support in the specification) to provide strong and high-quality protection for your client's technology. However, if you meet the criteria just set out when drafting the patent claims, you will be ahead of the game by far, regardless of the precedent the court chooses to follow.

---

192. 262 F.3d 1258 (Fed. Cir. 2001).
193. *See* Chapter 4.
194. *See id.*
195. *See id.*
196. See later in this chapter.

Use Words in the Claims Consistent with Their Understood Meaning

A reason to use words consistent with their understood meaning, quite simply, is because that is precisely how those words are likely to be construed. A relatively impressive body of Federal Circuit law has developed, as has been shown, to the effect that words of a claim are to be given their ordinary and customary meaning, unless it is relatively clear that the words are not intended to have that meaning. This principle is stated in *Phillips*[197] and *Vitronics*.[198] Furthermore, after *Vitronics*, a number of cases, beginning with *Johnson Worldwide Associates v. Zebco Corp.*,[199] recite that this is not simply a presumption but rather a *heavy* presumption. The Federal Circuit has never recanted this principle, although they cite it much less frequently after *Phillips*. A helpful case, cited in *Phillips*, is *CCS Fitness v. Brunswick Corp.*[200] Thus, ordinary and customary meaning is a presumption and, according to case law that has not been rejected or overturned, it is a heavy one.

Of course, it is not absolutely guaranteed that claim terms will receive their ordinary and customary meaning. However, good practice suggests that you would do far better to *use terms in a manner consistent* with their ordinary and customary meaning, rather *than in a manner inconsistent* with or that departs from that meaning.

Vitronics itself is a wonderful example of what might happen if you fail to follow this simple principle. As is now well-known,[201] in *Vitronics*, the patent drafter employed the terminology "solder reflow temperature" in the specification and claims in a manner not consistent with the art. While it is true that the drafter made it clear in the specification the special meaning he intended those words to have, the meaning he intended was not consistent with the established meaning in the relevant art. This gave opposing counsel a basis to dispute the meaning of these terms.

Therefore, while the specification clearly intended that these words mean the peak reflow temperature, the peak temperature the solder may reach as a

197. See earlier in this chapter.

198. See earlier in this chapter.

199. 175 F.3d 985, 989 (Fed. Cir. 1999).

200. 288 F.3d 1359 (Fed. Cir. 2002). This case provides a logical framework for analyzing when it is appropriate to depart from the ordinary and customary meaning of a claim term and when such a departure is not appropriate. The typical reason is because the drafter has demonstrated an intent to depart from the ordinary and customary meaning in either the specification or the file history of the patent.

201. See earlier in this chapter.

liquid, this was not the generally accepted meaning of solder reflow temperature. Instead, the generally accepted meaning of solder reflow temperature is liquidus temperature, the temperature at which the solder first begins to become liquid, something quite different. It is worth noting that the patentee eventually did prevail and convinced the Federal Circuit that the meaning demonstrated by the specification was the meaning intended in the claims; however, perhaps what practitioners should take from the case is the observation that Vitronics lost at the trial level, and it took an appeal to the Federal Circuit to obtain the proper construction under the law. Therefore, it took significantly more time and expense for Vitronics to obtain the proper claim interpretation, the claim interpretation that was intended by the drafter.

Use Words in the Claims with Broadly Understood Meanings Where Appropriate

In addition to the principle that words of a claim are presumed to have their ordinary and customary meaning, those words are entitled to a full scope of meaning[202]—the meanings associated with the term that are consistent with the use in the claims, unless it is clear that this is not what is intended (or if it leads to a ridiculous interpretation, which would not be a meaning consistent with the usage in the claims).[203]

To the patent drafter, this suggests that the best words to use for claim terms are those that generally encompass a broad understanding for the particular context.

In many ways, this is nothing new to the seasoned patent practitioner. The Federal Circuit has made part of the black letter law what patent drafters have known for years. Therefore, it should come as no surprise that some of the best words to employ in claims are *already an established part of the parlance of patent claim drafting, not unlike patent terms of art.*[204] A few examples are provided here, although, of course, many more such terms exist:[205]

202. *See, e.g.*, Liebel-Flarsheim Co. v. Medrad, Inc., 358 F.3d 898, 905–09 (Fed. Cir. 2004), *cert. denied*, 543 U.S. 925 (2004) (holding that claim terms are given the full breadth of their ordinary meaning unless a clear disavowal of scope is stated in the specification).

203. *See, e.g.*, Phillips v. AWH Corp., 415 F.3d 1303 (Fed. Cir. 2005) (en banc).

204. See earlier in this chapter regarding categories and examples of claim terminology.

205. *See* Kahrl & Soffer, *supra* note 170; see also earlier in this chapter regarding categories and examples of claim terminology.

Actuator
Adjust
Analog
Application
Arrangement
Assembly
Associate
Attachment
Base
Branch
Buffer
Card
Cell
Change
Channel
Chassis
Circuit
Code
Component
Conductor
Conduit
Configuration
Connection
Contact
Control
Converter
Corresponding
Coupled
Cycle
Decode
Derivative
Detector
Device
Digital
Direct
Discrete
Division
Encode
Feedback
Feed forward
Gate
Grouping
Hold
If (instead of "when")
Indirect
Initial
Insulator
Interface
Layer
Limit
Link
Location
Magnitude
Measurement
Medium
Member

Memory
Mode
Modulate
Module
Movement
Network
Node
Operation
Operative
Overlap
Part
Pass
Path
Peripheral
Physical
Port
Portion
Position
Processing
Processor
Product
Receive
Register
Regulator
Relation
Sensor
Separate
Shunt
Signal
Sink
Sort
Source
Spectrum
State
Store
Switch
System
Terminal
Terminate
Timing
Transform
Translate
Transmit
Unit
Update
Using
Value
Workpiece

As should be clear, although these words have discernible meanings, suggesting that they are not ambiguous, nonetheless, the full scope of their meaning may include a broad array of possibilities. Consider, for example, the word "interface." One may imagine myriad possibilities that such a word may conjure up across a broad array of technologies. It may likewise be appropriate to bolster this understanding with a consistent and broad (but not vague) definition in the specification, so that one may legitimately take the position that whether one applies the ordinary and customary meaning or one employs the meaning imparted by the specification, in either case, the accused product would be covered.

It is worth noting that even in particular technologies, although certain words have acquired a particularized meaning related to that technology, nonetheless, within that particular technology, the understanding of the word may still be somewhat broad and flexible, depending upon the circumstances. It is, therefore, helpful to be cognizant of such words and use them when working in such technologies. The key point is to think carefully when choosing words of the claim and use those words that have an inherent breadth and potentially wide scope, even where the word may, in some instances, have some particularized technological associations with it. For example, some of the preceding words illustrate this point—*signal*, *medium*, *layer*, *interface*, *detector*, *sensor*, *converter*, and so on. However, again, it will also be important to make sure that these terms are adequately supported in the specification through use in the description of multiple embodiments of varying scope to support the intended breadth and meaning.

Employ a Hierarchy of Claim Terms

For purposes of claim drafting and for specification drafting, it is desirable to create and employ a hierarchy of terms that relate to the subject matter of the invention. The point of doing so is to make clear the scope intended for certain terms and then support that with specification description. This is at least one reason that it usually makes sense to draft a set of claims before drafting the specification. That set of claims may be updated, modified, and grow as you draft the specification, but it crystallizes your thinking initially and creates a list of terms.

As should now be clear, how terms are used in the specification and claims is legally significant. Thus, creating an initial set of claims that may be viewed as hierarchical would be prudent. The hierarchy relates to narrower or more specific embodiments—that is, differing scope. In this manner, terms are able to be used consistently so as not to create ambiguity while still being clear regarding intended scope.

Let us begin with some simple examples.

Suppose an invention may be implemented with the following: an analog circuit, a digital circuit, a microprocessor, and so on. This is not such an unusual situation because for most types of electrical filters this is the case. Imagine, for example, a filter related to a medical application in which this is the case. For example, in medical imaging, filters are needed. Filters are also used for test equipment. So, as another example, imagine a filter uniquely designed for equipment that tests an optical waveguide. These are just two illustrative technical examples.

At a high level, the filter for an optical waveguide operates on signals. The signals may be optical or electrical, both of which are electromagnetic in nature. Likewise, the signals may be analog or digital. In addition, the signals may be binary, such as in a microprocessor, for example. Thus, one may imagine a hierarchy of terms such as shown in Figure 5.1 used to draft the following claims:

---

1. An apparatus comprising: a filter to process signal measurements for a waveguide, the signal measurements to be taken at angular focal positions of the waveguide relative to a transverse directional path of light to illuminate an object, wherein sum and difference patterns are to be formed from the signal measurements for the respective focal angular positions taken two at a time.

2. The apparatus of claim 1, wherein the signal measurements are to comprise optical signal measurements to form one or more spectra.

3. The apparatus of claim 2, wherein the optical signal measurements are to be converted to analog electrical signals and the filter to process the signal measurements comprises an analog filter to process the analog electrical signals.

4. The apparatus of claim 2, wherein the optical signal measurements are to be converted to digital electrical signals and the filter to process the signal measurements comprises a digital filter to process the digital electrical signals.

5. The apparatus of claim 4, wherein the digital electronic signals comprise binary digital electrical signals and the digital filter to process the signal measurements comprises a microprocessor programmed to process the binary digital electrical signals.

Figure 5.1 First Example Hierarchy of Claim Terms

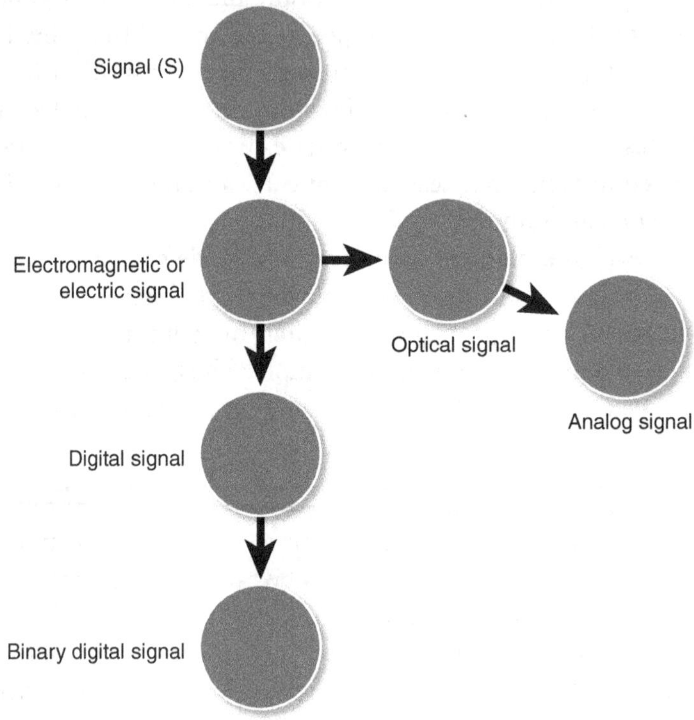

In another example, a metal oxide semiconductor (MOS) transistor body made from silicon may be biased in a manner to reduce noise for analog signals being transmitted, as in an electrical or electronic switch. Typically, the switch has a pass gate/path and a shunt gate/path in close proximity to each other. Assume an analog signal is passing through the pass gate transistor (ON transistor), for example. This may cause positively charged holes, for example if using NMOS transistors in the shunt and pass transistors, to gather under the gate of the shunt transistor because it is OFF (i.e., negative voltage applied to the gate). Furthermore, the analog signal being passed may cause the positively charged holes to oscillate, which then mutually induces an electromagnetic signal that corrupts the analog signal being passed. The result is that, in a cell phone, for example, the connection may drop.

However, if the body of the shunt transistor is biased properly to be below the lower of ground and voltages on the source and drain, for example, this moves the positively charged holes, in this example, so they do not gather near the gate and, therefore, reduces the mutual inductance effect.

As suggested, an electronic switch may comprise an RF switch, which is used, for example, in cell phones. A similar body biasing mechanism may be used in the MOS transistor of a modulator, as may be employed in radio communications, for example. The switch or modulator may be implemented in an IC and the IC may be part of a module. In addition to silicon, a transistor made from gallium arsenide (GaAs) may include body biasing to reduce noise as well for similar applications.

Typically, an electronic switch has multiple signal paths, such as a path to pass an analog signal, which may be implemented as a pass gate, and a path to not pass the analog signal, which may be implemented as a shunt gate. It is a transistor in the shunt gate that is electrically body biased when OFF while the pass gate is ON to pass an analog signal. This electrical body biasing of the transistor in the shunt gate reduces noise that might otherwise corrupt the analog signal passing through the pass gate of the switch.

These terms may be used in claims such as those illustrated here.

---

1. An apparatus comprising: a module; wherein the module comprises an integrated circuit (IC) chip;

   wherein a component of the IC chip comprises at least one field effect transistor, the at least one field effect transistor including a gate, a drain, a source, and a body;

   wherein, during at least a portion of an off state, the body of the at least one field effect transistor is to be electrically biased to have a voltage level substantially more negative than the lowest voltage level of the following: ground, the DC voltage level of the source of the at least one field effect transistor, and the DC voltage level of the drain of the at least one field effect transistor.
2. The apparatus of claim 1, wherein the component comprises at least one of the following: an electrical switch or a modulator.
3. The apparatus of claim 2, wherein the electrical switch comprises an RF switch including a pass gate and a shunt gate, wherein the shunt gate comprises the at least one field effect transistor.
4. The apparatus of claim 3, wherein the at least one field effect transistor comprises at least one of the following: a silicon metal oxide semiconductor (MOS) field effect transistor or a gallium arsenide (GaAs) field effect transistor.
5. The apparatus of claim 4, wherein the silicon MOS field effect transistor comprises an N-channel metal oxide semiconductor transistor (NMOS).
6. The apparatus of claim 4, wherein the silicon MOS field effect transistor comprises a P-channel metal oxide semiconductor transistor (PMOS).

These terms should be used in a manner in the specification to clarify the subject matter intended to be *included* (as opposed to excluding subject matter, unless a logical necessity). In some, if not all, cases, express definitions may be appropriate. In patent law, the terms "genus" and "species" are often used to explain relationships. For example, "silicon" is the genus for the species "PMOS" and "NMOS" in Figure 5.2. The terms "genus" and "species" are also used to describe claims, such as a genus claim or a species claim.

At times, it may be appropriate for certain terms to be used interchangeably. If so, it is recommended that this be made clear in the specification so as not to create a claim construction issue, since the use of different terms may suggest different scope. This is usually a matter of convenience and judgment that may vary with the particular technical subject matter, and so on. Varying terms may be fine as long as it does not create ambiguity; thus, it may be desirable to clarify whether a change in terminology means a change in scope or is merely an interchangeable term. For example, in Figure 5.2, a term is "component." At times, it may be convenient to refer to a "component" as a "part" without a change in meaning or loss of generality. Likewise, rather than "electrical switch," the term "electronic switch" may be used without a change in meaning or loss in generality. If this takes place in the claims, in particular, it would be highly desirable to clarify in the specification that these terms are used interchangeably and are intended to have corresponding scope. Some extra care is required if using terms interchangeably.

In the Patent Claims, Use Multiple Verbal Formulations or Approaches That Are Logically Consistent to Capture and Characterize the Inventive Concept

Trustees of Columbia University v. Symantec Corp.
811 F.3d 1359
United States Court of Appeals for the Federal Circuit
February 2, 2016, Decided

Questions

1. Observe that the trustees of Columbia University are suing Symantec. How do you think that came about?
2. What are the ways that Columbia argues the presumption of ordinary and customary meaning may be overcome? How strong is this argument? What is the Federal Circuit's position on this?

Figure 5.2 Second Example Hierarchy of Claim Terms

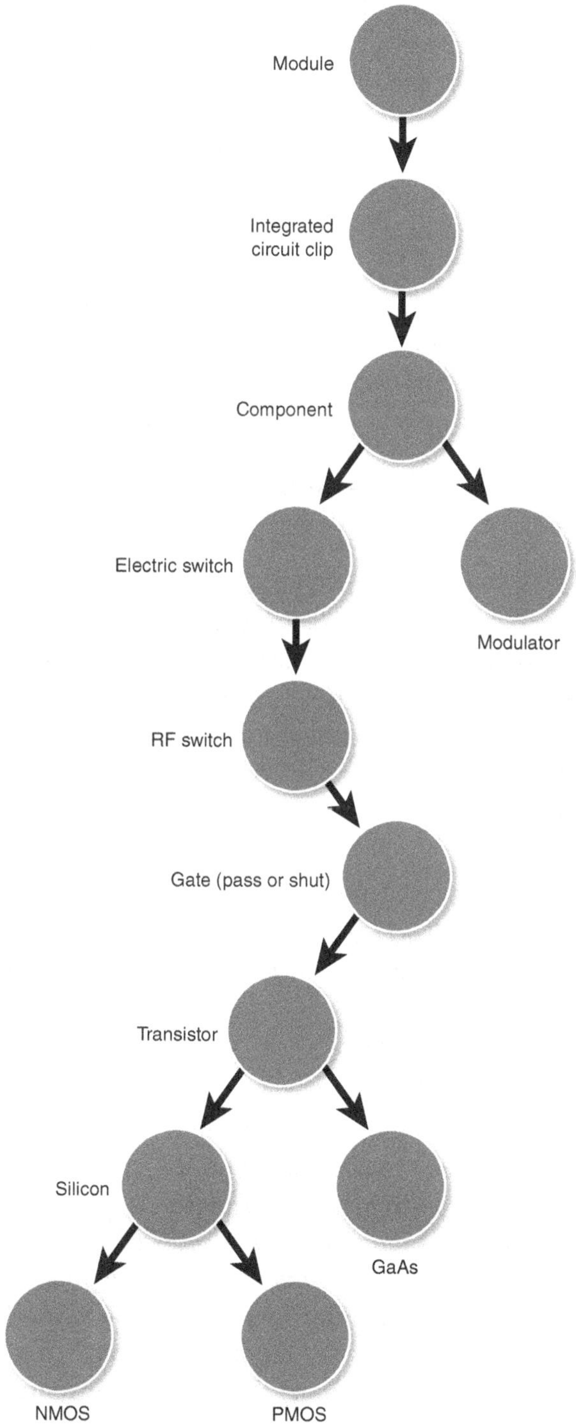

3. Columbia argued that the district court improperly interpreted "byte sequence feature." What was the appellate court's evidence that the district court construed the term correctly? How did the appellate court distinguish this from the term "feature"? Does this suggest a claim drafting approach? How do these terms relate to "resource information"?
4. Why did the appellate court agree that claims 1 and 16 of the '554 patent were indefinite? What do you think was the reason these issues of indefiniteness occurred based on the drafting of the specification and claims?
5. What was the construction issue regarding "probabilistic model of normal computer system usage"? Why did the appellate court not consider the material incorporated by reference?
6. Why did the appellate court treat the term "anomalous" differently than how it treated the term "probabilistic model of normal computer usage"? How did claim differentiation help Columbia's argument?

* * *

One of the issues that makes claim drafting a difficult enterprise is that the attorney drafting the claims is essentially required to describe with words something that, in theory, was not previously known or did not previously exist. Given that the invention is new, it is frequently difficult to know which aspects will become valuable in time versus which aspects, while still new, will not. The now-famous case *Autogiro Co. of America v. United States* recognized this conundrum quite eloquently:

> An invention exists most importantly as a tangible structure or a series of drawings. A verbal portrayal is usually an afterthought written to satisfy the requirements of patent law. This conversion of machine to words allows for unintended idea gaps which cannot be satisfactorily filled. Often the invention is novel and words do not exist to describe it. The dictionary does not always keep abreast of the inventor. It cannot. Things are not made for the sake of words, but words for things.[206]

Thus, by its very nature, the process of reducing an invention to words runs a risk of being flawed, incomplete, or at least, when the time comes to attempt to assert the claims, not particularly valuable or useful.

One way to attempt to mitigate this situation is to avoid being locked into a single particular mode of thought or single way of characterizing the invention. This usually will not happen automatically or without forethought, however. It is, therefore, recommended that you *affirmatively* take steps to avoid being locked into one particular way of thinking about or characterizing the invention.

206. Autogiro Co. of Am. v. United States, 384 F.2d 391, 397 (Ct. Cl. 1976).

This is another reason why it is good practice to disclose multiple embodiments and multiple ways of implementing specific features of the embodiments. Doing so will allow you to also claim the invention in multiple ways, reducing the risk that, when it comes time to prosecute the claims or assert the patent, you are stuck in a particular phraseology that ultimately proves to not advance your cause, but is too late to change.

Thus, it is specifically recommended that you not rely on only one particular set of phrases throughout the claims (and specification) to characterize what is inventive or unique about the subject matter being claimed. This may be accomplished several different ways.

One way is to include claims that are broad, intermediate, and narrow, and to use claim differentiation to potentially broaden the interpretation of the base claims. Another recommended technique is to include entirely different sets of claims that take entirely different approaches to the subject matter. It is important to recognize that the phrase or phrases you might otherwise exclusively rely upon may be construed against you, either from an infringement perspective or from a validity perspective. Thus, it is recommended that you develop several "fallback" verbal formulations to "cover" these possibilities.

In addition to the benefits discussed earlier, this approach also has the added benefit that it is likely to increase the breadth of the claims. Varying use of terminology with reference to different embodiments is likely to broaden the scope of the invention. In particular, the Federal Circuit has made it clear that use of claim terms in varying senses in the specification generally implies breadth.[207] Likewise, the Federal Circuit has implied narrow intent from use throughout the specification of the same term to mean the same thing.[208] Thus, using varying terminology, rather than simply employing varying senses, should also imply breadth.

It is noted, however, that using varying terminology is not the same as using synonyms for what may be essentially the same feature in a single family of dependencies. This last practice is to be avoided. It is likely that you will create ambiguity and/or other interpretation problems if you use different words to essentially refer to the same thing *unless* you clarify expressly that this is what you are doing. For example, you might state: "Without loss of generality and not intending to limit the scope of claimed subject matter, the following terms are used interchangeably throughout this patent application."[209] Likewise, again, it is good practice to use *varying* terminology when you intend *different* scope.

---

207. *See, e.g.*, Johnson Worldwide Assocs. v. Zebco Corp., 175 F.3d 985, 991 (Fed. Cir. 1999).

208. *See* Bell Atl. Network Servs., Inc. v. Covad Comm'cns Grp., Inc., 262 F.3d 1258, 1262, 1270 (Fed. Cir. 2001).

209. Even then, great care is warranted when trying to use words interchangeably. *See* Aqua-Aerobic Sys., Inc. v. Aerators Inc., 211 F.3d 1241 (Fed. Cir. 2000) (different phrases interpreted

When developing alternative formulations of the claims, it would also be wise to avoid being limited by the current state of the technology. Patents, of course, potentially have a 20-year-plus term. Many changes in technology and variations in implementation may occur during such an extended period, especially with the current pace of technological change. Consider, for example, a vacuum tube versus a transistor. Claims to a vacuum tube circuit, if properly drafted, would apply to the same circuit implemented with a transistor. As is well-known, both may, for example, be employed to implement an amplifier or an electronic switch. Thus, claims referring to amplification or an amplifier or to an electronic switch would arguably not be limited to a vacuum tube, assuming a patent written before the invention of the transistor remained in force after the transistor was invented.

Given the potential that state-of-the-art technology has to limit the scope of claims, it is, thus, worthwhile spending time considering potential current and future implementations of various aspects of the invention. It is also worthwhile to consider the maturity of the technology when drafting the claims. For example, is the technology in the research stage, the early development stage, the prototype stage, or the production stage, and so on? This consideration has the potential to impact not only the claim breadth, but also alternative applications of the technology and its patentability. For example, for technology in the research stage, the claims should be extremely broad; whereas for technology in the production stage, narrower claims may be acceptable and still provide valuable protection.

To illustrate the concept of multiple verbal formulations, consider the claim from Chapter 2 (also provided as Example 4.22 of Chapter 4):

I claim:

1. A method of forming a virtual private network comprising:

   communicating one or more signal packets between respective physically separate broadcast domains via a gateway device included in the respective physically separate broadcast domains, wherein the communicating the one or more signal packets comprises:

---

differently, even if the drafter intended them to have the same meaning); Epcon Gas Sys., Inc. v. Bauer Compressors, Inc., 279 F.3d 1022 (Fed. Cir. 2002) (construing "substantially below" and "substantially constant" differently because of what the court found to be "subtle differences" in the way the terms were used in the claim).

encapsulating the one or more signal packets in the respective physically separate broadcast domains to be communicated; and

communicating the encapsulated signal packets between the respective gateways and at least one tunnel server so that the one or more signal packets are communicated between the respective physically separate broadcast domains.

Following is a different method claim based on the same technology.[210] Observe that while the same technology is at issue, really this new claim employs a different approach to capturing the concept of the technology than the previous claim. The previous claim is more about encapsulation and transmission via a tunnel server. This claims the technology at a higher level and is more about bypassing network address translation, although the tunnel server is also mentioned.

I claim:

1. A method comprising:

overlaying at least one private network on networking infrastructure and/or computing infrastructure via network connectivity, wherein the at least one private network comprises two or more separate logical broadcast domains and a controller, the controller being outside the two or more separate logical broadcast domains;

communicating selected signal packets from one network device in one of the two or more separate logical broadcast domains transmitted to one network device in another of the two or more separate logical broadcast domains via at least one tunnel server outside the two or more separate logical broadcast domains, the at least one tunnel server provisioned by the controller;

wherein the communicating selected signal packets further comprises communicating the selected signal packets from the one network device in the one of the two or more separate logical broadcast domains transmitted to the one network device in the another of the two or more separate

210. See earlier technology description in Chapter 2.

logical broadcast domains as if the logical broadcast domains are not separate, which comprises communicating the selected signal packets in a manner to bypass network address translation.

Thus, here, at least two distinct approaches to capturing essentially the same technology is demonstrated.

Identify Features of the Invention Independent of the Embodiment

When drafting claims from the information in an invention disclosure, it can be important to identify features of the invention that are innovative independent of many of the specific implementation details for a particular embodiment. This may sound easier said than done, but it is a facility that one acquires from drafting claims for different inventions from scratch. A crucial aspect involves interviewing the inventor and having him or her explain the state of the art, the innovative aspects of the invention, and why he or she sees those aspects as innovative.

Often, inventors will believe to be innovative it is sufficient that the invention has never been done before. Inventors think that if it would have been obvious, the invention would have been implemented by someone. Unfortunately, this reasoning will not convince the PTO. That it has not been previously implemented and/or was not previously known really goes to novelty rather than nonobviousness. However, it may be a starting point. What are the technical reasons the invention was not previously implemented? This may help explain the innovation in a manner that might be divorced from a particular embodiment.

One of the more important skills to develop is the ability to interview the inventor and with a series of questions get him or her to articulate the innovation, although before coming to see you, the inventor may have had no idea of what that might be. One helpful technique is to take a somewhat practical approach to the invention using the problem-solution approach mentioned in Chapter 2.

One might begin by asking about a problem the invention is intended to address. Is it an existing and known problem or is it a new, unrecognized problem? It might be both depending how one looks at it, but that is useful information as well.

A known problem might be a device that uses too much power or uses too much memory. These are typically known technical problems, depending on context. The invention might relate to reducing electrical interference. You get the idea. If it is a known problem, the next question is why not use off-the-shelf approaches to this problem? There may be deficiencies in the existing off-the-shelf approaches. Now the innovation is taking shape. The invention solves an existing, known problem, but it does so in a manner that has an advantage over state-of-the-art approaches. Now we are getting somewhere.

If it does not solve a known, existing problem, then it may, instead, solve an otherwise unrecognized problem—a problem that is not yet known in the prior art because it has not yet been recognized. On this point, there is well-established law that the mere recognition of a previously unaddressed problem may be sufficient to impart patentability to an invention, even if once the problem is recognized, the solution employed might have been obvious.[211] Of course, it might also be that the problem is unrecognized *and* the solution would not have been obvious. However, the point is that this line of questioning should uncover the innovation if the other line of questioning does not.

It is not the case, of course, that how the invention is implemented is unimportant. Rather, the claims should cover the implementation. However, it should more typically be handled with dependent claims so that the independent claim is *not* limited to the particular embodiment.

To, perhaps, gain a better appreciation of trying to identify an innovation not necessarily limited to a particular embodiment, let us return to a previous example from Chapter 2. Consider Example 2.1, now Example 5.2. Also, recall our drafting principle: a good claim is an appropriate balance between breadth, vagueness, and precision.

EXAMPLE 5.2

I claim:

1. An apparatus comprising:

   a substantially horizontally oriented, rectangularly shaped seat including four corners;

   wherein attached to a respective corner of the seat are four substantially vertically oriented legs such that the legs point in the same direction away from the seat, are oriented to be substantially mutually parallel, and are of substantially the same length.

211. *See, e.g.*, Eibel Process Co. v. Minn. & Ontario Paper Co., 261 U.S. 45 (1923).

This sample claim has precision and some breadth. More to the point, however, what is the innovation sought to be captured? It is not clear from the claim language. By focusing on the innovation, the aspects involving breadth and vagueness, which are better able to be balanced, along with balancing precision, may also perhaps be better developed.

It is important, however, in performing such an evaluation, to consider the closest *known* prior art. This is a hypothetical situation. In this hypothetical world, chairs have not been invented yet. So, what did people use to sit in groups or to sit on after becoming tired from a lot of walking, and so on? Perhaps they used very large rock formations, the ground, or trees that had fallen due to windstorms and the like. Of course, these "prior art" approaches are not convenient. To sit in groups, for example, you would need a bunch of fallen trees or boulders close together.

So, with this background, what might one conclude is innovative about a chair? It appears to be that it is portable. It provides a place to sit that is easily and conveniently portable. What would that look like in a patent claim body? Perhaps something like Example 5.3.

EXAMPLE 5.3

I claim:

An apparatus comprising: a portable seat.

Of course, this is a stylized example and, hence, here results in a possibly overly broad claim, but it *does* begin the process of formulating the claim, primarily the claim body. A portable seat seems like it might have been novel and unobvious in light of prior art such as the ground or fallen trees. Also, it is useful.

Appreciate, however, if allowable, what this potentially captures compared with the previous claim. Many potential follow-on improvements—wheelchairs, swivel chairs, ergonomic chairs, even exercise balls, and so on. Many things that the previous claim would not have captured. Patents have a 20-year term. With the pace of technical change, it might be surprising how quickly products built on a fundamental concept, such as this example, might develop.

Someone, a lawyer most likely, may argue that a small boulder could be a portable seat. That may be a good point; again, Example 5.3 was a starting point. Perhaps, to distinguish from the known prior art, the claim should be:

EXAMPLE 5.4

I claim:

1. An apparatus comprising: a portable seat;

   wherein the portable seat includes a back oriented to be roughly perpendicular to the portable seat.

So, the claim body now includes elements (seat and back) and limitations ("portable," "oriented to be roughly perpendicular"), which provide relationships between the elements.[212]

Avoid Overly Specific Term Modifiers in the Independent Claims

One tendency when drafting claims that is best avoided is the use of relatively specific and often unneeded modifiers, particularly in the independent claims. Using an unnecessarily specific modifier in the claims, particularly in the independent claim, is likely to be construed as an attempt by the drafter to limit claim scope. Good practice, therefore, would indicate that it would be best to omit such highly specific modifiers or, at a minimum, introduce them through dependent claims rather than employing them in the independent claims to take advantage of claim differentiation.[213] In this way, claim differentiation suggests that the independent claim is intended to have a meaning that is broader than the dependent claim that includes the specific modifier.[214] Thus, structuring claims in this manner, in effect, "bootstraps" the independent claim to have a broader implied meaning. Following are a few simple examples to illustrate how easy it may be to limit a claim term unintentionally. Furthermore, if one considers, instead, using those modifiers in a dependent claim, the bootstrapping effect of such an approach may be striking.

212. Alternatively, perhaps, Example 5.3 is claim 1 and Example 5.4 is a claim 2 that is dependent, providing additional features.

213. See Chapter 4's treatment of claim differentiation in the context of dependent claims.

214. *See, e.g.*, Interdigital Commons v. Int'l Trade Comm'n, 690 F.3d 1315, 1324 (Fed. Cir. 2012) (The doctrine of claim differentiation disfavors reading a limitation from a dependent claim into an independent claim.).

Examples:

Use "signal" instead of "digital signal"; thus, one may imagine a dependent claim 2: "wherein the signal of claim 1 comprises a digital signal."

Use "waveguide" instead of "optical waveguide"; thus, one may imagine a dependent claim 2: "wherein the waveguide of claim 1 comprises an optical waveguide."

Use "frequency" instead of "radio frequency"; thus, one may imagine a dependent claim 2: "wherein the frequency of claim 1 comprises a radio frequency."

Use "conductive material" instead of "electrically conductive"; thus, one may imagine a dependent claim 2: "wherein the conductive material of claim 1 comprises an electrically conductive material."

Use "radiation" instead of "electromagnetic radiation"; thus, one may imagine a dependent claim 2: "wherein the radiation of claim 1 comprises electromagnetic radiation."

These are simply a few examples; however, they are sufficient to illustrate this basic principle of claim drafting.

Draft Short Claims

It may seem deceptively simple; however, the best claims are almost always the shortest ones. Of course, there are many examples of valuable claims that are not short; nonetheless, this does not mean that, even for those valuable claims, a better claim could not have been drafted that would have been shorter. On the contrary, to be quite blunt, more words provide a greater opportunity for a clever opponent to argue that additional limitations are present, or for an unfavorably disposed judge to interpret the claim or claims more narrowly.[215] It is quite simple. Short claims are broad claims.[216] Use dependent claims to narrow scope.

215. It may also give someone an opportunity to argue that the claim is not properly supported for want of written description.

216. Of course, this approach assumes that prior art is not a problem and, thus, narrower claims are not as desirable. This is an issue that will certainly be fleshed out in patent prosecution and, as suggested in Chapter 4, good PCDP strongly recommends claims of varying scope, from broad to intermediate to narrow. In the absence of any particular knowledge about troubling prior art, broad claims are generally accepted to be preferred over narrow claims; however, this issue, as well, was treated in Chapter 1.

Always endeavor to reduce the number of words in your claims, particularly the independent ones. It is probably a good practice to review each word of a claim to make sure that each and every word is absolutely necessary. In fact, review each word of the claim with the inventors themselves to see if they consider each word to be necessary. This is an excellent practice that is often overlooked or skipped.

As most patent attorneys are aware, shorter claims also typically bring more heartache from the PTO. This, of course, is not a reason to write longer claims. To the contrary, where is the challenge as a practitioner in writing long, narrow claims that you know will sail through the PTO because the examiner has not even bothered to read the entire claim? Ultimately, an examiner is usually more than willing to allow an overly narrow claim since the examiner knows that such a claim will not bother anyone (meaning it is unlikely to be infringed).[217]

The goal, of course, is not to get claims allowed that are so broad that the issued claims will generate snickering from an opponent when presented (because the opponent knows that claim is so broad that it is probably invalid). Rather, the goal is to get claims allowed that generate value for your client. However, be aware that patent examiners apply the BRI to patent claims during prosecution.[218] The "broadest reasonable interpretation," even when properly applied, by design is necessarily broader than the interpretation that a federal court will apply to the claim. It is not unusual for what an examiner considers to be the "broadest reasonable interpretation" to actually be an *unreasonably* broad interpretation. Even the BRI is supposed to be an interpretation that is in light of the specification.[219] The point simply is this: expect that examiners will be pushing for claims that are narrower than may be appropriate in light of the prior art. Thus, as an advocate, it is important for you to push for claims having a scope *that is appropriate* in light of the prior art.

Ultimately, patent prosecution is a type of negotiation. In any negotiation, strategically you should at least initially be asking for more than you are willing to take. (Assuming you can do so ethically—without reading on the *known* prior art.[220]) That is simply good negotiating. If you initially ask for *only* what you are seeking *and no more*, it will almost certainly be the case that *you will*

---

217. Such narrow claims may also undermine patent infringement under the DOE. See treatment later in this chapter.

218. See Chapter 1's treatment of BRI.

219. *See In re* Smith Int'l, Inc., 872 F.3d 1374 (Fed. Cir. 2017).

220. Knowingly submitting a claim that reads on prior art may result in an ethical violation. *See* 37 C.F.R. § 1.56 (2024). For each claim, there should be a good faith argument for patentably distinguishing from the known prior art. *See* Chapter 6.

end up with less than that. Thus, one way you can help your client's position in this "negotiation" with the PTO is by making sure that the claims you initially present are short.

It is correct conventional wisdom that a short claim is more likely to be rejected by the PTO than a long claim. That is just the way the PTO works. Still, if the examiner does not have the prior art to support the rejection (and you know of none), does it matter that he or she has a visceral reaction because your claim is short? Part of the point of the process, in fact, is to ferret out the closest prior art. You do that by presenting short claims and seeing what art the examiner is then able to apply to reject them. Under the law, at least in theory, you should prevail in getting your claim allowed, unless the examiner has the evidence, in the form of prior art, to support the position that the claim is unpatentable. The prior point says "in theory" because, unfortunately, examiners do not always follow the law or do not always fully grasp the technology. In addition, they have limited time and they usually have to get their boss to approve their recommendations. So, yes, in some situations, it may be prudent to give in to an examiner who does not have the art to make his or her case. Yet another negotiation advantage of short claims, however, is that you may add language to address the examiner's desire for a longer claim without necessarily introducing significant limitations to overall claim scope. Furthermore, if you do believe it is appropriate to concede despite an examiner not providing prior art to support his or her position, this should be done only if your client approves and only if by doing so you are still able to get claims of a sufficient scope to meet your client's needs.[221] Again, this is a negotiation and you are entitled to present claims that you believe are patentable over the known art. Years of experience have shown that you are better off starting with short claims, even if you ultimately give in to the examiner and add some language. If you start with overly narrow claims, it is more likely than not that the examiner will still want you to narrow those claims further.

It is a bit of PTO lore that if a claim can be covered by two or three outstretched fingers of one hand, then it receives an automatic rejection from the examiner, whether he or she has the prior art to support the rejection or not. No official confirmation of this bit of "wisdom" exists; however, it is true that exceedingly short claims are nearly always rejected. However, those rejections also are usually quite weak on substantive grounds. Thus, instead, a countervailing tenet for claim drafting may be adopted as a sort of drafting challenge.

---

221. In addition, you may want to file a continuation, once you have gotten allowed claims, so you are still able to seek broader claims, assuming the prior art suggests such broader claims should be patentable.

If the independent claim you draft cannot be covered by two or three outstretched fingers, then consider that there probably exists a way to rewrite the claim that will protect the invention, avoid the prior art you are aware of, and put the claim below the two- or three-finger maximum. One reason to do this is because the rewritten claim will likely be broader. Again, the shorter the claim is, the broader it is. Likewise, of course, such broad claims must be adequately supported with multiple embodiments of varying scope to reduce the risk of a court reading limitations into the claims or finding the claims invalid for want of written description, although, again, this is treated in Chapter 6.

In the Patent Claims, Follow Rules of Grammar

This simple rule is an important one. Endeavor to follow the rules of good grammar. This may seem like a challenge given how claims are constructed. Typically, claims violate a basic rule of grammar because a claim looks a lot like a run-on sentence. However, aside from that, because a claim is, in effect, a sentence starting with "I claim," "We claim," or something similar and ending in a period, generally rules of grammar should be followed to avoid creating interpretive ambiguities. For example, a clause of a claim should have a subject, a verb, and potentially an object.

Good grammar is what judges, especially those less familiar with reading claims, would expect. To the extent that rules of grammar (and punctuation) are not followed, it may either lead to an unexpected interpretation or to indefiniteness in an extreme case.[222]

Avoid Sloppy Claim Drafting Practices

There are innumerable sloppy techniques for drafting claims. The problem, of course, is that sloppiness increases the potential for problems when interpreting claims, potentially resulting in noninfringement or, perhaps, invalidity, such as for indefiniteness.

In 2014, the U.S. Supreme Court issued a decision changing the standard used to determine whether claims are indefinite. This standard should be kept in mind when preparing patent claims. In *Nautilus, Inc. v. Biosig Instruments, Inc.*,[223] the new standard for indefiniteness became "failing to inform those of

---

222. *See* SIMO Holdings v. H.K. uCloudlink Network Tech. Ltd., 983 F.3d 1367 (Fed. Cir. 2021) (see Chapter 3); Grace Instrument Indus., LLC v. Chandler Instruments Co., LLC, 57 F.4th 1001 (Fed. Cir. 2023) (see earlier in this chapter).

223. 134 S. Ct. 2120 (2014).

ordinary skill regarding the scope of the claim with reasonable certainty." The Court stated: "In place of the 'insolubly ambiguous' standard, we hold that a patent is invalid for indefiniteness if its claims, read in light of the specification delineating the patent, and the prosecution history, fail to inform, with reasonable certainty, those skilled in the art about the scope of the invention."[224] The Court's holding affects whether the claims particularly point out and distinctly claim the invention, as required by statute.

A few of the more common sloppiness problems are discussed next.

Double Inclusion

One common problem is referred to as "double inclusion." This refers to including the same element in a claim twice under two different names. For example, the following:

---

1. An apparatus comprising:

   a bottle having a neck with a cylindrical-shaped opening; and a cork stopper sized to fit securely within the cylindrical-shaped opening.

2. The apparatus of claim 1, and further comprising:

   means for corking the cylindrical-shaped opening.

As should be apparent, this is likely to create difficulties of various sorts, most likely invalidity for indefiniteness. For example, is the "cork stopper" of claim 1 the "means for corking" of claim 2?

Singular and Plural Elements

Another example of sloppy claim drafting relates to whether claim elements are plural or singular. It is wise to take care and ensure that singular and plural elements are *only* used where appropriate in claim language. Sometimes a specification may include boilerplate language directed to this issue.

Realize that a plural claim element may provide a wonderful noninfringement argument where the particular element is singular in the accused product.[225] This may seem like a simple point; however, consider the case *Superior*

224. *Id.* at 2124.

225. *See* Apple Inc. v. MPH Techs. Oy, 28 F.4th 254 (Fed. Cir. 2022) (a plural term is presumed to refer to two or more absent a clear disclosure to the contrary).

Fireplace v. Majestic Products.[226] This case may be an example of a patent attorney's worst nightmare.

The invention related to a fireplace, and the submitted claims included a reference to a firebox with a "rear wall." During prosecution, the attorney and the examiner had several interviews, which resulted in amendment of the claims. Although it appears from the record that the portion of the claim relating to the "rear wall" had not specifically been amended by Superior, nonetheless, due to an examiner's amendment, an "s" was inserted, resulting in issued claims that referred to "rear walls" rather than "rear wall." After suing Majestic on the patent, Superior submitted a certificate of correction to make the term singular, as had been originally intended, and the PTO issued the certificate. However, the Federal Circuit declared the certificate of correction invalid, as although filed and corrected within two years of issuance, it was not clearly evident from the specification, drawings, and prosecution history how the error should appropriately be corrected. Thus, Superior was stuck with the plural "rear walls," which, of course, in this case, the accused product did not meet.

Redundant Terms

Redundancy in claims often happens; however, this is also some small risk at least that redundancy may lead to interpretation issues. "Double inclusion" discussed earlier is one type of redundancy; however, it is not the only example. For example, it is not uncommon to see the following formulation in a patent claim: "a receiver for receiving signals." On its face, perhaps this formulation might be harmless; however, it would be better if, instead, this element had been recited as: "a signal receiver."

In addition, a current concern when drafting claims is to avoid unintentionally invoking 35 U.S.C. subsection 112(f). Current Federal Circuit law indicates it is possible for a claim to be interpreted under this provision even without express use of the word "means" in the claim. If this occurs, the claim typically receives a narrower interpretation.

The former claim language, reciting "a receiver for receiving signals," thus would probably be an example in which an opponent, hoping for a narrow construction, would attempt to argue that subsection 112(f) should apply, based at least on its similarity to "means for receiving signals," arguing that if this had been intended to be structure, the language "signal receiver" would have been used; whereas the formulation "receiver for receiving" implies function. Of course, a court may not necessarily apply subsection 112(f) to interpret such language, if it were argued; nonetheless, good practice suggests that it would be

226. 270 F.3d 1358 (Fed. Cir. 2001).

better to avoid the risk. Thus, this is another reason to avoid the formulation "receiver for receiving signals." On the other hand, if the intent is to invoke subsection 112(f), then perhaps it would be better to recite: "means for receiving signals," rather than "a receiver for receiving signals," making the intention clearer.

Lack of Antecedent Basis

Another common problem is lack of antecedent basis. This is not always a problem, depending on the context. There are Federal Circuit cases that state that lack of antecedent basis does not *necessarily* make a claim indefinite.[227] For example, elements that are considered inherent are often recited without creating antecedent basis, but this should not create an indefiniteness issue. Nonetheless, out of an abundance of caution, it seems wise to provide antecedent basis rather than make a claim susceptible to an indefiniteness argument.

For example, consider:

---

1. An apparatus comprising:

   a bandgap circuit;

   the bandgap circuit to produce a fixed voltage, the fixed voltage to correspond to the size of the bandgap.

Here, no formal antecedent basis for "size" was provided. Nonetheless, there is probably no harm or ambiguity because it is inherent that a bandgap has a particular size. However, in other circumstances, failing to provide antecedent basis can create problems. For example:

---

1. An apparatus comprising:

   a cylindrical-shaped container including an opening at an end of the cylindrical-shaped container.

2. The apparatus of claim 1, wherein the opening at the other end includes a cover.

---

227. *See, e.g.*, Bose Corp. v. JBL, Inc., 274 F.3d 1354, 1359 (Fed. Cir. 2001); Slimfold Mfg. Co. v. Kinkead Indus., Inc., 810 F.2d 1113, 1117 (Fed. Cir. 1987).

Again, the potential issues should be apparent. Claim 2 may not necessarily be indefinite despite the lack of antecedent basis for "the opening at the other end," but why take the risk?

Inconsistent Use of "Said" or "The"

Another problem similar in kind to the preceding examples is the inconsistent use of "the" and "said" in connection with a claim element. It is probably best to choose one (that is, either use "the" or use "said") and stick with it throughout the claims. Otherwise, an opponent may argue that these refer to two different elements rather than the same element, potentially creating indefiniteness. *We generally recommend using "the" throughout.*

Some practitioners profess to prefer using "the" so that a patent claim is easier to be understood by a lay person, such as members of a jury, for example. However, some prefer "said" due to its historical roots.

Here, however, "the" is recommended over "said" for a different reason. For a set of claims with dependencies, especially during a prosecution that may have many months (or even years) between office action responses, it becomes surprisingly easy to inadvertently intermix the use of "said" with "the," potentially raising difficult and undesired questions of interpretation.

Inconsistent Use of Term Modifiers

Another common situation of sloppy drafting is improperly adding a modifier. For example:

---

1. An apparatus comprising:

   a container and a platform;

   wherein the container is attached to the platform.

2. The apparatus of claim 1, wherein the circular platform is capable of rotating.

From these claims, we can infer that the platform in claim 1 is circular; however, again, this sloppy drafting may leave this open to interpretation if an opponent wished to challenge that construction. Perhaps claim 1 is intended to be broader than having a circular platform. Hence, this is a good case for finding indefiniteness. Sometimes this is referred to as inferential claiming, although not all inferential claiming should necessarily be avoided.[228]

228. See Chapter 3 discussing inferential claiming.

Sloppy Use of Conjunctions and Disjunctions

We previously discussed issues related to use of "and" versus "or," particularly in conjunction with Markush groups. It is quite important to review claims and make sure the proper language is employed. Often, this issue is addressed at least partially with patent application boilerplate. However, even with application boilerplate, there are situations that may trip up a patent claim drafter.

As one example, the following claim would be interpreted in a manner so that it would probably not be infringed:

> An apparatus comprising: a substance including a halogen comprising at least one of the following: chlorine, fluorine, and iodine.

The reason is because the use of "and" indicates the substance must include all three halogens.[229] Again, for such situations, it is not uncommon to see boilerplate in the specification to assist in addressing the issue. Here, it is recommended to, in general, use "and/or" in claims except where it makes no sense and to address this in the specification. For example, language such as the following may be employed in the specification:

Unless otherwise indicated, in the context of the present patent application, the term "or" if used to associate a list, such as A, B, or C, is intended to mean A, B, and C, here used in the inclusive sense, as well as A, B, or C, here used in the exclusive sense. With this understanding, "and" is used in the inclusive sense and intended to mean A, B, and C; whereas "and/or" can be used in an abundance of caution to make clear that all of the foregoing meanings are intended, although such usage is not required.

Thus, the claim could be written:

> An apparatus comprising: a substance including a halogen comprising at least one of the following: chlorine, fluorine, and/or iodine.

---

229. *See* SuperGuide Corp. v. DirecTV Enters., Inc., 358 F.3d 870 (Fed. Cir. 2004).

Claim Drafting Problems IV

<u>Problem 1</u>. <u>Pez Dispenser</u>—Draft one independent apparatus claim and four dependent claims.

<u>FIGURES:</u>

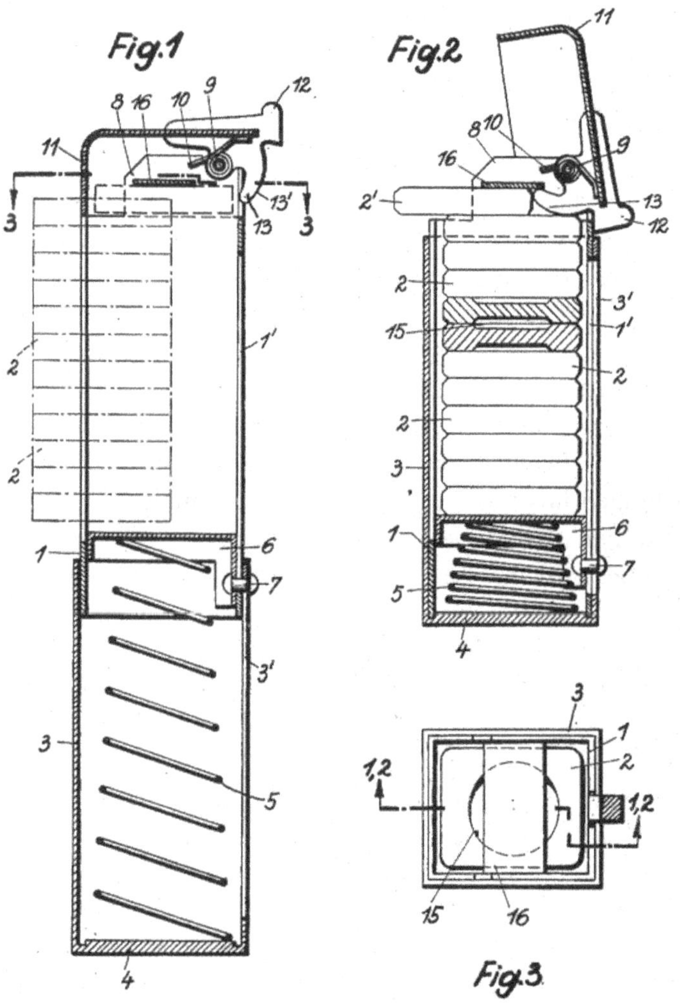

OSKAR UXA, INVENTOR.

BY

ATTORNEY

DESCRIPTION:

The invention relates to a pocket container having a hinged lid and adapted for the delivery of articles, such for example as pastilles, tablets, sweetmeats, and cigarettes, which containers, can be opened or closed with one hand, and present the merchandise to the user in a hygienic and unspoilt condition. The possibility of operation by one hand only is important not only for persons having only one hand but also persons, who often, have only one hand free (for example motor-vehicle drivers), or whose occupation causes their hands to become smeared with dirt.

Known pocket containers for the delivery of tablets singly and that are provided with hinged lids can be opened by one hand, but it is necessary to grasp the uppermost articles with the fingers. This is only made possible by opening the container to render the top article accessible and inserting a knife or similar implement laterally beneath it in order to raise it slightly. These operations can obviously be effected only by using both hands. By contrast the container according to the present invention is so constructed that the opening operation can be effected with one hand and not only frees the tablets but, also, displaces each of them laterally sufficiently far over the edge to enable it to be gripped between the lips and so placed in the mouth in a hygienic and unspoilt condition.

This lateral displacement is achieved by providing a thrust member attached to the lid that, on opening the lid, presses laterally against the upper most article in the container thus displacing it from its central position and over the container edge. The thrust member may be formed in the shape of a finger, in which case its lower edge is so curved that, on opening the lid, the article following the one being delivered is prevented from moving upward and so rendering closing the lid difficult.

The diagrammatic drawings illustrate by way of example several embodiments of pocket containers according to the invention.

Fig. 1 is a cross section on line 1-1 in Fig. 3 of a container with the lid closed and in which the component parts are shown extended for refilling.

Fig. 2 is a section on line 2-2 of Fig. 3 of the same container, in use, delivering an article.

Fig. 3 is a section on line 3-3 of Fig. 1.

The embodiment shown in Figs. 1 to 3 has an oblong container 1 with an opening in front. The container 1 is made of synthetic resin, metal, or the like, and is adapted to contain the loose articles 2, which in this case consist of oblong pastilles (sweetmeats or pharmaceutical tablets). Surrounding the inner container 1 is a movable base 6 above the floor 4 inside the container under which is fixed a spring 5 acting against the movable base 6 of the container 1. Secured to the base 6 is a stud 7 arranged to slide in the slots 1' and 3' provided in the surrounding component parts 1, 3 of the container. By this means the parts 1, 3 can be arranged at will either in the position for filling (Fig. 1) or in the position for use (Fig. 2) without completely dismantling the container. Free movement of the base 6 is kept within the required limits, however, by virtue of the stud 7 being rigid with the base 6 and slidable only in the slots 1' and 3'. In the upper extension of the wall of the container 1 is mounted a pin 9 about which the lid 11 is rotatable against the action of a spring 10, one end of which is fixed to the extension 8.

The lid carries a fixed thumb piece 12 including a thrust member 13, the lower edge 13' (Fig. 1) of which is curved. Holding the container, with one hand, the lid can be opened by depressing the thumb piece 12 with the thumb, whereupon the thrust member 13 laterally displaces the uppermost article 2' into the position shown in Fig. 2. Owing to the curved form of the lower edge 13' of the member 13 the articles thrust upwards by the action of the spring 5 are prevented from following the article 2' being delivered. As soon as the pressure on the thumb piece 12 is sufficiently relaxed, the lid 11 is automatically returned to the closed position by the spring 10. The thrust member 13 is thus removed out of the way of a new top article and thus allows the latter to take up a position ready for next opening operation (Fig. 1).

The lid may also be arranged in a known manner so as to be permanently spring-loaded in the direction tending to open it, the lid moving smartly to the open position on release of a locking device and thus ejecting or pushing out an article 2. The articles are formed with recesses 15 in order to facilitate lateral displacement with respect to one another.

When it is desired to fill the container, the parts 1, 3 are moved into the position shown in Fig. 1, whereupon the new stack of tablets 2 (shown by dotted lines in Fig. 1) is inserted through the front of the open container 1. By collapsing the parts 1, 3 the base 6 is displaced downwards and the spring compressed (Fig. 2), whereupon the container is ready for use. The uppermost article presses against the bridge piece 16 carried by the extension 8 of the container 1.

When dealing with articles having a sticky surface, it is advisable to separate the individual articles by interposing spacers of different material, for example separation could be effected by means of wafers or by covering the articles with a non-adhesive wrapper.

Problem 2. Camera—Draft one independent apparatus claim and one independent method claim.

FIGURES:

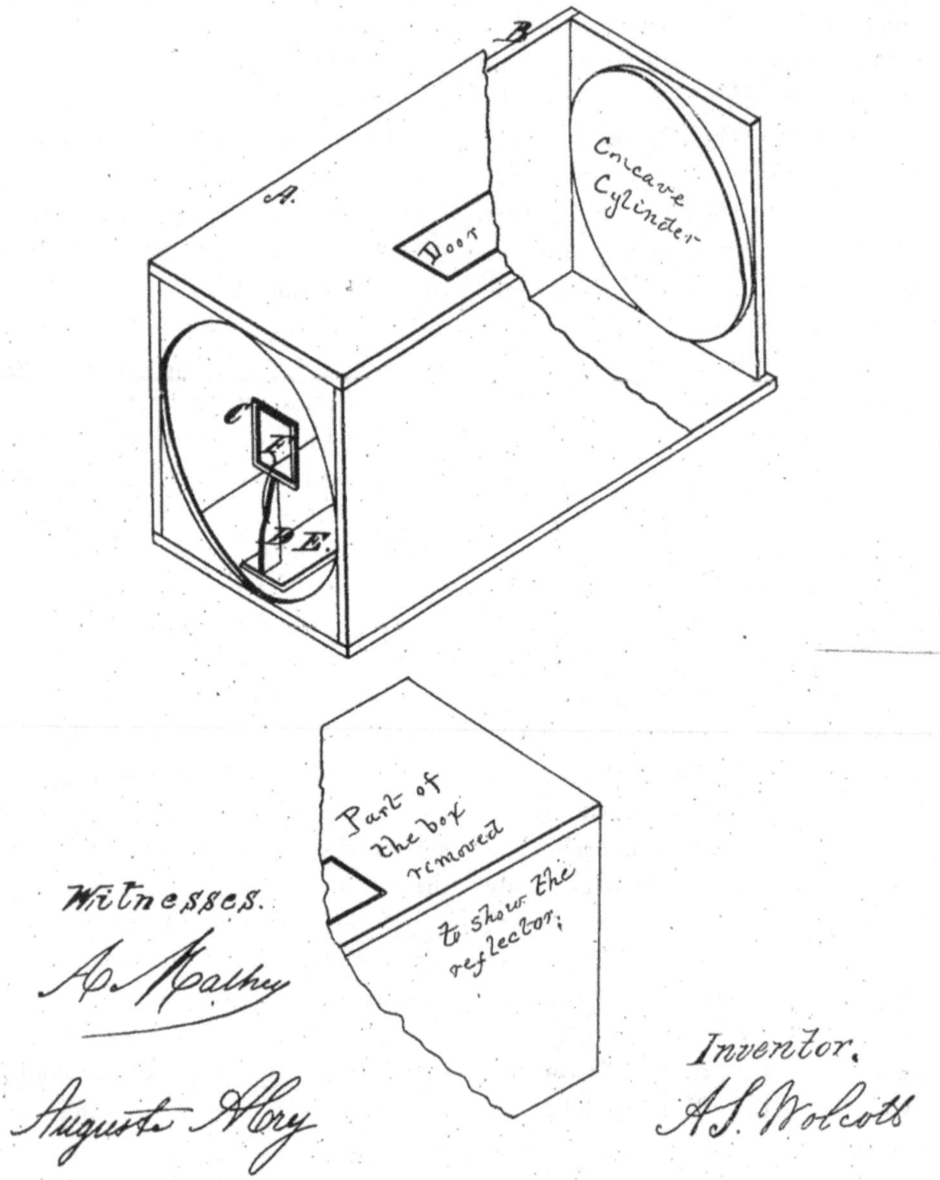

DESCRIPTION:

A is a box, inside of which, at the end B, a concave reflector (which may either be a piece of solid metal or glass silvered) is placed, with the reflecting-surface facing the other end, which has an opening corresponding to the size of the reflector.

C is a light metal frame fixed by a thin support D to a piece of wood or other material E, with which it slides on the bottom of the box, in a direction perpendicular to the face of the reflector and lengthwise of the box. This frame is intended to carry the metallic plate, paper, or other material on which the impression is to be made. The plate, paper, or other material may be retained in the proper position against the frame by a small spring F, pressing the plate, paper, or other material on the back, and between which spring and the frame C the plate, paper, or other material is slid.

A small door should be made on the top of the box for the purpose of observing the focal image. The box A should be placed on a table or other support at such height that the center of the reflector may be as high as that part of the person who is intended to be in the middle of the picture. When a very small picture of the person is intended to be taken, the focus may be adjusted by a microscope, which may be introduced through a hole in the top or side of the box or held by the hand at the doorway on the top.

When the camera—that is the box A with the reflector—is to be used, the person whose likeness is to be taken should be placed in a chair, to which some suitable support for the head is attached to enable him to remain perfectly still. The camera should then be placed with the open end immediately opposite to the person. A trial plate is then to be placed or put against the frame C and the focus adjusted by sliding the piece E. The trial plate is then to be removed and the plate, paper, or other material (prepared in any of the well-known methods for being acted on by luminous or other rays) put into its place and allowed to remain as long as required to form the image. A convenient size for such camera would be as follows: box A, inside fifteen inches long, eight and a half inches high, and eight inches wide; reflector, seven inches clear diameter and twelve inches focus.

The plate, paper, or other material on which the picture is to be formed is two and a half inches long by two inches wide.

For taking likenesses for breast pins the reflector may be about two and a quarter inches diameter and four inches focus and all the other parts of the camera of proportionate size.

Problem 3. Method of making foil—Draft one independent method claim and seven dependent claims.

DESCRIPTION:

This invention relates generally to the making of copper and copper alloy foil and, more particularly, to the making of ultra-thin foil using a copper or copper alloy carrier.

BACKGROUND INFORMATION

Copper foil has been widely used for many years in the manufacture of printed circuits. The raw material for printed circuits usually consists of a laminate of a copper foil and a resinous substrate. In recent years, it has been found desirable to make such laminates for printed circuits using copper foil that is much thinner than formerly used. Ultra-thin foils of thicknesses of less than 18 microns (0.5 ounces per square foot) and on the order of 5–9 microns are now being used. One reason for the use of thinner foil is the demand for printed circuits with good dimensional precision, especially in circuitry with narrow width lines and short distances between the conductors. With the use of thinner copper foils, decrease of the so called "undercut" is obtained. By undercut it is meant the elimination of copper under the etch resist caused by the etching solution that while dissolving the unprotected portions of the copper layer also eats into the copper covered by the etch resist.

Further, there is also a desire to reduce the amount of copper removed by the etching process that forms the circuit conductor pattern so as to reduce the cost of etchant as well as reducing copper recovery costs or, alternatively, a reduction of copper loss if no such recovery is effected.

When copper foil is made by itself in thicknesses of less than 0.5 ounce per square foot or less, it becomes very difficult to handle. During processing it often wrinkles and tears unless extreme care is exercised. Thus, according to current practice, the desired ultra-thin copper foil layer is conventionally formed on a temporary carrier surface of aluminum. The foil is then laminated onto an insulating support such as a glass fiber reinforced epoxy resin. Thereafter, the temporary carrier is removed, either by mechanically peeling the carrier off, or chemically by etching it off, leaving a copper foil surface on the support. The copper foil may then be etched or otherwise treated to produce the electrical circuit. Examples of making thin copper foil supported on an aluminum alloy substrate are described in U.S. Pat. Nos. 3,886,022; 3,936,548; 4,088,544; 4,113,576; 4,234,395; and 4,323,632.

SUMMARY OF THE INVENTION

The present invention is directed to the use of copper or copper alloy foil as the carrier for making thin copper foil. As compared to aluminum, copper foil has better mechanical strength and, as a result, the composite sheet will be less likely to rip or tear. Further, in order to obtain uniform plating of the copper on the disposable aluminum foil carrier, special surface treatment such as etching of the aluminum foil is required. Additionally, the use of aluminum foil as a carrier presents recycling problems. The aluminum is relatively soft and is generally not removed as a usable strip. Generally, the copper foil manufacturers are not equipped to reuse aluminum. On the other hand, if copper is used as the carrier, the foil maker can either reuse the peeled strip, or reclaim the copper for use as scrap material for use in the deposition process.

If the copper foil carrier is made by an electrodeposition process, the surface finish can be controlled. The condition of the surface of the carrier is important because the ultra-thin foil will mirror the surface of the carrier.

In accordance with the present invention, the copper or copper alloy foil is pretreated in order to render it strippable from the thin layer of foil that is deposited thereon. The pretreatment process includes cleaning the surface of the carrier foil and thereafter treating the foil with an aqueous solution of chromic and phosphoric acid to apply a film to the foil that will render a subsequent deposit of copper or copper alloy on the foil strippable therefrom. The foil may then be used as the carrier for thin foil deposition.

DESCRIPTION OF THE PREFERRED EMBODIMENT

More specifically, the present invention contemplates the use of a copper or copper alloy foil as a carrier for this foil deposition. The copper or copper alloy foil carrier may be either wrought foil or electrodeposited foil and may have a thickness of 18 microns or greater. The thickness of the foil should be such as to provide the mechanical strength necessary to support the ultra-thin layer to be deposited thereon. Foil in the conventional one ounce (35 microns) thickness is preferred.

In the case of electrodeposited foil to be used as the carrier, such foil may be produced according to any of the methods disclosed and with any of the apparatus shown in U.S. Pat. Nos. 4,529,486; 4,532,014; 4,549,950; and 4,568,431. In general, such an electrodeposition system for producing a copper or copper alloy foil comprises a plating tank designed to hold an electrolyte. A rotating metal drum is connected to a negative terminal of a direct current power supply and serves as the cathode. An anode of arcuate shape is connected to the positive terminal of the power supply and is mounted in the tank in such a way that a substantial uniform inner-electrogap is formed with the drum cathode. An electrolyte solution is present within the tank and generally comprises an aqueous solution containing a concentration of metal ions to be deposited on the cathode plating surface of the rotating drum. For the production of copper foil, it would contain a concentration of copper ions. Preferably, such electrolyte solution comprises a copper sulfate-sulfuric acid solution. The compositional specifics of a copper sulfate-sulfuric acid solution and the temperature ranges with which it may be used are more fully described in the Polan et al., U.S. Pat. No. 4,529,486. When a current is applied, metal is deposited on the rotating drum. The metal deposit generally takes the form of a relatively thin, relatively smooth continuous strip of metal foil that is removed from the drum plating surface after it emerges from the electrolyte.

The foil constituting the carrier is preferably cleaned prior to undergoing treatment. Any suitable cleaning process may be used to remove oxides and contaminants from the foil. In general, the cleaning process may include treatment of the surfaces of the carrier foil with an aqueous acidic solution that may contain an oxidizer. Any suitable acid may be used that is capable of cleaning the foil and that does not have a deleterious effect on the foil and does not present environmental problems. Preferred acids include H_2SO_4 and HNO_3 and suitable oxidizers include $Na_2S_2O_8$ and H_2O_2. When HNO_3 is used, a separate oxidizer ingredient may be omitted as the HNO_3 is an oxidizer.

Concentration of the solution may vary according to the components being used. For example, when H_2SO_4 is used with $Na_2S_2O_8$, the solution may contain from about 1 to about 5 volume percent of H_2SO_4 and about 10 to about 30 weight percent of the $Na_2S_2O_8$. In the case of solutions of H_2SO_4 and H_2O_2, concentrations of from about 10 to about 20 volume percent H_2SO_4 and from about 1 to 3 volume percent H_2O_2 may be used. When an aqueous solution of nitric acid is used, its concentration may be from about 1 to 30 volume percent.

While the cleaning solution may be applied in any appropriate manner such as by dipping or spraying, it is preferred that the foil be immersed in a tank containing the cleaning solution. The time of the immersion of the foil in the solution may be from about 5 to about 20 seconds. The cleaning process may be carried out at any desired temperature though it is preferred that the solution be maintained at an ambient temperature.

After the cleaning treatment, the foil is rinsed to remove any loose particles on the foil and wash away any unwanted chemicals left during the cleaning treatment. Such rinsing may be achieved by using spray nozzles to spray ionized water on both sides of the foil. Alternatively, the rinsing may be achieved by using a tank containing the rinse solution and through which the foil is passed.

After cleaning and water rinsing, the foil is treated with a chromic acid-phosphoric acid solution to apply a film to the foil. Solutions that may be used in accordance with the present invention contain chromic acid in a concentration of about 0.002 grams per liter to about 3.0 grams per liter and phosphoric acid in a concentration in the range of about 0.002 grams per liter to about 3.0 grams per liter. Generally this solution contains no other constituents besides water and some minor impurities. The preferred embodiment of the solution may consist essentially of from 0.1 grams per liter to about 0.5 grams per liter of chromic acid, from about 0.1 grams per liter to about 1.0 gram per liter of phosphoric acid and the balance essentially water.

It is preferred that the chromic acid-phosphoric acid solution treatment be applied by immersing the foil in a tank containing the phosphoric-chromic acid solution. The treatment of the foil may be applied with the phosphoric-chromic acid solution at any desired temperature although it is preferred that the solution be maintained at a temperature in the range of from about 20° C to about 100° C.

It is also preferred to keep the foil immersed in the solution for a time in the range of from about 3 seconds to about 3 minutes and most preferably from about 20 seconds to about 60 seconds. When other techniques such as spraying are used to apply the treatment, the foil should be exposed to the solution for similar time periods.

After immersion of the foil carrier in chromic acid-phosphoric acid solution, the carrier may be rinsed with H_2O or preferably a dilute caustic solution may be applied. This step may be omitted depending upon the concentration of the chromic acid-phosphoric acid solution. If a dilute caustic solution is used, such solution may comprise an aqueous solution having a pH of at least about 8. Solutions of particular benefit are those having a pH in the range of about 9 to 11.5. Any suitable addition agent may be employed to adjust the pH of this solution. Generally, the addition will be selected from the group consisting of the salts of alkali metals, the salts of alkaline earth metals, the hydroxides of the alkali metals, and the hydroxides of the alkaline earth metals. A preferred addition agent is one selected from a group consisting of sodium hydroxide, calcium hydroxide, potassium hydroxide, and ammonium hydroxide. While the amount of addition agent present in the solution will be a function of the desired pH level for the solution, generally the addition agent will be present in the concentration of greater than 1 ppm, and preferably about 50 ppm.

The temperature of the basic solution may be maintained at a temperature in the range of from about room temperature to about 100° C. While the time of immersion in the basic solution may vary from about 1 second to about 120 seconds, most preferably, it is immersed for about 5 seconds to about 30 seconds.

The foil may then be dried and is ready for use as a carrier for thin foil deposition. If it is desired to dry the foil, such drying may be accomplished by any suitable method. Numerous drying processes are known in the art. One such process that may be used embodies a water blow-off stage followed by a hot-air tunnel drying stage. An alternative process utilizes heat as well as air for both bulk and evaporative water removal. In this latter process, the hot air can be directed against the foil when it is lying on drum rollers in the processing line. In still another alternative process, at least one internally heated drum roller or infra-red heating may be used to dry the foil.

As mentioned, after the above-described treatment, the foil is ready to be used as a carrier for depositing ultra-thin foil. The thin foil may be deposited on the copper carrier by either D.C. plating or pulse plating, both of which are well known in the art. In both processes, the foil is immersed in electrolyte containing a source of copper ions and an electric current is passed through the foil and an anode to cause the electrodeposition of the copper on the foil.

To show the feasibility of such a process, a 1 ounce ED foil was cleaned in an aqueous solution containing 1 volume percent H_2SO_4 and 20 weight percent $Na_2S_2O_8$ for 30 seconds followed by an H_2O rinse. The foil was then immersed in a chromic acid-phosphoric acid solution for 30 seconds at 60° C. The concentration of the solution was 0.2 grams per liter chromic acid and 0.5 grams per liter phosphoric acid. The foil was then dried and a copper nodule layer was deposited on this treated ED foil utilizing a process of the type disclosed in U.S. Pat. No. 4,468,293 to Polan et al. that uses a current having regularly recurring pulses. In this process copper dendrites are formed on the surface of the copper foil during a first portion of each pulse and are bonded to the surface during the second portion of each pulse. The resulting deposited foil had its free surface laminated to an FR-4 substrate. It was found that the nodule layer was easily separated from the ED foil carrier member after lamination. The peel strength of the foil was 1.6 lbs/in as determined by specification IPC 2.4.8 of the Institute for Interconnecting and Packaging Electronic Circuits.

Indirect Infringement

A Claim for Indirect Infringement Is Harder to Prove; Thus, Attempt to Draft Claims That Will Be Directly Infringed

It requires knowledge of the patent and knowledge that the acts contributed to or induced would be infringing.

35 U.S.C. § 271(a)–(d)

(a) Except as otherwise provided in this title, whoever without authority makes, uses, offers to sell, or sells any patented invention, within the United States or imports into the United States any patented invention during the term of the patent therefor, infringes the patent.

(b) Whoever actively induces infringement of a patent shall be liable as an infringer.

(c) Whoever offers to sell or sells within the United States or imports into the United States a component of a patented machine, manufacture, combination or composition, or a material or apparatus for use in practicing a patented process, constituting a material part of the invention, knowing the same to be especially made or especially adapted for use in an infringement of such patent, and not a staple article or commodity of commerce suitable for substantial noninfringing use, shall be liable as a contributory infringer.

(d) No patent owner otherwise entitled to relief for infringement or contributory infringement of a patent shall be denied relief or deemed guilty of misuse or illegal extension of the patent right by reason of his having done one or more of the following: (1) derived revenue from acts which if performed by another without his consent would constitute contributory infringement of the patent; (2) licensed or authorized another to perform acts which if performed without his consent would constitute contributory infringement of the patent; (3) sought to enforce his patent rights against infringement or contributory infringement; (4) refused to license or use any rights to the patent; or (5) conditioned the license of any rights to the patent or the sale of the patented product on the acquisition of a license to rights in another patent or purchase of a separate product, unless, in view of the circumstances, the patent owner has market power in the relevant market for the patent or patented product on which the license or sale is conditioned.

Nalco Co. v. Chem-Mod, LLC
883 F.3d 1337
United States Court of Appeals for the Federal Circuit
February 27, 2018, Decided

Questions

1. Why is direct infringement so important to the other case allegations (i.e., indirect infringement) that the district court was able to dismiss the complaint under Federal Rule of Civil Procedure 12(b)(6) primarily because it concluded a plausible claim of direct infringement had not been pled? Why is direct infringement one of the elements of a claim of indirect infringement when it is not an element specified in the statute?
2. Nalco is the exclusive licensee rather than the assignee or the patentee. What significance, if any, does this have in a lawsuit generally? Did it matter here?
3. What is the legal standard to survive a motion to dismiss under Rule 12(b)(6)? What does the appellate court say is the plausibility standard to be determined? What confused the district court so that it believed a sufficient pleading of direct infringement had not occurred? How should the district court have understood the pleading? What do you think about this statement by the appellate court: "Nalco's pleading clearly exceeds the minimum requirements under Rule 12(b)(6), especially as 'the Federal Rules of Civil Procedure do not require a plaintiff to plead facts establishing that each element of an asserted claim is met.'"?[230]
4. Is there a difference between "flue gas" and "coal combustion flue gas"? Why or why not? How does this potentially impact the sufficiency of the pleading of direct infringement?
5. What is pleading yourself out of court? Why did that not happen here?
6. What is the divided infringement claim the appellate court references and how is it relevant to this case and to direct infringement? What is the issue regarding section 45 of the tax code with respect to divided infringement and why did the district court deem it to be insufficient? What must be shown legally to prove direct infringement under such circumstances referred to as "divided infringement"? Why and how was this shown here? What were the sources of the evidence relied upon by the plaintiffs?
7. What is the substance of plaintiff's claim of infringement under the DOE? Is this a type of direct infringement or a type of indirect infringement in this case? Would direct infringement under the

230. Nalco Co. v. Chem-Mod, LLC, 883 F.3d 1337, 1350 (Fed. Cir. 2018).

DOE be sufficient to support a claim of indirect infringement if the other elements required were proven?

8. What were other deficiencies in the pleadings regarding indirect infringement according to the district court? Why did the appellate court conclude this was an error? Note this statement by the appellate court regarding inducement:

> Nor was Nalco required to plead that a named Defendant engaged in the underlying direct infringement; Nalco's allegations that, in certain circumstances, a non-Defendant power plant operator or testing facility is the direct infringer who actually performs the injection of the thermolabile bromine precursor into flue gas is sufficient to state a claim for indirect infringement. *Nalco 4AC*, at 27.[231]

Why is this the case?

9. Why did the defendants argue a finding of direct infringement is needed for a claim of willful infringement? What is willful infringement and how does it relate to direct and indirect infringement?
10. Do the issues surrounding pleading in this case, particularly regarding proving direct infringement to make out a claim of indirect infringement, give you any guidance regarding drafting patent claims for litigation? Why is indirect infringement asserted?

* * *

Basically, making, using, selling, importing, or offering to sell a product that literally meets all the elements and limitations recited in a patent claim amounts to literal, direct infringement. Making, using, selling, importing, or offering to sell a component of a patent claim in which the patent claim recites several components, as an example, or in which the claim is a method claim involving the component, as another example, may result in indirect infringement, if other requirements, as discussed later, are met.

As mentioned, a claim of direct infringement is a much easier claim to assert. Indirect infringement requires intent and has additional requirements. Thus, a component claim is generally more valuable against a component manufacturer, as a direct patent infringement claim, and a system-level claim is generally more valuable against a system integrator, as a direct patent infringement claim.[232]

The current legal basis for indirect patent infringement is statutory subsections 271(b) and (c), which state:

231. *Id.* at 1354.
232. See Chapter 2 discussion.

> (b) Whoever actively induces infringement of a patent shall be liable as an infringer;
>
> (c) Whoever offers to sell or sells within the United States or imports into the United States a component of a patented machine, manufacture, combination or composition, or a material or apparatus for use in practicing a patented process, constituting a material part of the invention, knowing the same to be especially made or especially adapted for use in an infringement of such patent, and not a staple article or commodity of commerce suitable for substantial noninfringing use, shall be liable as a contributory infringer.

In general, these sections are directed to someone who in some manner aids and abets a direct infringer but does not otherwise directly infringe the patent claim at issue. Hence, the name "indirect infringement." As with direct infringement, this infringement may occur literally or nonliterally.

The rationale for liability for indirect infringement is that an indirect infringer furthers direct infringement and should be jointly and severally liable as a joint tortfeasor. Hence, unlike direct infringement, which has no intent requirement, indirect infringement does have an intent requirement. That is, to be liable, one has to at least knowingly aid and abet direct infringement by a direct infringer. The logical basis for this comes from the basic principles of tort law.

In general, there are two types of indirect patent infringement:[233] contributory patent infringement and inducing patent infringement. The latter is governed by subsection 271(b) and the former is governed by subsection 271(c), both of which were introduced in the 1952 patent statute, a major milestone in terms of the statutory origins of U.S. patent law. The legislative history of these provisions indicates that they are a codification of previous case law.[234]

If possible, it is best to draft claims that are directly infringed rather than indirectly infringed. Cases for indirect infringement are much harder to establish in federal court. In general, for a claim of indirect infringement, you must prove the same case elements as direct infringement *and* also additional

---

233. This is distinguished from imputed patent infringement, which is yet another type of patent infringement. For example, if an employee infringes a patent, that infringement may be imputed to the employer. Likewise, acts of a subsidiary company may be imputed to the parent company. *See* Emma Tracy, *Imputed Liability: How to Determine When Parent Companies Should Be Held Liable for the Patent Infringements of Their Subsidiary Companies*, 82 Mo. L. Rev. 571 (2017), https://scholarship.law.missouri.edu/mlr/vol82/iss2/13.

234. *See, e.g.*, Hewlett-Packard Co. v. Bausch & Lomb Inc., 909 F.2d 1464 (Fed. Cir. 1990).

case elements. It is well established that direct infringement must *necessarily* be present to have a claim for indirect infringement.[235]

Appreciate that without direct infringement, there would be no patent infringement that the indirect infringer induced or contributed to; hence, it is fundamental that direct infringement must necessarily be shown to make out a case for indirect infringement.[236] However, direct infringement may be proven with circumstantial evidence.[237] Due to these additional case elements to establish a claim, there is much less case law regarding indirect patent infringement than direct patent infringement.

In addition, proving indirect infringement requires proving that the indirect infringer at least knowingly engaged in the acts that constituted the indirect infringement and knew that direct infringement would result.[238] Although, again, this may be proven by circumstantial evidence.[239]

Thus, it must be proven that the indirect infringer knew of the patent, and, further, that the acts being induced or contributed to would have resulted in infringement. Generally, contributory infringement requires knowledge. The statute, subsection 271(c), expressly states (emphasis added):

> Whoever offers to sell or sells within the United States or imports into the United States a component of a patented machine, manufacture, combination or composition, or a material or apparatus for use in practicing a patented process, constituting a material part of the invention, *knowing* the same to be especially made or especially adapted for use in an infringement of such patent, and not a staple article or commodity of commerce suitable for sub stantial noninfringing use, shall be liable as a contributory infringer.

In contrast, subsection 271(b) does not specify a level intent. It states: "Whoever actively induces infringement of a patent shall be liable as an infringer."

---

235. *Id.* However, it remains somewhat unclear whether the direct infringement must precede the indirect infringement. *See* Fina Rsch., S.A. v. Baroid Ltd., 141 F.3d 1479, 1485, 46 U.S.P.Q.2d 1461, 1467 (Fed. Cir. 1998) ("[W]e decline . . . to create a per se rule that an actual controversy predicated only on induced infringement may exist only if direct infringement has already occurred."). *Cf. Waymark Corp. v. Porta Systems Corp.*, 245 F.3d 1364 (Fed. Cir. 2001), regarding liability under subsection 271(f)(2) for exportation of a component, in which the court noted that "infringement without a completed infringing embodiment is not the norm in patent law, but it is reasonable in the context of 271(f)(2)."

236. *See, e.g.*, Aro Mfg. Co. v. Convertible Top Replacement Co., 377 U.S. 476 (1964).

237. Cases involving indirect infringement have permitted circumstantial evidence of direct infringement. *See, e.g.*, R&L Carriers, Inc. v. Pitt Ohio Express, Inc., 681 F.3d 1323 (Fed. Cir. 2012).

238. *See* Commil USA, LLC v. Cisco Sys., 575 U.S. 632 (2015).

239. *See* Water Techs. Corp. v. Calco, Ltd., 850 F.2d 660 (Fed. Cir. 1988).

Over the years Federal Circuit law has not been entirely consistent as to the level of intent needed for inducement; however, the Supreme Court appears to have resolved that contributory infringement and inducing infringement require the same level of intent—that is, knowledge rather than purposeful conduct.[240]

Contributory Infringement

35 U.S.C. § 271(c)

Whoever offers to sell or sells within the United States or imports into the United States a component of a patented machine, manufacture, combination or composition, or a material or apparatus for use in practicing a patented process, constituting a material part of the invention, knowing the same to be especially made or especially adapted for use in an infringement of such patent, and not a staple article or commodity of commerce suitable for substantial noninfringing use, shall be liable as a contributory infringer.

Fujitsu Ltd. v. Netgear Inc.
620 F.3d 1321
United States Court of Appeals for the Federal Circuit
September 20, 2010, Decided

Questions

1. What are the elements of a claim of contributory infringement according to the appellate court?
2. In this case why is Netgear asserted to be a contributory infringer rather than a direct infringer as to patent '952? Who, then, is the direct infringer?
3. What is the issue raised by Netgear regarding direct infringement of a standard covered by a patent (particularly with respect to the '952 patent)? Can one show that a product directly infringes a patent that covers a standard without necessarily applying the asserted patent claim to the accused product? If so, how? Why was U.S. Philips Corp. unable to show direct infringement regarding the '952 for most of the products at issue (other than four models for which there were genuine issues of material fact) even considering circumstantial evidence?

240. See *Life Technologies Corp. v. Promega Corp.*, 137 S. Ct. 734 (2017), in which the Supreme Court stated in a footnote that, in the *Global-Tech* case, it had "substantially equat[ed] the intent requirements for §§271(b) and 271(c)."

Is circumstantial evidence usually enough to show direct infringement when assessing contributory infringement?

4. What is the precise standard of knowledge required to show contributory infringement? Why is knowledge required for contributory infringement, when intent is not required for direct infringement? Why did the appellate court conclude there were genuine issues of material fact relating to the requisite knowledge for contributory infringement of the '952 patent?
5. What is the issue with respect to substantial noninfringing uses that relates to a "separate and distinct" feature versus the entire product? Which approach did the appellate court use and what was its ruling? Why did the appellate court treat the issue of whether the feature may be turned off differently for purposes of direct infringement than for determining the presence of substantial noninfringing uses? What would it mean for the feature at issue to have substantial noninfringing uses?
6. Why did the appellate court conclude that defragmentation is not a material part of the invention? Why do you think defragmentation was not claimed when it was clear that it would be needed? What would have been a good way to handle this issue via claim drafting?
7. Why did the appellate court conclude genuine issues of material fact remained regarding inducement to infringe for the four models but not for other models?
8. What is the marking issue in the case? What was the error by the district court?
9. Why did the appellate court agree that the '993 and '642 patents were not infringed?

* * *

As mentioned, contributory patent infringement is defined by statute. Typically, it involves sale of a component especially designed for use in a patented combination or process. 35 U.S.C. subsection 271(c) specifies the elements for a claim of such infringement:

> [1] a component of a patented machine, manufacture, combination or composition, or a material or apparatus for use in practicing a patented process, [2] constituting a material part of the invention, [3] knowing the same to be especially made or especially adapted for use in an infringement of such patent, and [4] not a staple article or commodity of commerce suitable for substantial noninfringing use . . . .

As mentioned, direct infringement is a perquisite for indirect infringement. If this is not capable of being proven, then there is no claim for indirect infringement, although direct infringement may be proven with circumstantial evidence.[241]

As the statute makes clear, contributory infringement relates to supplying a component of a patented invention (i.e., a component of a patent claim), typically as a sale, although the statute also recites offer for sale and importation. Likewise, the intent element requires that the party supplying the component for a patented combination, for example, know both that the combination is patented and is infringing.[242] Intent, however, may be proven by circumstantial evidence.[243]

The component must also (1) be specially made so as to result in infringement in the combination; (2) *not* be capable of substantial noninfringing use (i.e., not be a staple article of commerce); and (3) be a material part of the invention. Very few cases construe the material part requirement. Generally, if a component meets the requirements of being specially made to infringe and being not capable of substantial noninfringing use, it will likely constitute a material part.[244]

Staple and Non-Staple Articles of Commerce

Dawson Chemical Co. v. Rohm & Haas Co.
448 U.S. 176
Supreme Court of the United States
April 21, 1980, Argued; June 27, 1980, Decided

Questions

1. Subsection 271(d) exempts certain activities by a patent owner from the misuse doctrine. *Rohm & Haas (R & H)* construed subsection 271(d) enacted as part of the 1952 patent reform. However, in 1988, Congress added two more sections to the statute:

---

241. *See, e.g.*, Refac Int'l, Ltd. v. IBM, 798 F.2d 459, 460, 230 U.S.P.Q. 537 (Fed. Cir. 1986). *Cf. Waymark Corp. v. Porta Systems Corp.*, 245 F.3d 1364 (Fed. Cir. 2001), regarding liability under subsection 271(f)(2) for exportation of a component, in which the court noted that "infringement without a completed infringing embodiment is not the norm in patent law, but it is reasonable in the context of 271(f)(2)."

242. *See, e.g.*, Aro Mfg. Co. v. Convertible Top Replacement Co., 377 U.S. 476 (1964).

243. *See* Metabolite Laby's, Inc. v. Lab'y Corp. of Am. Holdings, 370 F.3d 1354, 71 U.S.P.Q.2d 1081 (Fed. Cir. 2004) (A "patentee may prove such intent through circumstantial evidence.").

244. *But see* Fujitsu Ltd. v. Netgear Inc., 620 F.3d 1321 (Fed. Cir. 2010) (in which an accused infringer's software product was not a material part of a patented invention, although the product was for use in a system that carried out the invention primarily because the software performed defragmentation whereas the claims only recited fragmentation, not defragmentation).

> No patent owner otherwise entitled to relief for infringement or contributory infringement of a patent shall be denied relief or deemed guilty of misuse or illegal extension of the patent right by reason of his having done one or more of the following: (1) derived revenue from acts which if performed by another without his consent would constitute contributory infringement of the patent; (2) licensed or authorized another to perform acts which if performed without his consent would constitute contributory infringement of the patent; (3) sought to enforce his patent rights against infringement or contributory infringement; (4) refused to license or use any rights to the patent; or (5) conditioned the license of any rights to the patent or the sale of the patented product on the acquisition of a license to rights in another patent or purchase of a separate product, unless, in view of the circumstances, the patent owner has market power in the relevant market for the patent or patented product on which the license or sale is conditioned.[245]

Parts (4) and (5) were added by the Patent Misuse Reform Act of 1988. Do these statutory updates codify or change the holding of *R & H*?

2. *R & H* clarified the distinction between staple and non-staple articles of commerce. The distinction remains a feature of U.S. patent law via the express wording of subsections 271(b) and (c). What is that distinction? How important is that distinction to the reasoning of *R & H*? Note that Justice Brennan in his dissent suggests that the holding of the case also implicates subsection 271(b). Do you agree or disagree? Why or why not?
3. Although subsection 271(c) provides a level of intent required, subsection 271(b) does not. The Federal Circuit and the Supreme Court have not been entirely consistent over the years. However, in a case written by Judge Rich, *Hewlett Packard v. Bausch & Lomb*,[246] he attempted to clarify the level of intent as more than simply "knowledge." Note that this is the same Rich cited in the *R & H* decision as testifying before Congress regarding the related subsections of § 271. One might expect, therefore, that he speaks with a level of authority. However, despite this, the Supreme Court seems to have decided the issue differently; in *Life Technologies Corp. v. Promega Corp.*,[247] the Supreme Court stated in a footnote that, in *Global-Tech*, it had "substantially equat[ed] the

245. 35 U.S.C. § 271(d) (2024).
246. 909 F.2d 1464 (Fed. Cir. 1990).
247. 137 S. Ct. 734 (2017).

intent requirements for §§ 271(b) and 271(c)."[248] Given the distinction between staple and non-staple articles of commerce, can one formulate a logical basis for a difference in level of intent, as suggested by Judge Rich? What about the act portion of these statutory torts? Might that be a basis for a higher level of intent for inducement than for contributory infringement? If so, why then does the Supreme Court require knowledge for both?[249]

4. Assume that the *R & H* decision does not directly affect subsection 271(b) (despite Justice Brennan's comment). Patent misuse is a judge-made affirmative defense to patent infringement. Subsection 271(d) does not define "patent misuse." Instead, it clarifies what is not patent misuse. The policy behind patent misuse appears to be to prevent the patentee from exploiting any rights under the patent beyond the legal rights granted by the patent. How might patent misuse potentially arise *with the sale of a staple article of commerce to a customer of a patentee that is to be used to practice the patentee's patent*?[250] How might a patentee arrange its sale of staple articles of commerce to a customer in a manner that associates a license under a patent without committing patent misuse? Does *R & H* change the result in the case *Morton Salt Co. v. G.S. Suppiger Co.*?[251] Why or why not?
5. *R & H* was a 5–4 decision. What issue has the Court so divided? Is there a logical difference between the first three subsections of 271(d) and the fourth subsection? If so, what is the logical distinction? What might be the policy justification for saying they should be treated the same under patent law? What might be an economic justification for saying they should be treated the same?
6. Antitrust policy (e.g., sections 1 and 2 of the Sherman Antitrust Act) and the patent misuse doctrine are close cousins. First, legally, what is the difference between violating the Sherman Act and committing patent misuse? Second, is there a different policy underlying each? If so, what is it?

---

248. *Id.* at 742 n.8.

249. *See* Global-Tech Appliances, Inc. v. SEB S.A., 563 U.S. 754 (2011).

250. *See* Switzer Bros. v. Locklin, 297 F.2d 39, 46, 131 U.S.P.Q. 405 (7th Cir. 1961), *cert. denied*, 369 U.S. 851 (1962); Dr. Salsbury's Laby's v. I.D. Russell Co. Laby's, 212 F.2d 414, 94 U.S.P.Q. 199 (8th Cir. 1952), *cert. denied*, 348 U.S. 837 (1954). *Cf.* Dawson Chem. Co. v. Rohm & Haas Co., 448 U.S. 176, 214, 206 U.S.P.Q. 385 (1980) ("§ 271(d) would afford no defense to a charge of misuse for an attempt to control staple materials"); Robintech, Inc. v. Chemidus Wavin Ltd., 628 F.2d 142, 149, 205 U.S.P.Q. 873 (D.C. Cir. 1980).

251. 314 U.S. 488, 52 U.S.P.Q. 30 (1942).

7. Under antitrust law, can it ever be a violation to unilaterally refuse to deal commercially with a party?[252] Is refusal to grant a patent license like this or not? Note that under antitrust law, having a patent created a presumption of having market power. However, the Patent Misuse Reform Act of 1988 changed that presumption for patent misuse and the Supreme Court then extended that change to antitrust law.[253]
8. The Court in *R & H* discusses the granting of an implied patent license with the sale of a non-staple article of commerce. What is that? How does it relate to contributory infringement?[254]
9. The Court also discusses "repair" versus "reconstruction" and the Supreme Court case *Aro I*.[255] How does this relate to contributory infringement? Does it relate to an implied patent license?[256]

* * *

If the component is capable of substantial noninfringing use, there would be no liability for contributory infringement; however, there may be liability for inducing infringement in that instance.[257] A use that is not unusual, far-fetched, illusory, impractical, occasional, aberrant, or experimental is a substantial noninfringing use.[258] The statutory language, legislative history, and case law indicate that if an article is not suitable for substantial noninfringing use, then the article is not a staple article or commodity of commerce.

A tricky issue relates to how to apply this test to a complex product that has several components, one of which is specially adapted to infringe, but in which other components are not. This issue, however, appears to have been resolved by the Federal Circuit. For example, in *Lucent Technologies, Inc. v. Gateway, Inc.*, the Federal Circuit indicated that the issue is "whether the 'material or apparatus' is the entire software package or just the particular tool (e.g., the calendar date-picker [the accused product in the case]) that performs the claimed method."[259] The Federal Circuit stated:

---

252. *See* Aspen Skiing v. Aspen Highlands Skiing, 472 U.S. 585 (1985).
253. *See* Ill. Tool Works Inc. v. Independent Ink, Inc., 547 U.S. 28 (2006).
254. *See* Met-coil Sys. Corp. v. Korners Unlimited, Inc., 803 F.2d 684 (Fed. Cir. 1986).
255. Aro Mfg. Co., Inc. v. Convertible Top Co., 365 U.S. 336 (1961).
256. *See, e.g.*, Kendall Co. v. Progressive Med. Tech., Inc., 85 F.3d 1570, 38 U.S.P.Q.2d 1917 (Fed. Cir. 1996).
257. See later in this chapter addressing inducing patent infringement; *see, e.g.*, Toshiba Corp. v. Imation Corp., 681 F.3d 1358 (Fed. Cir. 2012).
258. *See, e.g.*, Nalco Co. v. Chem-Mod, LLC, 883 F.3d 1337, 1357 (Fed. Cir. 2018) ("A substantial noninfringing use is any use that is 'not unusual, far-fetched, illusory, impractical, occasional, aberrant, or experimental.'").
259. 580 F.3d 1301, 1320 (Fed. Cir. 2009), *cert. denied*, 560 U.S. 935 (2010).

> One example illustrates the problem with Microsoft's approach. Consider a software program comprising five—and only five—features. Each of the five features is separately and distinctly patented using a method claim. That is, the first feature infringes a method claim in a first patent, the second feature infringes a method claim in a second patent, and so forth. Assume also that the company selling the software doesn't provide specific instructions on how to use the five features, thus taking potential liability outside the realm of § 271(b). In this scenario, under Microsoft's position, the software seller can never be liable for contributory infringement of any one of the method patents because the entire software program is capable of substantial noninfringing use. This seems both untenable as a practical outcome and inconsistent with both the statute and governing precedent.[260]

Thus, such a situation will generally not prevent contributory infringement from being applicable—for this particular case, the test was applied to the particular accused tool rather than the entire software program.[261]

To illustrate more clearly the benefits of direct infringement over indirect infringement, we will work through a few examples in the next few sections. As stated, one who knowingly sells a component of a claim that is a non-staple article of commerce (i.e., not capable of substantial noninfringing use) may be liable for contributory infringement. Typically, this may involve selling a component of an apparatus claim or selling an apparatus or component capable of performing a method claim.

If the component is capable of substantial noninfringing use there would be no liability for contributory infringement; however, there may be liability for inducing infringement.[262] Rather than a non-staple article, the component would be a staple article of commerce. An article capable of substantial noninfringing uses is a staple article of commerce.

Sale of a staple article by itself, even with knowledge that it will be used in a manner that will directly infringe a patent claim, is not sufficient to establish liability for inducing infringement.[263] However, additional activities may be sufficient. For example, encouraging use in a manner that will directly infringe

260. *Id.*

261. *Cf.* Vita-Mix Corp. v. Basic Holding, Inc., 581 F.3d 1317 (Fed. Cir. 2009) (regarding contributory infringement, use was in a noninfringing manner because the claim recited "not merely additional separable features" but, instead, "defining features of the device").

262. *See, e.g., Toshiba Corp.*, 681 F.3d 1358.

263. *See* Takeda Pharms. U.S.A., Inc. v. West-Ward Pharm. Corp., 785 F.3d 625 (Fed. Cir. 2015); Tegal Corp. v. Tokyo Electron Co., Ltd., 248 F.3d 1376, 58 U.S.P.Q.2d 1791 (Fed. Cir. 2001) ("Facilitation. . . . In the absence of a showing of control over another party, merely permitting that party to commit infringing acts does not constitute infringement, and it likewise cannot constitute 'facilitating infringing acts.'").

with the appropriate knowledge, such as via instructions, as one example, is sufficient.[264]

Thus, it is not required that a *non*-staple article of commerce be sold in order to make out a claim for indirect infringement.

Component of a Method Claim

Consider a situation involving method claim 1 from Example 2.7. This claim was introduced in Chapter 2.

EXAMPLE 5.5

I claim:

1. A method of forming a virtual broadcast domain by virtually linking at least a first broadcast domain with at least a second broadcast domain in which the at least a first broadcast domain and the at least a second broadcast domain are physically separate, the method comprising:

   communicating one or more signal packets between respective physically separate broadcast domains *via respective gateway devices* included in the respective physically separate broadcast domains, wherein the communicating the one or more signal packets comprises:

      encapsulating the one or more signal packets in the respective physically separate broadcast domains; and

      communicating the encapsulated signal packets between the respective gateway devices and at least one tunnel server so that the one or more signal packets are communicated between the respective physically separate broadcast domains.

Suppose a networking competitor, to the patentee who owns the patent that includes claim 1, sells a gateway device in accordance with claim 1. For example, the competitor may establish a network for a business customer. A gateway device is really a computer loaded with software that in operation

264. *See, e.g.*, Arthrocare Corp. v. Smith & Nephew, Inc., 406 F.3d 1465 (Fed. Cir. 2005) (affirming a "jury's induced infringement verdict where defendant distributed 'sales literature' and 'manuals' that instructed how to use product in infringing manner").

results in infringement of claim 1. Thus, in this hypothetical, the competitor sells the computers and software to establish the virtual broadcast domain recited in claim 1.

The business customer for whom the network was established is a direct infringer such that the aspect of a claim to contributory infringement requiring direct infringement is met. The patentee may sue both the business customer and the competitor. However, the patentee may be more interested in suing or stopping the competitor than the competitor's customer. Perhaps the patentee only sues the competitor, for example. Note that the competitor is fully liable for the customer's direct infringement. As joint tortfeasors, the customer and competitor are joint and severally liable.

The patentee must also establish that the competitor knew of the patent and knew that use of the component would result in infringement of the method claim. Unless the patentee specifically provided notice to the competitor previously, the patentee may be out of luck. It may be that the competitor did not know of the patent at the time it sold the gateway device and, perhaps, assembled the network. For example, the patentee may have found out about the network after it was created and then put the competitor on notice. *Of course, the direct infringement likely continues through use of the network by the customer (this is a method of using claim). However, direct patent infringement alone, of course, does not establish contributory infringement.* Unless the competitor sets up *another* network resulting in *use after* being put on notice or there is a basis to believe the competitor *will continue sales* of such networks/gateway devices that result in *use after* being put on notice, the intent needed would not be present. Thus, intent or knowledge is a significant hurdle to establish a claim for contributory infringement *even for continued direct infringement of the method claim if the direct infringement is use by the customer/direct infringer.*

It, however, is pretty clear that the gateway device is a material part of the invention since it implements much of the functionality claimed.

Even assuming "knowledge" could be established, there remains the issue of substantial noninfringing use. There is little doubt that a computer loaded with networking software is capable of doing things other than infringe claim 1. Thus, the competitor will argue that the product sold, the gateway device, is a staple article of commerce.

Fortunately, *Lucent v. Gateway*[265] supports the argument for contributory infringement despite the potential for these other capabilities. Likewise, one could simply take the position that the networking software, rather than the

265. See discussion of this case previously in this chapter.

gateway device, meets the elements for contributory infringement. However, it may be that the networking software itself has substantial noninfringing uses. This is clearly a factual issue needing resolution. Thus, contributory infringement here is not necessarily a slam dunk. There are significant factual issues that impact the legal analysis requiring investigation and resolution.

Now, compare the preceding situation with asserting a claim directed only to the gateway device or only to the software.

Claim Drafting Problem

See if you can draft an apparatus claim to a gateway device that would be directly infringed in the hypothetical and a claim to networking software that would be directly infringed in the hypothetical.[266]

Here, for such a claim, there would be no requirement of intent or of no substantial noninfringing use for these claims.

Such claims would be much easier to assert and prove regarding direct infringement than the method claim of Example 5.5 regarding contributory infringement. While claims for indirect infringement certainly have value, it should be apparent that to provide good representation one should try to craft claims, assuming the client approves and has available budget, of course, that would be directly infringed, even if those claims are directed to a component, rather than to the ultimate end product.

One should also appreciate that with respect to the initial method claim 1 of Example 5.5, the component sold (i.e., gateway device), even assuming it is a *non*-staple article of commerce *not* capable of substantial noninfringing use (it is a product that sale thereof may amount to contributory infringement), is technically an *unpatented* product. As such, before the 1952 act, attempting to assert a patent claim against such a product, such as a component of a claim, in some courts may have amounted to patent misuse. However, subsection 271(d) of the 1952 act (which remains in the current statute) clarified that bringing such a claim is no longer patent misuse.[267]

Component of an Apparatus Claim

Now consider a situation involving apparatus claim 1 from Example 2.6.[268]

266. See the examples in Chapter 2, specifically Examples 2.8 and 2.10.
267. *See* Dawson Chem. Co. v. Rohm & Haas Co., 448 U.S. 176 (1980).
268. This is another example from Chapter 2.

EXAMPLE 5.6

I claim:

1. An apparatus comprising:

   random access memory (RAM), a memory controller, a central processing unit (CPU), and a system transfer bus;

   wherein the memory controller is capable of initiating burst mode operation based, at least in part, on receipt of a request from the CPU;

   wherein the request is to include a memory address, a word count, and a read or a write control transfer designation; and

   wherein the memory controller is to process the request and take control of the system transfer bus.

For this situation, consider a competitor who is selling memory with a memory controller[269] that would infringe claim 1 of Example 2.6 from Chapter 2 (shown here as Example 5.6) if combined with the other claim elements in the manner recited in that claim. The analysis should be quite similar to the last example, although the facts may, of course, affect the analysis. First, imagine that a memory manufacturer who competes with a patentee memory manufacturer supplies the memory and memory controller to a company that integrates this into a computing system with a CPU, system transfer bus, and so on. Again, direct infringement is established by the activities of the company that is performing the integration. However, the patentee may not want to sue that party, who may even be a current customer. Rather, the patentee would prefer to sue its competitor, another memory manufacturer.

Now, a much trickier situation might be if the company performing integration is a foreign entity performing the integration outside the United States. Technically, there is no infringement under subsection 271(a) by virtue of the assembly abroad, thus meaning no indirect infringement under subsection 271(c).[270] However, fortunately, there are other subsections of § 271 to address this.[271]

---

269. The claim might have been limited to the memory controller, but it would be unusual to sell a memory controller without the memory it is intended to operate on the same IC.

270. *See* Deepsouth Packing Co. v. Laitram Corp., 406 U.S. 518, 528 (1972).

271. 35 U.S.C. § 271(f) (2024) states:

> (1) Whoever without authority supplies or causes to be supplied in or from the United States all or a substantial portion of the components of a patented invention, where such

Assuming this is not a foreign entity situation, much like the analysis regarding the component of the method claim, the patentee must establish that the competitor knew of the patent and knew that using the component in the recited combination would result in infringement of the apparatus claim in this example. Unless the patentee specifically previously provided notice to the competitor, again, the patentee may be challenged here. It may be that the competitor did not know of the patent. For example, the patentee may have found out about a system to implement burst mode using memory and a memory controller manufactured by someone else (here, perhaps even a customer) *after* the sale. However, in this situation, in comparison with the preceding method example, *if more direct infringement of the apparatus claim continues after notice is provided, such as via additional making and/or selling of the claimed combination by the customer, for example, then it may be possible to establish intent for contributory infringement.* The competitor may provide the memory and controller for an infringing system to be made and/or sold by the direct infringer *again after* the competitor has been put on notice. The difference from the previous example is that the claim directly infringed here is an apparatus claim rather than a method claim. In the previous example, the claim at issue, shown in Example 5.5, was a method claim. Thus, continued direct infringement, here, additional sales of infringing systems, after notice, necessarily results in the intent needed for contributory infringement. On the other hand, in the previous example, continued direct infringement of a method claim after notice does not necessarily implicate intent for contributory infringement. For the method claim example, the competitor may not necessarily engage in another sale to its customer resulting in a directly infringing use of the method claim for which the notice needed for contributory infringement had

---

components are uncombined in whole or in part, in such manner as to actively induce the combination of such components outside of the United States in a manner that would infringe the patent if such combination occurred within the United States, shall be liable as an infringer.

(2) Whoever without authority supplies or causes to be supplied in or from the United States any component of a patented invention that is especially made or especially adapted for use in the invention and not a staple article or commodity of commerce suitable for substantial noninfringing use, where such component is uncombined in whole or in part, knowing that such component is so made or adapted and intending that such component will be combined outside of the United States in a manner that would infringe the patent if such combination occurred within the United States, shall be liable as an infringer.

Section (1) is similar to inducement and section (2) is similar to contributory infringement. See also *Waymark Corp. v. Porta Systems Corp.*, 245 F.3d 1364 (Fed. Cir. 2001), regarding liability under subsection 271(f)(2) for exportation of a component, in which the court noted that "infringement without a completed infringing embodiment is not the norm in patent law, but it is reasonable in the context of 271(f)(2)."

been provided. Of course, in that example, another sale to *another* customer who then directly infringes after appropriate notice may result in contributory infringement.

For this apparatus claim, the memory and memory controller likely constitute a material part of the invention since they implement much of the functionality claimed.

Assuming knowledge could be established, as suggested, there remains the issue of substantial noninfringing use. For this situation, this issue may present a greater challenge than establishing "knowledge," discussed earlier, although it really depends on details regarding the memory controller. For example, could the memory and memory controller work with a system that does *not* implement burst mode? Have there been examples of such sales? Is it possible to turn burst mode operation *off* while still performing memory operations one cell at a time? These are all important questions for resolution. If the answers are yes, it may be that the memory and memory controller together are capable of substantial noninfringing use. Of course, all is not lost, because there may still be a basis for asserting a claim of inducing infringement.[272]

Now, compare the preceding situation with asserting a claim directed only to the memory and memory controller.

Claim Drafting Problem

See if you can draft an apparatus claim to memory and the memory controller that would be directly infringed in the aforementioned hypothetical.[273]

Here, for such a claim, there would be no requirement of intent or of no substantial noninfringing use for these claims.

Such a claim would be much easier to assert and prove regarding direct infringement than the apparatus claim of Example 5.6 regarding contributory infringement. While claims for indirect infringement certainly have value, it should be apparent that to provide good representation one should try to craft claims, assuming the client approves and has available budget, of course, that would be directly infringed, even if those claims are directed to a component, rather than to the ultimate end product.

---

272. See later in this chapter addressing inducing patent infringement.

273. See the examples in Chapter 2, specifically Examples 2.2 and further examples that follow. Observe that if the memory controller is sold stand-alone, then we would not have direct infringement, but, again, an indirect infringement claim. However, since memory is almost always sold with an *embedded* controller, this should not be an issue. Nonetheless, someone very conservative might prefer a claim only to the memory controller.

As suggested, a claim that meets the claim drafting problem mentioned earlier avoids the potential issues associated with asserting contributory infringement. There is no need to show knowledge or that there is no substantial noninfringing use. It should be much clearer now why there is less case law on indirect infringement than direct infringement. It may be a challenge to establish indirect infringement. If one has a claim of direct infringement, that claim is more likely to be pursued. Typically, of course, both are asserted in a lawsuit if the facts for both are present.

One should also appreciate that with respect to the initial apparatus claim 1 of Example 5.6, the component sold, even assuming it is a *non*-staple article of commerce *not* capable of substantial noninfringing use (it is a product that sale thereof may amount to contributory infringement), is technically an *unpatented* product, if sold by itself. As such, before the 1952 act, attempting to assert a patent claim against such a product, such as a component of a claim, in some courts may have amounted to patent misuse. However, subsection 271(d) of the 1952 act (which remains in the current statute) clarified that bringing such a claim is no longer patent misuse.[274]

Inducing Infringement

35 U.S.C. § 271(b)

Whoever actively induces infringement of a patent shall be liable as an infringer.

Global-Tech Appliances, Inc. v. SEB S.A.
563 U.S. 754
Supreme Court of the United States
February 23, 2011, Argued; May 31, 2011, Decided

Questions

1. For active inducement under subsection 271(b), does the Court require knowledge of the patent *and* knowledge that the acts of the tortfeasor would lead to direct infringement? The statutory language is unclear; what, therefore, would be an argument for such an interpretation? How compelling is it for the Court to rely on its prior interpretation of subsection 271(c)? Can you think of a policy reason why it may make sense to require knowledge of the patent?
2. What did the Court actually hold here? Note this language:

274. *See* Dawson Chem. Co. v. Rohm & Haas Co., 448 U.S. 176 (1980).

> This language [referring to subsection 271(c)] contains exactly the same ambiguity as § 271(b). The phrase "knowing [a component] to be especially made or especially adapted for use in an infringement" may be read to mean that a violator must know that the component is "especially adapted for use" in a product that happens to infringe a patent. Or the phrase may be read to require, in addition, knowledge of the patent's existence.[275]

3. Thus, while the Court is called upon to address whether knowledge of the patent is required for active inducement, the Court appears to treat it as given that the intent standard is that a violator must *know* that it induced the acts in question. However, might it be that active inducement requires the violator to purposefully induce the acts in question (but with knowledge of the patent, as the Court ultimately ruled)?[276] Are there any logical reasons why one might argue this aspect of the intent for active inducement should be higher than for contributory infringement? Reread the Court's description of the pre-1952 law. What level of intent do those cases appear to require for this aspect of active inducement?
4. How does one prove the requisite level of intent? Does this perhaps suggest the Court went further than needed when it chose to address willful blindness? If so, does this make the ruling on willful blindness in this context mere dicta? Why or why not?
5. Why do you think the Court may have chosen to address willful blindness even if it was not clearly required?
6. Note the dissent's impassioned view that the Court should not have addressed willful blindness. Yet, it does appear true that willful blindness is accepted as equivalent to knowledge in criminal cases. Does this suggest that it should be more likely or less likely to be the case in a civil suit? Why?
7. If the level of intent for active inducement had been ruled to require that one must purposefully intend to induce the acts in question, would willful blindness still arguably be sufficient? Why or why not? Is there still room to argue for a higher level of intent (i.e., that active inducement requires purposeful intent to induce the acts in question) as a requirement for inducement after this case? Why or why not?

---

275. Global-Tech Appliances, Inc. v. SEB S.A., 563 U.S. 754, 764 (2011).

276. *Cf.* Hewlett-Packard Co. v. Bausch & Lomb Inc., 909 F.2d 1464 (Fed. Cir. 1990) (opinion by Rich, J.).

Commil USA, LLC v. Cisco Systems, Inc.
575 U.S. 632
Supreme Court of the United States
March 31, 2015, Argued; May 26, 2015, Decided

Questions

1. Observe the Supreme Court's clarification of its *Global-Tech* decision. This was done in response to the government attempting to suggest a lower scienter requirement as to the infringing acts for active inducement (as opposed to knowledge of the patent). However, does the Supreme Court necessarily foreclose a higher scienter requirement or is it pretty clear that after this decision, the scienter requirement for the infringing acts is knowledge?
2. What the decision, of course, is known for is that good faith belief that a patent is invalid is not a defense to inducement. Note the dissent by Justice Scalia. Which opinion do you find more persuasive, the majority or the dissent? Why?
3. Either way, of course, the law is now clear that a good faith belief in invalidity is not a defense. Note the analogies with other areas of law. Do you find the analogies persuasive? Is this a mistake of law or a mistake of fact?
4. Also, how practical are the Court's suggestions that one could seek a ruling as to invalidity via declaratory judgment or reexamination? Does it seem odd that "any accused infringer who believes the patent in suit is invalid may raise the affirmative defense of invalidity," yet a good faith belief that a patent is invalid is not a defense? Why or why not?
5. Practically speaking, it is common for potential infringers to seek written opinions that a patent is invalid and/or not infringed. However, note that both for direct infringement and, in light of this case, for indirect infringement, those opinions are not exculpatory, meaning that if the opinion turns out to be wrong, it does not relieve the accused infringer of liability. So why are those opinions sought?[277]
6. It is not uncommon, if accused of infringing a patent, to reply that after careful study the accused infringer believes that it (as in an entity) "infringes no valid claim of the patent." However, the Supreme Court

277. *See* 35 U.S.C. § 384.

goes out of its way to say that patent invalidity and patent infringement are completely separate legal issues. It states:

> To say that an invalid patent cannot be infringed, or that someone cannot be induced to infringe an invalid patent, is in one sense a simple truth, both as a matter of logic and semantics. See *M. Swift & Sons, Inc. v. W. H. Coe Mfg. Co.*, 102 F.2d 391, 396 (C.A.1 1939). But the questions courts must address when interpreting and implementing the statutory framework require a determination of the procedures and sequences that the parties must follow to prove the act of wrongful inducement and any related issues of patent validity. "Validity and infringement are distinct issues, bearing different burdens, different presumptions, and different evidence." 720 F.3d, at 1374 (opinion of Newman, J.).[278]

Why then is it helpful to phrase it that way, and how does this relate to liability?

* * *

Subsection 271(b) states: "Whoever actively induces infringement of a patent shall be liable as an infringer." Thus, inducing patent infringement is actively and knowingly aiding and abetting the direct patent infringement of another.[279] As with contributory infringement, direct patent infringement is required for a claim of inducing patent infringement, but direct infringement may be established by circumstantial evidence.[280]

The intent requirement for inducing patent infringement has not been entirely consistent over the years but appears to have been resolved to be knowledge of the patent and knowledge that the acts induced would result in direct patent infringement.[281] Intent for indirect infringement may also be proven by circumstantial evidence.[282]

---

278. Commil USA, LLC v. Cisco Sys., 575 U.S. 632, 644 (2015).

279. *See* Nat'l Presto Indus., Inc. v. W. Bend Co., 76 F.3d 1185, 1194, 37 U.S.P.Q.2d 1685, 1691 (Fed. Cir. 1996) ("The statutory liability for inducement of infringement derives from the common law, wherein acts that the actor knows will lead to the commission of a wrong by another, place shared liability for the wrong on the actor.").

280. *See* Limelight Networks, Inc. v. Akamai Techs., Inc., 572 U.S. 915 (2014). Note that an act of indirect infringement by inducement could occur *outside* the United States and still result in liability if the induced activity was a direct infringement in the United States.

281. See *Life Technologies Corp. v. Promega Corp.*, 137 S. Ct. 734 (2017), in which the Supreme Court stated in a footnote that, in *Global-Tech*, it had "substantially equat[ed] the intent requirements for §§ 271(b) and 271(c)."

282. Metabolite Laby's, Inc. v. Lab'y Corp. of Am. Holdings, 370 F.3d 1354, 71 U.S.P.Q.2d 1081 (Fed. Cir. 2004) (A "patentee may prove such intent through circumstantial evidence.").

Legislative history suggests that inducement and contributory infringement should be seen as complementary causes of action.[283] Thus, while sale of a staple article of commerce will not result in liability under subsection 271(c), it may, in appropriate circumstances, result in liability under subsection 271(b).[284]

Subsection 271(b) sweeps in a broad range of acts. One court articulated it as follows:

> [C]ivil culpability need not stop with the dealer who does the final act of making, using or selling. The prohibition of the law, now codified in § 271(b), extends to those who induce that infringement. Of course inducement has connotations of active steps knowingly taken—knowingly at least in the sense of purposeful, intentional, as distinguished from accidental or inadvertent. But with that qualifying approach, the term is as broad as the range of actions by which one in fact causes, or urges, or encourages, or aids another to infringe a patent.[285]

Examples include advertising, such as advertising that communicates or encourages compliance with an infringing standard; providing instructions, such as distributing sales literature and manuals that instruct how to use a product in an infringing manner;[286] certain types of repair (e.g., that legally amount to reconstruction of a patented product) of an otherwise infringing product;[287] design of an infringing product;[288] and so on.

If the component is capable of substantial noninfringing use there would be no liability for contributory infringement; however, there may be liability for inducing infringement.[289] Rather than a non-staple article, the component

---

283. *See, e.g.*, Hewlett-Packard Co. v. Bausch & Lomb Inc., 909 F.2d 1464 (Fed. Cir. 1990).

284. *Compare* Warner-Lambert Co. v. Apotex Corp., 316 F.3d 1348 (Fed. Cir. 2003) ("Especially where a product has substantial noninfringing uses, intent to induce infringement cannot be inferred even when the defendant has actual knowledge that some users of its product may be infringing the patent."), *with* Toshiba Corp. v. Imation Corp., 681 F.3d 1358 (Fed. Cir. 2012) ("existence of a substantial non-infringing use does not preclude liability for active inducement").

285. *See* Fromberg, Inc. v. Thornhill, 315 F.2d 407, 411, 137 U.S.P.Q. 84 (5th Cir. 1963).

286. *See* Ericsson, Inc. v. D-Link Sys., Inc., 773 F.3d 1201 (Fed. Cir. 2014) (affirming a "jury's induced infringement verdict where defendant advertised compliance with an infringing standard"); Arthrocare Corp. v. Smith & Nephew, Inc., 406 F.3d 1465 (Fed. Cir. 2005) (affirming a "jury's induced infringement verdict where defendant distributed 'sales literature' and 'manuals' that instructed how to use product in infringing manner").

287. *See, e.g.*, Aro Mfg. Co. v. Convertible Top Replacement Co., 377 U.S. 476 (1964).

288. *See* Ricoh Co., Ltd. v. Quanta Comput. Inc., 550 F.3d 1325, 1342–43 (Fed. Cir. 2008), *cert. denied*, 129 S. Ct. 2864 (2009).

289. *See, e.g.*, *Toshiba Corp.*, 681 F.3d 1358.

would be a staple article of commerce. An article capable of substantial noninfringing uses is a staple article of commerce.

Sale of a staple article by itself, even with knowledge that it will be used in a manner that will directly infringe a patent claim, is not sufficient to establish liability for inducing infringement.[290] However, additional activities may be sufficient, such as the previous examples. Encouraging use in a manner that will directly infringe with the appropriate knowledge, such as via instructions, as one example, is sufficient.[291]

Thus, it is not required that a *non*-staple article of commerce be sold in order to make out a claim for indirect infringement.

Inducing Infringement of a Method Claim

Consider a situation involving method claim 1 from Example 5.7.

EXAMPLE 5.7

I claim:

1. A method of forming a virtual private network comprising:

   communicating one or more signal packets between respective physically separate broadcast domains via a computing device included in the respective physically separate broadcast domains, wherein the communicating the one or more signal packets comprises:

      encapsulating the one or more signal packets in the respective physically separate broadcast domains to be communicated; and

      communicating the encapsulated signal packets between the respective computing devices and at least one tunnel server so that the one or more signal packets are communicated between the respective physically separate broadcast domains.

---

290. *See* Takeda Pharms. U.S.A., Inc. v. West-Ward Pharm. Corp., 785 F.3d 625 (Fed. Cir. 2015); Tegal Corp. v. Tokyo Electron Co., Ltd., 248 F.3d 1376, 58 U.S.P.Q.2d 1791 (Fed. Cir. 2001) ("Facilitation. . . . In the absence of a showing of control over another party, merely permitting that party to commit infringing acts does not constitute infringement, and it likewise cannot constitute 'facilitating infringing acts.'").

291. *See, e.g.*, *Arthrocare Corp.*, 406 F.3d 1465 (affirming a "jury's induced infringement verdict where defendant distributed 'sales literature' and 'manuals' that instructed how to use product in infringing manner").

Again, suppose a networking competitor, to the patentee who owns the patent that includes claim 1, provides instructions to a business customer on implementation of a computing device in accordance with claim 1. The competitor may not necessarily sell the computers to establish the virtual broadcast domain recited in claim 1 but may direct a customer to a source along with implementation instructions or may perform the assembly, such as installing software, once the appropriate components are purchased.

Now, the business customer for whom this network is established is a direct infringer such that the aspect of a claim to inducing infringement requiring direct infringement is met. Thus, the patentee may sue various parties, including the business customer, the networking competitor, and the party supplying the hardware. Note that all these parties, some with requisite intent,[292] are fully liable, as joint tortfeasors. Still, the patentee gets to choose whether to sue one, some, or all.

The patentee must establish that the parties (other than the direct infringer) being sued knew of the patent and that assembly or implementing the instructions would result in infringement of the method claim. However, it may be that no one involved knew of the patent initially. If the patentee found out about the network after it was established and then put the parties on notice, the direct infringement may continue, as in prior examples.

However, this does not address the issue regarding intent or knowledge regarding the inducement claim. This element would not be met unless another network is set up and sold by the parties resulting in infringing use *after* being put on notice or if there is a basis to believe the parties will continue to perform assembly or distribute instructions resulting in infringing use *after* being put on notice. Thus, as with contributory patent infringement, intent or knowledge is a significant hurdle to establish a claim for inducing patent infringement.

Now, recall, in our previous example, it was not entirely clear whether a computing device (i.e., a gateway device in Example 5.5) or even the software installed necessarily has no substantial noninfringing uses. For example, there is little doubt that a computer loaded with networking software is capable of doing things other than infringe claim 1. Thus, the competitor will argue that the product sold is a staple article of commerce. Although *Lucent v. Gateway*[293] supports the argument for contributory infringement despite the potential for these other capabilities, it may be that even the networking software itself has substantial noninfringing uses.

---

292. No intent is required for the direct infringer.

293. See the discussion of this case previously in this chapter.

However, unlike contributory infringement, there is no need to establish the lack of substantial noninfringing uses. This is helpful here because factual issues remain, as previously described, regarding whether this could be satisfied to meet contributory infringement. Note therefore that for inducement, more is required than simply a sale with knowledge that it may be used in an infringing manner.[294] Rather, some act must occur to further the infringement, such as providing instructions on how to use the software in a manner that would infringe.

Claim Drafting Problem

See if you can draft an apparatus claim to a computing device or to networking software on a storage medium that would be directly infringed in the aforementioned hypothetical.

Here, for such a claim, there would be no requirement of intent, as in contributory patent infringement and inducing patent infringement. Such a claim would be much easier to assert and prove regarding direct infringement than the method claim of Example 5.7 with respect to inducing patent infringement, for example. While claims for indirect infringement certainly have value, it should be apparent that to provide good representation one should try to craft claims, assuming the client approves and has available budget, of course, that would be directly infringed, even if those claims are directed to a component, rather than to the ultimate end product.

As suggested, a claim that meets the previous claim drafting problem avoids the potential issues associated with asserting inducing patent infringement. There is no need to show knowledge of the patent and knowledge that the acts induced are infringing acts. It should be much clearer now why there is less case law on indirect infringement than direct infringement. It may be a challenge to establish indirect infringement. If one has a claim of direct infringement, that claim is more likely to be pursued. Typically, of course, both are asserted in a lawsuit if the facts for both are present.

---

294. *See Takeda Pharms.*, 785 F.3d 625; *Tegal Corp.*, 248 F.3d 1376, 58 U.S.P.Q.2d 1791 ("Facilitation. . . . In the absence of a showing of control over another party, merely permitting that party to commit infringing acts does not constitute infringement, and it likewise cannot constitute 'facilitating infringing acts.'").

Inducing Infringement of an Apparatus Claim

Now consider another situation involving apparatus claim 1 from Example 5.8.

EXAMPLE 5.8

I claim:

1. An apparatus comprising:

   random access memory (RAM), a memory controller, a central processing unit (CPU), and a system transfer bus;

   wherein the memory controller is capable of initiating burst mode operation based, at least in part, on receipt of a request from the CPU;

   wherein the request is to include a memory address, a word count, and a read or a write control transfer designation; and

   wherein the memory controller is to process the request and take control of the system transfer bus.

For this situation, consider, again, a competitor who is selling memory with a memory controller[295] that would infringe claim 1 if combined with the other claim elements in the manner recited. As before, a memory manufacturer who competes with a patentee memory manufacturer supplies the memory and memory controller to a company that integrates this into a computing system with a CPU, system bus, and so on. Again, direct infringement is established by activities of the company that performs the integration. However, again, the patentee may not want to sue that party, who may even be a current customer. Rather, the patentee would like to sue its competitor.

As before, if the company performing the integration is a foreign entity performing the integration outside the United States, technically, there is no infringement under subsection 271(a) by virtue of the assembly abroad, thus,

295. The analysis might be limited to the memory controller but it would be unusual to sell a memory controller without the memory if it is intended to operate embedded on the same IC.

meaning no indirect infringement under subsection 271(b).[296] However, fortunately, there are other subsections of § 271 to address this.[297]

Assuming this is not a foreign entity situation, for inducing infringement, as for contributory infringement, the patentee must establish that the competitor knew of the patent and knew that using the component in the recited combination would result in infringement of the apparatus claim in this example. It may be that the competitor did not know of the patent. For example, the patentee may have only *after* a sale found out about a system to implement burst mode using memory and a memory controller manufactured by someone else. Thus, the patentee may have provided notice after the sale. However, in this situation, in comparison with the previous method example, if direct infringement continues after notice is provided, which is reasonably likely, then it may be possible to establish intent. The competitor will likely provide the memory and controller for an infringing system again *after* being put on notice. Continued direct infringement of the previous method claim, in comparison, does not necessarily provide a basis for asserting inducement (unless by an infringing sale) if the knowledge was not present at the time of the inducement.

As was noted for subsection 271(c), assuming knowledge could be established, there may be decent arguments of substantial noninfringing uses for the memory and memory controller depending on the facts. Thus, there may

296. *See* Deepsouth Packing Co. v. Laitram Corp., 406 U.S. 518, 528 (1972).

297. 35 U.S.C. § 271(f) (2024) states:

> (1) Whoever without authority supplies or causes to be supplied in or from the United States all or a substantial portion of the components of a patented invention, where such components are uncombined in whole or in part, in such manner as to actively induce the combination of such components outside of the United States in a manner that would infringe the patent if such combination occurred within the United States, shall be liable as an infringer.
>
> (2) Whoever without authority supplies or causes to be supplied in or from the United States any component of a patented invention that is especially made or especially adapted for use in the invention and not a staple article or commodity of commerce suitable for substantial noninfringing use, where such component is uncombined in whole or in part, knowing that such component is so made or adapted and intending that such component will be combined outside of the United States in a manner that would infringe the patent if such combination occurred within the United States, shall be liable as an infringer.

Section (1) is similar to inducement and section (2) is similar to contributory infringement. See also *Waymark Corp. v. Porta Systems Corp.*, 245 F.3d 1364 (Fed. Cir. 2001), regarding liability under subsection 271(f)(2) for exportation of a component, in which the court noted that "infringement without a completed infringing embodiment is not the norm in patent law, but it is reasonable in the context of 271(f)(2)."

be no claim of contributory infringement. For example, could the memory and memory controller work with a system that does *not* implement burst mode? Have there been examples of such sales? Is it possible to turn burst mode operation *off*? These are all important questions for resolution. If the answers are yes, it may be that the memory and memory controller together are capable of substantial noninfringing use.

Nonetheless, this may be an inducing infringement situation, under subsection 271(b). It is likely that with the memory and memory controller instructions on use are provided. If so, it is well established, assuming the requisite knowledge, this is sufficient to establish inducing infringement.[298]

Claim Drafting Problem

Now, see if you can draft an apparatus claim directed only to the memory and a memory controller.[299] As suggested with the prior example, this claim avoids the potential issues associated with proving intent or active inducement.

Direct, Nonliteral Infringement

Previously, direct, literal patent infringement was discussed along with claim drafting principles that emanate from legal doctrines associated with direct, literal infringement and claim construction. Now, we discuss direct, nonliteral patent infringement, also known as the "doctrine of equivalents," and principles for claim drafting that emanate from legal doctrines around the DOE.

Doctrine of Equivalents and Its Limits

We begin with an overview of the DOE. As with indirect patent infringement, the DOE introduces more legal hurdles to finding patent infringement than direct, literal patent infringement. Thus, the latter is preferred. Nonetheless, the world of patent infringement is not always ideal. For example, a case filed as a claim for direct, literal infringement may become a DOE case after some discovery. Generally, claims under the DOE are today viewed as weaker than

---

298. *See, e.g.*, Arthrocare Corp. v. Smith & Nephew, Inc., 406 F.3d 1465 (Fed. Cir. 2005) (affirming a "jury's induced infringement verdict where defendant distributed 'sales literature' and 'manuals' that instructed how to use product in infringing manner").

299. If the memory controller is sold stand-alone, then we would not have direct infringement, but, again, an indirect infringement claim. However, since memory is almost always, if not always, sold with an embedded controller, this should not be an issue. Nonetheless, someone very conservative might prefer a claim only to the memory controller.

claims for literal infringement. Notably, however, recently some cases under the DOE have resulted in liability.[300]

When drafting patent claims, although literal infringement is most important, there are ways to potentially increase the chances of liability under the DOE, if that should be needed, as shall be discussed.

At a high level, there are three doctrinal legal considerations that affect whether there might be liability under the DOE. The first is the function-way-result (FWR) test or the insubstantial differences test, the second is prosecution history estoppel (PHE), and the third is how the prior art may limit the scope of the DOE. For example, the Federal Circuit in *Pennwalt Corp. v. Durand-Wayland, Inc.* stated:

> Under the doctrine of equivalents, *infringement may be found (but not necessarily) if an accused device performs substantially the same overall function or work, in substantially the same way, to obtain substantially the same overall result as the claimed invention. Perkin-Elmer Corp. v. Computervision Corp.*, 732 F.2d 888, 901–02, 221 USPQ 669, 679 (Fed. Cir.), *cert. denied*, 469 U.S. 857, 105 S. Ct. 187, 83 L. Ed. 2d 120 (1984); *Graver Tank*, 339 U.S. at 608, 70 S. Ct. at 856. That formulation, however, does not mean one can ignore claim limitations. As this court recently stated in *Perkin-Elmer Corp. v. Westinghouse Elec. Corp.*, 822 F.2d 1528, 3 USPQ2d 1321 (Fed. Cir. 1987):
>
> The doctrine of equivalents is limited in that the doctrine will not extend *(1) to cover an accused device in the prior art, and (2) to allow the patentee to recapture through equivalence certain coverage given up during prosecution. Loctite Corp. v. Ultraseal Ltd.*, 781 F.2d 861, 870, 228 USPQ 90, 96 (Fed. Cir. 1985).[301]

Hence, this quotation outlines the three legal considerations just discussed. Each is addressed in the following sections of this chapter.

Function-Way-Result versus Insubstantial Differences

Warner-Jenkinson Co. v. Hilton Davis Chemical Co.
520 U.S. 17
Supreme Court of the United States
October 15, 1996, Argued; March 3, 1997, Decided

---

300. *See* Eli Lilly & Co. v. Hospira, Inc., 933 F.3d 1320 (Fed. Cir. 2019) (narrowing amendment did not create prosecution history estoppel; no disclosure-dedication; district court did not err in finding insubstantial differences); Ajinomoto Co., Inc. v. Int'l Trade Comm'n, 932 F.3d 1342 (Fed. Cir. 2019) (affirming equivalents determination).

301. Pennwalt Corp. v. Durand-Wayland, Inc., 833 F.2d 931, 934 (Fed. Cir. 1987) (emphasis added).

Questions

1. In *Warner-Jenkinson*, what was the Court's reason for rejecting three of the petitioner's arguments that the DOE did not survive the 1952 patent reform passed by Congress? What was the fourth argument and why did the Court also reject that argument?
2. It is noted that prior to trial, Hilton Davis conceded that that the claim at issue was not literally infringed and so the case proceeded to trial based on the DOE. Can you think of an argument to be made that the claim was literally infringed? If so, why do you think that Hilton Davis, instead, went to trial relying on the DOE? Note that the jury determined that Warner-Jenkinson did infringe under the DOE and the Federal Circuit affirmed, apparently in a sharply divided *en banc* decision.
3. The *Warner-Jenkinson* decision cut back on the DOE in several ways because it had "taken on a life of its own, unbounded by the patent claims." The Court adopted an approach that was apparently discussed in Judge Nies's dissent to the Federal Circuit's ruling discussed later. The Court stated: "It is important to ensure that the application of the doctrine, even as to an individual element, is not allowed such broad play as to effectively eliminate that element in its entirety."[302] What is the approach adopted and how does this new approach ultimately "rein[] in" the DOE, so to speak?
4. Who determines whether something is an equivalent, the judge or the jury? Did the Court ultimately decide this issue or not? If the Court did not decide the issue, what did the Court decide?
5. What are circumstances in which the Court indicated that summary judgment as to no infringement under the DOE would be proper?
6. The Court states that "intent plays no role in the application of the doctrine of equivalents."[303] However, could intent play a role in determining whether there are insubstantial differences between the asserted equivalent and the claim? For example, could evidence of an attempt to design around the patent claim be evidence that is relevant to whether there are insubstantial differences?
7. The Court confirmed, as was stated in *Graver Tank & Manufacturing Co. v. Linde Air Products Co.*,[304] that known interchangeability may play a role in determining whether something is an equivalent.

---

302. Warner-Jenkinson Co. v. Hilton Davis Chem. Co., 520 U.S. 17, 29–30 (1997).
303. *Id.* at 19.
304. 339 U.S. 605 (1950).

However, what is the test the Court determined should be applied to make that determination? Legally, do you believe there is a difference between "insubstantial differences" and the triple identity test, or do you believe the triple identity test is simply one way of determining whether the differences are insubstantial? As of what time is the relevant time for making the determination? How does that compare with the time at which the Court determines the meaning of claim terms to decide whether a claim is infringed literally?

8. How does the Court say that PHE should generally be applied with respect to the DOE? If the reason for an amendment to narrow a patent claim is unable to be ascertained, how does the Court say that prosecution history should be applied? In determining or assessing the reason for an amendment, is that assessment limited to the written record before the PTO?
9. Does the Court address the application of the DOE and PHE where the claim is not amended, but a legal argument is made in the record to distinguish the claim from the prior art? Given the Court's reasoning for situations in which the patent claim is amended, how might you expect these doctrines to be applied in such situations?

* * *

Hilton Davis[305] is a Supreme Court case that reaffirmed the DOE as a fixture of U.S. patent law and also reaffirmed some principles that had emerged from the Federal Circuit; however, it also addressed PHE and introduced new principles around this latter doctrine, as discussed in the next section.

While the Court expressed no particular preference as to the legal test and both the FWR (called the triple identity test by the Court) and the insubstantial differences test have been used by the Federal Circuit, it appears that the FWR test is generally used more frequently.[306]

In general, regarding the FWR test, typically if there is a feature in the accused device argued to be an equivalent of a limitation, it may typically meet the "substantially the same function" component of the FWR test. However, more frequently, that feature fails the "substantially the same way" component of the FWR test.

305. *Hilton Davis*, 520 U.S. 17.

306. This is not based on a formal survey but is rather based on having read a number of DOE cases. *See also* Mas-Hamilton Grp. v. LaGard, Inc., 156 F.3d 1206 (Fed. Cir. 1998) ("One way to determine if substantial differences exist is to apply the function-way-result analysis of Graver Tank . . . .").

This approach by the FWR test is sometimes criticized because saying the feature does not meet "substantially the same way" may simply be little more than saying it does not literally meet the limitation at issue, which will by design usually fail if the criticism is accurate. It is true that the DOE is generally considered weaker than literal infringement; however, whether the equivalent meets "substantially the same way" amounts to a judgment that comprehends the claim language, the specification description, and the prosecution history.[307]

Likewise, whether the argued equivalent meets "substantially the same way," it still must also meet "substantially the same result." For example, the argued equivalent might provide an *inferior* or even a *superior* result compared with the literal claim limitation at issue.

One claim drafting guideline to deduce from the FWR test has been discussed previously in a different context. Previously, we discussed the legal issues associated with functional claiming.[308] Those considerations may be applied here.

As the discussion of the FWR test and the insubstantial differences test suggests, generally limitations that are functional are more likely to be satisfied by the accused device or service with respect to an accused device or service in which a feature is argued to be met by equivalence, assuming the functional language does not result in application of subsection 112(f). A similar observation may be made regarding the insubstantial differences test. To the extent that the limitation is more functional than structural, for example, it seems more likely that the insubstantial differences test may be met as to an accused device or service. Based on the face of the claim, functional limitations appear to be broader than structural limitations; however, it is not always easy to predict whether such limitations will be interpreted as the words appear in the claim due to subsection 112(f).

Resolving this issue requires the exercise of legal judgment. Some claim terms appear to be *sufficiently* structural so as to not invoke subsection 112(f). Further, in some other Federal Circuit cases, functional language was permissibly used and did *not* invoke subsection 112(f).[309] The cases suggest that

---

307. *See* Pennwalt Corp. v. Durand-Wayland, Inc., 833 F.2d 931 (Fed. Cir. 1987) (en banc).

308. *See* Chapter 4.

309. *See, e.g.*, K-2 Corp. v. Salomon S.A., 191 F.3d 1356, 1363 (Fed. Cir. 1999) (functional language "for substantially preventing movement" did not invoke subsection 112(6)); BASF Corp. v. Johnson Matthey Inc., 875 F.3d 1360 (Fed. Cir. 2017) (functional phrase "effective to catalyze" did not involve subsection 112(6)); *see also* Enzo Biochem, Inc. v. Applera Corp., 599 F.3d 1325, 1332–33 (Fed. Cir. 2010), *reh'g and reh'g en banc denied*, 605 F.3d 1347 (Fed. Cir. 2010) ("[W]hen a claim limitation is defined in 'purely functional terms,' a determination of whether

functional language may in some situations properly and appropriately be employed in claims without using the means-plus-function format of subsection 112(f) and without necessarily being interpreted under that subsection. Presumably, despite the functional language, the claim still recited *sufficient* structure to avoid invoking subsection 112(f).

With this in mind, it is suggested a mix of structural and functional language be used so that the claim language at issue is not entirely devoid of structure. Consider Example 2.2 from Chapter 2, although terminology "external" and "externally derived" are added, with claim language such as:

> wherein the memory controller is capable of initiating burst mode operation based, at least in part, on receipt of an externally derived request from an external central processing unit (CPU);
>
> wherein the request is to include a memory address, a word count, and a read or a write control transfer designation; and
>
> wherein the memory controller is to process the request and take control of an external system transfer bus.

The claim, here, recites "the memory controller is capable of initiating burst mode operation" and "the memory controller is to process the request and take control of an external system transfer bus." The term "memory controller" is likely structural, but the other recited limitations are more functional; however, a memory controller may be argued to support such functions.

Example 2.9 from Chapter 2 uses a similar approach reciting "network device," a potentially structural device, but adding functional limitations such as "to emulate," "to encapsulate," and "to communicate." Again, these could be

---

the limitation is sufficiently definite is 'highly dependent on context (e.g., the disclosure in the specification and the knowledge of a person of ordinary skill in the relevant art area).'"); Miken Composites, L.L.C. v. Wilson Sporting Goods Co., 515 F.3d 1331 (Fed. Cir. 2008) (court stated that while the term "insert" has "functional attributes," it was still a structural component); Plastic Container Corp. v. Cont'l Plastics of Okla., Inc., 607 F.2d 885 (10th Cir. 1979), *cert. denied*, 444 U.S. 1018 (1980), *on remand*, 515 F. Supp. 834, 214 U.S.P.Q. 530 (W.D. Okla. 1980), *aff'd in part, rev'd in part*, 708 F.2d 1554, 219 U.S.P.Q. 26 (10th Cir. 1983) ("the idea that functional language ipso facto cannot precisely define novelty in structure was laid to rest in *In re Swinehart*"); *In re* Swinehart, 439 F.2d 210, 212, 169 U.S.P.Q. 226, 228 (C.C.P.A. 1971) ("[T]here is nothing intrinsically wrong with [employing functional limitations] in drafting patent claims.").

argued to be operations a network device may support. With even more attention, these positions might be made even clearer through claim language and specification language. The point, here, is to pay attention to the use of structural versus function language in the claim and attempt to use *some* functionality to increase the chances of meeting the FWR or insubstantial differences test of equivalency due to the presence of functional language while not being so functional so that subsection 112(f) is invoked. Of course, easier said than done.

Prosecution History Estoppel

Festo Corp. v. Shoketsu Kinzoku Kogyo Kabushiki Co.
535 U.S. 722
Supreme Court of the United States
January 8, 2002, Argued; May 28, 2002, Decided

Questions

1. In *Festo*, the Court again takes up the DOE, but primarily to deal with PHE. It is fair to say that the Supreme Court clarified the scope of PHE in situations in which a claim is amended. Did the Court purport to address PHE by legal argument without an amendment?
2. What is the difference, if any, between estoppel that limits the DOE (i.e., PHE) and "estoppel" that limits the literal meaning and scope of claim terminology? Some people refer to the latter as "claim estoppel," although the Federal Circuit merely considers it part of the process of claim construction in which correspondence with the PTO may affect that claim construction.
3. In what sense is PHE (or even claim estoppel) truly an estoppel? For example, the elements of equitable estoppel are (1) representation as to a material fact that is contrary to a later-asserted position; (2) reliance on that representation; and (3) a change in position detrimental to the party claiming estoppel that is caused by the representation and reliance thereon. In the cases of PHE (or claim estoppel), a party has taken a position before the PTO and may now, in litigation, for example, be attempting to take a different position. An example might be as to the meaning of a claim term or what the claim should be interpreted to cover or not cover, for example, to avoid some prior art, either by amendment or, perhaps, by legal argument. However, it may be that no one necessarily relies on that, at least not at the time the position is taken. It may even be the case that the examiner rejects the argument

and, therefore, may not have truly relied on the position taken, in the sense of allowing a claim for example, which might be construed as a change in position if that occurs. However, nothing in the Court's opinion suggests that detrimental reliance is required to be shown to have occurred. However, an estoppel exists in this sense. The public is entitled to rely on the record before the PTO. So, while there is no requirement of proof that anyone has; nonetheless, the patentee is held to positions taken before the PTO that are a matter of public record.

4. The Court, consistent with *Warner-Jenkinson*, says it is placing the burden on the applicant. So, while the Court rejects the approach of the Federal Circuit, which would have been a complete bar as a result of an amendment, the Court, still, applies a pretty stiff rule compared to prior law. As the Court states: "We agree with the Court of Appeals that a narrowing amendment made to satisfy any requirement of the Patent Act may give rise to an estoppel."[310]

   Thus, the question is not whether there is estoppel, but rather its scope.

   Can you think of any situations where one could argue that their amendment was not to specifically satisfy a requirement of the Patent Act?

5. The Court's assumption that any narrowing must be more than cosmetic is a bit of an oversimplification. In the past, amendments that merely went to formal matters did not necessarily result in PHE, even if, as a technical matter, it could be said that the claim had been narrowed. For example, what if someone goes from a multiple dependent claim to one that is not multiply dependent (which happened in *Festo*)? According to the Court:

   > When the patentee has chosen to narrow a claim, courts may presume the amended text was composed with awareness of this rule and that the territory surrendered is not an equivalent of the territory claimed. In those instances, however, the patentee still might rebut the presumption that estoppel bars a claim of equivalence. The patentee must show that at the time of the amendment one skilled in the art could not reasonably be expected to have drafted a claim that would have literally encompassed the alleged equivalent.[311]

310. Festo Corp. v. Shoketsu Kinzoku Kogyo Kabushiki Co., 535 U.S. 722, 736 (2002).
311. *Id.* at 740–41.

What does this suggest regarding claim amendments, even as to matters of form?

6. Do you think evidence to rebut the presumption must be in the public record before the PTO? Why or why not? However, does it ever make sense not to clearly indicate on the record the reason for making an amendment?

* * *

As mentioned previously, *Hilton Davis* also addressed the issue of PHE. On this issue the Court stated:

> We are left with the problem, however, of what to do in a case like the one at bar, where the record seems not to reveal the reason for including the lower pH limit of 6.0. In our view, holding that certain reasons for a claim amendment may avoid the application of prosecution history estoppel is not tantamount to holding that the *absence* of a reason for an amendment may similarly avoid such an estoppel. Mindful that claims do indeed serve both a definitional and a notice function, we think the better rule is to place the burden on the patent holder to establish the reason for an amendment required during patent prosecution. The court then would decide whether that reason is sufficient to overcome prosecution history estoppel as a bar to application of the doctrine of equivalents to the element added by that amendment. *Where no explanation is established, however, the court should presume that the patent applicant had a substantial reason related to patentability for including the limiting element added by amendment. In those circumstances, prosecution history estoppel would bar the application of the doctrine of equivalents as to that element. The presumption we have described, one subject to rebuttal if an appropriate reason for a required amendment is established, gives proper deference to the role of claims in defining an invention and providing public notice, and to the primacy of the PTO in ensuring that the claims allowed cover only subject matter that is properly patentable in a proffered patent application.* Applied in this fashion, prosecution history estoppel places reasonable limits on the doctrine of equivalents, and further insulates the doctrine from any feared conflict with the Patent Act.
>
> Because respondent has not proffered in this Court a reason for the addition of a lower pH limit, it is impossible to tell whether the reason for that addition could properly avoid an estoppel. Whether a reason in fact exists, but simply was not adequately developed, we cannot say. On remand, the Federal Circuit can consider whether reasons for that portion of the amendment were offered or not and whether further opportunity to establish such reasons would be proper.[312]

312. Warner-Jenkinson Co. v. Hilton Davis Chem. Co., 520 U.S. 17, 33–34 (1997) (emphasis added).

In *Festo Corp. v. Shoketsu Kinzoku Kogyo Kabushiki*,[313] the Supreme Court again took up the relationship between the DOE and PHE. *Hilton Davis* and *Festo* together reset the law regarding PHE in the United States.

Regarding PHE, in this case the Court stated:

> Prosecution history estoppel ensures that the doctrine of equivalents remains tied to its underlying purpose. Where the original application once embraced the purported equivalent but the patentee narrowed his claims to obtain the patent or to protect its validity, the patentee cannot assert that he lacked the words to describe the subject matter in question. The doctrine of equivalents is premised on language's inability to capture the essence of innovation, but a prior application describing the precise element at issue undercuts that premise. *In that instance the prosecution history has established that the inventor turned his attention to the subject matter in question, knew the words for both the broader and narrower claim, and affirmatively chose the latter.*[314]

According to the Court, in such a situation, the question is not whether there is estoppel, but rather *the scope of the estoppel*. In this regard, the Court stated:

> Just as *Warner-Jenkinson* held that the patentee bears the burden of proving that an amendment was not made for a reason that would give rise to estoppel, we hold here that the patentee should bear the burden of showing that the amendment does not surrender the particular equivalent in question. This is the approach advocated by the United States, see Brief for United States as *Amicus Curiae* 22–28, and we regard it to be sound. The patentee, as the author of the claim language, may be expected to draft claims encompassing readily known equivalents. A patentee's decision to narrow his claims through amendment may be presumed to be a general disclaimer of the territory between the original claim and the amended claim. *Exhibit Supply*, 315 U.S., at 136–137 ("By the amendment [the patentee] recognized and emphasized the difference between the two phrases and proclaimed his abandonment of all that is embraced in that difference"). *There are some cases, however, where the amendment cannot reasonably be viewed as surrendering a particular equivalent. The equivalent may have been unforeseeable at the time of the application; the rationale underlying the amendment may bear no more than a tangential relation to the equivalent in question; or there may be some other reason suggesting that the patentee could not reasonably be expected to have described the insubstantial*

313. 535 U.S. 722.

314. *Id.* at 733–34 (emphasis added).

substitute in question. In those cases the patentee can overcome the presumption that prosecution history estoppel bars a finding of equivalence.[315]

Based on the ruling in *Festo*, it should be reasonably clear that (1) a claim should not be amended in a manner that is narrowing *unless* absolutely required, especially if addressing formalities unrelated to prior art; and (2) the record should clarify the rationale for an amendment, especially if a claim is being narrowed, so that it might be possible to later argue the estoppel is not a complete bar to all equivalents because "[t]he equivalent may have been unforeseeable at the time of the application; the rationale underlying the amendment may bear no more than a tangential relation to the equivalent in question; or there may be some other reason suggesting that the patentee could not reasonably be expected to have described the insubstantial substitute in question."[316]

Claim Language Excluding Equivalents

Dolly, Inc. v. Spalding & Evenflo Cos., Inc.
16 F.3d 394
United States Court of Appeals for the Federal Circuit
February 8, 1994, Decided

Questions

1. Although an older case, *Dolly* clarifies an important principle under the DOE that though easy to state may be a challenge to apply. Because each element and limitation of a claim is deemed material and substantive, each element and limitation must be met in some way, even under the DOE. Thus, a theory of equivalence that *vitiates* an element or limitation is not proper.[317] The challenge, of course, comes in determining whether that has occurred. How do we know that it has occurred in this case?

---

315. *Id.* at 740–41 (emphasis added).

316. *Id.* For a recent example of disclaimer, see *Genuine Enabling Technology LLC v. Nintendo Co., Ltd.*, 29 F.4th 1365 (Fed. Cir. 2022).

317. *See, e.g.*, *Hilton Davis*, 520 U.S. 17 n.8 ("Thus, under the particular facts of a case, if prosecution history estoppel would apply or *if a theory of equivalence would entirely vitiate a particular claim element*, partial or complete judgment should be rendered by the court, as there would be no further *material* issue for the jury to resolve.") (emphasis added).

2. According to the appellate court, one-to-one correspondence between the limitations of a claim and the features of an accused product is not a requirement. Rather, all the elements and limitations must be met, either literally or by equivalents. However, how do we know when we have gone too far and, in effect, *vitiated* a limitation?
3. Why could this not be a case where several elements together meet a single specified limitation? Does the Federal Circuit say that this may occur under the DOE? Likewise, apparently, one element may meet several limitations as well. If so, what is the difference here?
4. How does one distinguish the *Corning Glass Works v. Sumitomo Electric U.S.A., Inc.*[318] case? Apparently, the claim required a negative dopant be added to a cladding layer of an optical fiber. In the accused product, a positive dopant was added to a core layer. So, therefore, is not the accused product missing a limitation of the cladding layer? Who decides how to arrange the elements and limitations so that everything is met either literally or by equivalents? For example, one could say that a cladding layer and a core layer with negative dopant in the cladding layer is limitation-by-limitation equivalent to a cladding layer and a core layer with positive dopant in the core layer.
5. It appears that the answer necessarily resides in the particular claim language at issue. The appellate court tells us (quoting *Sun Studs, Inc. v. ATA Equipment Leasing Inc.*[319]): "Each case must be decided in light of the nature and extent of the differences between the accused device and the claimed invention, on the equitable principles of the doctrine of equivalents."[320] On the other hand, how much guidance does this really provide? Is there a principle here that one is able to apply?
6. Do you think one could dispose of a case under the DOE on summary judgment by arguing that the claim language itself excludes the accused product as an equivalent?
7. The appellate court tells us, specifically: "In short, the concept of equivalency cannot embrace a structure that is specifically excluded from the scope of the claims."[321] How is that necessarily the case here? Can you think of other examples where this principle might apply? For

318. 868 F.2d 1251, 9 U.S.P.Q.2d 1962 (Fed. Cir. 1989).

319. 872 F.2d 978, 10 U.S.P.Q.2d 1338 (Fed. Cir. 1989), *overruled on other grounds by* A.C. Aukerman Co. v. R.L. Chaides Constr. Co., 960 F.2d 1020, 1038–39, 22 U.S.P.Q.2d 1321, 1333 (Fed. Cir. 1992).

320. Dolly, Inc. v. Spalding & Evenflo Cos., Inc., 16 F.3d 394, 398–99 (Fed. Cir. 1994).

321. *Id.* at 400.

example, if a claim recited "only one widget," would one be able to reach via the DOE something otherwise equivalent that uses two widgets? Is the principle that one cannot extend claim language via equivalents to something inconsistent with what is claimed? Is this the same as saying a limitation is vitiated?

8. Do you think the nature of the invention here had any influence on the ultimate outcome? In other words, how inventive is the invention claimed by Dolly really?

Sage Products, Inc. v. Devon Industries, Inc.
126 F.3d 1420
United States Court of Appeals for the Federal Circuit
September 18, 1997, Decided

Questions

1. Does this case show the value of careful claim drafting?

   Note that the appellate court states: "Thus, for a patentee who has claimed an invention narrowly, there may not be infringement under the doctrine of equivalents in many cases, even though the patentee might have been able to claim more broadly. If it were otherwise, then claims would be reduced to functional abstracts, devoid of meaningful structural limitations on which the public could rely."[322] The court further states: "The claim at issue defines a relatively simple structural device. A skilled patent drafter would foresee the limiting potential of the 'over said slot' limitation. [footnote: This court does not imply that Sage's representation before the Patent and Trademark Office was inadequate. To the contrary, it appears that the claim precisely defines the structure elaborated in the written description and drawings. The public record reflects a manifest intention to claim this structure and no more. Whether actual or constructive, that intention now binds Sage.]"[323]

2. According to the appellate court, the patentee is the so-called "least cost avoider" in accordance with economic theory applied to law. It states: "However, as between the patentee who had a clear opportunity to negotiate broader claims but did not do so, and the public at large, it is the patentee who must bear the cost of its failure to seek protection

322. Sage Prods., Inc. v. Devon Indus., 126 F.3d 1420, 1424–25 (Fed. Cir. 1997).
323. *Id.* at 1425.

for this foreseeable alteration of its claimed structure."[324] More generally, the appellate court states:

> This court recognizes that such reasoning places a premium on forethought in patent drafting. Indeed this premium may lead to higher costs of patent prosecution. However, the alternative rule—allowing broad play for the doctrine of equivalents to encompass foreseeable variations, not just of a claim element, but of a patent claim—also leads to higher costs. Society at large would bear these latter costs in the form of virtual foreclosure of competitive activity within the penumbra of each issued patent claim. Because the doctrine of equivalents blurs the line of demarcation between infringing and non-infringing activity, it creates a zone of uncertainty, into which competitors tread only at their peril. *Cf. Markman v. Westview Instruments, Inc.*, 517 U.S. 370, 134 L. Ed. 2d 577, 116 S. Ct. 1384, 1396 (1996) (discussing the importance of certainty in defining the scope of exclusive rights). Given a choice of imposing the higher costs of careful prosecution on patentees, or imposing the costs of foreclosed business activity on the public at large, this court believes the costs are properly imposed on the group best positioned to determine whether or not a particular invention warrants investment at a higher level, that is, the patentees.[325]

Do you agree with this assessment? Note that at the beginning of the section, three legal hurdles to application of the DOE were suggested. As to Sage's '728 patent, in light of the appellate court's reasoning, which of these hurdles prevent application of the DOE here?

3. The appellate court then goes on to consider an additional patent that Sage asserted, the '849 patent, and states:

> However, "it is important to ensure that the application of the doctrine, even as to an individual element, is not allowed such broad play as to effectively eliminate that element in its entirety." *Warner-Jenkinson*, 117 S. Ct. at 1049. Thus, in cases where the patentee's theory of equivalents would "entirely vitiate a particular claim element, partial or complete summary judgment should be rendered by the court." *See id.* at 1053 n.8; *Pennwalt*, 833 F.2d at 935, 4 U.S.P.Q.2D

324. *Id.*
325. *Id.* at 1425–26.

> (BNA) at 1739 ("That [function-way-result] formulation, however, does not mean one can ignore claim limitations.").[326]

As to Sage's '849 patent, in light of the appellate court's reasoning, which of these hurdles prevent application of the DOE here?

4. Finally, the appellate court considers Devon's '592 patent, stating:

> A patentee is not free to retrade or renege on a deal struck with the PTO during patent prosecution. *See Mark I Mktg. Corp. v. R.R. Donnelley & Sons, Co.*, 66 F.3d 285, 291–92, 36 U.S.P.Q.2D (BNA) 1095, 1099–1100 (Fed. Cir. 1995), *cert. denied*, 516 U.S. 1115, 133 L. Ed. 2d 847, 116 S. Ct. 917 (1996). When an applicant distinguishes prior art by surrendering some previously-claimed subject matter, the patentee may not later seek to recover that surrendered subject matter by the doctrine of equivalents. *See id.*; *see also Warner-Jenkinson*, 117 S. Ct. at 1049–50.[327]

As to this patent, which of the hurdles does the appellate court reason do not permit application of the DOE?

5. In general, of the three hurdles, which do you think most frequently prevents application of the DOE? Which do you think least frequently prevents application of the DOE?

Ring & Pinion Service Inc. v. ARB Corp. Ltd.
743 F.3d 831
United States Court of Appeals for the Federal Circuit
February 19, 2014, Decided

Questions

1. This case is interesting in that due to its procedural posture it clarifies some aspects of the DOE and how it relates to means-plus-function elements of a claim. Specifically, the parties stipulated a number of things. What did the parties stipulate?
2. Despite the stipulation by the parties, the district court did not use it when it held that the DOE did not apply. On what legal basis, therefore, did the district court reach this conclusion? Do we know the logical basis for that conclusion by the district court?

326. *Id.* at 1429.
327. *Id.* at 1432–33.

3. Ring & Pinion (R and P) argues that foreseeability is a limit on the DOE. Do you think R and P may have reached such a conclusion based on language from *Festo* such as "[t]he equivalent may have been unforeseeable at the time of the application; the rationale underlying the amendment may bear no more than a tangential relation to the equivalent in question; or there may be some other reason suggesting that the patentee could not reasonably be expected to have described the insubstantial substitute in question."?[328] Assuming this is the case, why does this language not support R and P's position?
4. R and P also relies on *Sage Products v. Devon Industries*, a case we read. What in that case do you think led R and P to argue that foreseeability is a limit on the DOE? On the other hand, the appellate court ruled that this was a misreading of the case. What did the appellate court say was the reason the DOE did not apply in that case?
5. R and P also tried to argue that as to means-plus-function limitations in a claim, there is a foreseeability limit on the DOE, relying on the case *Chiuminatta Concrete Concepts, Inc. v. Cardinal Industries, Inc.*[329] The appellate court then explained that there are two primary differences between literal infringement under 112, 6 and infringement under the DOE for that same limitation. The primary differences are that the DOE may include after-arising technology that might qualify as an equivalent and that the function need not be identical for infringement under the DOE although it must be identical for literal infringement of a limitation under 112, 6. However, what R and P may have had in mind is this language from *Chiuminatta*:

> Due to technological advances, a variant of an invention may be developed after the patent is granted, and that variant may constitute so insubstantial a change from what is claimed in the patent that it should be held to be an infringement. Such a variant, based on after-developed technology, could not have been disclosed in the patent. Even if such an element is found not to be a § 112, 6, equivalent because it is not equivalent to the structure disclosed in the patent, this analysis should not foreclose it from being an equivalent under the doctrine of equivalents.
>
> That is not the case here, where the equivalence issue does not involve later-developed technologies, but rather involves technology

328. Festo Corp. v. Shoketsu Kinzoku Kogyo Kabushiki Co., 535 U.S. 722, 725 (2002).
329. 145 F.3d 1303 (Fed. Cir. 1998).

> that predates the invention itself. In such a case, a finding of non-equivalence for § 112, 6, purposes should preclude a contrary finding under the doctrine of equivalents. This is because, as we have already determined, the structure of the accused device differs substantially from the disclosed structure and given the prior knowledge of the technology asserted to be equivalent, it could readily have been disclosed in the patent. There is no policy-based reason why a patentee should get two bites at the apple. If he or she could have included in the patent what is now alleged to be equivalent, and did not, leading to a conclusion that an accused device lacks an equivalent to the disclosed structure, why should the issue of equivalence have to be litigated a second time? As indicated, this consideration does not necessarily apply regarding variants of the invention based on after-developed technologies.[330]

However, in context, the appellate court was discussing a situation in which there was no "structural equivalence" for purposes of determining literal infringement under 112, 6. The appellate court was pointing out that for nonstructural equivalents, if the patentee wanted those to be covered by the limitation under 112, 6, the patentee could have included those in the patent. Furthermore, the court made it clear that failing structural equivalence under literal infringement suggests there will not be structural equivalence under the DOE unless the variant might be after-developed technology. Thus, as the appellate court in R and P rules, this does not suggest a foreseeability requirement, but rather a structural equivalence requirement, which, of course, is the case for the DOE. This raises the question, how would a DOE analysis for a limitation under 112, 6 proceed in comparison to a literal infringement analysis for that limitation?

6. On what basis did the appellate court decide that foreseeability cannot be a limit on the application of the DOE?
7. However, despite there not being a foreseeability limit with respect to application of the DOE, again, the district court ruled that the DOE did not apply but did not rely on the stipulation. The appellate court ruled that this was legal error and reversed. Why did the appellate court rule this to be legal error? Why did the appellate court not conduct its own analysis regarding whether the limitation at issue would be vitiated if the DOE could reach the accused product?

330. *Id.* at 1411.

* * *

An important aspect related to claim drafting and the DOE is illustrated by *Dolly v. Spalding & Evenflo Cos.*[331] *Dolly* predates the Supreme Court decisions *Warner-Jenkinson* and *Festo*, but remains a feature of DOE jurisprudence that the Federal Circuit has repeated in various cases over the years. It illustrates that it is important to draft a good claim of literal scope not only because the DOE is generally a weaker claim than literal infringement, but also because drafting a narrow claim may also have the undesired effect of restricting the range of equivalents available, if any. After *Dolly*, the Federal Circuit in later cases has stated, a bit surprisingly after *Warner-Jenkinson* and *Festo*, that application of the DOE is the exception, rather than the rule.[332] These cases have consistent themes—it is that the precise claim limitations matter. The DOE is not a license to erase such limitations. Thus, the claim drafting principle, previously articulated in a different context,[333] is to *draft the broadest claim of literal scope that the prior art will permit (depending somewhat on context).*

At a high level, the principle at work in the cases in this section is that if a patent claim is overly narrow and/or if the invention barely gets over § 103 in terms of innovation, the patent claim will be given a restricted range of equivalents, if any.[334] Specifically, the Federal Circuit stated:

> The doctrine of equivalents cannot extend or enlarge the scope of the claims. *Wilson Sporting Goods Co. v. David Geoffrey & Assocs.*, 904 F.2d 677, 684, 14 USPQ2d 1942, 1948 (Fed. Cir.), *cert. denied*, 498 U.S. 992, 111 S. Ct. 537, 112 L. Ed. 2d 547 (1990). "The claims—i.e. the scope of patent protection as defined by the claims—remain the same and application of the doctrine expands the right to exclude to 'equivalents' of what is claimed." *Id.* The doctrine of equivalents is not a license to ignore claim limitations. *See Pennwalt Corp.*, 833 F.2d at 935.
>
> Claim 16's language requiring a stable rigid frame independent of seat and back panels is not a requirement solely for literal infringement. This limitation applies under the doctrine of equivalents as well. "Under the doctrine of equivalents, the accused device and the claimed invention cannot work in 'substantially the same way' if a limitation (including its equivalent) is missing." *Valmont Indus. v. Reinke Mfg.*, 983 F.2d 1039, 1043 n.2, 25 USPQ2d 1451, 1455

331. 16 F.3d 394.

332. *See, e.g.*, Schoell v. Regal Marine Indus., Inc., 247 F.3d 1202, 1210 (Fed. Cir. 2001).

333. *See* Chapter 2.

334. *See* Sage Prods., Inc. v. Devon Indus., 126 F.3d 1420 (Fed. Cir. 1997) ("[A]s between the patentee who had a clear opportunity to negotiate broader claims but did not do so, and the public at large, it is the patentee who must bear the cost of its failure to seek protection for this foreseeable alteration of its claimed structure.").

> n.2 (Fed. Cir. 1993). The Snack & Play chair lacks a stable rigid frame separate from the panels. The Snack & Play also lacks a structure to which additional components are added to form the body supporting feature. Rather, the Snack & Play chair achieves its function without a stable rigid frame independent of the various panels. In the absence of the stable rigid frame limitation or its equivalent, the Snack & Play chair does not infringe. . . .
>
> *In short, the concept of equivalency cannot embrace a structure that is specifically excluded from the scope of the claims.* A stable rigid frame assembled from the seat and back panels is not the equivalent of a separate stable rigid frame which the claim language specifically limits to structures exclusive of seat and back panels. The district court erred by failing to give effect to this claim limitation in applying the doctrine of equivalents to the Snack & Play chair.[335]

Dolly and similar cases, such as *Sage Products*,[336] therefore illustrate that where the innovation barely manages to get over § 103 and/or the claim language is apparently narrower than needed based on simple inspection of the patent claim, then the range of equivalents, if any, will be restricted.

Prior Art Limit on Equivalency

Wilson Sporting Goods Co. v. David Geoffrey & Associates
904 F.2d 677
United States Court of Appeals for the Federal Circuit
May 23, 1990, Decided

Questions

1. The case raises several issues regarding federal court procedure that we need not dwell upon. However, the ultimate substantive law question is a complex one. The question is whether the prior art in this case limits the scope of the DOE. Why is the DOE at issue, rather than literal infringement?
2. Why cannot infringement under the DOE be eliminated by the FWR test?
3. Why cannot PHE be employed to limit the DOE?

---

335. Dolly, Inc. v. Spalding & Evenflo Cos., Inc., 16 F.3d 394 (Fed. Cir. 1994) (emphasis added).

336. *See Sage Prods.*, 126 F.3d 1420 ("[A]s between the patentee who had a clear opportunity to negotiate broader claims but did not do so, and the public at large, it is the patentee who must bear the cost of its failure to seek protection for this foreseeable alteration of its claimed structure.").

4. Having evaluated these issues, we see that we must determine whether the prior art limits the scope of the DOE. Judge Rich first explains that as a technical matter, the DOE does not expand the scope of the claim at issue; instead, it expands the right to exclude. Why is this distinction legally important?
5. Does this analysis with respect to the prior art have any impact on the validity of the claim? If not, then what is the reason for conducting analysis with respect to the prior art?
6. Ordinarily, one might expect this analysis to be extremely difficult. Given the issued claim, the asserted equivalent, and prior art, a cogent analysis under § 102 and/or § 103 might be quite difficult for a court. However, Judge Rich proposes an approach to aid in the analysis (which may still be difficult, but at least makes the analysis more manageable). What is that approach and how would it help in terms of resolving the legal question regarding the DOE?
7. What is the key difference between the asserted claim—for example, claim 1—and the golf balls alleged to infringe under the DOE? How does Judge Rich go about analyzing this difference?
8. Judge Rich places the burden of persuasion on Wilson, the patentee. Why does this make sense both from a procedural position with respect to determining infringement and from the perspective of Judge Rich's so-called hypothetical claim analysis?
9. Judge Rich ultimately concludes that claim 1 of the patent is not infringed under the DOE by the golf balls at issue because a hypothetical claim that would cover those golf balls would also cover prior art golf balls. In other words, the prior art limits the scope of the DOE so that the accused product does not infringe under the DOE. Why does Judge Rich not stop there? Why does he go on to analyze the dependent claims as well? How is this different than the usual situation in which if the independent claim is not infringed then it should follow that the dependent claims are not infringed? Is it necessary to analyze the dependent claims as well as the independent claim in any DOE situation? Why or why not?

* * *

Wilson Sporting Goods[337] is an important case to understand in connection with the DOE. The facts and law are complex, but we should be able to simplify the facts for these purposes.

---

337. Wilson Sporting Goods Co. v. David Geoffrey & Assocs., 904 F.2d 677 (Fed. Cir. 1990). The case was written by the esteemed Judge Rich, who was a giant in the field of patent law in the United States.

Judge Rich begins with the question: Why should the prior art be a limitation on the range of permissible equivalents? According to Judge Rich:

> *The answer is that a patentee should not be able to obtain, under the doctrine of equivalents, coverage which he could not lawfully have obtained from the PTO by literal claims.* . . . Thus, since prior art always limits what an inventor could have claimed, it limits the range of permissible equivalents of a claim.
>
> Whether prior art restricts the range of equivalents of what is literally claimed can be a difficult question to answer. To simplify analysis and bring the issue onto familiar turf, it may be helpful to conceptualize the limitation on the scope of equivalents by visualizing a hypothetical patent claim, sufficient in scope to literally cover the accused product. The pertinent question then becomes whether that hypothetical claim could have been allowed by the PTO over the prior art. If not, then it would be improper to permit the patentee to obtain that coverage in an infringement suit under the doctrine of equivalents. If the hypothetical claim could have been allowed, then prior art is not a bar to infringement under the doctrine of equivalents.[338]

Hence, Judge Rich introduces hypothetical claim analysis, an invaluable tool to perform an evaluation of whether the prior art limits the scope of equivalents. The judge then states: "The specific question before us, then, is whether Wilson has proved that a hypothetical claim, similar to claim 1 but broad enough to literally cover Dunlop's balls, could have been patentable."[339] He answers that a hypothetical claim with respect to the one independent claim of the patent at issue would be unpatentable.

The judge then provides a dramatic insight regarding the dependent claims. The issue here is patent infringement. Normally, if the independent claim is not infringed that is the end of the matter. *However, Judge Rich realizes that principle only works for literal infringement, not infringement under the DOE.* The judge states:

> Before separately analyzing the asserted dependent claims, we should first explain why we are bothering to do so. This court has stated: "It is axiomatic that dependent claims cannot be found infringed unless the claims from which they depend have been found to have been infringed." *Wahpeton Canvas Co., Inc. v. Frontier, Inc.*, 870 F.2d 1546, 1553 & n.9, 10 USPQ2d 1201, 1208 & n.9 (Fed. Cir. 1989). While this proposition is no doubt generally correct, it does not apply in the circumstances of this case. . . . *The dependent claims, of course, are narrower than claim 1; therefore, it does not automatically follow that the*

338. *Id.* at 684 (emphasis added).
339. *Id.* at 685.

> *ranges of equivalents of these narrower claims would encompass the prior art, because of their added limitations. . . .*[340]

To comprehend the point raised in question 9 in the previous "Questions" section with respect to the dependent claims, consider this example. Suppose someone, cycle manufacturer A, has a patent claim on a cycle with three wheels in accordance with the following claims:

EXAMPLE 5.9

I claim:

1. An apparatus comprising:

   a cycle including a cycle frame and three wheels attached to the cycle frame in a manner to rotate, during use of the cycle, so that the cycle is able to move forward.

2. The apparatus of claim 1, further comprising: handlebars attached to the cycle frame and a hand brake attached to one of the handlebars for at least one of the wheels.

Suppose a competitor, cycle manufacturer B, comes out with a bicycle with handlebars and a hand brake. We assume, for the claims of Example 5.9, that the claims were allowed on the first office action and that there is at least a colorable argument, such that factual issues are present to be resolved, that two wheels are equivalent to three wheels (e.g., known to be interchangeable). We also assume two-wheeled cycles are in the prior art.

If a hypothetical claim were formulated from claim 1 of Example 5.9 to cover cycle manufacturer B's product, would the DOE be able to be extended that far for cycle manufacturer A's patent? It could not at least in light of our assumptions. However, what about dependent claim 2? Could claim 2 potentially be infringed under the DOE despite prior art showing a two-wheeled cycle necessarily limiting the scope of the DOE for claim 1? It depends, of course, on the prior art, but potentially it could.

This point leads to a claim drafting principle discussed previously[341] in an entirely different context. However, the same principle assists with potential

340. *Id.* at 686 (emphasis added).
341. *See* Chapter 4.

infringement under the DOE. The principle is to cover commercially desirable embodiments in the dependent claims. Here, this makes sense since features in dependent claims are not infrequently literally copied. Furthermore, however, if prior art were to limit infringement under the DOE of a base claim, this approach increases the chances of patent infringement under the DOE of these dependent claims.

Focus on Literal Infringement Rather Than the DOE When Drafting

Several principles for patent claim drafting emerge from the prior discussion of the DOE. First and foremost, when drafting patent claims, the focus should be on literal infringement and getting the broadest claim in terms of literal scope (depending somewhat on context), rather than focusing on the DOE. The DOE is the exception rather than the rule. It is a much harder case to make out and generally a weaker assertion than literal infringement in light of the multiple legal hurdles that exist. Understanding the DOE and being mindful about it may potentially avoid drafting overly narrow claims;[342] however, it would be the tail wagging the dog, so to speak, to sacrifice literal scope in favor of the DOE.

The principle to draft the broadest claim the prior art will allow (depending on context, of course) was previously articulated in another context.[343] Here, consideration of the DOE reaffirms that principle.

Use Dependent Claims for Commercial Aspects Most Likely to Be Copied

Another principle that emanates from our consideration of the DOE, also previously discussed in another context,[344] concerns drafting dependent claims. In general, it is prudent to include in the dependent claims commercial aspects related to the invention that are more likely to be copied.

Previously, this made sense as a fallback position in case the independent claims, for example, were of questionable validity, while potentially bolstering a claim for willful patent infringement in the right circumstances.[345]

342. See earlier in this chapter.
343. *See* Chapter 2.
344. See Chapter 4, addressing dependent claims.
345. *Id.*

Here, however, the previous analysis involving the DOE and hypothetical claims also suggests such an approach. For example, it may be that the prior art limits equivalents as to base claim features, which is the broadest claim with respect to literal scope. However, by including in the dependent claims features likely to be copied, it increases the chances of patent infringement under the DOE with respect to the dependent claims. A feature in the dependent claim that is copied may remove prior art from consideration that otherwise restricted the range of equivalents for the base claim.

Do Not Draft Claims in a Manner That Is Clearly Narrower Than Needed and Easily Designed Around by Inspection of the Patent Claims

Dolly and similar cases, such as *Sage Products*,[346] illustrate that where the innovation barely manages to get over § 103 and/or the claim language is apparently narrower than needed by simple inspection, then the range of equivalents, if any, will be restricted. In *Dolly*, the innovation was slight *and* the claim language used was easily designed around. In *Sage*, again, the innovation was slight *and* the claim language used was easily designed around. It is well established that the more innovative the invention, the greater the range of equivalents under the DOE.[347] Likewise, it is the limitations of a patent claim that define the invention.[348] Each limitation of a patent claim is considered material.[349] Form, in essence, becomes substance when dealing with patent claim language. Lazy or sloppy claim drafting will not only affect literal claim scope, it may also work against finding infringement by equivalents.

For example, here is an independent claim from one of the patents in *Sage Products*:

346. *See* Sage Prods., Inc. v. Devon Indus., 126 F.3d 1420 (Fed. Cir. 1997) ("[A]s between the patentee who had a clear opportunity to negotiate broader claims but did not do so, and the public at large, it is the patentee who must bear the cost of its failure to seek protection for this foreseeable alteration of its claimed structure.").

347. *See, e.g.*, Insta-Foam Prods., Inc. v. Universal Foam Sys., Inc., 906 F.2d 698, 704, 15 U.S.P.Q.2d (BNA) 1295, 1299 (Fed. Cir. 1990).

348. *See, e.g.*, Phillips v. AWH Corp., 415 F.3d 1303 (Fed. Cir. 2005) (en banc).

349. *See* Warner-Jenkinson Co. v. Hilton Davis Chem. Co., 520 U.S. 17 (1997).

1. A disposal container comprising:
   a. a hollow upstanding container body,
   b. *an elongated slot at the top of the container body* for permitting access to the interior of the container body,
   c. barrier means disposed adjacent said slot for restricting access to the interior of said container body, at least a portion of said barrier means comprising
      i. *a first constriction extending over said slot*, and
      ii. a complementary second constriction extending beneath said slot, and
   d. a closure disposed adjacent said slot.

The italicized portions represent those limitations that were argued to be infringed by equivalents.

Regarding the DOE, the Federal Circuit affirmed the district court ruling on summary judgment that there was no infringement by equivalents. The Federal Circuit stated:

> *A skilled patent drafter would foresee the limiting potential of the "over said slot" limitation. No subtlety of language or complexity of the technology, nor any subsequent change in the state of the art, such as later-developed technology, obfuscated the significance of this limitation at the time of its incorporation into the claim. . . .*
>
> *Instead, Sage left the PTO with manifestly limited claims that it now seeks to expand through the doctrine of equivalents. However, as between the patentee who had a clear opportunity to negotiate broader claims but did not do so, and the public at large, it is the patentee who must bear the cost of its failure to seek protection for this foreseeable alteration of its claimed structure. . . .*
>
> *This court recognizes that such reasoning places a premium on forethought in patent drafting. . . . Given a choice of imposing the higher costs of careful prosecution on patentees, or imposing the costs of foreclosed business activity on the public at large, this court believes the costs are properly imposed on the group best positioned to determine whether a particular invention warrants investment at a higher level, that is, the patentees.*[350]

350. *See Sage Prods.*, 126 F.3d at 1425 (emphasis added).

Rewriting Claims versus Amending Claims

A question may arise in the context of PHE whether it would be better to entirely rewrite a claim or to make a "surgically focused" amendment to the claim language. Before *Festo* and *Hilton Davis*, anecdotally, there was a view among some practitioners that rewriting a claim, although much more work, might potentially create less estoppel by narrowing some parts of a newly crafted claim while at the same time broadening the claim in other ways. Whether previously true, how might such an approach play out today?

Generally, the recommendation here is to *not* worry so much about PHE and, *instead*, focus on literal scope. If a better claim in terms of scope may result from rewriting the claim, then do so. How it likely will be analyzed is substantially in accordance with *Festo*. The portions narrowed may be analyzed for scope of estoppel in light of the remarks, including considerations mentioned by the Supreme Court, such as whether the rationale for amending is tangentially related to the equivalent in question. Perhaps, however, if the court is unable to figure these things out (e.g., associate the limitations between the unamended and rewritten claim), complete estoppel might be presumed. It may depend on a variety of issues tied to the language, the art, and the interaction between the PTO and the patentee's legal representative.

Regardless, instead, focus on literal scope. If a focused amendment is more likely to result in allowance of a claim of broad scope, then make a focused amendment. In either case, explain the rationale for the amendment or the claim rewrite so as not to create a presumption of complete estoppel.

Certainly, rewriting the claim is more difficult. In either case, the examiner will do a new search. It may be that rewriting the claim raises enough new issues so that ultimately a continuation to continue prosecution will be needed. Thus, the guidance is to do what is best to get the best patent claim of literal scope without introducing unnecessary delay due to prosecution.

Claim Drafting Problems V

Problem 1. Method of Plastic Encapsulation Using Irradiation—Draft an independent method claim and four dependent claims.

FIGURE:

Dec. 13, 1960 M. J. BROWN 2,963,747

METHOD OF PLASTIC ENCAPSULATION USING IRRADIATION

Filed May 15, 1957

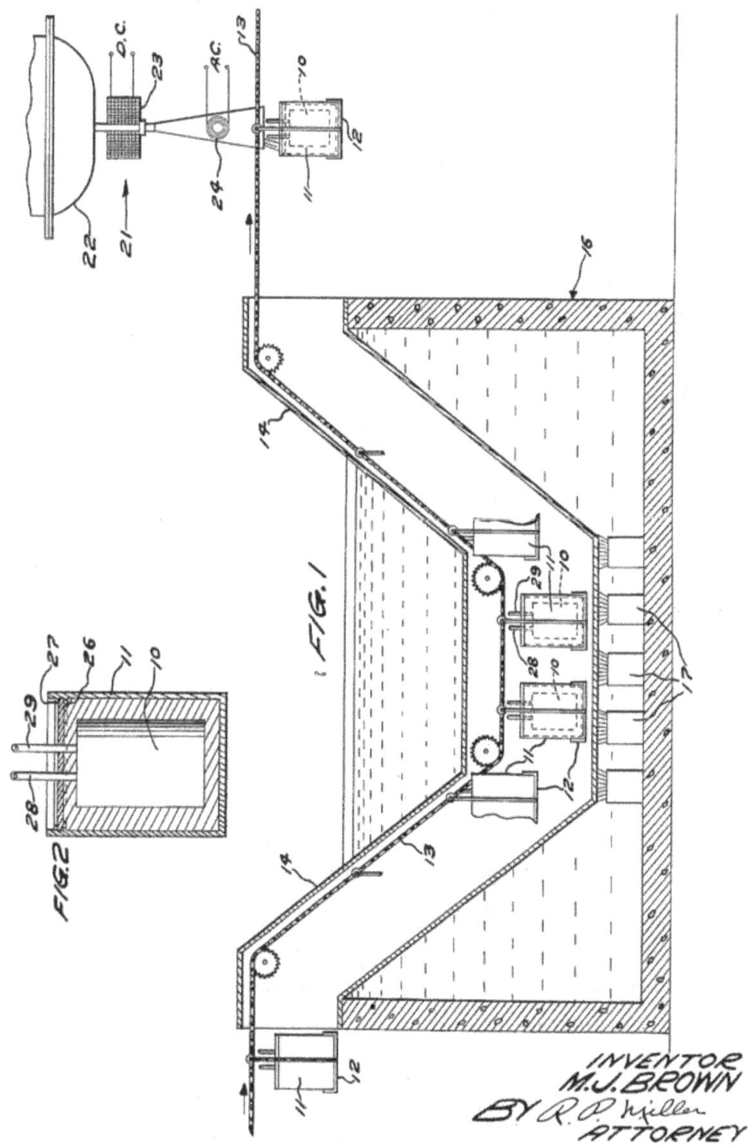

DESCRIPTION:

This invention relates to a method of plastic encapsulation using irradiation, and more particularly to a method of encapsulation wherein a styrene-polyester casting resin is initially polymerized by gamma irradiation to produce a partially poured gelatinous mass that is further surface cured by beta irradiation to produce a hard encasing shell.

In prior encapsulating processes wherein it was desired to produce an encapsulated electrical component having a shock-absorbing medium encasing the component surrounded by a wear resistant hard shell, it has been the practice to wrap or coat the component with a plastic material having shock-absorbing properties and then apply a second encapsulating coating of another plastic material that is polymerized to provide a hard shell by addition of curing agents, promoters, catalysts, or other initiators or inhibitors in combination with the application of heat. The resulting product has the property of resiliently supporting the encapsulated electrical component against external shock and internal stresses. However, these prior processes, using critical elevated temperatures and such catalytic agents as peroxides, require careful regulation and control to insure the attainment of the proper properties. Further, in the usual situation the catalyst is not all consumed in the process and as time passes the polymerizing action continues, causing undesirable physical, mechanical, and electrical properties to be imparted to the encapsulating materials.

A cardinal object of the invention is the provision of an improved method of encapsulating electrical components without attendant changes in electrical characteristics caused by the development of internal pressure.

It is another object of this invention to provide a method of producing an encapsulated electrical component having a gelatinous or viscous or resilient mass immediately surrounding the component and a hard wear resistant outer shell without the use of catalysts or heat.

A further object of the invention resides in an encapsulating process wherein a single encapsulating material is initially cured to a gelatinous state by relatively short exposure to gamma irradiation and then subjected to a beta irradiation to effectuate a substantially complete cure of the outer layer to form a hard wear resistant shell.

With these and other objects in view, the present invention contemplates a method of encapsulating electrical components by immersing said components in an unpolymerized styrene-polyester resinous liquid and then subjecting the resinous liquid to irradiation from a deep penetration gamma source until the liquid assumes a gelatinous or viscous state whereafter the gelatinous mass is irradiated from a shallow penetration beta ray source to completely cure the outer layer of encapsulating material into a hard wear resistant shell.

Other objects and advantages of the present invention will be apparent from the following detailed description when considered in conjunction with the accompanying drawing,

wherein Fig. 1 is a view of apparatus for subjecting encapsulated electrical components to gamma and beta radiations in accordance with the principles of the invention; and

Fig. 2 is a view of an electrical component that has been encapsulated by the apparatus shown in Fig. 1.

Referring to Fig. 1, an electrical component 10 such as a capacitor to be encapsulated is suspended in a container or mold 11 constructed of material that does not appreciably attenuate gamma rays. The mold can be constructed of aluminum, copper foil, thin walled glass, or other light metals or similar materials having low radiation absorbing properties. In a preferred embodiment of the invention, the mold is constructed of thermoplastic or thermosetting organic material similar to that used for purposes of encapsulation. It has been found that a satisfactory mold can be constructed of a commercially available styrene-polyester resin known as Selectron 5003. The aforementioned polyester resin comprises polymerizable polyesters or alkyds combined with approximately 34 percent of a reactive polymerizable monomer such as styrene or diallyl phthalate. The percentage of monomer present is varied slightly from time to time by the manufacturer to maintain a uniform viscosity of the product. The polyesters or alkyds contained in the resin are condensation products of polybasic acids (e.g., maleic acid, phthalic acid, etc.) and polyhydric alcohols (e.g., ethylene glycol, propylene glycol, etc.). Other electrical components such as resistors, cols, transistors, diodes, or networks of these components can also be encapsulated by the practice of the method encompassed by the invention.

Molds 11 having electrical components 10 suspended therein are filled with a liquid unpolymerized encapsulating compound such as Selectron 5003 and are then successively loaded on carriers 12 pivotally secured to a conveyor chain 13. Suitable drive means are provided to advance the carriers 12 into a thin wall steel tube 14 that runs through a well 16 having concrete walls. Submerged in water and positioned at the bottom of the well are a number of spent uranium fuel rods 17. The water acts as a shield to protect attendant personnel against the gamma rays emanating from the rods. Further, the water acts as a cooling medium for the fuel rods and any reactions induced by gamma radiation that happen to be exothermic.

As the molds 11 are carried by conveyor chain 13 past the fuel rods 17, the gamma radiation effectuates a polymerization of the encapsulating material. The time of exposure is controlled by the speed of the chain drive so that the reaction is only carried to such an extent as to set the material into a gelatinous state. Satisfactory polymerization can be obtained by use of radiation dose rates of from 0.75 x 10^6 to 2.5 x 10^6 roentgens per hour. A close rate of 2.0 x 10^6 roentgens per hour is considered to be particularly satisfactory. It is to be understood that other sources of gamma radiation such as Co^{60} or Cs^{134} may also be used to irradiate the encapsulating material so long as the reaction is controlled to place the material in a jelly or gelatinous state. It is not necessary that the molds 11 be carried by a conveyor so long as the molds and source of irradiation are only brought into proximity with each other for a sufficient length of time to set the encapsulating material in the gelatinous state. Obviously, the irradiation time required to effectuate the necessary setting or polymerization will be dependent upon such factors as the degree of gelatinization required, strength of the irradiating source, the composition and thickness of the mold, and the composition and volume of encapsulating material. The gamma rays have deep penetration abilities and as a consequence the entire mass of encapsulating material will be uniformly cured to a gelatinous state without the development of internal stresses and strains as is so often the situation in prior chemical and thermal polymerizing processes.

Next, the conveyor carries the molds from the tube 14 into close proximity to a source of beta radiation that in the drawing is disclosed as a well-known type of high voltage generator 21 susceptible of producing and accelerating a beam of high energy electrons but it could also be a source of direct radiation such as strontium-89 or -90 or some other type of artificial beta ray generator such as a Van der Graaff high energy electron accelerator.

The beta ray generator consists essentially of a source of beta rays 22, a D.C. focusing field winding 23 and an A.C. sweep control winding 24. As mold 11 is moved into register with the beta generator, the beta rays are caused to sweep the upper surface of the exposed gelatinous encapsulating material. Beta rays do not have the penetrating properties of gamma rays; consequently, only a shallow depth of the gelatinous material will be penetrated by the rays. These beta rays will, however, effectuate a continuation of the polymerizing action so that the upper portion of the gelatinous material will be transformed into a hard wear resistant mass. This hardened mass will be retained within the mold by a pair of lips 26 and 27 formed about the upper inner edges of each mold. The mold now becomes a casing or shell for the encapsulated component that is now suspended within the relatively soft gelatinous mass. The electrical component has terminals 28 and 29 that are held by the now hardened upper layer of encapsulating material and serve as a means for holding the component suspended in the mass.

If desired, the mold need not form a part of the completed encapsulated article. In this instance, a thin wall mold is provided of a material that will not appreciably attenuate beta rays, and both the exposed surface of the encapsulating material and the entire outer surface of the mold are exposed to beta irradiation. There is a hardened layer of encapsulating material formed not only at the upper exposed surface but also beneath all sections of the mold. These hardened layers act as a shell encasing the component suspended within the remainder of the encapsulating material that is in a gelatinous state. The encapsulated assembly may be then removed from the mold. As an alternative, the partially polymerized gelatinous mass with the component therein may be removed as a unit from the mold prior to exposure thereof to the beta radiation. It is only necessary that the partial polymerization effected by the gamma irradiation have proceeded to a point where the gelatinous mass will retain a coherent form upon removal from the mold.

It is to be understood that the above-described methods, arrangement of apparatus, and composition or matter are simply illustrative of an application of the principles of the invention and many other modifications may be made without departing from the invention.

Problem 2. Combination Masher and Fork—Draft an independent apparatus claims and three dependent claims.

FIGURES:

Dec. 11, 1956 C. D. SULLIVAN 2,773,530

COMBINATION MASHER AND FORK

Filed March 24, 1953

Fig. 1 Fig. 2

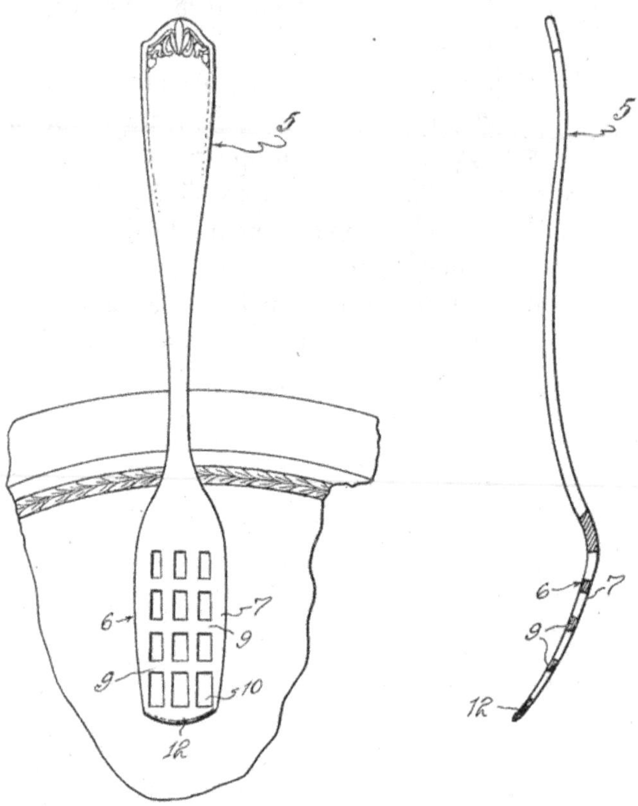

Inventor:
Cornelius D. Sullivan

BY Roy Griffith Jones
Attorney.

DESCRIPTION:

This invention relates to a combination masher and feeding fork intended especially for young children, but useful for adults under some circumstances and conditions.

It is known that young children between certain ages require that their foods be mashed, this due to the fact that they have not yet acquired molar teeth. This necessitates extra work by mothers in mashing the food before putting on the children's plates or other dishes, it being appreciated that it would be impractical for a child to perform this operation, especially considering that there may be several different kinds of foods served at any one meal that require mashing and that there may be a few such children in one family.

This invention eliminates the abovementioned operation, thus saving the mothers time in the preparation of meals, and additionally functions to train the young children themselves.

According to the invention, each child is enabled to mash his own food with a masher of convenient size and form and to use the same instrument with which to eat the food, as the article is a combination masher and fork. However, as the usual fork is rather sharp and pointed at the free ends of the tines, which may injure the young child, either during normal use or otherwise, I provide a guard across the ends of the tines, which is a valuable feature of my invention.

Another valuable feature is that the article may be economically manufactured, in that it is essentially the usual feeding or eating fork modified in a simple but effective way to accomplish the stated purposes.

A preferred form of the invention is shown in the accompanying drawings, in which Fig. 1 is a plan view of the article, and Fig. 2 is a side view of the same, partly in section.

Referring to the drawings for a more detailed description thereof, the article comprises a handle 5 and a functional portion 6 integral therewith. The functional part may be described as including tines 7 similar to those of a conventional eating fork, from which viewpoint, adjacent tines are connected by cross pieces 9, whereby to form a plurality of rows of openings 10 through which food may pass in mashing. As distinguished from the usual sharp-ended tines of the conventional fork, the present article is provided with a guard 12 at the ends of the tines, to make it safe for a child to use and handle. The whole article is preferably made in one piece and it is to be noted that neither the sides nor the end thereof have sharp edges. And it is to be understood that the drawing indicates only one form of the invention and that various modifications may be made within the scope of the inventive concept.

<u>Problem 3.</u> <u>System and method for providing dynamic high beam control</u>—Draft 10 patent claims.

<u>FIGURES:</u>

U.S. Patent **Jul. 20, 2021** **Sheet 1 of 4** **US 11,066,005 B2**

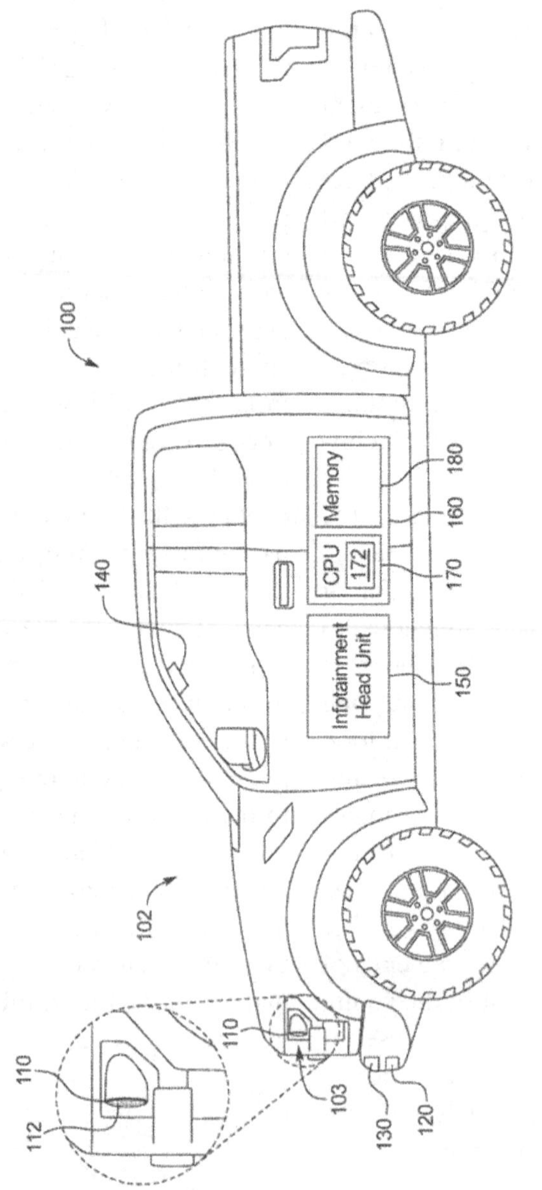

FIG. 1

U.S. Patent Jul. 20, 2021 Sheet 2 of 4 US 11,066,005 B2

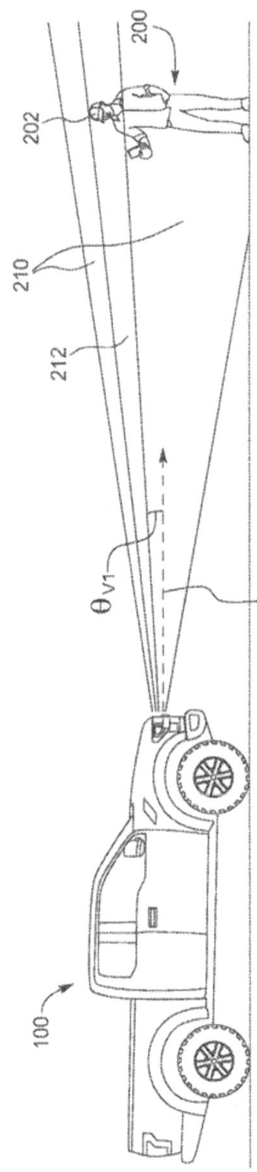

FIG. 2A

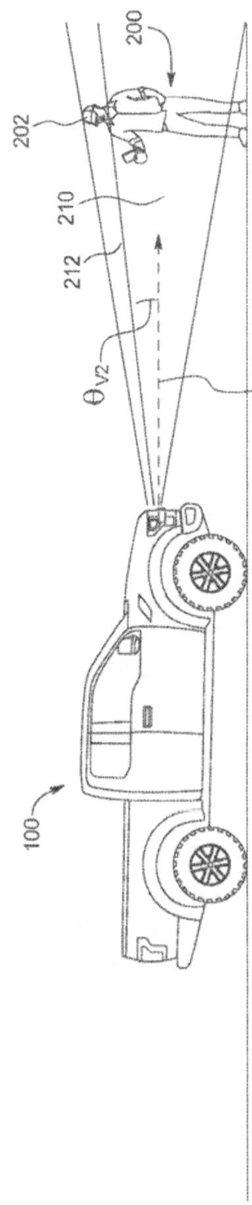

FIG. 2B

U.S. Patent Jul. 20, 2021 Sheet 3 of 4 US 11,066,005 B2

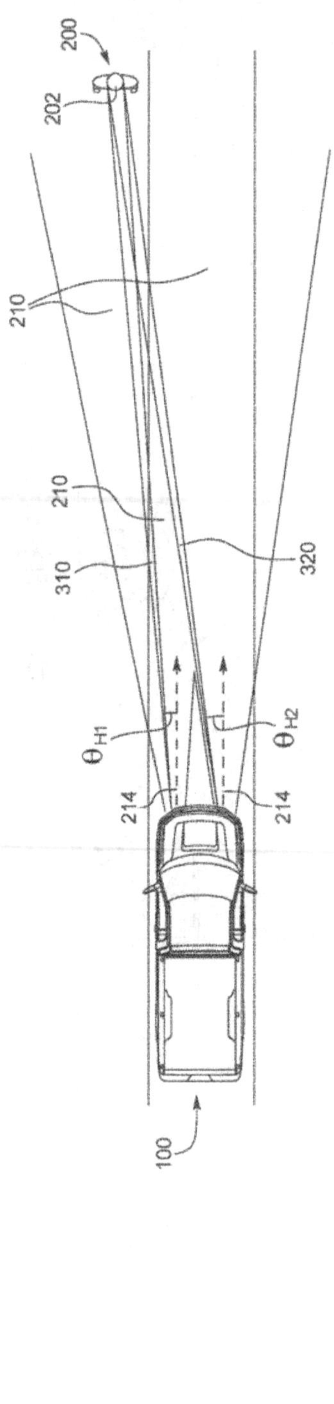

FIG. 3A

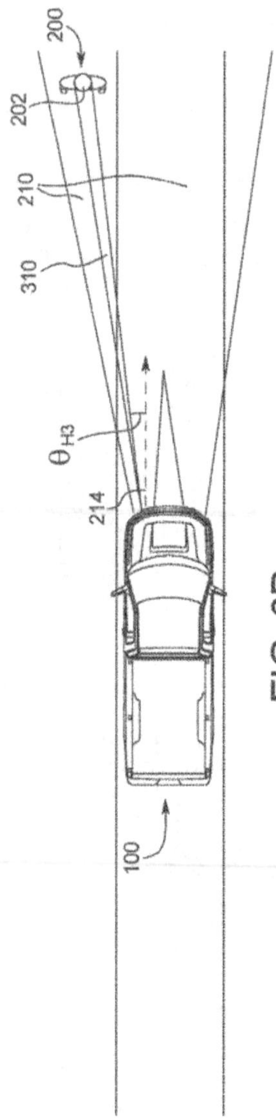

FIG. 3B

FIG. 4

U.S. Patent Jul. 20, 2021 Sheet 4 of 4 US 11,066,005 B2

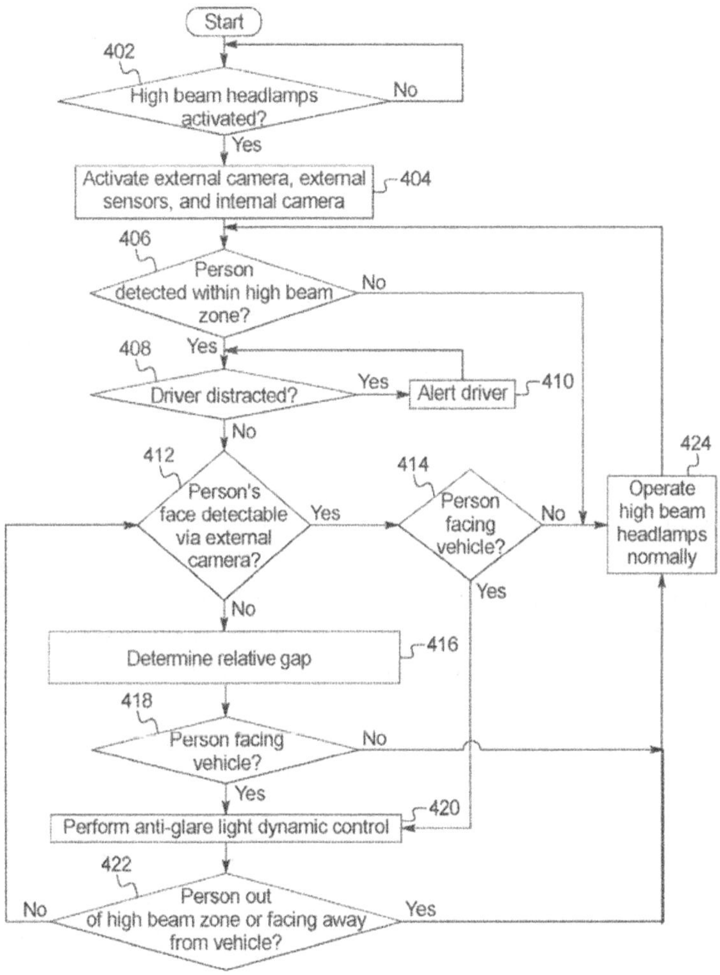

DESCRIPTION:

TECHNICAL FIELD

The present disclosure generally relates to a system and method for providing dynamic high beam control and, more specifically, a system and method for providing dynamic high beam control to mitigate dazzling effect caused by high beams.

BACKGROUND

High beams generated from a vehicle enable a driver to see further down a driving path in environments lacking ambient light. Since the intensity of high beams are generally greater than that of standard vehicle head lights, pedestrians facing the vehicle may experience discomfort.

SUMMARY

The appended claims define this application. The present disclosure summarizes aspects of the embodiments and should not be used to limit the claims. Other implementations are contemplated in accordance with the techniques described herein, as will be apparent to one having ordinary skill in the art upon examination of the following drawings and detailed description, and these implementations are intended to be within the scope of this application.

An example vehicle and method are disclosed. The example vehicle includes sensors, high beam headlamps comprising light pixels, and processors. The processors are configured to: determine, via the sensors, a direction in which a person is facing; and responsive to determining that the person is facing the vehicle: determine, via the sensors, a position of the person's face; and based on the position, adjust at least one of the light pixels projecting light to the person's face.

The example method is a method of controlling high beams generated from a vehicle. The method includes: determining, via sensors, a direction in which a person is facing; and responsive to determining that the person is facing the vehicle: determining, via the sensors, a position of the person's face; and based on the position, adjust at least one of the light pixels of high beam headlamps projecting light to the person's face.

BRIEF DESCRIPTION OF THE DRAWINGS

For a better understanding of the invention, reference may be made to embodiments shown in the drawings. The components in the drawings are not necessarily to scale and related elements may be omitted, or in some instances proportions may have been exaggerated, so as to emphasize and clearly illustrate the novel features described herein. In addition, system components can be variously arranged, as known in the art. Further, in the drawings, like reference numerals designate corresponding parts throughout the several views.

FIG. 1 illustrates a vehicle in accordance with this disclosure.

FIGS. 2A and 2B illustrate a side view of example scenarios in which the vehicle of FIG. 1 is approaching a pedestrian.

FIGS. 3A and 3B illustrate a plan view of the example scenarios as illustrated in FIGS. 2A and 2B, respectively.

FIG. 4 is a flowchart of a method for dynamically controlling high beams generated from the vehicle of FIG. 1.

DETAILED DESCRIPTION OF EXAMPLE EMBODIMENTS

While the invention may be embodied in various forms, there are shown in the drawings, and will hereinafter be described, some exemplary and non-limiting embodiments, with the understanding that the present disclosure is to be considered an exemplification of the invention and is not intended to limit the invention to the specific embodiments illustrated.

Vehicles include a headlight system for providing light to the road ahead. The headlight system typically includes headlamps providing high beams for enabling drivers to see further down a driving path in environments lacking ambient light (e.g., rural areas, mountain roads, tunnels, etc.). While the high beams facilitate drivers maneuvering vehicles in said environments, pedestrians facing a direction in which the high beams are projected may be dazzled and experience discomfort due to the light intensity thereof. Thus, there is a need for mitigating the dazzling effect of high beams projected on pedestrians while maintaining visual clarity in environments lacking ambient light.

As disclosed below, a vehicle includes a dynamic high beam control system for dynamically adjusting at least one pixel of high beam headlamps based on a heading of a pedestrian. As the vehicle traverses a driving path, the dynamic high beam control system dynamically adjusts one or more pixels of the high beam headlamps such that a portion of the high beams is prevented from being projected on to the pedestrian's face. The dynamic high beam control system includes at least one external sensor and/or camera, a processor, and high beam headlamps. Said external sensor and/or camera generates data by sensing and capturing images of a pedestrian. Based on the data, the processor determines whether the pedestrian is facing a direction in which the vehicle is approaching. If the pedestrian is facing the direction in which the vehicle is approaching the processor causes one or more pixels of the high beam headlamps to deactivate such that one or more portions of the high beams is prevented from being projected on to the pedestrian's face.

FIG. 1 illustrates a vehicle 100 in accordance with this disclosure. The vehicle 100 may be a standard gasoline powered vehicle, a hybrid vehicle, an electric vehicle, a fuel cell vehicle, and/or any other mobility implement type of vehicle. The vehicle 100 includes parts related to mobility, such as a powertrain with an engine, a transmission, a suspension, a driveshaft, and/or wheels, etc. The vehicle 100 may be a semi-autonomous vehicle (e.g., some routine motive functions, such as parking, are controlled by the vehicle 100), or an autonomous vehicle (e.g., motive functions are controlled by the vehicle 100 without direct driver input). In this illustrated example, the vehicle 100 includes a dynamic high beam control system.

The dynamic high beam control system includes high beam headlamps 110, external sensors 120, an external camera 130, an internal camera 140, an infotainment head unit 150, and an on-board computing platform 160. The high beam headlamps 110, the external sensors 120, the external camera 130, the internal camera 140, the infotainment head unit 150, and the on-board computing platform 160 may be communicatively coupled to each other via at least one bus (not illustrated) and/or via a wireless system (not illustrated).

The high beam headlamps 110 are positioned at the front side 102 of the vehicle. Each of the high beam headlamps 110 may be disposed within a vehicle head light 103. In some examples, the high beam headlamp 110 may be separately positioned from the vehicle head light 103. In some examples, each of the high beam headlamps 110 may include a plurality of light pixels 112. In such examples, each of the plurality of light pixels 112 may independently generate its own beam of light. The plurality of light beams generated from the plurality of light pixels 112 may form a single high beam. One or more of the plurality of light pixels 112 may be deactivated such that one or more portions of the high beam may be absent of light. It should be appreciated that each of the plurality of light pixels 112 may illuminate within a range of light intensity.

The external sensors 120 are disposed on the exterior of the vehicle 100 and on the front side of the vehicle 100. The external sensors 120 may be one or more of LiDAR sensors, radar sensors, ultrasonic sensors, and/or any other sensors capable of: (1) detecting an object; (2) determining a range between the vehicle and the detected object; and (3) determining the position of the detected object with respect to the vehicle 100. It should be appreciated that the position of the detected object with respect to the vehicle 100 may be determined by using a trilateration method or a triangulation method based on readings from the plurality of external sensors 120.

The external camera 130 is also disposed on the exterior of the vehicle 100 and on the front side of the vehicle 100. The external camera 130 may be a night vision camera. In some examples, one or more external cameras 130 may be disposed on the front side of the vehicle 100. By using image analysis techniques, images captured by the external camera 130 may be used to determine the distance and the position of an object with respect to the vehicle 100.

The internal camera 140 is disposed in the cabin of the vehicle 100 to face the driver side.

The infotainment head unit 150 provides an interface between the vehicle 100 and a user. The infotainment head unit 150 includes digital and/or analog interfaces (e.g., input devices and output devices) to receive input from the user(s) and display information. The input devices may include, for example, a control knob, an instrument panel, a digital camera for image capture and/or visual command recognition, a touch screen, an audio input device (e.g., cabin microphone), buttons, or a touchpad. The output devices may include instrument cluster outputs (e.g., dials, lighting devices), actuators, a heads-up display, a center console display (e.g., a liquid crystal display (LCD), an organic light emitting diode (OLED) display, a flat panel display, a solid state display etc.), and/or speakers. In the illustrated example, the infotainment head unit 150 includes hardware (e.g., a processor or controller; memory, storage, etc.) and software (e.g., an operating system, etc.) for an infotainment system (such as SYNC® and MyFord Touch® by Ford®, Entune® by Toyota®, IntelliLink® by GMC®, etc.). Additionally, the infotainment head unit 150 displays the infotainment system on, for example, the center console display.

The on-board computing platform 160 includes a processor or controller 170 and memory 180. In the illustrated example, the on-board computing platform 160 is structured to include a high beam controller 172. Alternatively in some examples, the high beam controller 172 may be incorporated into another electronic control unit (ECU) with its own processor and memory. The processor or controller 170 may be any suitable processing device or set of processing devices such as, but not limited to: a microprocessor, a microcontroller-based platform, a suitable integrated circuit, one or more field programmable gate arrays (FPGAs), and/or one or more application-specific integrated circuits (ASICs). The memory 180 may be volatile memory (e.g., RAM, which can include non-volatile RAM, magnetic RAM, ferroelectric RAM, and any other suitable forms); non-volatile memory (e.g., disk memory, FLASH memory, EPROMs, EEPROMs, non-volatile solid-state memory etc.), unalterable memory (e.g., EPROMs), read-only memory, and/or high-capacity storage devices (e.g., hard drives, solid state drives, etc.). In some examples, the memory 180 includes multiple kinds of memory, particularly volatile memory and non-volatile memory.

The memory 180 is computer-readable media on which one or more sets of instructions, such as the software for operating the methods of the present disclosure, can be embedded. The instructions may embody one or more of the methods or logic as described herein. In a particular embodiment, the instructions may reside completely, or at least partially, within any one or more of the memory

180, the computer-readable medium, and/or within the processor 170 during execution of the instructions.

The terms "non-transitory computer-readable medium" and "tangible computer-readable medium" should be understood to include a single medium or multiple media, such as a centralized or distributed database, and/or associated caches and servers that store one or more sets of instructions. The terms "non-transitory computer-readable medium" and "tangible computer-readable medium" also include any tangible medium that is capable of storing, encoding, or carrying a set of instructions for execution by a processor or that cause a system to perform any one or more of the methods or operations disclosed herein. As used herein, the term "tangible computer-readable medium" is expressly defined to include any type of computer-readable storage device and/or storage disk and to exclude propagating signals.

Operations of the high beam controller 172 with respect to the overall dynamic high beam control system will be described in detail below.

At the outset, it is assumed that the vehicle 100 is in motion, and the high beam headlamps, the external sensors 120, the external camera 130, and the internal camera 140 are activated.

While the vehicle 100 is traversing a driving path, the high beam controller 172 uses the external sensors 120 and/or the external camera 130 to detect any objects within a high beam zone. The high beam zone is defined by an area in which the high beams are projected. If an object is detected within the high beam zone, the high beam controller 172 determines whether the detected object is a person. To determine whether an object detected by the external sensors 120 is a person, the high beam controller 172 may compare readings from the external sensors 120 to a pre-stored data. For example, the high beam controller 172 may determine whether said reading indicating a size and shape of the detected object corresponds to that of a model representing a person. Further, to determine whether an object detected by the external camera 130 is a person, the high beam controller 172 may perform image analysis techniques on one or more images captured by the external camera 130.

Once the high beam controller 172 determines that the detected object is a person, the high beam controller 172 uses the internal camera 140 to determine whether a driver of the vehicle is distracted from driving. If the driver is distracted, the high beam controller 172 causes the infotainment head unit 150 to issue a visual and/or audible alert to the driver. It should be appreciated that the vehicle 100 may further include other subsystems for determining whether the driver is distracted. For example, other subsystems may include a steering system (not illustrated) for determining whether the vehicle 100 is swerving from the road, a wireless device detection system (not illustrated) for determining whether a mobile device is being used within the area around the driver's seat, etc.

The high beam controller 172 further determines a direction in which the person is facing. For example, using one or more images captured by the external camera 130, the high beam controller 172 may perform an image analysis technique to identity the face of the person and the heading of the person. In some examples, the high beam controller 172 may fail to identity the face of the person (e.g., the face is obscured, environmental factors, etc.), thus, failing to determine the heading of the person. In such examples, the high beam controller 172 may perform a heading algorithm to determine whether the person is facing the vehicle. The heading algorithm uses a plurality of images captured over a predetermined period and/or a plurality of readings measured by the external sensors 120 over the predetermined period to determine a direction in which the person is facing. Using said images and/or readings, the heading algorithm determines a direction in which the person is facing. Specifically using said images and/or readings, the heading algorithm determines a positional difference between the vehicle 100 and person over time by determining a relative gap G between the vehicle 100 and person by implementing various mathematical models including, but not limited to, a discrete function, a sound based method, a light reflection method, and a relative integrator approach.

For the discrete derivation, the heading algorithm determines: (1) a first vehicle speed V1 at a first time T1; (2) a first distance between the vehicle 100 and the person S1 at the first time T1; (3) a second vehicle speed V2 at a second subsequent time T2; and (4) a second distance between the vehicle 100 and the person S2 at the second time T2. The amount of time between the first time S1 and the second time S2 may be predetermined. Based on these variables, the heading algorithm determines a time difference Δt, which is modeled by the following equation:

$$\Delta t = T2 - T1 \qquad \text{[Equation 1]}$$

Based on Equation 1, the heading algorithm determines a discrete function $\Delta S_{vehicle}$ to determine the travel distance within a predetermined period. The discrete function $\Delta S_{vehicle}$ is determined, which is modeled by the following equation:

$$\Delta S_{vehicle} = ((V1+V2)/2)^{*}\Delta t \qquad \text{[Equation 2]}$$

Based at least in part on Equation 2, the heading algorithm further calculates a relative distance between the vehicle 100 and the person, or a relative gap G. For this variable, the heading algorithm assumes that the speed of the person is 0 m/s. The relative gap G is determined based on the following equation:

$$G = S1 - \Delta S_{\text{vehicle}} \quad \text{[Equation 3]}$$

If the second distance S2 between the vehicle 100 and the person is less than or equal to the relative gap G, the heading algorithm determines that the person is approaching the vehicle 100, thus, facing the vehicle 100. If the second distance S2 between the vehicle 100 and the person is greater than the relative gap G, the heading algorithm determines that the person is moving in the same direction as the vehicle 100, thus, not facing the vehicle 100.

For the sound based method, it is assumed that at least one of the external sensors 120 is a sound based sensor for determining a distance between an object and said sensor. Once a sound wave is generated by the external sensors 120, the heading algorithm determines a speed of the sound wave in aft. Based on said speed, the heading algorithm determines a distance traversed by the sound wave S_{sound}, which is modeled by the following equation:

$$S_{\text{sound}} = V_{\text{sound in air}} \times \text{time} \quad \text{[Equation 4]}$$

Based on said distance, the heading algorithm determines a distance between the vehicle 100 and the person $\Delta S_{\text{car,person}}$, which is modeled by the following equation:

$$\Delta S_{\text{car,person}} = 0.5 \times S_{\text{sound}} \quad \text{[Equation 5]}$$

The heading algorithm determines a distance between the vehicle 100 and the person $\Delta S_{\text{car,person}}$ for a first time T1 and a second subsequent time T2, and determines the relative gap G, which is modeled by the following equation:

$$G = \Delta S_{\text{car,person}}(T1) - \Delta S_{\text{car,person}}(T2) \quad \text{[Equation 6]}$$

If the distance between the vehicle 100 and the person $\Delta S_{\text{car,person}}$ at T2 (i.e. $\Delta S_{\text{car,person}}$ (T2)) is less than or equal to the relative gap G, the heading algorithm determines that the person is approaching the vehicle 100, thus, facing the vehicle 100. If $\Delta S_{\text{car,person}}$ (T2) is greater than the relative gap G, the heading algorithm determines that the person is moving in the same direction as the vehicle 100, thus, not facing the vehicle 100.

For the light reflection method, this method may be substantially similar to that of the sound based method, wherein the only difference is that the measurement is based on light instead of sound. Therefore, details thereof will not be described herein for sake of brevity.

For the relative integrator approach, it is assumed that at least one of the external sensors 120 is an accelerometer. The heading algorithm determines a first distance S1 at a first time T1 and a second distance at a second subsequent time T2 based on the following equations:

$$S1 = \iint \text{accelerometer output}(T1) \quad \text{[Equation 7]}$$

$$S2 = \iint \text{accelerometer output}(T2) \quad \text{[Equation 8]}$$

Based on the first distance S1 and the second distance S2, the heading algorithm determines the relative gap G, which is modeled by the following equation:

$$G = S1 - S2 \qquad \text{[Equation 9]}$$

If the second distance S2 between the vehicle 100 and the person is less than or equal to the relative gap G, the heading algorithm determines that the person is approaching the vehicle 100, thus, facing the vehicle 100. If the second distance S2 between the vehicle 100 and the person is greater than the relative gap G, the heading algorithm determines that the person is moving in the same direction as the vehicle 100, thus, not facing the vehicle 100.

It should be appreciated that other methods may be used to determine whether a person is facing the vehicle 100.

Moving on, if the high beam controller 172 determines that the person is not facing the vehicle 100, the high beam controller 172 maintains control of the high beam headlamps 110 under normal operations. If the high beam controller 172 determines that the person is facing the vehicle 100, the high beam controller 172 performs an anti-glare light dynamic control.

During the anti-glare light dynamic control, the high beam controller 172 determines the position of the person's face based on one or more images captured by the external camera 130. If the high beam controller 172 fails to identity the person's face to determine the position thereof, the high beam controller 172 calculates the overall height of the person and estimates a general region in which the person's face should be positioned. Based on the position of the person's face, the high beam controller 172 dynamically adjusts at least one of the plurality of light pixels 112 such that one or more portions of the high beams that would be directed to the person's face is deactivated. In some examples, the high beam controller 172 may dynamically adjust at least one of the plurality of light pixels 112 based on a prediction. For example, the high beam controller 172 may account for an average amount of delay for: (1) capturing an image of a person; (2) identifying the face of the person; and (3) deactivating at least one of the plurality of light pixels 112 directed to the person's face. Based on the average amount of delay, the velocity of the person, and the velocity of the vehicle, the high beam controller 172 may predict a position in which the person will be after the average amount of delay and deactivate at least one of the plurality of light pixels 112 directed to said position.

The high beam controller 172 continues to dynamically adjust at least one of the plurality of light pixels 112 until the person's face is outside the high beam zone.

It should be appreciated that the high beam controller 172 may adjust one or more portions of the high beams for each of the plurality of faces of persons detected within the high beam zone.

It should be appreciated that the dynamic high beam control system may provide the anti-glare light dynamic control to other living beings, such as animals.

FIGS. 2A and 2B illustrate a side view of example scenarios in which the vehicle 100 of FIG. 1 is approaching a pedestrian 200. In these example scenarios, the vehicle 100 performs the anti-glare light dynamic control such that one or more portions of the high beams 210 that would be directed to the pedestrian's face is deactivated.

FIG. 2A illustrates a first example scenario. In this scenario, the vehicle 100 and the pedestrian are separated at a first distance. Based on the position of the pedestrian's face 202, the vehicle 100 generates the high beams 210 such that one or more portions 212 of the high beams 210 that is absent of light is positioned at a first vertical angle θ_{V1} with respect to a reference line 214. Herein, the reference line 214 is parallel to a direction in which the vehicle 100 is traversing.

FIG. 2B illustrates a second example scenario. In this scenario, the vehicle 100 has moved closer to the pedestrian 200, and the vehicle 100 and the pedestrian 200 are separated at a second closer distance. Based on the position of the pedestrian's face 202, the vehicle 100 generates the high beams 210 such that one or more portions 212 of the high beams 210 that is absent of light is positioned at a second greater vertical angle θ_{V2} with respect to the reference line 214.

FIGS. 3A and 3B illustrate a plan view of the example scenarios as illustrated in FIGS. 2A and 2B, respectively.

In FIG. 3A, the pedestrian's face 202 is within both the left high beam and the right high beam. Thus, the vehicle 100 causes at least one of the light pixels 112 of the left high beam headlamp 110 to be deactivated such that the left high beam 210 includes a first portion 310 that is: (1) absent of light; and (2) positioned at a first horizontal angle θ_{H1} with respect to the reference line 214. The first portion 310 is one of the one or more portions 212. Further, the vehicle 100 causes at least one of the light pixels 112 of the right high beam headlamp 210 to be deactivated such that the right high beam 210 includes a second portion 320 that is: (1) absent of light; and (2) positioned at a second greater horizontal angle θ_{H2} with respect to the reference line 214. The second portion 320 is one of the one or more portions 212.

In FIG. 3B, the pedestrian's face 200 is only within the left high beam 210. Thus, the vehicle 100 only causes at least one of the light pixels 112 of the left high beam headlamp 112 to be deactivated such that the first portion 310 absent of light is positioned at a third horizontal angle θ_{H3} with respect to the reference line 214. Assuming that the pedestrian 200 was stationary and the driving path of the vehicle 100 was linear for both the first example scenario and the second example scenario, the third horizontal angle θ_{H3} is greater than the first horizontal angle θ_{H1}.

FIG. 4 is a flowchart of a method for dynamically controlling high beams generated from the vehicle 100 of FIG. 1, which may be implemented by the high beam controller 172 of FIG. 1.

At block 402, the high beam controller 172 determines whether the high beam headlamps 110 are activated. If so, the method continues to block 404. Otherwise, the method returns to block 402.

At block 404, the high beam controller 172 activates external camera 130, the external sensors 120, and the internal camera 140.

At block 406, the high beam controller 172 determines whether a person is detected within a high beam zone. If so, the method continues to block 408. Otherwise, the method continues to block 424.

At block 408, the high beam controller 172 determines whether the driver of the vehicle 100 is distracted.

At block 410, the high beam controller 172 causes the infotainment head unit 150 to generate a visual and/or audible alert to the driver.

At block 412, the high beam controller 172 determines whether the person's face is detectable from one or more images captured by the external camera 130. If so, the method continues to block 414. Otherwise, the method continues to block 416.

At block 414, the high beam controller 172 determines, based on said one or more images, whether the person is facing the vehicle 100. If so, the method continues to block 420. Otherwise, the method continues to block 424.

At block 416, the high beam controller 172 determines the relative gap G by implementing various mathematical models including, but not limited to, a discrete function, a sound based method, a light reflection method, and a relative integrator approach.

At block 418, the high beam controller 172 compares the relative gap G to a threshold value to determine whether the person is facing the vehicle 100. If the relative gap G satisfies a threshold value, the method continues to block 420. Otherwise, the method continues to block 424.

At block 420, the high beam controller 172 performs the anti-glare light dynamic control.

At block 422, the high beam controller 172 determines whether the person is out of the high beam zone or facing away from the vehicle 100. If so, the method continues to block 424. Otherwise, the method returns to block 412.

At block 424, the high beam headlamps 110 operate normally.

The flowchart of FIG. 4 is representative of machine readable instructions stored in memory (such as the memory of FIG. 1) that comprise one or more programs that, when executed by a processor (such as the processor of 1), cause the vehicle 100 to implement the example high beam controller 172 of FIG. 1. Further, although the example program(s) is/are described with reference to the flowchart illustrated in FIG. 4, many other methods of implementing the example high beam controller 172 may alternatively be used. For example, the order of execution of the blocks may be changed, and/or some of the blocks described may be changed, eliminated, or combined.

In this application, the use of the disjunctive is intended to include the conjunctive. The use of definite or indefinite articles is not intended to indicate cardinality. In particular, a reference to "the" object or "a" and "an" object is intended to denote also one of a possible plurality of such objects. Further, the conjunction "or" may be used to convey features that are simultaneously present instead of mutually exclusive alternatives. In other words, the conjunction "or" should be understood to include "and/or." As used here, the terms "module" and "unit" refer to hardware with circuitry to provide communication, control, and/or monitoring capabilities, often in conjunction with sensors. "Modules" and "units" may also include firmware that executes on the circuitry. The terms "includes," "including," and "include" are inclusive and have the same scope as "comprises," "comprising," and "comprise," respectively.

The above-described embodiments, and particularly any "preferred" embodiments, are possible examples of implementations and merely set forth for a clear understanding of the principles of the invention. Many variations and modifications may be made to the above-described embodiment(s) without substantially departing from the spirit and principles of the techniques described herein. All modifications are intended to be included herein within the scope of this disclosure and protected by the following claims.

Chapter 6

More Advanced Patent Claim Drafting Practice

Draft the Claims before the Specification

It is considered good practice, in general, to draft the claims before the specification. It permits you to make sure, when drafting the specification, that you have described the invention completely, both narrowly and broadly. In general, it is probably more difficult to broaden the specification once you have written it than it is to narrow it. This may explain at least partly the focus on getting a good initial independent claim that is as broad as is reasonably possible.[1] Thus, by formulating the claims before the specification, you "should" be able to ensure that you have support for your broadest claims.

The word "should" has quotes around it because the drafting process is more dynamic than simply first draft the claims, and then draft the specification. More typically, a working set of claims is drafted, then the specification is started. As the specification is fleshed out, a better understanding of the technology usually results, leading to changes to improve the claims along the way. Furthermore, once the specification is mostly written, there may be an attempt to draft additional claims to have a complete claim set of around 20 total claims and three independent claims.

However, by seeking to draft in the initially recommended order, you can endeavor to make sure that the exact same terminology that is employed in the claims is also employed in the specification. This is a good drafting practice because even slight changes in terminology may create interpretive problems or potentially even written description problems. If you were to write the specification first, you may be more likely to change and perhaps inconsistently employ the relevant terminology as you draft the claims. It then would be more problematic to attempt to ensure that the specification and claims are consistent.

1. However, as discussed in detail in Chapter 2, that is not necessarily always the chosen approach.

Another advantage of writing the claims before the specification is that it permits you to make sure that all key terms in the claims are clearly and carefully defined to provide the appropriate coverage. As has been previously discussed,[2] claim terms are given their ordinary and customary meaning, unless it is clear in the specification that they are intended to have a different meaning. One unfortunate result of this law is that unless you define your key terms in the specification, you may never be sure of the claim coverage until litigation ensues. You may want to rely on the ordinary and customary meaning, but it may not be entirely clear what that is. Therefore, it is recommended that once you have drafted the claims, you review them and pick out the key terms and make sure those terms are clearly and crisply defined to resolve potential ambiguities that might otherwise crop up later, such as in litigation.

As illustrations, consider these definitional questions: Is a set-top box a "computer"? Is a cell phone a "computer"? Is a microcontroller a "processor"? By defining the key terms of your claims in the specification, you are able to anticipate and answer questions, such as these, that otherwise might be unclear.

Furthermore, there are potential legal issues that are easier to address in this early drafting stage rather than later.

Avoid Potential Written Description Issues

Gentry Gallery, Inc. v. Berkline Corp.
134 F.3d 1473
United States Court of Appeals for the Federal Circuit
January 27, 1998, Decided

Lizardtech, Inc. v. Earth Resource Mapping, Inc.
424 F.3d 1336
United States Court of Appeals for the Federal Circuit
October 4, 2005, Decided

Questions

1. Although the decision in *Gentry Gallery* discusses infringement and invalidity under § 103 in detail, the case is more well known for its handling of the written description issue. This seems to be a case in which during prosecution the claims were modified to include some-

2. See discussion of claim interpretation in Chapter 5.

thing that was not necessarily supported by the specification. This is a real issue to watch when drafting patent claims. Here, this resulted in invalidating a number of claims. Apparently, the specification only described placing controls on the console. However, does it not seem straightforward that if they could be on the console, they could be anywhere? What does the Federal Circuit say about this with respect to this application?

2. The Federal Circuit observes that a narrow disclosure will lead to narrow claims. What do you think of this quote: "an applicant is entitled to claims as broad as the prior art *and his disclosure* will allow"?[3]
3. What was the standard of review applied by the appellate court? Why did the appellate court not remand the written description issue?
4. As the appellate court makes clear, the claims invalidated in *Lizardtech* were the original patent claims. This is not the same as in *Gentry Gallery*, in which the invalidated claims were broader than the initial disclosure because subject matter was added during prosecution. Why was this a surprise to the patent community at the time of the decision?
5. In *Lizardtech*, given that claim 21 was in the original disclosure, why was it held invalid for lack of written description support? Why did the patentee include claim 21? What does this suggest when drafting broad claims?
6. How does one know whether their disclosure enables patent scope beyond the embodiment described? Was Lizardtech's mistake not that it drafted a broad claim, but rather that it drafted a claim that covered any and all methods of generating a seamless discrete wavelet transform? What might have happened if, instead, Lizardtech included claim 21 and not claims 1 or 13? What then is suggested with respect to claim drafting?

* * *

Of course, many written description-type issues are possible. However, the focus here is primarily issues that relate to the process of drafting the claims of the patent application. Regarding claim drafting, one of the more common issues is to *modify* the claims in a way not ultimately reflected in the specification. This may occur as one refines a set of claims. It may be an oversight to not reflect some claim refinements in the specification itself.

Fortunately, if this happens and the examiner, for example, raises a written description issue, most of the time, it is correctible. Nonetheless, it would be

3. Gentry Gallery, Inc. v. Berkline Corp., 134 F.3d 1473, 1480 (Fed. Cir. 1998).

much better if this did not happen because there might be other legal issues from this oversight beyond written description support.

In general, the claim, if in the originally filed patent application, is usually considered to support itself. The originally filed claims are part of the written description.[4] In this case, the specification could be amended to include the claim language without raising a new matter issue. However, a risk, apart from the written description issue, is that the claim language may be unclear without more supporting description. Thus, for example, it may raise an indefiniteness issue.[5] Furthermore, there have been cases in which *an original claim* has been invalidated under the written description requirement. An example of this is the Federal Circuit case *Lizardtech, Inc. v. Earth Resource Mapping, Inc.*[6]

Much more deadly is to amend a claim in prosecution in a manner without written description support. Unfortunately, the contours of written description support are not precise. Typically, if this occurs, it may be that the attorney did not realize the claim was not supported, perhaps relying on his or her imperfect memory of the specification.[7]

Several well-known Federal Circuit cases, including *Gentry Gallery v. Berkline Corp.*,[8] *Tronzo v. Biomet, Inc.*,[9] and *Toro Co. v. Ariens Co.*,[10] have found patent claims to be invalid under 35 U.S.C. § 112 for failing to satisfy the written description requirement. In these cases, the appellate court determined that the specification failed to provide support for recited limitations in the claims. In these cases, the claims were amended in prosecution in ways that were not supported by the written description. This is a risk often associated with disclosing a single or only a few embodiments. By instead describing and claiming multiple embodiments from broadest to narrowest, as has been mentioned, the risk of lack of written description is reduced because explicit textual support is provided at the time of filing, at a minimum, by the claims themselves.

The apparent problem is that if not supported, the claim is invalid. However, a *more pernicious* problem also exists due to the America Invents Act (AIA). A real risk exists that, if this is a continuation claiming priority from a pre-AIA

4. *See, e.g.*, Mentor Graphics Corp. v. EVE-USA, Inc., 870 F.3d 1298 (Fed. Cir. 2017). *Cf.* Kennecott Corp. v. Kyocera Int'l, Inc., 835 F.2d 1419 (Fed. Cir. 1987) (claim supported because although words are missing from the specification, the specification provided inherent support).

5. See discussion of indefiniteness later in this chapter.

6. 424 F.3d 1336 (Fed. Cir. 2005).

7. Suggesting that a reread of the specification is always a good idea if amending claims.

8. 134 F.3d 1473.

9. 156 F.3d 1154 (Fed. Cir. 1998).

10. 232 F.3d 915 (Fed. Cir. 2000) (nonprecedential).

patent application, that is now post-AIA rather than pre-AIA, law applies to the continuation. This issue was discussed in Chapter 1.[11] It relates to AIA transition provisions for situations where a post-AIA-filed patent application claims priority to a pre-AIA original patent application filing.

The upshot of the AIA transition provisions may be summarized as follows: if a patent claim is added *at any time* that does not have written description support in the original pre-AIA patent application filing, all the claims of a patent application filed on or after March 16, 2013, are subject to *post*-AIA § 102 and *post*-AIA § 103. Furthermore, once such a patent claim is added, this consequence cannot be undone. These statutory sections apply to all the claims of a patent application as a result of adding new subject matter without written description support in the original pre-March 16, 2013, filing. Those statutory sections will continue to apply to all of the claims of the patent application filed on or after March 16, 2013, even if the new matter is later removed. Furthermore, recent Patent Trial and Appeal Board (PTAB) cases support this interpretation.[12]

Now let us think for a moment about the potential consequences of the post-AIA provisions applying to a continuation application for the preceding scenario. For one thing, more prior art may now be citable against the patent claims. For example, if the date of invention under subsection 102(g)(2) (pre-AIA) is much earlier than cited prior art, one will be legally foreclosed from arguing that the invention predates the prior art because it was conceived and reduced to practice before the date of the prior art.[13]

This is "in theory" because this all may happen inadvertently. For example, claims may be added that a judge in *later litigation* concludes do not have written description support in the original filing. At that time, then, the consequences of this on the validity of a patent that issued from the continuation patent application would need to be evaluated. This provides an additional reason to make sure that drafted patent claims have written description support in a patent application or claim amendment to be filed.

---

11. See Chapter 1, discussing claiming priority and the AIA.

12. *See* Microsurgical Tech., Inc. v. Regents of the Univ. of Colo., No. PGR2021-00026, Paper 12 (P.T.A.B. June 16, 2021); Rockwool Int'l A/S v. Knauf Insulation, Inc., No. PGR2022-00022, Paper 10 (P.T.A.B. July 6, 2022).

13. Note, however, that by statute subsection 102(g) does apply to transition patent applications; however, it is believed that this is only if subsection 102(g) is used to challenge the validity of the patent, not if the patentee could swear behind a cited piece of art.

Of course, if you add new subject matter to a claim you might also get a rejection under § 132[14] for having new matter; however, primarily the issue is really one of lack of written description support.

With respect to written description, another possible issue may arise under subsection 112(f) regarding the claims that relates to the specification—although the issue is characterized as indefiniteness, it is really a matter of not providing enough description.[15] For example, it may be that a functional claim without the word "means" (or, perhaps, with the word "means") may be held to include a limitation that is to be construed under subsection 112(f). Therefore, it is a good idea to be mindful of the consequences should, despite your best drafting efforts, your claim be construed under subsection 112(f) during examination or in litigation.

In the event subsection 112(f) is invoked, the specification *must* provide sufficient *corresponding* structure for the recited function. That is, for the function or functions recited in the claim, the specification *must* describe *corresponding* structure able to perform the recited function or functions or the claim will be held invalid if tested. Here, *corresponding* suggests that the specification is written to clearly associate the function of the claim and the structure in the description in a manner such that one of ordinary skill would comprehend the association.

If an element is construed under subsection 112(f) and the statutory requirements regarding corresponding structure are satisfied, then the claim covers, by express statutory direction (emphasis added): "the *corresponding* structure, material, or acts described in the specification *and equivalents*." Thus, the claim, by statute, construed *literally* under subsection 112(f) may be infringed by embodiments in your specification that *correspond* to the functional language or by a *112(f) equivalent* of what is shown in the specification; however, the scope of such *112(f) equivalents* is generally exceedingly narrow.[16]

In the area of software, in particular, the software algorithm is considered the structure at issue under subsection 112(f).[17] For this reason, not infrequently, claims interpreted under subsection 112(f) that relate to software are held invalid as not appropriately describing structure or enough

14. 35 U.S.C. § 132 (2024) states, in pertinent part: "No amendment shall introduce new matter into the disclosure of the invention."

15. See discussion later in this chapter regarding indefiniteness.

16. *See, e.g.*, Valmont Indus., Inc. v. Reinke Mfg. Co., 983 F.2d 1039 (Fed. Cir. 1993).

17. *See, e.g.*, Eon Corp. IP Holdings, LLC v. AT&T Mobility, LLC, 785 F.3d 616, 621 (Fed. Cir. 2015).

structure. They are invalidated as being indefinite, under § 112, second paragraph.[18] However, in reality, insufficient description has been provided. That is, generally it is *not* sufficient to merely provide a functional description.[19] Enough detail must be described to, in effect, show possession. This means sufficient detail of *how to perform the function* so that one of ordinary skill *would know the scope being claimed* with respect to implementing the function or operation claimed.[20]

If a function is claimed under subsection 112(f) that is not described to this level, the claim will be held invalid if tested. Therefore, in drafting claims, care is warranted to not inadvertently claim a function that is believed to be well understood, such as "transmit a signal" or "receive a signal," but for which the specification does not provide an implementation description because it is not appreciated that the claims will be interpreted under subsection 112(f).[21]

The *Lizardtech*[22] decision is a groundbreaking one for the written description requirement, although it was not entirely unexpected that such a decision might eventually be handed down. Earlier Federal Circuit cases, such as *Gentry Gallery, Inc. v. Berkline Corp.*[23] and *Toro Co. v. White Consolidated Industries, Inc.*,[24] suggested that that the written description may limit claim scope. Essentially, the *Lizardtech* case held that a claim that was originally filed with the patent application failed to have written description support because the scope of the claim exceeded what was described in the specification (and file history). The claim at issue was a valiant attempt by the claim drafter to capture more scope, but it ultimately did not succeed.

In hindsight, at best, what the drafter might have done was to have the inventors come up with additional embodiments and then draft different claims to these embodiments that might have potentially "snagged" the infringer in this case. Though feasible, such is usually considered above and beyond the duty of the drafter, unless the client has indicated that the application should receive "special" treatment and additional budget is provided to support such activities.

---

18. Section 112, second paragraph (pre-AIA) is § 112(b) (post-AIA).

19. *See* Blackboard, Inc. v. Desire2Learn, Inc., 574 F.3d 1371, 1383–85, 91 U.S.P.Q.2d 1481, 1491–93 (Fed. Cir. 2009); Noah Sys., Inc. v. Intuit Inc., 675 F.3d 1302 (Fed. Cir. 2012).

20. *See Blackboard, Inc.*, 574 F.3d at 1383–85, 91 U.S.P.Q.2d at 1491–93; *Noah Sys., Inc.*, 675 F.3d 1302.

21. *But see In re* Katz *Interactive Call Processing Patent Litig.*, 639 F.3d 1303 (Fed. Cir. 2011).

22. Lizardtech, Inc. v. Earth Res. Mapping, Inc., 424 F.3d 1336 (Fed. Cir. 2005).

23. 134 F.3d 1473 (Fed. Cir. 1998).

24. 383 F.3d 1326 (Fed. Cir. 2004).

Many good reasons, in addition to written description support, exist to define claim terms expressly in the specification.[25] Previously, we discussed this recommendation from the perspective of claim interpretation, which is quite important. In addition, however, as suggested, doing so provides clear written description support.

Federal Circuit jurisprudence has held that claim terms may be defined in the specification expressly or by implication. We recommend that all *important* claim terms be expressly defined in the specification. Of course, once this has been done, the claims must be properly drafted to implement the definition provided, an important and still challenging claim drafting exercise.

One problem with defining claim terms by implication, rather than with express language, is that whether this has occurred (e.g., the claim terms are defined) may be arguable. The ultimate decision is usually left to someone else other than the patentee, such as a judge in a suit, a competitor in a negotiation, and so on. Furthermore, what is required to define a claim term by implication is not entirely clear.

Cases in which claim terms were found to be defined in the specification by implication[26] include *Covad Communications*[27] and *SciMed.*[28] On the other hand, *Thorner v. Sony Computer Entertainment America*[29] suggests that the Federal Circuit may, instead, be reluctant to conclude a claim term has been defined by implication. As suggested previously,[30] the line may be a fine one between reading limitations from the specification into the claims, highlighted in *Phillips v. AWH Corp.*[31] as something to avoid, and impliedly providing a special meaning to a claim term. It also appears that different panels of judges may reach different conclusions, further confounding the issue.

Thus, it is recommended that important claim terms be expressly defined; however, in a manner consistent with ordinary and customary meaning. In

---

25. See discussion in Chapter 5 of expressly defining claim terms.

26. *Id.*

27. Bell Atl. Network Servs., Inc. v. Covad Commc'ns Grp., Inc., 262 F.3d 1258 (Fed. Cir. 2001).

28. SciMed Life Sys., Inc. v. Advanced Cardiovascular Sys., Inc., 242 F.3d 1337 (Fed. Cir. 2001). *See also* Microsoft Corp. v. Multi-Tech Sys., Inc., 357 F.3d 1340, 1347 (Fed. Cir. 2004), *cert. denied*, 543 U.S. 821 (2004) (citing and applying *SciMed*); Alloc, Inc. v. Int'l Trade Comm'n, 342 F.3d 1361, 1370, 68 U.S.P.Q.2d 1161 (Fed. Cir. 2003), *cert. denied*, 541 U.S. 1063 (2004) (citing and applying *SciMed*).

29. 669 F.3d 1362 (Fed. Cir. 2012); see discussion in Chapter 5.

30. See discussion in Chapter 5.

31. 415 F.3d 1303 (Fed. Cir. 2005).

this way, two risks are addressed. One risk relates to whether the patentee has imparted a special meaning to the claim term. The other risk relates to whether the ordinary meaning includes the intended meaning. Again, by following this approach, either position may be argued. It may turn out, depending on the circumstances, one position is preferred. However, by an approach that supports either position, the opportunity is preserved to take a preferred position later.

Negative Limitations

MPEP § 2173.05(i)

Negative Limitations

The current view of the courts is that there is nothing inherently ambiguous or uncertain about a negative limitation. So long as the boundaries of the patent protection sought are set forth definitely, albeit negatively, the claim complies with the requirements of 35 U.S.C. 112(b) or pre-AIA 35 U.S.C. 112, second paragraph. Some older cases were critical of negative limitations because they tended to define the invention in terms of what it was not, rather than pointing out the invention. Thus, the court observed that the limitation "R is an alkenyl radical other than 2-butenyl and 2,4-pentadienyl" was a negative limitation that rendered the claim indefinite because it was an attempt to claim the invention by excluding what the inventors did not invent rather than distinctly and particularly pointing out what they did invent. In re Schechter, 205 F.2d 185, 98 USPQ 144 (CCPA 1953).

A claim which recited the limitation "said homopolymer being free from the proteins, soaps, resins, and sugars present in natural Hevea rubber" in order to exclude the characteristics of the prior art product, was considered definite because each recited limitation was definite. In re Wakefield, 422 F.2d 897, 899, 904, 164 USPQ 636, 638, 641 (CCPA 1970). In addition, the court found that the negative limitation "incapable of forming a dye with said oxidized developing agent" was definite because the boundaries of the patent protection sought were clear. In re Barr, 444 F.2d 588, 170 USPQ 330 (CCPA 1971).

Any negative limitation or exclusionary proviso must have basis in the original disclosure. If alternative elements are positively recited in the specification, they may be explicitly excluded in the claims. See In re Johnson, 558 F.2d 1008, 1019, 194 USPQ 187, 196 (CCPA 1977) ("[the] specification, having described the whole, necessarily described the part remaining."). See also Ex parte Grasselli, 231 USPQ 393 (Bd. App. 1983), aff'd mem., 738 F.2d 453 (Fed. Cir. 1984). In describing alternative features, the applicant need not articulate advantages or disadvantages of each feature in order to later exclude the alternative features. See Inphi Corporation v. Netlist, Inc., 805 F.3d 1350, 1356–57, 116 USPQ2d 2006, 2010–11 (Fed. Cir. 2015). The mere absence of a positive recitation is not basis for an exclusion. However, a lack of literal basis in the specification for a negative limitation may not be sufficient to establish a prima facie case for lack of descriptive support. Ex parte Parks, 30 USPQ2d 1234, 1236 (Bd. Pat. App. & Inter. 1993). "Rather, as with positive limitations, the disclosure must only 'reasonably convey[] to those skilled in the art that the inventor had possession of the claimed subject matter as of the filing date.' . . . While silence will not generally suffice to support a negative claim limitation, there may be circumstances in which it can be established that a skilled artisan would understand a negative limitation to necessarily be present in a disclosure." Novartis Pharms. Corp. v. Accord Healthcare, Inc., 38 F.4th 1013, 2022 USPQ2d 569 (Fed. Cir. 2022) (quoting Ariad Pharm. Inc. v. Eli Lilly & Co., 589 F.3d 1336, 1351, 94 USPQ2d 1161, 1172). Any claim containing a negative limitation which does not have basis in the original disclosure should be rejected under 35 U.S.C. 112(a) or pre-AIA 35 U.S.C. 112, first paragraph, as failing to comply with the written description requirement. See MPEP § 2163–§ 2163.07(b) for a discussion of the written description requirement of 35 U.S.C. 112(a) and pre-AIA 35 U.S.C. 112, first paragraph.

Novartis Pharmaceuticals Corp. v. Accord Healthcare, Inc.
38 F.4th 1013
United States Court of Appeals for the Federal Circuit
June 21, 2022, Decided

Questions

1. The history of this case is a point of interest. The original opinion affirmed the district court and was written by Judge O'Malley with a dissent by Judge Moore. However, Judge O'Malley retired while a rehearing request was pending. Judge Hughes replaced Judge O'Malley and apparently sided with Judge Moore. Thus, a new opinion issued written by Judge Moore with a dissent by Judge Linn. What is the dispute between Judge Moore and Judge Linn?
2. According to Judge Moore, it is required that a particular limitation always be understood as necessarily excluded from a particular method or apparatus to qualify as written description support for a negative claim limitation. She states, "Rather, as with positive limitations, the disclosure must only 'reasonably convey[ ] to those skilled in the art that the inventor had possession of the claimed subject matter as of the filing date.'"[32] What is her position?

32. Novartis Pharms. Corp. v. Accord Healthcare, Inc., 38 F.4th 1013, 1020 (Fed. Cir. 2022).

3. What is Judge Linn's objection to the majority opinion? On the facts, do you agree with Judge Moore or Judge Linn?
4. If you needed to include a negative limitation in a claim, how would you make sure it had written description support?

EPO—Sufficiency and Claim Support—Articles 83 and 84

Article 83

Disclosure of the invention

The European patent application shall disclose the invention in a manner sufficiently clear and complete for it to be carried out by a person skilled in the art.

Article 84

Claims

The claims shall define the matter for which protection is sought. They shall be clear and concise and be supported by the description.

One situation that has potential to create a written description issue is a negative limitation. There was a time that negative limitations were not permitted, at least by the U.S. Patent and Trademark Office (PTO). Rather than saying what is covered, they recited what is not covered.[33] Although they are not verboten any longer, they may present tricky issues compared with other types of limitations. Negative limitations may be overly broad, so clarification in the specification is a good idea. That is, perhaps a narrower embodiment that could be covered with a positive recitation could be described and included as a dependent claim. Negative limitations might also create written description issues, primarily if not expressly described.

However, the law seems to be, as with other limitations, express language may not *necessarily* be required to satisfy written description. It is sufficient that one of ordinary skill upon reading the specification would conclude that the claim language reflects what has been invented.[34] However, best to avoid such a situation by being express regarding the negative limitation since then

33. *See* U.S. Patent and Trademark Office, Manual of Patent Examining Procedure § 2173.05(i) (9th ed. 2023) [hereinafter MPEP].

34. *See* Almirall, LLC v. Amneal Pharms. LLC, 28 F.4th 265 (Fed. Cir. 2022); *Novartis*, 38 F.4th 1013; Inphi Corp. v. Netlist, Inc., 805 F.3d 1350, 1356 (Fed. Cir. 2015) (there is no "new and heightened standard for negative claim limitations"); Santarus, Inc. v. Par Pharm., Inc., 694 F.3d 1344, 1350–51 (Fed. Cir. 2012); Nike, Inc. v. Adidas AG, 812 F.3d 1326, 1348 (Fed. Cir. 2016); All Dental Prodx, LLC v. Advantage Dental Prods., Inc., 309 F.3d 774, 779 (Fed. Cir. 2002) ("[T]he failure of the specification to specifically mention a limitation that later appears

whether the negative limitation is supported should not be arguable with the decision left to another. It is also worth noting that whether prior art shows a negative limitation appears to be just as, if not more, lenient.[35]

Avoid Potential Indefiniteness Issues

Aristocrat Technologies Australia Pty Ltd. v. International Game Technology
521 F.3d 1328
United States Court of Appeals for the Federal Circuit
March 28, 2008, Decided

Nautilus, Inc. v. Biosig Instruments, Inc.
572 U.S. 898
Supreme Court of the United States
April 28, 2014, Argued; June 2, 2014, Decided

Niazi Licensing Corp. v. St. Jude Medical S.C., Inc.
30 F.4th 1339
United States Court of Appeals for the Federal Circuit
April 11, 2022, Decided

Questions

1. *Aristocrat* is an important means-plus-function case because for software it clarifies to some extent what it needed for equivalent structure. What is the rationale used by the appellate court to conclude that even if one of ordinary skill is provided enough information to program the claimed function, the disclosure may still not be sufficient to make the claim definite?
2. It seems like the appellate court tells us what is not sufficient rather than what is sufficient. Is it clear what is required for a means-plus-function claim for software to be definite? Based on *Aristocrat*, what do you think is required? What does the case say is the legal standard?[36]

---

in the claims is not a fatal one when one skilled in the art would recognize upon reading the specification that the new language reflects what the specification shows has been invented.").

35. *See* Daniel Hanson, *Proving a Negative Claim Limitation: A Tale of Three Nonprecedential Cases*, IPWatchdog (Sept. 12, 2019, 1:15 PM), https://www.ipwatchdog.com/2019/09/12/proving-a-negative-claim-limitation-a-tale-of-three-nonprecedential-cases/id=113260/.

36. *See also* Noah Sys., Inc. v. Intuit Inc., 675 F.3d 1302 (Fed. Cir. 2012).

3. The parties agreed that the claim limitation at issue was a means-plus-function claim. Is there any argument that it was not? Such a construction would have likely changed the outcome of the case. This also suggests the danger of relying only on means-plus-function claims without a non-means-plus-function claim.
4. The appellate court draws a distinction in the case between a general microprocessor and the software to program it. Are there situations where this distinction may not hold up completely?[37]
5. In *Nautilus*, according to the Court, what was the real issue with the standard of definiteness articulated by the Federal Circuit?
6. Is claim definiteness an issue of law or an issue of fact? What did the Court say?
7. What was the language being argued as indefinite and why? What was the argued response to that assertion?
8. Do you agree that the different linguistic approaches might make a difference for lower courts or are lower courts smart enough to read Federal Circuit rulings to assess what the terms used by the Federal Circuit mean? Do you find "spaced relationship" indefinite on its face? Do you agree with the Federal Circuit reasoning regarding why "spaced relationship" was not indefinite, at least under the standard used before the Court altered the standard? What guidance can we take from this case?
9. In *Niazi*, although the case raised issues of induced infringement and evidentiary rulings, the main issue in the case concerned the definiteness of the terms "resilient" and "pliable." Do you find these words to be indefinite on their face?
10. What is it about the terms "resilient" and "pliable" that make them objects of an indefiniteness argument, according to the appellate court? Both the district court and St. Jude rely on a sentence in the written description to say these terms are indefinite because the sentence suggests inconsistent term usage. What is that sentence? How did the Federal Circuit resolve the question regarding inconsistency? Do you think without the intrinsic evidence pointed to by the appellate court that the claims at issue would have still been found definite? Why or why not?

---

37. *See In re* Katz Interactive Call Processing Patent Litig., 639 F.3d 1303, 1316, 97 U.S.P.Q.2d 1737, 1747 (Fed. Cir. 2011) (The appellate court identified a situation in which a general-purpose computer may be sufficient as the corresponding structure if the claims merely recite a "general computing function," such as a "means for storing data.").

EPO—Clarity—Article 84

> Article 84
>
> Claims
>
> The claims shall define the matter for which protection is sought. They shall be clear and concise and be supported by the description.

In more recent years, indefiniteness has become a much more important issue than many years ago although, in general, the Federal Circuit tends to find claims definite. A watershed event was the *Nautilus* case in which the U.S. Supreme Court altered the legal standard for indefiniteness.[38] The standard had been whether the claim language was "insolubly ambiguous" considering the claims, the specification, and the file history. The Supreme Court modified the standard, recognizing the inherent limits of language, to whether the language, again, considering the claims, the specification, and the file history, "fails to inform, with reasonable certainty, those skilled in the art about the scope of the invention."[39]

We have mentioned several ways indefiniteness might become as issue. A common situation might be to amend a claim in prosecution and use words not in the specification, claims, or file history. Although it is not a guarantee that such language will be found indefinite, such a situation is not a desirable one.

Other typical situations include use of language to suggest a subjective standard rather than an objective one, or simply nonsensical language.[40] In this regard, words of degree may create indefiniteness issues without clarification as to how the language is to be applied.[41] Another problematic situation may be in which several equally valid measures to evaluate a claimed property exist and the specification does not identify the one that should be used.[42] It is

38. *See* Nautilus, Inc. v. Biosig Instruments, Inc., 134 S. Ct. 2120 (2014).

39. As stated, the Federal Circuit tends to hold claims definite. *See, e.g.*, Niazi Licensing Corp. v. St. Jude Med. S.C., Inc., 30 F.4th 1339 (Fed. Cir. 2022) (reversing district court finding claims indefinite); Univ. of Mass. v. L'Oreal S.A., 36 F.4th 1374 (Fed. Cir. 2022) (vacating district court finding claims indefinite); ImmunoGen, Inc. v. Hirshfeld, No. 2021-1939, 2022 WL 885774, at *2 (Fed. Cir. Mar. 25, 2022) (vacating district court holding "adjusted ideal body weight" (AIBW) indefinite); ClearOne, Inc. v. Shure Acquisition Holdings, Inc., 35 F.4th 1345 (Fed. Cir. 2022) (affirming PTAB determination that newly added claim language was not indefinite); Dyfan, LLC v. Target Corp., 28 F.4th 1360, 1364 (Fed. Cir. 2022) (claimed "code" was not in means-plus-function format and not indefinite for lack of structural equivalents in the specification).

40. *See* Interval Licensing LLC v. AOL, Inc., 896 F.3d 1335 (Fed. Cir. 2018); Halliburton Energy Servs., Inc. v. M-I LLC, 514 F.3d 1244, 1251 (Fed. Cir. 2008).

41. See discussion in Chapter 5 regarding words of degree.

42. *See* Dow Chem. Co. v. Nova Chems. Corp. (Can.), 803 F.3d 620, 633–35 (Fed. Cir. 2015).

worthy of mention that the PTO employs a different standard for indefiniteness than in *Nautilus* based on the rationale that there is no presumption of validity in prosecution.[43]

Previously, indefiniteness issues with respect to means-plus-function claims were discussed and this may be an issue, particularly with respect to software, as mentioned.[44]

Likewise, we have previously pointed out that claims that leave unclear the statutory category of the claimed subject matter may be indefinite.[45] We discuss this latter issue in more detail later in this chapter.

Finally, simply sloppy drafting may lead to indefiniteness. Examples are included in Chapter 5.[46]

Avoid Potential Patent Eligibility Issues

MPEP § 2106

Patent Subject Matter Eligibility

I. TWO CRITERIA FOR SUBJECT MATTER ELIGIBILITY

First, the claimed invention must be to one of the four statutory categories. 35 U.S.C. 101 defines the four categories of invention that Congress deemed to be the appropriate subject matter of a patent: processes, machines, manufactures and compositions of matter. The latter three categories define "things" or "products" while the first category defines "actions" (i.e., inventions that consist of a series of steps or acts to be performed). See 35 U.S.C. 100(b) ("The term 'process' means process, art, or method, and includes a new use of a known process, machine, manufacture, composition of matter, or material."). See MPEP § 2106.03 for detailed information on the four categories.

Second, the claimed invention also must qualify as patent-eligible subject matter, i.e., the claim must not be directed to a judicial exception unless the claim as a whole includes additional limitations amounting to significantly more than the exception. The judicial exceptions (also called "judicially recognized exceptions" or simply "exceptions") are subject matter that the courts have found to be outside of, or exceptions to, the four statutory categories of invention, and are limited to abstract ideas, laws of nature and natural phenomena (including products of nature). Alice Corp. Pty. Ltd. v. CLS Bank Int'l, 573 U.S. 208, 216, 110 USPQ2d 1976, 1980 (2014) (citing Ass'n for Molecular Pathology v. Myriad Genetics, Inc., 569 U.S. 576, 589, 106 USPQ2d

43. *See* MPEP, *supra* note 33, § 2173.
44. *See* Chapter 4.
45. See discussion later in this chapter.
46. See discussion in Chapter 5.

1972, 1979 (2013)). See MPEP § 2106.04 for detailed information on the judicial exceptions.

Because abstract ideas, laws of nature, and natural phenomenon "are the basic tools of scientific and technological work", the Supreme Court has expressed concern that monopolizing these tools by granting patent rights may impede innovation rather than promote it. See Alice Corp., 573 U.S. at 216, 110 USPQ2d at 1980; Mayo Collaborative Servs. v. Prometheus Labs., Inc., 566 U.S. 66, 71, 101 USPQ2d 1961, 1965 (2012). However, the Court has also emphasized that an invention is not considered to be ineligible for patenting simply because it involves a judicial exception. Alice Corp., 573 U.S. at 217, 110 USPQ2d at 1980–81 (citing Diamond v. Diehr, 450 U.S. 175, 187, 209 USPQ 1, 8 (1981)). See also Thales Visionix Inc. v. United States, 850 F.3d. 1343, 1349, 121 USPQ2d 1898, 1902 (Fed. Cir. 2017) ("That a mathematical equation is required to complete the claimed method and system does not doom the claims to abstraction."). Accordingly, the Court has said that integration of an abstract idea, law of nature or natural phenomenon into a practical application may be eligible for patent protection. See, e.g., Alice, 573 U.S. at 217, 110 USPQ2d at 1981 (explaining that "in applying the § 101 exception, we must distinguish between patents that claim the 'buildin[g] block[s]' of human ingenuity and those that integrate the building blocks into something more" (quoting Mayo, 566 U.S. at 89, 110 USPQ2d at 1971) and stating that Mayo "set forth a framework for distinguishing patents that claim laws of nature, natural phenomena, and abstract ideas from those that claim patent-eligible applications of those concepts"); Mayo, 566 U.S. at 80, 84, 101 USPQ2d at 1969, 1971 (noting that the Court in Diamond v. Diehr found "the overall process patent eligible because of the way the additional steps of the process integrated the equation into the process as a whole," but the Court in Gottschalk v. Benson "held that simply implementing a mathematical principle on a physical machine, namely a computer, was not a patentable application of that principle"); Bilski v. Kappos, 561 U.S. 593, 611, 95 USPQ2d 1001, 1010 (2010) ("Diehr explained that while an abstract idea, law of nature, or mathematical formula could not be patented, 'an application of a law of nature or mathematical formula to a known structure or process may well be deserving of patent protection.'" (quoting Diamond v. Diehr, 450 U.S. 175, 187, 209 USPQ 1, 8 (1981)) (emphasis in original)); Diehr, 450 U.S. at 187, 192 n.14, 209 USPQ at 10 n.14 (explaining that the process in Parker v. Flook was ineligible not because it contained a mathematical formula, but because it did not provide an application of the formula). See Diamond v. Diehr, 450 U.S. 175, 209 USPQ 1 (1981); Gottschalk v. Benson, 409 U.S. 63, 175 USPQ 673 (1972); Parker v. Flook, 437 U.S. 584, 198 USPQ 193 (1978).

The Supreme Court in Mayo laid out a framework for determining whether an applicant is seeking to patent a judicial exception itself, or a patent-eligible application of the judicial exception. See Alice Corp., 573 U.S. at 217–18, 110 USPQ2d at 1981 (citing Mayo, 566 U.S. 66, 101 USPQ2d 1961). This framework, which is referred to as the Mayo test or the Alice/Mayo test, is discussed in further detail in subsection III, below. The first part of the Mayo test is to determine whether the claims are directed to an abstract idea, a law of nature or a natural phenomenon (i.e., a judicial exception). Id. If the claims are directed to a judicial exception, the second part of the Mayo test is to determine whether the claim recites additional elements that amount to significantly more than the judicial exception. Id. citing Mayo, 566 U.S. at 72–73, 101 USPQ2d at 1966). The Supreme Court has described the second part of the test as the "search for an 'inventive concept'". Alice Corp., 573 U.S. at 217–18, 110 USPQ2d at 1981 (citing Mayo, 566 U.S. at 72–73, 101 USPQ2d at 1966).

The Alice/Mayo two-part test is the only test that should be used to evaluate the eligibility of claims under examination. While the machine-or-transformation test is an important clue to eligibility, it should not be used as a separate test for eligibility. Instead it should be considered as part of the "integration" determination or "significantly more" determination articulated in the Alice/Mayo test. Bilski v. Kappos, 561 U.S. 593, 605, 95 USPQ2d 1001, 1007 (2010). See MPEP § 2106.04(d) for more information about evaluating whether a claim reciting a judicial exception is integrated into a practical application and MPEP § 2106.05(b) and MPEP § 2106.05(c) for more information about how the machine-or-transformation test fits into the Alice/Mayo two-part framework. Likewise, eligibility should not be evaluated based on whether the claim recites a "useful, concrete, and tangible result," State Street Bank, 149 F.3d 1368, 1374, 47 USPQ2d 1596, 1602 (Fed. Cir. 1998) (quoting In re Alappat, 33 F.3d 1526, 1544, 31 USPQ2d 1545, 1557 (Fed. Cir. 1994)), as this test has been superseded. In re Bilski, 545 F.3d 943, 959–60, 88 USPQ2d 1385, 1394–95 (Fed. Cir. 2008) (en banc), aff'd by Bilski v. Kappos, 561 U.S. 593, 95 USPQ2d 1001 (2010). See also TLI Communications LLC v. AV Automotive LLC, 823 F.3d 607, 613, 118 USPQ2d 1744, 1748 (Fed. Cir. 2016) ("It is well-settled that mere recitation of concrete, tangible components is insufficient to confer patent eligibility to an otherwise abstract idea"). The programmed computer or "special purpose computer" test of In re Alappat, 33 F.3d 1526, 31 USPQ2d 1545 (Fed. Cir. 1994) (i.e., the rationale that an otherwise ineligible algorithm or software could be made patent-eligible by merely adding a generic computer to the claim for the "special purpose" of executing the algorithm or software) was also superseded by the Supreme Court's Bilski and Alice Corp. decisions. Eon Corp. IP Holdings LLC v. AT&T Mobility LLC, 785 F.3d 616, 623, 114 USPQ2d 1711, 1715 (Fed. Cir. 2015) ("[W]e note that Alappat has been superseded by Bilski, 561 U.S. at 605–06, and Alice Corp. v. CLS Bank Int'l, 573 U.S. 208, 110 USPQ2d 1976 (2014)"); Intellectual Ventures I LLC v. Capital One Bank (USA), N.A., 792 F.3d 1363, 1366, 115 USPQ2d 1636,

1639 (Fed. Cir. 2015) ("An abstract idea does not become nonabstract by limiting the invention to a particular field of use or technological environment, such as the Internet [or] a computer"). Lastly, eligibility should not be evaluated based on whether the claimed invention has utility, because "[u]tility is not the test for patent-eligible subject matter." Genetic Techs. Ltd. v. Merial LLC, 818 F.3d 1369, 1380, 118 USPQ2d 1541, 1548 (Fed. Cir. 2016).

Examiners are reminded that 35 U.S.C. 101 is not the sole tool for determining patentability; 35 U.S.C. 112, 35 U.S.C. 102, and 35 U.S.C. 103 will provide additional tools for ensuring that the claim meets the conditions for patentability. As the Supreme Court made clear in Bilski, 561 U.S. at 602, 95 USPQ2d at 1006:

> *The § 101 patent-eligibility inquiry is only a threshold test. Even if an invention qualifies as a process, machine, manufacture, or composition of matter, in order to receive the Patent Act's protection the claimed invention must also satisfy "the conditions and requirements of this title." § 101. Those requirements include that the invention be novel, see § 102, nonobvious, see § 103, and fully and particularly described, see § 112.*

II. ESTABLISH BROADEST REASONABLE INTERPRETATION OF CLAIM AS A WHOLE

It is essential that the broadest reasonable interpretation (BRI) of the claim be established prior to examining a claim for eligibility. The BRI sets the boundaries of the coverage sought by the claim and will influence whether the claim seeks to cover subject matter that is beyond the four statutory categories or encompasses subject matter that falls within the exceptions. See MyMail, Ltd. v. ooVoo, LLC, 934 F.3d 1373, 1379, 2019 USPQ2d 305789 (Fed. Cir. 2019) ("Determining patent eligibility requires a full understanding of the basic character of the claimed subject matter"), citing Bancorp Servs., LLC v. Sun Life Assurance Co. of Can. (U.S.), 687 F.3d 1266, 1273–74, 103 USPQ2d 1425, 1430 (Fed. Cir. 2012); In re Bilski, 545 F.3d 943, 951, 88 USPQ2d 1385, 1388 (Fed. Cir. 2008) (en banc), aff'd by Bilski v. Kappos, 561 U.S. 593, 95 USPQ2d 1001 (2010) ("claim construction . . . is an important first step in a § 101 analysis"). Evaluating eligibility based on the BRI also ensures that patent eligibility under 35 U.S.C. 101 does not depend simply on the draftsman's art. Alice, 573 U.S. 208, 224, 110 USPQ2d at 1984, 1985 (citing Parker v. Flook, 437 U.S. 584, 593, 198 USPQ 193, 198 (1978) and Mayo, 566 U.S. at 72, 101 USPQ2d at 1966). See MPEP § 2111 for more information about determining the BRI.

Claim interpretation affects the evaluation of both criteria for eligibility. For example, in Mentor Graphics v. EVE-USA, Inc., 851 F.3d 1275, 112 USPQ2d 1120 (Fed. Cir. 2017), claim interpretation was crucial to the court's determination that claims to a "machine-readable medium" were not to a statutory category. In Mentor Graphics, the court interpreted the claims in light of the specification, which expressly defined the medium as encompassing "any data storage device" including random-access memory and carrier waves. Although random-access memory and magnetic tape are statutory media, carrier waves are not because they are signals similar to the transitory, propagating signals held to be non-statutory in Nuijten. 851 F.3d at 1294, 112 USPQ2d at 1133 (citing In re Nuijten, 500 F.3d 1346, 84 USPQ2d 1495 (Fed. Cir. 2007)). Accordingly, because the BRI of the claims covered both subject matter that falls within a statutory category (the random-access memory), as well as subject matter that does not (the carrier waves), the claims as a whole were not to a statutory category and thus failed the first criterion for eligibility.

With regard to the second criterion for eligibility, the Alice/Mayo test, claim interpretation can affect the first part of the test (whether the claims are directed to a judicial exception). For example, the patentee in Synopsys argued that the claimed methods of logic circuit design were intended to be used in conjunction with computer-based design tools, and were thus not mental processes. Synopsys, Inc. v. Mentor Graphics Corp., 839 F.3d 1138, 1147–49, 120 USPQ2d 1473, 1480–81 (Fed. Cir. 2016). The court disagreed, because it interpreted the claims as encompassing nothing other than pure mental steps (and thus falling within an abstract idea grouping) because the claims did not include any limitations requiring computer implementation. In contrast, the patentee in Enfish argued that its claimed self-referential table for a computer database was an improvement in an existing technology and thus not directed to an abstract idea. Enfish, LLC v. Microsoft Corp., 822 F.3d 1327, 1336–37, 118 USPQ2d 1684, 1689–90 (Fed. Cir. 2016). The court agreed with the patentee, based on its interpretation of the claimed "means for configuring" under 35 U.S.C. 112(f) as requiring a four-step algorithm that achieved the improvements, as opposed to merely any form of storing tabular data. See also McRO, Inc. v. Bandai Namco Games America, Inc., 837 F.3d 1299, 1314, 120 USPQ2d 1091, 1102 (Fed. Cir. 2016) (the claim's construction incorporated rules of a particular type that improved an existing technological process). Claim interpretation can also affect the second part of the Alice/Mayo test (whether the claim recites additional elements that amount to significantly more than the judicial exception). For example, in Amdocs (Israel) Ltd. v. Openet Telecom, Inc., where the court relied on the construction of the term "enhance" (to require application of a number of field enhancements in a distributed fashion) to determine that the claim entails an unconventional technical solution to a technological problem. 841 F.3d 1288, 1300–01, 120 USPQ2d 1527, 1537 (Fed. Cir. 2016).

III. SUMMARY OF ANALYSIS AND FLOWCHART

Examiners should determine whether a claim satisfies the criteria for subject matter eligibility by evaluating the claim in accordance with the following flowchart. The flowchart illustrates the steps of the subject matter eligibility analysis for products and processes that are to be used during examination for evaluating whether a claim is drawn to patent-eligible subject matter. It is recognized that under the controlling legal precedent there may be variations in the precise contours of the analysis for subject matter eligibility that will still achieve the same end result. The analysis set forth herein promotes examination efficiency and consistency across all technologies.

As shown in the flowchart, Step 1 relates to the statutory categories and ensures that the first criterion is met by confirming that the claim falls within one of the four statutory categories of invention. See MPEP § 2106.03 for more information on Step 1. Step 2, which is the Supreme Court's Alice/Mayo test, is a two-part test to identify claims that are directed to a judicial exception (Step 2A) and to then evaluate if additional elements of the claim provide an inventive concept (Step 2B) (also called "significantly more" than the recited judicial exception). See MPEP § 2106.04 for more information on Step 2A and MPEP § 2106.05 for more information on Step 2B.

The flowchart also shows three pathways (A, B, and C) to eligibility:

- *Pathway A: Claims taken as a whole that fall within a statutory category (Step 1: YES) and, which may or may not recite a judicial exception, but whose eligibility is self-evident can be found eligible at Pathway A using a streamlined analysis. See MPEP § 2106.06 for more information on this pathway and on self-evident eligibility.*
- *Pathway B: Claims taken as a whole that fall within a statutory category (Step 1: YES) and are not directed to a judicial exception (Step 2A: NO) are eligible at Pathway B. These claims do not need to go to Step 2B. See MPEP § 2106.04 for more information about this pathway and Step 2A.*
- *Pathway C: Claims taken as a whole that fall within a statutory category (Step 1: YES), are directed to a judicial exception (Step 2A: YES), and recite additional elements either individually or in an ordered combination that amount to significantly more than the judicial exception (Step 2B: YES) are eligible at Pathway C. See MPEP § 2106.05 for more information about this pathway and Step 2B.*

Claims that could have been found eligible at Pathway A (streamlined analysis), but are subjected to further analysis at Steps 2A or Step 2B, will ultimately be found eligible at Pathways B or C. Thus, if the examiner is uncertain about whether a streamlined analysis is appropriate, the examiner is encouraged to conduct a full eligibility analysis. However, if the claim is not found eligible at any of Pathways A, B or C, the claim is patent ineligible and should be rejected under 35 U.S.C. 101.

Regardless of whether a rejection under 35 U.S.C. 101 is made, a complete examination should be made for every claim under each of the other patentability requirements: 35 U.S.C. 102, 103, 112, and 101 (utility, inventorship and double patenting) and non-statutory double patenting. MPEP § 2103.

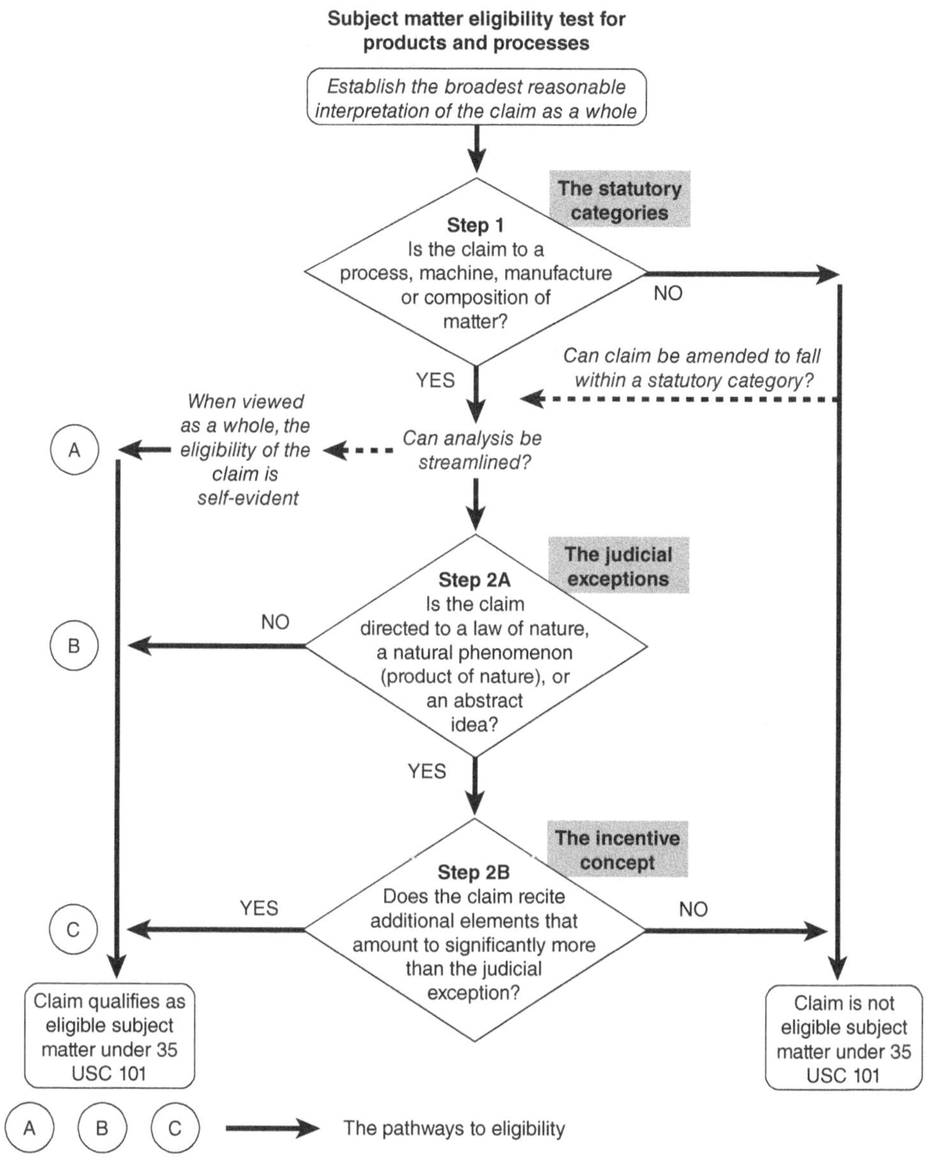

MPEP § 2106.04

Eligibility Step 2A: Whether a Claim is Directed to a Judicial Exception

I. JUDICIAL EXCEPTIONS

Determining that a claim falls within one of the four enumerated categories of patentable subject matter recited in 35 U.S.C. 101 (i.e., process, machine, manufacture, or composition of matter) in Step 1 does not end the eligibility analysis, because claims directed to nothing more than abstract ideas (such as a mathematical formula or equation), natural phenomena, and laws of nature are not eligible for patent protection. Diamond v. Diehr, 450 U.S. 175, 185, 209 USPQ 1, 7 (1981); Alice Corp. Pty. Ltd. v. CLS Bank Int'l, 573 U.S. 208, 216, 110 USPQ2d 1976, 1980 (2014) (citing Association for Molecular Pathology v. Myriad Genetics, Inc., 569 U.S. 576, 589, 106 USPQ2d 1972, 1979 (2013)); Diamond v. Chakrabarty, 447 U.S. 303, 309, 206 USPQ 193, 197 (1980); Parker v. Flook, 437 U.S. 584, 589, 198 USPQ 193, 197 (1978); Gottschalk v. Benson, 409 U.S. 63, 67–68, 175 USPQ 673, 675 (1972). See also Bilski v. Kappos, 561 U.S. 593, 601, 95 USPQ2d 1001, 1005–06 (2010) ("The Court's precedents provide three specific exceptions to § 101's broad patent-eligibility principles: 'laws of nature, physical phenomena, and abstract ideas'") (quoting Chakrabarty, 447 U.S. at 309, 206 USPQ at 197 (1980)).

In addition to the terms "laws of nature," "natural phenomena," and "abstract ideas," judicially recognized exceptions have been described using various other terms, including "physical phenomena," "products of nature," "scientific principles," "systems that depend on human intelligence alone," "disembodied concepts," "mental processes," and "disembodied mathematical algorithms and formulas." It should be noted that there are no bright lines between the types of exceptions, and that many of the concepts identified by the courts as exceptions can fall under several exceptions. For example, mathematical formulas are considered to be a judicial exception as they express a scientific truth, but have been labelled by the courts as both abstract ideas and laws of nature. Likewise, "products of nature" are considered to be an exception because they tie up the use of naturally occurring things, but have been labelled as both laws of nature and natural phenomena. Thus, it is sufficient for this analysis for the examiner to identify that the claimed concept (the specific claim limitation(s) that the examiner believes may recite an exception) aligns with at least one judicial exception.

The Supreme Court has explained that the judicial exceptions reflect the Court's view that abstract ideas, laws of nature, and natural phenomena are "the basic tools of scientific and technological work", and are thus excluded from patentability because "monopolization of those tools through the grant of a patent might tend to impede innovation more than it would tend to promote it." Alice Corp., 573 U.S. at 216, 110 USPQ2d at 1980 (quoting Myriad, 569 U.S. at 589, 106 USPQ2d at 1978 and Mayo Collaborative Servs. v. Prometheus Labs. Inc., 566 U.S. 66, 71, 101 USPQ2d 1961, 1965 (2012)). The Supreme Court's concern that drives this "exclusionary principle" is pre-emption. Alice Corp., 573 U.S. at 216, 110 USPQ2d at 1980. The Court has held that a claim may not preempt abstract ideas, laws of nature, or natural phenomena, even if the judicial exception is narrow (e.g., a particular mathematical formula such as the Arrhenius equation). See, e.g., Mayo, 566 U.S.

at 79–80, 86–87, 101 USPQ2d at 1968–69, 1971 (claims directed to "narrow laws that may have limited applications" held ineligible); Flook, 437 U.S. at 589–90, 198 USPQ at 197 (claims that did not "wholly preempt the mathematical formula" held ineligible). This is because such a patent would "in practical effect [] be a patent on the [abstract idea, law of nature or natural phenomenon] itself." Benson, 409 U.S. at 71–72, 175 USPQ at 676. The concern over preemption was expressed as early as 1852. See Le Roy v. Tatham, 55 U.S. (14 How.) 156, 175 (1852) ("A principle, in the abstract, is a fundamental truth; an original cause; a motive; these cannot be patented, as no one can claim in either of them an exclusive right.").

While preemption is the concern underlying the judicial exceptions, it is not a standalone test for determining eligibility. Rapid Litig. Mgmt. v. CellzDirect, Inc., 827 F.3d 1042, 1052, 119 USPQ2d 1370, 1376 (Fed. Cir. 2016). Instead, questions of preemption are inherent in and resolved by the two-part framework from Alice Corp. and Mayo (the Alice/Mayo test referred to by the Office as Steps 2A and 2B). Synopsys, Inc. v. Mentor Graphics Corp., 839 F.3d 1138, 1150, 120 USPQ2d 1473, 1483 (Fed. Cir. 2016); Ariosa Diagnostics, Inc. v. Sequenom, Inc., 788 F.3d 1371, 1379, 115 USPQ2d 1152, 1158 (Fed. Cir. 2015). It is necessary to evaluate eligibility using the Alice/Mayo test, because while a preemptive claim may be ineligible, the absence of complete preemption does not demonstrate that a claim is eligible. Diamond v. Diehr, 450 U.S. 175, 191–92 n.14, 209 USPQ 1, 10–11 n.14 (1981) ("We rejected in Flook the argument that because all possible uses of the mathematical formula were not pre-empted, the claim should be eligible for patent protection"). See also Synopsys v. Mentor Graphics, 839 F.3d at 1150, 120 USPQ2d at 1483; FairWarning IP, LLC v. Iatric Sys., Inc., 839 F.3d 1089, 1098, 120 USPQ2d 1293, 1299 (Fed. Cir. 2016); Intellectual Ventures I LLC v. Symantec Corp., 838 F.3d 1307, 1320–21, 120 USPQ2d 1353, 1362 (Fed. Cir. 2016); Sequenom, 788 F.3d at 1379, 115 USPQ2d at 1158. Several Federal Circuit decisions, however, have noted the absence of preemption when finding claims eligible under the Alice/Mayo test. McRO, Inc. v. Bandai Namco Games Am. Inc., 837 F.3d 1299, 1315, 120 USPQ2d 1091, 1102–03 (Fed. Cir. 2016); Rapid Litig. Mgmt. v. CellzDirect, Inc., 827 F.3d 1042, 1052, 119 USPQ2d 1370, 1376 (Fed. Cir. 2016); BASCOM Global Internet v. AT&T Mobility, LLC, 827 F.3d 1341, 1350–52, 119 USPQ2d 1236, 1243–44 (Fed. Cir. 2016).

The Supreme Court's decisions make it clear that judicial exceptions need not be old or long-prevalent, and that even newly discovered or novel judicial exceptions are still exceptions. For example, the mathematical formula in Flook, the laws of nature in Mayo, and the isolated DNA in Myriad were all novel or newly discovered, but nonetheless were considered by the Supreme Court to be judicial exceptions because they were "'basic tools of scientific and technological work' that lie beyond the domain of patent protection." Myriad, 569 U.S. 576, 589, 106 USPQ2d at 1976,

1978 (noting that Myriad discovered the BRCA1 and BRCA[2] genes and quoting Mayo, 566 U.S. 71, 101 USPQ2d at 1965); Flook, 437 U.S. at 591–92, 198 USPQ2d at 198 ("the novelty of the mathematical algorithm is not a determining factor at all"); Mayo, 566 U.S. 73–74, 78, 101 USPQ2d 1966, 1968 (noting that the claims embody the researcher's discoveries of laws of nature). The Supreme Court's cited rationale for considering even "just discovered" judicial exceptions as exceptions stems from the concern that "without this exception, there would be considerable danger that the grant of patents would 'tie up' the use of such tools and thereby 'inhibit future innovation premised upon them.'" Myriad, 569 U.S. at 589, 106 USPQ2d at 1978–79 (quoting Mayo, 566 U.S. at 86, 101 USPQ2d at 1971). See also Myriad, 569 U.S. at 591, 106 USPQ2d at 1979 ("Groundbreaking, innovative, or even brilliant discovery does not by itself satisfy the § 101 inquiry."). The Federal Circuit has also applied this principle, for example, when holding a concept of using advertising as an exchange or currency to be an abstract idea, despite the patentee's arguments that the concept was "new". Ultramercial, Inc. v. Hulu, LLC, 772 F.3d 709, 714–15, 112 USPQ2d 1750, 1753–54 (Fed. Cir. 2014). Cf. Synopsys, Inc. v. Mentor Graphics Corp., 839 F.3d 1138, 1151, 120 USPQ2d 1473, 1483 (Fed. Cir. 2016) ("a ***new*** *abstract idea is still an abstract idea") (emphasis in original).*

For a detailed discussion of abstract ideas, see MPEP § 2106.04(a); for a detailed discussion of laws of nature, natural phenomena and products of nature, see MPEP § 2106.04(b).

II. ELIGIBILITY STEP 2A: WHETHER A CLAIM IS DIRECTED TO A JUDICIAL EXCEPTION

As described in MPEP § 2106, subsection III, Step 2A of the Office's eligibility analysis is the first part of the Alice/Mayo test, i.e., the Supreme Court's "framework for distinguishing patents that claim laws of nature, natural phenomena, and abstract ideas from those that claim patent-eligible applications of those concepts." Alice Corp. Pty. Ltd. v. CLS Bank Int'l, 573 U.S. 208, 217–18, 110 USPQ2d 1976, 1981 (2014) (citing Mayo, 566 U.S. at 77–78, 101 USPQ2d at 1967–68). Like the other steps in the eligibility analysis, evaluation of this step should be made after determining what the inventor has invented by reviewing the entire application disclosure and construing the claims in accordance with their broadest reasonable interpretation. See MPEP § 2106, subsection II for more information about the importance of understanding what has been invented, and MPEP § 2111 for more information about the broadest reasonable interpretation.

Step 2A asks: Is the claim directed to a law of nature, a natural phenomenon (product of nature) or an abstract idea? In the context of the flowchart in MPEP § 2106, subsection III, Step 2A determines whether:

- *The claim as a whole is not directed to a judicial exception (Step 2A: NO) and thus is eligible at Pathway B, thereby concluding the eligibility analysis; or*
- *The claim as a whole is directed to a judicial exception (Step 2A: YES) and thus requires further analysis at Step 2B to determine if the claim as a whole amounts to significantly more than the exception itself.*

A. Step 2A Is a Two-Prong Inquiry

Step 2A is a two-prong inquiry, in which examiners determine in Prong One whether a claim recites a judicial exception, and if so, then determine in Prong Two if the recited judicial exception is integrated into a practical application of that exception. Together, these prongs represent the first part of the Alice/Mayo test, which determines whether a claim is directed to a judicial exception.

The flowchart below depicts the two-prong analysis that is performed in order to answer the Step 2A inquiry.

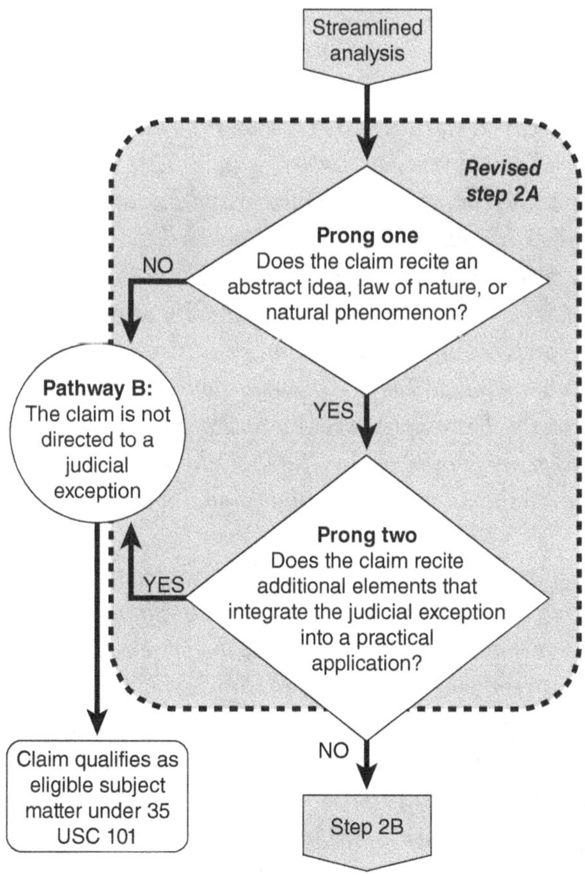

1. *Prong One*

Prong One asks does the claim recite an abstract idea, law of nature, or natural phenomenon? In Prong One examiners evaluate whether the claim recites a judicial exception, i.e. whether a law of nature, natural phenomenon, or abstract idea is set forth or described in the claim. While the terms "set forth" and "described" are thus both equated with "recite", their different language is intended to indicate that there are two ways in which an exception can be recited in a claim. For instance, the claims in Diehr, 450 U.S. at 178 n.2, 179 n.5, 191–92, 209 USPQ at 4–5 (1981), clearly stated a mathematical equation in the repetitively calculating step, and the claims in Mayo, 566 U.S. 66, 75–77, 101 USPQ2d 1961, 1967–68 (2012), clearly stated laws of nature in the wherein clause, such that the claims "set forth" an identifiable judicial exception. Alternatively, the claims in Alice Corp., 573 U.S. at 218, 110 USPQ2d at 1982, described the concept of intermediated settlement without ever explicitly using the words "intermediated" or "settlement."

The Supreme Court has held that Section 101 contains an implicit exception for "[l]aws of nature, natural phenomena, and abstract ideas," which are "the basic tools of scientific and technological work." Alice Corp., 573 U.S. at 216, 110 USPQ2d at 1980 (citing Mayo, 566 US at 71, 101 USPQ2d at 1965). Yet, the Court has explained that "[a]t some level, all inventions embody, use, reflect, rest upon, or apply laws of nature, natural phenomena, or abstract ideas," and has cautioned "to tread carefully in construing this exclusionary principle lest it swallow all of patent law." Id. See also Enfish, LLC v. Microsoft Corp., 822 F.3d 1327, 1335, 118 USPQ2d 1684, 1688 (Fed. Cir. 2016) ("The 'directed to' inquiry, therefore, cannot simply ask whether the claims involve a patent-ineligible concept, because essentially every routinely patent-eligible claim involving physical products and actions involves a law of nature and/or natural phenomenon"). Examiners should accordingly be careful to distinguish claims that recite an exception (which require further eligibility analysis) and claims that merely involve an exception (which are eligible and do not require further eligibility analysis).

An example of a claim that recites a judicial exception is "A machine comprising elements that operate in accordance with F=ma." This claim sets forth the principle that force equals mass times acceleration (F=ma) and therefore recites a law of nature exception. Because F=ma represents a mathematical formula, the claim could alternatively be considered as reciting an abstract idea. Because this claim recites a judicial exception, it requires further analysis in Prong Two in order to answer the Step 2A inquiry. An example of a claim that merely involves, or is based on, an exception is a claim to "A teeter-totter comprising an elongated member pivotably attached to a base member, having seats and handles attached at opposing sides of the elongated member." This claim is based on the concept of a lever pivoting on a fulcrum, which involves the natural principles of mechanical advantage and the law of the lever. However, this claim does not recite these natural principles and therefore is not directed to a judicial exception (Step 2A: NO). Thus, the claim is eligible at Pathway B without further analysis.

If the claim recites a judicial exception (i.e., an abstract idea enumerated in MPEP § 2106.04(a), a law of nature, or a natural phenomenon), the claim requires further analysis in Prong Two. If the claim does not recite a judicial exception (a law of nature, natural phenomenon, or abstract idea), then the claim cannot be directed to a judicial exception (Step 2A: NO), and thus the claim is eligible at Pathway B without further analysis.

For more information how to determine if a claim recites an abstract idea, see MPEP § 2106.04(a). For more information on how to determine if a claim recites a law of nature or natural phenomenon, see MPEP § 2106.04(b). For more information on how to determine if a claim recites a product of nature, see MPEP § 2106.04(c).

2. Prong Two

Prong Two asks does the claim recite additional elements that integrate the judicial exception into a practical application? In Prong Two, examiners evaluate whether the claim as a whole integrates the exception into a practical application of that exception. If the additional elements in the claim integrate the recited exception into a practical application of the exception, then the claim is not directed to the judicial exception (Step 2A: NO) and thus is eligible at Pathway B. This concludes the eligibility analysis. If, however, the additional elements do not integrate the exception into a practical application, then the claim is directed to the recited judicial exception (Step 2A: YES), and requires further analysis under Step 2B (where it may still be eligible if it amounts to an "inventive concept"). For more information on how to evaluate whether a judicial exception is integrated into a practical application, see MPEP § 2106.04(d)(2).

The mere inclusion of a judicial exception such as a mathematical formula (which is one of the mathematical concepts identified as an abstract idea in MPEP § 2106.04(a)) in a claim means that the claim "recites" a judicial exception under Step 2A Prong One. However, mere recitation of a judicial exception does not mean that the claim is "directed to" that judicial exception under Step 2A Prong Two. Instead, under Prong Two, a claim that recites a judicial exception is not directed to that judicial exception, if the claim as a whole integrates the recited judicial exception into a practical application of that exception. Prong Two thus distinguishes claims that are "directed to" the recited judicial exception from claims that are not "directed to" the recited judicial exception.

Because a judicial exception is not eligible subject matter, Bilski, 561 U.S. at 601, 95 USPQ2d at 1005–06 (quoting Chakrabarty, 447 U.S. at 309, 206 USPQ at 197 (1980)), if there are no additional claim elements besides the judicial exception, or if the additional claim elements merely recite another judicial exception, that is insufficient to integrate the judicial exception into a practical application. See, e.g., RecogniCorp, LLC v. Nintendo Co., 855 F.3d 1322, 1327, 122 USPQ2d 1377 (Fed. Cir. 2017) ("Adding one abstract idea (math) to another abstract idea (encoding and decoding) does not render the claim non-abstract"); Genetic Techs. v. Merial LLC, 818 F.3d 1369, 1376, 118 USPQ2d 1541, 1546 (Fed. Cir. 2016) (eligibility "cannot be furnished by the unpatentable law of nature (or natural phenomenon or abstract idea) itself."). For a claim reciting a judicial exception to be eligible, the additional elements (if any) in the claim must "transform the nature of the claim" into a patent-eligible application of the judicial exception, Alice Corp., 573 U.S. at 217, 110 USPQ2d at 1981, either at Prong Two or in Step 2B. If there are no additional elements in the claim, then it cannot be eligible. In such a case, after making the appropriate rejection (see MPEP § 2106.07 for more information on formulating a rejection for lack of eligibility), it is a best practice for the examiner to recommend an amendment, if possible, that would resolve eligibility of the claim.

B. Evaluating Claims Reciting Multiple Judicial Exceptions

A claim may recite multiple judicial exceptions. For example, claim 4 at issue in Bilski v. Kappos, 561 U.S. 593, 95 USPQ2d 1001 (2010) recited two abstract ideas, and the claims at issue in Mayo Collaborative Servs. v. Prometheus Labs. Inc., 566 U.S. 66, 101 USPQ2d 1961 (2012) recited two laws of nature. However, these claims were analyzed by the Supreme Court in the same manner as claims reciting a single judicial exception, such as those in Alice Corp., 573 U.S. 208, 110 USPQ2d 1976.

During examination, examiners should apply the same eligibility analysis to all claims regardless of the number of exceptions recited therein. Unless it is clear that a claim recites distinct exceptions, such as a law of nature and an abstract idea, care should be taken not to parse the claim into multiple exceptions, particularly in claims involving abstract ideas. Accordingly, if possible examiners should treat the claim for Prong Two and Step 2B purposes as containing a single judicial exception.

In some claims, the multiple exceptions are distinct from each other, e.g., a first limitation describes a law of nature, and a second limitation elsewhere in the claim recites an abstract idea. In these cases, for purposes of examination efficiency, examiners should select one of the exceptions and conduct the eligibility analysis for that selected exception. If the analysis indicates that the claim recites an additional element or combination of elements that integrate the selected exception into a practical application or that amount to significantly more than the selected exception, then the claim should be considered patent eligible. On the other hand, if the claim does not recite any additional element or combination of elements that integrate the selected exception into a practical application, and also does not recite any additional element or combination of elements that amounts to significantly more than the selected exception, then the claim should be considered ineligible. University of Utah Research Foundation v. Ambry Genetics, 774 F.3d 755, 762, 113 USPQ2d 1241, 1246 (Fed. Cir. 2014) (because claims did not amount to significantly more than the recited abstract idea, court "need not decide" if claims also recited a law of nature).

In other claims, multiple abstract ideas, which may fall in the same or different groupings, or multiple laws of nature may be recited. In these cases, examiners should not parse the claim. For example, in a claim that includes a series of steps that recite mental steps as well as a mathematical calculation, an examiner should identify the claim as reciting both a mental process and a mathematical concept for Step 2A Prong One to make the analysis clear on the record. However, if possible, the examiner should consider the limitations together as a single abstract idea for Step 2A Prong Two and Step 2B (if necessary) rather than as a plurality of separate abstract ideas to be analyzed individually. . . .

MPEP § 2106.05

Eligibility Step 2B: Whether a Claim Amounts to Significantly More
I. THE SEARCH FOR AN INVENTIVE CONCEPT

The second part of the Alice/Mayo test is often referred to as a search for an inventive concept. Alice Corp. Pty. Ltd. v. CLS Bank Int'l, 573 U.S. 208, 217, 110 USPQ2d 1976, 1981 (2014) (citing Mayo Collaborative Servs. v. Prometheus Labs., Inc., 566 U.S. 66, 71–72, 101 USPQ2d 1961, 1966 (2012)).

*An inventive concept "cannot be furnished by the unpatentable law of nature (or natural phenomenon or abstract idea) itself." Genetic Techs. v. Merial LLC, 818 F.3d 1369, 1376, 118 USPQ2d 1541, 1546 (Fed. Cir. 2016). See also Alice Corp., 573 U.S. at 217–18, 110 USPQ2d at 1981 (citing Mayo, 566 U.S. at 78, 101 USPQ2d at 1968 (after determining that a claim is directed to a judicial exception, "we then ask, '**[w]hat else** is there in the claims before us?'") (emphasis added)); RecogniCorp, LLC v. Nintendo Co., 855 F.3d 1322, 1327, 122 USPQ2d 1377 (Fed. Cir. 2017) ("Adding one abstract idea (math) to another abstract idea (encoding and decoding) does not render the claim non-abstract"). Instead, an "inventive concept" is furnished by an element or combination of elements that is recited in the claim in addition to (beyond) the judicial exception, and is sufficient to ensure that the claim as a whole amounts to significantly more than the judicial exception itself. Alice Corp., 573 U.S. at 217–18, 110 USPQ2d at 1981 (citing Mayo, 566 U.S. at 72–73, 101 USPQ2d at 1966).*

Evaluating additional elements to determine whether they amount to an inventive concept requires considering them both individually and in combination to ensure that they amount to significantly more than the judicial exception itself. Because this approach considers all claim elements, the Supreme Court has noted that "it is consistent with the general rule that patent claims 'must be considered as a whole.'" Alice

Corp., 573 U.S. at 218 n.3, 110 USPQ2d at 1981 (quoting Diamond v. Diehr, 450 U.S. 175, 188, 209 USPQ 1, 8–9 (1981)). Consideration of the elements in combination is particularly important, because even if an additional element does not amount to significantly more on its own, it can still amount to significantly more when considered in combination with the other elements of the claim. See, e.g., Rapid Litig. Mgmt. v. CellzDirect, 827 F.3d 1042, 1051, 119 USPQ2d 1370, 1375 (Fed. Cir. 2016) (process reciting combination of individually well-known freezing and thawing steps was "far from routine and conventional" and thus eligible); BASCOM Global Internet Servs. v. AT&T Mobility LLC, 827 F.3d 1341, 1350, 119 USPQ2d 1236, 1242 (Fed. Cir. 2016) (inventive concept may be found in the non-conventional and non-generic arrangement of components that are individually well-known and conventional).*

Although the courts often evaluate considerations such as the conventionality of an additional element in the eligibility analysis, the search for an inventive concept should not be confused with a novelty or non-obviousness determination. See Mayo, 566 U.S. at 91, 101 USPQ2d at 1973 (rejecting "the Government's invitation to substitute §§ 102, 103, and 112 inquiries for the better established inquiry under § 101"). As made clear by the courts, the "'novelty' of any element or steps in a process, or even of the process itself, is of no relevance in determining whether the subject matter of a claim falls within the § 101 categories of possibly patentable subject matter." Intellectual Ventures I v. Symantec Corp., 838 F.3d 1307, 1315, 120 USPQ2d 1353, 1358 (Fed. Cir. 2016) (quoting Diamond v. Diehr, 450 U.S. at 188–89, 209 USPQ at 9). See also Synopsys, Inc. v. Mentor Graphics Corp., 839 F.3d 1138, 1151, 120 USPQ2d 1473, 1483 (Fed. Cir. 2016) ("a claim for a new abstract idea is still an abstract idea. The search for a § 101 inventive concept is thus distinct from demonstrating § 102 novelty."). In addition, the search for an inventive concept is different from an obviousness analysis under 35 U.S.C. 103. See, e.g., BASCOM Global Internet v. AT&T Mobility LLC, 827 F.3d 1341, 1350, 119 USPQ2d 1236, 1242 (Fed. Cir. 2016) ("The inventive concept inquiry requires more than recognizing that each claim element, by itself, was known in the art. . . . [A]n inventive concept can be found in the non-conventional and non-generic arrangement of known, conventional pieces."). Specifically, lack of novelty under 35 U.S.C. 102 or obviousness under 35 U.S.C. 103 of a claimed invention does not necessarily indicate that additional elements are well-understood, routine, conventional elements. Because they are separate and distinct requirements from eligibility, patentability of the claimed invention under 35 U.S.C. 102 and 103 with respect to the prior art is neither required for, nor a guarantee of, patent eligibility under 35 U.S.C. 101. The distinction between eligibility (under 35 U.S.C. 101) and patentability over the art (under 35 U.S.C. 102 and/or 103) is further discussed in MPEP § 2106.05(d).

A. Relevant Considerations for Evaluating Whether Additional Elements Amount To An Inventive Concept

The Supreme Court has identified a number of considerations as relevant to the evaluation of whether the claimed additional elements amount to an inventive concept. The list of considerations here is not intended to be exclusive or limiting. Additional elements can often be analyzed based on more than one type of consideration and the type of consideration is of no import to the eligibility analysis. Additional discussion of these considerations, and how they were applied in particular judicial decisions, is provided in . . . MPEP § 2106.05(a) through (h).

Limitations that the courts have found to qualify as "significantly more" when recited in a claim with a judicial exception include:

i. *Improvements to the functioning of a computer, e.g., a modification of conventional Internet hyperlink protocol to dynamically produce a dual-source hybrid webpage, as discussed in DDR Holdings, LLC v. Hotels.com, L.P., 773 F.3d 1245, 1258–59, 113 USPQ2d 1097, 1106–07 (Fed. Cir. 2014) (see MPEP § 2106.05(a));*
ii. *Improvements to any other technology or technical field, e.g., a modification of conventional rubber-molding processes to utilize a thermocouple inside the mold to constantly monitor the temperature and thus reduce under- and over-curing problems common in the art, as discussed in Diamond v. Diehr, 450 U.S. 175, 191–92, 209 USPQ 1, 10 (1981) (see MPEP § 2106.05(a));*
iii. *Applying the judicial exception with, or by use of, a particular machine, e.g., a Fourdrinier machine (which is understood in the art to have a specific structure comprising a headbox, a paper-making wire, and a series of rolls) that is arranged in a particular way to optimize the speed of the machine while maintaining quality of the formed paper web, as discussed in Eibel Process Co. v. Minn. & Ont. Paper Co., 261 U.S. 45, 64–65 (1923) (see MPEP § 2106.05(b));*
iv. *Effecting a transformation or reduction of a particular article to a different state or thing, e.g., a process that transforms raw, uncured synthetic rubber into precision-molded synthetic rubber products, as discussed in Diehr, 450 U.S. at 184, 209 USPQ at 21 (see MPEP § 2106.05(c));*
v. *Adding a specific limitation other than what is well-understood, routine, conventional activity in the field, or adding unconventional steps that confine the claim to a particular useful application, e.g., a non-conventional and non-generic arrangement of various computer components for filtering Internet content, as discussed in BASCOM Global Internet v. AT&T Mobility LLC, 827 F.3d 1341, 1350–51, 119 USPQ2d 1236, 1243 (Fed. Cir. 2016) (see MPEP § 2106.05(d)); or*

vi. Other meaningful limitations beyond generally linking the use of the judicial exception to a particular technological environment, e.g., an immunization step that integrates an abstract idea of data comparison into a specific process of immunizing that lowers the risk that immunized patients will later develop chronic immune-mediated diseases, as discussed in Classen Immunotherapies Inc. v. Biogen IDEC, 659 F.3d 1057, 1066–68, 100 USPQ2d 1492, 1499–1502 (Fed. Cir. 2011) (see MPEP § 2106.05(e)).

Limitations that the courts have found not to be enough to qualify as "significantly more" when recited in a claim with a judicial exception include:

i. Adding the words "apply it" (or an equivalent) with the judicial exception, or mere instructions to implement an abstract idea on a computer, e.g., a limitation indicating that a particular function such as creating and maintaining electronic records is performed by a computer, as discussed in Alice Corp., 573 U.S. at 225–26, 110 USPQ2d at 1984 (see MPEP § 2106.05(f));

ii. Simply appending well-understood, routine, conventional activities previously known to the industry, specified at a high level of generality, to the judicial exception, e.g., a claim to an abstract idea requiring no more than a generic computer to perform generic computer functions that are well-understood, routine and conventional activities previously known to the industry, as discussed in Alice Corp., 573 U.S. at 225, 110 USPQ2d at 1984 (see MPEP § 2106.05(d));

iii. Adding insignificant extra-solution activity to the judicial exception, e.g., mere data gathering in conjunction with a law of nature or abstract idea such as a step of obtaining information about credit card transactions so that the information can be analyzed by an abstract mental process, as discussed in CyberSource v. Retail Decisions, Inc., 654 F.3d 1366, 1375, 99 USPQ2d 1690, 1694 (Fed. Cir. 2011) (see MPEP § 2106.05(g)); or

iv. Generally linking the use of the judicial exception to a particular technological environment or field of use, e.g., a claim describing how the abstract idea of hedging could be used in the commodities and energy markets, as discussed in Bilski v. Kappos, 561 U.S. 593, 595, 95 USPQ2d 1001, 1010 (2010) or a claim limiting the use of a mathematical formula to the petrochemical and oil-refining fields, as discussed in Parker v. Flook, 437 U.S. 584, 588–90, 198 USPQ 193, 197–98 (1978) (MPEP § 2106.05(h)).

It is notable that mere physicality or tangibility of an additional element or elements is not a relevant consideration in Step 2B. As the Supreme Court explained in Alice Corp., mere physical or tangible implementation of an exception is not in itself an inventive concept and does not guarantee eligibility:

> *The fact that a computer "necessarily exist[s] in the physical, rather than purely conceptual, realm," is beside the point. There is no dispute that a*

> *computer is a tangible system (in § 101 terms, a "machine"), or that many computer-implemented claims are formally addressed to patent-eligible subject matter. But if that were the end of the § 101 inquiry, an applicant could claim any principle of the physical or social sciences by reciting a computer system configured to implement the relevant concept. Such a result would make the determination of patent eligibility "depend simply on the draftsman's art," Flook, supra, at 593, 98 S. Ct. 2522, 57 L. Ed. 2d 451, thereby eviscerating the rule that "'[l]aws of nature, natural phenomena, and abstract ideas are not patentable,'" Myriad, 133 S. Ct. 1289, 186 L. Ed. 2d 124, 133.*

Alice Corp., 573 U.S. at 224, 110 USPQ2d at 1983–84 (alterations in original). See also Genetic Technologies Ltd. v. Merial LLC, 818 F.3d 1369, 1377, 118 USPQ2d 1541, 1547 (Fed. Cir. 2016) (steps of DNA amplification and analysis "do not, individually or in combination, provide sufficient inventive concept to render claim 1 patent eligible" merely because they are physical steps). Conversely, the presence of a non-physical or intangible additional element does not doom the claims, because tangibility is not necessary for eligibility under the Alice/Mayo test. Enfish, LLC v. Microsoft Corp., 822 F.3d 1327, 118 USPQ2d 1684 (Fed. Cir. 2016) ("that the improvement is not defined by reference to 'physical' components does not doom the claims"). See also McRO, Inc. v. Bandai Namco Games Am. Inc., 837 F.3d 1299, 1315, 120 USPQ2d 1091, 1102 (Fed. Cir. 2016) (holding that a process producing an intangible result (a sequence of synchronized, animated characters) was eligible because it improved an existing technological process).

B. Examples Of How Courts Conduct The Search For An Inventive Concept

Alice Corp. provides an example of how courts conduct the significantly more analysis. In this case, the Supreme Court analyzed claims to computer systems, computer readable media, and computer-implemented methods, all of which described a scheme for mitigating "settlement risk," which is the risk that only one party to an agreed-upon financial exchange will satisfy its obligation. In part one of the Alice/Mayo test, the Court determined that the claims were directed to the abstract idea of mitigating settlement risk. Alice Corp., 573 U.S. at 221, 110 USPQ2d at 1982. The Court then walked through part two of the Alice/Mayo test, in which:

- *The Court identified the additional elements in the claim, e.g., by noting that the method claims recited steps of using a computer to "create electronic records, track multiple transactions, and issue simultaneous instructions", and that the product claims recited hardware such as a "data processing system" with a "communications controller" and a "data storage unit" (573 U.S. at 224–26, 110 USPQ2d at 1984–85);*
- *The Court considered the additional elements individually, noting that all the computer functions were "'well-understood, routine, conventional activit[ies]' previously known to the industry," each step "does no more than require a generic computer to perform generic computer functions", and the recited*

hardware was "purely functional and generic" (573 U.S. at 225–26, 110 USPQ2d at 1984–85); and

- *The Court considered the additional elements "as an ordered combination," and determined that "the computer components . . . '[a]dd nothing . . . that is not already present when the steps are considered separately'" and "simply recite intermediated settlement as performed by a generic computer." 573 U.S. at 225 (citing Mayo, 566 U.S. at 79, 101 USPQ2d at 1972).*

Based on this analysis, the Court concluded that the claims amounted to "'nothing significantly more' than an instruction to apply the abstract idea of intermediated settlement using some unspecified, generic computer", and therefore held the claims ineligible because they were directed to a judicial exception and failed the second part of the Alice/Mayo test. Alice Corp., 573 U.S. at 225–27, 110 USPQ2d at 1984.

BASCOM provides another example of how courts conduct the significantly more analysis, and of the critical importance of considering the additional elements in combination. In this case, the Federal Circuit vacated a judgment of ineligibility because the district court failed to properly perform the second step of the Alice/Mayo test when analyzing a claimed system for filtering content retrieved from an Internet computer network. BASCOM Global Internet v. AT&T Mobility LLC, 827 F.3d 1341, 119 USPQ2d 1236 (Fed. Cir. 2016). The Federal Circuit agreed with the district court that the claims were directed to the abstract idea of filtering Internet content, and then walked through the district court's analysis in part two of the Alice/Mayo test, noting that:

- *The district court properly identified the additional elements in the claims, such as a "local client computer," "remote ISP server," "Internet computer network," and "controlled access network accounts" (827 F.3d at 1349, 119 USPQ2d at 1242);*
- *The district court properly considered the additional elements individually, for example by consulting the specification, which described each of the additional elements as "well-known generic computer components" (827 F.3d at 1349, 119 USPQ2d at 1242); and*
- *The district court should have considered the additional elements in combination, because the "inventive concept inquiry requires more than recognizing that each claim element, by itself, was known in the art" (827 F.3d at 1350, 119 USPQ2d at 1242).*

Based on this analysis, the Federal Circuit concluded that the district court erred by failing to recognize that when combined, an inventive concept may be found in the non-conventional and non-generic arrangement of the additional elements, i.e., the installation of a filtering tool at a specific location, remote from the end-users, with customizable filtering features specific to each end user. 827 F.3d at 1350, 119 USPQ2d at 1242.

II. ELIGIBILITY STEP 2B: WHETHER THE ADDITIONAL ELEMENTS CONTRIBUTE AN "INVENTIVE CONCEPT"

As described in MPEP § 2106, subsection III, Step 2B of the Office's eligibility analysis is the second part of the Alice/Mayo test, i.e., the Supreme Court's "framework for distinguishing patents that claim laws of nature, natural phenomena, and abstract ideas from those that claim patent-eligible applications of those concepts." Alice Corp. Pty. Ltd. v. CLS Bank Int'l, 573 U.S. 208, 217, 110 USPQ2d 1976, 1981 (2014) (citing Mayo, 566 U.S. 66, 101 USPQ2d 1961 (2012)). Like the other steps in the eligibility analysis, evaluation of this step should be made after determining what the inventor has invented by reviewing the entire application disclosure and construing the claims in accordance with their broadest reasonable interpretation. See MPEP § 2106, subsection II for more information about the importance of understanding what has been invented, and MPEP § 2111 for more information about the broadest reasonable interpretation.

Step 2B asks: Does the claim recite additional elements that amount to significantly more than the judicial exception? Examiners should answer this question by first identifying whether there are any additional elements (features/limitations/steps) recited in the claim beyond the judicial exception(s), and then evaluating those additional elements individually and in combination to determine whether they contribute an inventive concept (i.e., amount to significantly more than the judicial exception(s)).

This evaluation is made with respect to the considerations that the Supreme Court has identified as relevant to the eligibility analysis, which are introduced generally in Part I.A of this section, and discussed in detail in MPEP § 2106.05(a) through (h). Many of these considerations overlap, and often more than one consideration is relevant to analysis of an additional element. Not all considerations will be relevant to every element, or every claim. Because the evaluation in Step 2B is not a weighing test, it is not important how the elements are characterized or how many considerations apply from this list. It is important to evaluate the significance of the additional elements relative to the invention, and to keep in mind the ultimate question of whether the additional elements encompass an inventive concept.

Although the conclusion of whether a claim is eligible at Step 2B requires that all relevant considerations be evaluated, most of these considerations were already evaluated in Step 2A Prong Two. Thus, in Step 2B, examiners should:

- *Carry over their identification of the additional element(s) in the claim from Step 2A Prong Two;*
- *Carry over their conclusions from Step 2A Prong Two on the considerations discussed in MPEP §§ 2106.05(a)–(c), (e), (f) and (h);*
- *Re-evaluate any additional element or combination of elements that was considered to be insignificant extra-solution activity per MPEP § 2106.05(g), because if such re-evaluation finds that the element is unconventional or*

otherwise more than what is well-understood, routine, conventional activity in the field, this finding may indicate that the additional element is no longer considered to be insignificant; and

- *Evaluate whether any additional element or combination of elements are other than what is well-understood, routine, conventional activity in the field, or simply append well-understood, routine, conventional activities previously known to the industry, specified at a high level of generality, to the judicial exception, per MPEP § 2106.05(d).*

In the context of the flowchart in MPEP § 2106, subsection III, Step 2B determines whether:

- *The claim as a whole does not amount to significantly more than the exception itself (there is no inventive concept in the claim) (Step 2B: NO) and thus is not eligible, warranting a rejection for lack of subject matter eligibility and concluding the eligibility analysis; or*
- *The claim as a whole does amount to significantly more than the exception (there is an inventive concept in the claim) (Step 2B: YES), and thus is eligible at Pathway C, thereby concluding the eligibility analysis.*

Examiners should examine each claim for eligibility separately, based on the particular elements recited therein. Claims should not be judged to automatically stand or fall with similar claims in an application. For instance, one claim may be ineligible because it is directed to a judicial exception without amounting to significantly more, but another claim dependent on the first may be eligible because it recites additional elements that do amount to significantly more.

For more information on how to evaluate claims reciting multiple judicial exceptions, see MPEP § 2106.04, subsection II.B.

If the claim as a whole does recite significantly more than the exception itself, the claim is eligible (Step 2B: YES) at Pathway C, and the eligibility analysis is complete. If there are no meaningful limitations in the claim that transform the exception into a patent-eligible application, such that the claim does not amount to significantly more than the exception itself, the claim is not patent-eligible (Step 2B: NO) and should be rejected under 35 U.S.C. 101. See MPEP § 2106.07 for information on how to formulate an ineligibility rejection.

Diamond v. Diehr
450 U.S. 175
Supreme Court of the United States
October 14, 1980, Argued; March 3, 1981, Decided

Alice Corp. Pty. Ltd. v. CLS Bank International
573 U.S. 208
Supreme Court of the United States

March 31, 2014, Argued; June 19, 2014, Decided

Enfish, LLC v. Microsoft Corp.
822 F.3d 1327
United States Court of Appeals for the Federal Circuit
May 12, 2016, Decided

BASCOM Global Internet Services v. AT&T Mobility LLC
827 F.3d 1341
United States Court of Appeals for the Federal Circuit
June 27, 2016, Decided

Electric Power Group, LLC v. Alstom S.A.
830 F.3d 1350
United States Court of Appeals for the Federal Circuit
August 1, 2016, Decided

Questions

1. As should be clear, the issue regarding the patentability of software was and to some extent remains a controversial issue. On what legal basis is the patentability of Diehr's invention challenged?
2. *Diehr* is a watershed case. The dissent correctly points out some logical inconsistencies between *Diehr* and the predecessor cases *Benson* and *Flook*. *Flook*, in particular, is difficult to reconcile with *Diehr*. However, the principles of *Diehr* continue to apply. What is perhaps the most important principle announced by *Diehr*? What do you think may be the logical basis for that principle?
3. The dissent places great significance on the mental steps doctrine. Why does that doctrine not apply here? However, the dissent also says that the basis for *Benson* and *Flook* is that the subject matter at issue qualified as a law of nature. These cases are interpreted to stand for the "mathematical algorithm" doctrine, which is still valid today. What do you think is the policy basis for that doctrine? Why does the dissent believe that the claims in *Diehr* are not statutory? *Diehr* is sometimes said to stand for the principle that to be statutory subject matter, what is claimed must be physical. What do you think of this interpretation?[47] If that principle is correct, then what is the basis for concluding that Diehr's claims are statutory subject matter?

47. *See* Digitech Image Techs., LLC v. Elecs. for Imaging, Inc., 758 F.3d 1344 (Fed. Cir. 2014).

4. *Alice* combined with *Mayo* refers to the *Alice-Mayo* framework. This framework is described in *Alice* as follows:

> In *Mayo*, we set forth a framework for distinguishing patents that claim laws of nature, natural phenomena, and abstract ideas from those that claim patent-eligible applications of those concepts. First, we determine whether the claims at issue are directed to one of those patent-ineligible concepts. *Id.*, at 77, 132 S. Ct. 1289, 182 L. Ed. 2d 321, 337. If so, we then ask, "[w]hat else is there in the claims before us?" *Id.*, at 78, 132 S. Ct. 1289, 182 L. Ed. 2d 321, 337. To answer that question, we consider the elements of each claim both individually and "as an ordered combination" to determine whether the additional elements "transform the nature of the claim" into a patent-eligible application. *Id.*, at 79, 78, 132 S. Ct. 1289, 182 L. Ed. 2d 321, 337. We have described step two of this analysis as a search for an "'inventive concept'"—*i.e.*, an element or combination of elements that is "sufficient to ensure that the patent in practice amounts to significantly more than a patent upon the [ineligible concept] itself." *Id.*, at 72, 132 S. Ct. 1289, 182 L. Ed. 2d 321, 327.[48]

   What is the ineligible concept that it was alleged that Alice's claims are directed to? What does it mean that the claims are "directed to" an ineligible concept? What does it mean that the patent in practice amounts to "significantly more" than a patent upon the ineligible concept itself? Does the Court clearly articulate what "directed to" and "significantly more" mean?

5. The Court concludes that the claims in *Alice* are directed to an ineligible "abstract idea." Does the Court explain what makes something an "abstract idea"? What is the Court's basis for concluding an abstract idea is present here? How does one determine whether what a claim "is directed to" is an abstract idea?
6. In some respects, *Alice* is an easy case for the Court, especially in light of *Bilski*. The problem is that because it is an easy case, the Court's guidance for lower federal courts is minimal. What would be your understanding of *Alice* as a lower court or as a patent practitioner?[49]
7. After *Alice*, what subject areas do you think are likely to be subject to greater scrutiny as involving abstract ideas?

---

48. Alice Corp. Pty. Ltd. v. CLS Bank Int'l, 573 U.S. 208, 217, 110 U.S.P.Q.2d 1976 (2014).

49. *See* Howard Skaist, *Alice Corp. and Patent Claiming: A Simple Example*, PATENTLY-O (Aug. 28, 2014), https://patentlyo.com/patent/2014/08/claiming-simple-example.html.

8. *Benson*, *Flook*, and *Diehr* professed to be directed to the issue of non-statutory subject matter. What is the relationship between being "patent ineligible" and being "non-statutory subject matter"? Are they the same thing?
9. *Enfish* is a rather important case because it finally provided some meaningful guidance regarding how to apply the *Mayo-Alice* framework to software; however, it was a long time coming, being decided roughly two years after *Alice*. First, how does the appellate court clarify the "directed to" inquiry? What is the appellate court's guidance on identifying an abstract idea? Why did the appellate court conclude that simply because technology is software that does not necessarily make it an abstract idea?
10. Why did the district court in *Enfish* conclude the claims are directed to an abstract idea? This case points out a key problem in applying *Mayo-Alice* that is still present. Whether the claim turns out to be directed to an abstract idea turns very much on the level at which the claims are interpreted—that is, at a high level, or at the level of the language of the claim itself. Although the appellate court points out this danger, it does not really provide an approach to sufficiently guard against reading the claims at a level divorced from the language of the claims themselves.
11. Note that the appellate court in *Enfish* relies heavily on the specification's description of advantages and disadvantages. What does this suggest about the patent eligibility inquiry?
12. The appellate court provides several meaningful pronouncements in *Enfish* that suggest that software in many cases will be found to be patent eligible. What are those pronouncements?
13. What does the *Enfish* court tell us about the second step of the *Mayo-Alice* inquiry?
14. In *BASCOM*, what is the procedural posture of the case? Note that the district court dismissed the lawsuit based on § 101. What does that mean legally?
15. In *BASCOM*, the district court concluded the claims were directed to the abstract idea of filtering content. However, this is a pretty high-level view of the claims at issue. Nonetheless, the Federal Circuit agreed with the district court, stating:

    > We recognize that this court sometimes incorporates claim limitations into its articulation of the idea to which a claim is directed. *See Enfish*, 2016 U.S. App. LEXIS 8699, 2016 WL 2756255 at *6 (relying on a step of an algorithm corresponding to a means-plus-function

> limitation in defining the idea of a claim for step-one purposes). This case, unlike *Enfish*, presents a "close call[ ] about how to characterize what the claims are directed to." *See* 2016 U.S. App. LEXIS 8699, [WL] at *8. The *Enfish* claims, understood in light of their specific limitations, were unambiguously directed to an improvement in computer capabilities. *See* 2016 U.S. App. LEXIS 8699, [WL] at *5. *Here, in contrast, the claims and their specific limitations do not readily lend themselves to a step-one finding that they are directed to a nonabstract idea.* We therefore defer our consideration of the specific claim limitations' narrowing effect for step two.[50]

Could BASCOM have written its claims in a way that there would not have been a need to go to step two? What does the appellate court mean when it says that the claims are directed to an abstract idea? What was needed to make it clear that the claims were not directed to an abstract idea?

16. In *BASCOM*, how is the Federal Circuit applying the second step to determine whether there is an inventive concept?
17. From the information in the *BASCOM* case, can you formulate a claim that might have received a more favorable analysis under step one?
18. Do you agree or disagree with Judge Newman's concurrence in *BASCOM*?
19. Is *Electric Power Group* an example of a case in which the claims are quite detailed, yet still failed to claim a true innovation, making the claims patent ineligible?
20. What are some of the problems with the claims in *Electric Power Group*?
21. The abstract idea in *Electric Power Group* is stated to be collecting information, analyzing it, and displaying certain results of the collection and analysis. However, this is the nature of a lot of inventions. Are these inventions now necessarily patent ineligible? Why or why not?

* * *

Since the *Mayo*[51] and *Alice*[52] decisions from the Supreme Court, patent eligibility has increasingly become an issue that has proven to affect more types

---

50. BASCOM Glob. Internet Servs., Inc. v. AT&T Mobility LLC, 827 F.3d 1341, 1348–49 (Fed. Cir. 2016) (emphasis added).
51. *See* Mayo Collaborative Servs. v. Prometheus Lab'ys, Inc., 566 U.S. 66, 71, 101 U.S.P.Q.2d 1961, 1965 (2012).
52. *See Alice Corp.*, 573 U.S. at 216, 110 U.S.P.Q.2d at 1980.

of claims than expected. It is to the point where claims cannot be drafted and, likewise, a specification cannot be drafted, without serious consideration of whether this issue has been adequately handled.

There are several pieces to this puzzle to consider. Initially, one should at least understand the *Mayo-Alice* framework as articulated by the Supreme Court. It is articulated reasonably clearly in MPEP section 2106 (I) (2024), as follows:

> *2106 Patent Subject Matter Eligibility*
> *I. TWO CRITERIA FOR SUBJECT MATTER ELIGIBILITY*
>
> *First, the claimed invention must be to one of the four statutory categories. 35 U.S.C. 101 defines the four categories of invention that Congress deemed to be the appropriate subject matter of a patent: processes, machines, manufactures and compositions of matter. The latter three categories define "things" or "products" while the first category defines "actions" (i.e., inventions that consist of a series of steps or acts to be performed). See 35 U.S.C. 100(b) ("The term 'process' means process, art, or method, and includes a new use of a known process, machine, manufacture, composition of matter, or material."). See MPEP § 2106.03 for detailed information on the four categories.*
>
> *Second, the claimed invention also must qualify as patent-eligible subject matter, i.e., the claim must not be directed to a judicial exception unless the claim as a whole includes additional limitations amounting to significantly more than the exception. The judicial exceptions (also called "judicially recognized exceptions" or simply "exceptions") are subject matter that the courts have found to be outside of, or exceptions to, the four statutory categories of invention, and are limited to abstract ideas, laws of nature and natural phenomena (including products of nature). Alice Corp. Pty. Ltd. v. CLS Bank Int'l, 573 U.S. 208, 216, 110 USPQ2d 1976, 1980 (2014) (citing Ass'n for Molecular Pathology v. Myriad Genetics, Inc., 569 U.S. 576, 589, 106 USPQ2d 1972, 1979 (2013)). See MPEP § 2106.04 for detailed information on the judicial exceptions.*
>
> *Because abstract ideas, laws of nature, and natural phenomenon "are the basic tools of scientific and technological work," the Supreme Court has expressed concern that monopolizing these tools by granting patent rights may impede innovation rather than promote it. See Alice Corp., 573 U.S. at 216, 110 USPQ2d at 1980; Mayo Collaborative Servs. v. Prometheus Labs., Inc., 566 U.S. 66, 71, 101 USPQ2d 1961, 1965 (2012). However, the Court has also emphasized that an invention is not considered to be ineligible for patenting simply because it involves a judicial exception. Alice Corp., 573 U.S. at 217, 110 USPQ2d at 1980–81 (citing Diamond v. Diehr, 450 U.S. 175, 187, 209 USPQ 1, 8 (1981)). See also Thales Visionix Inc. v. United States, 850 F.3d. 1343, 1349, 121 USPQ2d 1898, 1902 (Fed. Cir. 2017) ("That a mathematical equation is required to complete the claimed method and system does not doom the claims to abstraction."). Accordingly, the Court has said that integration of an abstract idea, law of nature or natural phenomenon into a practical*

application may be eligible for patent protection. See, e.g., Alice, 573 U.S. at 217, 110 USPQ2d at 1981 (explaining that "in applying the § 101 exception, we must distinguish between patents that claim the 'buildin[g] block[s]' of human ingenuity and those that integrate the building blocks into something more" (quoting Mayo, 566 U.S. at 89, 110 USPQ2d at 1971) and stating that Mayo "set forth a framework for distinguishing patents that claim laws of nature, natural phenomena, and abstract ideas from those that claim patent-eligible applications of those concepts"); Mayo, 566 U.S. at 80, 84, 101 USPQ2d at 1969, 1971 (noting that the Court in Diamond v. Diehr found "the overall process patent eligible because of the way the additional steps of the process integrated the equation into the process as a whole," but the Court in Gottschalk v. Benson "held that simply implementing a mathematical principle on a physical machine, namely a computer, was not a patentable application of that principle"); Bilski v. Kappos, 561 U.S. 593, 611, 95 USPQ2d 1001, 1010 (2010) ("Diehr explained that while an abstract idea, law of nature, or mathematical formula could not be patented, 'an application of a law of nature or mathematical formula to a known structure or process may well be deserving of patent protection.'" (quoting Diamond v. Diehr, 450 U.S. 175, 187, 209 USPQ 1, 8 (1981)) (emphasis in original)); Diehr, 450 U.S. at 187, 192 n.14, 209 USPQ at 10 n.14 (explaining that the process in Parker v. Flook was ineligible not because it contained a mathematical formula, but because it did not provide an application of the formula). See Diamond v. Diehr, 450 U.S. 175, 209 USPQ 1 (1981); Gottschalk v. Benson, 409 U.S. 63, 175 USPQ 673 (1972); Parker v. Flook, 437 U.S. 584, 198 USPQ 193 (1978).

The Supreme Court in Mayo laid out a framework for determining whether an applicant is seeking to patent a judicial exception itself, or a patent-eligible application of the judicial exception. See Alice Corp., 573 U.S. at 217–18, 110 USPQ2d at 1981 (citing Mayo, 566 U.S. 66, 101 USPQ2d 1961). This framework, which is referred to as the Mayo test or the Alice/Mayo test, is discussed in further detail in subsection III, below. The first part of the Mayo test is to determine whether the claims are directed to an abstract idea, a law of nature or a natural phenomenon (i.e., a judicial exception). Id. If the claims are directed to a judicial exception, the second part of the Mayo test is to determine whether the claim recites additional elements that amount to significantly more than the judicial exception. Id. citing Mayo, 566 U.S. at 72–73, 101 USPQ2d at 1966). The Supreme Court has described the second part of the test as the "search for an 'inventive concept.'" Alice Corp., 573 U.S. at 217–18, 110 USPQ2d at 1981 (citing Mayo, 566 U.S. at 72–73, 101 USPQ2d at 1966).

The Alice/Mayo two-part test is the only test that should be used to evaluate the eligibility of claims under examination. While the machine-or-transformation test is an important clue to eligibility, it should not be used as a separate test for eligibility. Instead it should be considered as part of the "integration" determination or "significantly more" determination articulated in the Alice/Mayo test. Bilski v. Kappos, 561 U.S. 593, 605, 95 USPQ2d 1001, 1007 (2010). See MPEP § 2106.04(d) for more information about evaluating whether a claim reciting a judicial exception is integrated into a practical application and MPEP § 2106.05(b) and MPEP § 2106.05(c) for more information about how the machine-or-transformation test fits into the Alice/Mayo two-part framework. Likewise, eligibility should not be evaluated based on whether the claim recites a "useful, concrete, and tangible result," State Street Bank, 149 F.3d 1368, 1374, 47 USPQ2d 1596, 1602 (Fed. Cir. 1998) (quoting In re Alappat, 33 F.3d 1526, 1544, 31 USPQ2d 1545, 1557 (Fed. Cir. 1994)), as this test has been superseded. In re Bilski, 545 F.3d 943, 959–60, 88 USPQ2d 1385, 1394–95 (Fed. Cir. 2008) (en banc), aff'd by Bilski v. Kappos, 561 U.S. 593, 95 USPQ2d 1001 (2010). See also TLI Communications LLC v. AV Automotive LLC, 823 F.3d 607, 613, 118 USPQ2d 1744, 1748 (Fed. Cir. 2016) ("It is well-settled that mere recitation of concrete, tangible components is insufficient to confer patent eligibility to an otherwise abstract idea"). The programmed computer or "special purpose computer" test of In re Alappat, 33 F.3d 1526, 31 USPQ2d 1545 (Fed. Cir. 1994) (i.e., the rationale that an otherwise ineligible algorithm or software could be made patent-eligible by merely adding a generic computer to the claim for the "special purpose" of executing the algorithm or software) was also superseded by the Supreme Court's Bilski and Alice Corp. decisions. Eon Corp. IP Holdings LLC v. AT&T Mobility LLC, 785 F.3d 616, 623, 114 USPQ2d 1711, 1715 (Fed. Cir. 2015) ("[W]e note that Alappat has been superseded by Bilski, 561 U.S. at 605–06, and Alice Corp. v. CLS Bank Int'l, 573 U.S. 208, 110 USPQ2d 1976 (2014)"); Intellectual Ventures I LLC v. Capital One Bank (USA), N.A., 792 F.3d 1363, 1366, 115 USPQ2d 1636, 1639 (Fed. Cir. 2015) ("An abstract idea does not become nonabstract by limiting the invention to a particular field of use or technological environment, such as the Internet [or] a computer"). Lastly, eligibility should not be evaluated based on whether the claimed invention has utility, because "[u]tility is not the test for patent-eligible subject matter." Genetic Techs. Ltd. v. Merial LLC, 818 F.3d 1369, 1380, 118 USPQ2d 1541, 1548 (Fed. Cir. 2016).

Thus, as stated, the first part of the *Mayo-Alice* test is to determine whether the claims are directed to an abstract idea, a law of nature, or a natural phenomenon (i.e., a judicial exception or a patent-ineligible concept). If the claims are directed to a judicial exception, the second part of the test is to determine whether the claim recites additional elements that amount to significantly more than the judicial exception that transforms the judicial exception into patent-eligible subject matter.[53] This involves looking at the elements and limitations of the claim individually and as an ordered combination to determine, either individually or as an ordered combination, whether the claim amounts to more than simply known, routine, or conventional technology.

53. If the claims are not directed to a judicial exception, then the claims are patent eligible, as explained in the MPEP.

Illustrative Claim Example—Software: VisiCalc

More typically, in connection with the predictable arts, the issue under the first part of the test relates to whether the claim is directed to an abstract idea. The term "abstract" was not defined by the Court in *Alice*. Furthermore, the meaning imparted to the term from *Alice* and from subsequent Federal Circuit cases is likely different from what might be expected.

Rather, the language of *Alice* and certainly the direction of the jurisprudence since then has been *to assess whether an innovation is truly being claimed.*[54] One way to view this is that the Court is asking whether the innovation is abstract or concrete (meaning, largely, that it is identifiable, specific, technical, and innovative, as discussed in more detail later). Meaning, again, is this *truly* an innovation or just smoke and mirrors to make it look like there is an innovation? The subsequent case law seems to bear out this view.

Let us consider, as an example, the early days of computers and the creation of VisiCalc. If today's law were to have been applied then, in particular *Mayo-Alice*, would a patent claim covering VisiCalc be patent eligible? The answer truly depends on the claim itself. *So, unlike other countries, in the United States, how the claim is drafted may critically affect eligibility.*

Prior to *Alice* and *Mayo*, a claim drafter might have written the following claim:

EXAMPLE 6.1

I claim:

1. A method comprising: implementing a spreadsheet on a computer.

Appreciate, here, as we have suggested previously, most skilled practitioners tend to make sure that *a spectrum* of claims is included, at least for considerations related to § 103. Drafting a *spectrum* of claims around patent eligibility may *now* be a best practice to consider *for addressing § 101 issues.*

The preceding claim, thus, is in line with claims previously adjudicated before the Federal Circuit. That is, the claim on its face does not appear to communicate details about the innovation itself. Rather, this claim would likely be held patent ineligible under the *Mayo-Alice* approach.

54. *See* Skaist, *supra* note 49.

Spreadsheets are of long-standing use. The aspect of the claim calling out implementation on a computer likewise, on its face at least, does not constitute a sufficiently meaningful addition. It might be argued that computer implementation is faster than performing spreadsheet calculations on paper, but merely being faster is not sufficient, generally, to pass muster under *Mayo-Alice*.

How might such a claim, then, otherwise have been deemed patentable under §§ 102 and 103, *before* the *Alice* and *Mayo* decisions?

It is important to realize that when technology is implemented, rarely does it just result in being faster *and nothing more*. Usually, the implementation provides other advantages. *Here, referring to this simple example as an illustration, VisiCalc made a type of functionality possible via computer that had not existed before.*

Thus, there are quite reasonable arguments for patentability of claim 1 under §§ 102 and 103 (and *before Mayo-Alice*).

Under § 102, is the claim novel? It would seem so. While spreadsheets were known and computers were known, VisiCalc is likely the first spreadsheet to be implemented on a computer.

Section 103 is more challenging than § 102 in this example, as is usually the case; nonetheless, there are good arguments, such as the point articulated earlier. Per § 103 and case law, the claim must be viewed *as a whole*, and this includes advantages that would necessarily flow from the claim language as a whole. *Thus, implementing a spreadsheet on a computer permits new functionality, such as implementing user-selected operations within cells.* The power of this feature may not be understated. It is why spreadsheets have become largely essential tools throughout the world. They have literally changed how the world operates.

This example also demonstrates the *challenge* faced by the PTO and courts as well to evaluate broad claims under §§ 102 and 103 *before* the *Mayo-Alice* framework. With a doctrine like the one articulated for § 103, patent attorneys became quite adept at drafting broad patent claims because under § 103 *the innovation does not need to be recited in the claim language.* ***The key to understanding the power of § 103 is that claim language dissection is not permitted. This is well-established patent law.*** This is also part of the essence of viewing the claim "as a whole."

Enter § 101. Whereas viewing the claim "as a whole" under § 103 is statutory, viewing the claim as a whole under § 101 is judge-made and, consequently, capable of being changed.[55] Before *Alice* and *Mayo*, under § 101, claim

55. *See* Diamond v. Diehr, 450 U.S. 175 (1981).

dissection was already beginning to happen. For example, one doctrine, such as "extra solution activity," stated that such activity did not "make statutory" an otherwise non-statutory claim, and another doctrine stated that limiting a claim to a particular technology did not transform a non-statutory claim into a statutory one. These doctrines could be viewed as examples of claim dissection at the margin. However, appreciate also that while a large overlap between being statutory and being patent eligible exists, the two have become separate considerations. *Thus, one way to view the two-part test is as a type of claim dissection under § 101 despite the teachings of* Diamond v. Diehr. *Rather, the two-part test of* Mayo *and* Alice *effectively breaks the* Diehr *analysis into two parts to, in effect, permit claim dissection.*

The first part of the *Mayo-Alice* framework, to a first approximation, is the "dissection" part asking what the claim is "directed to." The second part, again, to a first approximation, is the "as a whole" part, which might find a claim patent eligible despite being too abstract if dissected. *Here, "abstract" means the proposed technical innovation based on the claim language is not sufficiently concrete, largely meaning not sufficiently identifiable, specific, technical, and innovative.*

Note also that "innovative" here is not the same as being unobvious. Rather, if there are no factual issues that arise in the analysis (e.g., via judicial or examiner notice, known art, or some other way), the innovative evaluation might be seen as "like" a judgment on the pleadings. We take what the patentee says as true in the evaluation of whether this claim is *sufficiently* technical, identifiable, specific, and innovative for § 101 patent eligibility. That is, under those assumptions, is the claim sufficiently concrete? If not, then it is deemed "abstract." This is one way to view the analysis at a high level.

Returning to our example, if such an aspect of VisiCalc, described earlier as the innovation, were *particularly claimed*, perhaps such a claim would be deemed eligible under the analysis in *Alice*. For example, consider the following claims, recognizing that this example is not intended to illustrate the best claims possible, but is just a simple example to illustrate considerations raised by the *Mayo-Alice* framework.

EXAMPLE 6.2

I claim:

1. A method comprising:

   generating and displaying a matrix of cells comprising an electronic spreadsheet on a computer, the electronic spreadsheet implementing one or more user-specified operations in which one or more operands for the one or more user-specified operations are entered in one or more particular cells of the matrix and results of performing the one or more user-specified operations on the one or more operands are retained in the particular cells and/or one or more other particular cells of the matrix with or without display thereof.

2. The method of claim 1, and further comprising: displaying on the computer, in the particular cells and/or the other particular cells, after the one or more operands are entered, the results of performing the one or more user-specified operations on the one or more operands.

3. The method of claim 1, wherein, the implementing comprises: implementing one or more other user-specified operations for the particular cells and/or the other particular cells on the results of performing the one or more user-specified operations on the one or more operands, which are retained in the particular cells and/or the other particular cells of the matrix with or without display thereof.

Observe these are method claims. Software tends to be more easily claimed as a method. Likewise, a benefit is that functionality typically is less of an issue for method claims. Claim 1 is intended to cover using cells to implement user-specified operations with or without display of the results. This is so that one dependent claim may cover displaying the results (claim 2), while another claim may cover using the results as operand inputs for one or more "other" user-specified functions (claim 3).

The first part of *Mayo-Alice* is to determine whether the claims are directed to an abstract idea, a law of nature, or a natural phenomenon (i.e., a judicial exception). If the claims are directed to a judicial exception, the second part of the test is to determine whether the claim recites additional elements that amount to significantly more than the judicial exception.

Analyzing these claims under the first part of Mayo-Alice, as we suggested, *if we take what the patentee says as true, is this claim* ***sufficiently*** *technical, identifiable, specific, and innovative (i.e., concrete; not abstract)*?

Arguably so. Probably the most challenging issue with these claims is whether they are sufficiently *technical*. That is, do they address a *technical* problem? Correctly characterizing this as a solution to a technical problem may be critical here.[56]

---

56. Note the similarity with European Patent Convention law, which requires a "technical effect." *See* European Patent Office, Guidelines for Examination in the European Patent Office pt. G, ch. II, § 3.6 (2024).

Keep in mind that this claim is for a time when the IBM personal computer, for example, was quite new; whereas today this invention may seem straightforward, it was not at the time VisiCalc was invented. The specification should describe the technical hurdles related to implementation of the claims. This is likely both a hardware and software problem and solution, which should be described. Such explanation would also provide written description support for narrower dependent claims.

One should be clear that this approach was not used previously in the prior art. That is, this is not a case of taking something previously done and simply implementing it by computer. *Rather, new computer functionality is enabled here.*

This distinguishes the case from *Alice*. Providing new computer functionality has also been shown to be an aspect of patent eligibility.[57] *Here, the new functionality is permitting or enabling user-specified operations within cells of a spreadsheet.* This functionality enables a user to program solutions to extremely complex problems much more quickly and much more easily. Whereas previously it might have taken someone with a degree in programming days to program and troubleshoot something reasonably complex, with this technology, someone with only a high school diploma may effectively generate a programmed solution to such a problem within hours.

Furthermore, this is not a case of preempting all possible solutions, which has also been shown to be an aspect of patent eligibility (that is, preemption of all possible solutions suggests patent ineligibility).[58] For example, programmable calculators exist, as does computer programming itself. Rather, this is a very particular implementation in which user-selected operations are implemented within cells.

One issue to also appreciate here is that although the desire is to have the PTO issue the claim, the courts and the PTO are not fully aligned on patent eligibility. Thus, it may be important when drafting claims to be patent eligible to provide a basis for eligibility that will be sufficient if the claim were to be tested in litigation. As we discuss later in more detail, it is not too

---

57. For example, the PTO-issued November 2, 2016, patent eligibility guidance states:

> An "improvement in computer-related technology" is *not limited to* improvements in the operation of a computer or a computer network per se, but may also be claimed *as a set of "rules" (basically mathematical relationships) that improve computer-related technology by allowing computer performance of a function not previously performable by a computer.*

Memorandum from Robert W. Bahr, Deputy Commissioner for Patent Examination Policy, PTO, to Patent Examining Corps, re: Recent Subject Matter Eligibility Decisions 2 (Nov. 2, 2016), https://www.uspto.gov/sites/default/files/documents/McRo-Bascom-Memo.pdf (emphasis added). *See also* McRO, Inc. v. Bandai Namco Games Am. Inc., 837 F.3d 1299 (Fed. Cir. 2016).

58. *See, e.g.*, *McRO, Inc.*, 837 F.3d 1299.

difficult to draft a claim that satisfies the PTO requirement of an application, per PTO guidelines. However, meeting that requirement may not satisfy a court.[59] Hence, we are focusing here on the two-part test and case law in connection with drafting a patent-eligible claim.

Thus, to summarize the prior discussion of the first part of the test, an important point under the *Mayo-Alice* framework is to appreciate that "not abstract'" does not mean "physical" (although the claim subject matter must be physical as well to be statutory). Rather, it means an "identifiable," "specific," "concrete," "technical," and "innovative" improvement recited on the face of the claim at issue.

---

59. See, for example, *In re* Killian, 45 F.4th 1373, 1382 (Fed. Cir. 2022) (citations omitted), which states the following:

> Although there is no single, inflexible rule for the abstract idea inquiry, our court has provided guidance as to what constitutes an abstract idea. We have explained that, first, "[t]he 'abstract idea' step of the inquiry calls upon us to look at the 'focus of the claimed advance over the prior art' to determine if the claim's 'character as a whole' is directed to excluded subject matter." Once we identify the "focus of the asserted claims," we may consider whether the claims "fall into a familiar class of claims 'directed to' a patent-ineligible concept."
>
> We have provided still further guidance for those "familiar class[es] of claims." For example, in the context of claims to results, we have explained that claims that "simply demand[] the production of a desired result . . . without any limitation on how to produce that result" are directed to an abstract idea. In the context of mental processes . . . we have explained that if a claim's steps "can be performed in the human mind, or by a human using a pen and paper," and the elements in the claim do not contain a sufficient inventive concept under *Alice/Mayo* step two, the claim is for a patent-ineligible abstract idea. And we have explained that "[i]nformation as such is an intangible"; accordingly, "gathering and analyzing information of a specified content, then displaying the results" without "any particular assertedly inventive technology for performing those functions" is an abstract idea. We have provided further guidance for "cases involving software innovations," where the abstract idea "inquiry often turns on whether the claims focus on 'the specific asserted improvement in computer capabilities . . . or, instead, on a process that qualifies as an "abstract idea" for which computers are invoked merely as a tool.'"
>
> Our case law also provides guidance as to "inventive concept," particularly in the context of claims for computer implementations of abstract ideas. We have explained that claims for methods that "improve[] an existing technological process" include an inventive concept at step two. And claims that "recite a specific, discrete implementation of the abstract idea" rather than "preempt[ing] all ways of" achieving an abstract idea using a computer may include an inventive concept. But claims to "an abstract idea implemented on generic computer components, without providing a specific technical solution beyond simply using generic computer concepts in a conventional way" do not pass muster at step two. "Neither 'attempting to limit the use of [the idea] to a particular technological environment' nor a 'wholly generic computer implementation' is sufficient."

An aspect of this, if responding to a § 101 rejection, for example, includes pointing out that the claim is not directed to any of the problematic areas, like a mathematical algorithm, mental steps, organizing human activities, and/or a fundamental or long-standing practice (especially economic or legal practices). Thus, one should draft the claim to avoid these problematic areas. If, under scrutiny, however, such arguments are weak or suspect in light of the drafted claim, then the claim language may need to be reformulated to more clearly recite an approach that, as an example, addresses a previously unaddressed *technical* problem or that addresses a *technical* problem in a way that is better than otherwise known approaches.

Thus, one should draft a claim in which it may be shown that what is being claimed is, again, an "identifiable," "specific," "technical," and "innovative" improvement.

If, again, responding to a rejection under § 101, often the examiner will overgeneralize the claim language and/or assert that the claim merely covers data processing, which is not generally patent eligible. It may be helpful to remind the examiner to not overly generalize the claim language, to point to the specific claim language at issue, and also to point out that the claim language and the specification explicitly refer to "signals and/or states,"[60] which qualifies as physical manifestations, unlike "data," which does not. Cases that support this include *Digitech*[61] and even older precedent like *Arrhythmia*.[62]

It may also be appropriate to point to and discuss (that is, distinguish) the case *Electric Power Group*.[63] The claims related to systems and methods for performing real-time performance monitoring of an electric power grid by collecting data from multiple data sources, analyzing the data, and displaying the results.

The appellate court went on to distinguish two cases, in particular *BASCOM*, which is discussed more later. It stated:

> Nor do the claims here require an arguably inventive distribution of functionality within a network, thus distinguishing the claims at issue from those

---

60. This assumes the specification is drafted to refer to physical signals and/or states rather than "data" or "information," which are not physical.

61. *See* Digitech Image Techs., LLC v. Elecs. for Imaging, Inc., 758 F.3d 1344 (Fed. Cir. 2014).

62. *See* Arrhythmia Rsch. Tech. Inc. v. Corazonix Corp., 958 F.2d 1053 (Fed. Cir. 1992). The case *Enfish, LLC v. Microsoft Corp.*, 822 F.3d 1327, 1333 (Fed. Cir. 2016), is also helpful to cite here due to its language (emphasis added):

> Much of the advancement made in computer technology consists of improvements to software that, by their very nature, may not be defined by particular physical features but rather *by logic structures and processes*. We do not see in *Bilski* or *Alice*, or our cases, an exclusion to patenting this large field of technological progress.

63. *See* Elec. Power Grp., LLC v. Alstom S.A., 830 F.3d 1350 (Fed. Cir. 2016).

> in *Bascom*, 827 F.3d 1341, 2016 U.S. App. LEXIS 11687, 2016 WL 3514158, at *6 (at pleading stage finding sufficient inventive concept in "the installation of a filtering tool at a specific location, remote from the end users, with customizable filtering features specific to each end user"). The claims in this case specify what information in the power-grid field it is desirable to gather, analyze, and display, including in "real time"; but they do not include any requirement for performing the claimed functions of gathering, analyzing, and displaying in real time by use of anything but entirely conventional, generic technology. The claims therefore do not state an arguably inventive concept in the realm of application of the information-based abstract ideas.[64]

Thus, unlike *Electric Power Group* and more like *BASCOM*, the claims here, one would argue, are specific and innovative as to the operations at issue.

In this manner, through argument, one may refocus the examiner's attention on more appropriate considerations for patent eligibility, such as the technical problems that are being addressed through express claim language and associated discussion contained in the specification describing the technical problem.

Usually when addressing an overgeneralization of claim language by an examiner, again, it may be helpful to highlight and repeat the exact language of the claim and point out the improvement over the state of the art to make the overgeneralization quite clear and specific for the examiner.

Likewise, as alluded to previously, one should draft the claim so that one may emphasize that the claim does not tie up fundamental scientific building blocks, again, through the specificity of claim language and how that language relates to a particular technical issue.

Thus, one may assert that, as a whole, the claim is patent eligible and not directed to an abstract idea. Because the improvement is identifiable, specific, technical, and innovative (such as not a long-standing practice), the discussion of the problem and the improvement distinguishes the claim from the one in *Alice*. Likewise, emphasizing that the subject matter claimed is not a long-standing practice further distinguishes *Alice*, not unlike how the *DDR*[65] court compared a website to a kiosk to conclude the subject matter to be patent eligible because of significant technical differences. That is, per *DDR*, mere analogies are inadequate in a discussion involving *specific* and *technical* improvements. The technical advances, such as new computer functionality, or the internet, as another example, create new problems that require new solutions.[66]

---

64. *Id.* at 1355–56.
65. *See* DDR Holdings, LLC v. Hotels.com, L.P., 773 F.3d 1245, 1258 (Fed. Cir. 2014).
66. On this point, *DDR Holdings*, 773 F.3d at 1258, states (emphasis added):

> The dissent suggests that the "store within a store" concept, such as a warehouse store that contains a kiosk for selling a third-party partner's cruise vacation packages, is the

However, for the sake of argument, this could also be a case, for example, in which whether the first part of the test is met is on the borderline. Case law suggests that the second part of the test is to address such situations.[67] Thus, under the second part of the test, the benefits that flow from the claim may also be important. That is, for the analysis to be conducted, the claim elements are viewed individually or in combination to determine whether they amount to more than the judicial exception. Here, meaning the claim elements viewed individually or in combination are more than simply well-known, routine, or conventional technology.

Thus, in our example, for claim drafting and for analysis, one should also consider the second step—which *BASCOM* clarifies is used for close call cases. That is, for example, even if the examiner might be "on the fence" on the first step (simply for the sake of legal argument), the claim *still* may pass muster through application of the second step. *BASCOM* clarifies (and it is reiterated in the PTO guidelines) that even if individual elements of a claim are known, conventional, and so on, nonetheless, a *nongeneric/nonconventional arrangement* of known elements is still able to be patent eligible. Thus, *DDR* and/or *BASCOM* provides a good basis for distinguishing the improvement as nonconventional.[68] *Amdocs (Israel) Ltd. v. Opennet Telecom, Inc.*[69] is also on point in this regard.

---

pre-Internet analog of the '399 patent's asserted claims. Dissenting Op. 1264. While that concept may have been well-known by the relevant timeframe, that practice did not have to account for the ephemeral nature of an Internet "location" or the near-instantaneous transport between these locations made possible by standard Internet communication protocols, *which introduces a problem that does not arise in the "brick and mortar" context.*

67. *See* BASCOM Glob. Internet Servs., Inc. v. AT&T Mobility LLC, 827 F.3d 1341 (Fed. Cir. 2016).

68. In *BASCOM*, 827 F.3d at 1340–50, the Federal Circuit disagreed with the district court's holding that the ordered combination of limitations was noninventive and held that the claimed technical improvement transformed the abstract idea into patent-eligible subject matter under the second step. The Federal Circuit recognized that courts commonly consider whether various claim elements simply recite "well-understood, routine, conventional activities." But the Federal Circuit further stated that "[t]he inventive concept inquiry requires *more than* recognizing that each claim element, by itself, was known in the art . . . *an inventive concept can be found in the non-conventional and non-generic arrangement* of known, conventional pieces" (emphasis added).

Amdocs (Isr.) Ltd. v. Opennet Telecom, Inc., 841 F.3d 1288, 1303 (Fed. Cir. 2016), is yet another decided Federal Circuit case suggesting that, even assuming the claim were directed to an abstract idea, other aspects of the claim transform it to be patent-eligible subject matter. For example, in that case, the court stated (emphasis added):

> Claim 1 involves some arguably conventional components (e.g., gatherers), but the claim also involves limitations that when considered individually and as an ordered combination recite an inventive concept through the system's distributed architecture. . . . *This arrangement is not so broadly described to cause preemption concerns.* Instead, it is narrowly circumscribed to the particular system outlined. As in *BASCOM*, this is a technical improvement over prior art technologies and served to improve the performance of the system itself.

69. 841 F.3d 1288.

It is worth pointing out that prior technical arguments made under the first part of the test may also come into play under the second part of the test, but with a different emphasis (e.g., viewed through a different lens, so to speak).[70] In this example, then, for a case such as this, and in general, one may draft the claim to provide technical arguments able at least in part to show that the technology at issue involves a computer-related technical problem. This assists to illustrate that the problem addressed does *not* relate to a problem addressed by a long-standing practice and, instead, provides new functionality. This further suggests that it is sufficiently identifiable, specific, technical, and innovative (i.e., concrete)—that it is not abstract.

Even assuming, without agreeing, this example is a close call case, nonetheless, the language used to draft this claim is intended to transform an otherwise arguably abstract idea to patent-eligible subject matter, such as through a nongeneric or nonconventional arrangement. That is, the claim should be drafted with this in mind. For example, in claim 1, the language

> the electronic spreadsheet implementing one or more user-specified operations in which one or more operands for the one or more user-specified operations are entered in one or more particular cells . . . and results of performing the one or more user-specified operations on the one or more operands are retained in the particular cells and/or one or more other particular cells . . .

could and should be argued to be a nongeneric and nonconventional arrangement that provides new functionality to the platform.

This part of the analysis, however, also involves some of the factual aspects of the inquiry, such as in the *Berkheimer*[71] case and the requirements set out by the PTO in the so-called *Berkheimer* memorandum, related to what is known, routine, or conventional.[72] Along these lines, an effective point to be made is

70. *See* Elec. Power Grp., LLC v. Alstom S.A., 830 F.3d 1350 (Fed. Cir. 2016).
71. Berkheimer v. HP Inc., 881 F.3d 1360, 1367 (Fed. Cir. 2018).
72. The *Berkheimer* memorandum provides:

> [A]n additional element (or combination of elements) is *not* well-understood, routine or conventional *unless* the examiner finds, and expressly supports a rejection in writing with, one or more of the following:
>
> A citation to an express statement in the specification or to a statement made by an applicant during prosecution that demonstrates the well-understood, routine, conventional nature of the additional element(s).
>
> A citation to one or more of the court decisions discussed in MPEP § 2106.05(d)(II) as noting the well-understood, routine, conventional nature of the additional element(s).
>
> A citation to a publication that demonstrates the well-understood, routine, conventional nature of the additional element(s).

that *Berkheimer* specifically says a feature shown in the prior art does not *necessarily* establish that the feature is conventional. Thus, for our example, one might point out that, *a fortiori*, the elements or limitations at issue cannot be conventional because (assuming this is accurate) the examiner has not even found prior art showing the elements or limitations at issue (e.g., in response to a rejection under § 102 or 103 made along with the rejection under § 101).

Likewise, when drafting the claim, it follows one would use claim language to provide linguistic support for legal arguments to distinguish the claim from known prior art. This may seem like simply drafting to avoid §§ 102 and 103; however, it is much more than that. It is drafting the claim to support arguments so that *on the face of the claim*, based on the language of the claim itself, it is clear that the subject matter is identifiable, it is specific, it is technical, and it is innovative. This is to support that when the elements and limitations are viewed individually and in combination, it is more than simply known, routine, or conventional technology.

Having provided an illustration of claim drafting and associated analysis to address § 101 patent eligibility in light of Federal Circuit case law, we now address drafting the claim to satisfy the PTO, based on its guidelines. To be more specific, how would the previous example claim *before Alice* (Example 6.1) fare under the current *subject matter eligibility guidance (i.e., published in January 2019)*?[73] Furthermore, how might that claim be redrafted to hopefully improve the chances that the claim will pass muster under that same new guidance?

One problem, however, as illustrated starkly by the previous hypothetical examples, is that claims drafted in light of the *Alice* decision are generally *narrower* than they would have been otherwise. Perhaps, for example, one could write better (e.g., broader) claims to pass muster under the *Mayo-Alice* framework in light of the PTO guidelines as a sort of hedge regarding breadth while at the same time increasing claim diversity.

To refresh, the "before" claim from earlier (Example 6.1) recited:

> A method comprising: implementing a spreadsheet on a computer.

> A statement that the examiner is taking official notice of the well-understood, routine, conventional nature of the additional element(s).

Memorandum from Robert W. Bahr, Deputy Commissioner for Patent Examination Policy, PTO, to Patent Examining Corps, re: Changes in Examination Procedure Pertaining to Subject Matter Eligibility, Recent Subject Matter Eligibility Decision (*Berkheimer v. HP, Inc.*) 3–4 (Apr. 19, 2018), https://www.uspto.gov/sites/default/files/documents/memo-berkheimer-20180419.PDF (emphasis added).

73. The PTO's current eligibility guidance is found in the MPEP and particularly sections 2103 through 2106.07(c). *See Subject Matter Eligibility*, PTO, https://www.uspto.gov/patents/laws/examination-policy/subject-matter-eligibility (last visited May 14, 2024).

The primary change under the January 2019 subject matter guidance was to so-called step 2A (using the terminology of the PTO; effectively the first part of the *Mayo-Alice* framework)—that is, whether the claim is directed toward a judicial exception, such as an abstract idea.

The *January 2019 subject matter guidance* adds a first prong and a second prong to step 2A of the PTO guidelines. Following the first prong of the PTO guidance, an examiner is to determine whether the claim recites a judicial exception, in this case an abstract idea, by referring to subject matter groupings. The subject matter groupings are specified as mathematical concepts, certain methods of organizing human behavior, and mental processes. These are essentially the areas discussed previously as problematic areas to avoid when drafting the claim.

The guidance is quite specific in saying that the claim must "recite" subject matter that falls within the enumerated groupings to raise an issue regarding patent eligibility. One could argue that the claim does not "recite" subject matter that falls into the enumerated groupings. Nonetheless, this claim is not going to get through the PTO unchallenged under § 101. One could easily imagine an examiner asserting that the claim recites a mental process despite the language directed to a computer. An examiner might say, for example, that implementing a spreadsheet can be a mental process and that the language "implementing . . . on a computer" is nothing more than clever patent drafting without a substantive limit on scope.

How, then, might the claim be redrafted to overcome such a rejection, but still retain some measure of breadth? Example 6.3 is one attempt, capturing the inventive concept of Example 6.2, while achieving some greater breadth.

EXAMPLE 6.3

I claim:

1. A method comprising: implementing a spreadsheet via a computer, including determining contents of one or more cells thereof, based at least in part on one or more user-specified operations to be applied to signals and/or states to be provided as operands for the one or more user-specified operations.

This redrafted claim at least arguably does not recite a mental process. Rather, the claim language is pretty specific to make it clear that physical processes are taking place. For example, it describes applying operations to signals and/or states. Often, the PTO will argue that the claim could be performed by a person in their head or with pencil and paper.[74] However, for a sufficiently complex problem, it could not be performed by a person.[75] For example, claim 1 of Example 6.3 could recite "*recursively* determining contents . . . ." Thus, at least two out of three groupings may have been drafted around, since it does not recite a mathematical process, as such.

However, the Manual of Patent Examining Procedure (MPEP) states:

> The phrase "methods of organizing human activity" is used to describe concepts relating to:
>
> - fundamental economic principles or practices (including hedging, insurance, mitigating risk);
> - commercial or legal interactions (including agreements in the form of contracts, legal obligations, advertising, marketing or sales activities or behaviors, and business relations); and
> - managing personal behavior or relationships or interactions between people (including social activities, teaching, and following rules or instructions).[76]

One could argue this does not fall into these categories. Still, an examiner might say that a spreadsheet is a long-standing, fundamental economic practice or one that is a method of organizing human activities, demonstrating one danger with this latter particular grouping. It is, by its very nature, a bit vague. At least partly due to its vagueness, it would not be *entirely* unreasonable for an examiner to suggest that a spreadsheet might fall into this grouping, even assuming the examiner was convinced that the claim was not an abstract idea because it does not qualify as a mental process. However, a spreadsheet is not merely or even necessarily an economic practice, which one could argue.

Fortunately, regardless, all is not lost. Even if one fails to pass muster under the first prong, an opportunity to satisfy § 101 under the second prong remains under the PTO guidelines. Here, the guidance says that if the recited exception is integrated into a practical application, then the claim is still patent eligible.[77]

---

74. Although courts have applied a similar analysis, this is not really the "mental steps" doctrine. For that doctrine to apply, there must be mental steps recited in the claim. That is not the case here. However, perhaps the analysis is that if the claim could be performed by a person in their head or with pencil and paper, then it is not sufficiently identifiable, specific, technical, and innovative (i.e., concrete)—that it is abstract.

75. *See* MPEP, *supra* note 33, § 2106.04(a)(2)(III). However, it might be prudent to have dependent claims that recite limitations related to a complex problem that could not be solved by pencil and paper.

76. *See id.* § 2106.04(a)(2)(II).

77. *See id.* § 2106.04(d).

This is an area where one *cannot* be sure that meeting this will satisfy a federal court; however, if a claim is issued, it is presumed valid and previously we drafted *narrower* claims intended to be included and provide some comfort regarding satisfying § 101 for federal court litigation.

Specifically, the guidance says that to meet the second prong the claim is to integrate the judicial exception into a *practical application that imposes a meaningful limit* on the judicial exception, such that the claim is more than a drafting effort to monopolize the judicial exception. One could argue that Example 6.2 already does this. As suggested previously, this is not a case of preempting all possible solutions, which has also been shown to be an aspect of patent eligibility (that is, preemption of all possible solutions suggests patent ineligibility).[78] For example, programmable calculators exist, as does computer programming itself. Rather, this is a very particular implementation in which user-selected operations are implemented within cells.

However, to bolster such a position, we could, in addition to reciting "recursively," also via claim language make it clear that some sort of result is generated, stored for further processing, and displayed or printed, so that, *as a whole*, the claim comprises a significant improvement over a spreadsheet generated by hand, for example, as follows:

EXAMPLE 6.4

I claim:

> A method comprising: implementing a spreadsheet via a computer, including: recursively determining and displaying contents of one or more cells of a displayed matrix of the spreadsheet, based at least in part on one or more user-specified operations to be applied to signals and/or states to be provided as operands for the one or more user-specified operations; retaining in the particular cells and/or one or more other particular cells of the matrix of the spreadsheet results of performing the one or more user-specified operations on the one or more operands for further recursive processing by one or more additional user-specified operations; and generating output signals and/or states based at least in part on the recursively determining, wherein the generating includes generating a report or a display that comprises at least a table portion or a sub-portion of the matrix of the spreadsheet.

78. *See* McRO, Inc. v. Bandai Namco Games Am. Inc, 837 F.3d 1299 (Fed. Cir. 2016).

Now, it seems that it would be challenging to assert that a practical application with meaningful limits has *not* been claimed.[79] Furthermore, if needed, more dependent claims could be used to flesh out more application-specific features. For example, a claim along the lines of claim 3 of Example 6.2 could be added. Thus, it would seem, we have successfully written or could successfully write a claim that is patent eligible under the PTO guidance.

Medical Diagnostic Methods

After *Mayo*, claims directed to medical diagnosis became another area that had problems related to patent eligibility. Often, a diagnosis claim relates to measuring something, for example, regarding the human body, and making a diagnosis based on the measurement. Because the first part of the test asks whether the claim is directed to a judicial exception, these types of claims are determined to be patent ineligible because ultimately this diagnosis at least in part is based on a measurement of the human body. This is viewed by courts as tantamount to claiming a law of nature.

The result has been the invalidation of patents claiming medical diagnostic methods that make use of commonly known laboratory and analytical techniques to diagnose naturally occurring physical phenomena, even where the diagnosis itself might be novel. That is, the measurement involves measuring something that occurs in nature and drawing a conclusion (e.g., making a diagnosis) based on a correlation of some sort between the measurement and a medical condition. Medical diagnostic patents might do better regarding eligibility by claiming innovative methods and/or practical applications, rather than the observation of biological or other physical effects using known techniques, not unlike the approach described earlier.

Specifically, courts have found that diagnostic method claims directed primarily to a correlation that exists in nature related to a natural phenomenon are not patent eligible. A good example is the *Ariosa Diagnostics, Inc. v. Sequenom, Inc.*[80] decision. The Federal Circuit held that claims directed to a method of detecting fetal DNA in a mother's serum or plasma sample were patent ineligible, as being directed to a natural phenomenon. The court acknowledged that the discovery of cell-free fetal DNA (cffDNA) present in a mother's circulating blood was a major scientific breakthrough; nonetheless, the claims were ultimately found to be primarily directed to a natural phenom-

79. *See* PTO, Subject Matter Eligibility Examples: Abstract Ideas exs. 37–42 (2019), https://www.uspto.gov/sites/default/files/documents/101_examples_37to42_20190107.pdf.

80. 788 F.3d 1371 (Fed. Cir. 2015).

enon—the presence of fetal DNA in a mother's serum or plasma. The claims recited conventional techniques for detecting the DNA. This, therefore, failed to transform the claims into patent-eligible subject matter.

A *claiming approach to address this issue is to draft a claim that uses the measurement in a manner that is more than simply making a diagnosis*. For example, perhaps the measurement leads to a new and innovative *treatment* or perhaps the measurement leads to a new and innovative *preparation of a sample* of some sort. That is, the claim is drafted in a manner so that the claim does not amount to simply a law of nature or little more than a law of nature when viewing the elements and limitations either individually or as an ordered combination.

Analogously, as discussed previously with software, as just discussed, this means drafting the claim in a manner to show that the claim recites a technique that is identifiable, specific, technical, and innovative (e.g., concrete), meaning, here, that the claim is more than simply a diagnosis based upon a measurement.

For example, some court decisions illustrate that method of treatment claims may be patent eligible. For example, in *Vanda Pharmaceuticals v. West-Ward Pharmaceuticals International*,[81] the claim at issue was directed to the *identification* of a genetic variant regarding individuals as poor metabolizers of a compound used to treat schizophrenia, and *administering* specific and different amounts of the compound to individuals, depending on whether they harbor the genetic variant. Thus, the administering the compound amounted to more than simply diagnosis and claiming a law of nature.

Similarly, in *Endo Pharmaceuticals v. Teva Pharmaceuticals USA*,[82] the claims were directed to treating pain in a renally impaired patient with a compound, in which the creatinine clearance rate of the patient was *measured*, and *a lower dosage of the compound was administered* to the patient, depending on the patient's clearance rate. The Federal Circuit found the claims at issue to be patent eligible, as being directed to "a specific method of treatment for specific patients using a specific compound at specific doses to achieve a specific outcome."[83]

Hence, a drafting technique here is to incorporate additional features related to treatment so that the claims represent practical applications of underlying natural phenomena. Again, this is similar to the approach, just discussed in the prior section, to draft the claim so that the claim covers a practical application in a manner that is identifiable, specific, technical, and innovative (e.g., concrete), as previously discussed.

81. 887 F.3d 1117 (Fed. Cir. 2018).
82. 919 F.3d 1347 (Fed. Cir. 2019).
83. *Id.* at 1354.

More recently, the Federal Circuit, in *Illumina v. Ariosa Diagnostics*,[84] deemed claims to be patent eligible and distinguished them from the claims in *Ariosa Diagnostics v. Sequenom*. The court stated: "This is not a diagnostic case. And it is not a method of treatment case. It is a method of preparation case."[85] Similar to our criteria regarding identifiable, specific, technical, and innovative, the claims involved *specific processing* of size discrimination, *selecting* DNA fragments above a specified size threshold, and *physical* processing that *changed the composition* of the mixture, resulting in a DNA fraction different from that occurring naturally.

Thus, again, following the analogy with the software area, conventional techniques may be used in an unconventional approach. If the method a patent applicant seeks to protect uses conventional operations, for example, perhaps the claims may be tailored in a way to exploit a new observation or to generate a new result.

Some additional suggestions include, similar to preceding suggestions regarding the software illustrative examples, focus the claims on actions (instead of correlations, for example); describe the method with specificity; focus the claims on the particular technology or systems at issue; and, in general, do not concede or state that an aspect of the claim is conventional or routine.

Avoid Potential Enablement Issues

MPEP § 2164.01(a)

Undue Experimentation Factors

There are many factors to be considered when determining whether there is sufficient evidence to support a determination that a disclosure does not satisfy the enablement requirement and whether any necessary experimentation is "undue." These factors include, but are not limited to:

(A) The breadth of the claims;
(B) The nature of the invention;
(C) The state of the prior art;
(D) The level of one of ordinary skill;
(E) The level of predictability in the art;
(F) The amount of direction provided by the inventor;
(G) The existence of working examples; and
(H) The quantity of experimentation needed to make or use the invention based on the content of the disclosure.

In re Wands, 858 F.2d 731, 737, 8 USPQ2d 1400, 1404 (Fed. Cir. 1988) (reversing the PTO's determination that claims directed to methods for detection of hepatitis

84. 952 F.3d 1367 (Fed. Cir. 2020).
85. *Id.* at 1371.

B surface antigens did not satisfy the enablement requirement). In Wands, the court noted that there was no disagreement as to the facts, but merely a disagreement as to the interpretation of the data and the conclusion to be made from the facts. In re Wands, 858 F.2d at 736–40, 8 USPQ2d at 1403–07. The court held that the specification was enabling with respect to the claims at issue and found that "there was considerable direction and guidance" in the specification; there was "a high level of skill in the art at the time the application was filed;" and "all of the methods needed to practice the invention were well known." 858 F.2d at 740, 8 USPQ2d at 1406. After considering all the factors related to the enablement issue, the court concluded that "it would not require undue experimentation to obtain antibodies needed to practice the claimed invention." Id., 8 USPQ2d at 1407.

It is improper to conclude that a disclosure is not enabling based on an analysis of only one of the above factors while ignoring one or more of the others. The examiner's analysis must consider all the evidence related to each of these factors, and any conclusion of nonenablement must be based on the evidence as a whole. 858 F.2d at 737, 740, 8 USPQ2d at 1404, 1407.

A conclusion of lack of enablement means that, based on the evidence regarding each of the above factors, the specification, at the time the application was filed, would not have taught one skilled in the art how to make and/or use the full scope of the claimed invention without undue experimentation. In re Wright, 999 F.2d 1557, 1562, 27 USPQ2d 1510, 1513 (Fed. Cir. 1993).

The determination that "undue experimentation" would have been needed to make and use the claimed invention is not a single, simple factual determination. Rather, it is a conclusion reached by weighing all the above noted factual considerations. In re Wands, 858 F.2d at 737, 8 USPQ2d at 1404. These factual considerations are discussed more fully in MPEP § 2164.08 (scope or breadth of the claims), § 2164.05(a) (nature of the invention and state of the prior art), § 2164.05(b) (level of one of ordinary skill), § 2164.03 (level of predictability in the art and amount of direction provided by the inventor), § 2164.02 (the existence of working examples) and § 2164.06 (quantity of experimentation needed to make or use the invention based on the content of the disclosure).

Trustees of Boston University v. Everlight Electronics Co.
896 F.3d 1357
United States Court of Appeals for the Federal Circuit
July 25, 2018, Decided

Amgen Inc. v. Sanofi
143 S. Ct. 1243
Supreme Court of the United States
March 27, 2023, Argued; May 18, 2023, Decided

Questions

1. Enablement is typically a specification drafting issue rather than a claim drafting issue; however, it may be that how the claims are drafted raises an enablement issue. In most cases, this is a known risk; however, one should be aware of the issue before drafting claims. How did an enablement issue arise in the *Boston University* case?
2. Could Boston University have avoided this legal question, even after the patent issued? If so, how? If so, why did Boston University choose the course that it did?
3. Is the warning from this case a claim construction issue or a claim drafting issue?
4. Assuming the claim was drafted intentionally the way it was interpreted, how might the risk of lack of enablement have been reduced? Why do you think that did not occur here?
5. The appellate court said that the enablement issue was of Boston University's own making. Do you think the university realized it was creating an enablement issue either via claim drafting and/or claim construction?
6. *Amgen* is another case where whether the full scope of the claims is enabled is an issue. Did Amgen use dependent claims to cover its risk, as suggested previously?
7. Why was there a question as to enablement with respect to the full scope of the claims? Is this a case that puts Markush group-type claims or functional claims under higher scrutiny?
8. This case is in the unpredictable arts but may also affect the predictable arts. How does one know whether they have enabled the full scope of the claims?
9. If this case does put either Markush-type claiming or functional claiming under greater scrutiny, what is a way to handle this increased risk for those claims?
10. The Court provides as a rationale that once the patent expires, the public is free to practice the invention. Is that entirely accurate? Is it possible that once a patent expires, the public is still not free to practice the invention?

* * *

Like written description, other issues, like enablement, though mostly about the specification, still have the potential to render claims invalid or to result in rejection during examination. It is well beyond the scope of this work to address these issues in any comprehensive manner since the focus here is about drafting patent claims. Rather, the point is to alert a claim drafter to a few of the pitfalls.

In the predictable arts, if there is full written description support for all the claims and if the claims cover the full range of embodiments, it is likely that enablement has been met. One way, perhaps, to tell is to make sure you, the drafter, could implement the invention from the specification description. Typically, but not necessarily, patent attorneys are probably below ordinary skill or just barely make it, particularly with respect to the most relevant technology for the invention. Patent attorneys simply cannot be experts in everything. Also, because this is the predictable arts, some "play" should be present at the margins. That is, there are many things that may not need to be described since some technical matters are within the knowledge of one of ordinary skill. On the other hand, as suggested by the cases and questions, a prudent practitioner would consider whether the broadest claims are fully enabled and would also include dependent claims to cover the risk that the broad claims may not be fully enabled.

What may be most important is enabling the feature or features that make the invention innovative. Most description provided for an invention in the predictable arts is known and the description is provided for written description support and for claim interpretation, rather than enablement. However, the feature or features that make the invention innovative is critical to describe. Thus, in the predictable arts, enablement is usually not an issue unless the invention is not enabled regarding the best mode and/or regarding what is believed to be the true innovation. However, implied by *Amgen*, if that feature is largely functional, then claims that are more structural should also be included.

Furthermore, significant confidence regarding enablement may not be as appropriate with respect to the unpredictable arts. In that case, the inventors may provide the best insights into whether enablement has been met. Furthermore, the level of detail needed for enablement is expected to vary with technical area. It is common to provide actual working examples or even prophetic examples, suitably identified as such, in the unpredictable arts. Satisfying enablement and written description may be challenging issues in some areas of the unpredictable arts. Thus, care is warranted.

Draft Claims in Anticipation of the First Office Action and in Light of Expected Obviousness Arguments

Consistent with the idea of drafting the claims before the specification is the notion of drafting claims in anticipation of a first office action. This is one reason it may be desirable to be aware of prior art at least as good as will be cited by the examiner, if possible. By anticipating the first office action and drafting the claims appropriately, the need to amend may potentially be avoided. That is, you may already have formulated an argument for patentability and drafted a claim reflecting that argument before the application is even filed.

This potentially reduces estoppel, results in quicker prosecution, saves the client money, and increases the patent term. In addition, if done properly, it also potentially reduces the risk that limitations will be imported from the specification or that written description problems will occur.

It should not be difficult from being aware of the closest *known* prior art to anticipate a typical § 103 rejection. The rejection anticipated is under § 103 because the claims should be written to clearly distinguish over any *known* § 102 art, although it is expected that *known* § 102 art may figure prominently in a § 103 rejection.

To make out a *prima facie* case under § 103, the examiner must establish (1) that the proposed combination of prior art references includes all the limitations of the rejected claim in the manner recited in the rejected claim; and (2) that there is motivation in the prior art to make the proposed combination.[86]

Typically, showing that element (1) is not met is the strongest argument against a § 103 rejection. Often, the examiner will cite art that might be analogous in some way to the language of the claim or it may in some hypertechnical way appear to meet the elements, but *not* in the manner expressly recited in the claim.

If you review your claims, you probably will be able to figure out those aspects of the claims the examiner would easily locate from searching. Likewise, you should be able to deduce those aspects that you think should be more challenging to locate from searching or that the examiner simply will not find. Thus, of course, focus on the latter over the former in terms of anticipating how you might respond.

It might, however, be that all the elements would not be difficult to locate and that you believe the strongest argument is that there should not be a motivation in the prior art to make the proposed combination. The prior art may not recognize the desirability and advantages of making the proposed combination. This, unfortunately, does tend to be a more challenging argument to make successfully. Examiners tend to not take such arguments as seriously, despite that such arguments are legitimate ones for patentability. As well, having the particular art that the examiner may be relying upon to make

86. *See* MPEP, *supra* note 33, § 2141.

a rejection will help (which is highly unlikely, if not impossible, when merely anticipating the rejection). It may be that the aspects of the documents the examiner seeks to combine are not readily combinable. Likewise, it may be that how the elements are depicted in the cited documents does not resemble the manner in which the examiner has sought to combine the elements. This further suggests that the prior art does not truly provide the appropriate motivation for the combination.

In anticipation of such a rejection, it may be helpful to consider why you think the prior art may not provide motivation for the proposed combination. It may be helpful to consider why others have not hit upon the invention. Typically, there is an underlying fact or several underlying facts that are not well known in the art and that often provide some basis for the invention. It is helpful to try to uncover from interviewing the inventor(s) this basis or these bases for later argument. It would also be a good idea that these notions, once explained by the inventor(s), be articulated reasonably clearly with respect to a "particular embodiment" in the specification. This should be possible since when anticipating this first office action, you are drafting the patent claims and, therefore, have not yet filed the patent application.

However, it is not required that prior art necessarily motivate one to combine the elements *for the exact reason that the elements are combined in the invention at issue*. Yet, despite this, the invention may be unpatentable as having been obvious. Any legitimate reason for one of ordinary skill in the art to make the proposed combination is sufficient for a § 103 rejection.[87] *Nonetheless, there must be a legitimate reason for one of ordinary skill to be motivated to combine the cited references in the manner asserted by the examiner*. Often, therefore, the examiner will come up with a straw man, not well-thought-out, or possibly not true technical reason to make the proposed combination. Also, sometimes the examiner fails to provide any motivation at all. Either way, the examiner's motivation, if provided in the office action, and not a truly legitimate and technical basis for making the combination of references in the manner recited in the claim, should be attacked as not sufficient. However, in anticipation, the specification should describe the actual motivation, again, with respect to a "particular embodiment." Depending on the details of the invention and the references cited, this description may demonstrate to the examiner that his or her proposed motivation is lacking in substance compared with a real or true technical motivation.

87. *See In re* Dillon, 919 F.2d 688 (Fed. Cir. 1990) (en banc).

Likewise, to the extent the dependent claims may be crafted to bring out such a motivation, one may try to do that.

As an example, consider the following claim:

EXAMPLE 6.5

I claim:

1. A method comprising: implementing a spreadsheet on a computer.[88]

Previously, we suggested that such a claim might be attacked as patent ineligible under § 101. However, the examiner may see this as such an easy rejection under § 103, he or she may not raise § 101. Or, perhaps, this claim is presented in a patent application participating in the pilot program in which § 101 rejections are not handled until all other rejections are resolved.[89] Either way, it is possible that such a claim may receive a rejection under § 103.[90]

A typical rejection would cite a document with a computer and a document with a spreadsheet and assert that the motivation to combine them is speed, accuracy, convenience, and so on. Thus, here is one example of anticipating the first office action.

One way to respond might be to point out that none of the documents show "implementing" on a computer. However, the examiner may have a document showing something being implemented. However, one may argue, quite legitimately, *even with these references before him or her, it would not have made obvious to one of ordinary skill in the art how to implement a spreadsheet on a computer*. One may also argue the benefits that flow from the claim as a whole.

However, it would be far more persuasive to add limitations directed to the functionality that one may believe will not be found in the prior art—that is, performing operations within cells.[91] Thus, including claims with such limitations in the dependent claims may be another way to anticipate the first office action. So that, if the examiner provides such a rejection, without amendment,

88. See earlier discussion in this chapter regarding potential eligibility issues.

89. *See Deferred Subject Matter Eligibility Response (DSMER) Pilot Program*, PTO, https://www.uspto.gov/patents/initiatives/patent-application-initiatives/deferred-subject-matter-eligibility-response (last visited May 14, 2024) (regarding deferred subject matter eligibility response).

90. Patent eligibility might not be raised also because we assumed that VisiCalc has not been invented or that this patent application is for VisiCalc.

91. See previous patent eligibility examples on how to frame such limitations.

those dependent claims may be argued. Consequently, such limitations, such as in Example 6.2, may be of value both to respond to a rejection under § 101 and to respond to a rejection under § 103. This is not an uncommon occurrence for subject matter subject to a patent eligibility challenge, such as software. The § 101 considerations and the § 103 considerations often overlap.

Have the Closest Known Prior Art in Mind When Drafting the Claims

Understanding Potential Inequitable Conduct Issues

37 C.F.R. § 1.56

Duty to disclose information material to patentability.

(a) A patent by its very nature is affected with a public interest. The public interest is best served, and the most effective patent examination occurs when, at the time an application is being examined, the Office is aware of and evaluates the teachings of all information material to patentability. Each individual associated with the filing and prosecution of a patent application has a duty of candor and good faith in dealing with the Office, which includes a duty to disclose to the Office all information known to that individual to be material to patentability as defined in this section. The duty to disclose information exists with respect to each pending claim until the claim is cancelled or withdrawn from consideration, or the application becomes abandoned. Information material to the patentability of a claim that is cancelled or withdrawn from consideration need not be submitted if the information is not material to the patentability of any claim remaining under consideration in the application. There is no duty to submit information which is not material to the patentability of any existing claim. The duty to disclose all information known to be material to patentability is deemed to be satisfied if all information known to be material to patentability of any claim issued in a patent was cited by the Office or submitted to the Office in the manner prescribed by §§ 1.97(b)–(d) and 1.98. However, no patent will be granted on an application in connection with which fraud on the Office was practiced or attempted or the duty of disclosure was violated through bad faith or intentional misconduct. The Office encourages applicants to carefully examine:

(1) Prior art cited in search reports of a foreign patent office in a counterpart application, and

(2) The closest information over which individuals associated with the filing or prosecution of a patent application believe any pending claim patentably defines, to make sure that any material information contained therein is disclosed to the Office.

(b) Under this section, information is material to patentability when it is not cumulative to information already of record or being made of record in the application, and

(1) It establishes, by itself or in combination with other information, a prima facie case of unpatentability of a claim; or

(2) It refutes, or is inconsistent with, a position the applicant takes in:

(i) Opposing an argument of unpatentability relied on by the Office, or

(ii) Asserting an argument of patentability.

A prima facie case of unpatentability is established when the information compels a conclusion that a claim is unpatentable under the preponderance of evidence, burden-of-proof standard, giving each term in the claim its broadest reasonable construction consistent with the specification, and before any consideration is given to evidence which may be submitted in an attempt to establish a contrary conclusion of patentability.

(c) Individuals associated with the filing or prosecution of a patent application within the meaning of this section are:

(1) Each inventor named in the application;

(2) Each attorney or agent who prepares or prosecutes the application; and

(3) Every other person who is substantively involved in the preparation or prosecution of the application and who is associated with the inventor, the applicant, an assignee, or anyone to whom there is an obligation to assign the application.

(d) Individuals other than the attorney, agent or inventor may comply with this section by disclosing information to the attorney, agent, or inventor.

(e) In any continuation-in-part application, the duty under this section includes the duty to disclose to the Office all information known to the person to be material to patentability, as defined in paragraph (b) of this section, which became available between the filing date of the prior application and the national or [Patent Cooperation Treaty] international filing date of the continuation-in-part application.

37 C.F.R. § 1.98

Content of information disclosure statement.

(a) Any information disclosure statement filed under § 1.97 shall include the items listed in paragraphs (a)(1), (a)(2) and (a)(3) of this section.

(1) A list of all patents, publications, applications, or other information submitted for consideration by the Office. U.S. patents and U.S. patent application publications must be listed in a section separately from citations of other documents. Each page of the list must include:

(i) The application number of the application in which the information disclosure statement is being submitted;

(ii) A column that provides a space, next to each document to be considered, for the examiner's initials; and

(iii) A heading that clearly indicates that the list is an information disclosure statement.

(2) A legible copy of:

(i) Each foreign patent;

(ii) Each publication or that portion which caused it to be listed, other than U.S. patents and U.S. patent application publications unless required by the Office;

(iii) For each cited pending unpublished U.S. application, the application specification including the claims, and any drawing of the application, or that portion of the application which caused it to be listed including any claims directed to that portion; and

(iv) All other information or that portion which caused it to be listed.

(3)

(i) A concise explanation of the relevance, as it is presently understood by the individual designated in § 1.56(c) most knowledgeable about the content of the information, of each patent, publication, or other information listed that is not in the English language. The concise explanation may be either separate from applicant's specification or incorporated therein.

(ii) A copy of the translation if a written English-language translation of a non-English-language document, or portion thereof, is within the possession, custody, or control of, or is readily available to any individual designated in § 1.56(c).

(b)

(1) Each U.S. patent listed in an information disclosure statement must be identified by inventor, patent number, and issue date.

(2) Each U.S. patent application publication listed in an information disclosure statement shall be identified by applicant, patent application publication number, and publication date.

(3) Each U.S. application listed in an information disclosure statement must be identified by the inventor, application number, and filing date.

(4) Each foreign patent or published foreign patent application listed in an information disclosure statement must be identified by the country or patent office which issued the patent or published the application, an appropriate document number, and the publication date indicated on the patent or published application.

(5) Each publication listed in an information disclosure statement must be identified by publisher, author (if any), title, relevant pages of the publication, date, and place of publication.

(c) When the disclosures of two or more patents or publications listed in an information disclosure statement are substantively cumulative, a copy of one of the patents or publications as specified in paragraph (a) of this section may be submitted without copies of the other patents or publications, provided that it is stated that these other patents or publications are cumulative.

(d) A copy of any patent, publication, pending U.S. application or other information, as specified in paragraph (a) of this section, listed in an information disclosure statement is required to be provided, even if the patent, publication, pending U.S. application or other information was previously submitted to, or cited by, the Office in an earlier application, unless:

(1) The earlier application is properly identified in the information disclosure statement and is relied on for an earlier effective filing date under 35 U.S.C. 120; and

(2) The information disclosure statement submitted in the earlier application complies with paragraphs (a) through (c) of this section.

Therasense, Inc. v. Becton, Dickinson & Co.
649 F.3d 1276
United States Court of Appeals for the Federal Circuit
May 25, 2011, Decided

Questions

1. In *Therasense*, the majority explains that it is making a major change in inequitable conduct law. Summarize the specific features of this change.
2. There is a rift on the court regarding this change to inequitable conduct law. What is the primary reason for the rift?
3. It is suggested that the majority is not being consistent with Supreme Court precedent while the majority indicates otherwise. Is the majority being consistent or not?
4. What happened in this case that raised the allegation of inequitable conduct?

Do Not Draft Claims That Read on Known Prior Art

Knowingly submitting claims that read on the prior art violates one's ethical duties before the PTO, even if that prior art has been disclosed appropriately.[92] This should also be considered an example of an affirmative act of egregious misconduct because you are representing that you believe presented claims are patentable when you know that at least one presented claim reads on prior art.[93]

Of course, it must be done knowingly. However, state of mind is inferred from the circumstances.[94] Is a jury likely to believe it was done inadvertently?

92. *See* 37 C.F.R. §§ 1.56, 1.57 (2024).
93. *See* Therasense, Inc. v. Becton, Dickinson & Co., 649 F.3d 1276, 1290 (Fed. Cir. 2011) (en banc).
94. *Id.*

In other words, taking an aggressive posture as an advocate may be warranted, but be careful not to take an *overly* aggressive posture.[95]

One way to do this is to review the broadest claims and make sure that you have *reasonable* arguments that distinguish the claim from the closest *known* art under §§ 102 *and* 103. If it turns out later the claims read on prior art *not* known by you or the inventors, no violation has occurred. If a claim issues that later is found to read on prior art that was *not* known to anyone involved in the prosecution (e.g., you, the inventors, and the examiner), the claim may be invalid but no inequitable conduct is present. Furthermore, until proven to be invalid, once issued, the claim is presumed valid.

Thus, the sin is not obtaining a patent with invalid claims, but rather having done so by not disclosing known material art and/or by knowingly (or perhaps, more accurately, by deliberately) submitting a claim that reads on known prior art. Appreciate, again, that for a violation the prior art must be *known*.

An analogy may be helpful here. Suppose you are putting your house on the market for sale. Suppose it has the original roof. You may wonder if the roof should be replaced. However, at this point, other than the fact that it is the original roof (e.g., other than pure speculation), you have no reason to believe it needs to be replaced. So, you have nothing to disclose about it to a perspective buyer other than it is the original roof, which should be apparent from your realtor's documents and disclosures.

However, suppose on your own initiative, you have a roofer come look at the roof before you put your house on the market. Suppose he tells you the roof is damaged and in need of significant repair or in need of replacement. Now, if you do not tell this to a perspective buyer, you have committed common-law fraud. Inequitable conduct is a type of common-law fraud committed before the PTO.

Thus, if you submit a broad claim and, for example, have not performed a search, then you have breached no duty. You may wonder why the claimed subject matter has not been done before, but if you otherwise have no reason to believe it has been done previously, then you have breached no duty. You have not committed inequitable conduct. On the other hand, if you or the inventors know of material art that you or they deliberately withhold because of concern that the examiner may not allow the broad claims, you may have committed inequitable conduct under the standards of *Therasense*. If your claim *deliberately* reads on prior art you are submitting (and perhaps you believe the examiner will not look closely enough at the submitted art to

95. In general, the underlying principle is to not let your client's problem become your problem.

appreciate it), then you have committed inequitable conduct under the standards of *Therasense*.

Generally, most lawyers are not about to commit inequitable conduct. Why should they? It is the client's invention and they get paid whether the patent issues or not. So, how is it that inequitable conduct is asserted in so many litigations? It is advocacy by the attorneys representing the defendant/alleged infringer. Therefore, it is important in your conduct before the PTO to consider borderline situations that someone may later assert was deliberately withholding material prior art or deliberately submitting a claim that reads on a known reference. In general, err on the side of caution by submitting more rather than less prior art. Of course, there have also been a few cases of inequitable conduct with allegations around *deliberately burying a material reference* in a lot of submitted prior art, but such cases are quite rare and, in balancing the risk, are not worth the worry.

Have a Good Faith Argument to Patentably Distinguish the Broadest Claims

As previously indicated, having a good faith argument for patentably distinguishing the claimed invention under §§ 102 and 103 from prior art known at the time of filing is a good practice. One advantage of doing this is that it forces the drafter to rigorously determine whether the claims being submitted are either too narrow or too broad.

A review with the inventors would be a good idea. This may accomplish several things. It will assist you in determining that you have successfully formulated appropriately distinguishing technical arguments. It should also potentially ferret out prior art that may not have come up previously that you would be better off disclosing to the PTO. Seeing the words of the claim and how it could be interpreted tends to trigger the inventors' minds in new ways. That is, the language of the claims tends to assist the inventors in seeing their invention in a way perhaps not fully appreciated previously, potentially leading to additional prior art to be disclosed. *On this point, consider that a patent is stronger if closer prior art is considered during examination*. Thus, while we are not necessarily recommending that a search needs to be performed,[96] it is important to disclose all the *known* art that is material at the time of patent application filing.

96. See Chapter 1, discussing advantages and disadvantages of performing a search.

Another advantage of a review with the inventors, consistent with the preceding point, is that it may uncover deficiencies in claim scope. For example, it would be a good idea to ask the inventors about potential design around opportunities[97] to see if the claim may be modified to cover those situations.

Avoid Drafting Claims in a Manner That Leaves the Statutory Class Unclear

IPXL Holdings, L.L.C. v. Amazon.com, Inc.
430 F.3d 1377
United States Court of Appeals for the Federal Circuit
November 21, 2005, Decided

Rembrandt Data Technologies, LP v. AOL, LLC
641 F.3d 1331
United States Court of Appeals for the Federal Circuit
April 18, 2011, Decided

Questions

1. Claim 25 was held indefinite by the district court and affirmed by the Federal Circuit. What was the claim in *IPXL* that raised an indefiniteness issue? The Federal Circuit said that this was an issue of first impression for the court although the Board of Patent Appeals had dealt with this issue. What was the reasoning employed by the Board of Patent Appeals?
2. Why did the Federal Circuit agree that the claim was indefinite? What about the claim would have been unclear to one of ordinary skill in the art such that the claim had unclear scope? Is this merely a formalist rule or is the claim really indefinite? Do you think one of ordinary skill in the art would be unable to ascertain whether the claim was infringed? How is this claim substantively different from a method claim with recitations to the apparatus needed to perform the method? Is the latter claim also indefinite?
3. In *Rembrandt*, why do you think Rembrandt is suing HP and Canon? How do you think Rembrandt came to own the patents in suit?

97. See Chapter 4, discussing addressing potential design around opportunities.

4. Note that this case raises issues of patent licensing and exhaustion. These are considerations to keep in mind when drafting patent claims. Why is it that the licensing granted by AT&T remains despite the patents changing hands several times? How would you know whether a particular patent is licensed?
5. The court ultimately agrees that the AT&T license applies to Conexant. Why does that mean Conexant's customers do not infringe?
6. Given that ultimately the court determined the license applies, why did the court nonetheless go on to resolve invalidity and, furthermore, remand to the district court to resolve the validity of claims 1 and 2?
7. Regarding claim 3, why was it found to be indefinite? Any ideas on why the claim was drafted that way? Is there any way that Rembrandt might attempt to "fix" the indefiniteness issue with respect to the claims? Note that claim 3 ultimately invalidated the remaining dependent claims of the patent. Does this suggest an approach to claim drafting to potentially address an issue that may arise as to a dependent claim so that not all the dependent claims are affected?
8. Given the ruling as to claim 3, do you see any argument with respect to claim 2? Assuming claim 2 is not invalid, what does the language of the claim suggest as to infringement? Does this suggest an approach to claim drafting for apparatus claims?
9. Why does the court say that there is a material issue of fact when claim construction is a pure question of law? Note that *Teva* was not decided until 2015.

Avoid Apparatus-Type Limitations in Method Claims and Avoid Method-Type Limitations in Apparatus Claims

Method claims may, if well drafted, provide one possible advantage over apparatus claims in that the subject matter of the claim may be covered quite broadly using method language, whereas apparatus claims tend to include more specific limitations that are often narrower. This may be because, in many instances, method elements tend to be more functional in nature.[98] Consider, for example, a corkscrew. To claim the apparatus, one may need to be rather specific in describing particular elements, such as the screw itself.

98. See discussion in Chapter 4.

However, a method claim directed to its operation may be broader since it may simply recite "attaching securely" to the wine cork or some similarly broad characterization, and then "applying a force" to remove the cork.

For this reason alone, it is recommended that apparatus limitations in method claims be avoided as much as possible. Including such limitations ultimately undermines the potential breadth of using method claims. *Hence, attempt to include **only** those apparatus limitations needed to perform the claimed method.*

Of course, it is not always easy to remove the apparatus limitations and still have a claim that is distinguishable from the art; nonetheless, it is certainly worth the effort to try. It may be surprising how much we tend to let apparatus limitations slip into such claims when they are either unnecessary or may, with only modest effort, be drafted around. It generally requires focusing on what the apparatus does functionally and how it operates, rather than its structure. As an intermediate step, for example, it might be helpful to first try to draft a means-plus-function claim to the apparatus.

As a reminder, since we are discussing method claims, in addition to the overuse of apparatus-type limitations, there are other pitfalls associated with the use of method claims. For example, it is important to avoid embedding an implied order in the elements of the claim unless that order is intended and is necessary. Black letter law dictates that the elements of a method claim do not need to be performed in a particular order to infringe the claim, unless the order is expressly or impliedly included in the claim.

Consider, for example, baking a cake:

> A method of baking a cake comprising:
> placing dry ingredients together in a container;
> mixing wet ingredients together with the dry ingredients in the container to produce batter;
> pouring the batter from the container into a baking pan;
> heating the baking pan holding the batter until the batter solidifies and rises.

As is apparent in this simple example, the claim appears to require that the dry ingredients be mixed before the wet ingredients. This may be the most logical order, the natural order, or the preferred order; however, it is probably not necessary that it be done in this order to bake the cake. Therefore, it is important to make sure to draft such a claim so that this order is not necessary, at least in the broadest claim. For example, the placing and mixing operations may be combined in one action or the first action may be omitted entirely, as follows.

A method of baking a cake comprising:
mixing wet ingredients together with dry ingredients in a container to produce batter;
pouring the batter from the container into a baking pan;
heating the baking pan holding the batter until the batter solidifies and rises.

Also, as a reminder regarding method claims, it is also wise when employing method claims to not overlook other related method claiming opportunities. For example, it is important to be aware that a method claim can cover a new use for an old device or apparatus.[99] For example, a new use for a composition of matter or a new application of a known circuit may be claimed.

Likewise, when preparing a method claim, it is always worth considering whether a subset of what is being claimed might be independently patentable. For example, if a method of manufacturing a plastic coating is being claimed, it may include a novel method of annealing that is independent of the overall manufacturing process. Therefore, both could be independently claimed as patentable inventions.

Also, it is helpful to be cognizant that 35 U.S.C. subsection 271(g) provides potential foreign coverage for methods that are performed abroad if the product produced is imported into the United States. This subsection provides the ability to sue a foreign competitor in the United States that may be manufacturing the patented invention abroad[100] using a patented process. Therefore, you may be well advised to include such method claims in an application where foreign competitors are known to exist.

Just as apparatus-type limitations should be avoided with method claims, method-type limitations should be avoided with apparatus claims. One advantage that apparatus claims have over method claims is that the subject matter of the claim does not need to be in operation to infringe. To be more specific, apparatus claims potentially cover making, using, selling, offering to sell, or importing the claimed invention. However, in addition to creating a risk of indefiniteness, including method-type limitations may undermine the ability to capture this broad set of rights by narrowing scope unnecessarily.[101] The

99. See Chapter 4, discussing claiming a new use of an old device.
100. See Chapter 4's discussion regarding subsection 271(g).
101. *Cf.* INVT SPE LLC v. Int'l Trade Comm'n, 46 F.4th 1361 (Fed. Cir. 2022) (distinguishing between actual operation and capability of operating or performing for apparatus claims, particularly for software on a device, which tends to be functional, without discussing indefiniteness issue of mixing method and apparatus limitations). See discussion in Chapter 3.

case *IPXL Holdings v. Amazon*[102] is a good example regarding how mixing statutory classes may create indefiniteness.

In this example, we demonstrate reducing hardware limitations for a method claim. Following are two method claims, denoted as Example 6.6, previously provided. Furthermore, the method claims even take different approaches to handling the apparatus limitations.[103] However, the scope is somewhat similar to the apparatus claim discussed in the sections of this chapter addressing component and system claims.[104] This might be considered a weakness here because these claims are not taking full advantage of the opportunity to use a method claim to capture greater scope than an apparatus claim.

EXAMPLE 6.6

I claim:

1. A method of operating a radio frequency (RF) module comprising at least one integrated circuit chip, the method comprising:

   inputting an RF signal and one or more control signals to the RF module;

   outputting an RF signal from the RF module;

   controlling, based at least in part on the one or more control signals, a silicon-on-insulator (SOI) N-type metal oxide semiconductor (NMOS) field effect transistor (FET) series connected stack configuration to either an OFF state or an ON state, the SOI NMOS FET stack configuration, comprising a plurality of NMOS FET transistors, being implemented on the at least one integrated circuit chip; and

   electrically biasing, based at least in part on the one or more control signals, a body of at least one NMOS FET transistor of the plurality of NMOS FET transistors of the SOI NMOS FET stack configuration with a bias voltage substantially more negative than ground during at least a portion of the OFF state of the at least one NMOS FET transistor.

102. IPXL v. Amazon, 430 F.3d 1377 (Fed. Cir. 2005).
103. See Chapter 4, discussing method of using claims.
104. See Chapter 4, discussing component- and system-level claims.

I claim:

1. A method of operating a module, the module including at least one integrated circuit chip comprising a plurality of N-type metal oxide semiconductor (NMOS) field effect transistors in a series connected stack configuration that comprises at least one NMOS field effect transistor including a body, the at least one NMOS field effect transistor either to pass a radio frequency (RF) signal in an enable state or to not pass the RF signal in a disable state, the method further comprising:

   electrically biasing the body of the at least one NMOS field effect transistor of the module in the disable state to have a voltage level substantially more negative than the lowest voltage level of the following: ground, a DC voltage level of a source of the at least one NMOS field effect transistor of the module, and a DC voltage level of a drain of the at least one NMOS field effect transistor of the module.

Here, however, is another claim, Example 6.7, demonstrating a method claim with fewer hardware limitations and, thus, greater scope.

EXAMPLE 6.7

I claim:

1. A method of reducing nonlinearity for an analog signal comprising:

   passing the analog signal through at least one N-type metal oxide semiconductor field effect transistor (NMOSFET) in the ON state; and

   negatively biasing a body of at least another NMOSFET in an OFF state to reduce the nonlinearity of the analog signal, the at least another NMOSFET proximate to the at least one NMOSFET.

This claim has stripped the claimed subject matter to bare essentials. The only hardware limitations relate to the two NMOSFETs. Likewise, the actions are "passing" and "negatively biasing." Also, appreciate that here the technology is quite intimately tied to hardware. That is, it is difficult to claim the technology without at least reciting the two NMOSFETs. Still, this claim significantly reduces the hardware limitations, resulting in a much broader claim. We also could write the claim so that the hardware is in the preamble, but this would not seem to "buy" much since, again, the transistors need to be mentioned in the actions performed.

Example 6.8 is a simple example of reducing method language for an apparatus claim. It is easy to see in this example how method language may inadvertently find its way into an apparatus claim, which, again, may be quite risky, as demonstrated by the *IPXL* case. The italicized language has a risk of making the claim indefinite or limiting claim scope since it may be interpreted to suggest that the circuit is operating rather than being capable of operating.

EXAMPLE 6.8

I claim:

1. An apparatus comprising:

   a bandgap circuit;

   the bandgap circuit *producing a fixed voltage*, the fixed voltage *corresponding* to the bandgap.

A better approach would be:

EXAMPLE 6.9

I claim:

1. An apparatus comprising:

   a bandgap circuit;

   the bandgap circuit *being capable of producing a fixed voltage*, the fixed voltage *to correspond* to the bandgap.

Or, perhaps, even more simply:

---

1. An apparatus comprising:

   a bandgap circuit;

   the bandgap circuit *to produce a fixed voltage*, the fixed voltage *to correspond* to the bandgap.

Here, the claim is drafted to make it clear that the circuit is not operating, but, rather, that the circuit has the capability of operating in a particular manner.[105]

Draft Claims to Avoid Covering Multiple Independent Parties Operating Together

Single Infringer Doctrine

BMC Resources, Inc. v. Paymentech, L.P.
498 F.3d 1373
United States Court of Appeals for the Federal Circuit
September 20, 2007, Decided

Akamai Technologies, Inc. v. Limelight Networks, Inc.
797 F.3d 1020
United States Court of Appeals for the Federal Circuit
August 13, 2015, Decided

Questions

1. Is it clear in *BMC* from reading the claims that this situation might result in divided infringement? Why or why not?
2. The Federal Circuit in *BMC*, essentially for the first time, dealt with divided infringement or joint infringement. What did the Federal Circuit hold?

---

105. *See INVT SPE LLC*, 46 F.4th 1361 (distinguishing between actual operation and capability of operating or performing for apparatus claims, particularly for software on a device, which tends to be functional, without discussing indefiniteness issue of mixing method and apparatus limitations). See discussion in Chapter 3.

3. What would BMC need to show to make out a claim of direct infringement by Paymentech?
4. The court states:

   > This court acknowledges that the standard requiring control or direction for a finding of joint infringement may in some circumstances allow parties to enter into arms-length agreements to avoid infringement. . . . The concerns over a party avoiding infringement by arms-length cooperation can usually be offset by proper claim drafting.[106]

   What does the court mean by arms-length cooperation? How might that avoid direct infringement?
5. Is there a way the claim in *BMC* might have been drafted to avoid the divided infringement issue?
6. How did *Akamai* alter the approach provided in *BMC*? What do you think caused the court to revisit its approach?
7. On what basis did the appellate court find Limelight liable for patent infringement?
8. What is another basis for finding multiple parties liable for patent infringement? What is the logical basis for this, do you believe?

* * *

Surprisingly, the single infringer doctrine, also referred to as divided infringement, does not have a long historical pedigree in case law. However, before Federal Circuit cases addressing it were handed down, patent claim drafters at least instinctively knew that a single entity must, in effect, perform all the elements and limitations of a claim for direct infringement liability. This follows logically from the All Elements Rule and from 35 U.S.C. subsection 271(a).

We have previously emphasized the point that claims should cover a single infringer because it is a common claim drafting error, and it may be fatal to any claim for patent infringement. Now, we discuss some of the cases behind the doctrine.

The widely known Federal Circuit case to directly state the principle appears to be *BMC Resources v. Paymentech*,[107] a case from 2007. The appellate court did acknowledge the corner case where the actions of one party are directed by another.

However, if the parties are operating independent of one another, then there would be no liability. For this reason, as the appellate court suggests, claims

106. BMC Res. Inc. v. Paymentech, L.P., 498 F.3d 1373, 1381 (Fed. Cir. 2007).
107. 498 F.3d 1373.

should be written from the perspective of a single party that will perform every element and limitation. Not long after *BMC Resources*, the court decided *Muniauction*.[108] In *Muniauction*, the question involved whether there was "direction and control" by one party of another, an issue alluded to by the court in the *BMC* case. Observe that a similar "direction and control" test arises under use infringement of a system claim.[109] However, it is noted that in *Akamai Technologies v. Limelight Networks*,[110] the appellate court, *en banc*, made what is required for divided or joint infringement more clear. Either direction and control or joint enterprise was sufficient for liability under subsection 271(a). However, the appellate court made a clarification on direction and control, stating that "liability under § 271(a) can also be found when an alleged infringer conditions participation in an activity or receipt of a benefit upon performance of a step or steps of a patented method and establishes the manner or timing of that performance."[111]

The divided infringement issue may arise in a host of possible situations; however, it has become particularly prevalent because a variety of technologies require client and server interactions in which the client and the server are operated by otherwise independent parties. For example, long before Apple Music and similar services, there was Napster. Napster is credited with being the first peer-to-peer network for sharing music. Putting copyright issues aside, before Napster, others had the idea for peer-to-peer sharing of digital music and attempted to obtain patent protection. Thus, consider Example 6.10.

EXAMPLE 6.10

I claim:

1. A method of sharing digital music comprising:

   initiating and establishing a network connection between a first computer and a second computer; and

   sharing one or more digital music files on the first computer with the second computer via the network connection so that the second computer is able to independently play the shared one or more digital music files.

Of course, this claim might raise a number of issues today, including, perhaps, patent eligibility. Even at the time of Napster, there might have been a

108. *See* Muniauction, Inc. v. Thomson Corp., 532 F.3d 1318 (Fed. Cir. 2008).
109. See Chapter 4, discussing use infringement of a system claim.
110. 797 F.3d 1020 (Fed. Cir. 2015) (en banc).
111. *Id.*

question of whether the claim was obvious. However, we put those issues aside for purposes of illustration.

It would also not be fair to say that *no one* necessarily infringes this claim. Rather, an entity or person that owns or directs and controls both the first and the second computer might infringe. Of course, detecting such infringement is problematic. It might be possible to argue with evidence that Apple infringes if Apple is transporting digital music between its servers, for example.

Could one argue that Apple infringes when a user downloads music from its servers? Apple provides software to assist in downloading the music. However, could it be argued that Apple initiates and establishes the network connection? It seems it is the user that initiates the network connection, granted that the details of the technology may matter here. Is the user under Apple's direction and control? Unlikely. However, Apple probably performs the second operation of sharing the one or more digital music files.

Thus, it should be clear from this example that it might have been possible to draft a claim that would more clearly be infringed had it properly been written from the perspective of the first computer.

Have Damages Issues in Mind When Drafting Patent Claims

35 U.S.C. § 284

Upon finding for the claimant the court shall award the claimant damages adequate to compensate for the infringement, but in no event less than a reasonable royalty for the use made of the invention by the infringer, together with interest and costs as fixed by the court.

When the damages are not found by a jury, the court shall assess them. In either event the court may increase the damages up to three times the amount found or assessed. Increased damages under this paragraph shall not apply to provisional rights under section 154(d).

The court may receive expert testimony as an aid to the determination of damages or of what royalty would be reasonable under the circumstances.

Entire Market Value Principle/Smallest Saleable Patent Practicing Unit Principle

Finjan, Inc. v. Blue Coat Systems, Inc.
879 F.3d 1299
United States Court of Appeals for the Federal Circuit
January 10, 2018, Decided

Exmark Manufacturing Co. v. Briggs & Stratton Power Products Group, LLC
879 F.3d 1332
United States Court of Appeals for the Federal Circuit
January 12, 2018, Decided

Questions

1. The theory of damages under patent law is to compensate the patentee to an extent that it is as if the infringement had never occurred. What are the ways the court can do that? The statute specifies:

   Upon finding for the claimant the court shall award the claimant damages adequate to compensate for the infringement, but in no event less than a reasonable royalty for the use made of the invention by the infringer, together with interest and costs as fixed by the court.[112]

   What was the legal issue the appellate court in *Exmark* and *Finjan* needed to resolve with respect to damages?
2. Sometimes damages involve lost profits, but more often damages involves a reasonable royalty calculation, as indicated by the court. What was the situation in *Finjan* in this regard? What is the entire market value rule and how does it relate to the smallest saleable patent practicing unit? Why did the appellate court reject the argument that because Finjan had accounted for the smallest saleable patent practicing unit with respect to the '844 patent, no further allocation was necessary, but then accepted the allocation by the expert with respect to the '731 and '633 patents? What is being allocated in this case?
3. How did the claims figure into the damages analysis in *Finjan*, if at all?
4. Briggs made several arguments regarding the damages award; however, the issue that relates most to claim drafting is the argument that the district court erred by permitting Exmark to use the sales price of the accused mowers as the royalty base instead of the sales price of the flow control baffles. What were the reasons the appellate court rejected the argument? Do any of the reasons relate to claim drafting?
5. What do these cases tell you about damages based on the claims and apportionment? How might the claims be drafted to benefit the patentee?

* * *

112. 35 U.S.C. § 284.

Generally, the value of a patent relates to how it might be used. There are three things at a high level that one may do with a patent.[113] One may rely on its exclusive power to increase barriers to entry for a market in which one sells a product or service, one may license it for value, or one may trade it for access to someone else's patented technology. The last two things could also be viewed as one, so that ultimately, one may rely on its exclusionary power or one may effectively trade it for value.

This is similar in principle to how the remedies in federal court mostly work as well. One may seek and obtain an injunction or one may seek and obtain monetary damages, or both.

The question for the claim drafter is how a formulation of the claims may affect these options or remedies. The options available in federal court serve as a backdrop to patent assertion, but typically the patent value is realized in private negotiations assuming rational parties and an enforceable patent.

The injunction side of remedies or exclusionary power is understood and reasonably predictable. This remedy has, in effect, guided much of our discussion. The process of reading a claim on an accused process or product captures this option. An injunction will foreclose making, using, and selling anything within the scope of the claims (and, potentially, something falling within the doctrine of equivalents, if raised and won).

The damages, trade for value, or royalty revenue side of remedies is less certain and less predictable unfortunately. It is driven in many cases by aspects beyond the control of the claim drafter, such as previous licenses or licenses by others for similar technology, markets, costs, profits, the relation of the parties, and a host of other factors. Here, there are not many hard and fast rules because these factors vary significantly with the situation. This also tends to make the legal principles less clear as well.

Nonetheless, the law does impose some structure here. Under 35 U.S.C. § 284, one may recover lost profits and "in no event less than a reasonable royalty."[114] The fundamental notion is to adequately compensate the patent holder as if the infringement had not taken place.[115] In general, if the

113. See discussion in Chapter 2 of patent strategy.

114. 35 U.S.C. § 284 (2024) states in part: "Upon finding for the claimant the court shall award the claimant damages adequate to compensate for the infringement, but in no event less than a reasonable royalty for the use made of the invention by the infringer, together with interest and costs as fixed by the court."

115. *See, e.g.*, Aro Mfg. Co. v. Convertible Top Replacement Co., 377 U.S. 476, 507 (1964) (stating a plaintiff can recover as damages "the difference between his pecuniary condition after the infringement, and what his condition might have been if the infringement had not occurred").

infringement had not taken place, then the patent holder would have had more profits. Hence, the patent holder is entitled to lost profits. Typically, lost profits is also the greater recovery than a reasonable royalty, but, in general, is a greater challenge to prove in many situations. It must be proven that "but for" the infringement, the patent holder would have made more sales and/or would not have had to lower its prices.[116] In a two-supplier market, this may be relatively easy to show, but that type of simple market is relatively unusual. Thus, in many situations, sufficient evidence to make out a strong or credible lost profits case is not available because of the complexity of the market and the availability of reasonable alternative noninfringing substitutes.[117] Where there are reasonable alternative substitutes, it is difficult to prove "but for" causation, as required to recover lost profits.

Fortunately, the statute provides a damages floor, which is the reasonable royalty measure of recovery. Here, the notion is, again, that the patent holder should be adequately compensated as if the infringement did not take place. Hence, the patent holder should be compensated as if the defendant had taken a license.

This brings us to the made-up world of the hypothetical negotiation. Here, the landmark case is the *Georgia-Pacific*[118] decision which lists 15 factors that continue to this day to drive damages recovery based on a reasonable royalty. These factors are:

1. The royalties received by the patentee for the licensing of the patent in suit, proving or tending to prove an established royalty.
2. The rates paid by the licensee for the use of other patents comparable to the patent in suit.
3. The nature and scope of the license, as exclusive or non-exclusive; or as restricted or non-restricted in terms of territory or with respect to whom the manufactured product may be sold.
4. The licensor's established policy and marketing program to maintain its patent monopoly by not licensing others to use the invention or by granting licenses under special conditions designed to preserve that monopoly.
5. The commercial relationship between the licensor and the licensee, such as whether they are competitors in the same territory in the same line of business, or whether they are inventor and promoter.

---

116. *See* RICHARD CAULEY, WINNING THE PATENT DAMAGES CASE (2009).

117. *Id.*

118. Georgia-Pacific Corp. v. U.S. Plywood Corp., 318 F. Supp. 1116 (S.D.N.Y. 1970), *modified and aff'd*, 446 F.2d 295 (2d Cir. 1971), *cert. denied*, 404 U.S. 870 (1971).

6. *The effect of selling the patented specialty in promoting sales of other products of the licensee; the existing value of the invention to the licensor as a generator of sales of his non-patented items; and the extent of such derivative or convoyed sales.*
7. The duration of the patent and the term of the license.
8. The established profitability of the product made under the patent; its commercial success; and its current popularity.
9. *The utility and advantages of the patent property over the old modes or devices, if any, that had been used for working out similar results.*
10. *The nature of the patented invention; the character of the commercial embodiment of it as owned and produced by the licensor; and the benefits to those who have used the invention.*
11. *The extent to which the infringer has made use of the invention; and any evidence probative of the value of that use.*
12. The portion of the profit or of the selling price that may be customary in the particular business or in comparable businesses to allow for the use of the invention or analogous inventions.
13. *The portion of the realizable profit that should be credited to the invention as distinguished from non-patented elements, the manufacturing process, business risks, or significant features or improvements added by the infringer.*
14. The opinion testimony of qualified experts.
15. The amount that a licensor (such as the patentee) and a licensee (such as the infringer) would have agreed upon (at the time the infringement began) if both had been reasonably and voluntarily trying to reach an agreement; that is, the amount that a prudent licensee who desired, as a business proposition, to obtain a license to manufacture and sell a particular article embodying the patented invention would have been willing to pay as a royalty and yet be able to make a reasonable profit and which amount would have been acceptable by a prudent patentee who was willing to grant a license.[119]

It is the last factor, number 15, that summarizes the concept of the hypothetical negotiation itself:

The amount that a licensor (such as the patent owner) and a licensee (such as the infringer) would have agreed upon (at the time the infringement began). This assumes both had been reasonably and voluntarily trying to reach an agreement. There is the amount that a prudent licensee would have been willing to pay as a royalty. This assumes the licensee desired, as a

119. *Id.* at 1120.

business proposition, to obtain a license to manufacture and sell a particular article embodying the patented invention and yet be able to make a reasonable profit. There is also the amount acceptable to a prudent patent owner who was willing to grant a license.

As suggested, these factors eschew hard and fast rules and relate in many cases to aspects beyond the control of the claim drafter, such as previous licenses under the patent, licenses by others for similar technology, markets, costs, profits, the relation of the parties, when the infringement took place, the time remaining on the patent, and a host of other factors.

Nonetheless, there are some factors that do appear to have the potential to be influenced by how the claims are drafted. These factors have been italicized, in particular, factors 6, 9, 10, 11, and 13. However, even here, how these factors translate into claim language is difficult to intuit.

Also, one should not lose sight of the practical reality that the possibility of an injunction may also affect the damages analysis.[120] That is, between a willing licensor and a willing licensee, the royalty will be higher to the extent that the possibility of an enforceable injunction limits the options available to the prospective licensee. Similarly, it is also clear that claim language and claim construction may potentially affect damages recovery.[121] Thus, we attempt to uncover the few principles that might be emergent from the case law.

It seems clear that the "entire market value" principle cuts across all approaches to damages recovery. The entire market value principle might be viewed as a sort of exception in damages law. Despite the patented feature being only a portion of the product sold with many unpatented features, it permits recovery for lost profits, for example if it can be shown that the patented feature drives consumer demand for the end product (or that the patented features and unpatented features of an end product worked together as a single functional unit).

Courts are not always clear regarding the damages theory being applied—that is lost profits, a reasonable royalty, or both. In *Del Mar Avionics, Inc. v. Quinton Instrument Co.*,[122] however, the Federal Circuit noted that "in appropriate circumstances the patentee may prove the extent of its lost profits by the 'entire market value rule,' . . . based on a showing that the patentee could

120. *See* Cauley, *supra* note 116; Mark Lemley & Carl Shapiro, *Patent Holdup and Royalty Stacking*, 95 Tex. L. Rev. 1991 (2007).

121. *See* Metabolite Lab'ys, Inc. v. Lab. Corp. of Am. Holdings, 370 F.3d 1354, 1364 (Fed. Cir. 2004) ("the invitation to apply a different claim construction for computation of damages than for infringement liability" was rejected by the court).

122. 836 F.2d 1320 (Fed. Cir. 1987).

reasonably anticipate the sale of the unpatented components together with the patented components. . . ."[123] Notably, a similar "entire market value" principle applies with respect to recovery based on a reasonable royalty damages measure.[124]

Clearly, the plaintiff prefers application of this principle while the defendant would prefer that it not be applied. Again, the goal is to compensate the patent holder for the infringement. Thus, to the extent one or more patented features influences the price or sale of other unpatented components or features, it seems an argument exists to apply the entire market value principle.[125] Ultimately, it likely will come down to how persuasive the evidence is for its application or non-application.

On the other hand, cases also recognize that to the extent this principle may overcompensate the plaintiff, that may potentially be handled via an appropriate royalty rate.[126] Thus, a line of Federal Circuit cases suggest that the problem of apportionment—that is, valuing a patented feature or component of a complex multicomponent—may be handled in this manner.[127]

The view we have come to, therefore, is that an argument for application of an entire market value principle, either on its own or as a step in an apportionment analysis, will be stronger to the extent that the claim covers the entire accused end product rather than merely a particular feature or improvement. Even to the extent that the royalty rate would be adjusted for a larger base, we still believe from a damages recovery or a negotiation standpoint, one would be better off with the larger base because typically the whole has more value than the sum of the parts.

---

123. *Id.* at 1327.

124. *See, e.g.*, Lucent Techs., Inc. v. Gateway, Inc., 580 F.3d 1301, 1324 (Fed. Cir. 2009). *See, e.g.*, Lucent Techs. Inc. v. Microsoft Corp., 544 F. Supp. 2d 1080, 1105–06 (S.D. Cal. 2008) (discussing Federal Circuit cases).

125. *See, e.g.*, Deere Co. v. Int'l Harvester Co., 710 F.2d 1551 (Fed. Cir. 1983) ("[T]he district court did nothing more or less than take into account the impact of anticipated collateral sales of an admittedly noninfringing product line on the respective bargaining positions of the parties engaged in theorized licensing negotiations. We consider this an eminently reasonable approach to the willing seller-willing buyer analysis . . . .").

126. *See Lucent Techs., Inc.*, 580 F.3d at 1338–39 ("Although our law states certain mandatory conditions for applying the entire market value rule, courts must nevertheless be cognizant of a fundamental relationship between the entire market value rule and the calculation of a running royalty damages award. Simply put, the base used in a running royalty calculation can always be the value of the entire commercial embodiment, as long as the magnitude of the rate is within an acceptable range (as determined by the evidence). Indeed, '[a]ll running royalties have at least two variables: the royalty base and the royalty rate.'").

127. *See, e.g.*, *id.* at 1324. *See, e.g.*, *Lucent Techs. Inc.*, 544 F. Supp. 2d at 1105–06 (discussing Federal Circuit cases).

On the other hand, as has been discussed, if the infringer only makes the component, as opposed to the end product, this approach may represent the difference between a case for direct infringement versus indirect infringement.[128] For this and other reasons, we have emphasized *both* component- and system-level claims with the recognition that different situations may prefer one or the other.[129]

For illustrative claim examples, one may simply look to the several component- and system-level claim examples discussed in prior chapters.[130]

The smallest saleable patent practicing unit developed in the case law for situations where it was expected, even with adjusting for apportionment via the royalty rate, still using the entire market value would tend to overcompensate the plaintiff.[131]

A similar strategy may be employed with this principle as described regarding the entire market value principle. That is, assuming the smallest saleable patent practicing unit is larger than the particular feature to be patented, draft the claim so that it at least covers the smallest saleable patent practicing unit. This strategy was alluded to previously in examples in which it was suggested that a patent claim be written to cover an integrated circuit or a module, as an example.[132] These examples involve situations in which the integrated circuit or module would likely be used in a computer or a cell phone. However, it might be a stretch to expect a royalty base of a computer or cell phone using the entire market value principle. Thus, instead, an integrated circuit or module is used, as the largest likely royalty base for an infringing commercial embodiment. That is, we assume for this strategy the patented feature would likely be a small part thereof.

In general, the difference in treatment of apportionment lies in the Federal Circuit's view of the scope of the claims compared to the accused products.[133] Where a claim covers an entire product, apportionment is required to account for the value the novel features add to the conventional features covered by the claim. One will argue for the entire market value principle based on the claim itself, consumer demand, and/or whether the patented and conventional features form a functional unit. *In this case, conventional features that are included in the claim are included in the royalty base where the claim covers a complete product and*

128. *See* Chapter 5.

129. See discussion regarding system versus component claims in Chapters 2 and 4.

130. *Id.*

131. *See, e.g.*, Ericsson, Inc. v. D-Link Sys., Inc., 773 F.3d 1201, 113 U.S.P.Q.2d (BNA) 1001 (Fed. Cir. 2014).

132. See, for example, discussions in Chapters 1 and 4.

133. *Compare* Exmark Mfg. Co. v. Briggs & Stratton Power Prods. Grp., LLC, 879 F.3d 1332 (Fed. Cir. 2018), *with* Finjan, Inc. v. Blue Coat Sys., Inc., 879 F.3d 1299 (Fed. Cir. 2018).

the royalty rate may, consequently, be apportioned to account for what the patented feature may add. Where a claim covers only a portion of a multicomponent product, apportionment may be required in the royalty base to account for the patented and unpatented features in the smallest saleable patent practicing unit as well as in the royalty rate. In other words, *if a claim covers only part of a product, both the royalty base and the royalty rate may be apportioned.* Furthermore, the royalty rate calculation must tie the facts of the case to the royalty rate determination. Hence, as suggested in the previous section, if one is able to draft a claim in a manner to make the entire market value royalty base more likely at the margin, that appears to be a laudable goal because it may lead to apportionment of the royalty rate without apportionment of the royalty base.

Draft Claims to Reduce the Risk of Exhaustion or Implied Patent Licensing

Met-Coil Systems Corp. v. Korners Unlimited, Inc.
803 F.2d 684
United States Court of Appeals for the Federal Circuit
October 8, 1986, Decided

Quanta Computer, Inc. v. LG Electronics, Inc.
553 U.S. 617
Supreme Court of the United States
January 16, 2008, Argued; June 9, 2008, Decided

Questions

1. What was the claim that Met-Coil made against Korners as the basis for the lawsuit? Factually, what is Met-Coil asserting that infringes its patent?
2. What does the appellate court say are the two requirements for an implied patent license? What do you think is the legal basis for those requirements?
3. One of the requirements relates to no noninfringing use. Do you think that is the same or different than no substantial noninfringing use? How do you think implied patent licenses relate to contributory infringement? Why do you think this condition is needed?
4. One of the requirements is that the circumstances of the sale must "plainly indicate that the grant of a license should be inferred." Why do you think this condition is needed?

5. Note that the appellate court expressed no opinion for the situation in which the notice from Met-Coil had been provided at the time of sale. Do you think that would have been sufficient so that an implied patent license would not have been inferred from the sale of product?
6. How do you think the requirements of an implied patent license might influence claim drafting?
7. Is there a distinction between exhaustion and an implied patent license before *Quanta*? Is there a distinction after *Quanta*? Why doctrinally does this matter since either way there is no infringement?
8. What do you think of the Court's handling of method versus apparatus claims?
9. What is the legal underpinning of the Court's ruling here?
10. What is the proper test after *Quanta* to determine when you sell a product or provide a license whether this may result in patent exhaustion?
11. Is the *Quanta* decision procompetitive or anticompetitive? Why or why not?
12. Did the *Quanta* decision overrule the Federal Circuit's *Mallinckrodt v. Medipart*[134] decision? Why or why not?
13. Does *Quanta* simply represent a corner case in line with *United States v. Univis Lens*,[135] or it is much broader than that?

* * *

When attempting to protect technology with various types of patent claims, such as a component and a system, different methods, or a method and apparatus, the doctrine of patent exhaustion and the doctrine of implied patent licenses may come into play. Doctrinally, the notion of exhaustion is that if you sell (or license a manufacturer who then sells) a product that is "covered" by a claim in a patent (i.e., reads on the product), then the patent that includes the claim that covers (i.e., reads on) the product is "exhausted," meaning that you may not ever assert the patent against that specific product item sold.[136]

Technically, exhaustion applies to an entire patent. That is, one may either sell product under the patent or license another to sell under the patent.[137] Once a sale of a product occurs in which a claim of the patent reads

134. 976 F.2d 700 (Fed. Cir. 1992).
135. 316 U.S. 241 (1942).
136. *See, e.g.*, Quanta Comput., Inc. v. LG Elecs., Inc., 553 U.S. 617 (2008).
137. Although through express language a license may be limited to specific patent claims so that there may be a question as to whether all the claims are exhausted if a product is sold in which one of the licensed claims reads on the product. *Cf. Quanta*, 553 U.S. 617; Gen. Talking

on the product, the patent with those claims is exhausted.[138] However, after the Supreme Court decision in *Quanta*, what constitutes patent exhaustion became understood to be more than having a claim read on the product sold. For example, the sale of a component of a claim typically was viewed previously as not necessarily creating exhaustion as to the patent claim, but as a possible implied license situation.[139] However, this latter situation was clarified by the Supreme Court to potentially constitute patent exhaustion as well, depending on the facts.

An implied patent license need not apply to all the claims of a patent since its doctrinal underpinnings rely on contract law. Thus, the doctrine of implied patent licenses, in general, is not the same legal doctrine as patent exhaustion. This former doctrine may arise, for example, if a component of a patent claim was sold or if a method claim covered use of a product sold. That is, depending on the circumstances, a license to certain patent claims might be implied by the sale. One requirement, however, was (and is) that the product sold not be capable of substantial noninfringing uses with respect to a claim or claims at issue.[140]

Years ago, by using different statutory classes and/or by using the same statutory class to cover different sets of rights, such as a combination and subcombination, as discussed in the preceding section, it was believed that these doctrines might be avoided or at least the risk of these doctrines being applicable in a given situation could be reduced through claim drafting in combination with contractual provisions. Thus, in addition to clever drafting of patent claims, attempts were made to limit both of these doctrines with contractual provisions. So-called post-sale contractual restrictions, for example, were used in an attempt to limit the scope of exhaustion. In yet another scenario, if you were to sell a component covered by a patent claim in which either a system claim or a method claim recited the component itself, typically, it would be argued that the system or method claims were not necessarily exhausted in some situations.[141] However, several Supreme Court cases have all but made it clear that many of these attempts will not work legally. Furthermore, today, the distinction between patent exhaustion and an implied patent license is blurrier than it was previously.

A primary consideration for drafting patent claims to reduce the risk of granting an implied patent license through the sale of a patented product is to

---

Pictures Corp. v. W. Elec. Co., 304 U.S. 175 (1938); Gen. Talking Pictures Corp. v. W. Elec. Co., 305 U.S. 124 (1938).

138. *See Quanta*, 553 U.S. 617. It is as if the entire patent is expressly licensed.

139. *See* Met-Coil Sys. Corp. v. Korners Unlimited, Inc., 803 F.2d 684 (Fed. Cir. 1986).

140. *Id.*

141. Often, these situations were accompanied by contractual provisions that expressly stated no intent to grant an implied patent license.

ensure that suitable or "reasonable"[142] noninfringing uses of the product sold are present. That is, the *product* as sold should be capable of substantial noninfringing uses with respect to the patent *claim or claims* at issue. Notably, if accomplished, this may eliminate potential for the patentee to bring a charge of contributory infringement based on the patent claims. This may not be desirable, so choices will need to be made. Should claims be drafted so that contributory infringement is possible or so that an implied patent license is not granted by a sale of a component of a claim?[143] Furthermore, this might be a real challenge because as a claim drafter, one may not know what future products the patentee might sell or license others to sell. However, with that said, there is no real harm in asking the patentee and taking that information into consideration in drafting the claims.

To illustrate this drafting approach, consider, for example, the situation for a graphics processor manufacturer. Let us simplify this complex analysis by assuming exhaustion of a component may be handled by claiming more than a component. For traditional exhaustion, a claim is exhausted if the claim reads on the product sold by the patentee or his or her licensee. Before *Quanta*, this was believed to be the case; however, today, exhaustion is much more complex in accordance with *Quanta*. However, with this more simplified approach as a start, a system claim may look like:

EXAMPLE 6.11

I claim:

1. A system comprising: a graphics processor coupled to memory.

In this example, the manufacturer probably has not managed to avoid an implied patent license, even assuming *Quanta* does not apply here. The reason an implied license is not avoided is that the processor cannot be used without coupling it to memory. Thus, the product sold—that is, the graphics processor—does not have substantial noninfringing uses. Suppose, however, the claim recited:

142. *See, e.g.*, Glass Equip. Dev. v. Besten, Inc., 174 F.3d 1337, 1343 (Fed. Cir. 1999).
143. Although a claim for inducing infringement may still be available. *See* Chapter 5.

EXAMPLE 6.12

I claim:

1. A system comprising: a graphics processor coupled to random access memory (RAM), wherein the RAM has an access time of 50 nanoseconds or less.

Assuming that the processor could be coupled to other more generic types of memory and/or RAM with slower access times, then arguably no implied license is granted;[144] however, because most of the valuable uses of the processor will be with RAM having relatively high speed (e.g., above 50 nanoseconds access time), little may have been given up in this example—that is, restricting the scope of the claim in this manner covers the valuable uses with fast memory while making it arguable that sale of the graphics processor does not impliedly license the claim.

This approach may be counterintuitive to most patent attorneys. It suggests that claims should be drafted to deliberately leave some uses not covered by the patent claims, rather than to cover as much with the claims as possible. However, also recognize that this is being suggested in a unique situation—that is, to avoid granting an implied patent license.

The suggestion is that when patenting a product that will be sold (or expressly licensed as a product that will be manufactured and sold), include claims that cover *more than* the product itself, which may assist in reducing the risk of exhaustion, as discussed later. Further, include claims such that noninfringing uses of the product sold exist to reduce the risk of an implied patent license. Of course, the uncovered uses should preferably be inferior or less valuable uses than those covered by the patent claims.

To explain the analysis further, the idea here is to avoid the implication *in law* of a grant of an implied patent license. If one sells a product (or licenses a product for manufacture and sale) and all its reasonable uses will result in patent infringement, then a court will likely conclude that a patent license is implied in law, if not, also, in fact.[145]

This entire approach, however, is merely to give the patent more vitality than to simply protect the product, a situation that may also be viewed with

144. It is also a good idea to include labels on the product or language in applicable order forms or agreements that clarify that no implied patent license is intended to be granted; however, that issue is not one related to claim drafting. *See Met-Coil Sys. Corp.*, 803 F.2d 684.

145. *See id.*

suspicion by a court. For example, if the goal were merely to protect the product itself, then the patent becomes diminished in value once a large market for the product develops based on the patentee's own sales. That is, if the patentee has flooded the market with its product, then a patent on the product should be less valuable; the patentee may have through sales already obtained most of its value for the product. Thus, such attempts as described here to reduce the risk of an implied patent license or exhaustion may be viewed by a court as an attempt to, in effect, "double dip." Courts view such attempts with extreme suspicion. It seems that this is how the Court viewed the situation in *Quanta*. That is, LGE got its value from licensing its technology to Intel and, thus, was not permitted to seek additional value from use of Intel's licensed product with non-licensed memory.

Hence, for this situation, one should not cover the product as sold with a claim of the patent or risk exhausting the entire patent.[146] If it is unclear whether protecting the product would be more valuable, one approach might be to have separate patents, one directed to the product as sold and one with claims directed to more than the product as sold, such that there are substantial noninfringing uses with respect to the claim that covers more than the product as sold, such as just described and as further explained later. If later it becomes clear that the patent with claims that cover more than the product is more valuable, then the patent with claims that cover the product as sold can be disclaimed, if needed, so that there arguably are substantial noninfringing uses (or vice versa).

As an example, consider the claim drafting principle "batteries not included." This refers to the notion that it is usually best to not claim the power source in connection with a particular technology. One reason, of course, is that it provides an easy design around for those interested in using the technology without infringing the patent claims. In fact, most technology is sold without the power source anyway. However, a claim that includes the power source may likewise grant an implied license with the sale of the product. If you include the power source in the claim, then, perhaps, at least arguably, the product sold has no noninfringing uses, assuming that there is no feasible way to use the product without a power source.[147] However, after *Quanta*, the claim with the power source may be exhausted, which is a potentially more powerful defense than an implied patent license, since all someone needs to do is to connect the product as sold to a power source. That situation is very similar to *Quanta*, suggesting the claim to the product and the power source is exhausted.

146. Later in this section, approaches to draft claims to address exhaustion are discussed.
147. *Cf.* Anton/Bauer, Inc. v. PAG, Ltd., 329 F.3d 1343 (Fed. Cir. 2003).

Consequentially, we must address the thorny issue of exhaustion. As mentioned previously, *Quanta*, to some extent, made less-clear differences between situations that might result in patent exhaustion and situations that might result in an implied patent license. Prior to *Quanta*, what we refer to here as "traditional exhaustion" required that a patent claim "read" on a product as sold, whether sold by a licensee or by the patentee. However, *Quanta* clarified the concept of a product that "substantially embodies" a patent (in the language of the Supreme Court), so that this latter principle, as previously understood, can no longer be maintained. Therefore, we introduce here the terminology of "*Quanta*-type exhaustion" to refer to a situation, such as in *Quanta*, where a claim does not read on the product sold, but nonetheless the product sold may be held to "substantially embody" a patent, such that the entire patent is exhausted. We refer to the situation where a claim of a patent reads on a product as sold, such that the entire patent is exhausted, as "traditional exhaustion."

It may not always be possible to avoid patent exhaustion. However, limiting the potential scope of exhaustion via claim drafting, if possible, remains beneficial, such as by not exhausting claims of related patents with respect to one's competitors. Although it may vary significantly depending on products, markets, and technologies, it is believed that the situation in *Quanta* may not be a typical technology situation. If this belief is correct, *Quanta* probably creates less risk regarding patent exhaustion than may be perceived.

For example, one might have the perception that, as a result of *Quanta*, any product sale has the potential to exhaust significant portions of one's patent portfolio. It is believed, however, that these perceptions, although in any given situation are possible, may be an overstatement of the impact of the decision and that the decision may, instead, represent a so-called corner case. *Quanta* addresses what may be a narrowly circumscribed factual situation.

In *Quanta*, LGE was asserting its patents against Quanta. Quanta was a system integrator that provided complete systems that included Intel processors and chipsets connected to system memory. Thus, the Intel processors and chipsets when connected to memory were able to implement the patented features. LGE had granted a license to Intel. However, the license agreement contained language that clarified that LGE did not grant Intel an implied license. Since Intel did not have an implied license to connect its product to unlicensed memory, neither did Quanta.

However, the district court ruled that patent exhaustion applied, although the patent claims did *not* read on the Intel product as sold. Thus, this was *not* a case of traditional exhaustion. The Federal Circuit reversed based on its understanding of the principles around patent exhaustion. However, the

Supreme Court reversed the Federal Circuit, concluding that the license to Intel exhausted the asserted patent claims, although the claims at issue did *not* read on the Intel product as sold.

Specifically, the Supreme Court, in explaining the situation at hand in *Quanta*, stated:

> Like the Univis lens blanks, the Intel Products constitute a material part of the patented invention and *all but completely practice the patent*. Here, as in *Univis*, the incomplete article substantially embodies the patent because *the only step necessary* to practice the patent is *the application of common processes or the addition of standard parts*.[148]

The Court further stated:

> Naturally, the Intel Products cannot carry out these functions unless they are attached to memory and buses, *but those additions are standard components in the system*, providing the material that enables the microprocessors and chipsets to function. The Intel Products were *specifically designed to function only when memory or buses are attached; Quanta was not required to make any creative or inventive decision when it added those parts*.[149]

Therefore, Quanta had to do no more than connect processors, chipsets, and memory. Rather, according to the Court, Quanta did not modify the Intel products at all: "*Quanta does not modify the Intel components* and follows Intel's specifications to incorporate the parts into its own systems."[150]

More typically, however, a company may bundle its own technology along with components that it may purchase to produce a complete or final product for market. *This product may, at times, involve significant technical modifications made to the purchased components, such as, for compatibility*, in comparison with the situation of *Quanta* or even *Univis Lens*[151] (a predecessor Supreme Court case relied upon in *Quanta*).

The Court's language in *Quanta* implies some possible factual differences, which, perhaps, may be used in claim drafting to provide a distinction from the facts of *Quanta*. One potential distinction suggests that *Quanta*-type exhaustion may be limited to situations in which a product is being "finished." For example, in explaining the reasoning of *Univis Lens*, the *Quanta* Court, quoting in part the *Univis Lens* Court, stated:

---

148. Quanta Comput., Inc. v. LG Elecs., Inc., 553 U.S. 617 (2008) (emphasis added).
149. *Id.* at 633–34 (emphasis added).
150. *Id.* at 624 (emphasis added).
151. 316 U.S. 241 (1942).

The Court assumed that the Univis patents containing claims for finished lenses were practiced in part by the wholesalers and finishing retailers who ground the blanks into lenses, and held that the sale of the lens blanks exhausted the patents on the finished lenses. *Univis*, 316 U.S., at 248–249. The Court explained that the lens blanks "embodi[ed] essential features of the patented device and [were] without utility until . . . ground and polished as the finished lens of the patent." *Id.*, at 249. The Court noted that:

> "where one has sold an uncompleted article which, because it embodies essential features of his patented invention, is within the protection of his patent, and has destined the article to be finished by the purchaser in conformity to the patent, he has sold his invention so far as it is or may be embodied in that particular article." *Id.*, at 250–251.[152]

In sum, the Court concluded that *the traditional bar on patent restrictions following the sale of an item applies when the item sufficiently embodies the patent. This latter principle applies even if the item as sold does not completely practice the patent. However, it should be that the only and intended use of the item sold is to be made complete in a manner that would infringe a claim of a patent owned by someone who either manufactured the item or licensed the manufacture of the item.*

Likewise, later in the *Quanta* opinion, the Court stated:

> First, *Univis* held that "the authorized sale of an article which is capable of use only in practicing the patent is a relinquishment of the patent monopoly with respect to the article sold." *Id.* at 249. The lens blanks in *Univis* met this standard because they were "without utility until [they were] ground and polished as the finished lens of the patent." *Ibid.* Accordingly, "*the only object of the sale [was] to enable the [finishing retailer] to grind and polish it for use as a lens by the prospective wearer.*" *Id.*[153]

The language of the Court cited here suggests a possibility that exhaustion may be limited to situations in which the "only and intended use" of the product sold is to be finished. This may be a situation in which the product "substantially embodies" the patent. Again, this could be a situation in which the product is sold to someone who integrates their own technology with the product sold. Perhaps, in that case, the product does not substantially embody the patent claim at issue. For example, suppose a product is a chip or module that is used in a cell phone, but requires many other components within the cell phone to also be present within the cell phone in order perform its function. Furthermore, instead, the chip or module could be used with a radio, for

152. *Id.* at 627–28.
153. *Id.* at 631–32 (emphasis added).

example, but, again, the radio requires other components as well for the chip to perform its function. In that case, if you claim the chip or module as part of a radio or as part of a cell phone with a bunch of other components, does the chip as sold substantially embody the patented invention so that sale exhausts such a patent claim?

Likewise, the Court stated:

> But we think that the nature of *the final step*, rather than whether it consists of adding or deleting material, is the relevant characteristic. In each case, *the final step to practice the patent is common and noninventive*: grinding a lens to the customer's prescription, or connecting a microprocessor or chipset to buses or memory.[154]

The Court later stated:

> But this is simply a rephrasing of its argument that combining the Intel Products with other components adds more than *standard finishing to complete a patented article. As explained above, making a product that substantially embodies a patent is, for exhaustion purposes, no different from making the patented article itself.* In other words, *no further "making" results from the addition of standard parts—here, the buses and memory—to a product that already substantially embodies the patent.*[155]

Again, these passages might imply that some type of ministerial "product finishing" may be a feature of exhaustion in situations like this. If so, reducing risk of exhaustion may involve drafting a claim that covers more than the product, but in which the covered combination is created by adding significant technology.

However, other language may suggest that if what is sold embodies the essential features of the invention, then exhaustion applies. The following are sample passages from the *Quanta* opinion:

> We agree with Quanta that *Univis* governs this case. As the Court there explained, exhaustion was triggered by the sale of the lens blanks because *their only reasonable and intended use* was to practice the patent and *because they "embodie[d] essential features of [the] patented invention."* 316 U.S., at 249–251. Each of those attributes is shared by the microprocessors and chipsets Intel sold to Quanta under the License Agreement. . . .
>
> Second, the lens blanks in *Univis "embodie[d] essential features of [the] patented invention." Id.*, at 250–251. The essential, or inventive, feature of the

154. *Id.* at 634 (emphasis added).
155. *Id.* at 637 (emphasis added).

> Univis lens patents was the fusing together of different lens segments to create bi- and tri-focal lenses. . . .
>
> The Intel Products *embody the essential features* of the LGE Patents *because they carry out all the inventive processes* when combined, according to their design, with standard components. . . .
>
> The relevant consideration is whether the Intel Products that partially practice a patent—*by, for example, embodying its essential features*—exhaust *that* patent. . . .
>
> Intel's microprocessors and chipsets *substantially embodied* the LGE Patents *because they had no reasonable noninfringing use and included all the inventive aspects* of the patented methods.[156]

However, some of the language cited here may be read to instead suggest that exhaustion applies where there are no reasonable noninfringing uses, not unlike the approach applied in *Met-Coil*, which relates to implied patent licensing. Additional language in the opinion may also be cited to support that view:

> Here, LGE has suggested *no reasonable use* for the Intel Products other than incorporating them into computer systems that practice the LGE Patents. Nor can we can discern one: A microprocessor or chipset cannot function until it is connected to buses and memory. And here, as in *Univis*, the only apparent object of Intel's sales to Quanta was to permit Quanta to incorporate the Intel Products into computers that would practice the patents. . . .
>
> Intel's microprocessors and chipsets substantially embodied the LGE Patents *because they had no reasonable noninfringing use and included all the inventive aspects of the patented methods.*[157]

Still other language, however, in addition to some of the language cited earlier, suggests that if something creative or inventive was required to be added based on the patent claim language, again, as suggested earlier by some hypotheticals, then exhaustion might not apply. The Court stated:

> Here, as in *Univis*, the incomplete article substantially embodies the patent *because the only step necessary to practice the patent is the application of common processes or the addition of standard parts*. . . .
>
> Quanta *was not required to make any creative or inventive decision* when it added those parts. . . .[158]

---

156. *Id.* at 631–38 (emphasis added).
157. *Id.* at 631–32 (emphasis added).
158. *Id.* at 633–34 (emphasis added).

In light of the passages from the *Quanta* opinion cited earlier, one might craft claims along the following lines in an attempt to avoid exhaustion from the sale of a product related to the claims of the patent. First, *the claims should cover more than the product as sold* so that *the claims do not literally cover what is sold*. Second, the claims should meet one or more (perhaps even all, if possible) of the following:

(1) What is covered by the claims is something that is a complete product and what is sold is either a different complete product or an incomplete product that requires much more than some type of common, well-known, or merely ministerial type of finishing or completion to provide the complete product that is claimed, such as discussed with the aforementioned radio and cell phone example.
(2) What is covered by the claims is something that has particular features of the patented invention and what is sold does not embody *all* of those features.
(3) What is sold is intended to be substantially modified by the purchaser and in a manner that may possibly be covered by the claims (and perhaps such modifications are creative or inventive modifications[159]).
(4) What is sold has reasonable alternative uses beyond practicing what is covered by the claims.

Again, the concept is to have what is sold by the patentee or licensee be different from the claims in a technically substantive manner, rather than a technically ministerial manner. These specific points, of course, focus on the situation in *Quanta*. There may be other ways to accomplish this in other situations. Drafting such claims might, however, be a real challenge because, as a claim drafter, one may not know what future products the patentee might sell or license others to sell. However, with that said, there is no real harm in asking the patentee and taking that information into consideration in drafting the claims. Consider, for example, a scenario in which a company might patent its software executing on a standard computing platform; however, other companies may purchase/license that software and modify it by adding their own technology to produce a special-purpose computing platform. For example, the software sold may be integrated with other software to provide a host of different features and patent claims may cover the software sold integrated on a hardware platform with software that provides other features. Does sale of the software alone exhaust such a patent claim? Does the patent

159. Software might be a good example.

claim necessarily embody the essential features of the invention? Likewise, hardware system integrators may similarly take flash memory and load bios or other low-level programs, add other software, and integrate the chip into a motherboard of a computing platform, which may then be sold. These may be scenarios where the claims cover something other than a product as sold, but what is sold does not "substantially embody" the invention of the claims. These claims, therefore, may otherwise have value if not exhausted. Claims might likewise be drafted so that a reasonable noninfringing alternative use of the product is present. This latter point is similar to the approach that has been suggested to reduce the risk that claims may be impliedly licensed by the sale of a component, for example. As was suggested, an approach may be to have a patent claim cover the product as sold included in one particular arrangement for which it may be purchased, while recognizing the product may be purchased for other arrangements not necessarily covered by the claim, as well.

Index

About the ABA Section of Intellectual Property Law

From its strength within the American Bar Association, the ABA Section of Intellectual Property Law (ABA-IPL) advances the development and improvement of intellectual property laws and their fair and just administration. The Section furthers the goals of its members by sharing knowledge and balanced insight on the full spectrum of intellectual property law and practice, including patents, trademarks, copyright, design, and trade secrets. Providing a forum for rich perspectives and reasoned commentary, ABA-IPL serves as the ABA voice of intellectual property law within the profession, before policy makers, and with the public.

Books from the ABA Section of Intellectual Property Law (ABA-IPL)

ABA AMERICAN BAR ASSOCIATION Intellectual Property Law Section

Title	Regular Price	ABA-IPL Member Price
ADR Advocacy, Strategies, and Practices for Intellectual Property and Technology Cases, 2nd Ed. (5370231)	$149.95	**$119.95**
ANDA Litigation, 3rd Ed. (5370243)	$379.00	**$295.95**
Antitrust Issues in Intellectual Property Law, 2nd Ed. (5370263)	$149.95	**$119.95**
Arbitrating Patent Disputes (5370229)	$89.95	**$74.95**
Biosimilars Litigation and Client Counseling (5370267)	$169.95	**$139.95**
Careers in IP Law (5370204) (The ebook is complimentary with ABA-IPL Section membership)	$24.95	**$16.95**
Commercialization of IP Rights in China (5370241)	$119.95	**$95.95**
A Comprehensive Patent Practice Form Book (5370260)	$139.95	**$109.95**
Computer Games and Immersive Entertainment, 2nd Ed. (5370239)	$89.95	**$69.95**
Copyright Litigation Strategies (5370228)	$369.00	**$285.00**
Copyright Remedies (5370208)	$89.95	**$74.95**
Crash Course on U.S. Patent Law (5370221)	$39.95	**$34.95**
The DMCA Handbook, 2nd Ed. (5370234)	$79.95	**$64.95**
The Essential Case Law Guide to PTAB Trials (5370233)	$249.95	**$199.95**
The Essentials of Japanese Patent Prosecution (5370245)	$149.95	**$119.95**
Intellectural Property and Technology Due Diligence (5370236)	$219.95	**$179.95**
The Intellectual Property Law Handbook, 2nd Ed. (5620154)	$139.95	**$109.95**
IP Attorney's Handbook for Insurance Coverage in Intellectual Property Disputes, 2nd Ed. (5370210)	$139.95	**$129.95**
IP Protection in China (5370217)	$139.95	**$109.95**
IP Strategies for Medical Device Technologies (5370238)	$149.95	**$119.95**
IP Valuation for the Future (5370237)	$89.95	**$59.95**
The Law of Trade Secret Litigation Under the Uniform Trade Secrets Act, 2nd Ed. (5370242)	$369.95	**$295.95**
A Lawyer's Guide to Section 337 Investigations before the U.S. International Trade Commission, 5th Ed. (5370266)	$139.95	**$109.95**
Legal Guide to Video Game Development, 2nd Ed. (5370227)	$74.95	**$59.95**
A Legal Strategist's Guide to Trademark Trial and Appeal Board Practice, 4th Ed. (5370247)	$179.95	**$144.95**
New Practitioner's Guide to Intellectual Property (5370198)	$89.95	**$69.95**
Patent Claim Drafting Practice (5370259)	$179.95	**$144.95**

Title	Regular Price	ABA-IPL Member Price
Patent Freedom to Operate Searches, Opinions, Techniques, and Studies (5370230)	$139.95	**$109.95**
Patent Trial Advocacy Casebook, 3rd Ed. (5370124)	$149.95	**$119.95**
Patently Persuasive (5370206)	$129.95	**$99.95**
The Practitioner's Guide to the PCT, 2nd Ed. (5370261)	$139.95	**$109.95**
The Practitioner's Guide to Trials Before the Patent Trial and Appeal Board, 3rd Ed. (5370258)	$169.95	**$139.95**
Pre-ANDA Litigation, 3rd Ed. (5370256)	$349.00	**$259.00**
Preliminary Relief in Patent Infringement Disputes (5370194)	$119.95	**$94.95**
Principles of Patent Claim Drafting and Patent Claim Analysis (5370268)	$159.95	**$127.95**
Right of Publicity (5370215)	$89.95	**$74.95**
Settlement of Patent Litigation and Disputes (5370192)	$179.95	**$144.95**
Starting an IP Law Practice (5370202)	$54.95	**$34.95**
Summary of Covenants Not to Compete (5370244)	$179.95	**$144.95**
The Tech Contracts Handbook, 3rd Ed. (5370248)	$42.95	**$33.95**
Trademark and Deceptive Advertising Surveys, 2nd Ed. (5370255)	$189.95	**$151.95**
What Is a Copyright, 4th Ed. (5370257)	$19.95	**$16.95**
What Is a Patent, 4th Ed. (5370262)	$19.95	**$16.95**
What Is a Trademark, 5th Ed. (5370254)	$19.95	**$16.95**
What Is a Trade Secret (5370265)	$19.95	**$16.95**

Find these and other ABA-IPL books at ShopABA.com

Thank you for your order!

Jeff Salyards
Executive Editor, ABA Publishing
jeff.salyards@americanbar.org

Tax, shipping and handling charges may apply.
See web store for complete details and current shipping and handling rates and information.

2 EASY WAYS TO ORDER **ShopABA.org** OR **(800) 285-2221**

ABA-IPL Books Editorial Board 2024–25